STRATEGIC INTELLIGENCE

D1457965

STRATEGIC INTELLIGENCE

4

COUNTERINTELLIGENCE AND COUNTERTERRORISM: DEFENDING THE NATION AGAINST HOSTILE FORCES

Edited by

Loch K. Johnson

Intelligence and the Quest for Security

PRAEGER SECURITY INTERNATIONAL
Westport, Connecticut • London

Library of Congress Cataloging-in-Publication Data

Strategic intelligence / edited by Loch K. Johnson.
      p. cm.—(Intelligence and the quest for security, ISSN 1932-3492)
   Includes bibliographical references and index.
   ISBN 0-275-98942-9 (set : alk. paper)—ISBN 0-275-98943-7 (vol. 1 : alk. paper)—
ISBN 0-275-98944-5 (vol. 2 : alk. paper)—ISBN 0-275-98945-3 (vol. 3 : alk. paper)—
ISBN 0-275-98946-1 (vol. 4 : alk. paper)—ISBN 0-275-98947-X (vol. 5 : alk. paper)
1. Military intelligence.   2. Intelligence service—Government policy.   I. Johnson,
Loch K., 1942–

UB250.S6385 2007
327.12—dc22   2006031165

British Library Cataloguing in Publication Data is available.

Library of Congress Catalog Card Number: 2006031165
ISBN: 0-275-98942-9 (set)
     0-275-98943-7 (vol. 1)
     0-275-98944-5 (vol. 2)
     0-275-98945-3 (vol. 3)
     0-275-98946-1 (vol. 4)
     0-275-98947-X (vol. 5)
ISSN: 1932-3492

First published in 2007

Praeger Security International, 88 Post Road West, Westport, CT 06881
An imprint of Greenwood Publishing Group, Inc.
www.praeger.com

Printed in the Untied States of America

The paper used in this book complies with the
Permanent Paper Standard issued by the National
Information Standards Organization (Z39.48-1984).

10 9 8 7 6 5 4 3 2 1

CONTENTS

Preface   vii

1. Definitions and Theories of Counterintelligence   1
   Stan A. Taylor

2. VENONA and Cold War Counterintelligence Methodology   15
   Nigel West

3. Catching Spies in the United States   27
   Katherine A. S. Sibley

4. The Successes and Failures of FBI Counterintelligence   53
   Athan Theoharis

5. The Idea of a European FBI   73
   Rhodri Jeffreys-Jones

6. Washington Politics, Intelligence, and the Struggle
   Against Global Terrorism   99
   Glenn Hastedt

7. The Intelligence War Against Global Terrorism   127
   Richard L. Russell

8. Intelligence to Counter Terror: The Importance
   of All-Source Fusion   139
   Jennifer Sims

9. Women in Religious Terrorist Organizations:
   A Comparative Analysis   157
   Katharina von Knop

Appendixes

A. CIA Counterintelligence: An Excerpt from the Church
   Committee Report   183

B. The Huston Plan   192

C. The Senate Select Committee on Intelligence Reports on the
   Aldrich Ames Counterintelligence Failure, 1994   220

D. Counterterrorism, Intelligence, and the Hart-Rudman
   Commission, March 2001   238

E. The 9/11 Commission Recommendations on Intelligence
   and Counterterrorism, 2004   243

F. The Silberman-Robb Commission Recommendations on
   Intelligence and WMDs in Iraq, 2005   302

G. The Butler Report on Weapons of Mass Destruction
   in Iraq, 2004   330

Glossary   349

Index   355

About the Editor and Contributors   367

PREFACE

THIS FIVE-VOLUME SERIES IN INTELLIGENCE IS SOMETHING of a landmark in the study of intelligence. Thirty years ago, one would have been hard-pressed to find enough good articles on the subject to fill two volumes, let alone five. In those three decades since 1975, however, the study of intelligence has grown considerably. Today there are several solid professional journals in the field, including the premier publications *Intelligence and National Security* (published in the United Kingdom), *International Journal of Intelligence and Counterintelligence* (the United States), and *Studies in Intelligence* (from the Central Intelligence Agency, in both classified and unclassified form). In just the past two years, bulging anthologies on the general topic "strategic intelligence," as well as a "handbook" on intelligence and a collection of chapters within the more specialized niche of "intelligence and ethics" have appeared, along with a tidal wave of books and articles on one aspect or another of this subject (see the bibliographic essay in volume 1).

Except in times of scandal (Watergate in 1973, CIA domestic spying in 1974, the Iran-*contra* affair in 1987), one could find in this earlier era little newspaper coverage of intelligence activities, so tightly held were these operations by the government. Now, fueled by the events of the September 11, 2001, terrorist attacks and the erroneous prediction in 2002 that weapons of mass destruction (WMDs) were being developed and stockpiled by Iraq, hardly a week goes by without reports on intelligence in the *New York Times* and other leading newspapers. These days, the *Atlantic Monthly* and the *New Yorker*, America's top literary magazines, visit the subject with some regularity, too. The latter has hired Seymour M. Hersh, the nation's most well-known investigative reporter with an intelligence beat.

Intelligence studies has come of age.

Certainly the chapters in these volumes display a breadth of inquiry that suggests an admirable vibrancy in this relatively new field of study. Presented here are empirical inquiries, historical treatments, theoretical frameworks, memoirs, case studies, interviews, legal analyses, comparative essays, and ethical assessments. The authors come from the ranks of academe (twenty-five); the intelligence agencies (thirteen); think tanks (seven); Congress, the State Department, and the National Security Council (three); and the legal world (three).[1] Over a quarter of the contributors are from other nations, including Canada, England, Germany, Israel, Scotland, Switzerland, and Wales. The American writers come from every region of the United States. As a collective, the authors represent a wide range of scholarly disciplines, including computer science, history, international affairs, law, sociology, political science, public administration, public policy studies, and strategic studies. Many of the contributors are from the ranks of the top intelligence scholars in the world; a few young ones stand at the gateway to their academic careers.

Notable, too, is the number of women who have entered this field of study. Thirty years ago, it would have been rare to find one or two women writing on this subject. Seven have contributed chapters to these pages, and another two wrote documents that appear in the appendixes. This is still fewer than one would like, especially in light of the major contribution women have made as intelligence officers. One thinks of the heroic efforts of British women in code breaking and in the Special Operations Executive during World War II, and the American women who contributed so much to the analytic efforts of the Office of Strategic Studies (OSS) during that same war. At least, though, the number attracted to the scholar study of intelligence appears to be rapidly expanding.

The end result of this mix is a landscape illuminated by a variety of methods and appreciations—a rich research trove that examines all the key aspects of intelligence. In addition, each of the volumes contains backup materials in the appendixes. These documents provide the reader with access to significant primary and secondary sources referred to in the chapters.

The volumes are organized according to the major topics of studies in the field. The first volume, titled *Understanding the Hidden Side of Government*, introduces the reader to methods commonly used in the study of intelligence. It imparts, as well, a sense of the "state of the discipline," beginning with a bibliographic essay (by the editor) and continuing with an examination of specific approaches scholars have adopted in their inquiries into this especially difficult discipline, where doors are often shut against outsiders.

In the bibliographic essay that opens the volume, I argue that the literature on intelligence has mushroomed over the past thirty years. Some of this literature is unreliable, but much of it is of high quality. Amy B. Zegart follows my chapter with an important caveat: the literature may be more voluminous these days, but intelligence studies as an academic field has yet to be accepted as a vital part of national security scholarship. The mainstream journals of history, international affairs, and political science have still regarded the study of intelligence as a marginal pursuit. In this regard, Zegart points out, there is a major disconnect between academic scholarship and those who make decisions in Washington, London, and other capitals around the world.

Following this introduction, Len Scott and Timothy Gibbs look at methods that have been used to study intelligence in the United Kingdom; Stuart Farson and Reg Whitaker in Canada; and Michael Warner in the United States. The volume then turns to a more specific inquiry into the central question of how intelligence is interpreted by professionals—the issue of analysis—explored by John Hollister Hedley. An overview of the sometimes turbulent relationship between intelligence officers and the policy makers they serve is explored by James J. Wirtz; and British scholar Peter Gill recalls the failures associated with the 9/11 attacks and the poor judgments about Iraqi WMDs, in hopes of extracting lessons from these intelligence disasters. In the next chapter, the youngest scholar represented in this collection, Harold M. Greenberg, takes us back in time with a remembrance of the legendary CIA officer and Yale history professor Sherman Kent, often known as the dean of CIA analysts. Kristin Lord rounds out the first volume with a look forward into future prospects for a more transparent world—the ultimate goal of intelligence.

As with each of the books, Volume 1 has a set of appendixes designed to supplement the original chapters with supportive materials from government documents and other sources. Appendix A contains the relevant intelligence excerpts from the National Security Act of 1947—the founding charter for the modern American intelligence establishment. Appendix B provides a history of U.S. intelligence since 1947, prepared for the Aspin-Brown Commission in 1995–96 by staff member Phyllis Provost McNeil. These two documents present a contextual backdrop for the Volume 1 chapters. Appendix C provides "wiring diagrams" of the intelligence community, that is, organizational blueprints for the sixteen agencies and related entities. One chart displays the community as it is today, and another displays how it looked in 1985. As the contrast between the two illustrates, the events of September 11, 2001, have led to a larger and more complex intelligence apparatus in the United States. Appendix D shows a photograph of the CIA Headquarters Building, as an example of what one of the secret agencies actually looks like from an aerial perspective. The white dome in the foreground is an assembly hall seating around 600 people and to its left is the main entrance to the original CIA headquarters, built during the Eisenhower years. Behind this older wing is the new green-glass structure erected during the Reagan administration, often known as the Casey addition because William J. Casey was the Director of Central Intelligence (DCI) at the time of its construction during the 1980s.

Appendix E lists the top leadership in the America's intelligence community: the DCIs from 1947–2005 and today's DNI. Included here as well are the leaders in Congress who have been responsible for intelligence accountability in the past, along with the current members of the two congressional Intelligence

Committees: the Senate Select Committee on Intelligence (SSCI, or "sissy" in the unflattering and sometimes true homophone of Capitol Hill vernacular) and the House Permanent Select Committee on Intelligence (HPSCI or "hipsee"). Appendix F presents a 1955 statement from historian and CIA analyst Sherman Kent about the need for a more robust intelligence literature. He would probably be amazed by how much is being written on this subject now. Appendix G offers an overview on the purpose and challenges of intelligence, drawn from the introductory chapters of the Aspin-Brown Commission Report. Finally, Appendix H provides an opening glimpse into the subject of counterintelligence, a world of counterspies and betrayal taken up more fully in Volume 4.

With the second volume, titled *The Intelligence Cycle: The Flow of Secret Information From Overseas to the Highest Councils of Government*, the focus shifts from a broad overview of intelligence to a more detailed examination of its core mission: the collection, analysis, and dissemination of information from around the world. The National Security Act of 1947, which created America's modern intelligence establishment, made it clear that the collection, analysis, and dissemination of information would be the primary duty of the intelligence agencies. As Allen Dulles—the most famous DCI (America's top intelligence official, until this title changed to director of National Intelligence or DNI in 2005)—put it, the intelligence agencies were expected "to weigh facts, and to draw conclusions from those facts, without having either the facts or the conclusions warped by the inevitable and even proper prejudices of the men whose duty it is to determine policy."[2] The collection and interpretation of information, through espionage and from the public record, would be the primary responsibility of America's secret agencies.

At the heart of this mission lies the so-called intelligence cycle. Professional intelligence officers define the cycle as "the process by which information is acquired, converted into intelligence, and made available to policymakers."[3] The cycle has five phases: planning and direction, collection, processing, production and analysis, and dissemination (see Appendix A in Volume 2 for a depiction). As former CIA officer Arthur S. Hulnick notes, however, in the opening chapter, the idea of a "cycle" fails to capture the complexity of how intelligence is collected, assessed, and distributed by intelligence officers.

The next five chapters in Volume 2 take us into the world of the "ints," that is, the specialized "intelligences" (methods) used by intelligence officers to collect information. Patrick Radden Keefe and Matthew M. Aid probe the method of signals intelligence or SIGINT, a generic term used to describe the interception and analysis of communications intelligence and other electronic emissions, from wiretapping telephones to studying the particles emitted by missiles in test flights. Both authors are sensitive to the possible abuse of these techniques, which can be and have been used to spy on Americans without a proper judicial warrant. Jeffrey T. Richelson explores the IMINT domain, that is, imagery intelligence or, in simple terms, photographs taken by surveillance satellites and reconnaissance airplanes (piloted and unpiloted). Telephone conversations can be revealing, but in the old saying, a picture can be worth a thousand words. (Appendix B provides photographic examples of these spy platforms, and Appendix C offers illustrations of the IMINT data they can collect.)

Important, too, is information that can be acquired by human agents ("assets") guided by case officers inside the CIA or the Defense Department, the topic of human intelligence or HUMINT, examined by Frederick P. Hitz. Not all the information needed by policy makers is acquired through SIGINT, IMINT, or HUMINT; indeed, the overwhelming majority—upward of 95 percent—is already in the public domain. This open-source intelligence (OSINT) must be sorted through, organized, and integrated with the secretly gained information. Robert David Steele's chapter looks at OSINT and its ties to the other ints.

In the next chapter, Daniel S. Gressang IV dissects some of the technological challenges faced by intelligence agencies in sorting through the avalanche of data that pours into their headquarters from various intelligence collectors around the world. Here is the Herculean task of sorting out the wheat from the chaff (or the signal from the noise, in another widely used metaphor) in the search for information that may warn the nation of impending peril. Here is the vital task of providing "indicators and warnings" (I&W) to a nation's leaders.

One of the most difficult relationships in the complex process of collection, analysis, and dissemination of information comes at the intersection between intelligence professionals and policy makers—groups of individuals that often have very different training, aspirations, and cultures. Jack Davis sheds light on this often turbulent relationship in the United States, and Michael Herman tackles the same topic in the United Kingdom. Minh A. Luong offers a case study on economic intelligence that underscores some of the difficulties encountered as information travels from the collectors and analysts (the "producers" of intelligence) to the policy makers (the "consumers"). Finally, Max M. Holland takes a look at how intelligence agencies examine their own mistakes ("postmortems") and attempt to make corrections—and how political consideration enter into the process.

By way of supporting documentation, in addition to the appendixes already mentioned, Appendix D outlines the general types of reports prepared by the producers of intelligence, along with a listing of specific examples. Appendixes E and F provide samples of key intelligence products: National Intelligence Estimates (NIEs)—the most important long-range and in-depth forecasting carried out by the U.S. secret agencies ("research intelligence," in contrast to shorter intelligence reports that tend to focus on near-term events, or "current intelligence"); Special National Intelligence Estimates (SNIEs), which concentrate on a narrow, high-priority information requirement (say, the capabilities of the Chinese military); and the *President's Daily Brief* (PDB), the most exclusive current intelligence report prepared by the intelligence agencies for the consumption of the president and a few other high-ranking officials.

In light of the fact that every study of the 9/11 and Iraqi WMD intelligence failures find fault, in part, with America's capacity for human intelligence—

especially in the Middle East and Southwest Asia—Appendix G presents one of the most searing critiques of this int. The critique, by the House Permanent Select Committee on Intelligence, has become all the more significant because the panel's chairman, Representative Porter Goss (R-FL), soon after the completion of the report rose to the position of the DCI. Last, Appendix H provides an excerpt from a key report on the Iraqi WMD mistakes, prepared by the "Roberts Committee": the Senate Select Committee on Intelligence, led by Pat Roberts (R-KS).

The third volume, titled *Covert Action: Behind the Veils of Secret Foreign Policy*, enters an especially controversial compartment of intelligence: the means by which the United States attempts to not just gather and analyze information about the world—hard enough—but to manipulate global events through secret activities in the advancement of America's best interests. An ambiguous passage of the National Security Act of 1947 charged the National Security Council (NSC), the boss over the sixteen U.S. secret agencies, to "perform such other functions and duties related to intelligence [over and beyond collection-and-analysis] affecting the national security as the National Security Council may from time to time direct."[4] The phrase "other functions and duties" left the door open for launching the CIA (and more recently the Pentagon) on a wide range of covert actions around the world.

Covert action (CA), sometimes referred to as the "quiet option," is based on the supposition that this secret approach to foreign affairs is likely to be less noisy and obtrusive than sending in the Marines. Sometimes professional practitioners also refer to covert action as the "third option," between diplomacy and open warfare. As former Secretary of State and National Security Adviser Henry Kissinger once put it: "We need an intelligence community that, in certain complicated situations, can defend the American national interest in the gray areas where military operations are not suitable and diplomacy cannot operation."[5] Still others prefer the euphemism "special activities" to describe covert action. Whatever the variation in terminology, the goal of covert action remains constant: to influence events overseas secretly and in support of American foreign policy.

Covert action operations are often grouped according to four broad categories: propaganda, political, economic, and paramilitary (PM) activities. An example of a propaganda operation was the CIA's use of Radio Free Europe during the Cold War to transmit anti-communist themes into nations behind the Iron Curtain. A political CA during the Cold War was the CIA's clandestine funneling of funds to the anti-communist Christian Democratic Party in Italy. An economic example: the CIA attempted to destroy electric power stations in Nicaragua during the 1980s, as a means of undermining the Marxist-oriented *Sandinista* regime. PM operations can including everything from assassination plots against foreign heads of state to arming and guiding pro-American insurgent armies in one country or another. Little wonder this has been a controversial subject.

Gregory F. Treverton introduces the reader to covert action in the first chapter of Volume 3. He is followed by Kevin A. O'Brien and Ephraim Kahana, who discuss the use of covert action by other nations. The next four chapters illuminate certain aspects of CA, with James M. Scott and Jerel A. Rosati providing an overview of CA tradecraft (that is, the tools used to implement such operations); Michael A. Turner evaluating the merits of CIA covert propaganda operations; William J. Daugherty looking at political and economic examples of covert action; Jennifer D. Kibbe exploring the entry of the Defense Department into this domain; and former diplomat John D. Stempel contrasting the uses of covert action to diplomatic initiatives. Winding up the volume is Judge James E. Baker's legal analysis of covert action.

Supporting documents include excerpts from the Church Committee Report on the evolution of covert action as carried out by the CIA (Appendix A). The supervision of covert action went from an informal to a highly formal process, as a result of a law known as the Hughes-Ryan Act, passed on December 31, 1974. The language of this statute is presented in Appendix B, and the covert action procedures that resulted from the law are outlined in Appendix C. At the center of the covert action decision process since the Hughes-Ryan Act is the *finding*, a term of art that stems from the passage in the law that requires the president to "find" that a particular covert action proposal is important and has the president's approval. Appendix D contains two findings from the Iran-*contra* era in the mid-1980s. Covert actions must have an organizational apparatus to carry them out, and Appendix E displays what that apparatus looked like during the Cold War (and in basic form remains the organizational chart today, with a few name changes in the boxes).

One of the most controversial forms of covert action has been the assassination of foreign leaders. Appendix F presents a case study from the Church Committee on the CIA assassination plot hatched against the leader of the Republic of Congo, Patrice Lumumba, in 1960. The Committee's exposé of this and other plots led President Gerald R. Ford to sign an executive order prohibiting assassination as an instrument of American foreign policy (see Appendix G). The executive order has been waived in times of authorized warfare against other nations, however, leading to failed attempts to assassinate Saddam Hussein in the first and second Persian Gulf Wars (he was eventually captured alive in 2004, hidden away in a hole near his hometown in Iraq) and Al Qaeda leader Osama bin Laden during the Clinton administration. Considerable ambiguity exists regarding the current status of the executive order and under what conditions it might be waived by administrations. Finally, Appendix H—drawing on a presidential commission study and congressional hearings—examines covert action at its lowest state: the Iran-*contra* affair of the 1980s, when this approach to foreign policy subverted the U.S. Constitution and several laws (including the Hughes-Ryan Act).

A third intelligence mission, after collection-and-analysis and covert action, is counterintelligence (CI) and its associated activity, counterterrorism (CT).

Here is the concentration in Volume 4, titled *Counterintelligence and Counter-terrorism: Defending the Nation Against Hostile Forces*. Like covert action, CI went without specific mention in the National Security Act of 1947. By the early 1950s, however, it had similarly achieved a status of considerable importance as an intelligence mission. CI specialists soon waged nothing less than a secret war against antagonistic intelligence services (especially the Soviet KGB); and, after the Cold War, CT specialists would focus on efforts to block terrorists who targeted the United States and its allies. Explaining why the mission of counterintelligence/counterterrorism evolved, a CI expert has pointed out that "in the absence of an effective U.S. counterintelligence program, [adversaries of democracy] function in what is largely a benign environment."[6]

The practice of counterintelligence consists of two matching halves: security and counterespionage. Security is the passive or defensive side of CI, involving such devices as background investigations, fences, sentries, alarms, badges, watchdogs, and polygraphs (lie detection machines). Counterespionage (CE) is the offensive or aggressive side of CI. The most effective CE operation is the infiltration of an American agent or "mole" into the enemy camp, whether a hostile intelligence service or a terrorist cell—a ploy called a penetration. Thus, the practice of security is, according to one of America's top counterintelligence experts, "All that concerns perimeter defense, badges, knowing everything you have to know about your own people," whereas the CE side "involves knowing all about intelligence services—hostile intelligence services: their people, their installations, their methods, and their operations."[7]

Stan A. Taylor and Nigel West clarify these issues in the first two chapters of this volume, then in the next two chapters Katherine A. S. Sibley and Athan Theoharis examine the challenges of keeping the United States spy-free. Rhodri Jeffreys-Jones looks at the efforts in Europe to create a counterintelligence capability similar to that practiced by America's Federal Bureau of Investigation (FBI). Glenn Hastedt takes the reader into the counterterrorism thicket in Washington, DC, explaining how politics influences CI and CT operations. Richard L. Russell and Jennifer Sims discuss the ups and downs of trying to establish an effective counterterrorism response in the United States, complicated by the fragmentation of authority and widely differing cultures among the sixteen U.S. intelligence agencies. Finally, Katharina von Knop looks at the rising role of women in terrorist organizations.

The back-of-the-book documents in Volume 4 begin with a look at the Church Committee findings regarding counterintelligence in 1975 (Appendix A), followed by the notorious Huston Plan—a master counterintelligence spy plan drafted by White House aide Tom Charles Huston in 1970, in response to a nation at unrest over the war in Vietnam (Appendix B). The Huston Plan is a classic illustration of overreaction in a time of domestic strife. In Appendix C, the Senate Select Committee on Intelligence summarizes its findings about the Aldrich H. Ames counterintelligence disaster. Next the appendixes include a series of U.S. commission conclusions about how to improve intelligence in the struggle against global terrorism, whether locating and penetrating their cells in advance of a terrorist attack or thwarting the ability of terrorists to acquire WMDs. The panel reports include: the Hart-Rudman Commission of 2001 (Appendix D); the 9/11 or Kean Commission of 2004 (Appendix E); and the Silberman-Robb Commission of 2005 (Appendix F). For purposes of comparison, the final appendix (G) examines the conclusions reached by a British commission that also probed the Iraqi WMD failure: the Butler Report of 2004.

The fifth volume in the series, titled *Intelligence and Accountability: Safeguards Against the Abuse of Secret Power*, stems from a concern that secret power might be misused by those in high office. This danger was underscored in 1975 when Congress found the U.S. intelligence agencies guilty of spying against law-abiding American citizens, and again in 1987 during the Iran-*contra* affair when some elements of the intelligence community violated the public trust by ignoring intelligence laws. The United States has been one of the few nations in the world to conduct an ongoing experiment in bringing democratic accountability to secret government activities. Democracy and spying don't mix well. Secrecy runs counter to democratic openness, while at the same time openness possesses a threat to the success of espionage operations. Democracies need intelligence agencies to acquire information that may protect them, but thoughtful citizens worry about having secret agencies in an open society.

Until 1975, the nation's remedy for the tension between intelligence gathering and democracy was to trust the intelligence agencies and hope for the best. Elected officials treated the secret services as exceptional organizations, immune from the checks and balances envisioned by the framers of the Constitution. Lawmakers were satisfied with this arrangement, because if an operation went awry they could duck responsibility. When James R. Schlesinger, DCI in 1973, attempted to inform John Stennis (D-MS), a key member of the Senate Armed Services Committee, about an approaching operation, the Senator stopped him short: "No, no, my boy, don't tell me. Just go ahead and do it, but I don't want to know."[8]

This attitude on Capitol Hill—overlook rather than oversight—underwent a dramatic turnabout in December 1974, however, when the *New York Times* reported on allegations of CIA spying at home and questionable covert actions in Chile. Congress might have waved aside the revelations about Chile as just another Cold War necessity in the struggle against regimes leaning toward Moscow, but spying on American citizens—voters—was another matter altogether. In January 1975, President Ford created the Commission on CIA Activities Within the United States (the Rockefeller Commission, led by his vice president, Nelson Rockefeller). Later that month the Senate established a select committee to investigate intelligence activities. The committee was headed by Frank Church, D-ID, and became known as the Church Committee (the editor served as Church's assistant). A counterpart House committee, led by Representative Otis Pike (D-NY), began investigations the following month.

These various panels, especially the Church Committee, found many more improprieties than they had expected. Not only had the CIA engaged in domestic spying in violation of its charter, so had the FBI and several military intelligence units. Furthermore, the FBI had carried out secret operations, known collectively as COINTELPRO, against thousands of civil rights activists, members of the Ku Klux Klan, and Vietnam War dissenters. The objective was to make their lives miserable by disrupting their marriages and employment. The Bureau even attempted to blackmail Dr. Martin Luther King Jr. into committing suicide. Church Committee investigators also discovered CIA assassination plots against foreign leaders and efforts to topple President Salvador Allende of Chile, even though he had been democratically elected.

These revelations convinced lawmakers that the time had come to bring accountability into the dark recesses of government. Congress established intelligence oversight committees in both chambers—the Senate in 1976 and the House a year later—and, by 1980, required by law timely reports on all secret intelligence operations. The new Committees pored over intelligence budgets, held regular hearings (mostly in closed session to protect spy sources and methods) and seriously examined the performance of America's intelligence agencies. No other nation has ever so thoroughly applied democratic principles to its secret services, although a number are now beginning to follow the leadership of the United States toward greater intelligence supervision.[9]

Since 1975, this effort has evolved in fits and starts. Sometimes lawmakers have insisted on close accountability, as when they enacted the Intelligence Oversight Act of 1980 with its stringent reporting requirements for covert operations, or when a series of laws in the 1980s sought to end covert actions in Nicaragua. At other times, members of Congress have loosened the reins—for example, repealing in 1985 a prohibition against covert action in Angola. On still other occasions, Congress has concentrated on helping the intelligence agencies improve their security and performance, as with a law in 1982 that prohibited exposing the names of undercover officers. The Iran-*contra* scandal of 1987 was a major setback to this new oversight, as the Reagan administration bypassed most of these rules and statutes in its conduct of a covert war in Nicaragua against the will of Congress. The scandal was an alert to lawmakers. The Intelligence Oversight Act of 1991 further tightened intelligence supervision by clarifying reporting requirements. Lawmakers also set up an Office of Inspector General in the CIA, confirmed by and accountable to Congress.

The pulling and tugging has continued, most recently over whether President George W. Bush violated the Foreign Intelligence Surveillance Act (FISA) of 1978 by conducting warrantless wiretaps as part of the war against terrorism in the aftermath of the 9/11 attacks. The FISA required warrants, but the White House claimed (when the secret operation leaked to the media) the law had become to cumbersome and, besides, the president had inherit authority to conduct the war against terrorism as he saw fit. This debate aside for the moment (several authors address the issue in these volumes), one thing is certain: the intelligence agencies in the United States are now very much a part of the nation's system of checks and balances. Americans want and deserve both civil liberties and a secure defense against threats; so the search continues for an appropriate balance between liberty and security, democracy and effectiveness—precisely the topic of Volume 5.

The set of chapters on intelligence accountability are introduced with a chapter by David M. Barrett, the foremost authority on the history of accountability in the early years of modern U.S. intelligence (1947 to 1963). The chief counsel of the Church Committee, Frederick A. O. Schwarz Jr., then reflects back on the effects of that watershed inquiry. Next, the editor offers a previously unpublished interview with DCI William E. Colby, who stood at the helm of the intelligence community as it weathered the storm of the investigations into domestic spying during 1975. Mark Phythian presents a chapter on the British experience with intelligence accountability; and, comparing British and American oversight, Lawrence J. Lamanna contrasts the responses on both sides of the Atlantic to the faulty Iraqi WMD assessments in 2002.

The next chapter, written by Cynthia M. Nolan, looks at contemporary issues of intelligence oversight in the United States. Hans Born and Ian Leigh follow with a comparative dimension by contrasting intelligence accountability practices in a variety other nations. Finally, A. Denis Clift and Harry Howe Ransom, who have witnessed the unfolding of intelligence accountability over the past four decades, offer their appraisals of where the experiment stands today.

The first supporting document in this volume is a succinct legislative history of intelligence accountability from 1947 to 1993, prepared by the Senate Select Committee on Intelligence (Appendix A). Then come a series of important oversight laws, beginning with FISA in 1978. With this law, members of Congress sought to rein in the open-ended authority of the executive branch to wiretap and otherwise spy on individuals considered risks to the national security—a privilege abused by a number of administrations from the 1930s forward. Henceforth, FISA required a warrant from a special court (the FISA Court, whose members are appointed by the Chief Justice of the Supreme Court) before such intrusive measures could be carried out. This law, a hot topic in 2005–6 when critics charged the second Bush administration with violation of the warrant requirement, can be found in Appendix B.

The Intelligence Oversight Act of 1980 is presented in Appendix C. This is a brief but nonetheless far-reaching law, enacted by Congress as an attempt to become an equal partner with the executive branch when it came to intelligence. The 1991 Intelligence Oversight Act (Appendix D) emerged after the Iran-*contra* scandal and provided a tightening and clarification of the language in its 1980 precursor, especially with respect to the approval and reporting rules for covert action. The political tug-of-war over the drafting of this currently prevailing oversight statute was intense, leading to the first and only presidential veto of an intelligence act. President George H. W. Bush found the proposal's insistence on prior reporting of covert action objectionable in times of emergency. Lawmakers entered into a compromise with the chief executive, settling on a two-day reporting delay in emergencies. The bill passed Congress again, this time without a presidential veto.

In 1995, the House Permanent Select Committee on Intelligence launched an inquiry into a wide assortment of intelligence issues, stimulated initially by counterintelligence concerns (Aldrich Ames's treasonous activities at the CIA had recently been discovered) but turning into an opportunity for a broad review of new challenges that faced the secret agencies now that the Cold War had ended. In Appendix E, an excerpt from the Committee's final report examines the state of intelligence accountability in the mid-1990s. The next document, in Appendix F, carries the examination into the twenty-first century, with the appraisal of the 9/11 Commission on the same subject. The commissioners were unimpressed, referring to intelligence accountability as "dysfunctional."

At the center of any efforts to maintain accountability for the secret agencies lies the question of funding—the mighty power of the pursue, held in the hands of lawmakers. Appendix G draws on the findings of the Aspin-Brown Commission to provide official documentation about how the United States spends money for spying. Finally, in Appendix H, DCI Robert M. Gates (1991–93) offers observations about oversight from the perspective of the intelligence community management team, located at that time on the Seventh Floor of the CIA.

Here, then, is what the reader will find in these five volumes. The editor and the contributors hope the chapters and documents will help educate the public about the importance of intelligence agencies, as well as stimulate scholars around the world to further the blossoming of this vital field of study. I am pleased to acknowledge my gratitude to Praeger's Heather Staines, senior project editor, and Anne Rehill, development editor, each a pleasure to work with and most helpful in their guidance; Julie Maynard at the University of Georgia for her administrative assistance; Lawrence J. Lamanna, my graduate research assistant, for his good counsel and logistical help; Leena S. Johnson for her indispensable encouragement and support; and the contributors to these volumes for their outstanding scholarship and their much appreciated cooperation in keeping the publishing train running on time.

These volumes are enthusiastically dedicated to Harry Howe Ransom, who has done so much in the United States to lead the way toward a serious discipline of intelligence studies.

Loch K. Johnson

NOTES

1. Some of the authors have had multiple careers, so in categorizing them I have counted the place where they have spent most of their professional lives.

2. Quoted by Senator Frank Church (D-ID), in *Congressional Record* (January 27, 1976), p. 1165.

3. *Fact Book on Intelligence* (Washington DC: CIA Office of Public Affairs, April 1983), p. 17.

4. National Security Act of 1947, signed on July 26, 1947 (P.L. 97-222; 50 U.S.C. 403, Sec. 102).

5. Comment, "Evening News," NBC (January 13, 1978).

6. Editor's interview with a FBI counterintelligence specialist, Washington, DC (May 16, 1975).

7. Editor's interview with Raymond Rocca, CIA/CI specialist, Washington, DC (November 23, 1975).

8. Editor's interview with James R. Schlesinger, Washington, DC (June 16, 1994).

9. See Hans Born, Loch K. Johnson, and Ian Leigh, *Who's Watching the Spies? Establishing Intelligence Service Accountability* (Washington, DC: Potomac Books, 2005).

1

DEFINITIONS AND THEORIES
OF COUNTERINTELLIGENCE

STAN A. TAYLOR

Counterintelligence is to intelligence as epistemology is to philosophy. Both go back to the fundamental question of how we know things, both challenge what we are inclined to take most for granted and both offer heavy advantage in debate to those who are skeptical of appearances.

—Thomas Powers[1]

INTRODUCTION

THEORIES ARE DEVELOPED AND USED IN SCIENCE to present conceptual frameworks that allow one to understand and explain phenomena. Theories also generate questions that are useful in research. These frameworks normally consist of assumptions (often called hypotheses) and statements, usually described as necessary and sufficient, for both explanation and prediction. However, in social sciences, the explanatory function is somewhat more important than the predictive function of theory because all of the controls necessary for a predictive theory are not available. Theories in the social sciences can be very useful in *explaining* phenomena but only moderately useful as *predictive* tools in what are called post hoc predictions that are much the same as explanations of historical events. This chapter presents a counterintelligence (CI) theory that explains (to some extent) the existence of counterintelligence practices in any state. The theory is drawn from broader intelligence theories of which counterintelligence is a part.

This attempt to theorize about counterintelligence begins with a brief discussion of intelligence theories and then derives counterintelligence theories from them.

DEFINITIONS AND THEORIES
OF INTELLIGENCE

Intelligence scholars argue about definitions of intelligence, but the primary difference between these efforts is merely the expansiveness of the definitions. In its most expansive application, *intelligence* refers to:

- The process that begins when national decision makers identify what information is needed to help them make better informed decisions regarding any entity with which they must deal.
- The prioritization, collection, analysis, production, and use of that information.
- The organizations and groups that actually collect, analyze, and produce the information.
- The other activities of various groups who participate in the intelligence cycle.
- The information and insights that flow from this process.

As defined, intelligence differs from the general use of information by human beings in everyday social intercourse in, at a minimum, six ways:

- The fate of ideologies, nations, economies, and people may depend on how effectively the information or intelligence is utilized.
- The information desired is usually (although not always) information that other individuals, groups, and nations do not want revealed.
- The information desired is about individuals, groups, or nations who often (but not always) are hostile or potentially hostile toward the collecting nation.
- The collection of this information is usually, although not always, done clandestinely.
- Individual, group, or national rights may be violated in the collection of this information.
- The broader intelligence process may generate secret special activities meant to influence the foreign or domestic policies of other states without revealing the source of the influence.

The Latin origins of the word *intelligence* are revealing. The prefix *inter* means between or among. Thus, the term *international relations* refers to the relations between or among nations. The remainder of the word *intelligence* comes from the Latin word *leger*—the gathering of fruit or vegetables. Over time, these two terms were combined into one word referring to the knowledge and skills necessary to distinguish between good and bad fruit and vegetables. Gradually, the meaning of *intelligence* came to connote the skills and aptitudes needed to make wise and productive choices about any aspect of one's life. It is used in this chapter to refer to the knowledge and information necessary to make informed decisions about statecraft.

Although some scholars stress the difference between intelligence as used by psychologists and intelligence as used by national strategists, in reality they come from the same origins. The word *intelligence* in "intelligence quotient" (IQ) really refers to the human ability to process environmental information into usable and productive knowledge. That is not substantially different from the ability to collect and process information about the interstate environment as a necessary prelude to informed statecraft.

National Security and Intelligence

At the outset, it is useful to understand the relationship between security and intelligence. Two early pioneers in the analysis of state power, Harold and Margaret Sprout of Princeton University, argued that there were five functions or variables by which the power of any state could be analyzed or measured.[2]

1. The information-providing function. How well do states define a need for information and then collect, analyze, and utilize that information?
2. The decision-making function. Can a nation coordinate all of its resources into an effective strategy?
3. The means-providing function. How well can states provide the elements of power needed to achieve strategic goals?
4. The means-utilizing functions. How well can a government utilize or effectively organize all of the means it may possess?
5. The resistance-to-demands function. How resilient is a state to the demands and challenges of other states?

Intelligence operations are critical in the first function, but also play a significant role in the fifth. Demands are more easily resisted when the intentions and capabilities of a threatening state are known. In sum, intelligence is a significant part of state power, and power—the ability to influence other states in a predictable way—is a crucial and critical key to national security.

Theories of Intelligence

Humans use theories to explain observed reality. They are necessary for the development of any discipline. However, only a few scholars have attempted to develop theories of intelligence; among them are David Kahn and Loch K. Johnson.[3] Kahn believes his theory meets the requirements of all theories—it is both explanatory and predictive. He begins with the assumption that all biological organisms, from amoebas to nation-states, need to sense their environment sufficiently to protect their existence. This leads him to his notion that intelligence, by its very nature, is for protection or for defense. That is, it is "essential to survival, but not to dominance."[4] He discusses both the antiquity and ubiquity of intelligence but notes the changing relative importance between physical intelligence (for example, information about physical objects—tanks, troops, etc.), whose importance is in relative decline, and verbal intelligence (for example, captured communications that may reveal enemy plans), which is increasing in importance. Kahn believes intelligence is increasing in importance, but he acknowledges that it will never be perfect. He also believes that the greatest contemporary and future problem intelligence faces is to be accepted by generals and heads of state whose minds are often set before they view intelligence information.

Johnson's approach is less of a general theory and more specific to strategic intelligence—that is, intelligence needed to support foreign policy and national strategy. He modestly calls his effort a "preface" to a theory and addresses the question of how much of a nation's scarce resources should be devoted to intelligence. He argues that such variables as a nation's global involvement, foreign policy goals, perceived threats, number of intelligence targets, and its ability to consume intelligence information will need to be studied more closely to construct an explanatory and predictive theory of intelligence. Johnson's greatest contribution is his insistence that intelligence must be viewed in the overall context of a nation's global strategy and threats.

A third and more general theory of intelligence, one into which both Kahn's and Johnson's theories would fit quite comfortably, can be drawn from cybernetics, a discipline developed in 1947 by mathematician Norbert Weiner and others.[5] The word *cybernetics* comes from a Greek word meaning helmsman or governor—one who steers a ship. A helmsman must use skill, intuition, and constant feedback from the environment to achieve accurate steerage of the vessel.

Cybernetics is a complex science drawn from biology, neural modeling, psychology, mathematics, electrical engineering, as well as other disciplines. It is the science of feedback—the study of how information can maintain or alter any biological, social, mechanical, or artificial system. Cybernetics has contributed to the development of general systems theory, artificial intelligence, and robotics, as well as significant developments in psychology and learning theories.

It is a perfect paradigm or theory for the role of intelligence applied to statecraft. Decision makers are the helmsmen, the governors, who must use skill, intuition, and a constant flow of information or intelligence to optimize efficiency (defined as the most security at the least cost) for the state. Cybernetics is the iterative flow of information that allows thermostats to maintain temperature in a building, computers to manufacture goods, guided missiles to reach their targets, and human beings to function in an often hostile world. It is about goal-oriented behavior at all levels of living systems. It allows these systems to reach defined goals based on information flows. It is a unifying theory that runs through all levels of human interaction. Though not frequently acknowledged, it played a role in the development of constructivism, particularly social constructivism—the notion that social institutions adapt through the constant processing of stimuli (information) from the environment.

Intelligence, defined as process, product, or people, collects and analyzes stimuli from the international environment. This information is used by decision makers as they act as helmsmen in steering the ship of state through the hazardous waters of international politics.

It should be obvious that all theories of intelligence or counterintelligence are overlaid on the traditional realist approach to international affairs. That is, it is the anarchic nature of global affairs that forces states to look out for their own interests, knowing that no others will look out for those interests for them. As long as states are sovereign, and as long as there is no ultimate authority among states, intelligence will be collected by all states, and counterintelligence efforts will be taken to protect state secrets.

COUNTERINTELLIGENCE

Counterintelligence "refers to the efforts taken to protect one's own intelligence operations from penetration and disruption by hostile nations" or groups and to protect state secrets.[6] Its primary functions are to:

- Protect classified information from unauthorized disclosure.
- Collect information about foreign intelligence services to prevent them from obtaining classified information from your nation.
- Collect information about hostile or potentially hostile group or state sponsored intelligence services to prevent them from disrupting or compromising your own operations through penetration, disinformation, or other means.
- Identify and recruit foreign intelligence agents to feed false and misleading information through them; that is, to "double" them and use them for your own purposes.

Counterintelligence Techniques

Several techniques, practices, and procedures are necessary to perform the primary functions.[7]

PRE-EMPLOYMENT PERSONNEL SECURITY

All intelligence community (IC) employees, as well as all people who handle classified information, are subject to background checks. These background checks begin with biographical information but include interviews with people who have known the applicants. For many IC agencies, this background check may also involve a polygraph or lie detector test. Although some scholars doubt the validity of the polygraph, few doubt that the fear of "being put on the box" has a deterring effect. While the Central Intelligence Agency (CIA), the National

Reconnaissance Office (NRO), the Defense Intelligence Agency (DIA), and the National Security Agency (NSA) have used the polygraph for many years, the Federal Bureau of Investigation (FBI) only began to polygraph employees after the disastrous Robert Hanssen case. Hanssen had spied for both the Soviet Union and Russia for about twenty-two years and would most likely have continued had his treason not been revealed by another spy who knew of his activities.

IN-SERVICE PERSONNEL SECURITY

Each agency also monitors its own employees during their period of employment. Many require periodic polygraph tests during which the employees are asked questions about their lifestyles as well as about foreign contacts and classified material they have handled. Other aspects of employee lifestyles—such as dramatic changes in financial worth, changes in spending habits, or aberrant sexual practices—are also observed independently and may provide questions for future polygraph sessions as well as act as warning signs to counterintelligence officers.

FACILITY SECURITY

Successful counterintelligence is impossible if facilities where secrets are produced and stored are not secure. Every agency in the IC as well as government offices, institutes, businesses, and contractors that handle classified information are responsible for facility security. Often this will also include computer security. Facility security varies widely from location to location, and some of America's worst security breaches have occurred at defense contractor facilities. It is the responsibility of IC counterintelligence officers to monitor security at all of these sites and to takes actions when that security is lax.

COMMUNICATIONS SECURITY

Overall communications security in the United States is the responsibility of the NSA, which provides, maintains, and verifies secure communications equipment at most IC agencies and other offices that handle classified information. However, each agency also carries out some communications security functions within its own facilities.

CLASSIFICATION AND COMPARTMENTATION

Information that might reveal sensitive national security secrets is classified by the government. Information may be classified both vertically and horizontally. There are three horizontal levels of classified information—confidential (used with decreasing frequency), secret, and top secret. Top secret information may be divided into vertical divisions called codeword compartments. The information in each compartment usually comes from a unique and specific intelligence collection source. That is, top secret/codeword material derived from a particular human source will be classified top secret and given a unique codeword. Information derived from intelligence intercepts of encrypted Soviet government communications throughout the 1950s, for example, was classified as top secret/Venona. A person's access to compartmented information is given on a need-to-know basis. That is, is knowledge of the particular information necessary for the performance of the person's official duties?

Issues of classification and compartmentation are continual thorns in the side of democratic governments. Virtually no one believes they protect classified information as they should, but virtually everyone agrees that governments have a legitimate right to keep sensitive national security information secret.

SIGNALS INTELLIGENCE

All intercepted communications are searched for clues that might reveal foreign agents operating in the United States or that might reveal U.S. persons working under foreign control. For example, the Venona project, already mentioned, was begun in 1941 by Army security and taken over by the NSA when it was created in 1952. The names of many well-known American and British traitors—Klaus Fuchs, Kim Philby, Alger Hiss, Julius and Ethel Rosenberg, just to name a few—were revealed through Venona decrypted information.

PROSECUTING TRAITORS

Antiespionage laws are not effective unless penalties exist for revealing or stealing secret information. Foreign agents in the United States who are caught stealing secrets or receiving classified information will be jailed if they do not have official cover, or they will be declared persona non grata and deported if they are in the country as a representative of their governments under official cover. U.S. citizens or U.S. persons who are caught revealing classified information are subject to federal prosecution.

Catching foreign agents or their American assets is a complicated task, primarily under the direction of the FBI. The Bureau, on the one hand, has a long history of detecting law breakers, gathering solid evidence against them, and then relying on the Department of Justice for prosecution. The CIA, on the other hand, prefers to detect traitors, monitor their activities, and use them as leads to other traitors and spies of whom they might not be aware. Rather than prosecuting them, they might wish to double them or supply them with misleading information. The clash between these two cultures has created a strained relationship between these two agencies marked by an absence of collaboration and cooperation of legendary proportions. And as has often been said, the success of counterintelligence in America rises or falls with the level of cooperation between the FBI and the CIA.

The counterintelligence techniques and practices listed here constitute an arsenal of no small significance. Nevertheless, the record of counterintelligence within the United States is not particularly distinguished. As William Webster, former director of both the FBI and the CIA, stated before U.S. Senate hearings in 2002, "Almost every spy that we have found both in the CIA and the FBI, has been found with the aid of recruited sources of our own in other hostile intelligence agencies."[8] In fact, from William Sebold, the German American recruited by German intelligence in 1939 who voluntarily became a double agent for the FBI, down to the most recent Americans caught in the act of treason, the information revealing them generally has come from defectors or from security files obtained from foreign states.

The testimony of former senior Soviet military spymaster Stanislav Lunev before the U.S. House of Representatives does not add any luster to the record of American counterintelligence. According to Lunev, "Despite the tireless work of the men and women of [US intelligence agencies], I must honestly report to you that obtaining highly sensitive and classified information was not very difficult."[9] In his testimony, Lunev went on to describe that while posing as a Soviet journalist, he attended the official unveiling of the Stealth aircraft, took photographs of highly sensitive parts of the aircraft, and sent them to Soviet military analysts to see what they could learn from them.

Assumptions of Counterintelligence Theory

Counterintelligence arises from the existence of four conditions or assumptions. First, it assumes that a nation has a decision-making system that deals with information that in the hands of hostile groups or nations, could jeopardize national security. Second, it assumes that a nation has one or more intelligence services that collect that information and then try to prevent it from falling into enemy hands. Third, it assumes that foreign intelligence services will attempt to obtain other nations' classified information through normal intelligence procedures (human intelligence and signals intelligence) as well as attempting to identify some who possess classified information and enticing them to reveal it. Fourth, a theory of counterintelligence assumes a very low level of trustworthiness in virtually all people. This last assumption will be discussed at greater length shortly.

These assumptions add up to a theory of counterintelligence that explains the existence of CI activities in the intelligence services in all internationally active nations. The first three assumptions fit nicely into each of the theories of intelligence discussed earlier. Counterintelligence is primarily defensive—it attempts to protect national secrets from other groups or nations in whose hands that information might be harmful. Kahn's theory of intelligence stresses its defensive value, a subsidiary function of which is counterintelligence. Johnson's theory is also useful in understanding counterintelligence. Among other things, it suggests that the extensiveness of a nation's global involvements explains the extensiveness and the costs of intelligence services. And the scope and extensiveness of a nation's intelligence services also explains both the efforts and the funds necessary to protect the security of the information collected.

The cybernetic theory of intelligence is what is called a "grand theory"—it explains a large variety of human behavior from which more narrow and specific activities can also be explained. As applied to the field of intelligence and counterintelligence, this theory also works very well. Nations require information so that decision makers can steer the ship of state safely through the hazardous waters of international politics. That information or intelligence diminishes in value if it is known to other nations or groups, particularly hostile ones. In fact, counterintelligence is essential for intelligence to be useful. Revealed classified information is more dangerous than the absence of information because it means that the steering of the ship of state may be based on false information, on information describing conditions that no longer exist, or on information deliberately revealed to deceive. Uncertainty about a state's environment may be better than unwarranted certainty, and the illusion of security may be worse than the absence of any intelligence services at all. As Thomas Powers has written,

> An insecure [intelligence] service is not merely useless; it is positively dangerous, because it allows a hostile agency to manipulate the penetrated organization, as the British, for example, manipulated German intelligence during World War II. MI 5 turned German agents in Britain, used them to feed false information to Germany, and thereby thoroughly confused the Germans as to the probable site and nature of the invasion of Europe. The Germans would have done better with no agents in Britain at all.... It is better to have no intelligence service at all than to have one which is insecure.[10]

Trust

More must be said about the fourth assumption of counterintelligence—the absence of trust—because it is particularly critical to an understanding of counterintelligence. Were all people fully trustworthy, many CI functions would be unnecessary. Most elements of personnel security and certain aspects of facility security (checking briefcases and packages that leave secure facilities, for example) would be unnecessary, and there would be few or no traitors to prosecute. Communication lines would still need to be made secure, and captured communications of other states would still have to be mined to see if foreign agents had penetrated any agencies or facilities, but it is the absence of trust that makes much of counterintelligence necessary.

This assumption is a human-level application of realism. It is based on that notion that for whatever reasons, humans possess an inherent dark side that causes them to doubt the goodness of others. Human nature is flawed, as Niebuhr and other realists have argued. Thus, they must always take steps to see that they are not hurt by their trust of others. When sixteen-year veteran CIA officer Harold Nicholson attempted to justify selling classified information to the Soviet Union, he explained that because his work had kept him away from his family and prevented him from being a good father, he thought he needed to look out for his own interests for once and earn some extra money for his family.

Not only is distrust the basis of much counterintelligence, but its very practice magnifies its presence. It is a curious conundrum—an automatic and self-feeding cycle that ultimately degenerates into paranoia and worse. The act of counterintelligence quite literally feeds feelings of suspicion, which in turn create greater distrust. And a culture of distrust spawns disgruntled employees who are ripe for recruitment by foreign intelligence services. In his 1953 play *Camino Real*, Tennessee Williams has the following dialogue:

John: "Why does disappointment make people unkind to each other?"

Marguerite: "Each of us is very much alone."

John: "Only if we distrust each other."

Marguerite: "We have to distrust each other. It is our only defense against betrayal."

As two former CIA employees have written, "The function of the counter-espionage officers is to question and verify every aspect of CIA operations; taking nothing at face value, they tend to see deceit everywhere. In an agency full of extremely mistrustful people, they are the professional paranoids."[11] Counterintelligence officers must distrust their fellow employees, look suspiciously at the good faith of—and even challenge—defectors, and study foreign intelligence entities so thoroughly so they begin to think like foreign intelligence agencies and officers.

James Jesus Angleton, the legendary and controversial director of CIA counterintelligence for over twenty years, described the landscape of counterintelligence as "a wilderness of mirrors," an "ever-fluid landscape where fact and illusion merge."[12] It is not an easy environment in which to work. Rebecca West has noted that "people who work in a self-contained [counterintelligence] unit are apt to develop theories which develop none the better for never being subject to open discussion."[13]

It is widely believed that Angleton's culture of distrust pervaded the CIA for so long that counterintelligence gained a very bad reputation within the agency—a reputation that lingered long after Angleton's forced resignation in 1974. In reaction to this culture of distrust, employees tended to question the need for both counterintelligence functions and officers. They tended to believe that their fellow officers who had been vetted and cleared and were in the service of their country could be trusted. It was a notion somewhat like joining a community service or business club; once a Rotarian, for example, one could be trusted forever.

This anticounterintelligence culture may have contributed to the failure to detect subsequent traitors throughout the entire IC. For example, the treason of Aldrich Ames, a CIA officer who spied for the Soviet Union and then for Russia for nine years, was nurtured partially by this culture. Information he sold resulted in the betrayal and death of nearly all of the CIA's most productive Soviet assets at the height of the Cold War. Time and time again, a failure to take counter-intelligence seriously, in part a reaction against the Angleton years, resulted in ignoring clear signals of Ames's treason.

On his just under $70,000 a year salary, Ames paid cash for a $540,000 home, purchased a $40,000 red Jaguar automobile (which he drove to work), and had money left over for cosmetic dental surgery. Ames once even cited Angleton's legacy as a reason for his decision to spy.[14] Whether this statement is true or merely his attempt to blame someone else for his actions, it is undoubtedly true that counterintelligence was not taken as seriously as it should have been at that time.

Sources of Treason

This trust-distrust paradox was first stated by first-century Roman philosopher and statesman Seneca in his *Letters to Lucilius*: "It is a vice to trust all, and equally a vice to trust none." But whom can you trust? This dilemma has provoked many to study the causes of betrayal and treason. It turns out that although many traitors on both sides of the Iron Curtain, particularly during the early years of the Cold War, were motivated by ideology, money has been the primary motivation of treason since the mid-1970s.[15] But if one examines secondary motives, that is, motives that led to ideological betrayal or selling out for monetary gain, the role of disgruntlement is growing. If one "considers those who, though not completely disgruntled, were not entirely 'gruntled' (to borrow from Oscar Wilde), then disgruntlement becomes a more prevalent motive" for treason.[16]

If the "trust assumption" aspect of counterintelligence theory is correct, then it may well be that a substantial part of the defense against treason in the future may be played by the human resources personnel in each intelligence agency. The ability to keep personnel satisfied with their employment may be one of the better defenses against treason, particularly against treason for financial gain. How to accomplish that is not the purpose of this chapter, however; enlightened and responsive leadership and management, collegial work conditions, the absence of cronyism in salary and advancement decisions, fair rewards for quality service, work equality, and employees who have bought into the mission of the agency for whom they work are certainly beginning points. Perhaps Andrew Roberts captured a glimpse of what was coming when he wrote in 1997, "Tomorrow's traitors are more likely to be driven to betray not from ideological convictions but from whining complaints about poor pension provisions or underfunded performance-related pay."[17]

SUMMARY AND CONCLUSION

This chapter began by defining intelligence, discussing how intelligence relates to national security, and then offered a brief review of three compatible and interrelated theories of intelligence. This was followed by a definition of counterintelligence, a summary of the primary functions of counterintelligence, and a review of CI techniques. Following that, four assumptions about counterintelligence were presented. These four assumptions provide a basis for a counterintelligence theory. At a general level of activity, this theory explains the existence of the practice of counterintelligence in virtually all states. The level of both intelligence and counterintelligence activities, as Johnson argues, depends on the extensiveness of a state's global activities and obligations.[18]

The absence of trust within societies appears to be the primary assumption in the theory of counterintelligence. Were all people trustworthy, much counterintelligence work would be unnecessary. That being the case, those who guard government secrets need to devote more time and energy into developing and nurturing trustworthiness within their employees. At the same time, a related effort needs to be made to reduce the rather high levels of disgruntlement among the custodians of national secrets.

This is a difficult task when, of necessity, the functions of counterintelligence are dispersed and decentralized throughout the IC and when the very practice of counterintelligence tends to alienate some employees. Clearly, the counterintelligence staff in every agency needs to take their work more seriously. Both routine as well as random security investigations need to be standard procedure rather than something done only when a traitor has been revealed. Perhaps the advice of the Countess to Bertram in Act I, Scene I, of Shakespeare's *All's Well That Ends Well* ought to be followed: "Love all, trust a few, do harm to none."

Counterintelligence personnel need to be well trained. There is a tendency to assume that any intelligence professional can be moved in and out of counterintelligence without additional training. And counterintelligence needs to be done in the field as well as at the home office. CI officers need to be rewarded within their field of specialization. Many feel that they need to get out of CI and into better career tracks or even to leave their agency and work in private industry. Counterintelligence is taken seriously in the United States only after a traitor has been revealed. After FBI agent Robert Hanssen was caught, the FBI acknowledged that it did not take security seriously. After CIA officer Aldrich Ames was caught, CIA officials acknowledged the same.

Finally, counterintelligence is the most difficult of all intelligence work. It is a thankless task where practitioners are in a lose-lose situation. If spies are found within U.S. agencies, it is called a counterintelligence failure. If they are not found, it may also be called a counterintelligence failure. What is often called the Law of Invisible Phenomena must be kept in mind: The absence of evidence is not evidence of absence.

NOTES

I thank the following for their help at various stages of the writing of this chapter: Kara Norman, Eric Lindsay, and Victoria Taylor.

1. Thomas Powers, *The Man Who Kept the Secrets: Richard Helms and the CIA* (New York: Knopf, 1979), cited in Charles E. Lathrop, *The Literary Spy* (New Haven: Yale University Press, 2004), 54.

2. Harold and Margaret Sprout, *Foundations of National Power: Readings on World Politics and American Security*, 2nd ed. (New York: Van Nostrand, 1962), 167–75.

3. David Kahn's theory is found in "An Historical Theory of Intelligence," *Intelligence and National Security* 16 (2001): 79–92; Loch K. Johnson's theory is found in "Preface to a Theory of Strategic Intelligence," *International Journal of Intelligence and Counterintelligence* 16 (2003–2004): 638–63.

4. Kahn, "An Historical Theory of Intelligence," 80.

5. This section is drawn from Stan Taylor, "Security and Intelligence," chapter 14 in Alan Collins, ed., *Contemporary Security Studies* (Oxford: Oxford University Press, 2006).

6. Mark M. Lowenthal, *Intelligence: From Secrets to Policy*, 2nd ed. (Washington, DC: CQ Press), 113.

7. The best available list of all counterintelligence techniques is found in Frederick L. Wettering, "Counterintelligence: The Broken Triad," *Intelligence and National Security* 13 (2000): 265–300.

8. Cited in Lathrop, *The Literary Spy*, 58.

9. Lunev's testimony was before the House National Security Committee on August 8, 1998, and is cited in Lathrop, *The Literary Spy*, 55.

10. Powers, *The Man Who Kept the Secrets*, as cited in Lathrop, *The Literary Spy*, 49.

11. Victor Marchetti and John Marks, *CIA and the Cult of Intelligence* (New York: Knopf, 1974), cited in Lathrop, *The Literary Spy*, 52.

12. The phrase actually comes from T. S. Eliot's 1920 poem "Gerontion." It has also been used as the title of several books, including one by former CIA officer David Martin in 1980 about Angleton. The subsequent quotation comes from Norman Polmar and Thomas B. Allen, *Spy Book: The Encyclopedia of Espionage*, 2nd ed. (New York: Random House Reference, 2004), 685.

13. *The New Meaning of Treason* (New York: Time, 1966), cited in Lathrop, *The Literary Spy*, 51.

14. Pete Early, *Confessions of a Spy* (New York: Putman's Sons, 1997), 146.

15. See Stan A. Taylor and Daniel Snow, "America's Cold War Spies: Why They Spied and How They Got Caught," *Intelligence and National Security* 12 (1997): 101–25. The best work on treason is done by the Defense Personnel Security Research Center in Monterey, California. See, for example, Susan Wood and Martin F. Wiskoff, *Americans Who Spied Against the Country Since World War II* (Monterey, CA, 1994); Lynn F. Fischer, "Espionage: Why Does It Happen," at http://www.hanford.gov/oci/maindocs/ci_r_docs/whyhappens.pdf, accessed (December 20, 2005); as well as Theodore R. Sabin and others, *Citizen Espionage: Studies in Trust and Betrayal* (Westport, CT: Praeger, 1994).

16. Taylor and Snow, "America's Cold War Spies," 110.

17. Andrew Roberts, *Sunday Times* (London), May 25, 1997, as cited in Lathrop, *The Literary Spy*, 398.

18. Johnson, "Preface to a Theory of Strategic Intelligence."

2

VENONA AND COLD WAR COUNTERINTELLIGENCE METHODOLOGY

NIGEL WEST

THE ROLE PLAYED BY VENONA IN COUNTERINTELLIGENCE operations conducted during the Cold War has been well documented since the decrypts were declassified and released to the public in July 1995. We now know, for example, that Alger Hiss was a Soviet spy, both Ethel and Julius Rosenberg were guilty of espionage, and such important figures in the Roosevelt administration as Harry Dexter White at the Treasury Department and Lauchlin Currie in the White House were part of a massive network directed from Moscow. VENONA proved to be the Holy Grail for British and American counterintelligence specialists to the extent that it provided leads to and offered links between hundreds of suspects. It also served to corroborate information from other sources, such as the testimony of Elizabeth Bentley, the NKVD (Narodnyy komissariat vnutennikh del, the Soviet foreign intelligence service) defector who was the catalyst for more than 100 FBI investigations following her statement made to special agents in September 1945.[1]

The attraction of VENONA is that in a sometimes murky counterespionage environment, it is as close to empirical evidence as can be found, but the paradox is that in legal terms the material was completely worthless and was never adduced in any criminal trial. The decrypts were, after all, the subjective application of cryptanalytical processes that could easily be refuted or undermined by defense counsel in any trial. In addition there was concern about maintaining secrecy of the nature of the source. At the time, the code breakers had narrowed the field of potential traitors to Klaus Fuchs and his friend the physicist Rudolf Peierls, who both appeared to fit the profile prepared by the mole hunters, VENONA remained an active source, with the Soviets continuing to rely on a compromised cipher system. Not surprisingly the Anglo-American teams working on the project were anxious not to alert their adversaries to the scale of the security breach, so even after the source appeared to terminate, with the Soviet introduction of new procedures, there was a keen desire to keep what had been achieved thus far as secret as possible. We now know that the Soviets received at least three warnings that their communications had been jeopardized. First, there is the recollection from Bentley that Currie had conveyed a message from his post in the White House as early as 1944 alerting the NKVD to the fact that the Americans had broken some of their traffic. Then, in 1947, a VENONA text concerning Judith Coplon indicated that the Americans had learned some of the code names routinely used for certain Washington institutions, such as the FBI (HUT) and the State Department (BANK).[2]

How could they have learned this? The most probable source of the leak was William Wiesband, a Russian linguist employed at Arlington Hall as an interpreter who had been indoctrinated into the project in 1945, as had his wife. Because neither were ever charged with espionage, Wiesband's status as one of the most important spies of the twentieth century has gone largely unrecognized outside of the Allied signals intelligence community, where he is still regarded as the discipline's most damaging traitor. The extent to which his wife assisted him, consciously or unconsciously, is unresolved. However, KGB retirees, such as Yuri Modin, have acknowledged that Wiesband tipped them off to the breakthrough accomplished by the Armed Forces Security Agency.[3] And equally certainly, it is acknowledged by all concerned that Kim Philby received a briefing on the project before he left London to take up his liaison role in Washington, DC, in September 1949.[4]

Indeed, Philby boasted in his 1968 memoirs, *My Silent War,* that he had immediately conveyed a message to his Soviet contact about the lapse, although his version suggests Soviet censors had a hand in concealing the precise details, doubtless to avoid embarrassment by admitting the appalling blunder that had allowed their opponents a window of opportunity which had been exploited so successfully. Certainly VENONA played a key role in the identification of Klaus Fuchs, and although he was convicted and imprisoned in 1950, neither he nor his MI5 interrogator, Jim Skardon, knew anything about the cryptographic source that had compromised him. Skardon was never indoctrinated into VENONA and knew only that the physicist had definitely spied for the Soviets while working on the Manhattan Project during World War II. This absence of doubt gave him a significant advantage, as did Fuchs's naiveté (bordering on intellectual arrogance) in his belief that his actions had not been criminal. During several interviews conducted over three months, Skardon persuaded Fuchs to confess that he had passed classified information to his Russian contacts, and the scientist proved so cooperative that he had subsequently identified an FBI surveillance photograph of Harry Gold as his principal Soviet contact in the United States. Nevertheless, it was VENONA that had supplied the first clues to the existence of a spy at Los Alamos in 1944 code-named REST and CHARLES, and it had taken five years of investigation to narrow the suspects down to Fuchs.

The Fuchs case (known to and filed by the FBI as FOOCASE) raises an interesting issue because Philby kept abreast of the investigation as it closed in on the physicist, and even before his departure for the United States he had sent a warning to the Soviets that the spy code-named CHARLES was in grave danger. He had been unable to deliver this vital message personally because his last meeting with his contact in London, Mikhail Shishkin, code-named ADAM, had taken place on September 21, before his indoctrination, so he had entrusted the information to Guy Burgess who, inexplicably, failed to pass it on for five months. When the news finally reached the London *rezidentura* on February 10, 1950, Fuchs had been under arrest for eight days. This was an astonishing lapse on the part of Burgess, then drifting in and out of an alcoholic haze, but it also served to suggest to the British and American mole hunters that the integrity of their source was intact, whereas in fact Moscow had made the necessary changes to their ciphers in 1949, unaware than Fuchs was already in dire peril. This all too human blunder on Burgess's part had the severest consequences, for as a result of Fuchs's arrest and confession, Harry Gold was identified, and thereafter the domino effect led to the electric chair for the Rosenbergs.

If, alternatively, Philby's warning had been relayed properly by Burgess, and Fuchs had been withdrawn before he could be interrogated, their subsequent history would have been very different indeed, with Gold and the Rosenbergs probably escaping, too. Understandably, this episode caused consternation in Moscow.

According to Philby's message to Burgess, the Americans had worked on the Soviet traffic for years, with minimal success, but the British Government Communications Headquarters (GCHQ) had achieved impressive results recently. Burgess later insisted that he had included Philby's tip in a personal note that had been photographed by Anthony Blunt, together with other documents, and then handed to Yuri Modin. Naturally, Moscow was alarmed by this news, particularly when Shishkin confirmed that Philby had said nothing about the decryption effort when they had met on September 21. Certainly Modin had received three rolls of film from Blunt on October 11, but when the pictures had been developed they had been found to be overexposed and out of focus. As for Burgess's personal note, it was re-examined in Moscow and found to say nothing about CHARLES.[5]

At their subsequent meeting, held on October 25, 1950, Burgess had promised to recopy the documents, and on December 7 had produced 168 documents, totaling 660 pages, but no personal note. Thus a combination of Blunt's camera error and Burgess's forgetfulness had ensured that the warning about Fuchs failed to reach Moscow. Burgess had said nothing to Modin, and Philby had been out of contact with his handlers while he had settled into his new post in America. Fuchs, of curse, could have been exfiltrated in September or even December 1949, and at the very least he could have been briefed on how to resist an MI5 interrogation, although the *rezidentura* had been out of direct touch with the spy since mid-1949. Although Fuchs seemed quite oblivious to the gravity of his situation and his imminent peril, there was actually no solid evidence against him, so his confession was vital to MI5. A simple, persistent denial would have stymied his adversaries.

According to Modin, reporting on their meeting on February 10, 1950, Burgess reacted with "calm and composure" to the news of the physicist's arrest but accepted that a mistake had been made. Soviet intelligence immediately suspended contact with Burgess and Blunt for six weeks, but Burgess failed to turn up at the next scheduled rendezvous on March 20, 1950, nor did he show up at any of the prearranged back-up meetings. However, at the beginning of April he left emergency signals for Modin and contact was restored on April 17. "Instead of YAN, PAUL came to the meeting without materials," reported the *rezidentura* (referring to Blunt and Burgess, respectively), which submitted a lengthy report on the crisis to Moscow by courier rather than cipher.[6]

Apparently Burgess had not attended the meetings in March because Philby (code-named STANLEY) had been summoned to London by the British Secret Intelligence Service (SIS) to discuss the Fuchs affair. Philby's account of the VENONA project, as he understood it, is illuminating:

> STANLEY asked to communicate that the Americans and the British had constructed a deciphering machine which in one day does "the work of a thousand people in a thousand years," Work on deciphering is facilitated by three factors: (1) A one-time pad was used twice; (2) Our cipher resembles the cipher of our trade organisation in the USA; (3) A half-burnt codebook has been found in Finland and passed to the British and used to decrypt our communications. They will succeed within six to twelve months. The CHARLES case has shown the counter-intelligence service the importance of knowing the past of civil servants. Although STANLEY is trusted, [Valentine] Vivian considers that STANLEY's past is not entirely clear. A role in establishing STANLEY's past may be played by his first wife who is somehow connected to the CHARLES case. STANLEY, PAUL and YAN consider that the situation is serious. A long meeting is needed to discuss it.[7]

The meeting was arranged for May 15, and Modin was instructed to calm Burgess and arrange a further meeting for him with the *rezident*, Nikolai Korovin, for June 4. Modin's meeting with Burgess was "businesslike" and he was "very calm, self-possessed, unhurried."

When Burgess offered to give Korovin at the next meeting a bundle of Foreign Office documents about the recent conference of the three foreign ministers, Modin forbade him. The second meeting with Korovin was held in a quiet suburban park and lasted six and a half hours. The marathon length was accounted for by the anxieties of the Cambridge spy-ring about the threat posed to them by the new menace, described as the "decryption machine," which was the latest generation of GCHQ's computers, then completely unknown to the wider public, that had only recently become aware of relatively primitive automated data processors and card sorters. Korovin admitted that mistakes had been made in the Soviet cipher procedures but tried to reassure Burgess that the errors had been limited and only occurred in wartime. He insisted that no "supermachine" existed capable of cracking the Soviet codes.

Korovin's reassurance is curious and raises the question of whether he was attempting to blithely calm the Cambridge Five or convey an informed message from Moscow. In fact, of course, the mole hunters were by then on the trail of both CHARLES and another quarry, code-named HOMER, who was revealed in April 1951 as Donald Maclean.

The most immediate worry in 1950 was Philby's safety. Burgess relayed to Korovin that Blunt had explained how, during the period in 1940 when the network had been out of direct contact with the *rezidentura*, their communications had been maintained through Edith Tudor-Hart, who had passed information to Bob Stewart of the Communist Party of Great Britain (CPGB). Blunt had recalled that during his conversations with Litzi Philby, she had mentioned the desirability of recruiting an atomic scientist, and he had gained the impression that she had found a suitable candidate. He was worried that if her nominee had been Klaus Fuchs, he might compromise her. It followed that if Fuchs exposed Litzi, the entire network would be put in jeopardy, but Korovin had assured Burgess that Fuchs was unconnected with Litzi. He subsequently submitted a report on the meeting for the *rezidentura*, which reached Moscow.

Before Burgess bade Korovin farewell, he returned to his preoccupation about exposure:

> Before leaving for the United States STANLEY asked PAUL to communicate to us his personal request for granting him political asylum in the USSR in case of obvious danger. PAUL added that essentially it was also a question of granting asylum to him, PAUL. YAN, like STANLEY and PAUL, was strongly alarmed by recent events but showed no signs of cowardice and made no hasty conclusions. In PAUL's opinion, if serious danger threatens, YAN will commit suicide. PAUL said that YAN's moral qualities are not like STANLEY's and PAUL's. STANLEY and PAUL think themselves politicians who have gone through the hard school of life, know what struggle is and know they should achieve their aim. PAUL considers YAN a good comrade, entirely devoted to our cause, but the spirit of an intellectual which is characteristic of YAN's profession is still firm in him, and this spirit makes him accept the inevitable and he doesn't mobilise for the struggle.[8]

Dismayed by Blunt's gloomy prognosis, Korovin asked Burgess to point out the senselessness of Blunt's frame of mind and persuade him to "abandon all thoughts of suicide." Burgess, Philby, and Blunt "can certainly count on our help," insisted Korovin, but when he announced that further personal meetings would have to be suspended, Burgess replied that he "saw no signs of danger" and that he was ready to resume passing documents, either originals, on film, or in the form of personal notes. Korovin declined the offer and provided a new procedure for establishing contact. He concluded the meeting on an optimistic chord: "PAUL was in a good mood. He came to the meeting sober. He thanked me for a long time for my conversation with him and asked to assure the Centre [Soviet intelligence] that everything was all right with him and that he would wait for instructions about passing over material to us."[9]

This meeting was something of a milestone, and it was not until July 1, 1950, that Ivan Chichayev (code-named ROSS) and Mikhail Shishkin had prepared "a summary of ROSS's talk with PAUL." Its conclusion, endorsed by the London rezidentura, was:

> Taking into account the absence of any dangerous signs concerning THE FIVE to conduct the prearranged meeting with PAUL in the first half of July at which to arrange for a meeting with YAN in a month's time for receiving materials. In future to receive documents from PAUL and YAN only on undeveloped film and at personal meetings. To give consent to the *rezidentura*'s suggestion about continuing work with PAUL and YAN and to receiving materials from them.[10]

On July 1, it was Burgess, not Blunt, that went to the arranged meeting and, in accordance with instructions, he arrived empty-handed. He gave an oral account of the war in Korea and said that he would be departing to the United States on July 28. At his next meeting, held on July 8, he passed over a film of Foreign Office papers and received instructions on how to establish contact with the Soviets in Washington, D.C.

Thus, as the mole hunters had disposed of Fuchs and were closing in on Maclean, the Soviets seemed oblivious to the escalating dangers posed by the VENONA project and more concerned about the security of personal meetings with rezidentura personnel. Fuchs had pleaded guilty to charges of breaches of the Official Secrets Act, so his trial had taken only a matter of hours for sentence to be pronounced, and no mention had been made of how MI5 identified him as a spy in the first place. In any event, the Soviets could not have harbored any illusions about how Fuchs had been caught, and their apparent complacency in letting the net narrow around Maclean is chilling. Philby had given what would prove to be a very accurate forecast of the progress that would be achieved by the cryptanalysts, yet his controllers seemed willing to allow both him and Burgess to remove themselves from London, where they might have been in a position to influence events or protect Maclean. It may be that the Soviets felt unable to intervene when their two best spies announced their new postings, and Philby's transfer from SIS's Istanbul station to Washington must have seemed to them like hitting the intelligence jackpot. Nevertheless, the ineptitude with which Soviet intelligence handled the deteriorating situation does seem breathtaking, especially when one considers that Philby hardly knew Maclean and had to guess for himself the true identify of the mole code-named HOMER.

From Philby's perspective, Burgess's arrival in Washington must have been quite a relief and at the very least a welcome opportunity to discuss the growing crisis with him privately. Burgess, of course, was the Cambridge Five's puppetmaster and knew the full ramifications better than anyone else. Alone, the two men would have been bound to consider their options, talk about the likelihood of Blunt's suicide, and debate tactics to save Maclean.

The Fuchs example demonstrated how easily a network could unravel and the skill of the FBI, which had zeroed in on Harry Gold and enabled the scientist to identify him from a photograph when he had never learned his true name. Fuchs probably had not realized the likely consequences of this identification, and it is obvious he tried to protect his original contact, Ursula Kuczynski, whose true name was also unknown to him. She was, however, already familiar to MI5 as an espionage suspect because she had been denounced by Allan Foote in 1947 and had been interviewed by Jim Skardon on that occasion. The encounter had proved unproductive—she had denied any involvement in Soviet espionage in England, and at the time MI5 had no choice but to accept her denials. Nevertheless, she had fled the country as soon as Fuchs's arrest had been announced.[11]

If Maclean had cracked under questioning in the same way, what might he have disclosed? He knew nothing incriminating about Kim Philby or the other member of the Cambridge Five, John Cairncross, but apart from Burgess and Blunt he could have exposed Kitty Harris, his former lover and NKVD handler in prewar London and Paris. By 1951 Harris was safely back in the Soviet Union, having completed her last assignment as an illegal in the United states, so Maclean really only represented a threat to Burgess and Blunt, and of course his own wife, Melinda, in whom he had confided shortly before their marriage in France in 1940.[12]

While the mole hunters had been searching for CHARLES, other VENONA texts, eight in all, implicated Judith Coplon, who had appeared in the traffic with the code name SIMA. These intercepts made the FBI realize in 1948, as the first text of January 1945 had indicated, that a spy had been at work in the Justice Department in Washington. As soon as Special Agent Bob Lamphere extracted the vital date of the spy's commencement in her new post, February 15, 1945, on an internal transfer from New York, Coplon's identity was confirmed by Inspector Leo Lauchlin in consultation with the assistant attorney-general as SIMA, for she was the only person to have switched from the Justice Department's Economic Warfare section to Washington, as had been mentioned in the traffic.[13]

Preliminary inquiries into Coplon's background showed that her parents were living in Brooklyn, and she had graduated in 1943 from Barnard College, where she had been involved briefly with the Young Communist League. The question for the FBI was how she could be caught on a charge of espionage, bearing in mind that her position gave her access to files on the FBI's current investigations, which doubtless was why no prosecutions had resulted from the allegations made by Elizabeth Bentley. By the time the FBI had gone in pursuit of the members of Nathan Silvermaster's network, there was absolutely no incriminating evidence to be found, even in the extensive photographic laboratory discovered in the basement of his suburban home. Quite obviously, Coplon had allowed the NKVD to remain one step ahead of the FBI, tipping off the Soviets each time a new suspect came under the FBI's scrutiny, so the only action to be taken was the removal of suspects from their jobs. This had effectively eliminated the spy-rings headed by Silvermaster and Victor Perlo but had allowed their subordinate members to evade prosecution. As Coplon was routinely handling internal security dossiers at her office in the Foreign Agents Registration section of the Justice Department, her hand in their escape was all too obvious. The only advantage to the FBI was to learn which personalities currently under investigation were of interest to the Soviets. In this way suspicion hardened against Joseph Bernstein, a courier whose name appeared on one of the FBI files compromised by Coplon.

Coplon was placed under discreet surveillance, which revealed that she was having an illicit affair with Harold Shapiro, a Justice Department attorney, and that she made two trips a month to New York to visit her parents. When she was followed to Manhattan on January 14, 1949, she was seen to meet a man for dinner who subsequently was identified as Valentin A. Gubitchev, an employee of the United Nations secretariat, and they were watched at two further meetings, on February 18 and March 4. At this latter rendezvous, both were arrested, and Gubitchev was found to be carrying an envelope containing $125, and Coplon's handbag revealed a wealth of classified data, including some documents that had been prepared by the FBI as a barium meal to test whether she gave them to her Soviet contacts.

At her trial, the FBI concealed the exact nature of the "confidential informant" that had led the investigation of Coplon, and she deployed the defense that her relationship with Gubitchev was entirely romantic and the information she had been carrying was nothing more than notes she had prepared for writing a novel. The prosecution neatly destroyed the "innocent liaison" ploy by disclosing details of her affair with Shapiro, so she was convicted and received a sentence of between forty months and ten years' imprisonment for conspiring to pass classified secrets to Gubitchev, who was also convicted.

Coplon's conviction was later overturned on appeal on the technicality that the FBI's telephone intercept had been unlawful. Because the clear impression had been left that the FBI had begun its investigation as a consequence of a wiretap on Coplon's office line, all the evidence that flowed from that source was deemed inadmissible. The alternative was to reveal that the FBI had been led to Coplon by VENONA, but that expedient was considered too high a price to pay, so she was freed to marry one of her lawyers, Albert H. Socolov, and settle in Brooklyn, where she opened several restaurants.

As well as losing Coplon, the FBI also missed Flora Wovschin, code-named ZORA, the daughter of Russian immigrants who had been responsible for Coplon's recruitment in the first place. She, too, had joined the Communist Youth League at Barnard College and later went to work for the Office of War Information in Washington. In 1947 she had resigned from the civil service to marry an Amtorg engineer, but by the time the FBI had started to look for her in 1949 she had moved to Moscow. No action was taken against her mother and stepfather, but the FBI did attempt to identify the other members of her network. The fact that Flora had continued to be active after the war was revealed in a VENONA text from Moscow dated March 11, 1945, marking Stepan Apresyan's appointment to be *rezident* in San Francisco, which designated Vladimir Pravdin (code-named SERGEI) as her controller, with a *referentura* clerk, Olga V. Khlopkova (code-named JULIA), responsible for processing her information:

[16 groups unrecoverable] in San Francisco the work of ALBERT's [Iskhak Akhmerov] office. The operational direction of ZORA [6 groups unrecovered] JULIA [Olga Khlopkova] will deal with his documents under SERGEI's [Vladimir Pravdin] direction.

The scale of Wovschin's activities can be judged by this cable, sent from Moscow two days later:

Your 203. ALAN—Ralph Bowen, works in the BANK [State Department] as assistant [3 groups unrecovered] economics. He and his wife Sue are acquaintances of ZORA and together with the latter were members of the GYMNASTIC organisation [Young Communist League]. In so far as ZORA works in the BANK, [5 groups unrecovered] with them the former friendly relations.

DROP—Philip E. MOSELEY. Up to 1943 worked in the Russian Section of the HUT [OSS]. Since 1943 has been in the BANK in the Division of Territorial Studies. In 1932–34 has [2 groups unrecovered] member of the staff of HARVARD University and [42 groups unrecovered] friend of BLERIOT. According to the latter's information is progressively inclined.

DUVER—our PROBATIONER [agent] in VADIM's office.

ROBERT—connected with the NEIGHBOURS.

OSWARD—Benjamin GERIG [6 groups unrecovered] in the BANK. We have no other data on [1 group unrecovered].

Whether Wovschin remained active until her departure for Moscow is uncertain, but her absence ensured the FBI made no further progress in its pursuit of her. According to the CIA, she participated in anti-American propaganda operations during the Korean War and died soon afterward.

The parallel cases against Fuchs and Coplon serve to illustrate the way in which the VENONA source fitted into the investigative jigsaw puzzle, and while offering an unrivaled glimpse into the adversary's activities, most certainly did not guarantee a criminal conviction or even ensure that espionage could be disrupted. In the example of Coplon, the central figure, Wovschin, was never even interviewed by the FBI, and some of the other personalities mentioned as her recruits were never identified.

The two best-known cases of Soviet espionage exposed by VENONA were those of Klaus Fuchs and Donald Maclean, although the latter defected to Moscow in May 1951 before he could be confronted. Other spies, who might have achieved similar notoriety, also escaped justice. Lauchlin Currie, Joel Barr, and Al Sarant moved abroad. Harry Dexter White died of a heart attack in 1948, and Laurence Duggan, formerly Roosevelt's aide, committed suicide. Although plenty of other spies were to emerge in the VENONA material, among them Ted Hall, Kim Philby, Morris and Lona Cohen, and Bill Wiesband, none of these names were broken by the cryptographers in time to ensure the mole hunters could take full advantage of the information. Indeed, Wiesband's identification as LINK was not made until the declassification process was under way, more than two decades after his death in May 1967. Actually, the only VENONA traffic directly relevant to contemporaneous counterintelligence operations were the cables exchanged between Moscow and Canberra in 1948, which were read within days of their interception.

Close study of VENONA's counterintelligence value reveals that the raw texts were a component in a larger canvas constructed with contributions from defector testimony (mainly from Elizabeth Bentley, Whittaker Chambers, and Hede Massing), physical and technical surveillance conducted by the FBI, and confidential information extracted from informants whose identities are still protected. These bland categories give no clue to the dramas they concealed: the illicit wiretaps routinely carried out by FBI technicians; the black-bag jobs performed by teams of skilled burglars whose illegal activities were authorized at the highest levels of government; the vast photo libraries of espionage suspects that accrued during street investigations; the monitoring of the vehicle registration plates of cars parked in the vicinity of suspected subversive gatherings; the wholesale penetration of the Communist Party of the United States of America (CPUSA) by legions of paid informants. Only the tiny tip of this investigative iceberg ever surfaced, so it is hard to assess the precise proportion any one indicator gave in the identification of a VENONA code name. Some of the identities were obvious, with the cover names proving semi-transparent or the real name being referred to in plain text, whereas others were much more elusive, and some were demonstrably wrong. The best example of error is the famous blunder in which RELAY was named as Morton Sobell, whereas Professor Philip Morrison was the more likely candidate.

Unquestionably VENONA deserves its reputation as the keystone of Anglo-American counterintelligence investigations, and the fact that the project was not closed down until 1979 suggests its long-term utility, but its longevity conceals some stark realities: VENONA did not implicate Philby or Burgess until it was too late to exploit it. Only Klaus Fuchs was imprisoned as a direct consequence of the source, and his conviction could have been avoided if the Soviets had acted on the information that we now know was available to them at the time.

NOTES

1. Elizabeth Bentley's *Out of Bondage* did not include all the names of spies she identified in her November 1945 statement to the FBI, which has now been declassified.

2. Judith Coplon's prosecution is best described by Marcia and Thomas Mitchell in *The Spy Who Seduced America* (New York: Invisible Cities Press, 2002).

3. In his autobiography *My Five Cambridge Friends* (London: Hodder Headline, 1995), Modin incorrectly identified the source of the NKVD's information about VENONA.

4. Kim Philby, *My Silent War* (London: McGibbon & See, 1968).

5. Nigel West and Oleg Tsarev, *Crown Jewels* (New Haven, CT: Yale University Press, 1999).

6. Ibid.

7. Ibid.
8. Ibid.
9. Ibid.
10. Ibid.
11. Ruth Werner, *Sonia's Report* (London: Chatto & Windus, 1991).
12. Kitty Harris, *The Spy with Seventeen Names* (London: St Ermin's Press, 2001).
13. Robert Lamphere, *The FBI-KGB War* (New York: Random House, 1986).

BIBLIOGRAPHY

Adamson, Iain. *The Great Detective.* London: Frederick Muller, 1966.

Albright, Joseph, and Marcia Kunstel. *Bombshell.* New York: Random House, 1997.

Bamford, James. *The Puzzle Palace.* Boston: Houghton, Mifflin, 1982.

Belfrage, Cedric. *Something to Guard.* New York: Columbia University Press, 1978.

Benson, Robert Louis, and Michael Warner. *VENONA: Soviet Espionage and the American Response 1939–1957,* Washington, DC: National Security Agency, 1996).

Bentley, Elizabeth. *Out of Bondage.* New York: Devin-Adair, 1951.

Bly, Herman O. *Communism: The Cold War and the FBI Connection.* New York: Huntingdon House, 1998.

Burt, Leonard. *Commander Burt of Scotland Yard.* London: Heinemann, 1959.

Carpozi, George. *Red Spies in Washington.* New York: Trident Press, 1965.

Clark, Ronald. *J.B.S.* London: Quality Books, 1968.

Clubb, O. Edmund. *The Witness and I.* New York: Columbia University Press, 1974.

Dallin, David. *Soviet Espionage.* New Haven, CT: Yale University Press, 1955.

Foote, Alexander. *Handbook for Spies.* London: Museum Press, 1964.

Haldane, Charlotte. *Truth Will Out.* London: Vanguard Press, 1950.

Harris, Kitty. *The Spy with Seventeen Names.* London: St Ermin's Press, 2001.

Huss, Pierre J., and George Carpozi. *Red Spies in the UN.* New York: Coward-McCann, 1965.

Kahn, David. *The Codebreakers.* London: Wiedenfeld & Nicolson, 1966).

Kalugin, Oleg. *The First Directorate.* New York: St Martin's Press, 1994.

Klehr, Harvey. *The Secret World of American Communis*m. New Haven, CT: Yale University Press, 1995.

Klehr, Harvey, and Ronald Radosh. *The Amerasia Spy Case.* Charlotte: University of North Carolina Press, 1996.

Knightley, Philip. *The Hack's Progress.* London: Bloomsbury, 1997.

Kuczynski, Ruth. *Sonia's Report.* London: Chatto & Windus, 1991.

Lamphere, Robert. *The FBI-KGB War.* New York: Random House, 1986.

Mitchell, Marcia and Thomas. *The Spy Who Seduced America.* New York: Invisible Cities Press, 2002.

Modin, Yuri. *My Five Cambridge Friends.* London: Hodder Headline, 1995.

Montagu, Ivor. *The Youngest Son.* London: Lawrence & Wishart, 1970.

Moorhead, Alan. *The Traitors.* London: Harper & Row, 1952.

Moynihan, Daniel Patrick. *Secrecy.* New Haven, CT: Yale University Press, 1998.

Peake, Hayden. *OSS and the VENONA Decrypts, 12 Intelligence & National Security* (July 1997), pp. 14–34.

Peierls, Rudolf. *Bird of Passage*. Princeton, NJ: Princeton University Press, 1985.

Philby, Kim. *My Silent War*. London: McGibbon & Kee, 1968.

Radosh, Ronald, and Joyce Milton. *The Rosenberg File*. New York: Holt, Rinehart & Winston, 1983.

Rees, David. *Harry Dexter White*. New York: Coward, McCann & Geoghegan, 1973.

Report of the Royal Commission, Canada, 1946.

Report of the Royal Commission, Australia, 1956.

Smyth, Henry D. *Atomic Energy for Military Purposes*. Princeton, NJ: Princeton University Press, 1945.

Stone, I. F. *The War Years, 1939–45*. Boston: Little, Brown, 1988.

Werner, Ruth. *Sonia's Report*. London: Chatto & Windus, 1991.

West, Nigel, and Oleg Tsarev. *Crown Jewels*. New Haven, CT: Yale University Press, 1999.

Wright, Peter. *Spycatcher*. New York: Viking Penguin, 1987.

3

CATCHING SPIES IN THE UNITED STATES

KATHERINE A. S. SIBLEY

FROM THE MOMENT OF THE AMERICAN REVOLUTION, when plotters like Benedict Arnold and John André attempted to snuff out the nascent republic, through the aftermath of September 11, 2001, when terrorists' attacks on the World Trade Center and the Pentagon stunned Americans and created a crisis that is still unfolding, national anxiety over the domestic influence of foreign spies and conspirators has seldom disappeared from American political culture. Catching them has remained a high priority.

John André was perhaps the first spy to be executed by Americans. Sneaking through American lines holding a passport for "John Anderson," with Arnold's plans for the British to take West Point hidden in his stockings, André was intercepted by Continental troops, who turned him in rather than accept proffered bribes of his steed or his watch. André was sentenced to death and hanged on October 2, 1780. Yet despite some celebrated espionage cases in the next major American conflict, the Civil War—including that of Confederate spy Rose O'Neal Greenhow, a well-connected Southerner who infiltrated Northern elite circles, continued spying from prison, and was eventually deported back to the Confederacy—more than a century passed after André's execution before the U.S. government set up intelligence agencies to look for spies. During the 1880s, in response to a growing imperialist push abroad as well as the increased value placed on "professional expertise" at home, the Navy and the War Department both set up intelligence offices, the Navy's in 1882, and the War Department's in 1885. By 1889, the War Department's new Division of Military Information was sending military attachés to five countries. Still, its intelligence-gathering role was rather passive until the Spanish-American War, when Division staff assisted in furnishing information about Cuba and uncovering insurgent plots in the Philippines. Afterward, this work once again was neglected as the Division suffered from a bureaucratic squeeze that banished it to a remote corner of the capital. Even so, the Justice Department went ahead and set up its Bureau of Investigation in 1909, which played a pivotal role in catching spies later.

For the military, another war was necessary for any revitalization of intelligence collection, and thus it was not until May 1917 that the indomitable Maj. Ralph Van Deman was able to overcome the resistance of top brass to create a newly powerful Military Information Section, despite his superiors being perfectly content with what intelligence the British and French deigned to share with the War Department. It was high time; espionage was already key to the U.S. war effort, thanks to the (British) discovery of the Zimmerman Telegram three months earlier, and its exposure of a German-Mexican plot against the United States. Van Deman also set up a Code and Cipher Bureau during the war to decode foreign cable traffic, which was led by Herbert Yardley and known as the Black Chamber.

The military's intelligence operation thus grew rapidly and included both positive and negative divisions: "positive," to gather information about other countries, and "negative," to stop them from picking up intelligence here. It was in the negative, or counterintelligence function that van Deman particularly excelled, setting up machinery to oversee both the armed forces and civilian populations, whom he deemed as riddled with subversive foreigners. Foreign agents were indeed active; as early as 1914, German military attaché Franz von Papen had organized a sabotage, espionage, and subversive campaign against the United States, which was discovered in 1915 when his agent, Dr. Heinrich Albert, foolishly left his briefcase—full of plans and money—on a train. Albert, von Papen, and other German and Austrian conspirators were soon thrown out of the country, but this did not prevent their successors from engineering the massive Black Tom explosion of 1916, blowing up millions of tons of munitions in northern New Jersey that were headed for Britain.

As the Army's efforts to find spies thus accelerated during the war, so did those of Congress. In 1917, it passed the Espionage Act, which included a $10,000 fine and twenty years' imprisonment for such acts as preventing the recruitment of armed forces personnel, refusing to enlist, or revealing information related to defense. The act sent nearly 1,000 Americans to prison in World War I, including Eugene Debs and Emma Goldman. (Debs was sentenced to ten years in 1918 for speaking out against the act and was pardoned by President Warren G. Harding in 1921; Goldman was sent to prison for opposing the draft, and was then deported to Russia in 1919.)

Van Deman's Military Information Section also officially encouraged private groups such as the American Protective League, also founded in 1917, to identify dissenters. Its thousands of members raided leftist groups like the International Workers of the World but unearthed few spies. Following the war, the Justice Department's Bureau of Investigation went on a massive raid of its own, otherwise known as the Red Scare, arresting more than 1,500 and sending nearly 250 back to Russia on the *Buford*.

A postwar cooling-off period followed the wartime hysteria, although this more relaxed atmosphere also permitted many spies to operate unheeded in the United States during the 1920s and 1930s. Ex-spy Whittaker Chambers believed that the 1930s were, in fact, the heyday of Soviet espionage: "To this period belongs the recruiting of the best Soviet sources. . . . The secret service rode along for almost a decade simply exploiting, and seldom seeking to amplify, this corps."[1] Chambers himself is best known for his filching of State Department documents supplied by Alger Hiss in the mid- to late 1930s, though he had contacts at numerous government departments. He even worked in military espionage, meeting a mathematician at the Aberdeen Proving Ground who supplied him classified materials on aircraft bombsights. Dwight D. Eisenhower later admonished his interwar predecessors for their largely nonexistent counterintelligence response to such practices and blamed it on domestic culture: "The American public has always viewed with repugnance everything that smacks of the spy."[2]

Yardley's outfit did continue for a time as part of the State Department; its most important achievement was spying on Japanese representatives at the Washington Naval Conference and thus learning their negotiating points. But much of the other intelligence work established by van Deman fell by the wayside, and the Black Chamber itself was abolished in 1929, owing in part to Secretary of State Henry Stimson's view that "Gentlemen do not read each other's mail." The Army was less scrupulous; in 1930, it set up the Signals Intelligence Service (SIS) to intercept signal traffic, break codes, and train cryptologists. It was this agency that began to collect secret Soviet communications in World War II, in a project code-named VENONA, which led to the later discoveries of atomic spies detailed below.

In 1930 Congress also conducted an investigation into communist activities, under the leadership of Hamilton Fish (R-NY). Upset by its findings, the Fish committee recommended that alien communists should be deported and Party members should be prevented from using the mails. In line with public opinion in this period, however, newspapers responded critically, arguing that Fish and company exhibited "symptoms of the sort of mental stampede that should be reined in by . . . long established American ideals."[3]

Despite the severe limitations on investigative activity in this era, spies were occasionally foiled. In 1931, William Disch, who designed firing control instruments for the Navy, met a man called Herb, posing as a German spy, who wanted to pay up to $2,000 for the technology. The Office of Naval Intelligence allowed Disch to supply Herb with obsolete blueprints. Bureau of Investigation agents soon spotted Herb taking the documents not into the German embassy but into Amtorg, the Soviet trading agency in New York. Even so, agents had no idea then about the far greater amounts of secret information being provided to Amtorg by Philadelphia chemist Harry Gold, who repeatedly raided the technology of his employer, Pennsylvania Sugar, preparing himself for a far more ambitious atomic espionage career in World War II. In this cautious era, not even J. Edgar Hoover, director of the newly named Federal Bureau of Investigation (FBI), was ready to have his agenda expanded into investigating "Communistic inner circles," especially if it placed the Bureau in the light of "Agents Provocateur."[4]

As a result, not only Soviet but German agents as well had a field day. In the mid-1930s, Dr. Ignatz Griebl, a German-born Nazi sympathizer living in Manhattan, recruited some of his German patients to spy for the fatherland; they succeeded in garnering blueprints from the Bath Iron Works, the Boston Navy Yard, and the Douglas Aircraft Corporation, among others. Griebl's work was part of a larger ring associated with Guenther Gustave Rumrich, an American educated in Austria. Thanks to a tip from British military intelligence, in 1938 the FBI arrested Rumrich and his associates; however, fourteen of the men charged escaped, including Griebl. This botch was only one of the FBI's missteps in the disastrous persecution of the case, which culminated in the firing of its chief investigator for signing a publicity contract. Despite the errors, the FBI's crime-fighting profile had already been considerably enhanced in this era with its successes in the Lindbergh kidnapping case and several celebrated bank robberies. When Europe's turn to war in August 1939 put the country in a state of emergency, the agency took on a new role in counterespionage work.

Hoover was now no longer shy in packaging his agency as a bulwark against the threatening clouds from abroad. That summer, Franklin D. Roosevelt set up an Interdepartmental Intelligence Committee made up of the FBI, the War Department's Military Intelligence Division, and the Navy's Office of Naval Intelligence and pronounced that "no investigation... into matters involving actually or potentially any espionage, counterespionage, or sabotage" could be undertaken except by those three agencies.[5] But Hoover quickly and effectively gained sole jurisdiction over domestic espionage and sabotage outside military personnel. His agency would brook no rivals; armed with its mandate from the White House, the FBI was intent "to head the Nation's attack against foreign spies, saboteurs, and subverters," as Hoover told the American Legion.[6]

The Bureau grew accordingly. Between 1940 and 1945, FBI agents mushroomed from 900 to almost 5,000. And from 1933 to 1945 the Bureau's budget expanded from $2.7 million to $45 million. The ineffectiveness of other agencies (like the State Department) to hinder their own species of spy also expanded the Bureau's purview abroad; in 1940, following the arrest for espionage of Tyler Kent, a disgruntled code clerk at the American embassy in London, FBI undercover agent Louis Beck came snooping and found incredibly lax disposal of secret materials and disturbingly intimate relations between embassy staff and local prostitutes.

Another success for the FBI was its crafty handling of a Nazi ring revealed in 1940 by defector William G. Sebold, an aircraft mechanic who had spied for Germany. Sebold's organization had been gathering military-industrial information in the United States since the 1920s, including the Norden bomb sight and Goddard's rocket technology. With Sebold's able help, the Bureau actually managed the ring, supplying fake but appetizing information that the mechanic radioed to his counterparts in Germany. When it was finally cashed in by the Bureau, the investigation brought thirty-three convictions and effectively ended German spying in the United States.

During the war, the heightened secrecy surrounding the atomic bomb made discoveries of Soviet espionage even more profoundly disturbing than the feckless attempts of the Germans. Indeed, as Hoover believed, during the war "American Communists...made their deepest inroads upon our national life."[7] Scholars have noted the heightened intensity of this wartime anti-Soviet campaign, but it has been judged a "counterintelligence failure" because the United States caught relatively few spies.[8] Yet FBI surveillance forced such Soviet representatives as Harry Gold's wartime handler Semyon Semyonov, NKVD agent Vassili Zarubin, and others to return to Russia, while U.S. officials effectively stymied such military-industrial spies as Clarence Hiskey, Andrei Shevchenko, Arthur Adams, Steve Nelson, and Joseph Weinberg. Soviet intelligence agents could ignore U.S. counterespionage activities only at their peril.

One of the first Soviet spies to be arrested was Gaik Ovakimian, an engineer who worked at Amtorg. Ovakimian was charged with being an unregistered representative of the Soviet government, but he was also known to be a spy; during his stay in the United States, he had paid handsomely for information on the production of gasoline- and on oil-refining processes. Yet after the German invasion of Russia, the State Department dropped the charges against Ovakimian, and he was allowed to return home in exchange for six others. While pursuing Ovakimian, FBI agents also bumped into Soviet master spy Jacob Golos, who had earlier also gotten in trouble as an unregistered foreign agent. The surveillance of Golos did lead the agency to a brief encounter with his lover and spy associate, Elizabeth Bentley, until she lost her pursuers in the Pennsylvania Station ladies' room.[9] Once the United States became firmly committed to helping the Soviet Union, surveillance of the couple ended. They, along with Julius Rosenberg's group of electrical engineers, Harry Gold's industrial and military contacts, Igor Gouzenko's revealed ring of radar and nuclear specialists in Canada, and of course, the large number of sources within the Manhattan Project itself, were largely unhindered participants in a huge haul of material for the Soviet Union in World War II.

Oblivious to all this, the government blundered even more strikingly with Gen. Walter Krivitsky, who actually presented himself as a source on Soviet espionage. Kritivsky, a senior GRU agent who had escaped to the United States in 1938, drew much interest in a series of articles he wrote for the *Saturday Evening Post*. Krivitsky told the State Department's Passport Office of the existence of hundreds of agents, but because there were as yet no procedures for handling defectors, little was done to delve seriously into his allegations. Hoover questioned Krivitsky's ideological leanings, and the Immigration and Naturalization Service was soon trying to deport him. He died in Washington in 1941 under mysterious circumstances.[10]

Krivitsky was not the only defector whose significance was overlooked. Whittaker Chambers had visited Assistant Secretary of State Adolf Berle in

September 1939 to tell him about a network in the State Department and other agencies involved in "Russian espionage." But Berle did not mention Chambers's story to the FBI until March 1940, and it took the Bureau another two years to even contact Chambers. Hoover, of course, could not pursue Soviet espionage to the extent he might have wished. As he told lawmakers, in his counterespionage program "emphasis was placed upon control of Axis agents operating in the US and upon the penetration and study of the Axis intelligence system."[11] In this, he was effective; German espionage was nearly nonexistent during the war. The handful of inept Abwehr spies who washed ashore on the Eastern Seaboard in 1942 (Long Island, Florida) and 1944 (Maine) were either executed or given long sentences. Another rarity in the United States, a spy for Japan called Velvalee Dickinson, a doll saleswoman who wrote messages about U.S. Navy ships in doll-code, was also captured by the FBI in 1944 after some of her letters were traced. She was sentenced to ten years in prison.

Despite these successes, the far more expansive and effective Soviet espionage operation remained largely unmolested. American officials were hampered in grasping the full dimensions of it by strategic considerations, namely, the alliance with Russia against Nazi Germany. Nevertheless, in 1943 intelligence officials discovered the work of California communist leader Steve Nelson, a Soviet spy interested in developments at the Berkeley Radiation Laboratory, where Ernest O. Lawrence and J. Robert Oppenheimer were conducting early atomic research for the War Department. Nelson's home was already under surveillance when one of Oppenheimer's graduate students came to tell the party leader about his secret work in fall 1942. Then, on March 29, 1943, Nelson was overheard at his home securing "some highly confidential data regarding the nuclear experiments" at the Radiation Lab from another lab scientist, Joseph Woodrow Weinberg.[12] Weinberg provided Nelson a formula that concerned the calutron, a separator that would enrich uranium. Soon after this meeting, Nelson was spotted passing information to Soviet vice consul Peter Petrovich Ivanov. Then, on April 10, the man who headed NKVD activities in the United States, Vassili Zarubin, stopped to visit Nelson and paid him for additional information.

With less justification, intelligence officials were also monitoring J. Robert Oppenheimer during the war. Lt. Col. Boris T. Pash believed that the physicist was passing on material to persons who, in Pash's estimation, "may be furnishing ... [it] to the Communist Party for transmission to the USSR."[13] As newly unearthed documents reveal, Oppenheimer was almost certainly a party member, but allegations of his involvement in espionage activity have never been convincingly demonstrated.[14] In August 1943, however, Oppenheimer told Army security officers of a breach at the lab. Sometime the previous winter he "had learned from three different employees of the atomic bomb project ... that they had been solicited to furnish information, ultimately to be delivered to the USSR." None of the men had cooperated, according to Oppenheimer, so he refused to name them; nor, for some months, would he identify the man who had solicited their espionage, whom he later divulged was Berkeley French professor Haakon Chevalier. That Oppenheimer did not get in more trouble over his reticence may be explained by his having "benefited from exceptional treatment," as one scholar has noted. Despite Oppenheimer's well-known left-wing past, it was only in the 1950s that he found himself subject to the security standards that had destroyed others, and his tale of the three contacts, which he later admitted he had invented, played a crucial role in the loss of his security clearance then.[15]

Occasionally, officials were able to successfully derail Soviet espionage during the war, as they did in their dealings with Soviet Purchasing Commission representative Andrei Shevchenko. On discovering his queries for secret documents, the FBI worked with a librarian and later an engineer at Bell Aircraft to give Shevchenko everything he had asked for on advanced airplanes in sanitized form.[16] The FBI was gratified to learn later that Soviet intelligence considered the doctored material supplied to Shevchenko "reliable." [17] But in December 1945, Shevchenko left the country with his wife and son. His escape had been facilitated not only by a tip from Moscow but also by the U.S. government's apparent reluctance to press charges in the wartime environment. Also departing that month, and for the same reason, was another longtime industrial spy, Arthur Adams.

The FBI had discovered Adams's meetings with Arthur Hiskey, a scientist in the Manhattan Project's University of Chicago laboratory, relatively late in the war. A break-in to Adams's dwelling on September 29, 1944, showed notes about the nuclear project, and these, the FBI declared, "reflect an intimate knowledge concerning highly secret phases" of the project. Indeed, Adams was "the most dangerous espionage agent yet discovered in the Comintern Apparatus."[18] At Chicago's Development of Substitute Materials Laboratory, Hiskey assisted in plans for plutonium production. To get him away from Adams, the Army drafted Hiskey in April 1944, sending him to the Yukon as property survey master or, as an army official put it, to "count underwear." At this remote posting, more notes on the atomic project were discovered in his effects.[19]

Yet a more dangerous spy than Nelson, Adams, or Hiskey was Klaus Fuchs, whom the FBI entirely missed. From the Los Alamos Laboratory, he provided Moscow with unparalleled information about the bomb project, including material on such topics as its construction, detonation, and the fission rates of certain types of plutonium. He continued to spy for the Soviets from Britain when he returned there after the war. The Atomic Energy Commission declared that Fuchs's information likely sped up Soviet atomic research by two years. Though the physicist's intelligence gathering at Los Alamos remained unknown until 1950, defector Igor Gouzenko revealed another significant espionage operation less than a month after the war ended. A clerk at the Russian embassy in Ottawa, Gouzenko secreted out 109 documents that illuminated Soviet successes in obtaining atomic, radar, and other military-industrial secrets, which he showed to British and American officials. One of the most active sources Gouzenko named was Allan Nunn May, a Cambridge-trained nuclear physicist, who gave the Soviets "a survey of the entire atomic bomb project." May made three trips to the

Chicago laboratory, from which he transferred uranium samples to Soviet military intelligence in 1944.[20]

Gouzenko's was not the only high-profile defection of 1945. Elizabeth Bentley walked into the FBI's arms that fall as well. After some initial disbelief at her allegations of high-level espionage within the U.S. government, the Bureau assigned twenty-five agents to her case, launching technical and physical surveillance of the eighty-odd individuals she named. Her defection had the effect of a *Titanic*-sized iceberg on Soviet operations in the United States, as the Soviet security agency, then known as the NKGB, stopped all communication with a number of agents and recalled others. Bentley told the FBI about sources like Nathan Gregory Silvermaster and William Ullman, among many additional spies, who supplied her with reams of material from the Pentagon and other departments beginning in 1941, much of it photographed in Silvermaster's basement.[21] Soviet cables, which identified her as "Good Girl," confirm this mass quantity; the material streamed in, on planes, munitions, and manpower, dwarfing the limited take of Chambers's earlier sources.[22] Unfortunately for the FBI, her testimony as an uncorroborated witness had very little value for prosecution purposes. Only one man, War Production Board staffer William Walter Remington, testified that he had given information to Bentley, and he claimed that he thought she was merely a journalist. Everyone else denied her charges or took the Fifth Amendment. Bentley sometimes exaggerated her story in ensuing congressional hearings, but the dearth of convictions does not reflect a lack of merit in her initial claims about Soviet espionage practices, which have been since demonstrated in both Soviet archives and American sources like VENONA.[23]

The government also had a hard time after the war prosecuting the atomic spies it had identified for the same reason. Released from his arctic purgatory, Hiskey claimed he had provided no secret information. Joseph Weinberg similarly denied his involvement in espionage, claiming he had never met Nelson or talked to him about the bomb. As for Nelson, he took the Fifth Amendment repeatedly. The wiretaps that confirmed these men's actual roles were not sufficient as courtroom evidence. Moreover, even where a willing eyewitness was available, espionage charges were difficult to prove. Whittaker Chambers, after waffling for some years about Alger Hiss's actual relationship with him, finally named Hiss as a former spy in 1948 after the latter tried to sue him for defaming Hiss as a communist. But the statute of limitations on Hiss's espionage had expired, and despite Chambers's possession of 1930s State Department documents connected with the former Foggy Bottom official, Hiss could only be charged with perjury for denying that he had known Chambers. Hiss served three and a half years in prison and the rest of his life trumpeting his innocence, garnering many believers.

The government did get significant help in identifying spies from the aforementioned VENONA project, the Army Security Agency's secret effort to decode wartime Soviet cables, although their secrecy and their hearsay nature prevented them from being of much value for legal purposes.[24] The first and only "live" American spy to be caught by VENONA was Judith Coplon, a political analyst at the Justice Department, arrested in March 1949 as she was supplying material to her Soviet handler, Valentin Gubitchev. Her 25-year sentence was overturned on appeal, owing to the FBI's missteps, including wiretapping her communications with her attorney. More significant, though, in 1949 cryptanalyists decoded a World War II cable on "Fluctuations and the Efficiency of a Diffusion Plant, Part III," written by Klaus Fuchs.[25] He soon confessed his espionage to British authorities. After a massive FBI manhunt, agents found Fuchs's American courier, Harry Gold, but he did not initially cooperate until his interviewers fished out a map of Santa Fe from his closet.

His New Mexican adventures now evident, an abashed Gold broke down. He was charged with "conspiracy to commit espionage on behalf of the USSR" on May 23, 1950; he got a 30-year sentence for his illicit information gathering. His sources had included not only Fuchs but engineer Abraham Brothman, chemist Alfred Slack, and Los Alamos machinist David Greenglass. Greenglass, too, soon talked with authorities, recounting the role of his sister and brother-in-law, Ethel and Julius Rosenberg, in recruiting him. They, of course, never cooperated.

In 1951, a congressional committee declared that the espionage of Fuchs, Greenglass, and others had "advanced the Soviet atomic energy program by 18 months as a minimum . . . if war should come, Russia's ability to mount an atomic offensive against the West will be greatly increased." This dire outlook certainly helps explain the extraordinary severity of Julius and Ethel Rosenberg's sentences.[26] Physicist Theodore Hall, a much more important source who had spied at Los Alamos, was luckier. He escaped because corroborating evidence outside of the classified VENONA intercepts was not available. Hall fled to England, where he lived nearly another fifty years; he only publicly admitted his role in 1998.

Cryptanalysts also used VENONA to develop information about Julius Rosenberg's ring of engineers, including Joel Barr, Alfred Sarant, and William Perl. Sarant and Barr alone produced over 9,000 pages of documents on radar and other technology with military applications. Perl, meanwhile, was given a prize for the lode of aircraft information he furnished.[27] As soon as Gold and Greenglass were apprehended in 1950, Barr escaped to Czechoslovakia. Sarant fled there also, via Mexico. Another of Rosenberg's engineers, Morton Sobell, also left the United States for Mexico on the day of Greenglass's arrest. Seized by the Mexican police, Sobell resisted, but eventually had a ".38 caliber pistol butt" smashed on his head.[28] He ended up on trial with the Rosenbergs, named by his former friend and roommate, Max Elitcher; he got a 30-year sentence and served eighteen years, five of them at Alcatraz. This was certainly an unusually harsh penalty for industrial espionage. Sobell, who is still alive, has always denied his role in Rosenberg's ring.[29]

Perl, on the other hand, did not flee, but because officials had really only the secret VENONA materials as evidence against him, he could not be charged as a spy. Instead, he was convicted of perjury, for denying that he knew both Rosenberg and Sobell, his former classmates at City College, and received two concurrent 5-year terms. Hoover, annoyed that Perl had not been charged with espionage, took cold comfort in his treatment at the New York Federal House of Detention, where the brilliant engineer was relegated to cleaning toilets.

The government didn't even get a perjury case against Steve Nelson. After the war, he was busy organizing immigrants in an unglamorous section of Pittsburgh. The House Un-American Activities Committee (HUAC), which was familiar with the FBI's wiretaps on Nelson, ordered him to appear in 1948 and 1949, but he refused to testify. Moreover, he flatly denied any role in espionage and continued to deny it for the rest of his life: "There may have been a Soviet espionage network operating in this country," Nelson wrote in 1981, "but common sense would dictate against recruiting prominent Party officials."[30] Congress charged him with contempt for his refusal to cooperate, but more troublesome for him was the Commonwealth of Pennsylvania's charge that he had violated a 1919 state sedition law. Authorities there sentenced him to twenty years in the ancient Blawnox workhouse, plus a fine of $20,000. After two appeals, he was finally vindicated by the U.S. Supreme Court in 1954; one could not be seditious to a state when the federal government had its own laws in the matter. Later in the decade, ironically, disgusted with Nikita Khrushchev's 1956 revelations about Josef Stalin, Nelson left the Communist Party.

By then, with only a few thousand members, this organization was riddled with FBI informants. Still, Hoover only planned to amplify his assault on the party through the COINTELPRO project. As one FBI staffer noted, "We were trying first to develop intelligence so we would know what they were doing [and] second, to contain the threat. . . . To stop the spread of communism, to stop the effectiveness of the Communist Party as a vehicle of Soviet intelligence, propaganda and agitation."[31] The 1956 COINTELPRO against the Communist Party proved such a successful model that the FBI set up similar efforts against organizations ranging from the Ku Klux Klan to the New Left in ensuing years.

The domestic party was unlikely to be doing much spying in the 1950s, of course, with the FBI's saturation of its ranks. Instead, Soviet agents bent on espionage focused increasingly on cultivating American spies overseas, especially men in uniform—an approach that proved successful throughout the Cold War and beyond. Of thirty-three U.S. espionage cases prosecuted between 1950 and 1975, fully twenty-three were either soldiers or civilians connected with the military abroad.[32] Though spy convictions abounded in the military sector, intelligence agency operatives who spied for Russia were seldom publicly revealed in this era. The CIA and the Justice Department had a pact, first signed in 1954, that allowed the intelligence agency to decide whether to send any of its agents suspected of illegal activities to Justice for prosecution. Not surprisingly, suspected personnel usually remained secret to the CIA for reasons of "national security."[33]

In 1957, the same year that the Soviet *Sputnik* satellite caught Americans off-guard, the United States was also surprised by a Russian spy living in Brooklyn, KGB illegal Rudolf Ivanovich Abel. Abel, who had been in the United States for almost ten years, was found guilty of conspiracy to obtain and transmit

CATCHING SPIES IN THE UNITED STATES   37

defense-related information to the Soviet Union, as well as for being an unregistered foreign agent. Authorities were assisted in finding him by a defector, Reino Hayhanen, himself a former KGB spy, along with a newsboy's earlier puzzling find of a hollowed-out nickel containing a secret code. Abel (whose actual name was Willie Fisher) was sentenced to serve thirty years in prison. But in 1962, after U-2 pilot Francis Gary Powers was caught red-handed when his spy plane crashed in a Russian field, the United States let Abel go in exchange for the downed flyer.

In 1960, Powers's exposure led two disgusted Americans, National Security Agency (NSA) mathematicians Bernon F. Mitchell and William H. Martin, to defect to Russia with their cryptographic secrets. In a public attack from Moscow, Mitchell and Martin vilified American secret missions over Soviet airspace. HUAC, however, blamed the men's supposed homosexuality for their betrayal.[34] Another NSA employee who also spied in the early 1960s, Jack Dunlap, was never caught. After failing a polygraph test in 1963, Dunlap made several attempts to kill himself; he completed the deed before authorities could unearth what he had stolen from the NSA. The same year, even as Kennedy and Khrushchev signed a comprehensive atomic test-ban treaty, an Air Force employee was successfully apprehended for furnishing the KGB the secrets of the Strategic Air Command's communications technology. John Butenko received a 30-year sentence for his spying.

Unfortunately for the United States, efforts to recruit its own moles to penetrate Moscow's intelligence agencies in this era remained stillborn owing to the paranoia of James Jesus Angleton, head of the CIA's Counterintelligence Staff, who became convinced that working with Soviet double agents would only involve the CIA in a deceptive KGB "monster plot." Persuaded by a defector, Anatoly Golitsyn, that the agency had been already penetrated, Angleton's agency was hamstrung—and yet no mole was disinterred.

By the 1970s, the diplomatic environment of détente prevented much spy catching. Here the story of Valery I. Markelov is revealing. In 1970, Markelov, a UN KGB operative, met a Grumman engineer and told him that he was very interested in that company's F-14 fighter jet. The engineer then contacted the FBI, and the Bureau monitored the two men's meetings over the next two years; at their last meeting, in February 1972, the FBI arrested Markelov with confidential documents in his hands. Soon indicted for espionage, Markelov saw his indictment dismissed by the Nixon administration. Eager to use Moscow's assistance in extricating itself from Vietnam, it claimed letting him go "would best serve the national and foreign policy interests of the United States."[35]

By 1975, however, with the United States' ignominious rout from Vietnam and Communism seemingly on the march around the globe, the bloom had faded from the détente rose. That June, the FBI arrested Sarkis O. Paskalian, one-time director of performing arts at the Armenian General Benevolent Union and a longtime KGB agent, along with his cousin, Sadag K. Dedeyian, a former mathematician at the Johns Hopkins Applied Physics Laboratory, who had supplied Paskalian with information about NATO's strength. Paskalian was given a

22-year sentence, and Dedeyian, a three-year term. The arrests prompted FBI Director Clarence Kelley, sounding much like his predecessor Hoover, to declare that the United States was a "prime target" for Soviet intelligence collection.[36] In summer 1977, the FBI fought back with a so-called dangle operation, sending retiring Navy Lt. Cmdr. Art Lindberg to schmooze aboard the Soviet tourist vessel *Kazakhstan* en route to Bermuda. On the trip, Lindberg snared three men from the Soviet UN Mission who eagerly took his Navy-screened materials on anti-submarine warfare and advanced helicopters until the FBI arrested them in May 1978. Two were tried and sentenced to fifty years in prison, although they were later exchanged for five Soviet dissidents. Not all the spies arrested in this era were working for the Soviet Union, however; Ronald Humphrey of the U.S. Information Agency had earlier provided information to the North Vietnamese delegation at Paris, hoping to free his wife and family from the communists. Unfortunately for him, his go-between was a double agent under FBI supervision. Humphrey and an accomplice got a 15-year term.[37]

Another spy identified in the post-détente Carter administration was CIA official David Barnett, who for nearly $100,000 provided names of agents, materials on submarines and missiles, and other information to the KGB. He was sentenced to eighteen years in jail. As his treatment suggests, the CIA-Justice gag rule had been quashed; in the mid-1970s, Frank Church's (D-ID) Senate Select Committee to Study Government Operations with Respect to Intelligence Activities, which was investigating intelligence agencies' abuses in the post-Watergate era, saw it as an abuse of executive power. President Gerald Ford thus axed the rule, but counterintelligence officials did not entirely drop their resistance to prosecution. When William Kampiles, a disgruntled CIA trainee, stole a top secret manual for a KH-11 military surveillance satellite in 1977 and sold it to the Soviets for $3,000, both the CIA and the Defense Department opposed his going on trial. The CIA was embarrassed by the laxity that Kampiles's espionage case would demonstrate, and the Pentagon worried about maintaining the secrecy of the satellite. As a result, the trial included closed sessions and limits on access to the material in question. Similar measures were employed in the prosecution of Christopher Boyce, a TRW employee who sold defense secrets from his firm to Moscow in 1977, and such provisions were enshrined in the Classified Information Procedures Act of 1980.

Boyce was one of the most famous spies arrested in this era, owing in part to Robert Lindsey's book about his case, *The Falcon and the Snowman* (1979). Though he earned $20,000 for his work, Boyce seems to have been motivated most by a strong disagreement with American foreign policy, especially its unequal relationship with client-states like Australia, which provided bases to support satellite intelligence collection without being furnished full data. Given a 40-year sentence, Boyce escaped from jail three years later—some believed he had been sprung by the KGB—and survived outside for almost two years, helped by a sympathetic woman friend. He hardly laid low; instead, he participated in sixteen bank robberies while on the lam. Upon capture, he got another twenty-eight years tacked on to his prison term. Boyce initially showed little remorse for his actions, telling an Australian TV audience in 1983: "I think that eventually the United States Government is going to involve the world in the next world war. And being a traitor to that, I have absolutely no problems with that whatsoever."[38] After being beaten up by members of the Aryan Brotherhood at Leavenworth prison, he was transferred to solitary confinement at Marion, Illinois, the federal system's most secure lock-up. This experience seems to have sobered him, for in 1985 he told the Senate Select Committee on Intelligence that espionage was "pretty dirty business ... it is not what you see on television." Spies, he noted, are "bringing down upon themselves heartache more heavy than a mountain. There is no exit from it."[39] Boyce was released in March 2003.

Not long after Boyce's arrest, lawmakers had authorized more controversial methods to catch even more spies. The Foreign Intelligence Surveillance Act of 1978 (FISA) allowed investigators to wiretap or otherwise secretly monitor suspected terrorists and espionage agents without worrying about violating the Fourth Amendment's protection of criminal defendants from unlawful search and seizure. Under this act, a panel of judges reviews the government's requests for surveillance and almost always accepts them: In 2004, for instance, the panel approved every one of the 1,758 requests put before it for secret surveillance (wiretap authorizations are somewhat more sparingly approved). The requests are much more frequent now than they were before September 11, 2001, not surprisingly. Just days after those attacks, in fact, Congress passed the USA-PATRIOT Act, which makes it even easier for the government to conduct surveillance on Americans and allows agencies to share the results of wiretaps and grand jury proceedings if they relate to foreign intelligence or counterintelligence. Nevertheless, the Bush administration drew an outcry when it began monitoring foreign phone calls of some Americans without FISA authorization in late 2005.[40]

With measures like FISA and the Classified Information Procedures Act in place, the 1980s saw a huge expansion in the number of espionage practitioners apprehended; authorities arrested sixty-two of them in the oft-named decade of the spy. Given the high-profile American defense buildup of this era, it is not surprising that much of the Soviet espionage at this time focused on military technology. It included, for example, the theft of radar at Hughes Aircraft in Los Angeles, the swiping of materials on the Minuteman Missile from Systems Control in northern California, and the pilfering of Stealth airplane technology at Northrop Advanced Systems. Declared FBI Director William Webster in 1984, "We have more people charged with espionage right now than ever before in our history."[41] Though the FBI deserves credit for cracking these cases, a good number of them originated with the revelations of defectors.

Even the hallowed halls of Congress were not immune from espionage in the 1980s. Randy Miles Jeffries, a stenographic messenger with a history of heroin abuse, twice supplied top secret materials from closed hearings of the House Armed Services Committee to Soviet military officials. He was arrested in 1985 on his third effort and was sentenced to serve from three to nine years. Jeffries, in fact, was the twelfth person charged with espionage in 1985, "the year of the spy." Among those apprehended that year also was Jonathan J. Pollard, a naval analyst who spied for Israel and remains in solitary confinement twenty-one years later. The exact information Pollard provided remains classified but included material on U.S. signals surveillance practices. His sentence was unusually harsh, similar to that meted out to top Soviet spy Aldrich Ames. As recently as February 2006, Pollard's attorneys had filed for the release of documents that would assist in a clemency petition; Pollard has been rejected, though, in every one of his appeals.

Another spy identified in 1985 who also got a life sentence was NSA communications specialist Ronald Pelton. He furnished Moscow agents information about Operation Ivy Bells, a top secret Navy program in which U.S. submarines placed bugging devices on Soviet undersea cables. Famed KGB defector Vitaly Yurchenko brought him to the FBI's attention. Yurchenko also identified CIA agent Edward Lee Howard, whom the agency, now freed from Angleton's anxieties, had hired in 1981 for the delicate task of managing Russians cooperating with the CIA inside the Soviet Union. Yet Howard, like Jeffries, had a history of substance abuse. Once fired, he began passing crucial information to the KGB, resulting in the death of at least one American agent. He averted arrest by escaping to the Soviet Union, the first CIA employee to do so. He died in Russia in 2002.

The most significant spy arrest in 1985 was that of John A. Walker Jr. Walker had first betrayed highly sensitive Navy codes in 1967, when he was a debt-ridden submarine officer, an unhappily married man with four children to support. The Soviets paid him $4,000 a month. Walker left the service in 1976, realizing he would not pass a background check if his ex-wife were interviewed. By then, he had firmly established his network by recruiting his friend Jerry Whitworth, a naval communications specialist, who supplied much cryptographic material. Walker also turned to his family, where his most productive source was his son Michael, a sailor on the U.S.S. *Nimitz* who stole numerous burn bags of classified information before they hit the ship's incinerator. Walker's arrest, too, was a family affair: His ex-wife turned him in.

Before it was rolled up, the Walker ring had provided a vast amount of information, including the codes needed to start nuclear weapons in war, keylists that allowed the Soviets to read naval messages, and the Navy's plans for possible war in Central America. Yurchenko contended that Walker's ring represented "the most important operation in KGB history," even more so than the World War II efforts to acquire nuclear secrets.[42]

Despite the discoveries, some notable new espionage operations began in 1985. It was then that FBI agent Robert Hanssen greatly accelerated his espionage work. It was also in that year that Aldrich Ames of the CIA's Soviet counterintelligence branch launched his nine-year career in Soviet service. While missing Ames, the CIA did discover in the 1980s that its own espionage operations in Cuba had been compromised for twenty years; all of its Cuban agents actually worked for the Direccion General de Intelligencia (DGI), Castro's secret service!

As these cases indicate, during an era of often tense Soviet-American relations, most of those charged with espionage worked for Moscow and its client-states. There were exceptions: In 1986, Michael H. Allen, a clerk at an American naval air station in the Philippines, stole classified documents that he handed over to the Manila government in exchange for assistance to his businesses, including a cockfighting enterprise. He got eight years in prison. Douglas Tsou, an FBI agent who had escaped from communist China in 1949, was arrested in 1986; he had spied for Taiwan and got a 10-year sentence. In 1988, Thomas J. Dolce received a similar prison term for spying for South Africa at the Aberdeen Proving Ground. At the same time, two Beijing diplomats, Hou Desheng, a military attaché, and Zang Weichu, a consular official, were tossed out of the country for trying to get NSA materials in an FBI sting operation. Similarly stung and chucked out was a Soviet military attaché, Yuri Pakhtusov, who had tried to get secret information from a defense contractor.[43]

The end of the Cold War drew an expanding range of countries into espionage against the United States. During the Gulf War in the early 1990s, Joseph G. Brown, a former member of the Air Force, was arrested for spying for the Filipino government, providing materials on Iraq as well as on the activities of insurgents in the islands. His material came from one of his karate students, a CIA secretary named Virginia Baynes. Indeed, it was the chance to become martial arts teacher at Langley that enticed Brown to return to the United States, where he was arrested as he deplaned in 1992; he got six months in jail. Meanwhile, Ronald Hoffman, an employee of Science Applications International, sold four different Japanese companies the software for designing missiles and identifying rockets from their exhaust trails and received more than $750,000. When his secretary discovered what he was doing, Hoffman quit his job, but then recklessly sneaked in after hours to get more material—and was recorded on camera. A government sting (which proffered the opportunity to sell the technology to South Africa) led to his arrest in June 1990, and he received a 30-month sentence for violating not only the Arms Export Control Act but the Comprehensive Anti-Apartheid Act, too.

This was relatively light compared to the thirty-four years at hard labor meted out to Army artillery specialist Albert Sombolay, who was apprehended the following year for offering his services to the Jordanians and Iraqis. Not all military personnel faced such a stiff sentence for spying for Middle Eastern governments. U.S. Navy Lt. Cmdr. Michael S. Schwartz had passed classified material to the Saudi navy in the early 1990s while stationed in Riyadh. Arrested in May 1995, he professed to have done it in a zealous attempt to assist Saudi—U.S. relations during the Gulf War. He avoided jail, suffering only the loss of military benefits.

The fall of the Berlin Wall also allowed U.S. authorities to discover spies for the defunct East Bloc. One of these, Jeffrey Carney, a former Air Force intelligence operative, had spied for East Germany since the early 1980s, defecting there in 1985. He continued to work for the Stasi on the other side, and was arrested in 1991 when the security service archive was opened; he was sentenced to thirty-eight years in prison, later reduced to twenty years. Another, more significant East Bloc case was the Lee Conrad spy ring, first cracked in 1988. Conrad, a U.S. Army sergeant in Germany, sold secrets to the Soviet bloc for thirteen years. Members of his extensive ring included Kelly Therese Warren, a secretary in the 8th Infantry Division headquarters in Germany. Arrested in 1997, she provided material to Conrad for Hungary, including NATO plans for the defense of Western Europe in case of a Soviet attack. For the mere $7,000 she'd earned, she got a 25-year sentence.

As these cases suggest, the military continued to be a prime recruiting ground for spies. But it had no monopoly on illicit intelligence gathering. John Lalas was a State Department officer who spied for the Greek government for more than a decade and a half before he was arrested in Virginia in 1993, after he had provided over 700 documents to Athens on everything from military strategy to the names of CIA agents. The United States was tipped off by the comments of a Greek embassy official, and Lalas got a 14-year sentence. Another State Department officer, Geneva Jones, was also arrested in 1993. With a top-secret clearance in the Bureau of Politico-Military Affairs, she gave thousands of secret State Department cables, mostly related to Somalia and Iraq, to a West African journalist named Dominic Ntube. The materials appeared in African magazines and got as far as the hideout of Liberian rebel leader Charles Taylor. She received a sentence of 37 months in prison for sneaking out documents (which she had wrapped up in grocery bags and newspaper) and "the unlawful communication of national defense information," a violation of the Espionage Act.

Government and military employees, though predominant, are hardly the only practitioners of espionage. Foreigners resident in the United States—like Jacob Golos, Andrei Shevchenko, and Arthur Adams earlier—still do their share. In 1993, an FBI sting caught Yen Men Kao, who along with other Chinese had tried to buy military technology that was illegal to export, including jet engines, jet radar, and plans for a Navy torpedo. He was deported, but not prosecuted, in the interest of preserving Beijing–Washington relations, leaving behind his family and two Chinese restaurants.

But certainly the most damaging clandestine information sharing in recent years has been carried out by employees of the nation's intelligence agencies—no surprise, given their privileged access. As head of the CIA's counterintelligence service in Europe, Aldrich Ames was officially charged with closely scrutinizing Soviet activities, and thus it is hard to think of a more valuable source for the Kremlin. He is reputed to have destroyed more than 100 U.S. anti-Soviet operations, as well as contributed to the deaths of 10 agents. The deaths were not hard to miss, and the CIA began a major effort to find their mole, soliciting the FBI's help for the first time. For too long, however, Ames's grandiose life style, supported by the $2.7 million he received from the Soviets, went unsuspected.

Finally nabbed in 1994, Ames got a life sentence with no chance of parole. His wife, Rosario, received five years for collaborating with him. Though the CIA fumbled here, the FBI itself took hundreds of agents out of counterintelligence operations in the late and post–Cold War era, deploying them instead in the fight against new threats such as drug-inspired violence. Such a focus allowed Soviet spies like Robert Hanssen to operate for years unsuspected within the Bureau.

The Ames arrest did spur Congress to pass the Violent Crime Control and Law Enforcement Act, which restored the death penalty for spying under certain conditions, including passing materials that resulted in the death of a U.S. agent. It also removed the 10-year statute of limitations on espionage. The Rosenbergs remain the only convicted U.S. spies to be executed, however. Prosecutors know that dead spies don't talk, and they have been loath to give up the opportunity to unearth details from them.

The new law allowed for the apprehending of espionage agents who had not been active for decades. In February 1996, the FBI arrested Robert Stephan Lipka in Millersville, Pennsylvania, after he was identified by Vasili Mitrokhin. As a 19-year-old NSA clerk thirty years earlier, Lipka had provided documents on communications intelligence to the Soviet Union and earned $27,000. With no statute of limitations in effect, Lipka received an 18-year sentence for this youthful malfeasance. A rather more impressive catch that year was Harold James Nicholson, former branch chief of the CIA's Counter-Terrorism Center, still the highest ranked CIA operative to be arrested. Between 1994 and 1996, he provided identities of CIA agents and sources, as well as everything else he could get from the CIA's secret computers. Nicholson agreed to cooperate, and his jail term was negotiated to 23½ years.

Though Jonathan Pollard remains the most famous, numerous spies have worked for allies of the United States, including Robert Chaegun Kim, a computer whiz at the Navy, arrested in 1996 for passing a large amount of classified military-intelligence material to South Korean naval attaché Baek Dong-Il. Kim, who apparently operated out of loyalty to his home country, got a 9-year sentence. Another man who attempted to spy for a friendly country was Jean-Philippe Wispelaere, who worked for the Australian Defense Intelligence organization, where he had access to highly classified U.S. materials derived from satellite spying. In 1999, he quit his job and tried to sell documents to the Singapore embassy in Thailand, whose staff told U.S. officials, enabling them to catch him in a sting. Flying into Dulles to receive his expected payment, he was arrested and ended up with a 15-year sentence.

Perhaps one of the more ambitious spy operations in the 1990s was orchestrated by Fidel Castro's government, itself the historic target of U.S. intelligence agents' sometimes obsessive plotting. Under the leadership of Cuban intelligence, the Red Wasp network, led by Gerardo Hernandez, infiltrated anti-Castro groups in Florida as well as U.S. defense installations like the Boca Chica Naval Air Station in Key West, in part to thwart possible U.S. attacks on Cuba. The group, which included both Cubans and Cuban Americans, was arrested in 1998;

three of the men got life sentences, though no secret information ever got back to Castro.

As this and other cases confirm, national loyalty continues to play a role in motivating spies. So, too, does ideology, as the case of Kurt Stand and his wife, Therese Marie Squillacote, suggests. Stand, a labor functionary, and his wife, who worked at the Department of Defense, were arrested with their friend James Clark in 1997 for spying for Russia and East Germany. Stand had been a spy for East Germany for twenty-five years, beginning in the early 1970s; all three had been leftist activists, even communists. Squillacote, who began her spying in 1980, indeed saw it as an "anti-imperialist" activity. Despite their political leanings, Stand earned $25,000. The FBI discovered them after Squillacote tried to offer her services to the South African Communist Party in 1995; the couple got lengthy sentences four years later.

Many Americans were eager to spy for the East Bloc, both within and without the United States, and Russian diplomats continued to assist in this task. In December 1999, the FBI found and arrested Stanislav Gusev dawdling in front of the State Department. Gusev, an attaché at the Russian embassy, was remotely controlling a listening device that had been secretly installed in a seventh-floor conference room down the hall from the offices of Secretary of State Madeleine Albright. Paul Redmond, former head of counterintelligence at the CIA, was surprised by this evidence of interest in State Department meetings, because the United States and Russia were no longer enemies. He thought that technology would be a better target for them: "If I were in Moscow, what I'd want to know is what's Microsoft going to do? What's Sun going to do?"[44]

Overall, however, it was Americans, not Russians like Gusev, who did the most damage. The well-publicized arrest of Robert Hanssen in 2001 capped a 15-year hunt for an agent who was responsible for the deaths of numerous U.S. sources in Russia, and who had sent thousands of documents to that country over a 22-year career in espionage, earning $600,000 in cash. Hanssen was the supervisor of the FBI's intelligence division—a perfect place to prevent himself from being discovered. He handed over extensive U.S. analyses on such subjects as Soviet nuclear strength and the American ability to withstand a nuclear attack, as well as top secret documents on U.S. intelligence activity, from satellites to radar to a prospective tunnel under the new Soviet embassy in Washington. He also supplied Moscow with the identities of fifty sources, several of whom were executed because of his betrayal, including one of the United States' most important agents, Dmitri Fedorovich Polyakov, or TOPHAT, executed in 1988. The government paid well to seal Hanssen's fate; the defector who produced crucial evidence in the case—including a garbage bag of documents with Hanssen's fingerprints—received $7 million and a new life in the United States. This generous remuneration was a far cry from the agency's bungling treatment of Krivitsky sixty years earlier. Hanssen was sentenced to life without parole in 2002.

Despite the fame of Hanssen, Russia has hardly been the only nation interested in American military technology in recent years. Peter H. Lee, a physicist at

Los Alamos, provided secret nuclear information in lectures to Chinese scientists during a 1985 visit to the PRC. Over a decade later, when he worked at TRW, he made another trip to China and provided more information about his work. He confessed in 1998 and got one year in prison, as well as 3,000 hours of community service. But when another Chinese physicist at Los Alamos named Lee was arrested in 1999, it turned out to be an embarrassing mistake. The FBI had learned that the Beijing government had obtained information about a highly advanced atomic weapon, a miniaturized warhead called the W-88, and suspicion fell on Wen Ho Lee, whose downloading of classified documents onto his own computer and associations with suspected spies had also drawn their suspicion. Lee, however, claimed he was innocent. He was nevertheless placed in solitary confinement for nearly a year, partly based on false information. When the case began to fall apart, Lee was freed in return for agreeing to a lesser charge rather than espionage. This blunder, along with the Hanssen debacle, contributed to the resignation of FBI director Louis Freeh.

The FBI's stumbles here, of course, paled in comparison to the intelligence community's shock at the terrorist attacks of September 11, 2001, a catastrophe that is still being dissected. The attacks, too, had a significant impact on the fate of accused spies who had nothing to do with these events. Caught before the attacks early in 2001, Hanssen's case never went to trial; his lawyers, like Ames's, plea bargained for him. By contrast, Brian P. Regan, a National Reconnaissance Office employee who was arrested in August 2001 for offering to sell information to Iraq, China, and Libya, did go on trial, where he faced the very real possibility of the death penalty. As legal analyst John Parry noted at the time, "Giving things to the Russians is bad, but not threatening in the same way as giving things to irrational terrorists." Defense lawyers, however, argued that a letter to Saddam Hussein found on Regan's computer was part of his "fantasy" of espionage rather than evidence of genuine spying. Regan's lawyers got him life in prison. Five months later, his effort seemed less of a fantasy when shovel-wielding FBI employees unearthed 20,000 pages of documents, as well as CD-ROMS and videotapes, that Regan had buried in nineteen different digs in two state parks in Virginia and Maryland.[45]

Another case affected by the post–September 11 environment demonstrated, too, that ideology has not died as a motive in espionage, despite the typical cash basis of the practice. That very September, authorities apprehended Ana Belen Montes, a Defense Intelligence Agency Cuban analyst who had spied for Cuba since 1985. She pled guilty to espionage in March 2002, her work based inspired by her beliefs "that U.S. policy does not afford Cubans respect, tolerance and understanding." Montes was sentenced to twenty-five years in prison.[46]

Although espionage is normally associated with governmental or military intelligence gathering, in the post–Cold War era Americans grew increasingly alarmed about commercial spying as well. "The threat of economic and industrial espionage looms over the horizon of the business world like a gray cloud threatening a placid sea," warned Congresswoman Ileana Ros-Lehtinen (R-FL) in 2000.[47] Congress had already taken action, passing the Economic Espionage Act in 1996. Within two years, the FBI had 700 economic espionage investigations in process; each field office, moreover, had a white-collar crime section to address this issue. Though some of the more notorious cases tried under this act involved foreign firms illicitly collecting American technology, most economic espionage continues to be conducted by employees.

One of the first cases tried under this law involved a Taiwanese firm, Yuen Foong Paper Manufacturing, in 1997, which had tried to gain technology for a treatment of ovarian cancer from Bristol-Myers Squibb. In a second case, also in 1997, another Taiwanese company, Four Pillars Enterprises, was discovered to have paid an employee of Avery Dennison for adhesive technology for nearly a decade, costing the company $50 million. But a recent case is more typical. In December 2005, Suibin Zhang, an ex-employee of Netgear, a Silicon Valley software company, was charged with stealing secrets from one of his former firm's vendors and providing them to his new employer across the Valley. He faces up to ten years in prison if convicted.

Despite the post-9/11 tightened security environment, military espionage cases have hardly disappeared in recent years. Indeed, this period has created a new enemy and potential perpetrator of espionage: Al Qaeda. In 2004, Ryan Anderson of the Washington State National Guard was arrested in an FBI sting operation for trying to sell military secrets to men he thought were Al Qaeda operatives, including information on how to kill his fellow soldiers inside Humvees. He had been discovered in an Islamic Internet chat room by another citizen monitoring these communications, on the eve of his guard unit's departure for Iraq in late 2003. His defense lawyers asserted that he was both autistic and manic depressive, but he still received a life prison term.

Along with the prospect of new enemies, old allies continue to spy on the United States. In October 2005, Leandro Aragoncillo, a member of Vice President Dick Cheney's staff, sent White House and FBI secret records to Filipino associates plotting a coup. The case's origination in the White House was notable, as the executive mansion has generally been free of spies. During that same month, the U.S. charged a Defense Department official, Lawrence A. Franklin, with spying for Israel. Franklin had provided secret materials to the American Israel Public Affairs Committee (AIPAC) as well as to an Israeli diplomat in hopes they would use it to affect U.S. policy. In a startling move, the government charged his AIPAC contacts with violating the Espionage Act because of their "unauthorized retention and transmission of national defense information." The lobbyists to whom Franklin spoke, Steven Rosen and Keith Weissman, are the first two people outside the government to be so indicted. A former Justice Department official, Viet D. Dinh, who himself assisted in drafting the USA-PATRIOT Act, condemned this action, declaring that it "presents a novel case because the listener has no [evidence] for knowing what relates to national defense."[48] Perhaps it is not so novel, considering how many were prosecuted for violating the espionage act in World War I for doing even less.

In sum, by the early twenty-first century, spies are drawing their motivation from more varied sources than ever, from political and ideological sympathies to nationalist inclinations to commercial gain. The countries involved are similarly diverse. Though the FBI no longer sees espionage as the country's "biggest threat," it is still the agency's second priority, after terrorism, as the Bureau's website indicates. No doubt only more unexpected challenges and crises await, and catching spies, especially in defense-related areas, is likely to remain a key government concern.[49]

NOTES

1. Whittaker Chambers, "Unpublished Ms. of 1938 on Soviet Espionage," in Sam Tanenhaus Papers, box 25, Herbert Hoover Institute on War, Revolution, and Peace, Stanford, CA.

2. Dwight Eisenhower, *Crusade in Europe* (Garden City, N.Y., 1948), 32, quoted in U.S. Army Intelligence Center, *History of the Counter Intelligence Corps: The Counter Intelligence Corps Between the World Wars, 1918–1941* (Fort Holabird, MD: U.S. Army Intelligence Center, 1960), 96.

3. Editorial Comment on Fish Committee Report, 88, Rossiskii Gosudarstvennyi Arkhiv Ekonomiki (Russian State Archive of the Economy), *fond* 413, *op.* 13, *del.* 101, Moscow; see also "Still the Fish Committee Nonsense!" ACLU pamphlet, May 1932, available at http://www.debs.indstate.edu/a505s75_1932.pdf.

4. Hoover to Attorney General, January 2, 1932, cited in Frank J. Rafalko, ed., *A Counterintelligence Reader,* Volume I: *American Revolution to World War II* (Washington: National Counterintelligence Center, 1996), 159.

5. Quoted in Raymond J. Batvinis, " 'In the Beginning' . . . An Investigation of the Development of the Federal Bureau of Investigation's Counterintelligence Program, 1936 to 1941" (Ph.D. dissertation, Catholic University, 2001), 46.

6. Quoted in Max Lowenthal, *The Federal Bureau of Investigation* (Westport, CT: Greenwood, 1950), 425. In 1940, he chided Military Intelligence as having "crossed into matters upon which this Bureau has already been conducting investigations." See Hoover to Roosevelt, June 3, 1940, Official File 10B, box 11, Franklin D. Roosevelt Library, Hyde Park, NY.

7. Hoover speaking at the American Legion's Annual Convention in San Francisco, September 30, 1946, American Civil Liberties Union Papers, file 2731, reel 235, Seeley Mudd Library, Princeton University, Princeton, NJ. These inroads were significantly reduced thereafter; from a height of 80,000 members during the war, the number of party members shrank by the late 1950s to about 3,000, in large part owing to FBI harassment and infiltration of the party.

8. Athan Theoharis, *Chasing Spies: How the FBI Failed in Counterintelligence but Promoted the Politics of McCarthyism in the Cold War Years* (Chicago: Ivan R. Dee, 2002), 34.

9. See Ralph D. Toledano and Victor Lasky, *Seeds of Treason: The True Story of the Hiss-Chambers Tragedy* (New York: Funk and Wagnalls, 1950), 131. As FBI special agent Robert Thelan noted, "According to the surveillance logs of this case, Bentley, on two occasions, was surveilled . . . when she went to Penn Station and entered the ladies

rest room there and the surveillance was lost." Perhaps the FBI should have hired some female agents!

10. See Gary Kern, *A Death in Washington: Walter G. Krivitsky and the Stalin Terror* (New York: Enigma Books, 2003). His appeal to extend his visa—"the Soviet Government... would take measures to finish me off"—did not spare him for long.

11. Report of the Director of the FBI for the Fiscal Year 1945, 6. Report supplied to author by John Fox.

12. On the surveillance of Nelson, see D. M. Ladd to the Director, April 16, 1943, Re: Communist Infiltration of Radiation Laboratories (CINRAD), FBI File 100-16847-201; Communist Infiltration of Radiation Laboratory, University of California, Berkeley, California, FBI File 100-16980, July 7, 1943, 1; FBI Steve Nelson File, August 20, 1945, 100-16847-NR, 8–20 passim. The FBI files used here come from either the FBI's Reading Room in Washington, DC, or originated in Freedom of Information Act requests by the author.

13. Pash to Lansdale, June 29, 1943, cited in U.S. Atomic Energy Commission, *In the Matter of J. Robert Oppenheimer: Transcript of Hearing before Personnel Security Board and Texts of Principal Documents and Letters* (Cambridge, MA: MIT Press, 1971), 822. Also see surveillance on Oppenheimer in Julius Robert Oppenheimer, February 17, 1947, FBI background, attached to Hoover to Vaughan, February 28, 1947, President's Secretary File (PSF), box 167, Harry S Truman Library, Independence, MO.

14. On his party membership, see FBI letter to David Lilienthal, April 23, 1947, and memo, April 21, 1947, cited in Jerrold and Leona Schecter, *Sacred Secrets: How Soviet Intelligence Operations Changed American History* (Washington, DC: Brassey's, 2002), appendix 1. Berkeley professor Haakon Chevalier reported his and Oppenheimer's membership in the same unit of the party from 1938 to 1942. See Chevalier to Oppenheimer, July 13, 1964, cited at http://www.brotherhoodofthebomb.com, the website for Gregg Herken's *Brotherhood of the Bomb: The Tangled Lives and Loyalties of Robert Oppenheimer, Ernest Lawrence, and Edward Teller* (New York: Henry Holt, 2002).

15. Report on J. R. Oppenheimer, February 5, 1950, Summary Brief on Fuchs, February 6, 1950, FBI Klaus Fuchs File 65-58805-1202, 3; Chevalier Conspiracy," Part II, Steve Nelson file, August 20, 1945, 100-16980, 36; Barton L. Bernstein, " 'In the Matter of J. Robert Oppenheimer,' " *Historical Studies in the Physical Sciences* 12, no. 2 (1982): 246.

16. Leona Franey testimony, *Soviet Espionage Activities in Connection with Jet Propulsion and Aircraft*, 81st Congress, 1st sess. (Washington, DC, 1949), 104–5, 127–28; see also references to Shevchenko's contacts in VENONA 705, New York to Moscow, May 18, 1943; VENONA 1151, New York to Moscow August 12, 1944; VENONA 1327, New York (signature unrecoverable) to Fitin, September 15, 1944; VENONA 1607–1608, Anton (Kvasnikov) to Viktor (Fitin), November 16, 1944. The VENONA files are at the National Archives, Washington, DC.

17. A. H. Belmont to D. M. Ladd, espionage memo, May 15, 1950, 5, available at http://foia.fbi.gov/VENONA/VENONA.pdf.

18. FBI Arthur Adams file, New York, June 20, 1950, 100-331280-715, 188, 433; San Francisco FBI Comintern Apparatus (COMRAP) Summary Report 100-203581-3702 for period covering March 29, 1943, to November 1, 1944, Dec. 15, 1944, 12. I am grateful to John Earl Haynes for a copy of this report.

19. U.S. Congress, Committee on Un-American Activities, *Report on Soviet Espionage Activities in Connection with the Atom Bomb*, cited in U.S. Congress, Joint Committee on Atomic Energy (JCAE), *Soviet Atomic Espionage*, 82nd Congress, 1st sess. (Washington, DC, 1951), 166.

20. FBI, "Soviet Espionage Activities," October 19, 1945, PSF FBI box 167, 8–9. May, who died in 2003, was sentenced to ten years at hard labor. He later moved to Ghana, where he taught physics and kept up with nuclear developments in Africa.

21. T. G. Spencer Report, FBI Silvermaster file 65-56402-220, 18–23. When the FBI explored the basement later, they discovered photoflood bulbs with attachments, the bellows of a camera, light reflectors, an enlarger, photographic developing equipment and fluids, pans, printing paper, drying frames, negatives, electric driers, photograph trimmings, and empty film cartons in the trash. See December 13, 1945, report in Silvermaster file, volume 7, 65-56402-234, 158–59.

22. See, for instance, VENONA 794–799, New York to Moscow, reporting Silvermaster's information, May 28, 1943.

23. Hayden Peake does an effective job of demolishing the claims of one of Bentley's accused, William H. Taylor, that she was substantially inaccurate. See Peake, Afterword, in Elizabeth Bentley, *Out of Bondage* (New York: Ivy Books, 1988), 237–47, as well as the FBI's own listing of her corroborating evidence in idem., appendix B. On the FBI's difficulties in proving her allegations of espionage, see Gary May, *Un-American Activities: The Trials of William Remington* (New York: Oxford University Press, 1994), 88–89. On her exaggerations, see, for instance, Kathryn S. Olmsted, *Red Spy Queen: A Biography of Elizabeth Bentley* (Chapel Hill: University of North Carolina Press, 2002), 162–63. For confirmation of her materials in Russian archives, see discussions in Allen Weinstein and Alexander Vassiliev, *The Haunted Wood: Soviet Espionage in America—The Stalin Era* (New York: Modern Library, 2000), chaps. 5, 10, 11; and Harvey Klehr, John Earl Haynes, and Fridrikh Igorevich Firsov, *The Secret World of American Communism* (New Haven, CT: Yale University Press, 1995), 309–17.

24. See Robert Louis Benson and Michael Warner, eds., *VENONA: Soviet Espionage and the American Response, 1939–1957* (Washington, DC: National Security Agency/Central Intelligence Agency, 1996), xxi–xxvii.

25. See Summary Brief on Fuchs and Gold, February 12, 1951, 65-58805-1494X, 53; Report, February 6, 1950, 65-58805-1202, 19. See, for example, VENONA message 850, Moscow to New York, June 15, 1944. A month later, the resident agent at the Soviet consulate recommended a $500 bonus for Fuchs.

26. JCAE, *Soviet Atomic Espionage*, 5.

27. On Perl's "highly valuable" contributions, see VENONA 154, Fitin (Moscow) to New York, February 16, 1945.

28. Ladd to Director, August 23, 1950, 100-2483-236. The Bureau gave no credit to the Mexican police in this manhunt, declaring that they "fall far short of the the the standards of reliability which a case like this requires." Yet it was the security police to whom fell the task of arresting the highly combative Sobell and then driving the Sobell family nonstop 750 miles to Laredo—except for "abrupt stops" so that the "extremely" carsick female Sobells could relieve themselves. Legation, Mexico City office, to Director, April 4, 1951, 100-2483-991, 7–12.

29. See Sobell, *On Doing Time* (New York: Scribner's, 1974), passim, and Sobell's discussions of the VENONA releases and his role, available at http://www2.h-net.msu.edu/~diplo/Sobell.htm.

30. Steve Nelson, James R. Barrett, and Rob Ruck, *Steve Nelson: American Radical* (Pittsburgh: University of Pittsburgh Press, 1981), 294.

31. U.S. Senate, Select Committee to Study Government Operations with Respect to Intelligence Activities, Intelligence Activities and the Rights of Americans; Supplementary Detailed Staff Reports on Intelligence Activities and the Rights of Americans, Book III, 94th Congress, 2nd sess. (Washington, DC, 1976), cited at http://www.icdc.com/~paulwolf/cointelpro/churchfinalreportIIIa.htm.

32. See discussion in Katherine L. Herbig and Martin F. Wiscoff, *Espionage Against the United States by American Citizens* (Monterey, CA: Defense Personnel Security Research Center, 2002), 7–8. A full list of U.S. espionage cases from 1945 to 1989 is in Nigel West, *Games of Intelligence: The Classified Conflict of International Espionage* (New York: Crown, 1989), 57–60.

33. See Griffin B. Bell with Ronald J. Ostrow, *Taking Care of the Law* (New York: William Morrow, 1982), 100–101.

34. James Bamford, *The Puzzle Palace: Inside the National Security Agency, America's Most Secret Intelligence Organization* (New York: Penguin Books, 1983), 177–96 passim. The two men, fed up with life in the socialist paradise, tried to return to the United States in the late 1970s but were not admitted.

35. "Espionage in the Defense Industry," available at http://www.fbi.gov/libref/historic/famcases/petrov/petrov.htm (this site gives Markelov the alias Sergei Viktorovich Petrov).

36. "2 Arrested by FBI on Spying Charges," *Washington Post*, June 28, 1975.

37. These and many of the recent cases discussed below are detailed at the Pentagon's Defense Security Service website, www.dss.mil/training/espionage/industry.htm.

38. See Court TV website at http://www.crimelibrary.com/terrorists_spies/spies/boyce_lee/8.html?sect=23.

39. Quoted in "The Falcon and the Fallout," *Los Angeles Times*, March 2, 2003.

40. See report of William E. Moschella, Assistant Attorney General, to Dennis Hastert, Speaker, House of Representatives, April 1, 2005, at http://www.fas.org/irp/agency/doj/fisa/2004rept.pdf; and the American Bar Association's condemnation of the Bush Administration's practices, available at http://www.abanews.org/docs/domsurvre commendationfinal.pdf, just one of many protests.

41. "Engineer Is Held in Scheme to Sell Secrets," *New York Times*, December 19, 1984.

42. Yurchenko quoted in Pete Earley, *Family of Spies: Inside the John Walker Spy Ring* (New York: Bantam Books, 1988), 358. After defecting and sharing so much, Yurchenko then redefected to the KGB, who claimed he'd been "drugged and kidnapped by American agents." More likely, he was upset by his treatment by American intelligence officials.

43. Newspaper digests of these cases are available at www.dss.mil/training/espionage/industry.htm.

44. *Sixty Minutes*, February 1, 2000, available at http://www.cbsnews.com/stories/2000/01/31/60II/main155216.shtml.

45. "Spy Trial Opens, Death Penalty Result Possible," Associated Press, January 28, 2003; "Convicted Spy Accepts Life Sentence: Sudden Sentencing Deal Will Prevent Prosecution of Ex-Air Force Analyst's Wife," *Washington Post*, March 21, 2003. Bush identified the governments of Iraq, Iran, and North Korea as part of an "axis of evil" in his State of the Union Address, January 29, 2002.

46. Ronald Radosh, "Cuba's Top Spy," Frontpagemagazine.com; *Washington Post*, March 20, 2002; *Miami Herald*, October 16, 2002.

47. "Corporate and Industrial Espionage and Their Effects on American Competitiveness," Hearing before the Subcommittee on International Economic Policy and Trade of the Committee on International Relations House of Representatives, 106th Congress, 2nd sess., September 13, 2000 (Washington, DC, 2000), 1.

48. See *Secrecy News*, from the Federation of American Scientists Project on Government Secrecy, no. 26 (February 23, 2006), and *Washington Post*, February 14, 2006.

49. FBI website, available at http://www.fbi.gov/priorities/priorities.htm.

4

THE SUCCESSES AND FAILURES OF
FBI COUNTERINTELLIGENCE

ATHAN THEOHARIS

RELYING ON DEPARTMENTAL CONTINGENCY FUNDS, ON June 29, 1908, Attorney General Charles Bonaparte established by executive order a special investigative force within the Department of Justice, the Bureau of Investigation (formally renamed the Federal Bureau of Investigation, FBI, in 1935). Bonaparte's decision in effect contravened recent congressional actions of 1907–1908 that first rejected the attorney general's request to fund a special agent task force and then barred the Justice Department from contracting for the services of Secret Service agents. Because his decision violated the intent of these actions (although the 1870 statute creating the Department of Justice authorized it to prosecute "and detect" federal crimes), Bonaparte was forced to assuage congressional concerns. During January 1909 testimony before a House Appropriations Subcommittee, the attorney general emphasized the need for such a force, stressed that it would only investigate violations of federal statutes, and pledged to monitor its operations closely to ensure that agents would not violate privacy rights or monitor political beliefs. The size of this agent force (thirty-four in 1909) and Bonaparte's assurances deterred congressional opposition. Congress nonetheless approved appropriations in 1909 confining the Bureau of Investigation to "detection and prosecution of crimes against the United States."

Congress revisited this restriction in 1910, empowering the newly created Bureau to conduct "such other investigations regarding official matters under the control of the Department of Justice as may be directed by the Attorney General." This more permissive standard was triggered by the enactment that year of the Mann (or White Slave Traffic) Act criminalizing the transportation of women across state lines "for the purpose of prostitution, or for any other immoral purpose." Not only had Congress thereby expanded the definition of interstate commerce crimes but a numerically larger force would be required with agents stationed outside Washington, D.C., subject to the supervision not of the attorney general but the bureau director.[1]

The belated (April 1917) U.S. military involvement in World War I did not fundamentally change the Bureau's role as a law enforcement agency. Its wartime investigations focused on alien residents, prominent antiwar critics, and radical activists. Those targeted included Socialist Party officials Charles Schenck and Eugene Debs, leaders of the radical Industrial Workers of the World Union, Senator Robert LaFollette, social reformer and pacifist Jane Addams, black nationalist leader Marcus Garvey, prominent Irish nationalist Eamon de Valera, and the anti-British and pro-Irish Hearst press and *Chicago Tribune*. The Bureau's most controversial actions, however, involved the arrests of hundreds of suspected "slackers" in New York City in 1918 and the arrests of 6,000–10,000 citizens and alien residents during dragnet raids of January 1920, the so-called Palmer raids. All were law enforcement operations, initiated on the suspicion that the targeted subject had violated either the Espionage Act of 1917, the Conscription Act of 1917, or the alien radical deportation provisions of the 1917 and 1918 immigration acts.[2]

Subsequent revelations that in the postwar years Bureau agents intensively monitored political and labor union activities and even investigated members of Congress instrumental in triggering a congressional investigation of the involvement of senior Harding administration officials in the Teapot Dome scandal, led President Calvin Coolidge to dismiss Attorney General Harry Daugherty in 1924. Harlan Fiske Stone, Daugherty's successor, in turn fired Bureau Director William Burns and issued a series of orders to preclude future FBI abuses. These included banning wiretapping and restricting investigations to violations of federal statutes. Investigations of political activities, though scaled back, were not wholly abandoned. Bureau Director J. Edgar Hoover (Burns's successor) encouraged concerned citizens to continue reporting on such activities while the FBI's agents were to report such information as coming not from their investigations but "sources." Bureau files on organizations such as the American Civil Liberties Union and the Communist Party (for a time during the 1920s renamed the Workers Party) continued to be developed.[3]

The real shift in the FBI's role occurred in the mid-1930s when it began to conduct intelligence investigations having no direct law enforcement purpose. The catalyst to this new role stemmed from twin domestic and international crises: the Great Depression at home and the international policies of Nazi Germany and the Soviet Union. The devastating economic crisis of the Great Depression caused many Americans to question the nation's economic and political institutions with some joining fascist and communist movements. Concurrently, as "subversive" powers committed to furthering their own international goals, German and Soviet officials sought to recruit American fascists and communists to conduct espionage.

President Franklin Roosevelt accordingly turned to the FBI to neutralize this perceived foreign-directed security threat. In May 1934, in a one-time response, the president directed the FBI to conduct "an intensive and confidential investigation of the [American] Nazi movement with emphasis on anti-American activities having any connection with German government officials." Then, in August 1936, he met with Hoover to discuss "the question of subversive activities in the United States, particularly Fascism and Communism." Roosevelt was particularly concerned that "some [domestic] organizations would probably attempt to cripple our war effort through sabotage." No U.S. agency was acquiring "general intelligence information" about such "subversive activities," Hoover responded but then claimed that a 1916 appropriation statute would provide the authority allowing the FBI to conduct such investigations at the request of the State Department. Roosevelt orally concurred while emphasizing the need for secrecy (for domestic political as much as for security reasons).[4]

The sensitivity of intelligence investigations (which lacked any law enforcement purpose) ultimately posed a bureaucratic problem for FBI officials, because the 1916 statute required a State Department request to trigger them. In response to FBI pressure, on June 26, 1939, Roosevelt assigned to the FBI and military and naval intelligence sole responsibility for all such investigations. Then, in a series of delimitation agreements concluded with military and naval intelligence in 1940–42, the FBI acquired a monopoly over all domestic intelligence investigations—with military and naval intelligence investigations confined to military personnel and base security (which would include weapons programs such as the Manhattan Project).[5] FBI officials also expanded authorized investigative techniques. To anticipate espionage and sabotage, Roosevelt secretly authorized FBI wiretapping in May 1940 during "national defense" investigations—even though the 1934 Communications Act banned wiretapping and the Supreme Court ruled in 1937 that this ban applied to federal agencies and in 1939 required the dismissal of any indictment based on evidence obtained through wiretaps. On his own, Hoover authorized FBI break-ins of targeted individuals and organizations to install microphones or photocopy records, a series of mail-opening programs (to intercept and open mail transiting through the United States from identified foreign countries), and the cooperation of telegraph and cable companies access to cable traffic involving thirteen identified foreign countries transiting to and from the United States.[6]

Roosevelt's concerns that German agents might seek to exploit anti-Yankee sentiments in Latin and South America also led him to expand the FBI's counterintelligence role. Dating from 1940, FBI officials worked out with William Stephenson, the head of the British Security Coordination (BSC) stationed in New York City, a liaison relationship to ensure that German agents active in Latin and South America would be closely monitored. Then, on June 24, 1940, Roosevelt authorized the FBI to conduct "foreign intelligence work in the Western Hemisphere on the request of the State Department." In response, Hoover created a Special Intelligence Service (SIS) with FBI agents assigned as "legal attachés" to U.S. diplomatic missions in the capitals of eighteen nations in the region. The combination of the FBI-BSC liaison program and the FBI's SIS led to the detection during World War II of 832 German espionage agents, the apprehension of 336, and the shutting down of 24 clandestine radio stations used by German agents to communicate with Berlin and with other agents in Latin America.[7]

In contrast to its successful counterintelligence role in Latin and South America, FBI counterintelligence operations within the United States had mixed results—striking successes and major failures.

In 1938 FBI agents arrested Guenther Rumrich and three other members of a German-directed espionage ring operating out of New York City (although another fourteen co-conspirators escaped arrest by fleeing to Germany). Dating from 1927, German intelligence operatives had recruited German American citizens and German alien residents to infiltrate defense plants (particularly those engaged in airplane and ship construction) and the U.S. military to obtain information about U.S. military technology and tactics, defense planning, and shipping operations in the port of New York. The acquired information was then relayed to Germany through couriers who were either passengers or employed in the shipping industry. In June 1941, moreover, FBI agents successfully shut down another German espionage operation, headed by Frederick Duquesne and involving thirty-three citizens and resident agents, that sought to relay sensitive defense information to Germany through a shortwave radio station in Centerport, Long Island. And in an even more dramatic success, FBI agents in 1942 arrested two four-man teams of German saboteurs, one that had landed in Amagansett, Long Island, and the second in Jacksonville, Florida. These teams' purpose was to sabotage American transportation and industrial facilities along the East Coast, an aluminum plant in Tennessee, and locks on the Ohio River.

The FBI's successes in the Rumrich, Duquesne, and German saboteur cases resulted more from good luck than FBI investigative prowess. In the Rumrich case, the original lead came in September 1935 when a customs officer apprehended William Lonkowski (a German agent sent to the United States in 1927) when boarding the liner *Europa* with film strips and letters concealed in a violin case. Alerted to German espionage plans, FBI officials received a further break when Rumrich blatantly attempted to obtain blank American passport forms in February 1938. Interviewed by military intelligence agents, Rumrich admitted his role. Military intelligence thereupon referred the matter to the FBI, and, in return for leniency, Rumrich identified the other participants in this operation. In the Duquesne case, German intelligence operatives had pressured William Sebold (an American citizen of German descent), during a family visit to Germany, to serve as a spy. When returning to the United States, however, Sebold contacted the FBI and agreed to participate in an elaborate sting operation. FBI agents assisted him in setting up a shortwave radio station to relay to Germany information obtained by their recruited spies. The apprehension of the German saboteurs was equally fortuitous, the byproduct of the inadvertent discovery of the landing of one of the four-man saboteur teams by Coast Guardsman John Cullen, when patrolling the beach near Amagansett. The saboteurs claimed to be fishermen and paid Cullen a bribe. Having overheard them speaking German, a suspicious Cullen returned the next morning to discover the equipment and uniforms that the four men had buried in the sand. He immediately brought this discovery to the attention of the FBI. In the interim one of the four saboteurs, George Dasch, fearing discovery, approached the FBI and told agents the cover names and possible contacts of the other members of his team and the second team that had landed in Florida.[8]

Ironically, the most serious security threat was posed not by a wartime adversary, Nazi Germany, but a wartime ally, the Soviet Union. The FBI, however, failed to discover the scope of Soviet espionage activities during the prewar and wartime years. Dating from the late 1930s and continuing after the United States and the Soviet Union became military allies in 1941, FBI agents closely monitored Soviet embassy and consular officials stationed in the United States (as well as Soviets assigned to the wartime Soviet Government Purchasing Commission) and high-level American Communist Party officials. The scope and intensity of this counterintelligence effort cannot be fully documented either because relevant FBI documents remain classified or when released are heavily redacted. At a minimum the FBI wiretapped the Soviet embassy, the headquarters of the American Communist Party, and a host of radical labor union and political organizations; bugged meetings that Soviet officials or American communists attended; intercepted the mail of communist officials and activists; and broke into the offices and residences of prominent American communists and other radical activists. In these efforts, FBI agents sought to uncover activities "detrimental to the national defense of the United States with respect to espionage, propaganda activities and otherwise."[9]

Nonetheless, despite the intensity of FBI counterintelligence operations, the Bureau's agents failed to uncover the involvement of American communists and Soviet officials in espionage during the World War II era. These included the pilfering of FBI files by Judith Coplon, a communist employed in the Department of Justice; the atomic espionage activities of David Greenglass and Theodore Hall; and the pilfering of classified information for delivery to the Soviets by two rings of communists employed in various wartime agencies, one headed by Victor Perlo and the second by Nathan Silvermaster.[10]

The FBI, it must be emphasized, had not been deterred from seeking to learn about Soviet and American communist espionage activities by a Roosevelt administration indifferent to the employment of communists and motivated to sustain U.S.–Soviet cooperation, or because of the priority of German counterintelligence operations. In fact, Attorneys General Robert Jackson and Francis Biddle approved all FBI requests to wiretap the Soviet embassy and Communist Party headquarters and identified communist and radical activists. Furthermore, dating from 1940, FBI officials assured the White House that they had the situation in hand. In a 1941 report, for example, FBI Director Hoover claimed that the FBI's "active and intensive [counterintelligence] operations are carried on in keeping under observation and constant study the operations of the German,

Italian, Soviet and Japanese Agents.... The identification of all major representatives of the Governments specified are known and their activities are under constant scrutiny." Earlier in 1940, Hoover reported that FBI agents were able to "maintain a careful check against the channels of communication, the sources of information, the methods of finance, and other data relative to" Soviet, German, French, and Italian agents.[11]

Hoover's 1940 and 1941 reports had been prepared at a time when the United States was neutral and when the Soviet Union and Germany still adhered to a 1939 nonaggression pact. FBI surveillance of Soviet officials and American communists, however, did not abate and instead intensified after the United States and the Soviet Union became allies following the Pearl Harbor attack. Indeed, in post-1941 reports to the White House, the FBI Director emphasized the possibility of Soviet (and communist) subversion. Yet the only information that he reported about Soviet officials and American communists involved their efforts to influence either U.S. policy toward the Soviet Union, individuals of Baltic or Eastern European descent, or congressional legislation. Alternatively, Hoover cited communist efforts to influence labor union, youth, and civil rights movements.[12] This total failure to uncover the reality of Soviet espionage is documented by a December 1944 report on FBI "espionage and counter-intelligence operations" having "ramifications within the United States" that only cited the actions of German agents or double agents.[13]

Two cases in particular highlight this counterintelligence failure. The first is a massive FBI investigation of planned Soviet espionage activities and the second is the response of senior FBI officials to the defection of Victor Kravchenko, a Soviet official employed in the Soviet Government Purchasing Commission.

Through a wiretap of Communist Party headquarters, FBI officials learned that Communist Party leader Earl Browder had alerted a West Coast Communist Party activist, Steve Nelson, about a forthcoming sensitive initiative. Bugging Nelson's residence in Oakland, California, FBI agents intercepted Nelson's meeting with Soviet embassy official Vassili Zubilin in April 1943, at which time Zubilin gave Nelson a large "sum of money" for the express "purpose of placing Communist Party members and agents in industries engaged in secret war production in the United States so that information could be obtained for transmittal to the Soviet Union." Thus alerted to a planned Soviet espionage operation involving the recruitment of American communists, FBI officials benefited further with the receipt in August 1943 of an anonymous letter to Hoover that identified by name a number of Soviet officials who were purportedly involved in espionage (some employed in the Soviet embassy and others in Soviet consulates, the Soviet trading company Amtorg, or the Government Purchasing Commission).

In response, Hoover ordered a massive FBI counterintelligence operation, code named COMRAP (Comintern Apparatus), one that had the advantage of focusing on identified Soviet and Communist Party officials. FBI agents followed these individuals and from them followed those with whom they were in contact, eventually totaling forty-six. Lasting two years, the FBI's COMRAP investigation (which extended beyond physical surveillance to include the extensive use of wiretaps, bugs, break-ins, and mail opening) failed to uncover a single instance of Soviet or American communist espionage. Indeed, a December 1944 report summarizing the results of this investigation claimed only that the suspects had distributed "pro-Russian propaganda" through the media and communist front groups to "influence the people and Government of the United States toward acceptance of Soviet foreign policy," to recruit new Communist Party members, to "collect political information of value to the USSR," to "secure information of value to the [Communist] Party," and to promote "the employment of Communists in Government work."[14]

This failure raises questions about FBI counterintelligence capabilities. In part, FBI efforts were neutralized by the safeguards adopted by Soviet officials, as trained professionals, to avert discovery. Equally important, FBI agents had focused on prominent communist leaders and not low-level functionaries (some of whom had severed contact with the Communist Party). FBI agents even failed to follow up on what could have been a promising lead—their discovery, through monitoring one of the COMRAP suspects, Louise Bransten, of her December 1944 meeting in Washington, D.C. with Nathan Silvermaster and Charles Flato. Silvermaster at the time was the subject of a Hatch Act investigation (authorizing the dismissal of any federal employee who was a Communist Party member). FBI officials first learned of Silvermaster's role as head of one of two Soviet espionage rings (and Flato's role as a contributing member) in November 1945 with the defection of the courier for these two rings, Elizabeth Bentley.[15]

A second FBI counterintelligence failure involved defector Victor Kravchenko. Alerted in February 1944 to Kravchenko's pending defection (formally announced in April 1944), FBI officials obtained Roosevelt's and Attorney General Francis Biddle's unqualified authorization to pursue this matter. (Hoover had sought such assurances in light of the potential impact on U.S.–Soviet relations.) Meeting with Kravchenko in March 1944, FBI agents learned that he was willing to brief them about the "espionage activity of Soviet representatives in the United States," about other "illegal conspiracies" between Soviet representatives and U.S. defense firms, about the "activities" of Soviet intelligence agents in the United States, and about the organization and plans of the Soviet Communist Party and the NKVD (the predecessor to the KGB). In return for this information, Kravchenko demanded personal protection (including transportation to a safe hiding place and a permit to carry a gun) and limited financial support (namely, "no monetary worries for about a year and a half"). Hoover immediately briefed Biddle about Kravchenko's demands. The attorney general again authorized the FBI Director to proceed as he saw fit. Biddle had concurrently secured Secretary of State Cordell Hull's approval, because this defection could adversely affect already delicate U.S.–Soviet relations. At first hesitant Hull concurred, convinced that this was a "matter of internal security and might involve sabotage," could provide insights into "what the Russians were doing here," and could serve as a "convenient card" that he could use "when he next conferred" with Soviet officials.[16]

FBI officials, however, failed to exploit this opportunity to learn about ongoing and planned Soviet espionage activities. Instead, they launched an intensive investigation of Kravchenko and those Americans whom he contacted (all prominent anticommunists), suspecting that he "may be an agent" of the NKVD and thus "part of a NKVD scheme to check on the Bureau's activities and attempt to lay some predication for possible embarrassment of the Bureau." In this investigation that lasted until 1945, FBI agents used wiretaps extensively, conducted break-ins, and opened the mail of Kravchenko and his American contacts, in addition to monitoring their activities closely.[17]

The FBI's counterintelligence failures in part resulted from the difficulty of anticipating espionage, but just as important was the essentially political criteria employed to target suspected subversives. In guidelines issued in September 1936, Hoover ordered FBI agents to target "Maritime Industry, Government affairs, steel industry, oil industry, newspaper field, clothing, garment and fur industry, general strike activities, Armed Forces, educational institutions, general activities—Communist and Affiliated Organizations, Fascists, Anti-Fascist movements, and activities in Organized Labor organizations." This focus on radical labor union and political activists was not revised after U.S. military involvement in World War II. Among those targeted were the radical American Youth Congress (during a 1942 break-in of the organization's New York headquarters FBI agents photocopied Eleanor Roosevelt's correspondence with its leaders); Mrs. Roosevelt's contacts with the International Student Association (another radical youth group); anti-Nazi refugees from Germany (Thomas Mann, Bertolt Brecht, Hanns Eisler, Ruth Berlau, Leonhard Frank, Berthold Viertel), suspect because of their Marxist political views; and communists employed in the Hollywood film industry (targeted in 1942 under a code-named COMPIC program). Ironically, the catalyst to the COMPIC investigation was Hollywood's production of antifascist and pro-Soviet films (such as *For Whom the Bell Tolls* and *Mission to Moscow*), confirming that FBI officials' underlying concern was that communists could influence the popular culture.[18]

The reality of Soviet espionage became publicly known with Elizabeth Bentley's congressional testimony in August 1948, with the congressional and grand jury testimony of another communist defector, Whittaker Chambers, in August/December 1948, with the arrest in March 1949 and subsequent trial of Judith Coplon, and with the arrest in 1950 and subsequent trial of the Rosenbergs.

These publicized Soviet espionage activities had occurred three to six years earlier in 1944–45 (with the exception of Coplon, who remained a government employee at the time of her arrest). During the resultant investigations and media exposés, however, no question was raised about a seeming FBI counterintelligence failure. The FBI instead was credited with having ensured the convictions of Coplon, Alger Hiss, and the Rosenbergs. And although Coplon's conviction was reversed on appeal, owing to the failure of FBI agents to have obtained a warrant and to having wiretapped her, even this reversal did not raise questions about methods or capabilities. The debate over Soviet espionage operations instead centered on the actions of the Roosevelt and Truman administrations, with the main accusation leveled by McCarthyites that these administrations' "softness toward Communism" had enabled disloyal communists to obtain federal employment and had also hamstrung the FBI from uncovering Soviet espionage.

This public debate was misplaced. In reality, the Roosevelt and Truman administrations had given FBI officials wide latitude to conduct counterintelligence operations (with Roosevelt authorizing FBI intelligence investigations as early as 1936, in 1940 secretly authorizing "national defense" wiretapping, and in 1942, reaffirmed by Truman in 1947, authorizing FBI investigations to effect the dismissal of disloyal federal employees). Ironically, the very cases that raised public doubts about these Democratic administrations and that had fostered a positive assessment of the FBI's investigative prowess underscore the Bureau's counterintelligence deficiencies.

The Bentley case indirectly documents this. Her November 1945 detailed account of her role as a courier for two wartime Soviet espionage rings, whose members she identified, first alerted FBI officials to this wartime Soviet espionage operation. The participants in this conspiracy had been able to retain their governmental positions despite a government screening program instituted in 1942 to preclude the employment of disloyal employees. (Under this program, an individual could be denied employment or dismissed should the FBI have uncovered evidence of "a reasonable doubt as to his loyalty to the Government of the United States.") The head of one of these two rings, Nathan Silvermaster, had escaped a Hatch Act firing and, in addition, Bureau agents did not launch an investigation to ascertain his involvement in espionage when learning of his (and Flato's) meeting with Bransten in December 1944.

Based on Bentley's disclosures in November 1945, FBI officials launched a massive investigation of those she identified as Soviet agents. A special squad of 200 agents intensively investigated her claims (concurrently urging her to renew her contact with her Soviet handler, Anatoly Gorsky). And because their main objective was to identify those involved in a suspected, ongoing espionage operation, FBI agents were authorized to employ a series of illegal investigative techniques: wiretaps, break-ins, and mail opening. Nonetheless, as recorded in a March 1970 FBI memorandum, despite having investigated Bentley's charges "over and over again," agents were unable to "substantiate and corroborate" them. An October 1946 report to the Truman White House, following up on the flurry of reports based on Bentley's November 1945 allegations that Hoover had sent to Truman administration officials between November 1945 and March 1946, offers further documentation of this failure. FBI officials then lamely justified their inability to corroborate Bentley's charges as due to the "time element," the alleged conspiracy having dated "back several years." This report continued, "The facts are strong in many instances and circumstantial in others principally because of the disparity in time between the date of these activities and the actual report of these activities to the authorities."[19] The FBI's "facts," however, only involved the confirmation that the accused individuals knew and met with each other, whether socially, at public meetings, or through correspondence—but not that they engaged in espionage.

In the final analysis, the FBI's failure was the product of bad luck:Soviet officials had been alerted to Bentley's defection by Kim Philby, a secret Soviet agent employed in British intelligence. Apprised by Philby of Bentley's defection, Soviet officials first ordered their operatives in New York and Washington to "cease immediately their connection with all persons known to Bentley in our work," "to warn the agents about Bentley's betrayal," and to return to Russia before they could be interviewed by the Bureau. The recruited American spies were also instructed to deny any involvement in espionage but to admit to having known Bentley because the FBI might already have observed such contact. Although the FBI had failed to confirm the involvement of those named by Bentley in espionage, Justice Department officials convened a grand jury in 1948 hoping to break one of the participants into admitting his involvement and implicating the others. This strategy failed; none of those identified by Bentley was indicted.[20]

FBI officials' immunity from critical scrutiny recurred in what was contemporaneously seen to be its most brilliant counterintelligence success—the uncovering of a Soviet conspiracy to steal atomic bomb secrets. At various times during 1950, FBI agents arrested the participants in this operation—Julius and Ethel Rosenberg, David Greenglass, Harry Gold, and Morton Sobell. Yet despite the fact that this espionage operation had occurred in 1944–45, no question was then raised about this after-the-fact apprehension or about how this conspiracy was belatedly uncovered.

The identification of the participants in this Soviet espionage operation was the consequence not of FBI investigative efforts but a wartime military intelligence program, subsequently code-named VENONA. Military intelligence first intercepted Soviet consular messages sent from New York and Washington to Moscow during the years 1940–48 and successfully deciphered them (with the important breakthrough occurring in 1949–50). Because Soviet operatives had assumed that their communications to Moscow could not be deciphered, their reports at times included background information about their sources, which enabled military and FBI officials to identify the recruits (Greenglass, Rosenberg, Gold) even though these consular messages concealed their identities through code names. The FBI's principal contribution to the resultant prosecution of the Rosenbergs involved pressuring Greenglass, Gold, and Max Elitcher to admit their own involvement and implicating the Rosenbergs and then developing circumstantial information that corroborated their testimony in specific instances.

Military intelligence was responsible for vetting the individuals employed in the Manhattan Project. Nonetheless, under the wartime delimitation agreements, the FBI should have alerted military intelligence officials about all information that FBI agents had developed about the potential disloyalty of any of the Manhattan Project's employees. In this case, the FBI's failure was secondary.

The intercepted VENONA messages, however, pinpoint a more serious FBI counterintelligence failure. In contrast to the Los Alamos project, where Julius Rosenberg's role was indirect (recruiting his brother-in-law David Greenglass, a military recruit assigned to Los Alamos), the VENONA messages confirm that Julius Rosenberg had personally stolen and in addition had recruited two others, Joel Barr and Alfred Sarant, employed in defense-related industries to steal information about sensitive military technology for transmission to the Soviets. The classified information pilfered by these three included information about radar systems, jet engine designs, analog fire-control computers, and the proximity fuse. Barr and Sarant copied and transmitted 9,000 pages of secret documents relating to over 100 weapons programs and the entire 12,000-page design for a U.S. jet fighter while Rosenberg provided the design for the proximity fuse. Military intelligence was again responsible for vetting individuals employed in defense industries, but in this case the FBI failed to follow up when Barr and Sarant switched jobs when denied an earlier clearance. At no time, moreover, did FBI officials authorize investigations to ascertain whether either Rosenberg or Barr had engaged in espionage even when discovering their employment in defense-related work.[21]

Portrayed as the crime of the century at the time, the Rosenberg case was not the sole known instance of Soviet atomic espionage. The deciphered VENONA messages also documented that Theodore Hall (and his friend Saville Sax, who served as his courier to the Soviets) had similarly provided the Soviets with atomic bomb secrets. FBI officials learned of Hall's and Sax's roles at the same time as the Rosenberg-Greenglass-Gold operation. Without assessing the significance of the information that Greenglass had provided the Soviets (he was only a high school graduate), Hall was a particularly valued recruit, having graduated from Harvard College with a degree in physics at the age of eighteen. On receipt of his submissions, Soviet officials in Moscow characterized them as of "great interest" and encouraged further submissions.

Alerted by military intelligence in 1950 to Hall's and Sax's espionage activities, FBI officials launched a massive investigation that included checking files on communist activities compiled during the 1930s and 1940s, breaking into their residences and opening their mail, and monitoring their contacts and activities in 1950–51. Then, in 1951 FBI agents conducted aggressive separate interviews of Hall and Sax, hoping to break one or both of them to admit to their past conduct and implicate the other. In these interviews, FBI agents asked questions based on the documentation of their activities in the deciphered Soviet consular messages. Unlike Greenglass, Gold, and Elitcher, however, both Sax and Hall denied any involvement in espionage. Sax, moreover, brazenly explained why he had traveled to Albuquerque in 1945 (planning to apply for admission to New Mexico University) or why he had visited the Soviet consular office in New York in 1944 (to assist relatives in the Soviet Union through Russian War Relief). Because FBI agents could not break Sax or Hall, this investigation was closed in 1952. "All outside leads have been exhausted," an FBI official reported, and the "only indication we have" of Hall's and Sax's "espionage activity" came from VENONA and such information "cannot be disseminated outside the Bureau."[22]

The Bentley, Rosenberg, and Hall cases were not the FBI's sole counter-intelligence failures. Another case, highly publicized during the Cold War era, involved former State Department employee Alger Hiss, indicted in December 1948 on two counts of perjury (for denying to a federal grand jury having given classified State Department documents to a known communist, Whittaker Chambers, in 1938). FBI officials first learned of this espionage operation not when it occurred in 1936–38 but when Chambers in November–December 1948 produced State Department documents that he claimed Hiss had given him.

Prior to this dramatic development, FBI officials had failed, first in 1941 and then in 1946, to pursue potential leads that could have uncovered the Hiss–Chambers relationship. In May–August 1941, an FBI informer, Ludwig Lore, told FBI agents of Chambers's "OGPU [Soviet intelligence] Activities in the United States" and his supervision of approximately seventy Soviet agents, and specifically of Chambers's contacts with two "private secretaries to Assistant Secretaries of State" and with another secretary employed by "one of the high officials of the Department of Commerce." Lore claimed that Chambers had obtained from the Commerce Department secretary "all necessary statistical data" and from the State Department secretaries "two extra copies" of the Roosevelt administration's diplomatic correspondence, which they had typed. FBI agents subsequently interviewed Chambers, who admitted only to having been in contact with an "underground group" of federal employees (identifying twenty, including Hiss but no secretaries) whose purpose was to influence government policy. FBI agents did not press him on the differences between his account and that of Lore–Chambers having endorsed their conception of the threat: communist influence on New Deal policy.

Then, in 1946, pressured by an FBI agent about his knowledge of Hiss's activities (the FBI had launched an investigation of Hiss in 1945 based on the suspicion that he might have engaged in espionage, during the course of which Hiss's phone was tapped and his mail opened), Chambers only claimed that Hiss was "favorably impressed with the Communist movement." When the interviewing agent asked Chambers if he possessed any documentary evidence that Hiss had been a Communist Party member, Chambers responded that he did not and then emphasized that he had "never purposefully held out any information and had always been forthright in relaying any information that he had in which the Bureau had shown an interest."[23] Ironically, much like Hiss himself, FBI officials were blindsided when Chambers produced in November–December 1948 documentary evidence (typed and handwritten documents and microfilm copies of State Department documents), which he only then admitted to having acquired from Hiss in 1938.

The FBI's principal contribution to Hiss's indictment, moreover, stemmed from the grand jury testimony of an FBI expert that the typed documents produced by Chambers had been typed on the same typewriter owned by the Hisses. A further FBI effort to enhance Chambers's credibility to the grand jury (essential because he had abruptly changed his grand jury testimony between October and December 1948, in October denying any knowledge of espionage activity and then in December claiming that Hiss had regularly given him State Department documents since 1936) involved an attempt to identify the individual (known to Chambers only as Felix) who in 1936–38 had photographed the classified documents that Chambers claimed to have received from his government sources. The result was a fiasco—an alleged Felix, Samuel Pelovitz, was produced in December 1948 as a grand jury witness. During his testimony, Pelovitz denied knowing Chambers or to having any photographic skills. Prosecutors then called Chambers who at first identified Pelovitz as Felix but recanted this identification when called back before the grand jury, lamely explaining that Felix was not Jewish, but Pelovitz was. The FBI had produced the wrong man; Pelovitz coincidentally was a former communist and had resided (but not in 1936–37) on the same street (Callow) and city (Baltimore) as Chambers's Felix.[24]

The Hiss case highlights the centrality of luck for FBI counterintelligence successes—in this instance the fact that a communist defector had since 1938 maintained what he described as a "life jacket." The limits of FBI capabilities are further highlighted by another seemingly successful FBI counterintelligence operation—the apprehension of Justice Department employee Judith Coplon as a Soviet spy.

As in the Rosenberg and Hall cases, Coplon's recruitment as a Soviet spy was discovered through the VENONA project. The deciphered messages confirmed that she had been recruited in 1944–45 at the time of her employment in the Department of Justice. Coplon, however, had escaped discovery of her disloyalty whether in 1944–45 or with the inception of the Federal Employee Loyalty Program in 1947. Having first learned of her disloyalty in 1949, FBI and senior Justice Department officials sought to ascertain whether she continued her espionage activities and to identify her Soviet contacts. In the course of this intelligence investigation, Bureau agents wiretapped both her office and home phones (and those of her parents in New York, with whom she frequently visited). Bureau and Justice Department officials eventually decided to launch a sting operation to ensure her conviction for espionage by making available to her carefully selected FBI records that would command her attention but would not compromise the nation's security. Coplon bit, and she was arrested in March 1949 when attempting to deliver twenty-eight FBI records to Valentin Gubitchev, a Soviet intelligence operative assigned to the United Nations staff in New York.

Coplon's attorney petitioned the court during her first trial, demanding the submission of the twenty-eight FBI reports as evidence. When the judge so ordered, FBI officials recommended dropping the case rather than honoring this order—claiming that their public release would harm the nation's security. Justice Department officials rebuffed this proposal. The released records, though not harming the nation's security, proved deeply embarrassing to FBI officials—confirming that agents monitored political activities and wiretapped extensively (fifteen of the reports were based on wiretaps). Coplon's attorney immediately demanded a hearing to ascertain whether his client had been tapped, a motion that the U.S. attorney prosecuting the case successfully rebuffed as a "fishing expedition." In Coplon's second trial, however, the presiding judge honored the defense's motion for a pretrial hearing resulting in the disclosure that Coplon's office and home phones had been tapped, that the FBI agent who denied any knowledge as to whether Coplon's phone had been tapped had in fact routinely received the results of these wiretaps, and that FBI officials had ordered the destruction of the Coplon wiretap logs "in view of the imminence of her trial." The combination of the revelations about FBI wiretapping activities and the failure of arresting agents to have obtained a warrant ultimately led to her conviction being overturned on appeal.[25]

The Coplon case underscores the problem of attempting to convict individuals when evidence had been illegally obtained through a counterintelligence operation. FBI and Justice Department officials were unwilling to disclose (in this case as in the cases of Hall and Sax) how they had learned of Coplon's espionage activities (and thus the reasonableness of the wiretaps and the failure to obtain an advance warrant). To do so would have publicly compromised the VENONA program.

These Cold War internal security cases had far-reaching political ramifications, lending support to a McCarthyite politics that blamed the Roosevelt and Truman administrations for Soviet espionage successes. Significantly, the McCarthyites never attempted to ascertain the reality of the FBI's responsibility and that FBI officials had been accorded broad latitude by both presidents. Just as important, Soviet recruitment of ideologically motivated federal employees had been foreclosed by the late 1940s owing to the stricter standards governing federal employment instituted by Truman in March 1947 under the Federal Employee Loyalty Program. Henceforth, Soviet officials were compelled to rely on their own agents or to recruit sources based on greed, not ideology.

Soviet officials also employed "illegals," that is, individuals not assigned officially to Soviet consular or embassy offices. One such was Rudolf Abel, a colonel in the Soviet Union's intelligence service, the KGB, who entered the United States from Canada in November 1948 on a false passport. The KGB's resident agent in New York, Abel was uncovered in 1957 due to the defection of another Soviet illegal, Reino Hayhanen. Recalled to the Soviet Union, Hayhanen interrupted his return upon arriving in Paris in May 1957, approaching the U.S. consulate and then advising a CIA officer of his role as a Soviet agent and how he had entered the United States in 1952 under a false passport. In return for a promise of resettlement, Hayhanen described Soviet intelligence activities, identified one of his recruits (Roy Rhodes), and provided background information that eventually led to Abel's apprehension. Hayhanen did not know Abel's cover name or residence but remembered meeting him in a photo studio in Brooklyn.

Based on this lead, FBI officials launched an intensive investigation that eventually led to Abel's arrest on June 21, 1957. Tried and convicted, Abel was released in 1962 in return for the Soviets' release of captured U-2 pilot Francis Gary Powers.[26]

Luck and solid investigation had led to Abel's apprehension. The same combination led to FBI uncovering another Soviet espionage ring headed by retired naval communications officer John Walker Jr., who dating from 1968 had provided the Soviets with sensitive information relating to naval communications. Walker's motives for spying were strictly mercenary; he was quite conservative politically—indeed his political beliefs and background as a private investigator and businessman enabled him to receive security clearances. Walker, moreover, recruited his brother (Arthur), son (Richard), and a friend (Jerry Whitworth) to pilfer classified information. FBI agents uncovered Walker's espionage activities and those of his ring fortuitously in 1984—their first awareness of possible espionage derived from an anonymous letter (written by Whitworth) to the FBI's San Francisco office and then from reports to the FBI's Boston field office from Walker's former wife, Barbara, and daughter, Laura. FBI agents were at first unable to identify the writer of the San Francisco letter and did not immediately follow up on Barbara's and Laura's reports on Walker's espionage activities. An intrepid FBI supervisor finally acted on these reports, triggering an intensive investigation that culminated in the arrests in May 1985 and resulting conviction of John, Arthur, and Richard Walker and Jerry Whitworth.[27]

If the Abel and Walker cases highlight the importance of luck to FBI counterintelligence successes, the FBI's delayed apprehension of Aldrich Ames was primarily the responsibility of officials in the Central Intelligence Agency (CIA). A career CIA officer, Ames was appointed in 1983 the head of the Agency's counterintelligence branch on the Soviet Union and then in 1990 was assigned briefly to the Agency's Counterintelligence Center. Disillusioned with the Agency and motivated by greed, in 1985 Ames approached the Soviets to sell secret information, particularly identifying Soviet officials whom the CIA had recruited as double agents. He continued thereafter, in return for large sums of money, to identify other double agents as well as providing sensitive CIA records. Troubled by the deaths (or disappearances) of these sources, CIA officials suspected a mole, although they did not focus on Ames until 1992 and only sought FBI assistance in 1991 to uncover the suspected spy—having ignored Ames's extravagant life style, sloppy work habits, and excessive drinking. When finally given free rein, the FBI's intensive investigation (including wiretapping and bugging Ames's residence, monitoring his credit card bills and trash, and following him) resulted in his arrest on February 21, 1994, and conviction.[28]

FBI officials experienced similar embarrassment owing to their failure over a 21-year period to uncover another U.S. intelligence official who had also identified to the Soviets the Russians whom the FBI and CIA had recruited as double agents. This spy, Robert Hanssen, was employed in the FBI's counterintelligence division. After joining the FBI in 1976, Hanssen was assigned to the Bureau's counterintelligence division in 1979 and then in 1983 to that division's Soviet analytical unit, where he had access to sensitive information about FBI counterintelligence programs, the identities of fifty recruited Soviet double agents, and thousands of pages of classified FBI, CIA, and NSA documents. Dating from 1979 he provided much of this information to the Soviets in return for large sums of cash and diamonds. As the result of the death of one of the FBI's recruited double agents in 1986, Bureau officials launched an investigation to identify the mole. Nonetheless, Hanssen escaped detection until late 2000, in part because of the precautions he had taken as a skilled counterintelligence officer (including not disclosing his identity to his Soviet contacts and successfully diverting attention from himself). His arrest on February 18, 2001, was the byproduct of the November 2000 defection of a Russian intelligence officer who, in return for a \$7 million payment, delivered to U.S. intelligence the Russian file on Hanssen. This file contained a tape of Hanssen's conversation with a Soviet official (enabling FBI agents to identify his voice) and a bag that he had used to provide documents to the Soviets that contained his fingerprints. Until acquiring this file, FBI investigators had focused on a CIA officer, Brian Kelley, as the suspected mole.[29]

This narrative does not recount the totality of FBI counterintelligence operations. Because of continued classification restrictions, it is impossible to ascertain whether these and other known counterintelligence operations are representative.[30] Nonetheless, the known history of FBI counterintelligence successes and failures permits some qualified observations.

First, FBI failures were not due to incompetence but to the difficulty of identifying carefully trained spies (or, for that matter, terrorists) who had an obvious interest in precluding discovery of their plans. The cases cited herein highlight the importance of luck (most notably the defection of Soviet intelligence operatives). These cases further confirm the impossibility of achieving absolute security. This is highlighted by the recent FBI investigation of the sender(s) of anthrax letters in October–November 2001. Despite the intensity of an FBI investigation that to date has lasted four years, the sender or senders of the anthrax letters remain unidentified. This failure occurred even though FBI investigators had three advantages: first, they knew that such letters had been sent (and did not need to anticipate this possibility); second, whoever sent the letters had to have access to a lab and the expertise to weaponize anthrax; and third, FBI agents had the vastly expanded surveillance authority provided by the 2001 USA-PATRIOT Act.[31]

The Ames and Hanssen cases further confirm the unreasonableness of an expectation of absolute security. Despite the repressive character of Soviet society, and although Soviet intelligence officials closely vetted potential recruits to ensure their ideological loyalty and were not constrained by a need to respect due process or privacy rights, FBI and CIA officials were nonetheless able to recruit Soviet intelligence officers to betray their nation's secrets.

Second, this history highlights that FBI agents either focused on the wrong suspects, ignored tantalizing leads, or (in the Kravchenko case) made unwarranted assumptions. The objective of anticipating espionage inevitably led to a form of profiling where suspects were targeted based on their politics and associations. This suspicion drove the COMRAP investigation, and, more recently, under-pinned a recommendation of FBI agent Kenneth Williams.

In a report of July 10, 2001, recommending that FBI headquarters launch a nationwide investigation focusing on Middle Eastern alien residents attending flight schools, Williams cited in particular an Al Qaeda sympathizer, Zakaria Soubra. Soubra had come to Williams's attention because of his public role in organizing demonstrations and meetings against U.S. and Israeli policy in the Middle East, his militant beliefs that the resort to violence in defense of Islam was justified, and his advocacy of a unitary Islamist state. When interviewing Soubra, Williams discerned in his apartment photographs of Osama bin Laden and Chechnyan *muhahedeen*. The FBI's subsequent (post-9/11) investigation of Soubra (and others whom Williams had identified in his July communication) uncovered no evidence that they either had advance knowledge of the September attacks or were co-conspirators. That radical political activism does not predict violence and that anticipating terrorism based on public political activities is nonpredictive is confirmed by Williams's failure to have identified Hani Hanjour as a prospective terrorist. Hanjour had, off and on over the previous five years, attended flight schools in the Phoenix area; but he was not a known public exponent of Islamist views. Yet on September 11, 2001, Hanjour (not Soubra) piloted one of the four commandeered jets, American Airline Flight 77, into the Pentagon.

The *President's Daily Brief* of August 6, 2001, captioned "Bin Ladin De-termined to Strike in the US," provides further evidence of the limitations of basing counterintelligence investigations on political criteria. The final paragraph of this document reported that the FBI was "conducting approximately 70 full field investigations throughout the US that it considers Bin Ladin related." None of these investigations, however, involved any of the nineteen terrorists who engineered the 9/11 attack. A July 2, 2001, communication from the FBI's Counterintelligence Division to federal, state, and local law enforcement agen-cies warning of possible terrorist attacks by groups "aligned with or sympathetic to Usama Bin Ladin [an alternative spelling of the Al Qaeda leader's name, often used by the U.S. government]," moreover, starkly admitted that "the FBI has no information indicating a credible threat of terrorist attack in the United States."[32]

Political (and as well ethno-religious) profiling has serious limitations—and carries the additional risk that such investigations could lead to violations of civil liberties and privacy rights. Indeed, one byproduct of the FBI's counterintel-ligence investigations of the World War II and Cold War years was the acquisition of information about the political and personal conduct of suspected subversives. Although this information could not be used for legitimate prosecution or national security purposes, FBI officials in time (on the strict condition that recipients not disclose their actions) purposefully disseminated this information to "reliable" reporters, members of Congress, and congressional committees for the purpose of "influencing public opinion." These covert, and extensive dissemination practices proved crucial to the promotion of a McCarthyite politics.[33]

NOTES

1. Willard B. Gatewood, *Theodore Roosevelt and the Art of Controversy: Episodes of the White House Years* (Baton Rouge: Louisiana State University Press, 1970), pp. 236–47, 249–54, 257–87; Vern Countryman, "The History of the FBI: Democracy's Development of a Secret Police," in Pat Watters and Stephen Gillers, eds., *Investigating the FBI* (Garden City, NY: Doubleday, 1973), pp. 33–38; Max Lowenthal, *The Federal Bureau of Investigation* (New York: William Sloane, 1950), pp. 3–17; Sanford Ungar, *FBI* (Boston: Atlantic Monthly/Little Brown, 1975), 38–41.

2. William Preston, *Aliens and Dissenters: Federal Suppression of Radicals, 1903–1933* (New York: Harper Torchbooks, 1966), pp. 6–7, 118–51, 208–38; Robert Murray, *Red Scare: A Study of National Hysteria, 1919–1920* (New York: McGraw-Hill, 1964), pp. 14, 18–32, 210–22; Charles McCormick, *Hopeless Cases: The Hunt for the Red Scare Terrorist Bombers* (Lanham, MD: University Press of America, 2005), pp. 14–141; Lowenthal, *Federal Bureau of Investigation*, pp. 24–35, 83–129, 147–98; Ungar, *FBI*, pp. 41–45; Curt Gentry, *J. Edgar Hoover: The Man and the Secrets* (New York: Norton, 1991), pp. 71–72, 79–105.

3. Athan Theoharis and John Stuart Cox, *The Boss: J. Edgar Hoover and the Great American Inquisition* (Philadelphia: Temple University Press, 1988), pp. 76–80, 82–86, 92–94; Gentry, *J. Edgar Hoover*, pp. 117–42; Ungar, *FBI*, pp. 45–49.

4. Ibid., Theoharis and Cox.

5. Ungar, *FBI*, p. 101; Theoharis and Cox, *The Boss*, pp. 148–54, 179–85.

6. Athan Theoharis, *Spying on Americans: Political Surveillance from Hoover to the Huston Plan* (Philadelphia: Temple University Press, 1978), pp. 97–99, 106, 125–26, 130; Gentry, *J. Edgar Hoover*, pp. 281–82.

7. Douglas Charles, " 'Before the Colonel Arrived': Hoover, Donovan, and the Origins of American Central Intelligence, 1940–41," *Intelligence and National Security* 20, no. 2 (June 2005), pp. 225–37; Leslie Rout and John Bratzel, *The Shadow War: German Espionage and United States Counterespionage in Latin America during World War II* (Frederick, MD: University Publications of America, 1986), pp. 29–40, 454–56; Thomas Troy, *Wild Bill and Intrepid: Donovan, Stephenson, and the Origins of CIA* (New Haven, CT: Yale University Press, 1996), pp. 33–40, 63–76; G. Greg Webb, "Intelligence Liaison Between the FBI and State, 1940–44," *Studies in Intelligence* 49, mo. 3 (2005), pp. 25, 29–38.

8. Athan Theoharis, *The FBI and American Democracy: A Brief, Critical History* (Lawrence: University Press of Kansas, 2004), pp. 50–52; Francis MacDonnell, *Insidious Foes: The Axis Fifth Column and the American Home Front* (New York: Oxford University Press, 1995), pp. 49–61, 127–28, 131–33.

9. Athan Theoharis, *Chasing Spies: How the FBI Failed in Counterintelligence But Promoted the Politics of McCarthyism in the Cold War Years* (Chicago: Ivan Dee, 2002), pp. 49–50, 56–94; Theoharis and Cox, *The Boss*, pp. 9–11, 13–15; Athan Theoharis, "A Creative and Aggressive FBI: The Victor Kravchenko Case," *Intelligence and National Security* 20, no. 2 (2005), pp. 324–28.

10. Not all Soviet espionage successes were the consequence of FBI counterintelligence failures. Under a 1943 delimitation agreement, military intelligence had exclusive responsibility for all personnel employed in the Manhattan Project. This agreement prohibited the FBI from initiating any investigation of "persons connected with the Atomic Bomb Project," although the FBI did have the responsibility of forwarding to military intelligence any information its agents had obtained in the course of other investigations. Katherine Sibley, *Red Spies in America: Stolen Secrets and the Dawn of the Cold War* (Lawrence: University Press of Kansas, 2004), p. 145.

11. Theoharis, *Chasing Spies*, pp. 60–61.

12. A representative sample of such FBI reports to the White House includes: Letters, Hoover to Watson, October 24, 1942, August 3, 1943, September 30, 1943, October 27, 1943, August 7, 1944, and December 28, 1944, OF 10-B; all in Franklin Roosevelt Presidential Library, Hyde Park, NY.

13. Letter, Hoover to Hopkins, December 22, 1944, and accompanying Quarterly Report on Espionage and Counterintelligence Activities Having United States Connections, November 1, 1944, OF 10 B, Roosevelt Library.

14. Theoharis, *Chasing Spies*, pp. 62—78.

15. Ibid., pp. 47–49, 77.

16. Theoharis, *Chasing Spies*, pp. 50–53.

17. Theoharis, "A Creative and Aggressive FBI," pp. 321–31.

18. Theoharis, *Chasing Spies*, pp. 57–60, 151–55; Theoharis and Cox, *The Boss*, pp. 13, 191–93; Alexander Stephen, *"Communazis": FBI Surveillance of German Emigre Writers* (New Haven, CT: Yale University Press, 2000), pp. 2, 20, 35–36, 43–45, 50, 67, 76–77, 85, 89, 117–29, 138, 190–99, 253–69, 271, 275–76.

19. Theoharis, *Chasing Spies*, pp. 42–43.

20. Theoharis, *Spying on Americans*, pp. 197–98; Theoharis, *Chasing Spies*, pp. 41–43, 54–55, 239–41; Allen Weinstein and Alexander Vassiliev, *The Haunted Wood: Soviet Espionage in America—The Stalin Era* (New York: Random House, 1999), pp. 103–7.

21. Theoharis, *Chasing Spies*, pp. 17–18, 31–32, 45–47, 81–83; Steven Usdin, "Tracking Julius Rosenberg's Lesser Known Associates," *Studies in Intelligence* 49, no. 3 (2005), pp. 13—19.

22. Theoharis, *Chasing Spies*, pp. 31–32, 81–84; Theoharis *The FBI and American Democracy*, pp. 84–85. The FBI's voluminous file on this investigation, FBI 65-59122, documents the intensity of the investigation of Hall and Sax; the 1952 decision to close this investigation is Memo, name deleted to Branigan, May 8, 1953, FBI 65-59122-403.

23. Theoharis, *Chasing Spies*, pp. 114–141.

24. Ibid., pp. 36–41, 114–31.

25. Ibid., pp. 48–49, 84–93; Theoharis, *Spying on Americans*, pp. 100–105.

26. Nigel West, *The Illegals: The Double Lives of the Cold War's Most Secret Agents* (London: Hodder and Stoughton, 1999), pp. 116–26; Robert Lamphere and Tom Shachtman, *The FBI-KGB War: A Special Agent's Story* (New York: Random House, 1986), pp. 273–77.

27. John Barron, *Breaking the Ring* (Boston: Houghton Mifflin, 1987), pp. 3–22, 40–137.

28. Tim Weiner, David Johnston, and Neil Lewis, *Betrayal: The Story of Aldrich Ames, an American Spy* (New York: Random House, 1995), pp. 3–9, 13–17, 32–43, 81–99, 110–20, 128–66, 190–95, 200–52, 276–91; Mark Riebling, *Wedge: The Secret War between the FBI and CIA* (New York: Knopf, 1994), pp. 413–15, 430–33, 441–47.

29. David Wise, *Spy: The Inside Story of How the FBI's Robert Hanssen Betrayed America* (New York: Random House, 2002), pp. 3–4, 7–8, 18–22, 24–27, 37–42, 50–68, 74–84, 94–99, 107–8, 117–19, 122–42, 159–60, 162–247.

30. Other known cases include Erich Gimpel, William Colepaugh, Gaik Ovakimian, Andre Shevchenko, William Remington, Kaarlo Tuomi, Ann and Robert Baltch, Ivan and Alexandra Egorov, Morris and Lona Cohen, James Harper, Daniel Richardson, Allen Davies, Jonathan Pollard, Edward Howard, Ronald Pelton, Wen Ho Lee, Richard Miller, Thomas Kavanaugh, Larry Wu-Tai Chin, David Barnett, Karl Koecher, Sharon Screnage, Nelson Drummond, Joseph Garfield Brown, Valery Markelov, William Whalen, Herbert Boekinhaupt, Felix Bloch, Earl Pitts, Harold Nicholson, Stanislau Gusev, Katrina Leung, Brian Regan, Ana Montes, Gennadi Zakharov, Christopher Boyce, Marian Zacharski, and Stephan Lipka.

31. *New York Times*, September 17, 2005, p. A1.

32. *The 9/11 Commission Report: Final Report of the National Commission on Terrorist Attacks upon the United States* (New York: Norton, 2004), pp. 225–27, 239, 258, 261–62, 272; U.S. Senate Select Committee on Intelligence and U.S. House Permanent Select Committee on Intelligence, *Report on Joint Inquiry into the Intelligence Community Activities Before and After the Terrorist Attacks of September 11, 2001*, 107th Cong., 2d sess. (2003), pp. 20–22, 325–35, Appendix: The Phoenix Electronic Communication (redacted text of Williams's July 10, 2001, report to FBI headquarters); *New York Times*, May 4, 2002, p. A10; May 9, 2002, p. A22; June 19, 2002, p. A18; September 25, 2002, p. A12.

33. For examples of such uses, see Theoharis, *Chasing Spies*, pp. 139–234 and Theoharis, *Spying on Americans*, pp. 133–95.

5

THE IDEA OF A EUROPEAN FBI

RHODRI JEFFREYS-JONES

THE IDEA THAT THE EUROPEAN UNION (EU) should create its own equivalent of the U.S. Federal Bureau of Information (FBI) has been in circulation for some years. Clearly, 21st-century terrorist attacks, such as those on September 11, 2001, the Madrid bombings of March 11, 2004, and the London bombings of July 7, 2005, have added zest to discussions of the issue. Attention has focused largely, if not exclusively, on the European Police Office, an EU agency founded in 1999, headquartered in The Hague, and universally known as Europol.

Although the phrase "European FBI" trips off tongues and keyboards with some frequency, the position is anomalous. Commentators are sometimes erudite on Europol and its history, but they have shown little knowledge of the FBI itself and of its suitability (or lack thereof) as a model for Europol. Officials in Europol or involved in its governance characteristically deny that any emulation is taking place. German Chancellor Helmut Kohl, a keen promoter of European police cooperation, apologized in 1997 for using the phrase "European FBI." Europol official Søren Kragh Pedersen noted in 2005 that there was no talk of the FBI at Europol headquarters, even if he hinted at some ambivalence because the FBI was "still a good brand name." Yves Joannesse, Europol desk officer at the European Commission, observed in the same year that some commentators were ignorant of Europol and designated the agency a European FBI only in a lazy act of "copy and paste."[1]

There are, then, several reasons for inquiring into the idea of a European FBI. One is simply a matter of originality: Such research has not previously been conducted in a rigorous fashion. Another is the need to explore the contradictions between popular rhetoric about a European FBI and the realities of Europol and the FBI, respectively. If misperceptions have occurred, the historian must dissect them and suggest the reasons they arose. Still another reason for the inquiry might be curiosity about the processes by which ideas are, in general, transmitted across the Atlantic. Finally, and more assiduously pursued in this chapter, there is the less arcane issue of what the Americans would call "public history," that is, the utilization of history for public betterment and improved government. In other words, on the evidence of contemporary history, what lessons for Europol-led police cooperation can be adduced from studying the history of the FBI?

On the face of it, Europol is a small organization with less than one-twentieth of the personnel of the FBI and a larger population base to serve, so the comparison may seem strained. However, this essay does posit a number of lessons to be learned from the American experience (as well as some areas in which the FBI could learn from Europol). The history of the FBI over a century or more suggests a need for an expanded Europol with at least some federal laws to uphold, for parliamentary oversight, for ethnic and racial diversity, for commitment to the promotion of the Charter of Fundamental Rights of the EU, for proactive analysis to supplement responsiveness to member state police forces in the field of intelligence collection and analysis, and for liaison with member states' intelligence services in anticipation of the development of that would-be phenomenon, a European foreign intelligence service.

The sources for this chapter, as one might expect, are a blend of printed and digital sources on one hand and, on the other hand, primary sources such as unpublished documents detailing the deliberations of Europol's governing body, the EU's Council of Ministers, and, given Europol's recent provenance, oral history interviews. To round out this preamble with a methodological observation, it seems appropriate to note that one is comparing slow and fast history: The United States is much older than the European Union, and the FBI evolved over a substantially longer period than Europol. If Europol has become an incipient FBI, it will have been as the result of accelerated history.

It remains to examine, in turn, various dimensions of the problem of Europol considered as a European FBI. The administrative history of Europol will not be dealt with here because it has been adequately traced elsewhere.[2] The politics of Europol in individual member states and the way in which the FBI issue has played out in those nations is rich and intriguing (in the United Kingdom, for example, there have been calls for a "British FBI"),[3] but such matters are left to future students of history and government. Here, attention will be given successively to the historical background to the international transmission of police intelligence lessons, impediments to understanding, the reception of foreign ideas, the anatomy of European perceptions of the FBI, enumerated facets of actual FBI history and practice of possible relevance to EU/Europol history and development, and, in conclusion, lessons and cautions suggested by the American experience.

To say that American ideas may have migrated to Europe is hardly revolutionary. From Copernicus to Karl Marx, the intra-European transmission of thought has been a self-evident fact, and European ideas have also traveled further afield. They have beaten a path to America, which, in being well trodden, has furnished a means for reverse intellectual migration. Just as the American founding fathers were recognizably creatures of the European Enlightenment, so the European Union, though largely a response to war and the product of local leadership, came about partly as the result of American encouragement of the idea of a "United States of Europe."[4]

European experiences of policing and intelligence inspired study and occasionally emulation in the United States. The FBI's precursor, the Bureau of Investigation, was established informally in 1908 and given its name the following year. It was also in 1909 that the British domestic security service, MI5, came into existence, but unaware of that, Congress looked to France and protested that the methods of Napoleon's police chief Fouché were being introduced to their country. Soon thereafter, the administration of President William Taft established a Commission on Industrial Relations that looked abroad for inspiration on how to police class violence, and its Research Division concluded that Germany provided the best model.

In the 1930s, FBI Director J. Edgar Hoover wanted to emulate Scotland Yard. According to one school of thought, the British model was the inspiration for the Office of Strategic Services (OSS, established in 1942) and its successor, the Central Intelligence Agency (CIA, established in 1947). In response to the 1960s race riots, a national commission sponsored work on international comparisons. Soon afterward, Princeton University initiated a study of the FBI that elicited comparisons with the Criminal Investigation Departments of British police forces. In the aftermath of September 11, 2001, there was a powerful agitation in the United States, still unsuccessful at the time of this writing, for the FBI to be scrapped in favor of an American equivalent of MI5 (principally on the ground that MI5 concentrates on intelligence work without the distraction of law enforcement duties). Meanwhile, Harvard University supported a study by Adrian Fortescue, formerly Director General for Justice and Home Affairs at the European Commission, on the new U.S. Department of Homeland Security, in which the author suggested that the "EU might learn, but also perhaps teach." Although Americans are prone to think of themselves as isolationist and anti-intellectual, they have been by no means incurious about intelligence and police practices in Europe.[5]

All this suggests a two-way highway. But the idea of a European FBI has provoked opposition. The citizens of member states have periodically suffered from bouts of xenophobia making them liable to oppose *any* foreign idea. Playing the role of big fish in little ponds, their leaders were prone to fight for the preservation of national sovereignty. Member state leaders like Chancellor Kohl had to curb their enthusiasm for European cooperation in police matters not just to appease their own citizens but also to preserve good diplomatic relations with their peers in other countries. They had to remember that it was only in 1991 that the Maastricht Treaty extended the EU's competences to create a legal basis for cooperation on justice and home affairs that included policy cooperation.

The cultural threat posed by the United States could raise hackles in non-Anglophone areas of Europe. The EU allocated funds to the preservation of minority languages like the author's own, Welsh, but there remained the problem of which language or languages should be used for official EU business. When the EU's Council of Ministers debated the first Europol convention, the working papers and minutes were mainly in English. The French lodged several objections. It is easy to see how people might unconsciously recoil from a policing solution that was pre-packaged in the English tongue and seemed to be modeled on solutions in a far-off English-speaking country.[6]

The issue of national sovereignty has been important in the debate. Not recognizing the analogy with state sovereignty in the United States, European federalists have tended to develop the view that the EU model for cooperation is unique, and perhaps instructive for the North American Free Trade Association (NAFTA) and other such entities. The European equivalent of what Americans call "exceptionalism" militates against receptiveness to the idea of a European FBI.

Other factors conspiring against the idea of a European FBI have been resentment of American power, and the unpopularity of the George W. Bush administration especially because of the Iraq war. Additionally, there is the problem of what one German scholar called the "not always glorious history" of Europol, which has had financial scandals. Perhaps even more damaging to the prospects of emulation were high-profile criticisms of the civil rights record of the FBI, and the concerted post-9/11 criticism of the FBI within the United States on the grounds that more than any other agency it had been responsible for failures in prediction and preemption in the months preceding the attacks on the Twin Towers.[7]

A profile of European perceptions of the FBI-Europol issue might appropriately start, then, with the denials of any link between the two agencies. One tendency has been denial by omission. For example, Europol Director Max-Peter Ratzel, in addressing the European chapter of the FBI National Academy in September 2005, circumspectly embraced the FBI as a partner, rather than as a model. Other denials have been more blunt. Willy Bruggeman, deputy director of Europol, stated in 2000, "Europol is *not* an FBI and is not intended to become a comparable instrument of the EU." In 2002, the sentiment found its way onto the frequently asked question section of the Europol website: "Is Europol a European FBI? No." Singly, it would be possible to take such statements at face value. Their frequent and emphatic repetition, however, brings to mind the words of the Danish prince: "The lady doth protest too much, methinks."[8]

That would certainly be the view of those who have opposed Europol outright on the grounds that it uses FBI practices that will lead Europe down the road to a police state. Prominent in this camp has been the British civil liberties group Statewatch. In 1995, Statewatch's Tom Bunyan greeted the adoption of the Europol convention with a pamphlet arguing that the new organization was the result of a 1980s conspiracy by British, German, and other police chiefs to promote "the idea of a European-style FBI." The convention had been "drawn up in secret," the European Parliament had not been consulted, and there was no provision for parliamentary oversight. By the time Statewatch's Ben Hayes wrote an additional pamphlet on the issue in 2002, Europol was installed in its offices in The Hague and had started work. The line of attack remained the same, Hayes's tract being subtitled "towards an unaccountable 'FBI' in Europe" and a section in the Statewatch website was titled "EU-FBI surveillance plan."[9]

According to Niels Bracke, a senior official at the General Secretariat of the EU's Council of Ministers charged with Europol and antiterrorist liaison, Bunyan and his colleagues grossly overestimated the powers of Europol and saw abuses where none existed. But Statewatch's critique won a sympathetic hearing in at least one conservative quarter, *The Daily Telegraph* (as this reminds us, conservatives have a claim to the libertarian tradition). Commenting on Statewatch in the wake of a 45.9 percent boost in Europol's budget post-9/11, a Brussels correspondent wrote that Europol seemed to be developing into "a sort of joint FBI/CIA wrapped together in The Hague." It was further acquiring the kind of powers that had "allowed the FBI in Washington to gain the whip-hand over the U.S. state and city police forces." Members of the British contingent in Brussels worried that any hint of an aggregation in Europol powers would provoke stories in the populist press about the return of "jackboot" (fascist) practices in Europe.[10]

The penultimate observation suggests an equivalence between the states' rights issue in America and the national sovereignty issue in Europe. Member states were wary of police integration. For example, in spite of strong support from the British police for the creation of Europol, in 1995 the Home Office shrank from the prospect of operational cooperation. In the words of its spokesman, Peter Wrench, "the original proposal for Europol envisages a sort of European FBI and that idea has not gone away on the part of some countries, but a clear majority are against going in that direction in the foreseeable future." A House of Lords report warned of the need to be on guard against "great dangers to individuals."[11]

As in the case of the United States, one might argue, a plea for citizens' rights could be a fig leaf for assertions of states' rights/national sovereignty. The United Kingdom, ever the South Carolina of European politics, decided not to sign the additional Europol Protocol of 1996, whereby the European Court of Justice could rule on interpretations of the Europol Convention. The election of a new Labour government in 1997 seemed to promise more openness to European cooperation, with Foreign Secretary Robin Cook endorsing police cooperation at European level. But in 2003 the House of Lords (the forum for Britain's senior judges) issued a further report that was critical of the 2002 Europol/United States agreement facilitating the exchange of personal data, complaining that "the draft agreement was deposited very late, when it appeared that the text had already been agreed with the United States."[12]

Other objections to the idea of Europol becoming a European FBI hinged on the matter of constitutional impracticality, with a perception of the problem having been compounded in 2005 by the failure of France and The Netherlands to ratify the new European Constitution.[13] The proposed constitution would have created European laws, ironed out local constitutional difficulties over the recently introduced European arrest warrant, increased parliamentary oversight, and improved police cooperation. Its defeat perpetuated what one academic study called a state of "legal limbo."[14] Early in 2006, the Austrian presidency emphasized the need to upgrade Europol as well as the general constitutional "architecture" of EU internal security.[15] But for a while, at least, the prospects for a more expansive role for Europol had looked bleak.

Fear of the unknown can be another factor, and here ignorance of the FBI plays a role. The dearth of studies that actually take account of the FBI's history in assessing its modularity for Europe is conspicuous. True, the field is not entirely barren. American political scientist John D. Occhipinti considered U.S.–Canadian police cooperation as a possible model; but what merits attention, surely, is not whether Canadian policemen can operate in the United States but the system whereby a policeman from Maine cannot arrest a suspect in New Mexico, whereas the FBI in a significant number of circumstances can. Another study, by Leuven-based law professor Frank Verbruggen, offered a valuable analysis of FBI–Drug Enforcement Agency (DEA) relations as a possible object lesson for Europol. However, neither scholar addressed the comparative history of police/intelligence federalism. In the absence of knowledge, copy and paste politics was too tempting.[16]

A further dimension of the profile of European perceptions of the FBI-Europol issue is, at least potentially, the paternity debate. After the Bay of Pigs debacle, President John F. Kennedy famously remarked "victory has a hundred fathers, and defeat is an orphan."[17] On the same principle, the stirrings of a debate over the paternity of an organization are one indication of that organization's rising prestige. There have been acute, even bitter disagreements over the origins of the CIA, and historians are beginning to think anew about the issue of whether the FBI originated in the presidency of Franklin D. Roosevelt, Theodore Roosevelt, or even Ulysses S. Grant. Just so, there are signs of dissent over the provenance of Europol.

Denials are legion of the assertion that the FBI fathered Europol. Malcolm Anderson, a pioneer of research into European police cooperation and Europol, reacted thus to the suggestion that following post-Hoover reforms in the previous decade, the FBI might have become an inspiring model for Europe by the 1980s: "It was Chancellor Kohl who launched the idea of a European FBI in the 1980s. It had nothing to with FBI reforms and was always used as a very vague label, given the very different circumstances of Europe and the USA."[18]

Kohl's role and the wider notion of German paternity have rightly attracted serious attention. Asserting "the Germans have always been the principal advocates of a reorganization of the police in the European Union," Verbruggen suggested some reasons. Germany's location at the heart of Europe bordering nine different countries together with its substantial immigrant population made it vulnerable to international crime and keen on international policing. As a federal nation with its own federal police agency, the Bundeskriminalamt, Germany thought it could offer its own system as a model. It pressed its case with some urgency because it regarded adequate federal policing as a *safeguard* against any return to a Nazi past—an analysis that put it poles apart from the Statewatch argument that Europol would be a *threat* to liberties.[19]

But even before the Europol convention had been signed in July 1995, the paternity debate had broadened. According to a 1993 study by French security expert Jean-Claude Monet, the ancient Athenians invented modern policing. Systematic French policing goes back to the 13th century, and, in the 18th century, the French system was under discussion as a model for Europe. The French inspired the conference in 1914 that gave rise to Interpol. That organization is still headquartered in a French city, Lyon (in the 1980s, the U.S. Secret Service mounted the first serious challenge to French dominance of Interpol, perhaps one reason for the growth of French support for an American-proof Europol).[20]

Monet asserted that enthusiasm for European police cooperation was never so strong as when politicians were exploiting mass hysteria. Examples of the latter included the advocacy of border controls to curtail international crime, with populists pressing the panic button when Schengen loosened border restrictions—a process that they claimed gave the green light to international criminals. What made nonsense of their rhetoric, Monet continued, was the fact that international crime had already been rampant before the EU reduced its internal barriers. Colorful language about crime waves and gangster syndicates was just one of Monet's bêtes noirs. Among the other inappropriate justifications of police integration that he cited were the "fifth column" rhetoric associated with the German police and the anticommunism of the French intelligence services. Monet actually favored European police cooperation but did not want it to come about for the wrong reasons. For him, although the federal German and American models were significant, the origins of cooperative policing in Europe were multinational.[21]

An example of outright advocacy serves to round out this profile of European perceptions of the FBI-Europol issue. In 2004, member of the European Parliament (MEP) Bill Newton Dunn issued a pamphlet, bearing the insignia of the United Kingdom Liberal Democrats but conveying his personal views, called *Europe Needs an FBI*. Newton Dunn had left the Conservative Party to join the Liberal Democrats because of the Tories' anti-European stance, and, with his political ambitions and even survival in question, felt he was free to an unusual degree to speak his mind.[22]

Newton Dunn had watched the American scene. He both knew and exchanged views with Bob Heibel, a former FBI deputy chief of counterterrorism who, since his retirement, had taught at Mercyhurst College (Erie, Pennsylvania), an institution that helped train intelligence analysts. Newton Dunn's pamphlet did not deal with the FBI extensively, but it did show an awareness of the Bureau's weaknesses, such as its fraught relations with the CIA, and of its tradition, such as leaving much of America's law enforcement to the local police. This last circumstance showed, Newton Dunn said reassuringly, that a European FBI would not "interfere in national policing."[23]

As his willingness to criticize reveals, Newton Dunn was no FBI dogmatist. Indeed, one development he urged was the creation of a European criminal assets bureau aimed at the confiscation of ill-gotten gains, an approach that the Irish government had pioneered. Much of his pamphlet was a litany of problems that needed to be tackled urgently, including cyber crime, trafficking in heroin and people, gangs, money laundering, car theft, currency forgery, and identity theft. In all these areas as well as in the realm of terrorism, criminals posing a threat to EU citizens were organized internationally, both within and outside Europe. European intelligence and policing could only succeed if organized on the federal principle. As this overview indicates, when Newton Dunn wrote of the FBI, he was using the term to describe both a specific phenomenon that might in some respects be emulated and a general need.[24]

Now I will discuss certain enumerated facets of actual FBI history and practice of possible relevance to EU/Europol history and development. In the manner of what the Americans would call the "public historian," the search will be utilitarian, a reflective exercise in the uses of history.[25] There are pitfalls here. In certain cases, lessons apparently transmitted or transmittable from America are not American at all, having been exported from Europe in the first place. In other cases, similar solutions may have arisen spontaneously and separately on each side of the Atlantic simply because the problems were similar, as was the cultural context within which problem solving took place. Nevertheless, while having due regard for such perils, it is possible to consider selected facets of FBI history, identify European equivalents offering appropriate comparisons, and identify lessons that have been or might be learned.

The constitutional and legal facets of FBI history are of special interest. In 2001 there were, according to one estimate, more than 3,300 federal crimes on the American statute books, with more in the offing as members of Congress saw political advantage in promoting "get tough" legislation.[26] Such a body of legislation gave the Bureau the legal basis for lots of work. It was, however, an outcome that had taken decades of effort and had come about not as a result of the founding fathers' plans, but *in spite of* their constitutional provision. After a period of loose confederation in the 1780s, the United States had adopted the Federalists' plan for a stronger Constitution. This contained at least a partial basis for the exercise of federal police powers. The federal government was charged with national defense, the preservation of the republican form of government in the several states, the protection of U.S. coinage, the administration of higher courts, and (Article 1, section 8) the regulation of commerce "among the several states." But in the compromise that allowed ratification of the Constitution, ten amendments were added, the American Bill of Rights. Here we have a potential complication in interpretation, because the U.S. Bill of Rights was partly based on the Magna Carta and the 1688 English Bill of Rights. However, the last of the amendments was, in the analysis of law professor Bernard Schwartz, American in origin.[27] And it did have a particular resonance for any federal polity. It "reserved to the States respectively, or to the people," those powers not assigned to the federal government by the Constitution.

For the first seventy years of the new republic, one antifederalist crisis followed another, with both New England and South Carolina threatening to secede from the Union, and the (federal) Bank of the United States being dissolved in 1836. But when the Confederate States did secede in 1861, the Union Army settled the matter by force. With the Union sealed in blood, President Abraham Lincoln's last Cabinet meeting in 1865 authorized the creation of the U.S. Secret Service. In the aftermath of the war, its agents—America's first nationally organized federal police force—operated against counterfeiters of the new "greenback" federal currency, with clear-cut constitutional authority. In the 1870s, on loan as special agents to the Department of Justice (newly formed in 1870), they penetrated the Ku Klux Klan, contributing to its demise (this is the origin of the term "special agent" to designate an FBI detective).

President Theodore Roosevelt decided to create a new Bureau of Investigation within the Justice Department instead of having recourse to the continuous borrowing of special agents. But the corpus of laws for the new Bureau of Investigation to enforce expanded slowly. The 1911 Mann Act (also known as the White Slavery Act) empowered it to operate against those who operated the vice trade across state lines, the interstate commerce clause of the Constitution here coming into its own. In World War I, it displaced the Secret Service as the nation's chief counterespionage agency, a function that it performed again in World War II, the Cold War, and at least until the advent of the Department of Homeland Security, in the recent war against terror. The Bureau's repertoire expanded in other respects, too, at least in the case of interstate crimes. By the 1920s, it was investigating automobile thefts. By the 1930s, it was hunting down kidnappers.

There was still no federal crime of murder. "Jumping the fence" became a standard ruse for gangsters on the run—they would reach the state line (or even just the county line) and the cops in hot pursuit would skid to a halt, with the FBI unauthorized to offer help except by circuitous means. Al Capone went to prison for tax evasion, not homicide. The National Association for the Advancement of Colored People's (NAACP) interwar campaign for a federal antilynching law seems irrational (why make murder a double offense?) until one realizes that Southern states were not enforcing their murder laws when the victims were black. But the NAACP failed in its effort to create a special federal crime of murder. In the case of many other serious crimes, too, FBI special agents simply advised on the basis of their specialist expertise or assisted at the scene under local supervision.

Here, however, it is appropriate to take note of a view expressed in 1950 by Edward S. Corwin, a Princeton University professor emeritus who had served in the Department of Justice and was America's leading authority on the

Constitution. He argued that the emergencies of the Depression and World War II had boosted the powers of federal government not just directly but also as the result of the provision of federal assistance in local cases. In positing that in recent cases the Supreme Court had "definitely discarded" the "enumerated powers" doctrine behind the Tenth Amendment he was, perhaps, overly sanguine.[28] Furthermore, following the exposure of an array of abuses of power by the FBI, both Congress and Attorney General Edward Levi took steps in the 1970s to rein it in. But first President Ronald Reagan and then post-9/11 reformers removed many of the restrictions. In summary, few can doubt that the FBI's powers expanded as a result of the imperatives of modern federal government.

Whereas the FBI acquired the duty of enforcing many federal laws, Europol has had not a single such law to enforce, because there is no such thing as a European statutory crime. In the original debate over Europol's remit, the Greek presidency proposed that the new federal police agency would fight drug trafficking and other serious international crime only where such activities occurred "within the territories of at least two Member States," a provision that remains embedded in the Europol convention. There is a parallel with the U.S. interstate commerce provision here, but the Greek presidency proposal went further. Europol would function only in cases where "the form of crime is liable to prosecution in *all* Member States."[29]

These principles were to endure. Noting that the European Union remained "almost always one step behind" in combating organized crime, the Council in 1997 adopted an action plan with the goal of "harmonization of laws" in the member states.[30] When a new European constitution was under discussion in 2005, it was envisaged that a European Public Prosecutor's Office would have powers to deal with "serious crime having a cross-border dimension," but only after unanimous authorization by the EU Council of Ministers and after obtaining the consent of the European Parliament. The British opposed even this measure, and the reverses in the French and Dutch referenda brought the whole constitutional project to a halt. According to Europol's Pedersen, after the constitutional setback, harmonization of member state laws had to remain the goal.[31]

To make the American analogy, it was as if the FBI could operate only with the passage of uniform legislation in every state in the Union. It might be added that unanimous governance through the EU's Council of Ministers resembles the hypothetical situation whereby American law enforcement would be run by a gubernatorial conference with every governor having to agree to each activity. Little wonder that when further protocols were drafted expanding Europol's functions in minor ways, ratification by member states was spotty. A protocol adopted by the Council of Ministers in November 2003 was to be "adopted by the Member States in accordance with their respective requirements," and they were to remember to notify the Secretary-General of the EU if and when they did so. With member states picking and choosing which protocols they wanted to observe, MEP Newton Dunn complained it was difficult to establish who had ratified what. In the aftermath of the 2005 constitutional setback, he predicted that a core of proactive member states would have to drive through police and intelligence cooperation, leaving the rest to join them later.[32]

On the constitutional front, the lessons of the American model might be separated from the lessons of American history, which are far from reassuring. It took a civil war to cement Lincoln's ideal of an "indissoluble union," and, lest that be considered a pessimistic reflection, let it be remembered that many Southerners still refer to the 1861–65 conflict not as the Civil War but as the war between the states. Hopefully, "member" states will not need that kind of transition. For those who believe that there must be an international solution to international crime and terrorism, the hope must be that European history will be both accelerated and peaceful. Perhaps some reassurance may be gleaned from an apparition of individuals wearing cagoules. These are marked "Europol," and their bearers now hover on the fringes of certain crime scenes and offer expert advice, for example, on the chemistry and likely provenance of new, synthetic narcotics.[33] As Corwin observed, the provision of local assistance can be a first step to greater federalization.

In 1954, J. Edgar Hoover concluded an article with the observation, "Local responsibility, recognized by our forefathers, remains the key to sound law enforcement."[34] Although this is testimony to the FBI director's recognition of the political need to continue to propitiate local sentiment, it belied significant developments over many decades in the powers and functions of American law enforcement. The Judiciary Act of 1789 had created the office of the attorney general, and President George Washington at that time appointed thirteen U.S. marshals, the first federal law officers. In 1870, the attorney general took responsibility for the newly formed Department of Justice, and, in enforcing law obedience in the turbulent South, had the support of U.S. marshals, U.S. district attorneys, and the U.S. Army, as well as the special agents on loan from Treasury. As the number of federal crimes increased, so did the powers of federal law enforcers—by the mid-1930s, special agents were able to make some types of arrest without requesting the presence of local sheriffs and, as all but the most sheltered will know, carried guns and used them.

The EU has no equivalent of federal marshals, federal attorneys, or a federal police force, and Europol staff can neither make arrests nor carry guns. According to Niels Bracke, there is no perception of any need for such practices, as the police forces of the EU member states are stronger and better organized than their equivalents in the states of the American Union. This is a topic that invites further research.[35]

One of the main features of U.S. intelligence history is boosterism. Ambitious agency leaders have been publicists. They converted America's woes into institutional blessings. Major augmentations in federal expenditure and responsibility followed in the wake of crises. It happened not just in the Civil War but in all subsequent wars, too. If no war was at hand, another crisis would suffice: the prostitution scare of 1911, the Red Scares of 1919 and the 1950s, the gangster scare of the 1920s/1930s, 1960s radicalism, crime waves, Chinese espionage in the 1990s, and Al Qaeda, the latest "threat du jour" as one U.S. intelligence veteran put it.[36] Money was sometimes poured into the solution of problems that had already passed or had been simply invented by some canny booster.

None was better at publicity than the FBI's long-time director, J. Edgar Hoover. But by way of qualification, even Hoover failed, in spite of his many real achievements and in spite of his exceptional gift for public relations, to become a national intelligence czar. That notion has been debated since the 1940s, yet has triumphed only recently, when both the congressional and the independent inquiry into 9/11 recommended the idea.[37]

There have been some glimmerings of such facets of the FBI's past in the relatively brief history of Europol. Newton Dunn recalled the strategic assessment of Jürgen Storbeck, Europol's director until 2004. Storbeck believed that Europol would achieve take-off only after some great crisis, perhaps a financial scam that threatened the stability of European banking.[38]

The prospects for such a shock may be quite real, not least psychologically. As Monet observed, red scares and apocryphal crime waves are no strangers to European history. MEP Claude Moraes, like Newton Dunn an active member of the European Parliament's Committee on Civil Liberties, Justice and Home Affairs, observed that police politics is "fashion driven." After the Madrid bombings, European Commission President Romano Prodi promised to increase EU spending on security research to 1 billion annually by 2007, matching the spending of the U.S. Department of Homeland Security. On July 12, 2005, in the wake of the London bombings, the EU's Justice and Home Affairs Council met in emergency session. Within two months came the announcement that, in August alone, €15 million had been pumped into security-related research. A cynic might be moved to observe that over twelve months, that would yield just €180 million, far short of the €1 billion mentioned by Prodi. Even the €15 million was contingent on budget agreement by the member states, which turned out to be a contentious issue under the British presidency the following year.[39]

European leaders, then, may be susceptible to gesture politics. But Europol is not. Storbeck, an unassuming man who reminded Newton Dunn of the U.S. television detective Columbo, was not the kind of person to "invent" a crisis where none existed. Even if Storbeck had wanted to issue sensational press releases, he would have been deterred from doing so. When the Europol convention was under discussion in 1994, the German delegation urged that "press briefings or any other form of public communication on matters concerning Europol . . . shall not be engaged in without . . . the consent of the relevant Member State authorities." Ten years later, Europol still took care to inform and consult member state police forces before issuing press releases on sensitive issues.[40]

Europol is not entirely unconscious of its image. It has responded to approaches from the film industry. In 2003, *Den Tredje Vågen* (The Third Wave), a thriller directed by Anders Nilssen and based on Europol, was the most expensive Swedish movie ever made. Its $4.5 million budget did not, however, match Hollywood extravaganzas. In 2004, *Ocean's Twelve* was a Hollywood thriller with a Europol dimension and featured a top-notch cast—Welsh actress Catherine Zeta Jones, together with Brad Pitt and George Clooney. Zeta Jones obligingly allowed herself to be photographed clad in a Europol T-shirt, and the portrait thereafter lifted the gloom in the corridors of Europol HQ. But *Ocean's Twelve* was a sequel movie made just to exploit the success of *Ocean's Eleven* and did not really succeed. Zeta Jones refused to allow her photograph to be used for publicity purposes. Staff at Europol HQ shook their heads and said real agents weren't like that, anyway. There was simply no comparison with the promotional impulse behind the G-men films Hoover encouraged in the 1930s, a genre that prompted a whole industry of FBI movies and even mutated, in a case of celluloid exceeding reality, into "The Postmodern G-Man," and "The New Age G-Man."[41]

Charismatic though Hollywood may be, the promotional lessons learned from America seem to have been mixed. Although European politicians can be opportunist, boosterism has not emanated from Europol directly. In 2004, New York–born Gijs De Vries, having served as Dutch deputy interior minister, was appointed to be what the BBC called Europe's new "terror tsar," and he did liaise through Bracke with Europol.[42] But this was hardly an outcome of long-term promotional activity orchestrated from The Hague. The lesson of American history is that overly robust agency promotion leads to distorted spending patterns with the money going to those gifted at publicity, not those who do their jobs well. The hard sell also led to mission distortion with resources being wasted on populist causes.[43] Boosterism is best avoided, and in this area the Americans would seem to have something to learn from Europe, not vice versa.

"Gestapo phobia" has been a further facet of FBI history of possible relevance to EU/Europol history and development. U.S. fear of the Gestapo is just one manifestation of a long trend—in the 20th century, Americans were deeply opposed also to manifestations of Fouché-style or NKVD/KGB-style political policing in their country. But in the immediate wake of Himmler's excesses, there were particular concerns, first that the OSS might become an American Gestapo, and then that the FBI might enact that role. The specter infused new life into American civil libertarianism. Of greater concern here, though, is the political administrative reaction. In spite of a dawning realization that poor intelligence coordination had contributed to America being caught unawares at Pearl Harbor, the Truman administration decided in 1947 to split the intelligence function, with the CIA being given the foreign job and prohibited from operating domestically and the FBI being stripped of its Latin American empire and restricted to domestic counterespionage and police work. The two agencies feuded, fought turf wars, and, in the run-up to 9/11, failed to exchange crucial data.

In Europe, too, there have been civil liberties concerns. Ironically, Statewatch depicted the FBI, at one time the victim of Gestapo-bogeyman politics, as a bogeyman in its own right. Monet complained about the lack of EU transparency in police matters. MEP Sarah Ludford and her civil liberties allies spoke out in 2002 against the dangers of personal data sharing between the Schengen

Information System (an internal EU crime data base) and Europol and between Europol and non-EU countries like Russia and the United States. It is here worth recalling the *Telegraph*'s complaint of Europol's being a "joint FBI/CIA wrapped together." Ludford continued to voice her concerns in 2005 warning about the dangers inherent in the retention of EU border-control personal details. But Ludford's fellow parliamentarian Claude Moraes reflected on the small size of Europol (just 535 staff in all categories in November 2005), which made it much too nonthreatening to be regarded as Gestapo-like. EU external intelligence work has also been relatively modest, with expenditure in 2000 running at approximately one-twentieth of the U.S. level.[44]

In December 2005, the European Parliament, Commission, and Council of Ministers agreed on a deal whereby intercepted telephone calls, text messages, and Internet connections could be retained for between six months and two years. U.K. Home Secretary Charles Clarke, who had been pressing for such a data retention measure, said he was "not so much offended by the use of the words 'police state' or drawing comparisons to Hitler or Stalin, I just regard them as absurd." Interviewees for this project concurred in the view that Europol was a most unlikely reincarnation of the Gestapo. It was partly modeled on modern German police practice, with German policemen prominent in its leadership— and one of the imperatives of postwar German policing had been to stamp out any semblance of Gestapo-like malpractices.

In the view of some of the interviewees, it was testimony to Europol's benign nature that the public had made little use of the EU freedom of information provision in regard to its activities. Also, there had been few complaints since the 1997 Amsterdam Treaty had made it possible for citizens to approach the European Ombudsman about maladministration at Europol. Between 1999 and 2003, for example, there were only eight complaints to the Ombudsman, most them about access to documents and staff issues and mostly upheld, but none of them particularly controversial in character.[45]

Bracke added a further type of rebuttal of the hypothetical Gestapo charge. Deprived, as it is, of arrest powers, Europol has been and remains an investigative, analytical intelligence agency. It does increasingly provide on-the-spot assistance in inquiries but otherwise leaves police operations to the forces in the individual member states.[46]

Europol, in short, is what the post-9/11 FBI is meant to aspire to: a coordinating intelligence agency. That is not to say that it has solved all the problems of analysis. For example, the challenge of recruiting intelligent and qualified analysts is as problematic in Europe as it is in America. The FBI has traditionally been staffed by brave men bearing guns, rather than by thinkers. Hoover wanted to offer measurable proof of the Bureau's efficacy, so he emphasized the need to make arrests and to secure convictions in court. This "arrest culture" often ran contrary to intelligence needs—should one arrest a terrorist suspect or follow him until he leads one to his controller? Post-9/11, the substitution of analysis for "getting a result" has been an uphill struggle.

The CIA, too, has had problems from its earliest days, as the 1950s Doolittle inquiry indicated. Talented members of the military did not want to waste part of their careers serving an agency lacking any power to promote them to a higher grade of general or admiral. Talented scholars shirked employment that would put their publications and academic promotion on hold and leave them tainted with a secret service stigma.[47]

Europol has had similar problems. Staff were seconded from the police forces of the member states, but when they returned to their own countries they found, like CIA agents, that they had marked time in terms of their careers and had to resume at their former ranks—this applied, for example, to Jürgen Storbeck on his return to the German police.[48] There was a danger that talented officers would be deterred from applying for Europol posts, and indeed Director Ratzel made a special plea at the January 2006 Council of Ministers in Vienna for Europol service to be recognized as a criterion for promotion in member state police forces.[49]

However, the fact that Europol has similar recruitment problems to the FBI and CIA does not detract from what many on both sides of the Atlantic would see as a structural superiority—there are no active police duties to contaminate its intelligence work. Though it seems unlikely that the FBI will ever give up its powers of arrest, perhaps here, too, the Americans can learn from Europol.

It is now time to turn to a further facet of FBI history and practice of potential relevance to EU/Europol history and development. The racial dimension of FBI history is notorious. For many years (1924–72), the Bureau was under the leadership of a racial conservative. Shortly after taking over, Hoover dispensed with the services of two of the few African American special agents in the FBI's employ, and thereafter he both resisted the hiring of blacks and persecuted leaders of the civil rights movement such as Martin Luther King Jr. More recently, questions have been asked about the FBI's apparent eagerness to investigate people of color and non-Christian faith and about its failure to recruit Arab American prospective agents in spite of a pressing need for diversity in the fight against terrorism.

But it must be emphasized that there is another side to all this. The first time the Justice Department hired special agents (in 1871), it was with the goal of suppressing Ku Klux Klan terrorism to the benefit of the African American population of the South. Again in the 1920s (and with Hoover playing a leading role), the Bureau moved effectively against the Klan. Between 1940 and 1952, special agents enforced the antilynching program of the Justice Department's new civil rights unit. In the 1960s, with Hoover still in charge, the FBI effectively (indeed ruthlessly) moved against what was a virtual reincarnation of the Klan, the White Hate movement. In making comparisons with Europe, then, both sides of the coin need to be considered.

In 2005, African Americans made up 9.7 percent of the U.S. House of Representatives—a shortfall in that they comprise 13.3 percent of the population. But the FBI was in a different league: blacks (as of 2003) composed just 5.5 percent of its special agent force.[50] Out of a total of 11,500 agents in the FBI in 2003, there were still only about 6 Muslims. The 2000 census listed 1.3 million Arab

Americans officially present in the United States, and the real number may have been three times as high. Yet a mere twenty-one agents were able to speak Arabic.

Europol, like the FBI and CIA, is composed of what one might call "officers" and "other ranks"—security guards, cleaners, secretaries, computer technicians, and so on. The equivalent of the FBI's "special agent" or the CIA's "intelligence officer" in Europol is the bold employee, so called because his or her job description is printed in bold, the requirement being that prior to joining Europol the holder of such a post must already be a policeperson in his or her own country. As of 2005, Europol did retain the nonbold services of multicultural Dutch citizens, a reflection of Netherlands legal requirements (in a visit to Europol headquarters, this researcher spotted two of the several people of color employed, a guard and a secretary). But the bold force was all white, with no Muslims. Following the EU's enlargement to the south and east, Europol was acquiring a capability in the new European languages, but there was much less emphasis on Arabic and Farsi, in spite of the importance of those languages to antiterrorist work.[51]

Europol (and its supporters) defended itself against the charge of prejudice on a number of grounds. Though it could advertise nonbold jobs in the local Dutch press, employees in the bold category were either seconded by the police forces in their own member states (in some cases being paid by their seconding employers) or successful applicants from police backgrounds in member states. Europol had no control over the hiring practices of those member state police forces. The suggestion was that, excepting the British police with its policy of proactive recruitment of minorities, the police forces of Europe were largely prejudiced against minorities, a circumstance that affected Europol's recruitment pool. Another defense, one of the type that is heard in America, too, is that a minority group applicant, for example, a Frenchman of Magreb ancestry, might be less qualified than a white candidate or less trustworthy because he would sympathize with Muslim terrorists. Such persons should not be appointed just because of political correctness.[52]

A further defense was that Europol is no worse than the EU's institutions as a whole, which are generally white and culturally Christian. This is true. I attended a plenary meeting of the Committee on Civil Liberties, Justice and Home Affairs. In an imposing and crowded committee room that would dwarf the entire parliaments of some nations, the back rows on that particular day were occupied by tourist groups from former European colonies, all black. A few rows in front of them sat privileged officials and observers, all white. The inner core consisted of committee members. Although the committee does contain MEPs of color (Claude Moraes and Saj Karim, a Muslim), the inner core, too, was on that day uniformly white. On that particular day, one could have been forgiven for thinking that the Third World had come to learn from its master.[53]

Both because of his concern for racial justice and because he thought jihadism was a real problem, Moraes has devoted thought to these problems and offered some additional reflections. Europol advertised posts, he thought, in places where ethnic minorities never looked. French postcolonial thinking prevailed—like

Spain and Portugal in their New World colonies, France maintained the fiction (even through the race riots of 2005) that every inhabitant of metropolitan France had equal citizenship and opportunity, regardless of ethnic or religious background. According to this mode of thought, actively seeking nonwhite bold appointments would have been illogical and quite unnecessary. For Moraes, the problem was not just a French one. In Eastern Europe with its newly acceded member states, there were ten million Roma (the gypsies that Hitler despised so much), but they were absent from the ranks of the local police and thus Europol. Why was there no agitation on such issues? Europol was a small organization that operated behind the scenes. It was because of this obscurity that its lack of diversity had not become a public symbol and remained less of an issue.[54]

Here is an instance where Europe can learn. Racial tolerance is a just goal in ethical terms. In social terms, it reduces divisiveness, and with it the likelihood of collective unrest, treasonable betrayal, and individual acts of terror. In functional terms, it enables police and intelligence agencies to recruit more widely, giving access both to a larger pool of talent and to people with special skills such as local knowledge or non-European languages and dialects. Post-9/11 investigations in the United States implicitly recognized such factors and recommended greater hiring diversity in the FBI and its sister agencies. The EU might consider a similar course of action.

Students of the drug addiction problem in America will be aware of another facet of FBI history having a potential bearing on Europol: the Two Prohibitions hypothesis. The prohibition of alcohol in the 1920s was then and is still regarded as having been an expensive failure. There are those, whether on the left of the political spectrum or neoconservatives like Milton Friedman, who would argue that the current narcotics prohibition is a mindless repetition of a historical error. Be that as it may, the American war on drugs fueled FBI expansion directly and, as Verbruggen noted, indirectly through the Bureau's absorption of the DEA.[55]

The parallel with Europol is plain, as the European Drugs Unit (established in 1994) preceded it. Other functions such as anticounterfeiting operations stimulated federal police work in Europe as they had in America, but the war against narcotics had a popular appeal that spread far beyond the banking fraternity. The new designer drugs penetrated suburbia and affected the offspring of politically influential middle-class parents. In the 1994 formative debate on Europol, the drug issue went from strength to strength. In March, the Greek presidency proposed that Europol should fight "1. Terrorism. 2. Other forms of crime." By May, the formula was "1. Terrorism. 2. Unlawful drug trafficking. 3. Other serious forms of international crime." Ten years later, Europol's annual report listed its crime priority as "drugs trafficking," followed by five other categories.[56]

Verbruggen saw the politics of drugs policing as playing a key role in the United States and Europe alike, with "Americanization" of European policing taking place and with the "over aggressive" crusade against drugs doing damage to police structures on both continents, even if Europol was "unlikely to become a European FBI." [57] However, another perspective might be that drug politics has been the engine of police cooperation, perhaps not a desirable phenomenon in itself, but a means to an end. Politicians may never admit that prohibition has been a mistake with a happy outcome, but historians on both sides of the Atlantic are free to speculate in that regard.

This brings us to another facet of the American experience—parliamentary oversight and politics. To legislators' fury, Theodore Roosevelt set up the FBI's precursor during a congressional adjournment. But that was for a special reason—the president's determination to target and root out corruption on Capitol Hill had provoked congressional opposition to his plans. In more normal times, the Bureau has been subject to abundant congressional oversight. Congress has held the purse strings, giving the Appropriations Committees a powerful say, and the heavyweight House and Senate Judiciary Committees, established in 1813 and 1816, respectively, have jurisdiction—the House committee having the FBI specifically in its remit, and the Senate committee being responsible for matters of concern to the Bureau, including espionage, counterfeiting, civil liberties, federal courts, antitrust policy, and revisions of the criminal code.[58] In addition to this, the FBI is subject to the perusal of special investigative committees, such as the Church and Pike inquiries of the 1970s. These in turn inspired new permanent intelligence committees in both houses of Congress that oversaw relevant aspects of the FBI's work.

More than this, the FBI is subject to the scrutiny of the Department of Justice. The attorney general of the United States is appointed by a democratically elected official, the president, and confirmed in office by Congress. Attorneys general have periodically reformed or reshaped the FBI; in their different ways, Charles Bonaparte, Harlan Fiske Stone, Bruce Cummings, Frank Murphy, Edward Levi, and John Ashcroft played roles that could be said to have been of greater strategic significance than those of the Bureau's directors. The Department of Justice also appointed inspectors general to scrutinize particular aspects of FBI performance, and they have sometimes been very critical. For example, in 2002 Inspector General Glenn Fine delivered devastating remarks, based on his audit of the FBI's counterterror performance, to a subcommittee of the Senate Judiciary Committee.[59]

In 1964, journalist Fred Cook published a critical study of the FBI, noting that the Bureau had been "created in secrecy, by executive order, in defiance of the will of Congress." But he added that it had been two "liberal" presidents, Republican Theodore Roosevelt and Democrat Franklin D. Roosevelt, who had created the "all-powerful" FBI.[60] Notwithstanding the fact that recently neoconservatives have made the Bureau their own, the FBI was the outcome of a 20th-century liberalism that, unlike its 19th-century namesake, was statist and thus federalist.

Here, one can detect the glimmerings of a European comparison. Newton Dunn estimated that approximately 90 percent of British Tories opposed the idea of Europol. More liberal parties did not always brim over with enthusiasm, but at least they were not opposed in principle. Looking at the European Parliament, his colleague Claude Moraes estimated that the center-left was broadly in favor of

Europol, especially as it pursued wealthy drug traffickers instead of making petty arrests. The center right, with the exception of the British Tories, was also supportive, but the far right was less keen on police cooperation except on matters like immigration restriction through border controls. Political generalizations and labeling are often unreliable, and it must be conceded that civil libertarian critics of the FBI and Europol are usually liberal/left in orientation, but with those qualifications, it may be said that both the FBI and Europol are the creations of liberal federalists.

But parliamentary oversight is also generally a liberal phenomenon, and this is as conspicuous by its absence from the European scene as by its presence in the United States. The EU's Council of Ministers controls Europol directly and through a management committee. This applies to both Europol's budget and the scope of its activities. The European Commission, which can be seen as a powerful civil service, might be expected to have a strong role, but it is less active than in other realms of EU activity. Europol reports annually to the European Parliament, but on an information-only basis. Europol would like to answer to parliament, and its director has testified before the Committee on Civil Liberties, Justice and Home Affairs on a voluntary basis. The committee is glad to perform this role and would like to expand it. Its members have visited Europol's HQ in The Hague, where they have been welcomed. But in spite of proposals for greater parliamentary oversight, little has happened. Instead, member states have floated the idea that there should be joint oversight by member states' parliaments, as distinct from the federal European Parliament.[61]

In short, by comparison with the United States, the EU has a democratic deficit in regard to the oversight of its federal police. The internal politics of the EU make the Council of Ministers reluctant to allow the Parliament a greater role in oversight of Europol. But the restrictions come at a price. Iron control by the member states may offer a guarantee that Europol will never become an instrument of a European police state, but it cannot offer reassurance to the public of the type that encourages social confidence and willing cooperation with police inquiries. Only parliamentary oversight and investigation can bring that about.

Europol is not a clone of the FBI. There are, however, parallels between the agencies that need to be discussed more fully and candidly. The similarities are sufficient in number to suggest that several lessons might be learned.

In an area like drug policing, neither America nor Europe seems equipped to teach the other. In other areas, in spite of Europol's small size and short history, there already appear to be lessons for America to learn. To this point, Europol boosterism has been kept firmly under control, an achievement that America might profitably emulate in the case of the FBI. If American commentary is to be heeded, Europe would seem to offer another lesson, too. Although it may aspire to a wider role, Europol remains essentially an intelligence agency, something to which the feds—or, at least, their political masters—profess to aspire.

The American Gestapo phobia resulted in an unfortunate domestic/foreign intelligence dichotomy. In the absence of any serious concern about an EU police state, there is a chance that Europe will be able to avoid this problem—early in 2006, for example, there was talk of an external role for Europol in the West Balkans.[62] Additionally, American mistakes would suggest the lesson that liaison with member state foreign intelligence services and with any EU equivalent that may develop should be a security prerequisite.

In other respects, though, the EU can learn from the FBI experience. While the diversity problem is still serious in America, present-day Europe faces a graver issue. The lack of diversity in policing in both member states and in Europol is an affront to Europe's sizable minority populations and a danger to Europe's whole self. Although Europol's liaison arrangements with member states remain essential, there does seem to be a need for direct hiring at bold level that is monitored according to diversity criteria.

American history offers many instances of the benefits of legislative oversight of intelligence functions, as well as examples of how lapses in oversight can cause things to go wrong. With the Council of Ministers monopolizing oversight, Europe has not yet dared to travel down that road, but should do so. On another didactic front, as the substantial corpus of federal criminal law attests, America has largely overcome the restrictions inherent in its constitutional doctrine of reserved powers. Europe may yet unravel that puzzle. However, a caution is appropriate here. Were the European Parliament to acquire greater powers and legislate in this way, it might give cause for Europol to expand from its intelligence function and become an agency with the power of arrest.

That is a dilemma that merits some thought. At some future point, it may be deemed appropriate for Europol officers to have the power of arrest in special cases, for example, where a local police force is failing in its duty. But there would appear to be a Euro-American convergence of viewpoint on the desirability of an agency that can concentrate on analysis and can cooperate with other intelligence and police agencies without being distracted by turf wars or the need to make frequent arrests to satisfy public opinion.

NOTES

Gwenda Jeffreys-Jones (Coreper Desk Officer, Secretariat General, European Commission) gave advice on this project as well as hospitality in Brussels. Terry F. Cole, a former colleague of the author's at the University of Edinburgh, helped with some German–English translation. EU officials and Members of Parliament, some credited by name in these notes and others anonymously, agreed to give interviews and advice. Staff at the EU Council Library, especially Rita Tuominen and (at the Transparency unit) Lino Liao, could not have been more helpful. A draft of this essay was delivered as a paper to the transatlantic seminar of the School of Social and Political Studies at the University of Edinburgh, where John Peterson and his colleagues offered valuable comments. Further advice came from academic colleagues Malcolm Anderson, Simon Duke, and Charles Raab and from Gustaaf Borchardt, director for Relations with the Council at the

Secretariat General of the European Commission. The United Kingdom's Arts and Humanities Research Council made an award to enable the author to undertake research both for a history of the FBI and for this project. The Leverhulme Trust awarded a Research Fellowship that defrayed the expense of overseas research trips. To all these individuals and institutions, the author is most grateful.

1. Frank Verbruggen, "Euro-Cops? Just Say Maybe. European Lessons from the 1993 Reshuffle of US Drug Enforcement," *European Journal of Crime, Criminal Law and Criminal Justice* 13, no. 2 (1995), p. 152; Jan Ellermann, "Vom Sammler zum Jäger: Europol auf dem Weg zu einem 'europäischen FBI'?" *Zeitschrift für europarechtliche Studien* 5, no. 4 (2002), p. 567; interview with Søren Kragh Pedersen (Public Relations Unit, Corporate Governance and Development, Europol), Europol headquarters, The Hague, November 17, 2005 (hereinafter Pedersen interview); interview with Yves Joannesse (Expert National Detaché, Lutte contre le terrorisme, le trafic et l'exploitation des êtres humains, et Cooperation policière, D.G. Justice et Affaires intérieures, Commission européenne), Justice and Home Affairs Building, Brussels, November 22, 2005 (hereinafter Joannesse interview).

2. See, for example, Malcolm Anderson, Monica den Boer, Peter Cullen, William Gilmore, Charles Raab, and Neil Walker, *Policing the European Union* (Oxford: Clarendon Press, 1995) and John D. Occhipinti, *The Politics of EU Police Cooperation: Toward a European FBI?* (Boulder, CO: Lynne Rienner, 2003). Occhipinti's book rarely mentions the FBI and is an administrative rather than a political study, but it provides reliable information both on the formation and development of Europol, and on its EU context.

3. When Home Secretary David Blunkett established the United Kingdom's Serious Organised Crime Agency, it prompted persistent speculation that the goal was a "British FBI": *Gloucestershire Echo*, April 1, 2004; *Independent*, November 24, 2004; *Guardian*, November 14, 2005.

4. See, for example, Thomas C. Fischer and Stephen C. Neff, "Some American Thoughts about European 'Federalism,' " *International and Comparative Law Quarterly* 44, no. 4 (October 1995), pp. 904, 910; John Killick, *The United States and European Reconstruction, 1945–1960* (Edinburgh: Keele University Press, 1997), pp. 9–10.

5. Both in this paragraph and in subsequent passages, a portion of the information is drawn from the author's forthcoming history of the FBI, to be published by Yale University Press. See also Rhodri Jeffreys-Jones, *Violence and Reform in American History* (New York: New Viewpoints, 1978), p. 168; Rhodri Jeffreys-Jones, "The Role of British Intelligence in the Mythologies Underpinning the OSS and Early CIA," in *American-British-Canadian Intelligence Relations 1939–2000,* eds. David Stafford and Jeffreys-Jones (London: Frank Cass, 2000), pp. 5–19; Courteney Ryley Cooper, "Introduction," in J. Edgar Hoover, *Persons in Hiding* (London: J. M. Dent, 1938), pp. vii, ix; Hugh Davis Graham and Ted Robert Gurr, eds., *Violence in America: Historical and Comparative Perspectives, A Report Submitted to the National Commission on the Causes and Prevention of Violence* (New York: Bantam Books, 1969), especially parts I, II, VI, and VII; C. H. Rolph, "The British Analogy," in *Investigating the FBI,* eds. Pat Watters and Stephen Gillers (New York: Ballantine for Princeton University's Committee for Public Justice, 1973), pp. 351–70; Todd Masse, *Domestic Intelligence in the United Kingdom: Applicability of the MI-5 Model to the United States* (Washington, DC: Congressional Research Service, 2003); "Intelligence at Home: The FBI, Justice, and Homeland

Security," chapter 10 in *Report of the Commission on the Intelligence Capabilities of the United States Regarding Weapons of Mass Destruction* (March 31, 2005), pp. 466–67; Adrian Fortescue, "The Department of Homeland Security: A Partner but not Necessarily a Model for the European Union," paper given at the Weatherhead Center for International Affairs, Harvard University, July 19, 2004, available at http://www.wcfia.har vard.edu/fellows/papers/2003–04/fortescue.pdf, p. 31. Sir Adrian died shortly after giving his paper, and in his honor the director general of Justice, Freedom and Security issued a new edition of it under the title *A European View of the U.S. Department of Homeland Security.*

6. For examples of French objections to English monoglotism, see General Secretariat (Council of the European Union), "Proceedings of the Europol Group on 29 and 30 March 1994," document 6018/94, Brussels, April 7, 1994, and General Secretariat (Council of the European Union), "Outcome of Proceedings of Europol Working Party," document 6200/94, Brussels, April 12, 1994.

7. Ellermann, "Vom Sammler zum Jäger," p. 584.

8. Max-Peter Ratzel, "Information Sharing—Developing the Framework to Engage Serious and Oganised Crime in the UK and Europe," address to the 23rd annual retraining event of the FBI National Academy Associates European Chapter, Edinburgh, September 27, 2005 (supplied by kind courtesy of Europol); Willy Bruggeman, "Europol—A European FBI in the Making?," lecture under the auspices of the Cicero Foundation, Paris, April 2000, availabe at http://www.cicerofoundation.org/lectures/p4bruggeman.html, p. 11; denial copyrighted in 2002 and still current in January 2006: http://www.europol.eu.int/index .asp?page=faq; William Shakespeare, *Hamlet* (1602–5), Act III, scene ii.

9. Tony Bunyan, *The Europol Convention* (London: Statewatch, 1995), pp. 1, 9; Ben Hayes, *The Activities and Development of Europol—Towards an Unaccountable "FBI" in Europe* (London: Statewatch, 2002); Statewatch website, http://www.state watch.org/eufbi.

10. Interview with Niels Bracke (principal administrator, General Secretariat, EU Council of Ministers), Caledonian Hilton Hotel, Edinburgh, November 28, 2005 (hereinafter Bracke Edinburgh interview); Ambrose Evans-Pritchard in *The Daily Telegraph*, April 27, 2002. On the jackboot fears, interview with Charles Williams (administrator, D-G Justice and Home Affairs, European Commission), Brussels, November 21, 2005 (hereinafter Williams interview), with a similar point being made by Bill Newton Dunn (member of the European Parliament), Brussels, November 22, 2005 (hereinafter Newton Dunn interview).

11. House of Lords, Select Committee on the European Communities, session 1994–95, 10th report, *Europol* (April 25, 1995), pp. 11, 25.

12. *Europol and the EU's Fight against Serious and Organised Crime* (Foreign and Commonwealth Office background brief, May 1997), front cover and p. 2; House of Lords, Select Committee on the European Communities, session 2002–03, 5th report, *Europol's Role in Fighting Crime* (January 28, 2003), p. 16.

13. The author's interviewees talked of constitutional difficulties, and it was Ellermann's concluding observation, "Vom Sammler zum Jäger," 585.

14. Elspeth Guild and Sergio Carrera, "No Constitutional Treaty? Implications for the Area of Freedom, Security and Justice," Centre for European Policy Studies Working Document 231 (October 2005), pp. 3, 5.

15. Press release from the Austrian presidency, January 14, 2006, net. According to BBC News, EU antiterror coordinator Gijs de Vries at this point referred to "a general desire to now see Europol take on an operational role," available at http://news.bbc.co.uk/go/pr/fr/-/2/hi/europe/4613508.stm.

16. Occhipinti, *Politics of EU Police Cooperation*, p. 1; Verbruggen, "Euro-Cops?," pp. 150–201.

17. Kennedy quoted in Arthur M. Schlesinger Jr., *A Thousand Days: John F. Kennedy in the White House* (London: André Deutsch, 1965), pp. 262–63.

18. Email, Anderson to author, November 9, 2005. Then professor of politics at the University of Edinburgh, Anderson headed a research project, financed by the United Kingdom Economic and Social Research Council and involving Monica den Boer, Bill Gilmour, Neil Walker, Peter Cullen, and Charles Raab, titled "Policing Europe after 1993." Anderson published widely in the field, the main outcome of the aforementioned project being *Policing the European Union* (Oxford: Clarendon Press, 1995), written in conjunction with his fellow researchers.

19. Verbruggen, "Euro-Cops?," p. 150n3.

20. Jean-Claude Monet, *Polices et Sociétés en Europe* (Paris: La documentation Française, 1993), p. 27; Malcolm Anderson, *The French Police and European Co-operation* (University of Edinburgh: Project Group European Police Co-operation, c. 1992), pp. 3, 5, 28–29.

21. Monet, *Polices et Sociétés en Europe*, pp. 301–5. Those who credit France with an input to proto-Europol thinking point to the work done by President Georges Pompidou (1969–74), who, though a Gaullist, tried to bring his nation out of its nationalist-isolationist shell in police matters. See, for example, Francis R. Monaco, "Europol: The Culmination of the European Union's International Police Cooperation Efforts," *Fordham International Law Journal* 19, no. 1 (October 1995), p. 267.

22. Bill Newton Dunn, *Europe Needs an FBI* (n.p.: Liberal Democrats, 2004. This pamphlet has no pagination, but is divided into enumerated sections and subsections); Newton Dunn interview.

23. Newton Dunn interview; Newton Dunn, *Europe Needs an FBI*, sections 6.2 and 8.6.

24. Newton Dunn, *Europe Needs an FBI*, section 8.3 and passim.

25. Dutch historian Pieter Geyl offered some respected thoughts and warnings in this area in *Use and Abuse of History* (New Haven, CT: Yale University Press, 1955), and, since 1978, the University of California Press has published a journal devoted to its eponymous field, *Public Historian*. Of special interest to readers of this chapter may be David J. Garrow, "FBI Political Harassment and FBI Historiography: Analyzing Informants and Measuring the Effects," *Public Historian* 10 (Fall 1988), pp. 5–18.

26. *Christian Science Monitor*, 25 June 2001.

27. Bernard Schwartz, *The Great Rights of Mankind: A History of the American Bill of Rights* (New York: Oxford University Press, 1977), p. 83.

28. Edward Corwin, "The Passing of Dual Federalism," *Virginia Law Review* 36, no. 1 (February 1950), p. 5.

29. Presidency (Council of the European Union) to Working Party on Europol, "Presidency Proposal Concerning Article 2," document 6016/94, Brussels, March 28, 1994 (emphasis added); *Europol Convention* (Luxembourg: Office for Official Publications of the European Communities, 2004), Title I, Article 2, p. 8.

30. "Action Plan to Combat Organized Crime," adopted on April 28, 1997 (97/C 251/01) in Council of the European Union, *Customs, Police and Judicial Cooperation in the European Union: Selected instruments* (Brussels, 1998), volume A, pp. 5–6.

31. David Phinnemore, "The Treaty Establishing a Constitution for Europe: An Overview," Royal Institute for International Affairs, London, 2004, available at http://www.chathamhouse.org.uk/pdf/research/europe/BN-DPJun04.pdf, p. 17; Pedersen interview. For the text of the constitution proposed in 2003, see http://european-convention.eu.int/docs/Treaty/cv00850.en03.pdf.

32. "Article 2, Protocol amending the Europol Convention adopted by the Council on 27 November 2003," *Official Journal of the European Union* (January 6, 2004), C 2/8; Newton Dunn interview.

33. Pedersen interview.

34. J. Edgar Hoover, "The Basis of Sound Law Enforcement," *Annals of the American Academy of Political and Social Science* 291 (January 1954), p. 45.

35. Telephone interview with Niels Bracke, November 9, 2005 (hereinafter Bracke telephone interview).

36. Arthur S. Hulnick, *Keeping Us Safe: Secret Intelligence and Homeland Security* (Westport, CT: Praeger, 2004), p. 189.

37. *Report of the Joint Inquiry into the Terrorist Attacks of September 11, 2001,* 107th Congress, 2nd sess. (2002), p. 3; *The 9/11 Commission Report* (New York: Norton, 2004), p. 411. For a general exposition of the publicity theme, see Rhodri Jeffreys-Jones, *Cloak and Dollar: A History of American Secret Intelligence,* 2nd ed. (New Haven, CT: Yale University Press, 2003).

38. Newton Dunn interview.

39. Interview with Claude Moraes, Brussels, November 22, 2005 (hereinafter Moraes interview); press release by the Xinhua News Agency, March 17, 2004; Keith Nuttall, "EU Gives £10m Boost to Security Research," *Times Higher Education Supplement,* September 2, 2005; anonymous interview.

40. Newton Dunn interview; German delegation to the ad hoc EU Council Working Group on Europol scheduled to meet on February 17 and 18, 1994, "Germany's Views," document 4776/94, Brussels, February 10, 1994.

41. Interview with Rainer Wenning (Corporate Communications, Europol), Europol headquarters, The Hague, November 17, 2005. For a dissection of the numerous movies made about the FBI, see Richard Gid Powers, "The FBI in American Popular Culture," in Athan G. Theoharis, ed., *The FBI: A Comprehensive Guide* (New York: Checkmark, 2000), pp. 261–307.

42. See http://news.bbc.co.uk/go/pr/fr/-/2/hi/europe/3567809.stm.

43. This is the theme of the author's book *Cloak and Dollar.*

44. Monet, *Polices et Societés,* p. 303; Ole R. Valladsen, "Prospects for a European Common Intelligence Policy," *Studies in Intelligence* 9 (Summer 2000), p. 87; Ludford quoted in *European Voice,* October 31–November 6, 2002; author's eyewitness notes on Ludford speech on the Visa Information System in plenary session of the European Parliament's Committee on Civil Liberties, Justice and Home Affairs, Brussels, November 23, 2005; Moraes interview; Pedersen interview.

45. Clarke quoted in *European Voice,* December 15–20, 2005; Pedersen interview, Williams interview; "The European Ombudsman Decisions Concerning Europol,"

available at http://www.euro-ombudsman.eu.int/decision/en/europol.htm. The author is grateful to Rosita Agnew of the Ombudsman's office for supplying this information.

46. Bracke telephone interview.

47. "Report on the Covert Activities of the Central Intelligence Agency," Doolittle Report, September 30, 1954, p. 26, in unlabeled box, Modern Military Headquarters Branch, National Archives, Washington, DC.

48. Newton Dunn interview.

49. Anonymous interview; telephone interview with Søren Kragh Pedersen, February 24, 2006.

50. Congressional Research Service, "Black Members of the United States Congress, 1870–2005," August 4, 2005, web, Table 5; 2003 FBI employee statistics for June 30, 2003, accessed June 2004 on FBI website; Table 13, "Resident Population by Sex, Race, and Hispanic Origin Status: 2000 to 2003," U.S. Census Bureau, "Statistical Abstract of the United States 2004–2005," census website (http://www.census.gov).

51. Bracke Edinburgh interview. On American concerns regarding Farsi and other non-European languages, see "Building Capabilities: The Intelligence Community's National Security Requirements for Diversity of Language, Skills, and Ethnic and Cultural Understanding," *Hearing of the Permanent Select Committee on Intelligence*, 108 Cong, 1 sess, 5 Nov 2003.

52. Interviewees who made these points said that they did not personally hold these prejudices, and they wished to remain anonymous.

53. Moraes interview; Newton Dunn interview; author's visit to plenary session of the European Parliament's Committee on Civil Liberties, Justice and Home Affairs, Brussels, November 23, 2005.

54. Moraes interview.

55. Milton and Rose Friedman, *Free to Choose* (Harmondsworth: Penguin, 1980), pp. 267–69; Verbruggen, "Euro-Cops?," p. 201.

56. Presidency (Council of the European Union) to Working Party on Europol, "Presidency Proposal Concerning Article 2," document 6016/94, Brussels, March 28, 1994; Presidency (Council of the European Union), Note, "Annex to Article 2 of the Draft Convention on the Establishment of Europol," document 7238/94, Brussels, May 26, 1994; *Europol Annual Report 2004* (The Hague: Europol, 2005), p. 6.

57. Verbruggen, "Euro-Cops?," p. 201.

58. Donald C. Bacon et al., eds., *The Encyclopedia of the United States Congress*, 4 vols. (New York: Simon and Schuster, 1995), vol. 3, pp. 1198–204.

59. Fine testimony to Subcommittee on Technology, Terrorism, and Government Information, October 9, 2002, LexisNexis.

60. Fred J. Cook, *The FBI Nobody Knows* (London: Jonathan Cape, 1965), p. 49.

61. Bracke telephone interview; Pederson interview; Williams interview.

62. EU Council of Ministers President Liese Prokop urged this. Press release from the Austrian presidency, January 14, 2006, net.

6

WASHINGTON POLITICS, INTELLIGENCE, AND THE STRUGGLE AGAINST GLOBAL TERRORISM

GLENN HASTEDT

Politics stops at the water's edge.
All politics is local.

NO GOLDEN RULE HAS YET BEEN FOUND that guarantees success in making American foreign and national security policy. Instead, we find the two competing imperatives presented in the epigraphs. According to the first, "politics stops at the water's edge," foreign and national security policy is made in response to events and forces beyond American borders. The nature of the situation confronting the United States, its internal logic and dynamics, and the actions of other international actors combine to establish the parameters of American foreign and national security policy. There is no room for partisan politics or bureaucratic infighting in shaping this policy. At best they are distracters that lessen the effectiveness of a policy; at worst they doom it to failure by injecting inconsistencies, unwarranted constraints, and contradictions into it. According to the second, "all politics is local," American foreign and national security policy is always made in response to domestic political considerations. It cannot be otherwise. Events beyond America's borders no more demand or dictate a certain policy response than do events inside it. Accordingly, foreign and national security policy does not operate according to a different set of political rules than does domestic policy. Success in each requires accommodating differences of opinion that are rooted as much in self-interest as in points of principle and building winning coalitions that are based on power considerations and not the elegance of an argument.

These two imperatives share an uneasy coexistence. They point in opposite directions, yet each contains elements of truth. Policy makers who fully embrace the reasoning of one imperative to the neglect of insights offered by the other risk policy failure. Intelligence policy is no exception. Conceptualizing intelligence solely in terms of unmasking conditions and threats beyond American borders so that the proper response can be crafted will not by itself ensure success in the struggle against global terrorism. Intelligence also needs to be understood in the context of the political dynamics that shape the policy process in Washington.

Conventional accounts of intelligence comfortably reside within the confines of the first imperative. Intelligence is discussed as a value-neutral activity whose defining purpose is to help policy makers better understand a situation by furnishing them with analyzed information. The most heated debates have been over whether the intelligence community correctly understands the capabilities and intentions of America's external enemies, whether it be international communism, the Soviet Union, Al Qaeda, or global terrorism. The most frequently employed framework for understanding how such judgments are arrived at is the intelligence cycle.[1] It breaks intelligence down into a series of functionally related steps beginning with setting "needs to know" and ending with the production of intelligence for policy makers.

Less common are accounts of intelligence that build on the second policy-making imperative. Viewed from this perspective, the essence of intelligence is its ability to enhance the political power of those who possess it. The most heated debates here have been over whether intelligence has become politicized. Obtaining an understanding of intelligence's internal dynamics from this second perspective requires a different analytical framework. Rather than see it as composed of a series of functionally related steps that follow one after the other, intelligence can be broken down vertically into a series of different political games or contests that are continuously being played out. Not all of these games are equally visible to the public due to the level of secrecy that surrounds them, nor is the level of activity the same in each game. Some political contests may be relatively quiet and in a state of equilibrium, whereas others may be hotly contested.

In the following sections, four political games that are continuously played out within the intelligence policy area will be introduced. For each I discuss what is being contested and why; I also identify the key political actors. The struggle against global terrorism provides the necessary policy context for the discussion because as the first policy-making imperative correctly notes American foreign and national security policy is designed with an eye toward dealing with a problem. Policy problems and politics cannot be totally separated.

SYMBOLIC POLITICS

Words and images matter in politics. By setting and controlling the language of the political debate and the images that frame it, policy makers are able to provide an inherent advantage to certain policy options over others and favor certain political institutions and actors over others.[2] As such, the words and images used in policy debates are often contested, but the political contest over symbols is not an even one. By virtue of their ability to command media attention, presidents possess an inherent advantage should they choose to use it. This is especially true in foreign and national security policy, where the president is looked on as the spokesperson for the nation and as the commander in chief. Entering into the arena of symbolic politics is not without risk. Words and images not only serve to control and direct political activity, they also raise expectations and can come to entrap policy makers that employ them.

Post-9/11 intelligence policy in the struggle against global terrorism has been shaped by symbolic politics in at least four different ways. First, it created a political context that favored aggressive collection policies. The George W. Bush administration moved quickly to define the terrorist threat as a war. Employing this imagery was easily understandable and well received by the American public. Both the location of the terrorist attacks of September 11, 2001, and the scale of the death and destruction they brought stunned Americans and produced a deep and palpable desire to reach out and punish those responsible for it. As natural as the war imagery seemed to most Americans, it was not the only way in which to symbolically frame the response to 9/11. Speaking of the British experience with terrorism in Northern Ireland, Michael Howard observed "a struggle against terrorism . . . is unlike a war against drugs or a war against crime in one vital respect. It is fundamentally a battle for hearts and minds. . . . Terrorists can be successfully destroyed only if public opinion, both at home and abroad, supports the authorities in regarding them as criminals rather than as heroes."[3]

From a political perspective, however, the war imagery offered something to the Bush administration that criminal imagery could not. It firmly centered decision-making power and authority on counterterrorism in the White House. It allowed the president to cast himself as a "war president" and in the process, at least for a time, politically disarmed his opponents who, in embracing the war imagery, were obliged to speak in the language of national unity. Just as significantly given the American approach to war, which sharply distinguishes periods of war and peace and favors unilateral action and is loathe to accepting restraints on the use of force, the war imagery allowed and perhaps encouraged the administration to think of intelligence activities in expansive terms. Wars are won or lost and presidents are held electorally accountable. Above all, winning the war on terrorism required preventing another attack on the American homeland, and to this end any and all information on the subject that could be collected needed to be collected.

Second, symbolic politics has been used extensively to reassure the public that the administration was in charge, all is well, and that progress in the war against terrorism was being made in the area of intelligence policy. Just nine days after the 9/11 terrorist attacks, Bush addressed a joint session of Congress and announced the creation of an Office of Homeland Security in the White House. Its director would report directly to the president and be advised by a Homeland Security Council. Tom Ridge, governor of Pennsylvania and a political confidante of the president was named director. The Office of Homeland Security was to oversee and coordinate the development of a comprehensive national strategy to safeguard the United States against terrorist attacks and take the lead in responding to any that might occur. Positioning Homeland Security and its director in the White House put it out of the reach of Congress both in terms of approving personnel and budget and being able to compel individuals to testify. Such requests, which quickly came, were met with invocations of executive privilege.

Intent on defending its prerogatives, Congress challenged the Bush administration by putting forward legislation to create a Department of Homeland Security whose head would be approved by Congress and whose budget would be authorized by it. In keeping with the war imagery, Congress did not present its plan in terms of Beltway politics but as a necessary move to give those charged with protecting the American homeland the power and resources it needed to do the job.

The Bush administration and Congress became locked in a serious political dispute over Homeland Security. As the conflict progressed, the political advantage was going to Congress. The Office of Homeland Security had not gotten off to a strong start. Positions were unfilled, and press accounts suggested that Ridge was not being consulted by other bureaucracies in their decision making on terrorism. Congress was also set to begin hearings into the performance of the intelligence community leading up to the terrorist attacks of 9/11. The star witness was to be an FBI whistle-blower who charged that the Bureau mishandled warning intelligence about those attacks. This revelation strengthened the hand of those who were calling for a Department of Homeland Security. Just hours after these accusations were made and only days before the congressional hearing was to take place, the Bush administration switched directions and endorsed the general concept of a Department of Homeland Security. In introducing his new plan, Bush again turned to symbolism, asserting that his proposal represented the most extensive reorganization of the Federal government since the 1940s.[4] Significantly, as we shall see, FBI and CIA intelligence activities were left virtually untouched by this reorganization. The Department of Homeland Security would not incorporate any of their activities, nor would it receive raw intelligence from them.

President Bush used similarly expansive and symbolic language two years later in signing the Intelligence Reform and Terrorism Prevention Act of 2004 that created the position of director of National Intelligence, calling it the "most dramatic reform of our nation's intelligence capabilities since President Harry S. Truman signed the national Security Act of 1947. Under this law our vast intelligence enterprise will become more unified, coordinated, and effective."[5] Establishing the position of Director of National Intelligence (DNI) had been one of the principal recommendations of the 9/11 Commission. In reality the Bush administration had shown little interest in having it come into existence.

With its attention riveted on waging the war against terrorism first in Afghanistan and then in Iraq, the Bush administration showed little interest in retrospective post mortems on how 9/11 came about. It preferred that such inquiries wait on the successful conclusion of the war on terrorism. Initially this position succeeded. It was only after victory in Afghanistan that in December 2001 Senators Joseph Lieberman (D-CT) and John McCain (R-AZ) introduced legislation to bring an independent investigatory commission into existence. The Bush administration argued this was unnecessary because the House and Senate had now agreed to their own separate investigations. Finding that the terms of reference to these investigations were too restrictive, the families of the victims of the terrorist attacks continued to lobby for an independent bipartisan investigation. On November 27, 2002, the Bush administration and the Republican-controlled Congress agreed. Of particular concern to the administration and its supporters was that the 9/11 Commission would issue a negative report in the midst of the 2004 presidential campaign. To prevent this occurrence, the administration set a May 2004 reporting date and followed a policy of noncooperation with the commission. Vigorous lobbying by the families of the 9/11 victims and negative press coverage compelled the administration into first cooperating more fully with the commission and then agreeing to its request for a two-month extension. When the commission's report and recommendations were made public in July 2004, Democratic presidential candidate John Kerry quickly endorsed all of them and urged rapid action, leaving Bush with little choice but to endorse the report as well. As was the case with establishing a Department of Homeland Security, however, we shall see that creating the position of Director of National Intelligence amounted to far less than the imagery and rhetoric of major reform suggested.

Symbolic politics is not a one-time affair. It requires constant attention and reaffirmation. It is thus no surprise that the imagery of a war against terrorism has been a constant feature of the Bush administration's rhetoric before, during, and after the 2004 presidential campaign. Here the symbolic need exists to reassure the public not only that the structure of the intelligence community has been strengthened but that progress is being made. Two symbolic moves were made in this direction in 2005. Both came on the heels of public reports issued by members of the 9/11 Commission criticizing the administration for failing to enact crucial reforms. In one move, President Bush sought to refocus attention on the war against terrorism by announcing that the United States and its allies had disrupted ten serious terrorist plots since 9/11. Bush mentioned Osama bin Laden by name five times in his speech and asserted that groups inspired by Al Qaeda were trying to "enslave whole nations and intimidate the world." In another move, in late October, Director of National Intelligence John Negroponte publicly released the new National Intelligence Strategy of the United States. In doing so he observed that this document "shows Congress and the public our commitment to building an intelligence community that is more unified, coordinated, and effective.[6] Ten goals were identified for the intelligence community, including bolstering the growth of democracy, countering terrorism, and preventing the spread of weapons of mass destruction. Previous versions of this document had been secret.

Third, symbolic politics was used by the Bush administration to deflect criticism for intelligence failures in the lead-up to the Iraq war, especially as they related to the charge that Iraq possessed weapons of mass destruction, a charge that was central to the administration's case for involvement. Central to this strategy was restricting the terms of reference given to bodies looking into these intelligence failures. The Senate Select Intelligence Committee investigated and reported its conclusions in July 2004 and stated that nearly every finding in the National Intelligence Estimate released prior to the war was wrong. As part of the agreement by Republicans and Democrats on the committee, the Senate's investigation was divided into two parts. Part I, reported here, dealt only with the quality of prewar intelligence. The investigation was not permitted to examine how intelligence was used by the Bush administration. The administration's handling of intelligence was to be Part II of the investigation. As 2005 ended, Part II had yet to begin, and Republicans and Democrats on the committee were sparring over the need to hear testimony from administration officials.

A second effort a deflecting attention from the administration to the intelligence agencies came with the terms of reference assigned to the Commission on the Intelligence Capabilities of the United States Regarding Weapons of Mass Destruction, also known as the Silberman-Robb Commission, after its co-chairs, Judge Laurence Silberman and former Senator Charles Robb (D-VA). Bush initially resisted efforts to establish such a commission. He changed his position in early February 2004 following the late January resignation of UN chief weapons inspector David Kay and his subsequent testimony to Congress that "we were almost all wrong" about Iraq's weapons program.[7] Bush had argued that creating a commission to look into this issue was premature and should wait on a more exhaustive search for weapons of mass destruction. But now fearful that the White House would lose control over the issue, Bush endorsed a commission but indicated that it would look at intelligence on weapons programs in Libya, Iran, and North Korea as well. He also indicated that he would appoint all of its members. This move angered congressional Democrats, who argued that the commission could no longer be considered independent.

Unlike the 9/11 Commission, whose deliberations the administration had failed to control, the Silberman-Robb Commission held closed-door hearings rather than public ones. It was also not authorized to examine how policy makers used the intelligence they received. The Commission released its report on March 31, 2005. Where the 9/11 Commission stated that President Bush saw repeated warnings about a potential terrorist attack prior to 9/11, the Silberman-Robb Commission concluded that the intelligence community was "dead wrong" in most of their assessments.[8] Press accounts describe Silberman and Robb standing next to Bush at the public release of the report looking like bodyguards. The report mentions the CIA 1,567 times, the White House eight times, and Vice President Dick Cheney twice.

Finally, symbolic politics can be used to place responsibility for future problems on others. Consumer safety alerts, foreign travel advisories, drug warning labels, and the like all say to citizens that the government is doing its job and now you must do yours. This is very much the case with issuing warnings about terrorist attacks. Lawrence Freedman notes that by communicating threat warnings, governments are able to shift responsibility for dealing with the risk of terrorism from governments to citizens, who are then the ones who make the decision on whether to ride the subways, go to work, or open their mail.[9]

As examples of this tendency, we have the October 2005 decisions to place police officers on every train, to have major shows of force at transportation centers in New York City, and to close the Baltimore Harbor Tunnel. All decisions were made in the aftermath of the London terrorist bombings in 2005, and the intelligence used consisted almost entirely of tips that a terrorist attack was possible in the immediate future. In the Baltimore case, the tip was described as uncorroborated. In the New York case, the threat was dismissed by Department of Homeland Security officials almost as soon as the alert was announced. On a more general level we have the color-coded alert system put in place by the Department of Homeland Security. Six times between its introduction after 9/11 and the presidential election of 2004, the system went into an orange or elevated alert level. Although issuing warnings holds the potential for shifting responsibility away from policy makers, it also has risks, especially when threats fail to materialize. Under these circumstances, policy makers are again trapped by their own symbols and run the risk of being accused of politicizing a situation or alarmism.

For intelligence, three consequences follow from the policy makers' desire to at least at a symbolic level protect themselves from charges that they are not doing their jobs. First, policy makers will demand greater specificity from intelligence than is possible. They will want the intelligence community to engage in fortune-telling.[10] One can see this outlook in President Bush's comment that the August 6, 2001, President's Daily Brief titled "Bin Laden Determined to Strike in US" did not contain specific enough information to take action.[11] Second, in the absence of concrete intelligence, policy makers tend to place greater emphasis on worst-case speculation about potential vulnerabilities and what terrorists might do rather than on the limited intelligence on hand about what terrorists are doing or planning. Finally, it heightens the tendency to engage in "sweepstakes" intelligence where the rush to a bottom-line conclusion takes precedence over sound analysis.[12] Taken together, these three tendencies work against the credibility of intelligence warnings over terrorist attacks but address the political imperative of shifting blame.

RESOURCE POLITICS

By its very nature and purpose, symbolic politics is a highly visible enterprise. Far less visible is the second political game or contest played out in Washington, DC: resource politics. Where the president is the principal political player in the symbolic politics arena, Congress and bureaucratic forces dominate resource politics. Successful symbolic politics actually provides a cover that shields this political game from public view by encouraging the general population to turn its attention to other matters because public statements, laws, investigations, or administrative reforms have taken place that have addressed the problem. The struggle against terrorism is no exception. Speaking of the 9/11 Commission's call to create a powerful Director of National Intelligence and locate the office in the White House, Congressman Jack Murtha (D-PA) commented in September 2004 that "public indifference will make Congress able to resist changes [to the intelligence community]."[13] Presidents traditionally have not been active players in these political arenas because they care less about reorganization than do legislators and bureaucrats and frequently employ them as bargaining chips.

Resource politics are concerned with the basic fiber of organizations: their structure, budgets, and areas of jurisdiction. All were key areas of contention in intelligence policy in Washington after 9/11 with the creation of the Department of Homeland Security and the post of director of National Intelligence.[14] As noted in the discussion of symbolic politics, they both were hailed as significant accomplishments in improving the quality of intelligence and winning the struggle against global terrorism. It bears noting, however, that as the reorganization process came to an end, no intelligence agency was abolished. Instead, the number of intelligence bureaucracies increased.

We can see the central role played by resource politics in setting up the Department of Homeland Security and the corresponding lack of importance of attached to intelligence concerns by the two struggles that began and ended this political contest. The policy debate began over whether a Cabinet-level Department of Homeland Security or an Office of Homeland Security in the White House should be created. This is a structural issue, and at its heart was the ability of Congress to influence how its funds were spent and who would run the department. A White House Office of Homeland Security would be beyond its reach, but not a Department of Homeland Security. The final policy debate was over the degree of civil service protection to be afforded to personnel assigned to the new department and the power of the Secretary of Homeland Security. Under Bush's proposal, the secretary would have the ability to reorganize the Department of Homeland Security without congressional approval as well as great flexibility in hiring and firing employees. It would have subjected only fourteen of twenty-eight senior officials to senatorial confirmation to hire and fire individuals and change their job responsibilities. The battle over implementing a new personnel system did not end with passage of the legislation creating the department. In August 2005, a U.S. District Judge argued that the system undermined employees' collective bargaining rights. Another judge issued a similar ruling in February 2006 over an attempt to extend such a system to the Defense Department.

As created, the Department of Homeland Security had three primary missions: (1) to prevent terrorist attacks within the United States, (2) to reduce the vulnerability of the United States to terrorism, and (3) to minimize the damage and assist in the recovery from terrorist attacks that do occur here. To accomplish these objectives twenty-two different agencies with some 170,000 employees were brought together in the new department. When President Bush publicly embraced the concept of a Department of Homeland Security in spring 2002, many inside and outside the administration speculated that it would become the primary intelligence center for the war on terrorism. Even the language establishing it suggested a major intelligence role. "Except as otherwise directed by the president the secretary [of Homeland Security] shall have such access to all information including reports . . . and unevaluated intelligence relating to threats of terrorism."[15] The reality proved to be quite different on both accounts.

The FBI and CIA were largely unaffected by the establishment of the Department of Homeland Security. Also remaining outside the new unit were the National Security Agency, the Defense Intelligence Agency, and the Northern Command, which is charged with the defense of American territory.

From the very outset, FBI Director Robert Mueller and Director of Central Intelligence (DCI) George Tenet spoke out against any rapid, major overhaul of the intelligence community, as did senior active and retired intelligence officials. Their opposition and uncertainty in Congress over how to proceed led to a decision to postpone intelligence reorganization and focus on reorganizing other aspects of Homeland Security, such as border and transportation protection, immigration, and disaster preparedness.

With intelligence agencies not subject to reorganization, the Department of Homeland Security became confined to the status of a consumer of intelligence and not a producer. Both the FBI and CIA pressed for strict limits on the information they had to share with the new department. One Senate aide close to the reorganization process stated that "there is real friction among these agencies. A lot of people want to put Homeland Security in a little box and not share much with them."[16] By mid-July Tom Ridge, still in his capacity as director of the White House Office of Homeland Security, was saying that the new department would limit its intelligence work to preparing warnings and leaving the central task of collecting intelligence to the FBI, CIA, and the Department of Defense intelligence agencies. Homeland Security was to be a coordinating center with access to the analytical production and information-gathering capabilities of the federal government. By the end of 2002, the administration's position retreated to the point where Ridge, now Secretary of Homeland Security, would only have access to unevaluated raw intelligence when he could make a case for it under yet-to-be-determined procedures.

These institutional and procedural arrangements did little to address the problem of intelligence sharing that the 9/11 Commission identified as a major deficiency in its report. Not only was the Department of Homeland Security limited in its access to intelligence from key agencies, but several units incorporated into its structure, notably the Coast Guard, Secret Service, Customs Service, and Immigration and Naturalization Service, retained their intelligence collection divisions.

The 9/11 Commission issued its report on July 22, 2004. Its central recommendation was the establishment of the position of Director of National Intelligence. This individual would oversee all-source national intelligence centers, serve as the president's principal intelligence advisor, manage the national intelligence program, and oversee the component agencies of the intelligence community. Included in his powers would be the responsibility for submitting a unified intelligence budget, appropriating fund to the intelligence agencies, and setting personnel policies for the intelligence community. The Director of National Intelligence's office would be in the White House.

The proposal to create a Director of National Intelligence, or DNI, became part of the Intelligence Reform and Terrorism Prevention Act of 2004. The House and Senate passed different versions of the bill with the Senate bill more closely following the 9/11 Commission's call for a strong DNI. The House bill provided for a far less powerful director. Under the Senate bill, the CIA director "shall be under the authority, direction, and control" of the national intelligence director. In the House version, the CIA director would only "report" to the National Intelligence Director. The House bill also only gave the National Intelligence Director the power to develop budgets and give "guidance" to intelligence community members. The Senate bill stated that he or she would "determine" the budget. The Senate bill would also make the intelligence budget public, require that most of the Director's high-ranking assistants be confirmed by the Senate, and create a civil liberties panel to prevent privacy abuses. Were the House version to prevail, which it largely did, some senators warned that Congress and the president would be creating a Potemkin Director of National Intelligence.

By fall, the House and Senate were deadlocked. Key opposition came from House Republicans led by Duncan Hunter (R-CA), chair of the House Armed Services Committee, who was adamant that the Pentagon should not loose control over its intelligence budget and that the overall intelligence budget should remain secret. To the consternation of the families of the victims of the 9/11 attacks and in the face of their pubic calls for action, President Bush remained on the sidelines as the battle dragged on. In fact, the administration from the outset had shown little interest creating the position of the position of DNI as outlined by the 9/11 Commission and was opposed to placing this office in the White House. Though the president did not speak out against the 9/11 Commission's recommendations, some argue he moved quietly to blunt the intent of the reforms through the issuance of executive orders and memos that in some cases did little more than reaffirm the system as it existed, including the secretary of Defense's operational control over defense intelligence agencies and intelligence priorities and in other cases advanced the commission's recommendations to established bureaucratic interests in a nonthreatening manner.[17]

Visible bureaucratic opposition to the 9/11 Commission's version of a DNI emerged soon after its report was released. Ridge opposed the idea, stating, "We don't need an intelligence czar."[18] Along with Secretary of Defense Donald

Rumsfeld and National Security Advisor Condoleezza Rice, he cautioned against moving too quickly. He also echoed Rumsfeld's warnings about creating a new layer of intelligence bureaucracy. Rumsfeld reportedly "blasted" the 9/11 Commission's report in classified hearings and stressed that centralizing intelligence outside of the Pentagon's control might undermine the military's ability to conduct the war against terrorism by placing barriers between Washington and battlefield commanders. The chairman of the Joint Chiefs of Staff, Gen. Richard Myers, made the same point in a letter he sent to congressional leaders. He asserted that if the Pentagon were to lose control of its spy satellites, troops on the ground would be endangered.

To these arguments were added partisan political concerns. Many Republicans in the House remained angry over what they considered to be the hostile treatment that administration officials received by the 9/11 Commission and the platform it provided to Bush's critics.[19] Republican opposition led by Hunter forced Speaker of the House J. Dennis Hastert to hold a Republican-only meeting in November to try to salvage a compromise bill. He failed, with Hunter winning an agreement that any bill should contain language that "directs the president to write regulations that protect the chain of command" regarding intelligence gathering aircraft and satellites.

In its final version, the Intelligence Reform and Terrorism Prevention Act of 2004 passed by Congress and signed by Bush followed far more closely the restricted vision of the Pentagon and its allies than it did the 9/11 Commission in establishing the DNI. Title I of the act stipulated that the DNI not be located in the executive office of the President. It gave the DNI the power to "develop and determine" an annual budget for the national intelligence program based on budget proposals provided by the heads of intelligence agencies and departments. The DNI is to ensure the "effective execution" of the annual budget and "monitor the implementation and execution of the National Intelligence Program." After consulting with department heads, the DNI is authorized to transform or reprogram a maximum of $150 million and no more than 5 percent of an intelligence unit's budget in any one fiscal year, but he or she may not terminate an acquisition program. He or she is also given the power to develop personnel policies and programs in consultation with the heads of other agencies and elements of the intelligence community.

Resource politics does not end in Washington with the passage of legislation but continues on a daily basis. Its effects at the Department of Homeland Security came into clear focus with its response to Hurricane Katrina. From the outset, fears were raised that the Federal Emergency Management Agency (FEMA) would experience a reduction in its ability to cope with natural disasters in the United States as a result of being placed in an organization whose primary mission was counterterrorism. Intelligence is not immune from these problems. In January 2006, Secretary of Homeland Security Michael Chernoff filled the position of chief intelligence officer with CIA veteran Charles Allen. Prior to his appointment, the position was vacant for seven months. Some half a dozen candidates turned down the position in 2003 when the Department of Homeland Security was set up. Moreover, the intelligence fusion center that was to bring together intelligence from all sources had been overtaken in importance by establishing the position of DNI and creating a National Counterintelligence Center in his office.

In April 2005, the Silverman-Robb Commission, now acting as a private watchdog organization over intelligence reform, warned Bush to expect existing intelligence agencies to try to undermine the authority of the new DNI. Modernization plans being put forward by the FBI and CIA were described as a "business as usual approach to intelligence gathering."[20] Evidence on this last point was not long in coming. In May 2005 it was revealed that the two army analysts whose work was key to the faulty argument that the aluminum tubes sought by Iraq were part of a nuclear weapons program had received job performance awards for the past three years. The Silverman-Robb Commission had criticized their work as a "serious lapse in analytic tradecraft" because they did not seek out confirming or disconfirming information from the Energy Department or other intelligence agencies on the matter. In October, new CIA Director Porter Goss announced that he would not hold any current or former agency officials, including former CIA Director George Tenet, responsible for pre-9/11 intelligence failures, despite a recommendation by the CIA's inspector general that he convene an accountability board to judge their performance.[21] He had supported such a review when he served as chair of the House Select Intelligence Committee but now cited a desire to avoid hurting the agency. Inspector generals in the State Department, Justice Department, and Defense Department conducted similar reviews and declined to take disciplinary action against anyone.

Other evidence surfaced in 2005 that supported the commission's fears. In June the FBI, under pressure from the White House and Congress, agreed to let DNI John Negroponte help select the FBI's intelligence chief. Veterans within the agency had resented this move as an unprecedented infringement on the FBI's independence. At the same time, press reports indicated that FBI Director Mueller had taken steps to prevent deeper changes at the FBI by undertaking a series or reorganization measures in thee areas of collection and intelligence analysis. For example, the FBI moved 96 percent of its intelligence budget into units not under the jurisdiction of the DNI.

September brought a public relations embarrassment to the CIA as Robert Richer, the second-highest ranking officer in the Directorate of Operations and a Goss appointee, resigned and testified before the Senate committee about morale problems within the agency and Goss's lack of leadership and vision. The next month it was announced that in spite of recommendations by the 9/11 Commission that responsibility for human intelligence be transferred to the DNI, the CIA would remain as the chief coordinator of overseas spying by intelligence agencies. A National Clandestine Service within the CIA was to be created under Goss. It would supervise and coordinate spying but not direct the espionage activities of the FBI or Department of Defense intelligence agencies. Though located at the CIA, the new National Clandestine Service and all overseas human intelligence collection programs will be overseen in the DNI's office by his deputy, Mary Margaret Graham, a former CIA intelligence official who left the Agency because of Goss.

The Intelligence Reform and Terrorism Act allowed the DNI to transfer up to 100 people from other intelligence agencies, including those in the Pentagon, but only in consultation with relevant congressional committees. The agreement reached with Congress at the time was that consultation meant approval from these committees. In June 2005 it was agreed that the House Armed Services Committee would not have veto power over personnel transfers. Instead Negroponte agreed to meet personally with Hunter to discuss any moves involving Pentagon personnel.

Resource politics potentially also has a second but more varied impact on those who produce intelligence. Richard Stoltz, former head of the CIA's clandestine service, suggests that the process of adding more layers to the intelligence bureaucracy will lead to a wait-and-see and risk-averse attitude among intelligence officials.[22] These are precisely the traits that drew so much criticism from the 9/11 Commission and other studies. At the same time, the process of redirecting resources, creating new units, and seeking to imbue them with a sense of urgency and purpose to their mission may also embolden some to act in ways that transgress the bounds of permissible behavior. After 9/11, the CIA came under pressure to capture members of Al Qaeda and their supporters. Renditions, the process of secretly capturing a suspect and transferring them to another country for interrogation, became a favored tool in the war on terrorism. Identifying candidates for rendition involved collaboration between analysts and operations officers sifting through tips and other pieces of circumstantial information as to a person's politics or identity. An estimated 3,000 people were captured. Unfortunately, not all of them had a connection with terrorism. Mistakes were made because of the fear of missing a case. And, in the process, the vetting and evaluating information suffered. It was "the Camelot of counterterrorism."[23]

AGENDA POLITICS

Policy makers are attracted to intelligence out of self-interest. They want to succeed, and to the extent that intelligence helps them succeed, they seek it out and use it. As one former diplomat noted, "I could not afford to read intelligence papers because this or that intelligence agency was empowered to produce them. . . . I could only read intelligence products tailored to help me through my substantive schedule."[24] This basic truth holds several important implications for intelligence. First, intelligence does not determine policy. Intelligence professionals recognize this. It is one ingredient in the mix of factors that determine what U.S. foreign and national security policy will be. The struggle against global terrorism is no exception. As Lawrence Freedman notes in speaking of the Iraq war, "This was not an intelligence driven crisis. The [9/11] attacks changed the terms of the security debate ... [policy] drew on intelligence information but could rarely be refuted or confirmed in a definitive manner."[25]

Second, intelligence is not always welcomed. Often it is inconvenient.[26] Typically policy makers seek to keep options open as long as possible, but the logic of intelligence is to close off options. Particularly problematic is intelligence that questions the wisdom of a policy after policy makers have publicly committed themselves to it. Intelligence may also be discounted when it suggests that a potential problem exists at a time when policy makers are focused on other issues. Again the struggle against terrorism provides examples. Planning within the State Department, the CIA, and nongovernmental organizations suggested that the rebuilding and occupation of Iraq would not follow the model of Germany or Japan (as administration officials suggested) but would be more difficult and require a much larger military force that was being planned for. These warnings were shunted aside.[27] The same can be said for the administration's response to doubts within the intelligence community about the soundness of the intelligence on which its pre-war policy rested; because the incoming Bush administration's agenda did not include terrorism as a prominent concern, attempts by Clinton administration holdover Richard Clarke and others to warn the administration about Al Qaeda fell largely on deaf ears.[28] For that matter, terrorism was also not a major issue in the Clinton administration. Prior to 9/11, the most comprehensive National Intelligence Estimate on terrorism was published in July 1995.

Third, to the extent that policy makers disagree over policy intelligence will become contested and competitive. Not only will policy makers seek out intelligence that supports their policy positions or undermines that of rivals, they will also seek to control its distribution. In some cases this will mean denying rivals access to it. In other cases it will mean going public with intelligence. Efforts by Bush administration officials to seek out supportive evidence in the struggle against terrorism prior to the Iraq war are well chronicled. Vice President Dick Cheney regularly visited CIA headquarters and challenged analysts on their sources and conclusions. Retired CIA official Michael Scheuer comments that the CIA received repeated inquiries from Undersecretary of Defense Douglas Feith's office at the Pentagon about Iraq–Al Qaeda links, causing the CIA to review over 70,000 documents.[29] Rumsfeld and Feith established the Office of Special Plans within the Defense Department to provide an alternative source of intelligence that would support their position.

The administration also sought to control access to intelligence. Defending its Iraq policy in 2005, the Bush administration argued that Congress had seen the same intelligence it had prior to the war. Yet the administration had far more intelligence available to it and did not share all it possessed. Doubts within the intelligence community were not shared, such as those expressed by the National Security Council four days before President Bush's 2003 State of the Union address, where he made the case for war against Iraq. The NSC had called for additional intelligence to support the claim that Saddam Hussein possessed chemical, nuclear, or biological weapons. In contrast to Director of Central

Intelligence George Tenet, who called the case for war "a slam dunk," the national intelligence officer for strategic and nuclear programs called the case "weak."[30] Similarly, doubts raised by a Defense Intelligence Agency analysis of the reliability of the administration's principal source establishing a link between Al Qaeda and Iraq were not shared nor reflected in Bush's October 2002 statement that "we know Iraq and al-Qaeda have had high level-contacts going back a decade."

Beginning in August 2002 and continuing through to the eve of war, the administration began a sustained and well-orchestrated campaign to promote public support for war against Iraq.[31] Central to this campaign was the release of intelligence (or references to intelligence) that supported its case. That month Cheney asserted that he was convinced Saddam Hussein possessed weapons of mass destruction. In support he cited information from defectors, including Hussein's son-in-law. Also in August, a White House Iraq Group under the direction of Chief of Staff Andrew Cord was set up to ensure that a unified front was being given by the administration on the need for war. In September, President Bush made several public references to Iraq's effort to obtain nuclear material and intelligence support for that assertion. In October he announced that Iraq was reconstituting its nuclear weapons program and that satellite photographs support this conclusion. He also asserted that the United States had discovered through intelligence that Iraq has a growing fleet of unmanned aircraft that might be targeted on the United States. In his January 2003 State of the Union address, Bush stated that the British government had learned of Iraqi efforts to obtain significant quantities of uranium from Africa. The next month, Secretary of State Colin Powell told the United Nations that his presentation of Iraqi efforts to obtain nuclear weapons was based on "solid intelligence." Twice more before war began, in March 2003 President Bush asserted that the United States possessed intelligence that "left no doubt" about Iraq's threat.

The fourth implication for intelligence of policy makers approaching it in a self-interested fashion is that they tend to view intelligence as a tool or instrument of policy. Intelligence is not supposed to have policy views of its own. It exists to serve them. Their basic approach is that they want "more, better and faster."[32] But in reality, intelligence officials are no more united in their views than are policy makers. The dividing lines separating intelligence officials are not necessarily partisan in the sense of Republican versus Democrat or realist versus neoconservative although such differences do exist. They are more likely to be centered on questions of institutional perspectives, control over information, the proper analytical frameworks employed, and definitions of professionalism. Thus, just as with policy makers, it is often necessary to find common ground to advance policy. In the case of the struggle against global terrorism, this common ground was the charge that Saddam Hussein possessed weapons of mass destruction. As Paul Wolfowitz acknowledged, "only the WMD issue had legs."[33] It was the only issue around which the bureaucracy could agree.

The failure to recognize that intelligence is not by definition neutral in its origins or infinitely malleable in its uses but that it reflects the thinking of individuals embedded in organizations that contain their own political dynamics can set the stage for a particularly bitter brand of agenda politics—one that pits the White House against the portions of the intelligence community. The primary weapons at the disposal of the disaffected segments of the intelligence community are leaks. The recipients of these leaks tend to be the media or members of Congress. Their purpose is to alter the complexion of the political landscape by bringing other groups into the political fray that might otherwise not be aware that a policy is being contested or even under discussion. In addition to principled disagreement over policy decisions, self-interest plays an important role in the decision to leak intelligence. Policy makers come and go, but intelligence agencies are permanent. Recalling the post-Vietnam experience of the American military, those who leak may fear that their agencies will bear the blame for policy failures, excesses, and illegalities long after the policy makers who ordered them have left Washington.

This is the pattern of Washington politics that emerged with the beginning of the occupation and reconstruction of Iraq. Leaks from the intelligence community and military personnel provided the impetus for revelations about Abu Ghraib prisons, the practice of secretly capturing and incarcerating suspected terrorist suspects abroad, the use of torture as an interrogation device, and electronic spying on American citizens in the United States. In each case, these revelations succeeded in widening the circle of those participating in the policy debate. Most notably it brought renewed attention to Senator McCain, a former prisoner of war and a potential Republican presidential candidate who opposed the use of torture. Leaks also brought European leaders into the policy debate as information about secret CIA renditions in Eastern European countries occurred on the eve of Secretary of State Rice's 2005 trip there.

For its part, the Bush administration continued to make secret intelligence public on a selective basis to further its position. DNI Negroponte released an inflammatory letter allegedly written by Ayman Zawahari just as President Bush was giving a speech on Iraq defending the administration's policy. In an October 6, 2005, news conference, Bush announced that ten unidentified Al Qaeda terrorist plots had been disrupted by the United States and allied intelligence agencies since 9/11. When pressed on the subject by reporters, the administration later released a list of those incidents. Intelligence officials commented off the record that the administration had overstated the gravity of those plots and that most were far from being in a position to be carried out.

ACCOUNTABILITY POLITICS

To whom is intelligence responsible? As we have just suggested, from the point of view of policy makers, intelligence is responsible to them. They expect intelligence organizations to provide them with information and assessments that will allow them to succeed. The conventional wisdom in Washington is that

Porter Goss was made director of the CIA in 2004 to bring it under control and end the series of anti-administration intelligence leaks emanating from it. Goss would not be the first Director posted to the CIA for that purpose. He brought with him highly partisan staffers from the House Select Intelligence Committee. In his first months in that position, between thirty and ninety senior CIA officials left, including some whom Goss had appointed to key positions, and someone who worked on the Bush-Cheney election campaigns was placed in charge of the CIA's public affairs unit. Goss also issued a memo to CIA employees (soon leaked) in which he stated "as agency employees we do not identify with support, or champion opposition to the administration or its policies."[34]

Intelligence officials are well aware that executive branch policy makers are not the only ones interested in the performance of the intelligence community. Congress though its powers of the budget, appointment, and oversight has a constitutionally defined role in evaluating and assessing its performance. The media is also interested in intelligence both for its ability to provide a good story and because of its fourth estate role as a watchdog for the people over governmental action. Also active in the area of oversight, but generally playing a much more limited role in holding intelligence agencies responsible for their actions, are private sector interest groups, such as the Electronic Privacy Information Center, which aggressively pursues national security–oriented freedom of information questions.

Secrecy is an obvious and major impediment to the ability of political actors, outside of the small group in the executive branch who make national security policy, to judge the performance of intelligence. But it is not the only factor affecting the ability and willingness of Congress, the media, or interest groups to scrutinize intelligence agencies and personnel and hold them accountable for their actions or inaction. Three other factors, all rooted in Washington politics, also play major if not more important roles. They are deference, partisanship, and self-interest.

The 9/11 Commission characterized congressional oversight of intelligence as "dysfunctional," a situation that can be traced to the three traits just noted.[35] Deference was long visible in the approach that Congress brought to oversight during early years of the Cold War. The national consensus focused on the need to combat communism, coupled with the widely held view that intelligence was an instrument of foreign policy to be exercised by the president at his discretion. During this period, congressional oversight served more to protect the CIA and other agencies than make them accountable for their actions. It was only in the mid-1970s, after revelations of CIA involvement in the coup to bring down Salvador Allende's government in Chile and spying on American citizens inside the United States, that congressional oversight became aggressive with the establishment of the Church and Pike Committees in the Senate and House, respectively. In the wake of the investigations carried out by these panels, each body established Select Intelligence Committees for purposes of continued oversight. They largely followed a model that stressed bipartisanship and deference to the president and his use of intelligence, with investigations being restricted to a examining problems only after they occurred rather than engaging in anticipatory or preventive oversight.

Deference to the president began to lessen during the Reagan years as the administration talked of "unleashing" the CIA and its Central American policies increasingly divided Republicans and Democrats. During the Clinton presidency, Congress (with Republicans leading the way) forced unwanted programs on the administration in the form of appropriating money for covert action programs against Saddam Hussein. In both administrations, as well as during Carter's term, the opposition party openly and successfully challenged the president's nominee to head the intelligence community. Deference returned briefly in the wake of the 9/11 terrorist attacks but soon faded as the United States moved from war in Afghanistan to war in Iraq. Partisanship became particularly intense in the House. Porter Goss, who chaired the House Select Intelligence Committee and was himself a retired intelligence officer who served in the clandestine service, had long acted as a protector of the CIA. Now he moved aggressively to protect the president. He often described the CIA as a mismanaged bureaucracy. He publicly supported the administration's position on weapons of mass destruction, and he blocked investigations into pre-war intelligence and the treatment of prisoners at Abu Ghraib as well as belittled the notion of an investigation into the leaking of undercover CIA official Valerie Plame's name to the press (linked by a special prosecutor to Lewis "Scooter" Libby in Vice President Cheney's office). During the presidential campaign, Goss also criticized Kerry's stance on intelligence in a speech on the House floor.

The 9/11 Commission rejected calls for tinkering with the system and urged a wholesale change that would establish a strong oversight committee in each chamber or a single joint committee. Congress reacted warily to the proposed reforms even while making support public statements. Of particular concern to legislators was the notion of giving one committee power over both setting program priorities and budget authority. This would produce a reduction in influence of the Appropriations, Armed Forces, and Foreign Relations committees. Senate Appropriations Chair Ted Stevens (R-AK) commented on the thrust of the 9/11 Commission calls for centralizing congressional authority: "I don't think it will fly."[36] House Appropriations Committee Chair C. W. Young (R-FL) observed that combining spending and authorization powers in one committee "is not part of this proposal" in discussing the House's response to the 9/11 Commission's plans. A Republican aide stated more bluntly that any such plan "doesn't have a snowball's chance in hell" of taking effect.

The same three factors emerge in media oversight of intelligence. Deference can be seen in how the press reports on intelligence. What the public tends to focus on are the sensational headlines of domestic spying, renditions, and the treatment of prisoners. Less often noticed is that the media is frequently in contact with the administration about the details of these stories and is sensitive to its concerns. In a November 2005 story revealing the covert prison system set up to hold and interrogate suspected terrorists outside of the United States without restrictions, the *Washington Post* agreed with a request from senior administration officials not to identify the Eastern European countries involved.[37] The next month, the *New York Times* reported on the program of domestic spying that President Bush had secretly authorized following the 9/11 attacks.[38] The paper reported that it had delayed publishing the story for one year after meeting with the White House and that some information that administration officials had argued could be useful to terrorists was omitted. When it was released, charges of partisanship were quickly raised. The story surfaced just as the Senate was nearly a final vote on extending the USA-PATRIOT Act. A compelling case for self-interest in the timing of the story can be made by pointing to competition between the *New York Times* and the *Washington Post* in breaking such stories and the imminent publication of a book on domestic spying by the article's author, James Risen.

For a brief period of time, one public affairs interest group played a key role in accountability politics. Its behavior deviated from the pattern of deference, partisanship, and self-interest exhibited by Congress and the media. After its report was issued on July 22, 2004, the members of the 9/11 Commission disbanded and formed a nonprofit organization, the 9/11 Public Discourse Project, to fulfill what they saw as the commission's original mandate of guarding against future terrorist attacks and promote a national debate on how future attacks can be prevented. To that end, the 9/11 Public Discourse Project issued a series of report cards from September to December 2005 on the extent to which the commission's recommendations had been acted on. While seeking to be nonpartisan, the negative tone of its evaluation (one A–, twelve B's, nine C's, twelve D's, five F's, and two incompletes) struck a partisan chord in Washington. The 9/11 Public Discourse Project ceased operation on December 31, 2005, with its ultimate impact on intelligence and the struggle against terrorism unclear.

CONCLUSION AND SYNTHESIS: DOMESTIC INTELLIGENCE GATHERING

To the casual observer, Washington politics frequently appears to be a game without rules, rhyme, or reason. It seems messy, unfocused, and unprincipled. On closer inspection, a different picture emerges. Reoccurring patterns to politics can be found. They are symbolic politics, resource politics, agenda politics, and accountability politics. National security policy is not exempt from these patterns. As discussed here, they are very much alive in intelligence policy. Not all of these political games or contests are equally visible. Each has its own inner dynamics and central set of political actors. These political games or contests are not self-contained. Activity in one feeds on and is influenced by the politics in the others. Washington politics becomes particularly intense and combative when simultaneous activity is occurring in all four political games or contests. Such was the case in late 2005 to early 2006 in the dispute over domestic spying on Americans as a means of gathering intelligence in the global struggle against terrorism.

In this case, agenda politics first came into public view. Controversy erupted in mid-December 2005 when the *New York Times* reported, on the basis of information leaked to it, that in February 2002 President Bush signed a secret order authorizing the National Security Agency (NSA) to monitor phone calls and other communications (such as faxes and e-mails) inside the United States by Americans identified by the NSA as having some connection to Al Qaeda or potential terrorist activities.[39] Published estimates placed the number of Americans being eavesdropped on at any one time as up to 500 and that all told, the number of Americans spied on may have reached into the thousands. The NSA, in turn, provided information to the Defense Intelligence Agency and others for use in carrying out its surveillance of people inside the United States. President Bush reportedly was deeply involved in the oversight of the program, reviewing it every forty-five or sixty days and reauthorizing it some thirty-six times.

The *New York Times* story broke the day before the Senate was to vote on reauthorizing the USA-PATRIOT Act. A key point of debate was whether the provisions of this act went far enough in protecting the civil liberties of Americans. The story appeared to have a significant impact and many senators expressed concern about the warrantless wiretapping. The next day by a vote of fifty-two to four-seven, with four Republicans voting with all but two Democrats, the Republican-controlled Senate refused to end the filibuster, signaling a setback for the act. Just days before, in an effort to ensure its passage, the Bush administration reversed its position and endorsed McCain's bill to ban the cruel, inhumane, and degrading treatment of prisoners in its custody. After extensive debate in the new year, Congress passed the renewed USA-PATRIOT Act on March 9.

The controversy that raged was not primarily over the value of this intelligence-gathering effort, although such questions were raised by some. Recall that what investigations of pre-9/11 intelligence revealed was not a failure to obtain intelligence per se but the inability to integrate it so that a meaningful pattern could be deciphered. After 9/11, a 2002 Senate Select Intelligence Committee report commented that "only a tiny fraction of the daily intercepts are actually ever reviewed by humans,, and much of what is collected gets lost in the deluge of data."[40] Experts on terrorism noted that terrorists were already well aware of the risks of phone, e-mail, and fax communications. They were now relying on ground couriers and the World Wide Web. The public was not overwhelmingly alarmed over domestic spying on Americans in the United States. The USA-PATRIOT Act had already given the FBI broad new powers to gather information on Americans. A January 2006 *Washington Post*/ABC News public poll found that almost two-thirds of Americans believed that the government's antiterrorism efforts were intruding on the privacy of American citizens, but less than one-third felt that this was unjustified.[41]

At the core of the issue was President Bush's authority to authorize this program on his own. And this moved intelligence politics squarely into the arena of symbolic politics with the outcome determining in large part which side would have the upper hand in the overall political contest. The president defended the program on the grounds that it was "limited, "a vital tool in the war on terrorism," and "critical to saving American lives." Most significant, he also stated that it was "consistent with U.S. law and the Constitution."[42] In making this last assertion, Bush was echoing the position taken by then Attorney General John Ashcroft who signed a brief on September 22, 2002, stating that "the Constitution vests in the President inherent authority to conduct wireless intelligence surveillance of foreign powers or their agents and Congress cannot by statue extinguish that constitutional authority."[43] Ashcroft's argument made no distinction between U.S. citizens or suspected foreign agents. In 2005, Attorney General Alberto Gonzales asserted that the administration's domestic eavesdropping was derived from the September 14, 2001, joint resolution authorizing the president to use "all necessary and appropriate force" to defeat Al Qaeda and the president's inherent powers as commander in chief. The Justice Department continued this line of argument, stating that because espionage is "a fundamental incident in the use of military force," even though it was not specifically mentioned, it was authorized by the resolution.[44] As the controversy grew, Bush engaged in symbolic politics again when he sought to redefine the program as "terrorist surveillance" and publicly presented an account of an Al Qaeda plot to crash a commercial jetliner into a Los Angeles skyscraper after 9/11. The significance of the revelation was quickly countered by unnamed intelligence officials who questioned whether the plot was anything more than loose talk.

Opponents countered with an argument heavily rooted in symbolism as well: American civil liberties were being violated, the rule of law had been broken, and neither Congress nor the Constitution provided such powers to the president. The Fourth Amendment to the U.S. Constitution protects citizens from unreasonable searches and seizures and stipulates that warrants can only be issued with probable cause. Opponents of Bush's policy assert that this prohibition has been interpreted by the courts to require a warrant and probable cause. Moreover, the Supreme Court has rejected the argument that national security considerations override this requirement. Opponents also challenged the stated limited nature of this program. The National Counterterrorism Center maintains a list of international terrorism suspects or those who might be providing them with aid. In early 2006, 325,000 names were on that list. Duplicate entries may reduce the total number of individuals listed to some 200,000. The number of U.S. citizens on the list has not been revealed. Names are provided by the CIA, NSA, FBI, and others and are given to the Transportation Security Administration and other agencies.[45]

Opponents continued that the rule of law was violated by Bush's failure to obtain permission from the U.S. Foreign Intelligence Surveillance Court to conduct surveillance on Americans inside the United States. This eleven-judge body, all of whose members were selected by the late Chief Justice of the Supreme

Court William Rehnquist, was set up by the Foreign Intelligence Surveillance Act (FISA) that was passed in the 1970s after revelations of widespread spying on Americans by the military and the NSA in the name of rooting out communist influence on the anti–Vietnam War movement. According to the Justice Department, in 2004 the secret court approved 1,754 warrants. By one account it had received over 5,600 requests since 2001 and rejected only four.[46] Provisions of the act also allow for emergency wiretaps without the consent of the court for up to seventy-two hours. The Bush administration's position was that FISA was not relevant because the September 14, 2001, resolution constitutes a statute that by the terms of the act can override its provisions. One of the judges resigned in protest following revelations that the program existed and the presiding judge of the secret court requested a briefing on why it was not consulted. Finally, former Senate Majority Leader Thomas Daschle (D-SD) stated that the Bush administration had requested war-making authority from the Senate in discussions over the wording of the September 14, 2001, resolution and that it was rejected.

The political battle over what symbolic reference points were to be used in judging the appropriateness of this intelligence-gathering policy set the stage for a renewed round of accountability politics. As noted above the Foreign Intelligence Surveillance Court was ignored. Only its presiding judge was informed, and she raised concerns in private that this program could undermine the secret court's work if information so obtained was later used to acquire warrants on terrorist suspects. In fact, twice since 9/11 the FISA court was told that information obtained by this program may have been improperly used to obtain wiretap warrants. Vice President Cheney informed leaders of both parties about the program after it started and later the administration informed key members of Congress. These congressional briefings are given to the Gang of Eight, the leadership of the House and Senate and the intelligence committees. Staff members are not present, and those briefed are prohibited from discussing the information with other members of Congress, including those who serve on the intelligence committees. The administration contends that with these briefings, Congress gave its approval to the domestic spying program. After it became public, John D. Rockefeller IV (D-WV), the ranking Democrat on the Senate Select Intelligence Committee, revealed that in 2003 he sent a letter to Cheney stating that the briefings were unsatisfactory. The letter stated, "Given the security restrictions associated with this information, and inability to consult staff or counsel on my own, I feel unable to fully evaluate, much less endorse, these activities."[47] House Minority Leader Nancy Pelosi (D-CA) expressed concerns about the legality of NSA domestic spying in a letter to Gen. Michael Hayden, who as head of the NSA in October 2001 briefed the House Select Intelligence Committee on its broadened domestic operations. She wrote, "I am concerned whether and to what extent the National Security Agency has received specific presidential authorization for the operations you are conducting."[48] Hayden's response remains classified, but an intelligence official indicated that he had not been referring to the new NSA domestic spying program.

Although the content of these briefings is the subject of debate, it is clear that congressional oversight was carried out with deference to the administration and far more in the spirit of putting out fires (which had not yet occurred) than patrolling for dangers. When the program became public, Congress quickly moved out of principle and self-interest to reassert its oversight powers as both Democrats and Republicans called for hearings and previously secret correspondence was made public. Partisanship was not completely absent, as many Republican members of Congress staunchly defended the program and the president's right to implement it. Cheney went so far as to suggest that the debate over spying on terrorists ought be an issue in the upcoming congressional campaign. The possibility that the NSA's domestic spying program might become an issue that Republicans could seize on led two leading congressional Democrats to acknowledge its importance in the war against terrorism while rejecting Bush's legal authority to act without congressional approval.

In additional to maintaining its right to conduct such a surveillance program, the administration also sought to deflect attention away from the question of presidential authority by returning to symbolic politics. Bush asserted that the story of the day was not the domestic intelligence-gathering program but the war in Iraq. The administration also called attention to the illegality of the leak and launched a Justice Department investigation into who leaked the information announcing in January 2006 that the NSA's inspector general would conduct an investigation into the matter. Critics observed that Bush had already maintained that the NSA's general counsel and inspector general had approved the domestic spying program, so little should be expected from this probe.

Lying beneath the surface of this controversy we can also find resource politics. During the Cold War, the NSA collected intelligence on the Soviet Union through electronic intercepts and controlled much of the intelligence community's secret budget. This mission no longer exists. The war on terrorism provided an opportunity for the NSA to reinvent itself, but doing so was not without challenges. As a former NSA director observed, "We've gone from chasing a slow-moving, technologically inferior, resource poor nation-state to chasing a communications structure in which an al Qaeda member can go into a storefront in Istanbul and buy for $100 a communications device that is absolutely cutting edge, and for which he has had to make no investment for development."[49]

The NSA has long been authorized to monitor international phone calls and e-mails of American citizens without a warrant when they originate overseas. Secret NSA intelligence gathering in the United States was limited to communications intercepts involving foreign embassies and missions and only then with a warrant. The major exception was when an individual was suspected of being an "agent of a foreign power" or a member of a terrorist group. Otherwise it generally fell to the FBI to carry out domestic eavesdropping operations. The expansion of the NSA's role after 9/11 was implemented with an eye to achieving results and not the imposition of controls. It was mid-2004 before voices of concern were raised. At that time, elements of the program were suspended and others recast after concerns were raised by national security officials and the head of the Foreign Intelligence Surveillance Court.

This was not the only expansion in domestic intelligence-gathering activities after 9/11. Also in late 2005, it was revealed that the Defense Department's new counterterrorism agency, the Counterintelligence Field Activity (CIFA), had expanded its efforts from a coordinating and oversight body into one with operational responsibilities. Its Directorate of Field Activities became responsible for disrupting adversaries, running roving patrols around military bases, and conducting surveillance on potentially threatening people and organizations inside the Untied States. CIFA also manages data bases that include Talon reports that consist of raw and unverified information collected by the military on suspicious activities. Talon reports are known to include information on peaceful civilian protests and demonstrations. In November 2005, the CIFA was given authority to task the domestic U.S. investigations and operations of the military counterintelligence units.

As promised by Senator Specter, hearings on the NSA's domestic surveillance program began in February 2006 after Congress returned from its winter recess. An all-out White House lobbying campaign plus a late-found willingness to brief House and Senate committees on the programs slowed down the momentum that had built for an investigation. The Senate rejected a Democratic attempt to launch an investigation into the matter through a procedural maneuver, which allowed time for a Republican working group appointed by Majority Leader Bill Frist (R-TN) to explore ways of changing the law to accommodate NSA's policy. Democrats were quick to criticize the formation of an all-Republican committee.

White House spokesman Scott McClellan sought to further calm the waters by outlining a new White House position. He stated that the NSA program does not require "congressional authorization" but that the administration is "open to ideas regarding legislation."[50] Two competing ideas became the center of attention. One, endorsed by the White House, was sponsored by Representative Mike DeWine (R-OH). It would provide additional congressional oversight for the NSA's domestic spying program but exempt it from FISA oversight. Such oversight would most likely come from a subcommittee of the intelligence committee with the full committee restricting itself to a review and modernization of the FISA. The second, opposed by the Bush administration, was introduced by Specter. It would require the NSA to obtain prior permission from the Foreign Intelligence Surveillance Court.

NOTES

1. For a CIA statement describing the intelligence cycle, see http://www.odci.gov/cia/publications/facttell/intelligence_cycle.html.

2. Murray Edelman, *The Symbolic Uses of Politics* (Urbana: University of Illinois Press, 1964).

3. Michael Howard, "What's in a Name? How to Fight Terrorism," *Foreign Affairs* 81 (2002), pp. 8–13.

4. *Weekly Compilation of Presidential Documents* (June 21, 2002). From 2002 Presidential Documents online via GPO Access at http://www.gpo.gov/nara/nara003.html; *Weekly Compilation of Presidential Documents* (December 17, 2004), from 2004 Presidential Documents online via GPO Access, http://www.gpo.gov/nara/nara003.html.

6. Office of the Director of National Intelligence, *The National Intelligence Strategy of the United States*: *Transformation through Integration and Innovation* (October 2005), Washington, DC.

7. http://www.Washingtonpost.com (January 28, 2004).

8. Katherin Shrader, "WMD Commission Releases Scathing Report," *Washington Post* (March 31, 2005), p. A1.

5. Lawrence Freedman, "The Politics of Warning: Terrorism and Risk Communication," *Intelligence and National Security* 20 (2005), pp. 379–418.

6. Shlomo Gazit, "Estimates and Fortunetelling in Intelligence Work," *International Security* 4 (1980), pp. 36–56.

11. See Dan Eggen, "Memo Not Specific Enough, Bush Says," *Washington Post* (April 12, 2004), p. A1.

12. Jack Davis, *Improving CIA Analytical Performance: Strategic Warning* (Washington, DC: Sherman Kent Center for Intelligence Analysis, Occasional Papers 1:1, Central Intelligence Agency, September 2002).

13. Charles Babington, "Hill Wary of Intelligence Oversight Changes," *Washington Post* (September 12, 2004), p. A5.

14. For a historical perspective on such politics, see Amy Zegart, *Flawed by Design: The Evolution of the CIA, JCS, and NSC* (Stanford, CA: Stanford University Press, 1999).

15. Walter Pincus, "Lesser Intelligence Role Seen for Security Dept.," *Washington Post* (July 18, 2002), p. A6.

16. Ibid.

17. Michael Turner, "Intelligence Reform and the Politics of Entrenchment," *International Journal of Intelligence and Counterintelligence* 18 (2005), pp. 383–97.

18. Dan Eggen and Dafna Linzer, "9/11 Commission Offers Critiques on Many Fronts," *Washington Post* (July 22, 2004), p. A1.

19. Helen Fessenden, "The Limits of Intelligence Reform," *Foreign Affairs* 84 (2005), p. 110.

20. Walter Pincus, "FBI, CIA Proposal to Retool Called 'Business as Usual,'" *Washington Post* (April 15, 2005), p. A6.

21. Dafna Linzer and Walter Pincus, "CIA Rejects Discipline for 9/11 Failures," *Washington Post* (October 6, 2005), p. A1.

22. Quoted in David Ignatius, "Danger Point in Spy Reform," *Washington Post* October 21, 2005, p. A3.

23. Dana Priest, "Wrongful Imprisonment: Anatomy of a CIA Mistake," *Washington Post*, December 4, 2005, p. A1.

24. Robert D. Blackwill and Jack Davis, "A Policymaker's Perspective on Intelligence Analysis," in *Strategic Intelligence: Windows into a Secret World*, eds. Loch K. Johnson and James Wirtz (Los Angeles: Roxbury, 2004), p. 122.

25. Lawrence Freedman, "War in Iraq: Selling the Threat," *Survival* 46 (2004), p. 38.

26. Jack Davis, *Strategic Warning: If Surprise Is Inevitable, What Role for Analysis?* (Washington, D.C.: Sherman Kent Center for Intelligence Analysis, Occasional Papers 2:1, Central Intelligence Agency, January 2003).

27. James Fallows, "Blind into Baghdad," *Atlantic Monthly* 293 (January/February 2004), pp. 52ff.

28. Richard Clarke, *Against All Enemies* (New York: Free Press, 2004).

29. Anonymous [Michael Scheuer], *Imperial Hubris* (Washington, DC: Brassey's, 2004).

30. The "slam dunk" remark is from Bob Woodward, *Plan of Attack* (New York: Simon & Schuster, 2004), p. 249; the "weak" remark from Walter Pincus, "Prewar Findings Worried Analysts," *Washington Post* (May 22, 2005), p. A1.

31. Glenn Hastedt, "Public Intelligence: Leaks as Policy Instruments—The Case of the Iraq War," *Intelligence and National Security* 20 (2005), pp. 419–39.

32. James Simon Jr., "Managing Domestic, Military, and Foreign Policy Requirements: Correcting Frankenstein's Blunder," in *Transforming U.S. Intelligence,* eds. Jennifer Sims and Burton Gerber (Washington, DC: Georgetown University Press, 2005), p. 154.

33. Lawrence Freedman, "War in Iraq: Selling the Threat," *Survival* 42 (Summer 2004), p. 26.

34. Robert Dreyfuss, "The Yes-Man," *American Prospect* 16 (November 2005), pp. 18–24.

35. On congressional oversight see L. Britt Snider, "Congressional Oversight of Intelligence After September 11," in Jennifer Sims and Burton Gerber, eds., *Transforming U.S. Intelligence* (Washington, DC: Georgetown University Press, 2005), pp. 239–58, and Loch K. Johnson, "Governing in the Absence of Angels: On the Practice of Intelligence Accountability in the United States," in *Who's Watching the Spies?* eds. Hans Born, Loch K. Johnson, and Ian Leigh (Washington, DC: Potomac Books, 2005), pp. 57–78.

36. This and the other quotations in this paragraph are from Charles Babington, "Hill Wary," p. A5.

37. David Johnston and Carl Hulse, "C.I.A. Asks Criminal Inquiry Over Secret Prison Article," *New York Times* (November 9, 2005), p. A18.

38. James Risen and Eric Lichtblau, "Bush Lets U.S. Spy on Callers Without Courts," *New York Times* (December 16, 2005), p. A1.

39. Eric Lichtblau and James Risen, "Spy Agency Mined Vast Data Trove, Officials Report," *New York Times* (December 24, 2005), p. A1.

40. Michael Hirsh, "The NSA's Overt Problem: So Many Conversations, So Few Clues to the Terrorist's Chatter," *Washington Post,* January 1, 2006, p. B1.

41. Dan Beltz and Claudia Deane, "Differing Views on Terrorism," *Washington Post,* January 11, 2006, p. A4.

42. Lisa Rein, "Bush Defends Spying Program as Necessary to Protect U.S.," *Washington Post* (January 2, 2006), p. A2.

43. Barton Gellman and Dafna Linzer, "Pushing the Limits of Wartime Powers," *Washington Post* (December 18, 2005), p. A1.

44. See "Legal Authorities Supporting the Activities of the National Security Agency Described by the President," Department of Justice (January 19, 2006).

45. Walter Pincus and Dan Eggen, "325,000 Names on Terrorism List," *Washington Post,* February 15, 2006, p. A1.

46. Suzzane Spaulding, "Power Play," *Washington Post,* December 25, 2005, p. B1.

47. Charles Babington and Dafna Linzer, "Senator Sounded Alarm," *Washington Post* (December 20, 2005), p. A10.

48. Dafna Linzer, "Secret Surveillance May Have Occurred Before Authorization," *Washington Post* (January 4, 2006), p. A3.

49. Quoted in Hirsh, "The NSA's Overt Problem."

50. Charles Babington and Carol Leonnig, "Senate Rejects Wiretapping Probe," *Washington Post*, February 17, 2006, p. A6.

7

THE INTELLIGENCE WAR AGAINST
GLOBAL TERRORISM

RICHARD L. RUSSELL

AMERICANS WERE HORRIFIED THAT THEIR INTELLIGENCE COMMUNITY (IC) failed to detect and disrupt the Al Qaeda surprise attacks of September 11, 2001. They rightly ask, "How is it possible that the intelligence community, which costs American taxpayers tens of billions of dollars per year, so miserably failed in protecting citizens and the homeland?"

The IC should have better been prepared to warn of Al Qaeda operations because the terrorist organization had been waging a war against the United States for some time. Al Qaeda bombed the American embassies in Kenya and Tanzania in 1998 as well as attacked the U.S.S. *Cole* in Yemen in 2000. These attacks should have signaled loud and clear that Al Qaeda had declared war on the United States, but American naiveté fueled the view that terrorist attacks were more a problem for law enforcement than for the military. Both civilian policy makers and the military hierarchy resisted moving the United States to a war footing to take head on the threat posed by Al Qaeda.[1] In response to the African embassy bombings, the United States could only muster half-hearted retaliatory cruise missile strikes against Al Qaeda–affiliated positions in Afghanistan and Sudan, which did little to blunt the network's capabilities to strike again against the United States.

The CIA, too, had not moved to a wartime footing to tackle Al Qaeda. Director of Central Intelligence George Tenet had warned in a December 1998 memorandum to his key lieutenants in the IC that the United States was at war with Al Qaeda and that he wanted no resources spared for the fight.[2] But Tenet's bravado was not matched by resources. The team inside the CIA's Counterterrorism Center (CTC) in the run-up to 9/11 only had five analysts assigned to track global Al Qaeda operations.[3] A handful of analysts is hardly commensurate with Tenet's call to "spare no resource." Within the CIA's Directorate of Operations (DO), responsible for collecting human intelligence, senior management believed that the Al Qaeda threat before 9/11 was being exaggerated and resisted assigning CIA resources to the problem, according to former White House official Richard Clarke.[4] The former head of the bin Laden unit in the CTC, Michael Scheuer, even believes that senior CIA officials "have made careers by keeping silent in the face of unfairness, avoiding risk, and refusing to make decisions."[5] The CIA's own inspector general has found senior CIA officials negligent for failing to competently orchestrate the Agency's resources against Al Qaeda prior to 9/11.[6]

But that, as they say, is all history. The challenge today for scholars, intelligence officers, policy makers, and the American public is to move beyond the blame game and take a hard, clear-eyed look at what went wrong. We need to find ways to sharpen the nation's intelligence capabilities for countering Al Qaeda—as well as loosely aligned affiliates and successor organizations that share a militant Islamic ideology and hatred of the United States, which they blame for most (if not all) of the failings of the Islamic world—in what regrettably promises to be a long-term struggle.

The term *terrorism* generates considerable debate and controversy, which sometimes boils down to the view that "one man's terrorist is another man's freedom fighter." Many observers in the United States tend to view operations conducted by terrorist groups against American military and diplomatic facilities and personnel as terrorist attacks, but they probably should be more accurately seen as insurgents using terrorist tactics to wage war. Today the news headlines are dominated by Iraqi insurgent use of terrorist tactics, especially roadside bombings, in their battle against American forces in Iraq. But in the past, other insurgent groups have used terrorist tactics against the United States, sometimes with nation-state sponsorship. Hezbollah, for example, benefited from Syrian and Iranian support in the 1980s in its bombings in Lebanon, which killed about 250 Marines and destroyed the American embassy in Beirut. The Saudi Hezbollah benefited from substantial assistance from Iran when it bombed the Khobar Towers in Saudi Arabia in 1996 and killed nineteen American servicemen.[7] In short, Al Qaeda is not the first militant Islamic movement to use terrorism against the United States, and they are not likely to be the last. To steer clear of that thicket of debate on the differences between terrorism and insurgency, this chapter views terrorism as the use of violence by transnational groups or organizations that is directed principally against civilians for political purpose.

The CIA has traditionally played the leading role in the IC along three major lines to support the president in the war on terrorism. First, the CIA runs human intelligence operations needed to penetrate the walls of secrecy behind which terrorists plot and plan against the United States. Second, the CIA performs analysis of terrorist groups to inform presidential decision making. And third, the CIA is also tasked to mount covert actions against terrorist groups to disrupt, prevent, and preempt their operations. This chapter critically examines the CIA's past performance in each of these areas against the terrorist adversaries, draws some lessons learned, and makes recommendations for strengthening future performance. This chapter acknowledges that the CIA's traditional position as the premier intelligence service in the community has been eclipsed by the creation of the Director of National Intelligence (DNI) and will conclude with some thoughts on how the DNI should best orchestrate the reorganized IC.

STEALING THE TERRORISTS' SECRETS

The IC taps a wide and deep array of sources of information to understand international terrorism. The United States uses diplomats and defense attachés posted abroad to collect information. It relies on publicly available information, such as newspapers, periodicals, and websites to analyze terrorist group memberships, propaganda, recruitment, and ideology. The IC also is able to use satellite imagery to identify terrorist training camps and state support for terrorist groups. The United States, for example, in 1998 used many of these sources of intelligence to identify Al Qaeda training camps in Afghanistan for retaliatory cruise missile strikes for the bombing of the two embassies in Africa.[8] The IC also clandestinely acquires information on terrorist groups and their plans from human sources (human intelligence, or HUMINT) and from intercepting communications such as radio, telephone, and e-mail (signals intelligence, or SIGINT). The primary responsibilities for these HUMINT and SIGINT operations fall, respectively, to the CIA and the National Security Agency (NSA) in the IC.

The CIA's Directorate of Operations, which was recently renamed the National Clandestine Service (NCS), is charged with running human intelligence operations intended to collect strategic intelligence on American adversaries.[9] The CIA's core human intelligence collection mission is to steal secrets that adversaries want to hide from the United States, secrets that could adversely affect American national interests.

The CIA's operational tradecraft for running human operations was honed during the Cold War. The Agency's operational officers working abroad under cover had used a method of spotting, accessing, developing, and recruiting Soviet diplomats and military officers primarily by trolling the diplomatic cocktail circuit. Though this is a proven method of human collection, the CIA's human operations against the Soviet Union were, on balance, less than impressive. Before the entire stable of CIA spies in the Soviet Union were exposed to the Soviet KGB by traitor Aldrich Ames, the Agency only had about a dozen spies inside the Soviet Union.[10]

The method is now deeply ingrained into the institutional culture at the CIA, and it has been stubbornly difficult for the Agency to move toward contemporary international terrorists targets. A former CIA case officer who was in the Agency's training class as late as 1999, nearly a decade after the Cold War, recalls that it was still focused on trolling the diplomatic cocktail party circuit.[11] Unfortunately, and quite obviously, members of Al Qaeda, Hezbollah, Hamas, Islamic Jihad, and their state sponsors in Syria and Iran do not regularly participate in diplomatic cocktail parties. Nor, for that matter, do the scientists and technicians with experience in weapons of mass destruction (WMDs) programs who might offer their talents to terrorist groups with or without the knowledge of their countries. Rogue Russian scientists trying to make a lucrative living are a particular problem on this score.

The CIA has done precious little to exploit alternative means of getting human intelligence information. Most notably, the Agency has a strong bureaucratic culture to run "agents in place" even though it has failed to do this with any consistency or reliability over a period of decades. The CIA and American security would much better off it the Agency were sparing no expense or effort to encourage defections from countries with pervasive and oppressive internal security apparatus, called "hard target" countries. The United States, for example, should be offering money and perhaps resettlement in the United States or the West for disaffected Al Qaeda and Hezbollah members and scientists and technicians laboring in North Korea's and Iran's suspected nuclear weapons programs, who all could offer significant intelligence to the United States. Dozens of defections would give CIA analysts snapshots of terrorist groups and plans, intentions, and capabilities, as well as disrupt WMD-related activities.

The CIA also significantly suffers in human operations against Middle East terrorist groups such as Al Qaeda and Hezbollah because it suffers from shortages of Arabic and Farsi speakers. Former CIA case officer Robert Baer lamented that he was one of only two Arabic speakers in the CTC when it was set up in the 1980s to track Hezbollah and Palestinian terrorist groups.[12] And judging from news reports today, the CIA is not gaining ground fast enough to address this gap. The chancellor of the University of California at Berkeley, for example, meet with CIA officials to discuss language capabilities and came away from the meeting with the understanding that "their needs are desperate."[13]

The CIA also is overly dependent on foreign intelligence liaison service information. Because the Agency lacks foreign language capabilities, it relies on foreign intelligence services, which do have hard languages such as Arabic and ethnic backgrounds needed to penetrate terrorists cells. The Senate-House investigation into 9/11 determined that the CIA is overly dependent on liaison reports and fails to deliver its own or "unilaterally" acquired human intelligence. It found that "the Intelligence Community depended heavily on foreign intelligence and law enforcement services for the collection of counterterrorism intelligence and the conduct of other counterterrorism activities. The results were mixed in terms of productive intelligence, reflecting vast differences in the ability and willingness of the various foreign services to target the Bin Ladin and al-Qa'ida network."[14] Unilaterally acquired intelligence is essential to compare and check against the information provided by foreign liaison services as well as other American sources of information.

There can be no gainsaying how important these liaison relationships are to human intelligence collection in the war on terrorism. But with that said, for all of the problems and shortcomings in the American intelligence community, they pale in comparison to the problems that plague many foreign liaison services. For example, these foreign services suffer from a deep subordination to vested policy interests, ingrained bureaucratic and cultural resistance to "speaking truth to power," personal fears of delivering bad news to their superiors, as well as worldviews—especially pronounced in the Middle East—that greatly hamper objective and critical analytic thinking and intelligence. There is also a significant risk that liaison services skew their human intelligence reports shared with the United States to influence the direction of American foreign policy. These tendencies all underscore the critical need for the CIA to acquire its own unilateral intelligence sources.

The NSA is charged with the responsibilities for intercepting the communications of terrorist groups. The United States has had better collection performance in strategic intelligence from the NSA than the CIA. Tragically, however, NSA operations against Al Qaeda appear to have suffered a major blow when word leaked by August 1998 that the United States was listening to Osama bin Laden's satellite telephone conversations, and he stopped using the satellite phone shortly after U.S. cruise missile strikes against his camps in Afghanistan in retaliation for the bombings of two American embassies in Africa.[15]

The NSA is now deeply embroiled in a domestic spying controversy with accusations that it was listening to American phone calls and e-mails domestically without the legal authority to do so.[16] Above and beyond today's news headlines, the NSA is up against the wall in reorienting its collection operations from the Cold War to the war on terrorism. Al Qaeda and other terrorist groups benefit enormously in the explosion in information and communication technology, and the NSA has not been able to keep pace. Al Qaeda can now purchase off-the-shelf encryption technology, making it difficult if not impossible for NSA to crack their communications. Al Qaeda can hide its communications in the billions of e-mails and cell phone calls made daily. And Al Qaeda operatives can easily and readily replace cell phones, making it extraordinarily difficult for the NSA to keep apace of small, nimble, and adaptive terrorist cells.

The shortcomings of CIA human operations and NSA communication interception operations were made painfully clear in the aftermath of the 9/11 attacks. The joint House-Senate investigation found that the CIA had no human agent placed inside Al Qaeda in a position to steal secrets on the 9/11 conspiracy.[17] Although the NSA did intercept some Al Qaeda communications related to the conspiracy, the intercepts were not sufficiently specific and not translated into English before the attacks because the NSA lacked the resources to translate all the communications it manages to intercept.[18] But even if these communications had been translated before 9/11, they would not have been sufficiently detailed to have allowed U.S. officials to wrap up the Al Qaeda cell that orchestrated the attack.

ANALYZING TERRORISTS INTENTIONS, PLANS, AND CAPABILITIES

Intelligence analysis does not hold the public's fascination nearly as well as human intelligence operations and covert action, which are the stuff of spy novels and adventure movies, but it plays no less a critical role in the war on terrorism. Even the best human intelligence and superb intelligence from other sources will come to naught if it not married with first-rate analysis.

The CTC has been the focal point for intelligence collection as well as analysis. The CTC was an exceptionally innovative organization that was created in the mid-1980s to grapple with the problems the United States was facing with Palestinian terrorism as well as Iranian-backed Hezbollah terrorism that was responsible for the bombings of the American embassy, the Marine Corps barracks in Beirut, and the kidnapping of American citizens, such as the CIA's station chief in the 1980s.[19] The creation of the CTC was a remarkable bureaucratic innovation because it located in one office both CIA case officers charged with running HUMINT operations with the CIA's Directorate of Intelligence (DI) analysts. The CIA had traditional fostered a bureaucratic barrier between case officers and analysts partly to protect disclosure of sources and methods, but the separation prevented the synergy of case officers working side by side with analysts. Analysts could identify blind spots and recommend avenues for case officers to gain access to individuals with access to information to fill intelligence gaps.

Despite these strengths, the CTC suffers from a lack of substantive analytic talent, a shortcoming that is a reflection of the CIA's entire analytic corps. The Senate-House inquiry discovered that "the quality of counterterrorism analysis was inconsistent, and many analysts were inexperienced, unqualified, undertrained, and without access to critical information. As a result, there was a dearth of creative, aggressive analysis targeting Bin Ladin and a persistent inability to comprehend the collective significance of individual pieces of intelligence."[20]

Notwithstanding these profound weaknesses, the CTC did indeed provide strategic intelligence warning to President Bush of the September 11 attacks. The CIA in its August 6, 2001, *President's Daily Brief*—a daily current intelligence document prepared for the president and his closest advisors—had warned Bush in an article titled "Bin Laden Determined to Strike in US."[21] The CIA's warning, however, was more a historical review than tactical intelligence needed to disrupt the conspiracy. In contrast, the FBI did have specific information coming from astute field offices in Arizona and Minnesota on suspected Al Qaeda members training on commercial aircraft, but Bureau headquarters lacked a robust analytic staff in Washington to "connect the dots."[22]

Although the strategic intelligence failure of 9/11 falls most heavily on the FBI, the CIA, for whatever reason, took the lion's share of public blame. As is the case with many reforms, the 9/11 Commission recommended changes that "threw the baby out with the bathwater" and recommended a new center under the auspices of the DNI for doing counterterrorism analysis, a recommendation that President Bush accepted.[23] The new National Counterterrorism Center (NCTC), however, will likely be inferior to the old CTC because it will not benefit from shoulder-to-shoulder relationships with the CIA's case officers.

COVERTLY KILLING AND DETAINING
SUSPECTED TERRORISTS

The collection of intelligence—via clandestine human sources, intercepted communications, and other means such as satellites and media monitoring—by far consumes the lion's share of the American intelligence community's budget, which now is running at $44 billion per year.[24] But public attention is captivated by covert action, which is designed to influence events abroad without exposing the hand of the United States, and special activities such as training foreign security services.[25]

These activities, which after many years tend to become publicly exposed, create political controversies in the United States and abroad. One of the largest covert action programs in the CIA's history was the military backing of the insurgency against the Soviet Union's occupation of Afghanistan during the Cold War. The CIA spent millions of dollars and provided tons of military arms and equipment to the Afghan insurgents over a period of years to substantially increase the costs of Soviet occupation and contributed to the Soviet decision to withdraw from Afghanistan. That less-than-covert war is heralded by CIA veterans as an exemplar of covert action that contributed to ending to the Cold War. Other commentators are not so sanguine and argue that the covert action program gave military training, expertise, and battlefield experience to militant Islamic extremists, who later went on to found Al Qaeda. The truth probably lies somewhere in between, but it is important to note that the United States never dealt directly with bin Laden during the Afghan war. Bin Laden's direct sponsors and benefactors were intelligence services of Saudi Arabia and Pakistan.[26]

Covert action has taken on an increasingly important role in the war on terrorism, which the public gets glimpses of by leaks. The CIA did a superb job in facilitating the U.S. Special Forces entry into Afghanistan in the 2001 war.[27] Covert actions such as the ones carried out in Afghanistan are carried out by the CIA and need to be authorized by a presidential order called a finding, which is shared with and approved by the House and Senate oversight committees to be legal in the American judicial system. Traditionally, the presidents have banned American assassination of foreign leaders under executive orders, a practice that has been perpetuated since President Ford's Executive Order 12333, which prohibited assassinations, a move to stem the tide of public criticisms against the CIA and the IC during a tumultuous period of history in American intelligence.[28] CIA Director Porter Goss recently told Congress in public testimony that the ban on assassinations by U.S. intelligence is still in force, but that it does not prohibit the CIA from killing terrorists.[29]

The CIA appears to be effectively using armed unmanned aerial vehicles (UAVs) to kill Al Qaeda operatives. The CIA has used armed UAVs to kill operatives in Yemen and Pakistan as well as in Iraq. "Several U.S. officials confirmed that at least 19 occasions since Sept. 11 on which Predators successfully fired Hellfire missiles on terrorist suspects overseas, including 10 in Iraq in one month last year [2005]. The Predator strikes have killed at least four senior Al Qaeda leaders, but also many civilians, and it is not known how many times they missed their targets."[30]

Some critics have faulted the CIA for falling to use the armed UAVs to target bin Laden or covert paramilitary operations to capture him prior to 9/11. The CIA's Directorate of Operations chief in 1998, for example, did not want to use his funds to sponsor a paramilitary operation to grab bin Laden from his farm in Afghanistan and "expressed concern that people might get killed" and that "the operation had at least a slight flavor of a plan for an assassination. Moreover, he calculated that it would cost several million dollars. He was not prepared to take the money 'out of hide,' and he did not want to go to all the necessary congressional committees to get special money."[31] Although civilians have been tragically killed in paramilitary operations, military strikes, or UAV attacks since 9/11, the strikes are probably still legitimate instruments of war—as long as there is a reasonable chance of killing Al Qaeda operatives and leaders who are sworn to kill as many American civilians and soldiers as they can as long as they live.

The CIA is also using covert teams to located suspected Al Qaeda operatives abroad—in areas where UAV attacks would not be politically viable options, such as in Europe—and in daring raids called renditions they sweep them off the streets and bring them to other countries for detention and interrogations. These operations have been embroiled in controversies. Italy, for example, is in a political uproar because a CIA team took a person off Italian soil.[32] Other European and Asian countries are in an uproar over the purported existence of a string of clandestine CIA detention facilities on their soil. The CIA also has been publicly condemned for blatant violations of the Geneva Conventions with the use of techniques that are commonly considered to be torture in its interrogations undertaken in U.S. military detention facilities in Afghanistan, Iraq, and Guantánamo Bay, Cuba.[33] These accusations include charges that the CIA is using a technique called water-boarding, which makes detainees believe they are drowning. Not only is this technique morally unacceptable, many professional interrogators judge that this technique produces bad intelligence because prisoners will say or make up anything to get interrogators to stop the water-boarding.[34]

The United States may have already fallen victim to this intelligence pitfall. According to journalist James Risen, the information the CIA got from debriefing one high-level Al Qaeda operational commander was fabricated because he wanted to stop water-boarding.[35] Another CIA detainee who was reported tortured after the CIA turned him over to Egyptian officials fabricated information on Iraq's links to Al Qaeda in the run-up to the 2003 Iraq war.[36]

STRENGTHENING INTELLIGENCE COLLECTION, ANALYSIS, AND COVERT ACTION FOR THE WAR ON TERRORISM

Lawyers could argue until the sun goes down whether water-boarding and other techniques the CIA is using constitute the legal definition of torture, but the average American using his or her common sense and moral compass would have little to no difficulty calling these techniques torture. And the American legalistic argument that Al Qaeda operatives are "enemy combatants" and not "prisoners of war" who are governed by the Geneva Conventions carries little weight with Americans and even less with the Middle Eastern populations, which the United States desperately needs to wean away from ideological support for Al Qaeda recruitment and operational support. Even the appearance of Geneva Conventions violations renders American calls for freedom and democracy in the Middle East as sheer hypocrisy and aids and abets our terrorist enemies by handing them ready-made justifications for their ruthless tactics, such as decapitating hostages. Even in its intelligence war on terrorism, the United States must uphold its own ethical standards and not stoop to those of the morally deprived barbarians it is fighting.

The CIA's use of paramilitary operations was a success story in the 2001 war in Afghanistan. But in the wake of the war, the 9/11 Commission recommended—on not very deep analysis or consideration—that these functions should all be controlled by the Pentagon and that CIA should get out of the business. The commission said, "Before 9/11, the CIA did not invest in developing a robust capability to conduct paramilitary operations with U.S. personnel. It relied on proxies instead, organized by CIA operatives with the requisite military training. The results were unsatisfactory."[37]

The recently announced Quadrennial Defense Review, which calls for a substantial beefing up of American Special Operations Forces, will likely work to further push the CIA out of paramilitary operations. The plan is to increase the number of special operations forces by 14,000 to about 64,000, the largest number since the Vietnam War, to fight small Al Qaeda cells dispersed across some eighty countries.[38] The Pentagon's new emphasis no doubt reflects in part the frustration of Defense Secretary Donald Rumsfeld over the lethargic response of the Special Forces to get into the 2001 Afghanistan war in comparison to the quick dispatch of CIA operatives into Afghanistan, which won high praise and respect from President Bush.[39] The push to remove the CIA from the paramilitary business will make sense as long as the Pentagon gives its Special Operations Forces room for operational ingenuity, a key ingredient of effective special operations. Unfortunately, creativity and ingenuity are often crushed by the weight of the Pentagon's bureaucracy.

The DNI, a post created by the president on the recommendation of the 9/11 Commission, will have his hands full trying to overcome the shortcomings of American strategic intelligence against terrorist groups. The DNI's activities so far have focused on recruiting a staff, leaving little time for substantive reforms to address strategic intelligence shortcomings all too evident to the American public in the aftermath of 9/11. The DNI, not the director of the CIA, is now the president's principal intelligence advisor. The DNI has established the National Clandestine Service, the Open Sources Center, and centers under his wing for counterterrorism and counterproliferation, as well as named IC collection managers for Iran and North Korea.[40] There is little evidence to show that these steps are anything more than renaming old organizations, however, and adding some new ones to respond to calls for reform, while in practice doing little to qualitatively improve America's intelligence performance in the war on terrorism.

These bureaucratic fixes run the risk of creating a false impression that the United States has "corrected" of all its strategic intelligence shortcomings in the war on terrorism. But the real, root causes of past failures lie in the quality of human intelligence collection and analysis. The creation of the DNI and new national support offices do nothing directly to correct the bureaucratic culture and failed business practices that are stubbornly rooted at the grassroots level of the CIA. Until reforms and profound changes in managerial business practices change at this level, all the reorganizing and changing of the bureaucratic wiring diagrams at the senior most rungs of the U.S. intelligence community will amount to little more than rearranging the deck chairs on the *Titanic*.

NOTES

The views expressed are those of the author and do not represent the policy or position of the National Defense University, the Department of Defense, or the U.S. government.

1. For an insightful analysis of the political and military obstacles against moving to a war footing against Al Qaeda before 9/11, see Richard H. Shultz Jr., "Showstoppers: Nine Reasons Why We Never Sent Our Special Operations Forces after al-Qaeda before 9/11," *Weekly Standard* (January 26, 2004).

2. House Permanent Select Committee on Intelligence and Senate Select Committee on Intelligence, *Report of the Joint Inquiry into the Terrorist Attacks of September 11, 2001* (Washington, DC, December 2002), p. 40. Hereafter referred to as the Joint House-Senate Inquiry.

3. Ibid., p. 59.

4. Richard A. Clarke, *Against All Enemies: Inside America's War on Terror* (New York: Free Press, 2004), pp. 205, 210.

5. Anonymous [Michael Scheuer], *Through Our Enemies' Eyes: Osama bin Laden, Radical Islam, and the Future of America* (Washington, DC: Brassey's, 2002), p. xiv.

6. Greg Miller, "CIA Plans No Discipline over 9/11," *Los Angeles Times* (October 6, 2005), p. A10.

7. For the most authoritative study of state sponsorship of terrorist groups, see Daniel L. Byman, *Deadly Connections: States that Sponsor Terrorism* (New York: Cambridge University Press, 2005).

8. On policy deliberations, see Clarke, *Against All Enemies*, pp. 184–89.

9. Walter Pincus, "CIA to Retain Coordinator of Overseas Spying," *Washington Post* (October 13, 2005), p. A4.

10. John Diamond, "CIA's Spy Network Thin," *USA Today* (September 22, 2004).

11. Lindsay Moran, "More Spies, Worse Intelligence?" *New York Times* (April 12, 2005).

12. Robert Baer, *See No Evil: The True Story of a Ground Soldier in the CIA's War on Terrorism* (New York: Three Rivers Press, 2002), p. 86.

13. Cited in Michael Janofsky, "Bush Proposes Broader Language Training," *New York Times* (January 6, 2006), p. A15.

14. Joint House-Senate Inquiry, p. 109.

15. Glenn Kessler, "On Leaks, Relying on a Faulty Case Study," *Washington Post* (December 23, 2005), p. A3.

16. On the controversy, see James Risen and Eric Lichtblau, "Bush Lets U.S. Spy on Callers Without Courts," *New York Times* (December 16, 2005), p. A1.

17. Joint House-Senate Inquiry, p. 90.

18. Ibid., p. 205.

19. For an account of the innovative creation of the CTC by its founding chief, see Duane R. Clarridge with Digby Diehl, *A Spy for All Seasons: My Life in the CIA* (New York: Scribner's, 1997), pp. 321–29.

20. Joint House-Senate Inquiry, 59.

21. *The 9/11 Commission Report* (New York: Norton, 2004), pp. 260–61.

22. See the Joint House-Senate Inquiry, pp. 325–35.

23. For the recommendation to establish the NCTC, see *The 9/11 Commission Report*, pp. 403–6.

24. The budget figure was revealed by a senior official in the DNI's office in 2005. See Scott Shane, "Official Reveals Budget for U.S. Intelligence," *New York Times* (November 8, 2005), p. A18.

25. For an insightful discussion of the differences between covert action and special activities, see William J. Daugherty, *Executive Secrets: Covert Action and the Presidency* (Lexington: University Press of Kentucky, 2004), pp. 12–16.

26. For a fascinating accounts of CIA's covert action program in Afghanistan, see Steve Coll, *Ghost Wars: The Secret History of the CIA, Afghanistan, and bin Laden, from the Soviet Invasion to September 10, 2001* (New York: Penguin Press, 2004) and George Crile, *Charlie Wilson's War: The Extraordinary Story of How the Wildest Man in Congress and a Rogue CIA Agent Changed the History of Our Times* (New York: Grove Press, 2003).

27. See Gary C. Schroen, *First In: An Insider's Account of How the CIA Spearheaded the War on Terror in Afghanistan* (New York: Ballantine Books, 2005).

28. For a concise history of congressional oversight of the CIA and covert action, see Loch K. Johnson, "Presidents, Lawmakers, and Spies: Intelligence Accountability in the United States," *Presidential Studies Quarterly* 34, no. 4 (December 2004), pp. 828–37.

29. Shaun Waterman, "Goss Says CIA Ban Excludes Terrorists," *Washington Times* (March 25, 2005), p. A5.

30. Josh Meyer, "CIA Expands Use of Drones in Terror War," *Los Angeles Times* (January 29, 2006), p. A1.

31. *The 9/11 Commission Report*, p. 113.

32. In a reflection of the anger surrounding the case, an Italian judge ordered the arrest of thirteen suspected CIA officers who participated in the rendition operation in 2003. See Stephen Grey and Don Van Natta, "In Italy, Anger at U.S. Tactics Colors Spy Case," *New York Times* (June 26, 2005), p. A1.

33. For an insightful treatment of the CIA's covert activity and ethical dilemmas with maintaining prison facilities for renditioned individuals, see Dana Priest, "CIA Holds Terror Suspects in Secret Prisons," *Washington Post* (November 2, 2005), p. A1.

34. James Risen, *State of War: The Secret History of the CIA and the Bush Administration* (New York: Free Press, 2006), pp. 32–33.

35. Ibid., p. 33.

36. Douglas Jehl, "Qaeda-Iraq Link U.S. Cited Is Tied to Coercion Claim," *New York Times* (December 9, 2005), p. A1.

37. *The 9/11 Commission Report*, p. 415.

38. Greg Jaffe, "Rumsfeld Aims to Elevate Role of Special Forces," *Wall Street Journal* (February 18, 2006), p. A1.

39. Bob Woodward, *Bush at War* (New York: Simon & Schuster, 2002), pp. 53, 78–80, 88, 99.

40. John D. Negroponte, "Intelligence Reform: Challenges and Opportunities," 25th Jit Trainor Award Speech, Georgetown University, February 17, 2006.

8

INTELLIGENCE TO COUNTER TERROR

The Importance of All-Source Fusion

JENNIFER SIMS

FROM 1934 TO 1937, THE BRITISH GOVERNMENT collected suspicious communications from its monitoring station at Camberwell.[1] Peeling back the encryption with the help of a well-placed mole and several émigrés, the government discovered the existence of an illicit Soviet spying and covert action network operating on British soil. It appeared to involve senior politicians and established political organizations. Direction-finding equipment owned by the Army intercept station at Fort Bridgewoods, the Air Ministry at Waddington, and at the Royal Navy's receiver at Flowerdown established the location of the network's transmission sites. MI5 used this knowledge to begin surveillance of the broad-based network, penetrate it with human intelligence assets, and gain advance notice of illegal activities. These counterintelligence efforts eventually established that the illicit British cells were connected to Vienna, Shanghai, Prague, Copenhagen, Zurich, Paris, Spain, and the United States. All were directed by Moscow and coordinated through the operations of Comintern or Communist International. According to British historian Nigel West, this huge counterintelligence operation, which intercepted a total of 1,571 messages, disrupted Moscow's efforts to influence British elections "on a massive scale."[2]

This is the story of MASK—the code name for MI5's penetration of the Communist Party of Great Britain during the period between the world wars. Although the details of the story are worth rereading in the post–September 11, 2001, political context, just the facts summarized above suggest three truths about counterintelligence operations directed against networks: first, they involve intrusive domestic operations, often against domestically based groups designed to "disappear" within the societies in which they operate; second, they require patient accumulation of data over a lengthy period of time; and finally, they depend on information fused from a variety of widely differing sources. These three ingredients, essential for such operations almost a century ago, are still important in the age of global, digitalized information flows and transnational threats. In fact, the new digital environment has made transnational crimes vastly easier to coordinate on a worldwide scale than was possible before World War II. It has also exacerbated a most serious challenge: governments (particularly democracies) attempting to stop terrorists are expected to do so without undermining the laws, representative principles, and informal confidences upon which a culture of democracy depends. Unfortunately, what Britain succeeded in doing against its domestic threat—to the satisfaction of the British public—was done even better within the militarized Nazi German state by Hitler's Gestapo and the Schutzstaffel, or SS ("Blackshirts"). If, as President Truman once promised the American people, we are not in the business of creating a Gestapo in this country, what are the proper limits of our counterintelligence business?

The purpose of this chapter is to examine the modern intelligence requirements for countering terror to appreciate this challenge in greater depth and develop a reasoned basis for balancing counterintelligence capabilities with civil liberties. What is meant by all-source data fusion in intelligence work, and how necessary is it against terrorists? How necessary are government-wide databases of digitalized information, and why does the idea of connecting them worry civil libertarians? If, as the post-9/11 commissions have suggested, one of the U.S. government's worst intelligence failures during this tragedy was the lack of adequate data fusion and analysis, what has been done about it, and can we do more without intolerable risks to our social and moral fabric?

To explore these questions, this chapter begins by considering the nature of the terrorists we face and the requirements for good intelligence operations against them. Historical examples will illustrate that there are lessons to be learned from the defeat of similar threats in the past, including the recurring ways in which challenges to civil liberties arise as democracies optimize intelligence in the name of security. Second, I run through the special opportunities and challenges modern technology presents. Third, I discuss an essential next step for democracies threatened by terrorists in their midst.

THE NATURE OF INTELLIGENCE AND COUNTERINTELLIGENCE IN THE AGE OF TERROR

As has been repeatedly pointed out, terrorism is a tool, not an adversary in and of itself. Yet adversaries who use this tool reveal much about themselves. They are ruthless, have strategies and tactics that require operational access to their victims, and they are able to organize in pursuit of their goals. Moreover, unless they are psychopathic, they use terror because they have no alternative that offers as much opportunity to win battles. Public access to national treasures and freedom to organize are integral to Western democracies' most vital interests. Democracies intent on fighting adversaries who exploit openness to kill massively, risk undermining themselves. Countering such adversaries at the strategic level may require understanding their larger purposes to deflect, overcome, or undermine them. But to defeat them at the tactical level, one must deny them access, disrupt their ability to organize, or deny them their "victories" even if their tactics succeed. One must know what they are doing and either catch them at it or refuse to flinch—ideally, both. Intelligence, in any case, is essential.

The Role of Intelligence

Intelligence is best understood as the collection, analysis, and dissemination of information by parties in conflict or competition. What turns the simple pursuit of information into the business of intelligence is its purpose: gaining competitive advantage over adversaries.[3] This goal fuels the desire for specific, urgent, and often secret knowledge as well as a systematic way of obtaining it in time to win the contest. Given that the context is competition, such decision advantages can be acquired in two ways: by getting better information for one's strategy than one's opponents gain for theirs, or by degrading the competitors' decision making through denial, disruption, deception, and surprise.[4] This latter category of activity is called *counterintelligence*. More than just security, counterintelligence involves discovering what opponents think they need to know and then using this information to block, disorient, confuse, and ultimately beat them. In virulent or hostile competitions, increasing the speed of one's own decision making and the mobility of the decision makers may unbalance the opponent more than trying to discern and defend all the information believed to be critical to that opponent's strategy—a process that can actually slow decision making and cripple one's offense. Of course, the best way to protect an intelligence system is to own the adversary's intelligence system through the use of moles, double agents, and the like.

Gangs, bureaucrats, and football teams all use a form of intelligence to gain advantages over their competitors.[5] The more intense and lawless the competition, such as in international politics, the more secretive intelligence operations tend to become and the more decisive the potential advantages they offer. In fact, for states, intelligence can be more than a life or death enterprise; it can entail the end of nations and cultures.[6] For these reasons, secrecy is often viewed as a necessary component of national or transnational intelligence efforts. It is more accurate, however, to think of secrecy as an attribute of a relatively good intelligence effort—not an essential requirement for it. Some contestants' counterintelligence capabilities are so poor that they are not aware of what information they should protect to beat their adversaries. Or they believe their relative agility makes such protection unnecessary. Trying to defeat such opponents by only looking for secrets they protect would lead to failure. Intelligence must instead work to collect the information that provides the competitor with a decision advantage over opponents—whether or not that information is secret—and to assume adversaries are doing likewise.

Arguably, a preoccupation with secrets cost the United States much before the devastation of 9/11. Although the terrorists' plans were indeed closely held, their operations were boldly open. Most used their true names when making airline reservations, used common addresses, and communicated on the Internet— not through privileged diplomatic pouches or hidden radios. The trick to catching them would have been to combine what we knew from the efforts of the Central Intelligence Agency (CIA) to track them overseas with what we could have known from the surveillance and unclassified information collected at home by the Federal Bureau of Investigation (FBI). Using classified sources to tip off the FBI and discern the unclassified information crucial for counterterrorist decision making is a critical part of the domestic intelligence enterprise.[7]

Traditionally, U.S. intelligence has used three types of collection to target opponents: technical intelligence (TECHINT), human intelligence (HUMINT), and open-source or unclassified intelligence (OSINT). TECHINT includes the collection of imagery, intercepted communications, electronic signals emitted by equipment, engineering data from captured electronics or weapons systems, and data from equipment or materials in the environment that leave signatures of their presence (such as radiation, effluent plumes, and noise) that trained analysts can discern using pre-existing data as reference.[8] The productivity of any of these collectors against a particular target will depend on that collector's access to the target's most vulnerable point. For example, if a network of spies uses wireless radios, picking up their electronic emissions (TECHINT) will be an effective way to find them; if they use couriers, human agents secretly opening the letters and packages (HUMINT) is likely to work best; if the adversary believes he is unobserved, collecting the names of those he visits from a phone book or the sites he visits while traveling as an ostensible tourist (OSINT) would be useful.

In any case, the best intelligence is obtained when the capabilities of all these collectors are quickly combined. Just as newspaper editors like to see multiple sources corroborating articles even from their best reporters, directors of national intelligence have greater confidence in intelligence that comes from multiple collectors. Better than simply hearing that Osama bin Laden has been sighted on a road in Pakistan would be seeing imagery of his convoy and receiving intercepts from his communications that each independently confirm the initial report.[9] As long as an opponent runs reasonably complex operations, some collectors will work best against certain aspects of those operations, whereas others will work best against the rest. Thus "all-source" collection can yield many pieces of a puzzle that analysts can then assemble, jumble up, and reassemble as the adversary moves, reacts to countermoves, and moves again.

Beyond corroboration, however, is the concept of collection boosting, in which the productivity of one collector depends on input from others.[10] The most obvious example of boosting within a single discipline is "direction finding" (DF), which may involve the use of multiple antennae to triangulate on a signal so that it can be not only identified but also geo-located with some degree of precision.[11] During World War II, the SS paired up with the Gestapo and used DF to locate the wireless radios used by a network of Stalin's spies in Europe. To their great chagrin, these radios were found in Berlin—some next to the most sensitive government ministries.[12]

Of course, boosting also works among collection disciplines, such as the use of spies (HUMINT) to steal the codes of adversaries so that analysts working on intercepted communications (TECHINT) can overcome the encryption methods and read the content of the messages.[13] In fact, the more tightly integrated collectors are in the decision-making process, the more likely an adversary's spoofing of a collector will work to deflect or deceive one's own decision makers. Because securing collectors can be a costly and seemingly never-ending endeavor, one good way to compensate for inevitable vulnerabilities is to ensure collection is "constructively redundant"—that is, sufficiently all-source that one collector's vulnerability to spoofing will not lead to misperception or miscalculation.

This kind of constructively redundant all-source collection was a linchpin of the Allied strategy to defeat Hitler during World War II; it was employed, for example, to determine whether covert and clandestine collection operations had been compromised and specifically in the running of the famous British counterintelligence operation known as the Double Cross System.[14] But the history of Double Cross also alerts us to the inherent dangers of redundant collection systems: Because collectors improve the reliability of each other's products by offering independent corroboration, they depend on good system-wide counterintelligence so an adversary can't defeat or spoof one of them and thus sow ambiguity, uncertainty and confusion throughout an interlaced collection system. If systemic counterintelligence is weak, collectors have good reason not to share their "take" lest it become tainted. Poor counterintelligence can lead to system-wide failure even when the majority of collection endeavors are robust and productive.[15]

In some respects, then, the business of all-source data fusion for countering terrorism follows what has been done in a traditional sense against other intelligence targets. What makes the counterterrorism a particularly challenging endeavor is the terrorists' objective of committing stealthy crime—often on the victim's home soil. This means that law enforcement information, including information on U.S. residents or citizens living in close proximity to terrorists, may be important intelligence information that needs to be shared with decision makers at the federal level working to thwart terrorist activities on a nationwide scale. Law enforcement agents, dedicated to preserving the information for the purposes of arrest and prosecution, realize the need to pass the information over to these officials but do not always know the best and most secure ways to do so. At times, in fact, the most important decisions must be made very quickly by state and local officials if they are to prevent an impending attack. In these cases, circulating information to Washington for recycling into intelligence products could delay action rather than assist it. The problem thus becomes the very nontraditional one of fusing all-source intelligence for a cop on the beat.

Intelligence for Counterterrorism

In other words, what makes terrorists particularly difficult intelligence targets for traditional intelligence systems is that they organize as networks, insinuate themselves into open societies, and kill suddenly. Whereas traditional collectors were designed to penetrate governments located in state capitals or military deployments located on discrete battlefields, terrorists specialize in operating in small numbers and under the skins of their adversaries—that is, wherever they can do the most damage. They fashion themselves to look like their targets and burrow into society to lie in wait. In this sense they occupy the same moral space as assassins, but without an assassin's traditional limits on targeting. Deceit is part of terrorists' stock in trade, and innocents are their intentional victims. Often free of the vertical command structures of their more bureaucratic opponents, they achieve agility through compartmented operations, often using minimal communications. Their offensive operations are also crucial to their defense; by instilling fear and panic, terrorists create sufficient confusion to enable their swift escape. For many of these reasons, analysts have long argued that it takes a network to fight networked organizations, such as Al Qaeda.[16]

Unfortunately for democracies, counterterrorism requires gaining access to the enemy where he operates, including on one's own soil. And because terrorists do not operate against a national security establishment but against an entire society, they will not necessarily be focused on any particular city or on stealing secrets from traditional national security establishments. This means that it may be necessary but no longer sufficient to use forms of collection appropriate to the Cold War, when the enemy was a highly bureaucratized state, targeting Washington and using a command-and-control system stretching halfway around the world. To stop terrorists, information from traditional intelligence collectors will need to be combined with information collected by those disconnected to the traditional national security community. Hospitals may be the first to see a spike in disease associated with a biological weapons attack; police may be the first to bust a document forger or stop a car carrying explosives; customs agents at a port may be the first to notice discrepancies between the scan of a shipping crate and its official manifest; a landlord may be the first to notice his building's security system is detecting toxic gases; and a shopper may be the first to notice someone in a mall or store pushing a heavy baby carriage with no baby inside.

Against this kind of threat, time is of the essence, yet indications and warning may come from untrained people just doing their day jobs. The intelligence these domestic collectors acquire, moreover, will often need to be analyzed and provided back to them. After all, they are likely to be the decision makers best placed to stop the attack itself. The first 9/11 counterattack was, in fact, carried out by passengers on an airliner—once they knew from collecting intelligence over their cell phones what they were up against and what was at stake.

In the modern era of the Internet and the global reach of broadband communications, terrorists have new capabilities beyond the reach of any one country.

By piggybacking on this information system, bolstered by highly effective private encryption, transnational terrorist groups can communicate instantaneously and largely anonymously, even to the extent of sending sensitive information embedded in pictures on websites or in e-mails, a practice known as steganography. For this reason, the intelligence gained by other states and their private sector collectors may be as potentially valuable as intelligence collected unilaterally; much depends on the confidence a state has in its liaison relationships—confidence that should fluctuate more with the capabilities of that state's counterintelligence capabilities than with the number of its perceived friendships.

The overall picture, then, is of proliferating intelligence sources, increasingly complex all-source analysis, and a maddeningly contingent list of those decision makers who not only need the results but must get them in record time. Preparation of a terrorist attack might take years, but its execution or prevention may take only hours or minutes. As bad as this situation sounds, it is not all that new. As with today's terrorists, past plotters have threaded themselves through the fabric of the societies they planned to attack. Catholics, intent on overthrowing the Protestant Queen Elizabeth I and installing her Catholic cousin, Mary, Queen of Scots, were distinguishable from Elizabeth's loyalists only by their faith. Sir Walsingham, Elizabeth's Secretary of State and chief spymaster, nonetheless caught them.[17] Kaiser Wilhelm's saboteurs infiltrated German immigrant communities in the United States prior to World War I so that they would have cover for their mission to blow up weapons depots, warehouses, and storage facilities. They, too, were countered—this time by a network of British liaison officers and U.S. law enforcement personnel, assisted by the intermittent incompetence of the saboteurs themselves.[18] Successful counterterrorist intelligence operations such as these have generally employed well-known principles: collect multisource intelligence, tighten borders, tap liaison services, conduct deception operations, and enlist law enforcement to interdict and "turn" the criminals so frequently but superficially aligned with terrorists, such as forgers and money launderers.[19]

What makes the current, post-9/11 effort so much more difficult than in times past is the nature of modern technology. Technology has affected the counterterrorist mission in a number of ways. For example, experts have discussed at length how advances in weapons technologies have rendered the scariest forms of attack—biologically engineered germs, toxins, and nuclear explosive or radiological devices—feasible for small numbers of nonexperts to execute. Perhaps less well understood among the general population is the extent to which advances in communications technology permit terrorist networks to exchange messages and plan attacks on a worldwide basis and to do so almost instantaneously.

The development and widespread use of commercial surveillance technologies mean that information on a developing terrorist attack that is acquired by private citizens or local businesses can in theory be handed off rapidly to local and federal officials even though it is "owned" by others. Individuals outside the traditional national security community may therefore not only be the first to get critical information about a coming terrorist attack but, with the proliferation of private surveillance technologies and personal communications capabilities, they could be empowered with the critical ability to decide what to do with it. Obviously, the national intelligence community has a stake in such decisions. But not surprisingly, the U.S. intelligence community has neither a roadmap for building the kind of domestic alliances that would facilitate such cooperation nor the deep and nuanced understanding of American political culture that makes such a task so difficult for the federal government to implement.[20]

Unfortunately, terrorists who recognize this trend in private sector surveillance and its potential connection to the nation's information infrastructure may use cyberattacks to facilitate their plans. According to James Gosler of Sandia Laboratory, these attacks are becoming increasingly feasible. His argument, in its simplest form, is that the distributed nature of the modern software and computer manufacturing industry makes modern information technologies inherently vulnerable.[21] Aware of both the threat in the private sector and its inherent vulnerability, the U.S. government decided after 9/11 to circumvent established procedures for domestic counterterrorist surveillance to permit rapid sampling of certain domestic communications as a counterintelligence measure.[22] This step at the federal level has proved highly controversial. Less controversial methods for improving domestic collection could involve building alliances with the private sector rather than simply tapping into it.[23]

DATA FUSION AND THE AGE OF TERROR: IMPLICATIONS FOR DEMOCRACY

The prominent role all-source intelligence and advanced technology have in countering terrorism presents special difficulties for democracies. Although the media have recently highlighted issues related to prisoner detention, rendition, and interrogation, these are not the only matters that trouble democracies fighting terrorists. Debates continue among civil libertarians, security officials and private citizens over the more obscure issues of domestic surveillance, data management and privacy. It is hard to promote freedom and liberty as antidotes for terror while at the same time encouraging allied governments to intrude more deeply into their own societies for the purpose of monitoring individuals and capturing fanatics before they act. Unfortunately, this is exactly the course that the US is now forced to take. Balancing security and pre-emption with restraint and freedom is difficult; terrorists likely hope the conundrum will prove paralyzing.

While some commentators have suggested that privacy may be one area where Americans may be willing to cede added power to authorities, others, including this author, have noted that suspicion of excess power in the hands of the federal government runs deep in American political culture. Although the issues prisoners' rights now before the courts are beyond the scope of this paper; these other issues of data fusion, control, and management are not.

The Domestic Context for Intelligence Collection and Data Fusion

Throughout the Cold War, the CIA, FBI, and certain military services were involved in domestic intelligence collection. When they over-reached, they were subjected to new legal constraints. By 1978, when the Foreign Intelligence Surveillance Act (FISA) was passed, the essential framework for domestic spying in the US had been established: on the one hand, the president's constitutional authority for the nation's defense gave him the prerogative to order domestic surveillance; on the other hand, his powers to spy on American citizens and residents were constrained by the requirement that the courts be convinced of these individuals' connections to foreign powers or terrorist causes in each case. It was understood, if not written into law, that information gathered in this secret way, that is, without the normal warrant process, was not to bleed into the criminal justice system to be used against citizens for other purposes—such as to convict them of a crime unrelated to espionage or terror. In this way, what has come to be called the "wall" between intelligence and law enforcement was deliberately and perhaps too impermeably erected.

After 9/11, lawmakers and national security experts criticized this framework as too tight a constraint on domestic intelligence gathering. While the president was secretly reasserting his perceived prerogatives to spy against domestic national security threats, Congress passed the Patriot Act. This act increased the FBI's ability to track and monitor terrorists using communications systems far more elaborate than those available when the original FISA law was passed. In addition, the "wall" between intelligence and law enforcement was torn down in the interests of intelligence sharing between agencies. The president also decided to consolidate within the Department of Homeland Security (DHS), those agencies responsible for border control, emergency response, and domestic security. While eschewing a new domestic intelligence gathering function, DHS began to consolidate databases and to generate related intelligence reports. The president created the Terrorism Threat Integration Center to fuse intelligence from all relevant agencies both inside and outside the formal intelligence community. Following the endorsement of the idea of data fusion centers by the 9/11 Commission, Congress passed legislation creating the National Counter Terrorism Center, the director of which gained authorities over overseas operations as well. Subsequently, its sister center was created under the new Director of National Intelligence to handle intelligence on weapons of mass destruction.

While these changes were under way at the highest levels in Washington, debate has continued on what appears to be a serious gap: Unlike Britain, the U.S. federal government continues to lack an institution specifically charged with conducting true domestic intelligence gathering and forging the kind of domestic alliances for intelligence networking already described. The FBI's expertise remains law enforcement and defensive counterintelligence—both arts involving the use of surveillance for arrests, not for strategic planning and the exploitation of decision advantages. The CIA and FBI—if not the NSA—have also remained boxed within the 1978 framework and thus prohibited from even thinking about how to develop knowledge on domestic activities. Without a deep domestic intelligence capability and the domestic consensus necessary to institutionalize it, data fusion at the federal level may remain inadequate to the counterterrorism task.[24]

Unwilling to wait for a federal agency to take an aggressive lead, law enforcement officials in cities such as New York, Los Angeles, and Chicago have begun to expand their capabilities to investigate domestic groups; consolidate the data from global, national, and local sources; and thus organize new and improved intelligence systems themselves. Data fusion is becoming a grassroots business. For example, Los Angeles has pioneered the Terrorism Early Warning Group, which fuses intelligence and directs it to first responders.[25] And New York City has gone so far as to establish liaison offices overseas. In the wake of the collapse of a local cable company, Chicago's Mayor Richard Daley bought up its fiber optic network and hooked hundreds of video cameras to it. He has also encouraged private companies to dump the returns from their surveillance cameras onto the network so that, for a fee, crimes could be rapidly reported to the city's police department.

Of course, the establishments wired for commercial security are becoming Chicago's platforms for law enforcement surveillance of criminal and gang-related behavior. The city's operations center has become the hub of a network for surveillance and monitoring in the name of citizen protection against crime and, simultaneously, natural disasters and terrorist attack. Not surprisingly, Chicago's innovation has been replicated in at least 150 other cities to a greater or lesser degree. New York, which reportedly plans a network of 3,000 cameras, is defending its right to archive the video files indefinitely.[26] Baltimore, whose cameras may soon have the ability to "talk," intends to deter crime as much as counter terrorists with its electronic network.[27]

Other first responders are adopting similar methods for different purposes. Hospitals have begun wiring themselves to keep track of the conditions of patients and the scarce medical equipment they may need to ensure efficiency of care. When more than one hospital participates, ambulances can make better decisions about where to transport emergency cases to ensure the swiftest medical care at emergency rooms. A system such as this, or the one in Chicago, could have assisted New Orleans in its efforts to respond to the emergency following Hurricane Katrina. It holds the promise of gathering data swiftly and analyzing it appropriately in the event of a terrorist attack as well.

Although public protests of increases in domestic surveillance at the local level have been light and sporadic, this level of tolerance has not been apparent when federal surveillance has been involved. National attention more readily focuses on federal moves, hesitant though they may be, to increase domestic surveillance. For example, the president's expansion of the Defense Department's Counterintelligence Field Activity (CIFA), including its surveillance activities nationwide, has triggered protests, including at least one congressional intervention.[28] Although CIFA was created to protect military facilities and personnel worldwide, it has significantly ramped up its domestic operations in recent years for the purpose of fusing intelligence, identifying and assessing threats, and retaining the results in a Pentagon database.

Perhaps even more notorious was the abbreviated effort to link databases at the federal level for similar purposes. In 2003 Adm. John Poindexter spearheaded an effort to link databases at the federal level for the purposes of querying them and drawing inferences about terrorists actions from their contents over time. The project, unfortunately dubbed Total Information Awareness (TIA), had an Orwellian quality that made many Americans' hair stand on end. Among them were a number of legislators who promptly killed the program. Along with it, they killed the only ongoing federally funded research in how to protect the privacy of citizens from advances in "inferencing" capabilities (discussed below), so crucial to anticipating, warning, and managing not just terrorist attacks but natural disasters and outbreaks of disease as well.

For reasons elaborated more fully elsewhere, Americans clearly have a particular distaste for federal government intrusion in their lives.[29] That the citizens of a small town in Vermont wire their streets with surveillance cameras or that Chicago and New York and Baltimore experiment in new law enforcement techniques does not mean that the American public will be willing to accept those kinds of domestic initiatives from the federal government. This attitude holds true even when the nation's security is arguably at risk. Although the relevant laws have been modified in the wake of 9/11, citizens are likely to demand that constitutional protections against unwarranted intrusion by the federal government stay intact even as they willingly cede these rights to commercial firms and local law enforcement.

WHAT IS TO BE DONE?

Britain's successful counterintelligence operation against communist infiltrators during the interwar period involved the use of domestic surveillance, communications intercepts, direction finding involving the military services, and the penetration of a domestic political party. Such an aggressive approach would be firmly resisted in the United States, constrained as it is by the electorate's deeply seated sense of domestic privacy and individual prerogatives. Yet without successful efforts to bring together all-source intelligence on domestic threats, a repeat of tragedy on the scale of 9/11 could bring the kind of domestic overreaction that leads to vigilantism and the undermining of the very constitutional protections that national security measures are meant to protect. So what can be done to balance the need for data collection and fusion with civil liberties?

Challenging as the technological political landscape seems, it also presents opportunities for domestic counterterrorist operations, provided secret breaching of democratically developed laws does not trigger public blowback. Terrorists have gained an advantage in operating within democracies because they have found ways to use technological innovations, such as the Internet and commercially available programs for communicating, hiding, and ferreting out new recruits. This penetration of liberal societies through the hijacking of the technologies they excel at creating is crafty. After all, Americans entrepreneurs rapidly employ their best commercial innovations in critical infrastructure, protecting them as national assets even as adversaries exploit them.

But technology is, by its nature, neutral. It is also constantly changing. The American public has proved itself both adaptable and tolerant of efforts to fuse intelligence for the purposes of interdiction, at least when done at the local level. The issue is whether those officials countering terrorism can be quicker and more innovative than the terrorists in recognizing what must be done in binding innovation to mission and whether citizens and officials at the local, state, and federal levels can find ways to embrace such innovation without doing violence to civil liberties.

Pursuing Total Information Awareness?

Although no one would suggest that American citizens should embrace an Orwellian world in which the federal government monitors their every move, most Americans probably do understand and even value society's ability to remember them when their lives and livelihoods are at stake. Insurers and pharmacists keep track of medical records; credit card companies and banks track credit histories so that people can borrow money to buy homes or send their kids to college.

What is at issue is the government's ability to access and combine these pools of data to uncover patterns of activity. Though such pooling might lower the risks to society, it could have unfortunate consequences for individuals in specific instances: a personal medical history falling into the hands of prospective employers; fallacious patterns that seem to implicate an innocent person in the activities of a gang; or the confusion of a name and profile of a suspected terrorist with that of a law-abiding citizen. At the same time, failure to establish such patterns may allow terrorists free rein in a society increasingly wired for their purposes.

Two avenues are open for addressing this dilemma. First, research institutions can delve more deeply into the question of data mining and analysis and educate the public about their results. Public understanding of the uses and limits of government held databases is currently minimal. And although institutions such as the Center for Strategic and International Studies have begun important initiatives to raise public awareness of the true nature of the data-mining question, much more needs to be done.[30]

Second, the U.S. government can more proactively align itself with domestic initiatives to fuse data for crisis management in the private sector and for local law enforcement purposes. In return for encouraging and even subsidizing those initiatives that have found support among local citizenry, the federal government could share federally researched techniques and standards for information processing and hand-off, while negotiating protocols for ensuring the threshold for federal access is appropriately restrictive.

Data Mining and Data Analysis: Thinking Ahead

An expert with the Center for Strategic and International Studies, Mary De Rosa, has conducted a carefully researched study of the data fusion and management problem confronting counterterrorism analysts.[31] Data mining has proved a particularly nettlesome area for domestic intelligence. In her published report, De Rosa makes important headway by drawing clear distinctions between data mining and data analysis. The former is a process that "uses algorithms to discover predictive patterns in data sets"; the latter "applies models to data to predict behavior, assess risk, determine associations or do other types of analysis."[32] Although both techniques simply exploit data that are already accessible, they also create new knowledge from these data faster and more accurately than human analysts can. Specifically, these techniques can help with the accurate attribution of records to individual people; establish connections between people, places, and things; and infer from existing data, using patterns of past illicit activities associated with known terrorist groups, the probable development of sleeper cells involving individuals with no known criminal records. What many of these systems do far less efficiently is discern data that no longer require archiving. The absence of such self-laundering systems means that inappropriate associations among data sets may linger. This means that innocent civilians may only notice that they have a problem when pulled out of lines at airports or encountering difficulties renewing their driver's licenses.

As these techniques are being developed in the private sector by commercial firms interested in increasing profits by understanding markets, the general public is intermittently outraged, perplexed, or delighted with the impact of these developments on their personal transactions. Most private citizens remain largely unaware of business and government investment in both data mining techniques and technologies designed to moderate their deleterious effects on privacy. De Rosa includes in her list of such advances anonymizing, auditing, and "permissioning" technologies. Investors are funding anonymizing techniques to allow data on individuals to be processed without using names. The second type of technology, auditing, allows those working on newly enabled data-processing techniques to be held accountable for their actions. Permissioning would ensure that rules established for handling data are fully respected.

Unfortunately, De Rosa concludes that even if the problems of inappropriate associations among data—that is, the problem of false positives—can be overcome, government mechanisms remain inadequate for controlling the use of the results. Among the issues that still need to be addressed are those related to mission creep, or the tendency to do more with information than the public has agreed to tolerate.

Enlisting the Private Sector: Smart Buildings?

It is not much of a stretch, given advances in data processing and the steps already taken in Chicago and New York, to see that in the event of a terrorist attack, the federal government would have potentially wide-ranging interest in information being generated in localities. Doctors, hospitals, and private surveillance cameras could become the new collectors in a nationwide intelligence effort to learn what the terrorists have done, where they have gone, and where they might attack next.

If such a system were developed and automated, the advantages would flow to both local crisis managers and the federal government. Doctors and hospitals could concentrate on care of the victims while an impersonal data hand-off of symptoms and geographic distribution could be provided to authorities responsible for determining if terrorists and biological weapons were involved. This would enable a quick, nationwide response. For example, if San Francisco, Houston, and Seattle were also equipped, the federal government would have instantaneous information from across the country should simultaneous attacks—the hallmark of terrorist groups such as Al Qaeda—occur. The capacity to learn about attacks and their nature early on would make the difference in the federal government's capacity to respond to such events.

Hospitals are not the only wired domains that might be lashed to such a nationwide 911 system. Indeed, technological innovations are moving swiftly toward a city landscape likely to differ greatly from the cities of today. Nanotechnology promises to offer micro-energy systems embedded in the skins of buildings that use solar power as energy for wireless sensing, lighting, and maintenance devices. Buildings already equipped with fiber optic cables of the kind laced through Chicago may soon have the ability to sense and control not only environmental conditions within them but the air quality and environmental conditions outside. In the event of disasters, these buildings may someday have the "sense" to seal themselves, control and clean air flows, and monitor the health, location, and well-being of their residents while sending this information to first responders and, if necessary, the federal government.

After all, the technologies that Chicago, New York, and now Baltimore are discovering turn on automated data analysis: "inferencing engines" that fuse sensor data from multiple inputs. These inferencing capabilities help assess not only what is happening at the moment but also what might be coming. In other words, by fusing lots of data simultaneously—far more data than a human analyst can cope with in a normal day—and applying sophisticated models, computers are able not just to see what has already happened but warn of coming events. From a counterterrorism standpoint, far better than hunkering down in buildings that protect their occupants from the effects of biological terrorism would be a system that sorts tremendous amounts of data and anticipates the attackers before they are able to act. This kind of data fusion for counterterrorism would permit consequence management as well as interdiction and protective actions prior to attack.

At the point where technology turns buildings into allies, the need to evacuate cities in the face of many kinds of disasters may pass. The trick, of course, would be to ensure that technology stays friendly and in the right hands. If technology is moving in this direction, and indications are that it is, the federal government needs to anticipate the wired society that is emerging and work to ensure that the protocols, access, and management of this information stays within the scope of tolerance for Americans not only protective of their families and well-being, but also of their freedoms and privacy as well. Such a legislative package would set the bounds for federal surveillance of domestic threats and the proper procedures for handing off information collected at local levels for civilian purposes, to the federal level in times of crisis or elevated threat.

CONCLUSION

In recognition of the rapid tempo of decision making so necessary for interdiction of terrorists—especially those possibly equipped with weapons of mass destruction—the intelligence community has organized centers for counterterrorism and nonproliferation that marry analysts with operators and technology specialists so that they can more rapidly fuse intelligence data, analyze it, and act. The military has employed a form of this approach since the first Persian Gulf War with its creation of National Intelligence Support Teams and now Joint Intelligence Operations Centers that fuse all collected data from tactical and national level sensors to support commanders' operations in the field.

What the federal government has been slower to do is to reach out to the private sector in support of initiatives such as those in Chicago and New York for the purpose of negotiating frameworks or protocols for the hand-off of information to the federal government under certain specified conditions.[33] Arguably, the best time to negotiate these solutions is now, before the next terrorist attack takes place and a spasm of reaction leads to measures not nearly as well thought out as the American polity deserves. At the same time, initial efforts to manage just the federally available information for such purposes has met with stunning political resistance from a poorly informed public. Burned once, the political will to bridge the Washington–locality divide may be hard to muster in the future.

To take these necessary steps, the United States needs to muster the will for a public debate on privacy—not seek to avoid it as a bothersome drag on the mission of law enforcement and counterterrorism experts. The need is now urgent. Between the great world wars of the last century, Britain succeeded in protecting its polity from the threats posed by an international network intent on penetrating and corrupting it. It did so by employing all-source data fusion—to include data from domestic sources still beyond the scope of what federal intelligence authorities are permitted under U.S. law. A great American debate awaits over the extent to which the federal government can ally with state and local governments and private industry to manage the new, secure information infrastructure that is already emerging to enable domestic intelligence authorities to do their job, within the law, as Americans expect them to.

NOTES

1. Nigel West, *MASK: MI-5's Penetration of the Communist Party of Great Britain* (London: Routledge, Taylor and Francis, 2005). This description of MASK and its accomplishments are derived from West's excellent work on the subject.

2. Ibid.

3. This argument on the nature of intelligence is expanded in my draft article, "Smart Realism: A Theory of Intelligence in International Politics," April 2006.

4. Surprise is properly understood as the extension of a counterintelligence effort because it involves learning how the opponent thinks and acts and then making a strategic or tactical move designed to exploit weaknesses in that decision-making process. Surprise can be achieved by simply getting inside the decision loop of the adversary: Even if intelligence provides warning, the victim cannot turn warning into effective action in time to stop his losses.

5. For more on the similarities of strategic decision making among gangs, mobs, and nation-states, see Thomas C, Schelling, *The Strategy of Conflict* (London: Oxford University Press, 1968), especially pp. 12–13.

6. I owe the insight on the connection between intensity of competition and the need for secrecy to enlightening discussions of intelligence theory with my friend and colleague Michael Warner, CIA historian, over the winter of 2005–2006. Getting any of this wrong is, of course, my responsibility, not his.

7. Most literature on open-source intelligence focuses on the role cheap, unclassified information can play in limiting the burden on precious, classified collection systems. But this leaves the comparative advantage for democracies partially unexploited and a fixation on the primacy of secrets intact. Speed may be more important than data source when stopping terrorists in our midst—and sifting huge quantities of data takes time. Intelligence managers should consider how classified information could be exploited to help target unclassified sources and databases to get the jump on an adversary. Creativity—and sloughing off old prejudices—is needed in thinking about the role of open sources in intelligence.

8. This last form of collection is known as measurement and signatures intelligence, or MASINT.

9. The importance of all-source collection for these purposes is discussed in Steve Coll, *Ghost Wars* (New York: Penguin Press, 2004), pp. 492–93.

10. The concept of boosting is discussed in greater detail in Jennifer E. Sims, "Smart Realism: A Theory of Intelligence in International Politics," paper presented to the Georgetown Intelligence Salon, April 2006. For more on this concept, see Michael Herman, *Intelligence Power in Peace and War* (London: Cambridge University Press, 1996), pp. 65–66.

11. This is a widely known technique for locating radio signals. In fact, amateurs engage in DF competitions under the sponsorship of the International Amateur Radio Union. For more on the term *DF*, see http://en.wikipedia.org/wiki/direction_finding.

12. For more on the Gestapo's efforts against Stalin's spies in Europe, including the use of DF against HUMINT cells, see V. E. Tarrant, *The Red Orchestra* (London: Wiley, 1996).

13. Michael Herman writes: "Espionage can also help other collection activities. Human sources are sometimes needed to plant bugging devices. Cipher-breaking has often been assisted by obtaining copies of codes and cipher material through human sources. Acquiring agents with this kind of cryptographic access was always one of the KGB's highest priorities." Herman, *Intelligence Power*, pp. 65–66.

14. See J. C. Masterman, *The Double-Cross System: The Incredible True Story of How Nazi Spies Were Turned into Double Agents* (Guilford, CT: Lyons Press, 2000). Also see Anthony Cave Brown, *Bodyguard of Lies* (New York: Harper & Row, 1975).

15. For an excellent history of the dangers of weak counterintelligence in an interlaced collection system, see Leo Marks, *Between Silk and Cyanide: A Codemaker's War* (New York: Touchstone, 1998).

16. John Arquilla and David Ronfeldt, eds., *Networks and Netwars: The Future of Terror, Crime, and Militancy* (Santa Monica, CA: RAND, 2001).

17. See Stephen Budiansky, *Queen Elizabeth I, Sir Francis Walsingham, and the Birth of Modern Espionage* (New York: Penguin, 2005).

18. Jeffrey T. Richelson, *A Century of Spies: Intelligence in the Twentieth Century* (New York: Oxford University Press, 1995), pp. 27–30.

19. Unfortunately, law-abiding citizens sometimes suffered discrimination, undeserved punishment, and retribution in the process.

20. The point about local empowerment may have been dramatically illustrated by the decisions of individual Finns to use their Nokia cell phones during the immediate aftermath of the 2004 tsunami in the Indian Ocean. Empowered by their individual communications devices, which offered a direct link back to Helsinki, Finnish citizens were able to provide critical information for their government's decision-making process. (Based on author's informal interviews with officials and Nokia personnel in Finland during June 2005.) The notion that U.S. intelligence has poor appreciation of domestic cultural issues related to its profession should not be controversial. After all, intelligence systems have long been suspect elements of democracies and, in any case, have focused their attentions against adversaries, not on deepening knowledge of the societies in which they operate. This may be changing now. For lengthier discussion of the American cultural context for intelligence, see Jennifer E. Sims, "Understanding Ourselves," in *Transforming US Intelligence,* eds. Jennifer E. Sims and Burton Gerber (Washington DC: Georgetown University Press, 2005).

21. James Gosler, "The Digital Dimension," in *Transforming US Intelligence,* eds. Jennifer E. Sims and Burton Gerber (Washington DC: Georgetown University Press, 2005), pp. 96–114.

22. These procedures were established in 1978 when Congress passed the Foreign Intelligence Surveillance Act (FISA). This act limits the president's authority to conduct wiretapping for national security purposes by requiring federal intelligence and law enforcement authorities to get warrants for such surveillance from a secret court. Some legal experts argue that the act is unconstitutional because it involved one branch of government (Congress) circumscribing the constitutional authorities of another branch (the president). In any case, many observers noted that FISA had been widely regarded as settled law and that challenges to it should have been publicly debated in the context of,

for example, the USA-PATRIOT Act, which was meant to amend previous domestic surveillance laws to post-9/11 circumstances. Others argued that such open debate would have revealed too much of our counterintelligence capabilities to the adversary.

23. For more on the idea of domestic alliances for intelligence purposes, see Henry C. Crumpton, "Intelligence and Homeland Defense," in *Transforming US Intelligence,* eds. Jennifer E. Sims and Burton Gerber (Washington DC: Georgetown University Press, 2005).

24. Ibid.

25. John P. Sullivan, "Terrorism Early Warning Group and Co-Production of Counterterrorism Intelligence," paper presented to the International Studies Association conference in San Diego, March 21–25, 2006. Also presented to the Canadian Association for Security and Intelligence Studies, 20th Anniversary International Conference, Montreal, Quebec, Canada, Panel 5, October 21, 2005.

26. Constituent Works, "Court Hears NYPD Surveillance Camera Case," March 27, 2006, available at http://www.officeoutlook.com/news/security/1147.htm (accessed April 7, 2006).

27. Associated Press, "Baltimore's Latest Crime Tool Is the Talking Camera," available at http://www.policeone.com/police-products/investigation/video-surveillance/articles/121178 (accessed April 7, 2006).

28. Walter Pincus, "Pentagon Will Review Database on U.S. Citizens: Protests Among Acts Labeled 'Suspicious,' " Washingtonpost.com, December 15, 2005, p. A01. Indeed, Senator Feinstein wrote a letter on January 10, 2006, to Secretary of Defense Rumsfeld requesting additional information on CIFA practices, including the retention of TALON reports on the activities of private citizens engaged in activities protected under the First Amendment.

29. The history of American skepticism of domestic surveillance is admirably covered by Christopher Andrew in his excellent history, *For the President's Eyes Only: Secret Intelligence and the American Presidency from Washington to Bush* (New York: HarperCollins, 1996).

30. Mary De Rosa, *Data Mining and Data Analysis for Counterterrorism* (Washington DC: Center for Peace and Security Studies, March 2004).

31. Ibid., p. v.

32. Ibid.

33. The Department of Homeland Security has provided some funding for these initiatives. However the development of privacy protocols, called "appliances" under the now-defunct TIA initiative, has languished. For more information, see "Chicago Moving to 'Smart' Surveillance Cameras," available at http://www.policeone.com/products.

9

WOMEN IN RELIGIOUS TERRORIST ORGANIZATIONS

A Comparative Analysis

KATHARINA VON KNOP

WOMEN HAVE BEEN ACTIVE IN VARIOUS TERRORIST groups throughout history. All of these women undermine the idea of who and what a terrorist is. What is generally not realized is the extent to which women are involved in terrorism.[1] The purpose of this chapter is to explore and analyze the multifaceted roles of women in religious terrorist organizations. My argument is that the role of women perceived by the world audience is one of a suicide bomber. However, the role of an ideological supporter and operational facilitator is even more important for the maintenance of operational capabilities, ideological motivation, and survival of a terrorist organization.

To verify these arguments, the chapter is divided in three parts. The first will look at what motivates women to participate in a terrorist organizations and what motivates a terrorist group to use women for its purposes. The second part will analyze the role of women in Palestinian terrorist organizations. Finally, the third part sheds light on the women of the global Salafi Jihad. For that purpose the female attacks of the global Salafi Jihad will be analyzed.

The findings of this chapter with regard to the involvement of women in Palestinian terrorist organizations and the Al Qaeda movement will bring us to conclude that women play a growing and essential role in these groups.

INTRODUCTION

The concept of terrorism, particularly against soft targets, is shocking enough to most liberal Western audiences; however, the use of female attackers exacerbates the already potent psychological effect of suicide terrorism. Women's involvement in terrorist organizations is long and established. They have been active in various terrorist groups in various positions throughout history. One of the most famous instances of modern international terrorism, and the first that received global media coverage, was led by a Palestinian women, Leila Khaled. This senior Popular Front for the Liberation of Palestine (PFLP) operative was involved in the hijacking of an Israeli plane in 1969 and a second one in 1970.[2] There have been other famous female terrorists, such as Ulrike Meinhof from the Red Army Faction and Patty Hearst from the Symbionese Liberation Army (SLA). Cases such as these, in which women act as leaders of terrorist organizations, are rare, but they do exist. In Germany, the Red Army Faction and the Red Brigades had women leaders and cofounders. Khaled is a member in the Leadership Council of the PFLP.[3] The current chief of staff of the Basque separatist organization Euskadi Ta Askatasuna (ETA) is reportedly a woman. The Japanese Red Army has also had women leaders. In various Latin American organizations, such as Peru's Sendero Luminoso (SL), women accounted for as much as 20 percent of the fighting force.

Every terrorist group in Western Europe has used women combatants. Other organizations that are currently composed of large numbers of women include the Tamil Tigers of Tamil Elam (LTTE) and the Fuerzas Armadas Revolucionarias in Colombia (FARC) among others. The first "successful" female suicide bomber was a 17-year-old Lebanese girl named Sana Mahaydali, who was known as the "the Bride of the South." In 1985, she was dispatched by the PPS, a pro-Syrian Lebanese organization, to blow herself up near some vehicles carrying Israeli soldiers in Lebanon. "This paved the way for several other Lebanese women acting on behalf of other terrorist organisations. From Lebanon, the use of female suicide bombers spread to other countries and within few years was adopted by the LTTE and the Kurdish PKK."[4] The women of the LTTE are responsible for one-third of all suicide bombings in Sri Lanka, whereas the female PKK (Kurdish Workers Party) members have carried out two-thirds of that group's suicide bombings. What these groups have in common, however, is that they are or were leftist or nationalist-separatist oriented.

During the past few years we have seen many changes occur within religiousterrorist organizations. One of the most surprising developments has been the way suicide terrorism by religious groups has opened the stage for entry of female combatants, who are increasingly involved in what was once an exclusively male-dominated area.

Over the past few years, women have played a central role in the Chechen campaign of suicide bombings directed against Russia, and since 2002 female suicide bombers have become an established force in Palestinian terrorist organizations. In April 2003, as a predictable surprise, the first female suicide bombers blew up their car at a coalition checkpoint in Iraq. One of the two women was pregnant. Al Qaeda claimed responsibility for the suicide attack carried out by a woman on September 28, 2005, in Talafa in northern Iraq against a U.S. military recruitment center, with the statement: "A blessed sister . . . carried out a heroic attack defending her faith. . . . May God accept our sister among the martyrs."[5] Even though the use of female suicide bombers in Iraq is still a relatively new trend, women will likely play a wider role in operations where terrorist groups mobilize an entire population.

For terrorist organizations as rational actors there are a number of operational advantages in the use of women as suicide bombers, supporters, and facilitators, because women undermine the idea of who and what a terrorist is. The intuitive assumptions presume that terrorists and terrorism is a man's domain. Most people still believe that women would not kill in such a barbaric and indiscriminate way that targets innocent people. This is why there is usually a public outcry of horror against women terrorists.

The function of women in religious terrorist groups and movements is multifaceted. The role that the world audience perceives is that of a suicide bomber; however, the role of an ideological supporter and operational facilitator is even more important for the maintenance of operational capabilities and ideological motivation. In sum, even when women are invisible to the world audience, they play an essential role in the short- and long-term survival of terrorist organizations.

THE MOTIVES OF THE WOMEN AND THE ORGANIZATION

Since 2002, female suicide attacks on behalf of religious terrorist organizations has been on the rise and is expected to increase in the future.[6] Though the personal motivations of female terrorists differ from the organizational motives for recruiting them, the two sides converge to produce an increased number of female terrorists. In these groups, the use of women in terrorist attacks is rare but not a new issue. Some of the most shocking recent incidents of female suicide terrorism have occurred during the current Israeli-Palestinian conflict. Suicide bombing, particularly during the present Intifada, has become one of the dominant features of the asymmetric campaign being waged against Israel by the Palestinian terrorists.

Female terrorism is increasing because women are motivated to engage in political violence and organizations are facing stronger incentives to recruit female operatives. To understand why female terrorism is on the rise, the societal, individual, and organizational motives must be explored. At this point, it should be mentioned that throughout history, women have played a relatively minor role in these terrorist groups.[7]

Media reporting has often suggested that most female suicide bombers, like their male counterparts, go eagerly to their deaths fueled by an unshakeable fervor; but the truth may be more complex. Although there are no concrete figures concerning the extent of women's current involvement, many commentators have observed that female participation in terrorism has significantly increased since 1976.[8]

The use of female suicide bombers could be found in many different kinds of terrorist organizations, but female terrorists share more then the use of terrorism as a fighting strategy. Female suicide bombings occur in the patriarchal societies from which these women originate and are the result of the deeply rooted values separating the women's roles from those of the men. Female terrorists are motivated by many of the same reasons men are, but the gender-based oppression they face creates additional motivation. Barbara Victor states that "the real reasons that motivate women, as opposed to the rational that creates male suicide bombers, are subtle and indicative of the second-class status of women in that part of the world."[9] All of the societies that have witnessed female suicide bombings are those where women are restricted to the private sphere. While women stay at home, men's tasks are conducted in the outer world. In traditional societies, gender defines acceptable activities and assigns particular roles to both men and women. Men hold a position of power and dominance, giving them full reign of the public domain. Women are relegated to the private sphere and are constrained in all areas of life. Rhiannon Talbot argues that women terrorists reject female roles and adopt the traditional male role of violent activity.[10] This violence occurs in the public realm from which women are otherwise excluded.[11] Female terrorists are thus able to pursue opportunities other than the limited ones available in traditional societies. This suggests that the existence of female subordination is linked to female participation in terrorism. As agents of violence, women are no longer defined according to their gender roles.

The PKK in Turkey also offered women an alternative to traditional gender roles and provided them access to the public domain. The Kurdish terrorist organization was the only structure that offered women a choice other than the traditional one of wife and mother. The group offered women the opportunity to be upgraded to the status of warrior. Within the organization, women would not be defined as a man's subordinate anymore, nor simply as wives or mothers.[12]

I argue that the scope of women's power interests are shaped by the society they live in. This scope in patriarchal society is normally the family. Encouraging and supporting the male relatives to participate in a terrorist organization gives women power and access to the public realm. Carrying out attacks allows women to fulfill traditional male duties: to carry out an political act and have the chance to be honored by the society they are living in. Talbot argues that this development is an act of female liberation and emancipation in these male-dominated societies. For instance, Yoram Schweitzer states: "The willingness of fundamentalist Islamic organisations to make use of women in their suicide operations contradicts the principle of religion as well as traditional social norms that preclude the involvement of women in 'masculine' activities that require close contact with men to whom they are not married."[13] I reject the argument that female suicide bombers in Islamist societies are acts of female liberation, because these women are recruited by men who are members of the terrorist organization. The explosives were provided by men, and the women were instructed by men on how to use them. This behavior is misinterpreted as female liberation or emancipation.

Being a suicide bomber is a learned behavior that results from the absence of other role models. Especially in Palestinian society, the only way to become a female hero is by carrying out a suicide attack.

However, in effect, being a suicide bomber amounts to total submission under a male-dominated terrorist organization. As mentioned, patriarchal societies, especially those that host terrorist groups, only offer two role models for women. The first is to be the mother of as many as children as possible, and the second is to be a suicide bomber. The only way to be honored by the society is to carry out a suicide attack in support of the ideology and the terrorist organization. The ideological goal and the struggle have priority over the battle of the sexes. These women adopt the masculine concept of Jihad for political reasons. Khaled brings it to the point: "So if this society doesn't mobilize all of its energy to face down the enemy, it can't achieve victory. A Palestinian woman is a Palestinian as well. As such, she has the same goals as the rest of our people."[14] This acceptance goes so far that religious leaders have found interpretations of the Koran to justify female suicide bombers and the supporting role of the women in this male-dominated ideology.

Attempts have been made to profile female suicide bombers in the hope of finding common threads in their backgrounds and motivations. However, it is very difficult to profile female suicide bombers or female facilitators and supporters because they come from very diverse educational, religious, social, and personal backgrounds.

Many women choose to join a terrorist organization to seek vengeance. Terrorism continues to be a male-dominated activity, and it is men who suffer the majority of casualties from counterterrorism, failed missions, and successful suicide bombing operations.[15] Faced with the loss of male family members, women are motivated to take up arms. This phenomenon is observable where women's participation in terrorism begins at a later stage than men's. In Chechnya, female terrorists are called Black Widows, and they are "prepared to kill and to die to avenge the deaths of fathers, husbands, brothers and sons at the hands of Russian troops in the current war or the one in the 1990s."[16] These female bombers are in part a direct reaction to Russian military tactics. The human rights group Memorial adds that another contributing factor is the routine rape of the Chechen women by the Russian soldiers. Although female participation was negligible throughout the 1990s, the Chechen groups suffered severe male casualties, and female suicide bombers have now become more common.[17] Women's active participation began in October 2002, and since that time Black Widows have been blamed for the deaths of over 200 people in nine attacks. These women are driven to terrorism by a desire to regain their personal or family honor.

As previously mentioned, women in traditional societies are governed by a strict set of social, cultural, and religious rules. In Palestine, for example, these rules prescribe the separation of men and women, and require women to be physically covered and chaperoned by a male family member when in public. If a woman breaks these rules, she is ostracized by society and brings shame on herself and her family. As a result of this marginalization, women may seek refuge in a terrorist organization. These groups offer a double benefit to these women by accepting them when they no longer have options in mainstream society and by allowing them to regain their honor by committing a terrorist act. By participating in armed struggle, these women are able to gain the dignity in death that they lost in life.

In Sri Lanka, terrorism is often seen as a viable option for Tamil women who are survivors of sexual violence. Following a rape, Tamil women are considered damaged goods, and social customs prevent them from getting married or bearing children.[18] The shame brought on by sexual violation is thus magnified by the humiliation of being unable to fulfill childbearing duties and desires. Many of these women join the LTTE because, unlike mainstream society, it does not condemn or marginalize women who have been raped.[19] Societal expectations of procreation are so fierce that families of rape survivors have been known to actively encourage these women to join the LTTE.[20] Tamil culture encourages women to advance their children's interests at the expense of their own welfare, but female self-sacrifice for her community by engaging in terrorism can serve as an acceptable substitute.[21] Their participation compensates for their inability to give birth to future generations and restores their personal and familial dignity.

Even today, when women are playing an increasing role in violent organizations, they still represent a minority of the total membership. To understand the low scale and the rise of female terrorism, organizational motives for recruiting women must be explored. Women may want to become actively engaged in the conflict, but the evolution of the role of women from supportive to active is initiated at the organizational level. There is a great disparity between what motivates women to join a terrorist group and what encourages a group to recruit women.[22] Regardless of a woman's individual motives, terrorist groups are rational actors acting on the basis of cost-benefit calculation. The use of terrorist violence is part of a political strategy and represents "a willful choice made by an organisation for political and strategic reasons."[23]

Changes in targets, perpetrators, and tactics can be understood under this framework. The use of female operatives in a male-dominated activity represents a tactical change by terrorist organizations. These groups "tend to adapt to high levels of external pressure by altering their techniques and targets."[24] Women provide many benefits to terrorist groups, and organizations are increasingly recruiting them as a strategic choice. The use of women provides a new media dimension, which the terrorist group intends for the media to interpret as an indication of a worsening situation. Media images of women terrorists serve as powerful propaganda tools. As we all know, suicide bombers provide a low-cost, low-technology, low-risk weapon that maximizes target destruction and instils fear. Women are even more effective at this with their increased accessibility and media shock value. Female terrorists tend to garner more media attention than men because the "thought of those who bring forth life actually destroying it, is disturbing."[25] The idea of women acting as agents of violence runs completely counter to expectations of femininity; images of female terrorists thus attract widespread publicity and disseminate the organization's message to a wider audience. Terrorism is a form of psychological warfare, and in this context, the use of women as terrorist operatives is simply a means of upping the ante.[26]

If organizations believe that increased female participation is advantageous, they are likely to encourage this participation in any way possible. Religious justifications, for example, have been manipulated to facilitate more women terrorists. Though the Islamic religious establishment has long opposed and actively condemned women's participation in violent struggles, it has dramatically changed its position more recently. Having seen the positive results and strategic benefits of allowing women's participation in terrorism, the religious establishment has gone so far as to provide an ex post facto justification for women's involvement in terror.

Finally, female terrorists have a greater capacity for mobilizing support than their male colleagues.[27] Female terrorists provide strong role models for other women who may then seek to emulate their heroine's actions. Female terrorism also increases male recruitment because men can be shamed into joining when women appear to be usurping their dominant role in conflict.[28] For example, following the first female Palestinian suicide attack in January 2002, the Egyptian Islamist weekly newspaper *Al-Sha'ab* taunted, "It is a woman, a woman, a woman who is a source of pride for the women of this nation and a source of honour that shames the submissive men with a shame that cannot be washed away except by blood."[29] In order to mobilise both men and women, female members are important for maintaining the recruitment mechanism of terrorist organisations.

Though terrorist organizations seek to achieve many goals, their primary objective is survival. Women are often recruited when membership is dwindling and there is a pressing need for more fighters to continue the struggle, for example, in protracted conflicts or following severe losses of male members. In Sri Lanka, for example, women have been actively involved in the LTTE since 1986, but the number of female fighters significantly increased after 1990. In June of that year, the LTTE suffered significant losses in the battle at Elephant Pass, and women were called to action to replace the losses.[30] The long-term survival of a terrorist group is often dependent on female participation to fill the ranks, either through direct involvement or by persuading men to join.

Female suicide bombers therefore provide many considerable advantages for terrorist organizations. First, they provide a tactical advantage: stealthier attack, an element of surprise, hesitancy to search women, and the stereotype of women as being nonviolent. Second, including women as suicide bombers increases the number of combatants. Third, this would increase the publicity of an attack and, finally, the psychological effect would be much higher.

Today, female participation in terrorist organizations is in its formative stages. But this development poses a challenge to national security services, because the participation of women in suicide bombings broadens the profile of who is considered to be a terrorist. Most counterterrorism measures focus on men. Women are still less suspicious among security staff around a guarded target; to preserve a woman's decency, security staff is generally more reluctant to subject her to as thorough a body search as they would a man. Some groups, such as the LTTE or the PKK, have allowed women to participate at every level of group activity. It could be just a question of time until we see a similar development in other terrorist organizations.

PALESTINIAN FEMALE TERRORISM

Even though it is still an exception when women carry out attacks in the name of Al Qaeda, we are able to observe some noteworthy developments in other Islamist-based terrorist groups like Hamas and Tanzim.

The women involved in Palestinian terrorism support their male relatives in following the ideology of the terrorist groups; they facilitate operations on a preparatory level, and they also carry out suicide attacks themselves. Looking at the suicide attacks carried out by Palestinian women, we can clearly see how the phenomenon has grown, both in scope and in the type of attack. In 2004, fifty-nine women have attempted attacks against Israelis.[31]

It is hard for many Westerners to understand how Palestinian mothers could sacrifice or push their children to die for "the cause." Creating a supportive social environment for terrorists has been a critical factor in the Palestinian Authority's (PA) successful promotion of suicide terrorism. To this end, PA policy has been to honor terrorists as *shahids* (martyrs for Allah), and to teach Palestinian mothers to celebrate when their children die as terrorist shahids.[32]

On several occasions, these mothers have been shown on television rejoicing over the death of their children. For instance, on November 17, 2004, a mother of two suicide attackers said in an interview with PA TV: "No. We do not encourage our sons to die. We encourage them to shahada [death for Allah] for the homeland, for Allah. We don't say to the mothers of the shahids, 'We come to comfort you,' rather, 'We come to bless you on your son's wedding, on your son's shahada. Congratulations to you on the shahada.' For us, the mourning is a wedding. We give out drinks, we give out sweets. Praise to Allah, our mourning is a wedding."[33]

Nahed Habiballah argues that there are several factors that complicate the role of these mothers.[34] Most of them admit that they venture out to the streets looking for their children and tried several times to prevent them from going to confrontation areas where the Israeli Defense Force is present. Patriotism hinders their effort, however, and they are caught between two extremes: on the one hand, they want to protect their children and prevent their deaths, but, on the other hand, the Intifada is a quest for freedom, and loss of life is possible in such situations. What complicates things even more is the fact that martyrdom has become ingrained in the Palestinian culture over the past two decades, and women have found themselves trapped in a society that provides support for mothers of martyrs while demanding that these mothers become public figures of steadfastness and pride. These mothers are unable to recover from their losses, because they are not allowed to grieve for their children. In Islam, martyrs are considered alive in heaven, and pious Muslims should not grieve the loss because, unlike the dead, these martyrs obtain the ultimate prize: being in heaven in the company of God and his prophets.

Al-Khansaa is considered the archetypal mother of shahids, a woman glorified by Palestinians for encouraging her sons to kill and die for Allah and rejoicing when they achieved their shahada deaths.[35] Promoting the Al-Khansaa ideal for Palestinians is a very powerful message for Muslims. This portrayal of the ideal Palestinian woman as one who willingly sacrifices her sons as shahids continues to represent official PA ideology. From a very young age, Palestinian girls are taught to adopt Al-Khansaa as a role model with her message of celebrating death in combat, which in contemporary Palestinian society includes death while committing acts of terror. A music video for children, broadcast hundreds of times over three years on PA TV, included the farewell letter of a child shahid, including the words: "Mother, don't cry for me, be joyous over my blood."

Here an additional point needs to be made: Palestinians have made their own cultural set of rules that markedly prescribe gender roles. These rules dictate the separation of the sexes and confine women to the private space of their homes. Their role as fertile mothers and reproducers of the nation marks their utility in the parameter of the conflict as a demographic war. The nationalistic discourse defines a Palestinian woman in terms of her reproductive capacity, thereby making her sexuality and fertility a patriotic and explicitly political issue. Their maternal sacrifice is a supreme political act that is translated into respect and prominent community stature.

The ideology becomes the tranquilizer: the assurance that their children did not die in vain. They died for their country and their ideology, and it is comforting for the mothers who struggle with the pain, loss, and the guilt of not being able to do more to protect their children. It seems that it is easier for mothers who have well-rooted faith to accept the fate that God has chosen for their children. According to the ideology, these mothers should be proud of their children because God chooses the purest people to be martyrs, as they are the ones who are privileged and worthy of his company.

The current trend in the use of Palestinian women as suicide bombers began in earnest in 2002. Wafa Idris, a 27-year-old Palestinian woman from the Al-Am'ari refugee camp near Ramallah, became the first female Palestinian suicide bomber on January 27, 2002, killing an Israeli civilian and wounding approximately 140 others. The military wing of Fatah, the Al-Aqsa Brigades, took responsibility for the attack three days later. This was the first female suicide attack in the Palestinian scene of the second Intifada. Until then, women were generally only employed to support and facilitate suicide operations. The ultimate honor of martyrdom was no longer reserved exclusively for men but had expanded to include women.

Several reasons for this development can be identified. During the current Intifada, as Israel's security forces enhanced their defensive measures against terrorist attacks, Palestinian militant groups were forced to adapt their tactics, and despite cultural and religious taboos, they began to make increasing use of female recruits. However, a decision to use women in suicide terrorism required clerical sanction, and the tactic was not universally accepted by Islamic militant groups. Indeed, the willingness by some groups to allow women to engage in such activities prompted furious theological debate among radical Muslim clerics. Using women as suicide bombers poses conflict with some leaders's fundamental religious beliefs, while serving a tactical need for a stealthier weapon. In January 2002, Shaykh Ahmed Yassin, the spiritual leader of Hamas, "categorically renounced the use of women as suicide bombers."[36] In March 2002, after the second Fatah bombing, he reported that "Hamas was far from enthusiastic about the inclusion of women in warfare, for reasons of modesty."[37] That position dramatically shifted in January 14, 2004, when the first Hamas female suicide bomber struck. Yassin defended this change as a "significant evolution in our fight. The male fighters face many obstacles,"[38] so women can more easily reach the targets. He concluded his statement by noting that "women are like the reserve army—when there is a necessity, we use them."[39] In addition, Abd al-Asis al-Rantissi, a senior Hamas leader, stated at the end of August 2001 in an interview with Abu Tibi Television that "there is no reason that the perpetration of suicide attacks should be monopolized by men."[40] Isma'il abi Shanab, a Hamas leader in Gaza, was also eager to see women as one more weapon to inflict harm on the enemy. He stated: "Jihad against the enemy is an obligation that applies not only men, but also women. Islam has never differentiated between men and women on the battlefield."[41] The head of the Women's Activist Division of the Palestine Islamic movement Jamila Shanti argued, "Islam does not prohibit a woman from sacrificing herself to defend her land and her honour. It is she who was attacked, and she has the right to defend herself in any way. It is not puzzling that Muslim sisters have been carrying out heroic operations with Palestine since 1948. On the other hand it would be strange if the Palestinian woman had not done so, as Jihad is a personal imperative for her and no one can prevent her from waging it.[42] Some Palestinian Muslim clerics provided the religious justification for female suicide bombers.[43] Searching for new ways to resist the security complications, the Palestinians discovered that women could be an advantage and religiously backed their use.

The Palestinian Islamic Jihad (PIJ) began to launch a public campaign in 2003 to recruit women. It has focused its recruitment efforts in the northern part of the West Bank, especially in the Jenin region. Its first recruit was nineteen-year-old Heiba Daragmeh, a student at Quds Open University. Standing in from of a shopping mall in Afula on May 19, 2003, she detonated an explosive charge strapped to her body. Three civilians died in the attack and another eighty-three were injured.

Many of the Palestinian female terrorists share the experience of having lost a male relative by Israeli countermeasures. By mapping the biographies of the women who participated in the early history of the Palestinian terrorism, we could assert that some of these females were professional women with above-average education and training, whereas others were young women with neither education nor career. Some of them were married and had children, others were single or divorced.

Two questions arise. Why did the women start to participate in the suicide bombing campaign at such a late point in time, and why are there so few females among the suicide bombers?

The answer for both questions is based partly on the generally patriarchal traditions of Muslim society, which as a whole does not promote the idea of females participating in warfare. Currently, Hamas and PIJ have enough male volunteers; and when these organizations have the chance to use a man for an attack, they prefer to do so.

It seems that Palestinian women in general have more rights and are allowed to choose political action. For instance, Rascha al-Rantissi, the widow of Hamas leader Rantissi, has run for office in Palestinian elections. Compared to other Muslim societies, Palestinian women have more opportunities and more freedom than their sisters in Iraq, Iran, Saudi Arabia, and other fundamentalist countries. They can vote, hold offices, drive cars, and own property. They also have equal access to universities. For decades, men have been fighting for the ideological goals of the terrorist organizations without having reached a substantial result. Every society has developed its identity over time and, in the Palestinian case, the concepts of a common enemy and the struggle have played a strong role in the construction of the Palestinian identity. Also, female Palestinians have learned to claim the full Palestinian identity even when that means carrying out a suicide attack. In the Muslim world, female suicide bombers have achieved immortality by becoming weapons against Israeli. When they were alive, the women who committed these actions were just women; however, from the moment they killed Israelis, they died as martyrs, achieving redemption. An important way to become a respected citizen in the Palestinian society is to kill and die.

The involvement of women in terrorism raises their awareness of the opportunities available outside the private domain. Women acquire a new understanding of their potential as political actors, and this can affect their demands within terrorist groups. Throughout the West Bank and Gaza, there are posters honoring female martyrs. Young girls no longer think of themselves as relegated to the private sphere; this in itself represents an important step toward female empowerment in Jihad.

Increased female terrorism affects women's personal and political development. Female terrorism demonstrates that traditional delineations along gender lines are unfounded and impermanent.

But this view is just one side of the coin. The phenomenon of the female suicide bomber is interconnected with a pathological misogynist culture in which young women are coerced and forced into suicide bombing in all kinds of violent and horrifying ways. Wafa Idris, for instance, couldn't bear children, and her husband divorced her. Discarded and shunned in a culture that sees a divorced barren woman as worthless, she became the obvious target of exploitation for terrorist groups. Tahani Titit, a 24 year old Tanzim operative, explained that she desired to end her life not for nationalistic reasons but because of her father, who repeatedly beat her, and because of failed love affairs at university. Thawiya Hamour, twenty-six, from Jaba was arrested in Tulkarm on her way to perpetrate a suicide attack in Jerusalem. During her questioning, she mentioned that four months prior to her arrest she had met Mounir Halwa, who proposed marriage. Hamour's family refused this offer and, as a result, she had decided to commit a suicide terrorist attack. Titi's and Hamour's cases are classic examples of the cynical exploitation of unstable young women by terrorist organizations.

Anat Berko states, "Often wishing to clear her name, the female suicide terrorist will carry out the mission, thereby upgrading the status of her family, earning them honour and preventing their humiliation or even murder."[44] Blowing oneself up is a way to achieve respect, honor, and self-esteem in Palestinian Society. Nancy Kobrin states, "These women seek honour (sharaf) that they desire and they will never really achieve it because they are bound by female honour—*ird* which means pelvis."[45]

To conclude this section, when a Palestinian woman carries out a suicide attack or supports a terrorist organization or her male relatives, she does it for several diverse reasons. She is fighting a five-front war. These fronts are of an ideological, national, gender-based, social, and individual nature.

The incidence of female suicide bombers in Palestinian society is still in its formative stages and the foregoing analysis has shown that there is generally no single overriding motivation for a female bomber's action. Many interrelated motivations work together and create an explosive mixture that only needs some traumatic event to release all its hidden destructive energy. "A skilful terrorist operative can easily identify a candidate in this emotional state, and coolly manipulate her into becoming a weapon for his organization."[46] Palestinian women have proved to be a valuable and precious terrorism weapon as bombers and supporters.

THE WOMEN OF AL QAEDA

The roles of women in the movement of the global Salafi Jihad are similarly multifaceted. Female acts of suicide play a minor role in the Al Qaeda terrorist movement, but bin Laden's "roses" function importantly as operational facilitators, supporters of their male relatives, and ideological educators of children. Too few terrorist operations have taken place where females have been involved to derive generalizations or to identify a profile of a female Al Qaeda suicide bomber. The majority of Al Qaeda's women operate invisibly; nevertheless, they have had a strong impact on the current and next generation of terrorists. To understand their role, it is helpful to start with an analysis of Osama bin Laden's *fatawa* and other publications made by followers of the ideology. Afterward, female terrorist attacks, the concepts of sisterhood, and of the female Jihad will be analyzed. Finally, the involvement of the women in the Al Qaeda–affiliated Jemaah Islamiah will be explained.

Until today, six *fatawa* have been identified that are allowing women to participate in martyrdom operations. The first one was issued by Yussuf al Qaradawi; three by faculty members at al-Azhar University Egypt; one by, Faysal al-Mawlawi of the European Council for Research and Legal Opinion based in Dublin; and one by Nizar Ábd al-Qadir Riyyam of the Islamic University of Gaza.[47] David Cook notes that it is significant that the more conservative Jordanian, Syrian, and Saudi religious leaders are completely absent from this list. "One can see that the question of women participating on suicide attacks has become associated with the Egyptian–Palestinian and consequently more progressive side of the Muslim world."[48]

But the ideology of the global Salafi Jihad has different functions for the women in mind than the one of a suicide bomber. The fatawa and some audiotapes of bin Laden express the role of women very clearly. In the fatwa "Declaration of War Against the Americans Occupying the Land of the Two Holy Places, Expel the Mushrikeen [infidels] from the Arabian Peninsula," he explains that women play an essential role as supporters, facilitators, and promoters in carrying out the Jihad.

> Our women had set a tremendous example for generosity in the cause of Allah; they motivate and encourage their sons, brothers and husbands to fight—for the cause of Allah in Afghanistan, Bosnia-Herzegovina, Chechnya and in other countries.... May Allah strengthen the belief—Imaan—of our women in the way of generosity and sacrifice for the supremacy of the word of Allah.... Our women instigate their brothers to fight in the cause of Allah.... Our women encourage Jihad saying: Prepare yourself like a struggler; the matter is bigger than the words.

However in the fatwa "Jihad Against Jews and Crusaders, World Islamic Front," published two years later, which became the manifesto of the full-fledged global Salafi Jihad, the role of women seems to be alleviated. They are mentioned once and then just addressed as being the victims of the United States and the Zionists. "Women and children, whose cry is: Our Lord, rescue us from this town, whose people are oppressors; and raise for us from thee one who will help!"

In the pledge of a training manual found by the Manchester Metropolitan Police during the search of an Al Qaeda member's home, women are also addressed as victims of the infidels: "To the sister believer whose clothes the criminals have stripped off. To the sister believer whose hair the oppressors have shaved. To the sister believer who's body has been abused by the human dogs." The ideology of the global Salafi Jihad says that a reason to carry out the defensive Jihad is when a Muslim woman is held by the *kufar* (infidels), to ensure her freedom is *fard* (duty) on the whole Muslim *ummah* (world Muslim community). But the women are also addressed as supporters "Covenant, O Sister ... To make them desire death and hate appointments and prestige" and perpetrators

"Covenant, O Sister . . . to slaughter them like lamb and let the Nile, al-Asi, and Euphrates river flow with their blood."

In an audiotape broadcast on October 18, 2003 by Al Jazeera, bin Laden said: "Our prudent Muslim women are also expected to play their role."

A recently found document, "The role of women in the Jihad against Enemies,"[49] on a Jihadist message board written by Yussuf al-Ayyiri, who was one of the ideological leaders of the Saudi Arabian branch of Al Qaeda,[50] encourages women to take an active role in Jihad. This role does not involve active fighting, but it calls for women to encourage and support men in their active quest to join the Jihad. While explicitly stating that women should not actively engage in physical combat, the document emphasizes the power that women hold over men, reminding them that their role in Jihad is a vital necessity for the entire Muslim ummah. "The reason we address women . . . is our observation that when a woman is convinced of something, no one will spur a man to fulfill it like she will . . . The saying behind every great man stands a women was true for Muslim women at these times, for behind every great Mujahid stood a women."[51] He focuses on women as fighters, rather than in a supportive role, but he avoids making the revolutionary call of women to join in suicide operations. In the final paragraph he destroys two of the principal blocks against women actually fighting Jihad: that they would need the permission of their parents, and that women's Jihad is the performance on the *hajj* ritual.[52] As for the idea that the hajj supercedes Jihad, he cites a tradition that enumerates the importance of various activities and lists them in the following order: prayer, Jihad, and respect toward parents. "With these two comments he has laid the intellectual ground for the full participation of women in Jihad among radical Muslims."[53]

The online periodical *al-Khansaa*, which is addressed to women who share the ideology of Al Qaeda, also shows very obviously the importance of female support. This magazine says it is published by an organization called Women's Information Bureau of Al-Qaeda in the Arabian Peninsula and claims that Abdul al-Murqrin, the leader of Al Qaeda in the peninsula, and Issa Saad Mohammed bin Oushan are among the founders. Al-Khansaa bint Omar was a poetess of the pre-Islamic period who converted to Islam during the time of the Prophet Muhammad, and she is considered "the mother of the shahids." When her four sons died in the Battle of al Qadissiya, she did not mourn but thanked Allah for honoring her with their death. It was already mentioned that this archetypal picture of a mother of shahids also exists in Palestinian society. The choice of the name al-Khansaa for the magazine was not without reason. The magazine aims to motivate women to participate in Jihad by bringing up their children to be good Jihadis and by being supportive of their husbands, brothers, and sons. The magazine teaches that the goal of the woman is also to become a shahid. An editorial in the magazine states: "We love Allah and his Messenger. We march in a single path, the path of Jihad for the sake of Allah, and our goal is Shahada for the sake of Allah, and our goal is [to gain] the pleasure of Allah and His Paradise."[54]

The perception of the women is that they are standing shoulder to shoulder with their men, supporting them, helping them, and backing them up. An article titled "Obstacles in the Path of the Jihad Warrior Woman," written by Umm Badr, included indoctrination and guidelines for the women. "My noble sisters . . . The woman in the family is a mother, wife, sister and daughter. In society she is an educator, propagator and preacher of Islam, and a female jihad warrior. Mohamed Salah states that 'What is new here is the use of the medium of the Internet to recruit women.'"[55] It should be mentioned at this point that the whole ideology of the global Salafi Jihad is to build a revival of the golden age, which took place in the few years between 632 and 661. For that reason, it is not surprising that the argumentation for the role of women also derives from history. "My sister you might hear these stories and think that they have been fabricated . . . but once you will learn that even today there are women similar to those of the past, you will believe the stories about (the women in) the past."[56]

For centuries, Muslim women in different struggles and communities have joined men on the front lines of war and have died alongside with them. The most prominent example of an early Muslim in Jihad in Nusayba bint Káb, who fought in the Battle of Uhud with her husband and two sons and during the Caliphate of Abu Bakr. She joined the Muslim troops, suffered eleven wounds, and lost one arm.[57] The Prophet's own female relatives took part in Jihad. His wife Ayesha led the Battle of the Camel, and his granddaughter Zaynab bint Al fought in the Battle of Karbala. Other women were recognized for tending to the wounded, donating their jewelery for the Jihad, and encouraging their male family members to fight to ensure the survival of Islam. The involvement of the early Arab women in Jihad is celebrated today throughout the Muslim world, and they serve as icons and a precedent for the contemporary Muslim women who choose suicide operations, who have lost a family member in Jihad, or who support the ideology.

In the past, a Muslim woman was seen as the responsibility of her male relatives. Militant organizations could not recruit women directly without transgressing familial and societal honor codes that require women to seek permission for every action they take outside the family home. To secretly recruit a woman as a suicide bomber or even as a courier of messages and weapons would be seen as an insult to the family's male honor. Increasingly, this seems to be changing, as evidenced by the *al-Khansaa* article saying that women need not ask for permission to become a Jihadi because it is their duty to do so. In fact, *al-Khansaa* exploits the woman's traditional role in family and society as mother and nurturer of her children to get women to play a larger role in the Jihad.

Extremist Islamic websites are generous with advices on how women can and should participate in the Jihad. There are many suggestions on how they should bring up children to be good shahids, and what books they should read to their children to make them devout Muslims and brave fighters. These websites provide advice on how mothers, wives, and sisters of Jihadi fighters should be supportive of decisions made by their husbands to become a shahid; and how they should provide food, shelter, and care for all shahids. That women must sacrifice their sons and husbands is a recurrent theme of much Jihadi literature.

Indeed, in some respects, females are considered to be the most effective and loyal supporters of terrorist organizations. When analyzing the women and their role in the Islamic organisation Hizb ut-Tahrir in Uzbekistan, an identical finding can be made.

Until today it has been difficult to profile female suicide bombers who have operated in name of the global Salafi Jihad, because very few cases have been observable, and there is not much known about theses women. The latest development of female suicide bombings started in Iraq in April 2003 under the command of Saddam Hussein's security forces. A car exploded in a terrorist attack at a U.S. checkpoint in western Iraq, killing three coalition soldiers. The Arabic TV station Al-Jazeera broadcast separate videotapes of the two female suicide bombers, one of them pregnant, each standing in front of the Iraqi flag, their right hands on the Korans placed on a table in front of them and their left hands brandishing automatic rifles. A woman who identified herself as "martyrdom-seeker Nour Qaddour al-Shammari" swore on the holy book of Islam "to defend Iraq . . . and take revenge from the enemies of the [Islamic] nation, Americans, imperialists, Zionists" and Arabs who have submitted to the foreigners. "We say to our leader and holy war comrade, the hero commander Saddam Hussein, that you have sisters that you and history will boast about," said the woman, who wore the red-checked *keffiyeh*, an Arab head scarf. In a separate video, another woman, who identified herself as Wadad Jamil Jassem, stood in a similar pose and declared, "I have devoted myself for Jihad for the sake of God and against the American, British and Israeli infidels and to defend the soil of our precious and dear country." The videotapes were similar to those distributed by Palestinian suicide bombers after attacks against Israelis.[58]

In September 2003, two 14-year-old girls named Imame and Sana Laghriff were arrested in Rabat, Morocco, and sentenced for terrorist offenses. According to various reports, the two were on their way to target a liquor store, with some sources suggesting this was a suicide attack plot. The twin teenagers were influenced by a branch of radical Islam advocates from a Salafia Jihadia cell.[59] It seems that the girls were highly manipulated by the male members of the cell.

Although there is little known about the other women and the intentions of their suicide attacks, the story of 19-year-old Uzbek woman, Dilnoza Holmuradova, who detonated explosives strapped to her body at Tashkent's Choru Market in March 2004, killing forty-seven people, illustrates her determination to participate in a suicide attack. Dilnoza came from a middle-class family and was an educated computer programmer and enrolled at the Tashkent police academy in 2001. She was able to speak five languages. In 2002 she began studying Islam with her elder sister, and both were greatly influenced by a meeting they had with teachers of the religion. They stopped wearing modern clothes, listening to music, and watching television. In January 2004, the sisters left their home with just two dresses and Islamic literature. Neither ever returned.[60] It is unclear when they were recruited by the Islamic Jihad Group, a radical offshoot of the Islamic Movement of Uzbekistan.

May 2005 was the first time women were directly involved in a terrorist attack in Egypt. Two women were involved in a shooting on a tourist bus. Both were in their twenties and were related to the male perpetrator, Ihab Yassin. Negat Yassin was the suicide bomber's sister and Iman Ibrahim Khamis, his fiancée. Both women shot themselves before they could be arrested. It remains unclear if the two women intended to commit suicide or chose the tactic to evade arrest. The Abdallah-Azzam Brigades, an Al Qaeda–affiliated group, claimed responsibility for this attack.[61] The Al Qaeda–affiliated Malik Suicidal Brigades claimed responsibility for the suicide attack carried out by a women on September 28, 2005, in Talafa in northern Iraq against a U.S. military recruitment center. The group issued the statement: "A blessed sister . . . carried out a heroic attack defending her faith. . . . May God accept our sister among the martyrs."[62] In an Internet posting by Al Qaeda in Iraq, led at the time by Abu Musab Zarqawi, a Jordanian and the most feared and wanted terrorist in Iraq until he was killed by U.S. forces in 2005, said the bomber attacked the center because it was a gathering spot "of converted volunteers." Residents said the building used to be an Iraqi army recruiting center.[63] The attack seems to represent a new tactic by the terrorist groups in Iraq to use women, who are rarely searched at checkpoints because of religious and social traditions that grant women special treatment. Until recently, women have not been suspected by the security forces, and this is demonstrated by the fact that the woman who carried out the attack was dressed in men's clothing—a factor that did not lead the soldiers to pay attention to her.

On November 9, 2005, three Iraqi suicide bombers carried out attacks in Amman, Jordan, in the lobby of the Grand Hyatt Hotel, at a wedding party at the Radisson SAS Hotel down the street, and at the Days Inn. They killed fifty-six people, severely injuring ninety-three. The Jordanian security services were able to arrest Sajida Mubarark al-Rishawi. The 35-year-old Iraqi woman was the fourth suicide bomber, but her trigger cord failed and she fled the wedding reception at the Radisson. Her husband, Ali Hussein al-Shumari, also part of the suicide squad, killed himself in the bombing.[64] Her brother is Mubarak Atrous al Rishawi, at the time a senior aide to Zarqawi in western Iraq. During her confession, she gave no indication of why she wanted to carry out the attack, saying only that her husband brought her from Iraq to Jordan, showed her how to use the explosives belt and fit it onto her, telling her that it would be used to attack a hotel.[65] The Abu Musab al-Zarqawi group, the Al Qaeda in Mesopotamia, took responsibility for the blast.

In November 2006, Muriel Degauque was the first European converted Muslim woman to carry out a suicide attack. She was raised as a Roman Catholic in a suburb near Brussels in Belgium. Degauque, thirty-eight, rammed an explosives-filled vehicle into an American military patrol in the town of Baquba in Iraq on November 9, wounding one American soldier. Her story supports fears among many law enforcement officials and academics that converts to Europe's fastest-growing religion could bring with them a disturbing new aspect in the war on terror. Women who marry Muslim men are now the largest source of religious conversions in Europe. Although a vast majority of those conversions are pro forma gestures for moderately religious in-laws, a small but growing number are women who willingly adopt the conservative comportment of their fundamentalist husbands or support them to follow the radical interpretation of Islam and join a terrorist organization belonging to the movement of Al Qaeda. French antiterrorism officials have been warning for several years that female converts represent a small but increasingly important part of the terrorist threat in Europe.

Degauque was born in the small suburb of Charleroi, a gritty coal and steel town where her father operated a crane at the sprawling smelter, according to neighbors and friends. Her parents sent her to the best local high school in the area at the time. The Belgian police say she became known as a drug user, though she was never arrested. Degauque's wayward streak took a decisive turn when her brother was killed in a motorcycle accident when she was twenty. Degauque said she should have died instead of her brother. She soon moved out of the house and began a troubled life in Charleroi. Degauque had several boyfriends after she was divorced. She eventually met an Algerian man who introduced her to Islam. She began appearing at the home of her parents wearing a head scarf. Her mother told neighbors that she was pleased because Islam had helped her daughter stop drinking and doing drugs. But her devotion became disturbing several years later after she met and married Issam Goris, the son of a Belgian man and a Moroccan woman. Goris with his long beard was already known to Belgian police as a radical Islamist. Degauque moved with him to Brussels and then to Morocco, where she learned Arabic and studied the Koran. When she returned, she wore not only a head scarf but the full-length robe. As she became increasingly rigid, she demanded that her parents follow Islamic customs when she and her husband visited.[66]

The Belgian police now say that Goris had fallen in with a group of Islamists focused on recruiting European Muslims to fight with Abu Musab al-Zarqawi's terrorist network in Iraq. The police had been monitoring the group for months when they intercepted phone calls from Goris indicating that he and his wife were already in Iraq. The police say the couple left Belgium by car and eventually entered Iraq from Syria. The Belgians didn't yet know the identities of Goris and Degauque, but they notified the United States and the Iraqi government that a Belgian couple was in the country intent on carrying out attacks. They turned over information on the telephone calls that would allow the Americans to find Goris, but Degauque struck before they found her. A day later, the Americans found Goris, who was also wrapped in explosives, apparently about to carry out an attack. They shot him before he could detonate his charges. Dismantling the network in Belgium that sent them to their deaths, police arrested another couple allegedly preparing to go to Iraq to become martyrs. The Belgian case has links to the youthful Dutch Hofstad group, a unique mix of extremist ferocity and modern European attitudes.

When analyzing these cases, it is difficult to profile female suicide bombers who operate under the banner of the global Salafi Jihad. What all these women have in common is that they were recruited and instructed by men. In three cases, the women carried out the attack shoulder to shoulder with a male relative. It could also be stated that the instance of female suicide bombers has increased over a relatively short period of time.

In addition, other findings support the observation that the involvement of women in terrorist operations is an emerging trend. In 2003, several factors led the Federal Bureau of Investigation (FBI) to prepare for the possibility that Al Qaeda might recruit women. In June 2003, the FBI started searching for a woman for the first time since the war on terror began: 31-year-old Aafia Siddiqui.[67] Along with her husband, she founded the Institute for Islamic Research and Teaching in 1999, and both were identified as suspected Al Qaeda agents. An additional indicator that the position of women is transforming is demonstrated by the warrant for a Tunisian woman, Bentiwaa Farida Ben Bechir. As a member of a cell in Italy, she was active in recruiting suicide bombers to be sent to Iraq.[68] As early as May 2003, France's famed antiterrorist investigating judge, Jean-Louis Bruguière, warned that European terrorist networks were trying to recruit Caucasian women to handle terrorist logistics, because they would be less likely to raise suspicion. On November 3, 2005, the Dutch police arrested a 21-year-old woman in Rijswijk, on suspicion of being involved in terrorist activities of the Islamist radical group Hofstad.[69] At the time of the arrest, she was on her way with her husband to kill a Dutch legislator, prominent Islam critical feminist Ayaan Hirsi Ali. The driver who brought both to the train station is also a women— a convert with cherubic Dutch looks and the former profession of police officer.[70] The women of the Dutch extremist network were new breeds of holy warriors on the front lines where Islam and the West collide. In the male-dominated world of Islamic extremism, they saw themselves as full-fledged partners in Jihad. The story of the Dutch network, fourteen members of which are on trial, reveals the increasing aggressiveness and prominence of female extremists in Europe. In a chilling trend in the Netherlands and Belgium, police are investigating the wives of militants, who are suspected of plotting suicide attacks with their husbands—or on their own. It looks like the primarily motivation of the women is to carry out a political act, and they do not follow their husbands blindly; they encourage them.

Women carry out the Jihad by educating, supporting, and encouraging their sons, brothers, and husbands. To reach this goal, they have to prepare themselves as strugglers. No less important for promoting the Salafi ideology is their role as the victims of the infidels, motivating their male relatives to carry out the Jihad. When a woman enters paradise, she will not find seventy-two male virgins waiting for her—she will sit beside her husband. A different interpretation says that the female martyr of the shahida is one of the seventy-two female virgins waiting for a male martyr. In the Shi'ite and Sunni tradition, the word *Jihad* is completely reinterpreted for the women; they might gain similar spiritual benefit for performing it, but the action performed is without topical connection to fighting.[71]

Marc Sageman discovered that 70 percent of the 400 terrorists he analyzed had been married. Every terrorist has a mother, and many of them at least one sister. Arranged marriages are a strong tradition in the Muslim world, and it would not be a mistake to assume that marriages in the global Salafi Jihad are arranged.

How intensive the women carry out the female Jihad is easy to see when analyzing the Al Qaeda affiliate Jemaah Islamiah. Sidney Jones from the International Crisis Group in Jakarta states that marriage alliances are the glue that holds Jemaah Islamiah together. "Oftentimes senior members of the organization will offer their sisters or sisters-in-law to new promising recruits so that they are not only drawn into the organization, but into the family as well." The result is that the members are much closer connected. In some cases they even had control of finances. They play a role as couriers in ensuring that, particularly after imprisonment, communication among different members of the organization is maintained. "It's not a role in actively taking part in bombing activities, the new way some of the women in Chechnya or in Sri Lanka have done. It's more ensuring that the organization stays solid."[72] The wife of the operational chief of the Jemaah Islamiah, Hambali, who was responsible for instance for the October 2002 Bali bombings, acted as his bookkeeper. The wife of Omar al-Faruk, also a key figure of the Jemaah Islamiah, translated and also acted as his bookkeeper. Both women played a crucial role in financing of the organization, as did Yazid Sufaat's wife.

Another insightful example is Malika Aroud. When her husband traveled to an Al Qaeda training camp in Afghanistan, Malika joined him. Two days before the September 11, 2001, attacks, her husband carried out a suicide bombing that killed Ahmed Shah Massoud, the leader of the north alliance in Afghanistan. Acquitted in the plot against Massoud, Malika moved to Switzerland, where she has been charged with operating a website that incited terrorism.

Women are often strongly involved in the financial issues of a terrorist organization. In the aftermath of the 9/11 attacks, the United States has closed several bank accounts of terrorist organizations or supporting institutions that were handled by women. The chance that the men will get arrested or die in combat or in an attack is much higher; so for the organization it makes sense that the individuals who take care of the financial issues have a stronger likelihood of survival. Dealing with the financial aspects could be done from home, the place where the women are usually restricted in these societies.

CONCLUSION

Over the past three years, religious terrorist groups have set the stage for the entry of female combatants. The role of women in terrorist organizations arises from the society in which they live. In patriarchal societies, women carry out attacks and support terrorist organizations as a way to have a chance to be honored by their society. But there are several motivations for women to carry out a terrorist attack, and these reasons are interconnected. Women are motivated because they follow a violent ideology; they want to carry out a political act; look forward to regaining personal or family honor; have lost a family member;or have been manipulated in some way. There is not single rational reason that motivates female suicide bombers.

These motivations also come into play when they "just" support their male relatives in following the ideology of a terrorist organization or facilitating terrorist operations. This behavior is widespread in Muslim and Western countries. In this case, the motivation arises mainly from a process of socialization conducted in the society in which they are living, whereas in other cases they have become radicalized by themselves.

Attempts have been made to profile female suicide bombers in the hope of finding common threads in their backgrounds and motivations. It is very difficult to profile female suicide bombers or facilitators and supporters because they come from diverse educational, religious, social, and personal backgrounds.

Terrorist organizations use women as suicide bombers because they provide several considerable advantages. First, they offer a tactical advantage: stealthier attack, an element of surprise, hesitancy to search women, and the stereotype of females as being nonviolent. Second, the inclusion of women as suicide bombers increases the number of combatants. Third, this increases the publicity of an attack. Finally, women suicide bombers carry a much greater psychological impact. Suicide bombers provide a low-cost, low-technology, low-risk weapon that maximizes target destruction and instills fear. Women are even more effective with their increased accessibility and media shock value. Until today, women could rarely be found as part of the suicide bombers of the global Salafi Jihad; however, when terrorism groups find women useful in their operations, they will find or create something in the Islamic theology to justify it.

Personal and organizational motivations converge to produce an increased number of female terrorists. To the extent that these motivations persist over time, the increase in female participation in religious terrorist organizations can be expected to continue. There is a need to understand their role as operational facilitators, organizational and personal supporters, and ideological educators, as a means to develop long-term effective and efficient counterterrorism.

NOTES

1. As the meaning and usage of the word *terrorism* have changed over time to accommodate the colloquial political language and discourse of each successive era, terrorism has proved increasingly elusive in the face of attempts to find a consistent definition. Boaz Ganor provides a very fruitful definition, which will be used in this article: "Terrorism is a form of violent struggle in which violence is deliberately used against civilians in order to achieve political goals (nationalistic, socioeconomic, ideological, religious, etc.)." Boaz Ganor, *The Counter-Terrorism Puzzle: A Guide for*

Decision Makers (Somerset, NJ: Transaction, 2005), p. 17. The second phrase that needs to be explained is "global Salafi Jihad." This broad-based ideology of Al Qaeda has its roots in the Egyptian Salafi Jihad, and today it is articulated in the global Salafi Jihad. The fatwa "Jihad against Jews and Crusaders," written by Osama bin Laden and published on February 23, 1998, has become the manifesto of the full-fledged global Salafi Jihad. In this document, bin Laden extended his previous concept of jihad from a defensive to an offensive one. The global Salafi Jihad now carried the fight to the "far enemy" (the United States and the West in general), on its own territory or in third-country territory. Today, Al Qaeda is a movement of uncountable terrorist organizations, groups, and cells. The term *global Salafi Jihad* will be used to describe this movement.

2. The Free Arab Voice, exclusive interview with Leila Khaled, February 2, 1999, available at http://www.freearabvoice.org (accessed November 5, 2005).

3. Ibid.

4. Yoram Schweitzer, "Female Suicide Bombers for God," *Telavivnotes* 88 (October 9, 2003).

5. BBC News, "Woman Suicide Bomber Strikes Iraq," September 28, 2005, available http://news.bbc.co.uk/1/hi/world/middle_east/4289168.stm (accessed November 5, 2005).

6. Karla J. Cunningham, "Cross-Regional Trends in Female Terrorism," *Studies of Conflict and Terrorism* 26 (2003), p. 172.

7. Leonard Weinberg and William Lee Eubank, "Italian Women Terrorists," *Terrorism: An International Journal* 9, no. 3 (1987), p. 242.

8. See Karla J. Cunningham, "Cross-Regional Trends in Female Terrorism," *Studies of Conflict and Terrorism* 26 (2003).

9. Barbara Victor, *Army of Roses: Inside the World of Palestinian Suicide Bombers* (New York: St. Martin's, 2003), p. 192.

10. Rhiannon Talbot, "Myths in the Representation of Women Terrorists," *Eire-Ireland* 35, no. 3–4 (Fall/Winter 2000), p. 171.

11. Sandy McEvoy, "Violent Women, Political Actors: A Feminist Analysis of Female Terror," paper presented at the International Studies Association 45th Annual Convention, March 17–20, Montreal. [AU: please cite year of presentation]

12. Clara Beyler, "Messenger of the Death: Female Suicide Bombers," International Policy Institute for Counter Terrorism, February 12, 2003, available at http://www.ict.org.il (accessed October 10, 2005).

13. Schweitzer, "Female Suicide Bombers for God."

14. Interview with Leila Khaled.

15. Weinberg and Eubank, "Italian Women Terrorists," p. 242.

16. Steven Lee Meyers, "Female Suicide Bombers Unnerve Russians," *New York Times*, (August 7, 2002), p. A1.

17. Ibid.

18. Karla J. Cunningham, "Cross-Regional Trends in Female Terrorism," *Studies of Conflict and Terrorism* 26 (2003), p. 180.

19. Vidyamali Samaranghe, "Soldiers, Housewives and Peace Makers: Ethnic Conflict and Gender in Sri Lanka," *Ethnic Studies Report* 14, no. 2 (July 1996), p. 211.

20. Ana Cutter, "Tamil Tigresses: Hindu Martyrs," Columbia University, 1998, available http://www.columbia.edu/cu/sipa/PUBS/SLANT/SPRING98/article5.html (accessed March 2, 2004).

21. Cunningham: Cross-Regional Trends in Female Terrorism," p. 181.

22. Ibid., p. 175.

23. Martha Crenshaw, "The Logic of Terrorism: Terrorist Behavior as a Product of a Strategic Choice," in *Origins of Terrorism,* ed. Walter Reich (Washington, DC: Woodrow Wilson Center Press, 1990), pp. 7–8.

24. Cunningham, "Cross-Regional Trends in Female Terrorism," p. 172.

25. Talbot, "Myths in the Representation of Women Terrorists," p. 180.

26. Ehud Talbot, "Rational Policy," *Eire-Ireland* (September–October 2000), p. 70.

27. Mia Bloom, "Feminism, Rape and War: *Engendering* Suicide Terror?" in *Dying to Kill: The Allure of Suicide Terror* (New York: Columbia University Press, 2005), p. 192.

28. Audrey Kurt Cronin, *Terrorist and Suicide Attacks*, CRS Report for Congress, Congressional Research Service, Library of Congress, August 28, 2003, Order Code RL32058, pp.14–15.

29. "It's a Woman!" *Al-Sha'ab*, February 1, 2002. cited in MEMRI Inquiry and Analysis Series, no. 84, February 13, 2002, available at http://memri.org/bin/opener.cgi?Page=archives&ID=IA8402 (accessed March 2, 2004).

30. Peter Schalk, "Women Fighters of the LTTE," *South East Asia Research* 14 (1990), p. 165.

31. Micah D. Halpern, "Terror: The Female Touch," *Israel Insider*, June 23, 2005.

32. Itamar Marcus and Barbara Crook, "The Joy of Killing Your Kids," *Palestinian Media Watch Bulletin*, March 16, 2005.

33. Ibid.

34. Nahed Habiballah, "Interviews with Mothers of Martyrs of the AQSA Intifada," *Arab Studies Quarterly* (Winter 2004).

35. Al-Khansaa was a poet in the early Islamic period. After she converted to Islam, she delivered a fiery speech encouraging her four sons to march into battle for Allah. When all four were killed, the poem she wrote was one of joy, rejoicing that Allah had honored her with deaths of her sons.

36. Armin Regular, "Mother of Two Becomes First Female Suicide Bomber for Hamas," *Haaretz* (January 16, 2004).

37. Ibid.

38. Ibid.

39. Ibid.

40. Israel Ministry of Foreign Affairs, "The Role of Palestinian Women in Suicide Terrorism," January 30, 2003, available at http://www.mfa.gov.il/MFA/MFAArchive/2000_2009/2003/1/The+Role+of+Palestinian+Women+in+Suicide+Terrorism.htm (accessed October 16, 2005).

41. Middle East News Online, January 28, 2002, available at http://www.mideasr web.org/mewnews.htm, (accessed November 6, 2005).

42. Ibid.

43. Islamic scholars continue to debate generally whether suicide attacks against Israelis are legitimate, regardless of whether the perpetrators are men or women. The religious among those who believe them to be a legitimate form of resistance, those who organize the attacks, and those who eventually carry them out are usually associated with the radical Islamist branch of the Muslim tradition. H. Malka, "Must Innocent Die? The Islamic Debate over Suicide Attacks," *Middle East Quarterly* 10, no. 2 (Spring 2003).

44. Interview with Anat Berko, "Symposium: The She Bomber," *Front Page Magazine* (September 9, 2005).

45. Interview with Nancy Kobrin, "Symposium: The She Bomber," *Front Page Magazine* (September 9, 2005).

46. Yoni Fighel, "Palestinian Islamic Jihad and Female Suicide Bombers," October 6, 2003, available at http://www.ict.org.il (accessed January 4, 2005).

47. David Cook, "Women Fighting Jihad?" *Studies in Conflict & Terrorism* 28 (2005), p. 380.

48. Ibid.

49. Yusuf al-'Ayyiri, "Dawr al-nisa'fi jihad al-'ada," available at http://www.epri sm.org/pages/5 (accessed March 4, 2006).

50. He was killed by Saudi security forces in May 2003.

51. SITE Institute, "Document on Jihadist Message Board Calls for Women to Take Active Role in Jihad," available at http://siteinstitute.org/bin/printerfriendly/pf.cgi (accessed October 16, 2005).

52. One of the five pillars in Islam is the pilgrimage to Mecca, the hajj.

53. Cook, "Women Fighting Jihad?," p. 382.

54. Intelligence and Terrorism Information Center at the Center of Special Studies, "Al-Qa'ida Women's Magazine: Women Must Participate in Jihad," available at http://www.intelligence.org.il/eng/memri/sep_e_04.htm (accessed October 16, 2005).

55. Rawya Rageh, "Islamist Women Use the Web for War with the Infidels," *Washington Times*, August 28. 2004, available at http://washtimes.com/world/20040827-110032-4232r.htm (accessed January 4, 2005).

56. Site Institute, Document on Jihadist Message Board.

57. Assad Nimer Busool, *Muslim Women Warriors* (Chicago: Al Huda, 1995), pp. 35–37.

58. Nicole Winfield, "Women Suicide Bombers Killed Three Soldiers," *Standard Times*, available at http://www.s-t.com/daily/04-03/04-05-03/a02wn020.htm (accessed November 5, 2005); Ibrahim Khalili, "Iraqi Women Suicide Bombers," *Shia News*, available at http://www.shianews.com/hi/middle_east/news_id/0000782.php (accessed November 5, 2005).

59. BBC news, U.K. edition, "Girls Guilty of Terror Charges," September 30, 2003, available at http://news.bbc.co.uk/1/hi/world/africa/3153110.stm (accessed January 4, 2005).

60. IWPR Staff in Central Asia, "Uzbek Suicide Bombers Don't Match Terrorist Profile," April 22, 2004, ISN Security Watch, available at http://www.isn.ethz.ch/news/sw/details.cfm?ID=8709 (accessed November 5, 2005).

61. Neue Züricher Zeitung, "Verhaftungswelle nach zwei Anschlägen auf Touristen in Kairo," *Erstmals verüben Frauen ein Selbstmordattentat* no. 226, (2005), p. 1.

62. BBC News, "Woman Suicide Bomber Strikes Iraq," September 28, 2005, available at http://news.bbc.co.uk/1/hi/world/middle_east/4289168.stm (accessed November 14, 2005).

63. Jackie Spinner, "Female Suicide Bomber Attacks U.S. Military Post," *Washington Post* (September 29, 2005), available at http://www.washingtonpost.com/wp-dyn/content/article/2005/09/28/AR2005092801631.html (accessed November 5, 2005).

64. Hassan M. Fattah, "Jordan Arrests Iraqi Woman in Hotel Blasts," *New York Times* (November 14, 2005), available at http://www.nytimes.com/2005/11/14/international/middleeast/14amman.html (accessed November 14, 2005).

65. Associated Press, "U.S. Held Iraqi With Same Name as Bomber," *New York Times* (November 14, 2005), available at http://www.nytimes.com/aponline/international/AP-Iraq-Jordan.html (accessed November 14, 2005).

66. Craig S. Smith, "Raised as a Catholic, She Died as a Muslim Bomber," *New York Times* (December 6, 2005).

67. FBI, "Seeking information, Aafa Siddiqui," available at http://www.fbi.gov/terrorinfo/siddiqui.htm (accessed January 4, 2005).

68. CNN, "Italy Terror Suspect Arrested" CNN, available http://edition.cnn.com/2003/World/Europe/11/29/italy.terror (accessed January 4, 2005).

69. AFP, "Dutch Police Arrest 21-Year-Old Female Terrorist Suspect," November 3, 2005.

70. Sebastian Rotella, "Jihadi Feminism," *Jerusalem Post* (January 15, 2006).

71. Cook, "Women Fighting Jihad?," p. 377.

72. Kelly McEvers, "The Women of Jemaah Islamiah," BBC News World Edition, 2004, available at http://news.bbc.uk/2/hi/asia-pacific/3382762.stm (accessed January 4, 2005).

CIA COUNTERINTELLIGENCE: AN EXCERPT FROM THE CHURCH COMMITTEE REPORT

IX. CIA COUNTERINTELLIGENCE

A. COUNTERINTELLIGENCE: AN INTRODUCTION

1. DEFINITION OF COUNTERINTELLIGENCE

Counterintelligence (CI) is a special form of intelligence activity, separate and distinct from other disciplines. Its purpose is to discover hostile foreign intelligence operations and destroy their effectiveness. This objective involves the protection of the United State Government against infiltration by foreign agents, as well as the control and manipulation of adversary intelligence operations. An effort is made to both discern and decive the plans and intentions of enemy intelligence services. Defined more formally, counterintelligence is an intelligence activity dedicated to undermining the effectiveness of hostile intelligence services. Its purpose is to guard the nation against espionage, other modern forms of spying, and sabotage directed against the United States, its citizens, information, and installations, at home and abroad, by infiltrating groups engaged in these practices and by gathering, storing, and analyzing information on inimical clandestine activity.[1]

Source: "Counterintelligence," in *Foreign and Military Intelligence, Final Report,* Select Committee to Study Governmental Operations with Respect to Intelligence Activities (the Church Committee), Book I, U.S. Senate, 94th Cong., 2d Sess. (April 26, 1976), pp. 163–71, written by Committee staffers John T. Elliff and Loch K. Johnson.

[1] Counterintelligence may also be thought of as the knowledge needed for the protection and preservation of the military, economic, and productive strength of the United States, including the security of the Government in domestic and foreign affairs against or from espionage, sabotage, and all other similar clandestine activities designed to weaken or destroy the United States. (Report of the Commission on Government Security Washington, D.C., 1957, pp. 48–49.)

In short, counterintelligence specialists wage nothing less than a secret war against antagonistic intelligence services. "In the absence of an effective U.S. counterintelligence program," notes a counterintelligence specialist, "[adversaries of democracy] function in what is largely a benign environment."[2]

2. THE THREAT

The adversaries of democracy are numerous and widespread. In the United States alone, 1,079 Soviet officials were on permanent assignment in February 1975, according to FBI figures.[3] Among these, over 40 percent have been positively identified as members of the KGB or GRU, the Soviet civilian and military intelligence units. Conservative estimates for the number of unidentified intelligence officers raise the figures to over 60 percent of the Soviet representation; some defector sources have estimated that 70 percent to 80 percent of Soviet officials have some intelligence connection.[4]

Furthermore, the number of Soviets in the United States has tripled since 1960, and is still increasing.[5] The opening of American deepwater ports to Russian ships in 1972 has given Soviet intelligence services "virtually complete geographic access to the United States," observes a counterintelligence specialist.[6] In 1974, for example, over 200 Soviet ships with a total crew complement of 13,000 officers and men called at 40 deep-water ports in this country.

Various exchange groups provide additional opportunities for Soviet intelligence gathering within the United States. Some 4,000 Soviets entered the United States as commercial or exchange visitors in 1974. During the past decade, the FBI identified over 100 intelligence officers among the approximately 400 Soviet students who attended American universities during this period as part of an East-West student exchange program.[7] Also, in the 14-year history of this program, more than 100 American students were the target of Soviet recruitment approaches in the USSR.

Other areas of counterintelligence concern include the sharp increase in the number of Soviet immigrants to the United States (less than 500 in 1972 compared to 4,000 in 1974); the rise in East-West commercial exchange visitors (from 641 in 1972 to 1,500 in 1974); and the growing number of Soviet bloc officials in this country (from 416 in 1960 to 798 in 1975).[8]

Foreign intelligence agents have attempted to recruit not only executive branch personnel, but also Congressional staff members. The FBI has advised the Committee that there have been instances in the past where hostile foreign intelligence officers have used the opportunity presented by overt contacts to attempt to recruit members of Congressional staffs who might have access to secret information.[9]

---

[2] Staff summary of interview, FBI counterintelligence specialist, 5/8/75.

[3] Staff summary of interview, FBI counterintelligence specialist, 3/10/75.

[4] FBI counterintelligence specialist (staff summary), 3/10/75.

[5] FBI counterintelligence specialist (staff summary), 5/8/75.

[6] *Ibid.*

[7] *Ibid*, 3/10/75.

[8] *Ibid.*

[9] FBI Memorandum for the Record, 10/30/75. Such recruitment approaches have been reported to the FBI by Congressional staff members. If the FBI otherwise learns of such recruitments, its policy is to report the facts to the appropriate Members of Congress.

The most serious threat is from "illegal" agents who have no easily detectable contacts with their intelligence service. The problem of "illegals" is summarized by the FBI as follows:

> The illegal is a highly trained specialist in espionage tradecraft. He may be a [foreign] national and/or a professional intelligence officer dispatched to the United States under a false identity. Some illegals [may be] trained in the scientific and technical field to permit easy access to sensitive areas of employment.
>
> The detection of . . . illegals presents a most serious problem to the FBI. Once they enter the United States with either fraudulent or true documentation, their presence is obscured among the thousands of legitimate emigres entering the United States annually. Relatively undetected, they are able to maintain contact with [the foreign control] by means of secret writing, microdots, and open signals in conventional communications which are not susceptible to discovery through conventional investigative measures.[10]

In several instances the FBI accomplished this most difficult assignment by carefully designed and limited mail opening programs which, if they had been authorized by a judicial warrant, might have been entirely proper. It is most unfortunate that the FBI did not choose to seek lawful authorization for such methods.[11]

This brief summary of the threat facing the American counterintelligence corps in this country is troubling enough, yet it does not take into account the worldwide scope of the problem. As an FBI counterintelligence expert states, hostile foreign intelligence services

> are alert for operational opportunities against the United States whether they occur within this country, abroad (in other countries) or in the home country itself. An operation might begin in the home country with recruitment of an American visitor; transfer to the United States with his return; and again, even later, might be transferred to a third country where the American agent may be met outside the normal reach of United States counterintelligence coverage. Regardless of the geographical location, the operation is still directed against the United States and can cause just as much damage from abroad as within our own borders.[12]

The espionage activities of the Soviet Union and other communist nations directed against the United States are extensive and relentless.[13]

To combat this threat, American counterintelligence officers have developed various sophisticated investigative techniques to (1) obtain information about foreign intelligence services, (2) protect our intelligence service, and (3) control the outcome of this sub-terranean struggle for intelligence supremacy. The task is difficult technically, and raises sensitive legal and ethical questions. As the CIA Deputy Director for Operations has testified, the

> U.S. counterintelligence program to be both effective and in line with traditional American freedoms must steer a middle course between blanket, illegal, frivolous and unsubstantiated

---

[10] FBI memorandum, "Intelligence Activities Within the United States by Foreign Governments," 3/20/75.

[11] Testimony of W. R. Wannall, Assistant Director, FBI, 10/21/75, p. 5; see Report on CIA and FBI Mail Opening.

[12] FBI Counterintelligence specialist (staff summary), 3/10/75.

[13] See Appendix III, Soviet Intelligence Collection and Operations Against the United States.

inquiries into the private lives of U.S. citizens and excessive restrictions which will render the Government's counterintelligence arms impotent to protect the nation from foreign penetration and covert manipulation.[14]

3. CI AS PRODUCT: INFORMATION ABOUT "THE ENEMY"

Counterintelligence is both an activity and its product. The product is reliable information about all the hostile foreign intelligence services who attack the United States by stealth. To guard against hostile intelligence operations aimed at this nation, a vast amount of information is required. It is necessary to know the organizational structure of the enemy service, the key personnel, the methods of recruitment and training, and the specific operations.

This information must be gathered within the United States and in all the foreign areas to which U.S. interests extend. Within the intelligence service, this acquisitive activity is referred to as intelligence collection. The resulting product—pertinent information on the enemy intelligence service—is often called "raw" intelligence data. The efforts of intelligence services through the world to conceal such information from one another, through various security devices and elaborate deceptions, creates the counterintelligence specialist what James Angleton, former Chief of CIA Counterintelligence, calls a kind of "wilderness of mirrors."

4. CI AS ACTIVITY: SECURITY AND COUNTERESPIONAGE

As an activity, CI consists of two matching halves: security and counterespionage. *Security* is the passive or defensive, side of counterintelligence. It consists basically of establishing static defenses against all hostile and concealed acts, regardless of who carries them out.

Counterespionage (CE) is the offensive, or aggressive, side of counterintelligence. It involves the identification of a specific adversary and a knowledge of the specific operation he is conducting. Counterespionage personnel must then attempt to counter these operations by infiltrating the hostile service (called penetration) and through various forms of manipulation. Ideally, the thrust of the hostile operation is turned back against the enemy. The security side of counterintelligence includes the screening and clearance of personnel and the development of programs to safeguard sensitive intelligence information (that is, the proper administration of security controls). The intelligence services try to defend three things: (1) their personnel, (2) their installations, and (3) their operations.

At the Central Intelligence Agency, the Office of Security is responsible for protection of personnel and installations, while actual operations are largely the preserve of the CI staff and the operating divisions. Among the defensive devices used for *information control* by intelligence agencies throughout the world are: security clearances, polygraphs, locking containers, security education, document accountability, censorship, camouflage, and codes. Devices for *physical security* include fences, lighting, general systems, alarms, badges and passes, and watchdogs. *Area control* relies on curfews, checkpoints, restricted areas, and border-frontier control.[15] Thus the security side of counterintelligence "is all that

---

[14] William Nelson testimony, 1/28/76, p. 5.

[15] Staff summary of interview, CIA security specialist, 8/20/75.

concerns perimeter defense, badges, knowing everything you have to know about your own people;" the counterespionage side "involves knowing all about intelligence services— foreign intelligence services—their people, their installations, their methods, and their operations. So that you have a completely different level of interest."[16] However, the Office of Security and the CI staff exchange information to assure adequate security systems.

5. THE PENETRATION AND THE DOUBLE AGENT

Several kinds of operations exist within the rubric of counterespionage. One, how-ever, transcends all the others in importance: the penetration. A primary goal of counter-intelligence is to contain the intelligence service of the enemy. To do so, it is eminently desirable to know his plans in advance and in detail. This admirable, but difficult, objective may be achieved through a high-level infiltration of the opposition service. As a Director of the CIA has written, "Experience has shown penetration to be the most effective re-sponse to Soviet and Bloc [intelligence] services."[17]

Moreover, a well-placed infiltrator in a hostile intelligence service may be better able than anyone else to determine whether one's own service has been penetrated. A former Director of the Defense Intelligence Agency (DIA) has observed that the three principal programs used by the United States to meet, neutralize, and defeat hostile intelligence penetrations are: (1) our own penetrations; (2) security screening and clearance of per-sonnel; and (3) our efforts for safeguarding sensitive intelligence information.[18] The im-portance of the penetration is emphasized by an experienced CIA counterespionage operative, with mixed but expressive similes: "Conducting counterespionage with pene-tration can be like shooting fish in a barrel;" in contrast, "conducting counterespionage without the act of penetration is like fighting in the dark."[19]

Methods of infiltrating the opposition service take several forms. Usually the most effective and desirable penetration is the recruitment of an agent-in-place.[20] He is a citizen of an enemy nation and is already in the employ of its intelligence service. Ideally, he will be both highly placed and venal. The individual, say a KGB officer in Bonn, is approached and asked to work for the intelligence service of the United States. Various inducements— including ideology—may be used to recruit him against his own service. If the recruitment is successful, the operation may be especially worthwhile since the agent is presumably already trusted within his organization and his access to documents may be unquestioned. Jack E. Dunlap, who worked at and spied on the National Security Agency (NSA) in the 1960s, is a well-known example of a Soviet agent-in-place within the U.S. intelligence service. His handler was a Soviet Air Force attaché at the Soviet Embassy in Washington. Of course, a single penetration can be worth an intelligence gold mine, as were Kim Philby for the Soviet Union and Col. Oleg Penkovsky for the United States.

Another method of infiltration is the double agent. Double agents, however, are costly and time-consuming, and they are risky. Human lives are at stake. Double agents

---

[16] Raymond Rocca deposition, 11/25/75, p. 19.

[17] Memorandum from John McCone to Chairman, President's Foreign Intelligence Advisory Board, 10/8/63.

[18] The Carroll Report on the Dunlap Case, 2/12/64.

[19] CIA/CI specialist, staff summary, 11/1/75.

[20] CIA/CI specialist, staff summary, 10/17/75.

also normally involve pure drudgery, with few dramatic results, as new information is checked against existing files. On top of this comes the difficulty of assuring against a doublecross.

Moreover, passing credible documents can be a major problem. The operations must be made interesting to the opposition. To make fake papers plausible, the genuine article must be provided now and again. Classified documents must be cleared, and this process can be painstakingly slow. Also, "this means letting a lot of good stuff go to the enemy without much in return," complains a CI officer with considerable experience.[21]

To accomplish each of these tasks, hard work, careful planning, and considerable manpower are necessary. The extraordinary manpower requirements of the double agent operation restricted the abilities of the British to run cases during the Second World War— approximately 150 double agents for the entire period of the war and no more than about 25 at any one time.[22] Moreover, their mission was eased greatly by the ability of the British to read the German cipher throughout most of the conflict.

6. THE DEFECTOR

Almost as good as the agent-in-place and less troublesome than the whole range of double agents is the "defector with knowledge." Here the procedure consists of inter-rogation and validation of bona fides, as usual, but without the worrisome, ongoing re-quirements for a skillful mix of false and genuine documents and other logistical support. Though an agent-in-place is preferable because of the continuing useful information he can provide, often a man does not want to risk his life by staying in-place, especially where the security is sophisticated; his preference is to defect to safety. In other words, agents-in-place are harder to come by in systems like the Soviet bloc countries; defection is more likely.[23] In contrast, agents-in-place are more easily recruited in so-called Third World areas.

Within the United States, the interrogation of intelligence service defectors who have defected in the U.S. is primarily the responsibility of the FBI, though the CIA may have a follow-up session with the individual. Sometimes the bona fides of a defector remain disputed for many years.

CIA-recruited defectors abroad are occasionally brought to the United States and resettled. The FBI is notified and, after the CIA completes its interrogation, FBI may interrogate. CIA does not bring all defectors to the United States; only those expected to make a significant contribution. CIA generally handles resettlement not only of defectors from abroad, but also (at the request of the FBI) of defectors in the United States.

7. THE DECEPTION

The penetration or double agent is closely related to another important CE technique: the deception. Simply stated, the deception is an attempt to give the enemy a false im-pression about something, causing him to take action contrary to his own interests. Fooling

---

[21] Rocca deposition, 11/25/75, pp. 33–34.

[22] Sir John Masterman, *Double Cross System of the War of 1939–45* (New Haven: Yale University Press, 1972).

[23] Bruce Solie, deposition, 11/25/75, pp. 26–27.

the Germans into the belief that D Day landings were to be in the Pas de Calais rather than in Normandy is a classic example of a successful deception operation in World War II.[24]

Deception is related to penetration because our agents operating within foreign intelligence agencies can serve as excellent channels through which misleading information can flow to the enemy. So double agents serve both as collectors of positive intelligence and channels for deception. However, there are opportunities for deception other than our own agents; in fact, "an infinite variety" exists, according to an experienced practitioner.[25] One example: the U.S. can allow penetration of its own intelligence service, and then feed false information through him.

8. Other CI Techniques

Other counterespionage operations include surreptitious surveillance of various kinds (for instance, audio, mail, physical, and "optical"—that is, photography), interrogation (sometimes incommunicado as in the case of one defector), and provocation. Decoding clandestine radio transmission and letters with messages written in secret ink between the visible lines is part and parcel of the CE trade, as is trailing suspected agents, observing "dead drops" (the exchange of material, like documents or instructions, between a spy and his handler), and photographing individuals entering opposition embassies or at other locations. At the recent funeral of CIA agent Richard Welch, two Eastern European diplomats were discovered among the press corps snapping photographs of CIA intelligence officers attending the burial ceremony.[26] Since the focus of offensive counterintelligence is disruption of the enemy service, provocation can be an important element of CE, too. It amounts, in essence, to harassment of the opposition, such as publishing the names of his agents or sending a defector into his midst who is in reality a double agent.

9. CI as Organization

Security at CIA is the responsibility of the Office of Security, a division of the Deputy Director for Administration. Counterespionage policy is guided by the Counterintelligence Staff of the Operations Directorate (Clandestine Service). Besides setting policy, the CI Staff sometimes conducts its own operations, though most CI operations emanate directly from the various geographic divisions as the CI field personnel—through the practice of the counterintelligence discipline—attempt to guard against enemy manipulation of espionage and covert action operations.

Structurally, counterintelligence services are usually composed of two additional sections which support Security and Operations. They are the Research and the Liaison sections. Good research is critical to a good counterintelligence effort, and it may take several forms. It can involve the amassing of encyclopedic intelligence on individuals, including American citizens associated—wittingly or unwitttingly—with hostile intelligence services. Specialists say that the hallmark of a sophisticated CI service is its collection of accurate records.[27] CI research personnel also produce reports on topics of interest

[24] Masterman, *Double Cross System.*
[25] CIA counterintelligence specialist (staff summary), 11/1/75.
[26] CIA counterintelligence specialist (staff summary), 1/15/76.
[27] *Ibid,* 6/27/75.

to the specialty, including guidelines for the interrogation of defectors and current analyses on such subjects as proprietary companies used by foreign intelligence services and the structure of Soviet bloc intelligence services. CI researchers also analyze defector briefs and, in the case of compromised documents, help ascertain who had access and what damage was inflicted.

Liaison with other counterintelligence services, at home and abroad, is also vital since no effective counterintelligence organization can do its job alone. The various CI units at home are particularly important, as counterintelligence—with all its intricacies and deceptions—requires coordination among agencies and sharing of records. Unlike the totally unified KGB organization, the American intelligence service is fragmented and depends upon liaison to make operations more effective. Coordination between CIA and FBI counterintelligence units is especially critical since, in theory at least, the former has foreign jurisdiction and the latter domestic, yet they must monitor the movements of foreign spies in and out of these two jurisdictions. Sometimes this coordination fails dramatically. In 1970, for example, J. Edgar Hoover of the FBI terminated formal liaison with the CIA and all the other intelligence units in the Government because of a disagreement with the CIA on a question of source disclosure (the Thomas Riha case).[28]

Liaison with foreign intelligence services overseas can undergo strain, too. As one CI specialist has said: "There are no friendly services; there are services of friendly foreign powers."[29] Each service fears the other has been infiltrated by hostile agents and is reluctant to see national secrets go outside its own vaults. Nonetheless, cooperation does take place, since all intelligence services seek information and, with precautions, will take it where they can get it if it is useful.

The CIA will work with friendly services to uncover hostile intelligence operations, including illegals, directed at the government of the friendly service. For example, a CIA-recruited defector may reveal Soviet agents in a friendly foreign government. This information is shared with the friendly government, if there is proper protection of the source. Protection of the CIA source is paramount.

FBI counterespionage activities within the United States are supervised by the Counterintelligence Branch of the FBI Intelligence Division. The Branch is made up of four Sections, three of which direct field operations conducted by the Bureau's field offices. The fourth handles liaison with other agencies and supervises the FBI's Legal Attaches assigned to serve in the embassies in several foreign countries.

The formal structure for counterespionage coordination between the FBI and the military intelligence agencies was established in 1939 and embodied most recently in a "charter" for the Interdepartmental Intelligence Conference in 1964.[30] This formal body, chaired by the FBI Director and including the heads of the military intelligence agencies, has not played a significant decisionmaking role in recent years.

As late as 1974, some FBI officials took the position that the Bureau's counter-espionage activities were not under the authority of the Attorney General, since the FBI was accountable in this area directly to the United States Intelligence Board and the National

---

[28] Staff summary of interview, former FBI liaison person with CIA, 8/22/75.

[29] Rocca deposition, 11/25/75, p. 43.

[30] Confidential memorandum from President Roosevelt to Department Heads, 6/26/39; memorandum from Attorney General Kennedy to J. Edgar Hoover, Chairman, Interdepartmental Intelligence Conference, 3/5/64.

Security Council. A Justice Department committee chaired by Assistant Attorney General Henry Petersen sharply rejected this view and declared

> There can be no doubt that in the area of foreign counterintelligence, as in all its other functions, the FBI is subject to the power and authority of the Attorney General.[31]

In recent years the FBI has taken steps to upgrade its counterespionage effort, which had been neglected because of the higher priority given to domestic intelligence in the late 60s and early 70s.[32] New career development and mid-career training programs have been instituted. FBI agents specializing in counterespionage begin their careers as criminal investigators and not as analysts; and Bureau officials stress that their role is accurate fact-finding, rather than evaluation. Nevertheless, counterespionage supervisory personnel have recently attended high-level training courses in foreign affairs and area studies outside the Bureau.[33]

Here, then, are the key elements of counterintelligence. Together they combine into a discipline of great importance, for the rock bottom obligation of an intelligence service is to defend the country; meeting this obligation is the very *raison d'être* of counterintelligence. The discipline also represents the most secret of secret intelligence activities—the heart of the onion. Its great importance and its ultra secrecy make counterintelligence an area of concern that cannot be ignored by policymakers and by those responsible for legislative oversight. As a review of current issues in CI attests, the discipline has several problems which demand the attention of those charged with the defense of the country and the reform of the intelligence community.

---

[31] Report of the Petersen Committee on COINTELPRO, pp. 34–35. The committee was especially concerned that the *ad hoc* equivalent of the U.S. Intelligence Board had approved the discredited "Huston Plan" in 1970. However, the committee complied with the FBI's request that it exclude from its review of domestic COINTELPRO activities the Bureau's "extremely sensitive foreign intelligence collection techniques." (Memorandum from FBI Director Kelley to Acting Attorney General Robert Bork, 12/11/73.)

[32] C. D. Brennan testimony, Hearings, Vol. 2, p. 117.

[33] W. R. Wannall testimony, 1/21/76, pp. 18–22.

APPENDIX B

THE HUSTON PLAN

Editor's note: In 1970, the Nixon administration assigned a young White House aide, Tom Charles Huston, to write a report on youthful anti–Vietnam War protesters and how intelligence could be gathered about their activities. The result was a master spy plan to conduct espionage against the protesters: opening their mail, wiretapping their telephone, shadowing their every move—all without proper warrants and in violation of their first amendment rights to peaceful dissent. The major intelligence chiefs at the time approved the plan, including the DCI (Richard Helms), the FBI Director (the legendary J. Edgar Hoover), the NSA director, and the DIA director, even though the envisioned activities were in violation of the law. The plan was rescinded by President Nixon when Hoover finally decided it was too risky and complained to the President. Many of these operations went on anyway, culminating in the 1975 investigations into illegal domestic surveillance after word of the CIA's mail-opening operations leaked to the *New York Times* in 1974. The Huston Plan represents domestic counter-intelligence at the extreme, just as Iran-*contra* represents the overzealous use of covert action.

Source: *Final Report,* Select Committee to Study Governmental Operations with Respect to Intelligence Activities (the Church Committee), Book I, U.S. Senate, 94th Cong., 2d Sess. (April 26, 1976).

SPECIAL REPORT INTERAGENCY COMMITTEE ON INTELLIGENCE (AD HOC)[1]

CHAIRMAN J. EDGAR HOOVER

JUNE, 1970

---

[1] Under criteria determined by the Committee, in consultation with the White House, the Department of Defense, the Department of Justice, the Central Intelligence Agency, and the Federal Bureau of Investigation, certain materials have been deleted from those documents, some of which were previously classified, to maintain the internal operating procedures of the agencies involved, and to protect intelligence sources and methods. Further deletions were made with respect to protecting the privacy of certain individuals and groups. These deletions do not change the material content of these exhibits.

JUNE 25, 1970

This report, prepared for the President, is approved by all members of this committee and their signatures are affixed hereto.

Director, Federal Bureau of Investigation
Chairman

Director, Central Intelligence Agency

Director, Defense Intelligence Agency

Director, National Security Agency

PREFACE

The objectives of this report are to: (1) assess the current internal security threat; (2) evaluate current intelligence collection procedures; identify restraints under which U. S. intelligence services operate; and list the advantages and disadvantages of such restraints; and (3) evaluate current interagency coordination and recommend means to improve it.

The Committee has attempted to set forth the essence of the issues and the major policy considerations involved which fall within the scope of its mandate.

TABLE OF CONTENTS

Page

PREFACE   i

PART ONE
SUMMARY OF INTERNAL SECURITY THREAT

I. MILITANT NEW LEFT GROUPS   1

   A. Assessment of Current Internal Security Threat   1
      1. Student Protest Groups   1
      2. Antiwar Activities   3
      3. New Left Terrorist Groups   4

   B. Assessment of Current Intelligence Collection Procedures   5
      1. Scope and Effectiveness of Current Coverage   5
      2. Gaps in Current Coverage   6
      3. Possible Measures to Improve Intelligence Collection   7

II. BLACK EXTREMIST MOVEMENT   9

   A. Assessment of Current Internal Security Threat   9
      1. Black Panther Party   9
      2. New Left Support for BPP   9
      3. BPP Propaganda Appearances   9
      4. Appeal to Military   10
      5. BPP Philosophy and Foreign Support   10
      6. Other Black Extremist Groups   10
      7. Black Student Extremist Influence   11
      8. Foreign Influence in the Black Extremist Movement   11

   B. Assessment of Current Intelligence Collection Procedures   12
      1. Other Black Extremist Organizations   13

III. INTELLIGENCE SERVICES OF COMMUNIST
      COUNTRIES   14

   A. Assessment of Current Internal Security Threat   14
      1. Intervention in Domestic Unrest   14
      2. Intelligence Operations   15

   B. Assessment of Current Intelligence Collection   17
      1. Scope and Effectiveness   17
      2. Gaps in Current Coverage   18

IV. OTHER REVOLUTIONARY GROUPS   20

   A. Assessment of Current Internal Security Threat   20
      1. Communist Party   20
      2. Socialist Workers Party and Other Trotskyist Groups   20

3. Pro-Chinese Communist Groups   21
4. Puerto Rican Nationalist Extremist Groups   21

B. Assessment of Current Intelligence Coverage   21
1. Scope and Effectiveness   21
2. Gaps in Current Coverage   22
3. Possible Measures to Improve Intelligence Collection   22

PART TWO
RESTRAINTS ON INTELLIGENCE COLLECTION

I. SPECIFIC OPERATIONAL RESTRAINTS   23

A. Interpretive Restraint on Communications Intelligence   23
B. Electronic Surveillances and Penetrations   26
C. Mail Coverage   29
D. Surreptitious Entry   32
E. Development of Campus Sources   34
F. Use of Military Undercover Agents   37

II. BUDGET AND MANPOWER RESTRICTIONS   40

PART THREE
EVALUATION OF INTERAGENCY COORDINATION

I. CURRENT PROCEDURES TO EFFECT COORDINDATION   42

II. SUGGESTED MEASURES TO IMPROVE THE
    COORDINATION OF DOMESTIC INTELLIGENCE
    COLLECTION   42

PART ONE
SUMMARY OF INTERNAL SECURITY THREAT

I. MILITANT NEW LEFT GROUPS

A. ASSESSMENT OF CURRENT INTERNAL SECURITY THREAT

The movement of rebellious youth known as the "New Left," involving and influencing a substantial number of college students, is having a serious impact on contemporary society with a potential for serious domestic strife. The revolutionary aims of the New Left are apparent when their identification with Marxism-Leninism is examined. They pointedly advertise their objective as the overthrow of our system of government by force and violence. Under the guise of freedom of speech, they seek to confront all established authority and provoke disorder. They intend to smash the U. S. educational system, the economic structure, and, finally, the Government itself. New left groups do not have a large enough number of rank-and-file followers, nor dry they have a unity of purpose to carry out massive or paralyzing acts of insurrection. They do, on the other hand, have the will to carry on more militant efforts in local situations and an inclination to utilize more extreme means to attain their objectives.

1. *Student Protest Groups*. The Students for a Democratic Society (SDS) has, in the past year, split into several factions, including the Revolutionary Youth Movement (RYM), which has control over 30 chapters; and the Worker Student Alliance (WSA), which consists of 63 chapters. The WSA faction, dominated by the Progressive Labor Party (PLP), aims to build a worker-student movement in keeping with the PLP's aim of developing a broad worker-based revolutionary movement in the United States.

There are some 85 unaffiliated SDS chapters generally sympathetic to revolutionary tactics and goals. The trend of increased radical campus organizations is noticeable at campuses where recognition of SDS has been refused or rescinded and SDS members have banded together, with or without sanction, under a new title to attract student support. In addition, numerous ad hoc groups have been established on campuses and elsewhere to exploit specific issues.

The National Student Strike (NSS), also known as the National Strike Information Center, was formed following the entry of the United States forces into Cambodia and the deaths of four students at Kent State University. NSS, which helped to coordinate the nationwide student strike in May, 1970, has three regional centers and includes among its leadership SDS members and other New Left activists. The NSS has established a nationwide communications system of "ham" radio stations on campuses to encourage student demonstrations and disruptions. This communications capability may have a significant impact on campus stability in the coming school year.

The Venceremos Brigade (VB), established to send United States youth to Cuba to aid in the 1970 harvests, has continually received favorable publicity in Cuban propaganda media. To date, over 900 members of the VB have visited Cuba and another group of approximately 500 members are expected to follow suit. While in Cuba, VB members were individually photographed and questioned in detail about their backgrounds. Because of their contacts with Cuban officials, these individuals must be considered as potential recruits for Cuban intelligence activities and sabotage in the United States.

The greatest threat posed to the security of the country by student protest groups is their potential for fomenting violence and unrest on college campuses. Demonstrations have triggered acts of arson by extremists against war-oriented research and ROTC facilities and have virtually paralyzed many schools. There has been a growing number of noncampus, but student-related, acts of violence which increase tensions between "town and gown" and which constitute a marked escalation of the scope and level of protest activities. Few student protests are currently related to exclusively campus issues; virtually all involve political and social issues. Increasingly, the battlefield is the community with the campus serving primarily as a staging area.

The efforts of the New Left aimed at fomenting unrest and subversion among civil servants, labor unions, and mass media have met with very limited success, although the WSA and its parent, the PLP, have attempted through their "Summer Work-Ins" to infiltrate and radicalize labor. The inability of these groups to subvert and control the mass media has led to the establishment of a large network of underground publications which serve the dual purpose of an internal communication network and an external propaganda organ.

Leaders of student protest groups have traveled extensively over the years to communist countries; have openly stated their sympathy with the international communist revolutionary movements in South Vietnam and Cuba; and have directed others into activities which support these movements. These individuals must be considered to have potential for recruitment and participation in foreign-directed intelligence activity.

2. *Antiwar Activists.* The impetus and continuity for the antiwar movement is provided by the New Mobilization Committee to End the War in Vietnam (NMC) and the Student Mobilization Committee to End the War in Vietnam (SMC). The NMC is a coalition of numerous antiwar groups and individuals including communist "old left" elements. The SMC is under the control of the Trotskyist Socialist Workers Party (SWP).

The NMC and SMC have announced a policy of "nonexclusion" which places no limitation on the type of individuals allowed to participate in demonstrations. This policy opens the door for violence-prone individuals who want to capitalize on the activities of these groups. Both groups profess to follow a policy of nonviolence; however, the very nature of the protests that they sponsor sets the stage for civil disobedience and police confrontation by irresponsible dissident elements. Various individuals in NMC and SMC are calling for more militant protest activities, a subject to be discussed at national meetings by both groups in late June, 1970.

Although antiwar groups are not known to be collecting weapons, engaging in paramilitary training, or advocating terrorist tactics, the pro-Hanoi attitude of their leaders, the unstable nature of many NMC advocates and their policy of "nonexclusion" underscore the use of the antiwar movement as a conduit for civil disorder. This is further emphasized by the NMC leadership's advocacy of civil disobedience to achieve desired objectives.

There is no indication that the antiwar movement has made serious inroads or achieved any more than a slight degree of influence among labor unions, the mass media, and civil servants. One group, however, the Federal Employees for a Democratic Society (FEDS), offers a means of protest for recent radical graduates employed by the Federal Government.

The military and educational institutions are the prime targets of the anitwar movement. In addition to vandalism, arsons, and bombings of ROTC facilities, there has been stepped-up activity to spread antiwar sympathy among American servicemen from within through sympathetic members in the military and from without through such programs as "GI Coffeehouses" and the proposed National GI Alliance. The increasing access by members of the military to the underground press, the establishment of servicemen's unions, and organizations which facilitate desertions, have contributed significantly to the increasing instances of dissent in the military services.

NMC and SMC leaders are constantly speaking before student groups and endeavoring to use student radicals to further the antiwar movement. They have called for an end to the ROTC and have demonstrated, often violently, to force universities to halt war-related research projects.

The NMC maintains close contact with the World Council for Peace and Stockholm Conference on Vietnam. A new organization dominated by NMC leaders, the Committee of Liaison with Families of Servicemen Detained in North Vietnam, emerged in January, 1970, after contacts with North Vietnamese representatives. It attempts to present a favorable picture of North Vietnamese treatment of American prisoners of war.

NMC leaders have frequently traveled abroad. It is therefore necessary to consider these individuals as having potential for engaging in foreign-directed intelligence collection.

The Central Intelligence Agency (CIA), in its analysis of bloc intelligence, is of the view that the Soviet and bloc intelligence services are committed at the political level to exploit all domestic dissidents wherever possible. This attack is being conducted through recruited agents, agents of influence, and the use of front groups. It is established bloc policy to deploy its forces against the United States as "the main enemy" and to direct all bloc intelligence forces toward ultimately political objectives which disrupt U. S. domestic and foreign policies.

3. *New Left Terrorist Groups.* The Weatherman terrorist group, which emerged from a factional split of SDS during the Summer of 1969, is a revolutionary youth movement which actively supports the revolutionary leadership role of the Negro in the United States. It has evolved into a number of small commando-type units which plan to utilize bombings, arsons, and assassinations as political weapons.

There has been evidence of Weatherman involvement in terrorist tactics, including the accidental explosion of a "Weatherman bomb factory" in New York City on March 6, 1970; the discovery of two undetonated bombs in Detroit police facilities on the same date; and the blast at New York City police installations on June 9, 1970.

While Weatherman membership is not clearly defined, it is estimated that at least 1,000 individuals adhere to Weatherman ideology. In addition, groups such as the White Panther Party, Running Dog, Mad Dog, and the Youth International Party (Yippies) are supporters of Weatherman terrorism but have no clearly definable ideology of their own.

Adherents to Weatherman ideology are also found within radical elements on campuses, among those living in off-campus communes, among New Left movement lawyers and doctors, and the underground press. Individuals who adhere to the Weatherman ideology have offered support and aid to hard-core Weatherman members, including 21 Weatherman members currently in hiding to avoid apprehension.

They identify themselves politically with North Vietnam, Cuba, and North Korea and consider pro-Soviet and pro-Chinese organizations as being aligned with imperialist powers. In addition, some of the Weatherman leaders and adherents have traveled to communist countries or have met in Western countries with communist representatives.

Weatherman leaders and other members of terrorist groups are not known at this time to be involved in foreign-directed intelligence collection activity. The fugitive and underground status of many of these people, as well as their involvement in activities which would likely bring them to the attention of American authorities, would be a deterrent to contacts by foreign intelligence organizations.

B. ASSESSMENT OF CURRENT INTELLIGENCE COLLECTION PROCEDURES

1. *Scope and Effectiveness of Current Coverage.* Although New Left groups have been responsible for widespread damage to ROTC facilities, for the halting of some weapons-related research, and for the increasing dissent within the military services, the major threat to the internal security of the United States is that directed against the civilian sector of our society.

Coverage of student groups is handled primarily through live informants and it is generally effective at the national level or at major meetings of these groups where overall policy, aims, and objectives of the groups are determined.

The antiwar movement's activities are covered through the FBI by live informants in all organizations of interest. This is supported by information furnished by all members of the intelligence community and other Federal, state, and local agencies. Key leaders and activists are afforded concentrated and intensified investigative coverage on a continuing basis and, in situations where there are positive indications of violence, electronic surveillances have been implemented on a selective basis. Informant and electronic coverage does not meet present requirements.

Although several SDS chapters on college campuses which adhere to Weatherman ideology have been penetrated by live informants, there is no live informant coverage at present of underground Weatherman fugitives. There is electronic coverage on the residence of a Weatherman contact in New York City and on the residence of an alleged Weatherman member in San Francisco; however, no information has been developed concerning the whereabouts of the 21 Weatherman fugitives.

2. *Gaps in Current Coverage.* Established, long-term coverage is not available within student protest groups due to the fact that the student body itself changes yearly, necessitating a constant turnover in the informants targeted against these groups. His idealism and immaturity, as well as thee sensitive issues of academic freedom and the right to dissent, all serve to increase the risk that the student informant will be exposed as such.

Generally, day-to-day coverage of the planned activities of student protest groups, which are somewhat autonomous and disjointed, could be strengthened. Advance notice of foreign travel by student militants is particularly needed. Campus violence is generally attributable to small, close-knit extremist groups among radical students. Coverage of these latter groups is minimal.

The antiwar movement is comprised of a great many organizations and people which represent varied political, moral and ethnic beliefs. Current manpower commitments preclude optimum coverage of all antiwar activities on a day-to-day basis.

Existing coverage of New Left extremists, the Weatherman group in particular, is negligible. Most of the Weatherman group has gone underground and formed floating, commando-type units composed of three to six individuals. The transitory nature of these units hinders the installation of electronic surveillances and their smallness and distrust of outsiders make penetration of these units through live informants extremely difficult.

Financially, the Weatherman group appears to be without a centralized source of funds. Wealthy parents have furnished funds to some of these individuals, including those in a fugitive status. Many members have also been involved in the thefts of credit and identification cards, as well as checks, and have utilized them for obtaining operating expenses.

3. *Possible Measures to Improve Intelligence Collection.* To establish effective coverage of student protest groups would require the expansion of live informant coverage of individual campus chapters of these organizations. This would entail extensive use of student informants to obtain maximum utilization of their services for the periods of their college attendance.

Because of the great number of individuals and groups in the antiwar movement, an increase in the manpower assigned to these investigations would facilitate more intensive coverage. In addition there are several key leaders involved in virtually all antiwar activities, including international contacts, against whom electronic surveillances and mail covers would be particularly effective.

Improvement of intelligence gathering against New Left terrorists depends on a combination of live informant coverage among key leaders and selective electronic surveillances. Because of the nature of the Weatherman groups, live informant coverage will most likely result through the defection of a key leader.

Extensive efforts have been undertaken which should produce of live informant capable of furnishing information as to the location of Weatherman fugitives and planned terrorist acts. In the event a commune is located, prompt installation of electronic coverage should produce similar results. Utilization of additional resources to expand and intensify this collection would be beneficial.

II. BLACK EXTREMIST MOVEMENT

A. ASSESSMENT OF CURRENT INTERNAL SECURITY THREAT

1. *Black Panther Party.* The most active and dangerous black extremist group in the United States is the Black Panther Party (BPP). Despite its relatively small number of hard-core members—approximately 800 in 40 chapters nationwide—the BPP is in the forefront of black extremist activity today. The BPP has publicly advertised its goals of organizing revolution, insurrection, assassination and other terrorist-type activities. Moreover, a recent poll indicates that approximately 25 percent of the black population has a great respect for the BPP, including 43 percent of blacks under 21 years of age.

The Panther newspaper has a current circulation of approximately 150,000 copies weekly. Its pages are filled with messages of racial hatred and call for terrorist guerrilla activity in an attempt to overthrow the Government. The BPP has been involved in a substantial number of planned attacks against law enforcement officers, and its leadership is composed in large part of criminally inclined, violence-prone individuals.

Weapons are regularly stockpiled by the Party. During 1968 and 1969, quantities of machine guns, shotguns, rifles, hand grenades, homemade bombs, and ammunition were uncovered in Panther offices.

2. *New Left Support for BPP.* The BPP has received increasing support from radical New Left elements. During 1970, the BPP formed a working relationship with radical student dissenters by injecting the issue of Government "repression" of Panthers into the antiwar cause. Students for a Democratic Society (SDS) supported the BPP in a 1969 "united front against fascism." The probability that black extremists, including the BPP, will work closely with New Left white radicals in the future increases the threat of esca-lating terrorist activities. It would be safe to project that racial strife and student turmoil fomented by black extremists will definitely increase.

3. *BPP Propaganda Appearances.* Despite its small membership, the BPP has scored major successes in the propaganda arena. In 1969, BPP representatives spoke at 189 col-leges throughout the Nation, while in 1967 there were only 11 such appearances. Although no direct information has been received to date indicating that the BPP has initiated any large-scale racial disorders, the year 1970 has seen an escalation of racial disorders across the Nation compared to 1969. This fact, coupled with an increasing amount of violent Panther activity, presents a great potential for racial and civil unrest for the future.

4. *Appeal to Military.* The BPP has made pointed appeals to black servicemen with racist propaganda. High priority has been placed on the recruitment of veterans with weapons and explosives training. The BPP has also called for infiltration of the Govern-ment. These activities, should they achieve even minimum success, present a grave threat.

5. *BPP Philosophy and Foreign Support.* The BPP relies heavily on foreign com-munist ideology to shape its goals. Quotations from Mao Tse-tung were the initial ideo-logical bible of the BPP. Currently, the writings of North Korean Premier Kim Il-sung are followed and extensive use of North Korean propaganda material is made in BPP pub-lications and training. The Marxist-oriented philosophy of the BPP presents a favorable environment for support of the Panthers from other communist countries.

BPP leaders have traveled extensively abroad including visits to Cuba, Russia, North Korea, and Algeria. International operations of the BPP are directed by Eldridge Cleaver, a fugitive from United States courts. Cleaver has established an international staff in Algeria, from where communist propaganda is constantly relayed to the BPP headquarters in Berkeley, California. He has also established close ties with Al Fatah, an Arab guerrilla organization, whose leaders have reportedly extended invitations to BPP members to take guerrilla training during 1970. Cleaver, in a recent conversation, indicated that North Koreans are conducting similar training for BPP members. Radical white students in Western Europe and the Scandinavian countries have organized solidarity committees in support of the BPP. These committees are the sources of financial contributions to the Party and provide outlets for the BPP newspaper.

6. *Other Black Extremist Groups.* The Nation of Islam (NOI) is the largest single black extremist organization in the United States with an estimated membership of 6,000 in approximately 100 Mosques. The NOI preaches hatred of the white race and advocates separatism of the races. The NOI as a group has, to date, not instigated any civil disorders; however, the followers of this semi-religious cult are extremely dedicated individuals who could be expected to perform acts of violence if so ordered by the NOI head, Elijah Muhammed. When Muhammed, who is over 70 years of age, is replaced, a new leader could completely alter current nonviolent tactics of the organization. For example, Muhammed's son-in-law, Raymond Sharrieff, now among the top hierarchy of NOI, could rise to a leadership position. Sharrieff is vicious, domineering, and unpredictable.

There are numerous other black extremist organizations, small in numbers, located across the country. There is also a large number of unaffiliated black extremists who advocate violence and guerrilla warfare. One particular group, the Republic of New Africa (RNA), headquartered in Detroit, Michigan, calls for the establishment of a separate black nation in the South to be protected by armed forces. These groups, although small, are dedicated to the destruction of our form of government and consequently present a definite potential for instigating civil disorder or guerrilla warfare activity.

7. *Black Student Extremist Influence.* Black student extremist activities at colleges and secondary schools have increased alarmingly. Although currently there is no dominant leadership, coordination or specific direction between these individuals, they are in frequent contact with each other. Consequently, should any type of organization or cohesiveness develop, it would present a grave potential for future violent activities at United States schools. Increased informant coverage would be particularly productive in this area. Black student extremists have frequently engaged in violence and disruptive activity on campuses. Major universities which made concessions to nonnegotiable black student demands have not succeeded in calming extremist activities. During the school year 1969–70, there were 227 college disturbances having racial overtones. There were 530 such disturbances in secondary schools compared with only 320 during the previous school year.

8. *Foreign Influence in the Black Extremist Movement.* Although there is no hard evidence indicating that the black extremist movement is substantially controlled or directed by foreign elements, there is a marked potential for foreign-directed intelligence or

subversive activity among black extremist leaders and organizations. These groups are highly susceptible to exploitation by hostile foreign intelligence services.

Currently the most important foreign aspect of the black extremist movement is the availability of foreign asylum, especially with regard to black extremists subject to criminal prosecution in the United States. Some foreign countries, such as Cuba, provide a temporary safe haven for these individuals. Information has been received that passports and funds for travel have also been furnished by countries such as Cuba, North Korea, [still-classified section missing here] and Communist intelligence services do not, at present, play a major role in the black extremist movement; however, all such services have established contact with individual black militants. Thus, the penetration and manipulation of black extremist groups by these intelligence services remain distinct possibilities. Communist intelligence services are capable of using their personnel, facilities, and agent assets to work in the black extremist field. The Soviet and Cuban services have major capabilities available.

B. ASSESSMENT OF CURRENT INTELLIGENCE COLLECTION PROCEDURES

There are some definite gaps in the current overall intelligence penetration of the black extremist movement. For example, although there appears to be sufficient live informant coverage of the BPP [still-classified section missing here] additional penetration [still-classified section missing here] is needed. High echelon informant coverage could conceivably prevent violence, sabotage, or insurrection if such activity was planned by BPP leadership. Insufficient coverage of [still-classified section missing here] BPP is offset to some extent by technical coverage [still-classified section missing here]. Penetration of leadership levels has been hindered in part by current BPP policies which prevent rank-and-file members from advancing to leadership roles.

Improvement in coverage of BPP financial activities could be made, particularly with regard to sources of funds and records. Information received to date indicates that financial support for the BPP has been furnished by both foreign individuals and domestic sources. Thus, a deeper penetration and correlation of foreign and domestic information received is essential to a full determination of BPP finances. Coverage of BPP finances has been hampered by fact that BPP leaders handle financial matters personally.

In view of the increased amount of foreign travel and contacts by BPP leaders abroad, there is a clear-cut need for more complete coverage of foreign involvement in BPP activities.

1. *Other Black Extremist Organizations.* Informant coverage of the NOI is substantial, enabling its activities to be followed on a current basis. Coverage of militant black student groups and individuals is very limited because of the sensitive areas involved. An effective source of such coverage would be reliable, former members of the Armed Forces presently attending college. Live informant coverage, particularly with respect to the activities and plans of unaffiliated black militants, needs to be increased. More sources both in the United States and abroad in a position to determine the amount of foreign involvement in black extremist activities need to be developed. Maximum use of communication interceptions would materially increase the current capabilities of the intelligence community to develop highly important data regarding black extremist activities.

III. Intelligence Services of Communist Countries

A. Assessment of Current Internal Security Threat

The threat posed by the communist intelligence services must be assessed in two areas: (1) direct intervention in fomenting and/or influencing domestic unrest; (2) extensive espionage activities.

Taken in complete context, these services constitute a grave threat to the internal security of the United States because of their size, capabilities, widespread spheres of influence, and targeting of the United States as "enemy number one." The largest and most skilled of these services is the Soviet Committee for State Security (KGB) which has roughly 300,000 personnel of whom some 10,000 are engaged in foreign operations.

1. *Intervention in Domestic Unrest.* There have been no substantial indications that the communist intelligence services have actively fomented domestic unrest. Their capability cannot, however, be minimized and the likelihood of their initiating direct intervention would be in direct relationship to the deterioration of the political climate and/or imminence of hostilities. The ingredients for a first-rate capability are present, including both the personnel and the ingrained philosophy and know-how for using such tactics.

Communist intelligence has shown a real capability to foment disorder in a number of trouble spots. The dissidence and violence in the United States today present adversary intelligence services with opportunities unparalleled for forty years. While fostering disorder and rebellion through communist parties and fronts is a potent weapon in the communist arsenal, their past success has been evident in clandestine recruitment efforts on campuses during times of unrest. H. A. R. (Kim) Philby, Guy Burgess, and Donald Maclean were all students at Cambridge during the depression period of the 1930's and were in the vanguard of what was then the New Left. Their recruitment and cooperation with Soviet intelligence wreaked havoc on British intelligence, and also compromised U. S. security in those sectors where they had authorized access.

[still-classified section missing here] For instance, about 900 members of the Venceremos Brigade, a group of American youths, recently completed a round trip to Cuba. This travel was financed by the Cuban Government. While in Cuba, they were exhorted to actively participate in United States revolutionary activities upon their return to the United States. [still-classified section missing here]

A sabotage manual, prepared in [still-classified section missing here] turned up in the hands of individuals responsible for recent bombings [still-classified section missing here]. While the potential for widespread, well-organized incidents of violence generated and controlled by the Cuban intelligence service is considered minimal, isolated occurrences of this nature must be considered probable. The [still-classified section missing here] services appear to have assumed the passive roles of observers and reporters.

The communist intelligence services maintain contacts and exert influence among a variety of individuals and organizations through the exploitation of ideological, cultural, and ethnic ties. Most of these liaisons are maintained with some degree of openness with individuals associated with the Communist Party, USA, various of its front groups, other pro-Soviet organizations, nationality groups, and foreign-language newspapers. These contacts are exploited as sources for and propaganda outlets of communist intelligence services. Regarded individually, these efforts cannot be considered a major threat to our internal security; however, in total, they represent a sizable element of our population which can be influenced in varying degrees by communist intelligence service operations.

2. *Intelligence Operations.* Persistent and pervasive intelligence operations which have their inspiration and direction supplied by communist intelligence services represent a major threat to the internal security.

B. ASSESSMENT OF CURRENT INTELLIGENCE COLLECTION

1. *Scope and Effectiveness.* The scope of overall intelligence efforts is encompassed in the threefold goals of penetration, intelligence, and prosecution. Domestic implementation of these goals is delimited by agreement among United States intelligence agencies. Intelligence components of the United States military services are immediately concerned with protecting the integrity of their personnel and installations. [still-classified section missing here]

Methods used in these endeavors, employed in varying degrees by U.S. intelligence agencies dependent upon their specific tasks are: penetrations; defectors; double agent operations; physical, technical, and photographic surveillances; examination and analysis of overt publications; information supplied by friendly intelligence services; and COMINT.

2. *Gaps in Current Coverage* [still-classified section missing here]

IV. OTHER REVOLUTIONARY GROUPS

A. ASSESSMENT OF CURRENT INTERNAL SECURITY THREAT

1. *Communist Party.* The Communist Party continues as a distinct threat to the internal security because of its extremely close ties and total commitment to the Soviet Union. There are many thousands of people in the United States who adhere to a Marxist philosophy and agree with the basic objectives of the Communist Party although they do not identify themselves specifically with the organization. The Party receives most of its finances from the Soviet Union, adheres to Soviet policies explicitly, and provides a major outlet for Soviet propaganda. The Party will without question continue to implement whatever orders it receives from the Soviets in the future.

There is little likelihood that the Communist Party, USA, will instigate civil disorders or use terrorist tactics in the foreseeable future. Its strong suit is propaganda. Through its publications and propaganda it will continue its efforts to intensify civil disorders, and foment unrest in the Armed Forces, labor unions, and minority groups. The Party is on the periphery of the radical youth movement and is striving to strengthen its role in this movement and to attract new members through a recently formed youth organization, but it does not appear this group will achieve any substantial results for the Party in the future.

2. *Socialist Workers Party and Other Trotskyist Groups.* These organizations have an estimated membership of [still-classified section missing here] The major Trotskyist organization, the Socialist Workers Party, has attained an influential role in the antiwar movement through its youth affiliate, the Young Socialist Alliance, which dominates the Student Mobilization Committee to End the War in Vietnam and which has more than doubled its size on college campuses in the past year. Trotskyist groups have participated in major confrontations with authorities both on and off campuses and have consistently supported civil disorders. At this time they do not pose a major threat to instigate insurrection or to commit terrorist acts. The propaganda of these groups, while emphasizing student unrest, is also aimed at creating dissatisfaction in labor organizations and in the Armed Forces. The Trotskyist organizations maintain close relations with the Fourth International, a foreign-based worldwide Trotskyist movement.

4. *Puerto Rican Nationalist Extremist Groups.* The radical Puerto Rican independence movement has spawned approximately ten violently anti-American groups committed to Puerto Rican self-determination. Revolutionary violence is a major aim of the estimated [still-classified section missing here] members of these groups and if sufficiently strong, they would not hesitate to mount armed insurrection. Since July, 1967, some 130 bombings in Puerto Rico and in the New York City area have been attributed to these extremists. American-owned businesses have been the main targets, but there has been a recent upsurge of violence against U.S. defense facilities in Puerto Rico.

B. ASSESSMENT OF CURRENT INTELLIGENCE COVERAGE

1. *Scope and Effectiveness.* Coverage of the Communist [still-classified section missing here]

Coverage of theTrotskyist and [still-classified section missing here] groups [still-classified section missing here]

Current live informant coverage can furnish information on the general activities of these groups and it should serve to warn of policy changes in favor of insurrection or sabotage.

Informant penetration of the Puerto Rican independence groups provides information on the objectives of most of these organizations as well as the identities of their members. However, these sources have limited ability to provide advance information regarding violence committed by these groups or by individual members.

2. *Gaps in Current Coverage.* [still-classified section missing here]

Closer coverage at the policy-making levels of the Puerto Rican independence groups is needed to obtain more comprehensive information on persons involved in terrorist activities. The small memberships of many of these organizations is a major reason for the limited coverage.

3. *Possible Measures to Improve Intelligence Collection.* The selective use of electronic surveillances would materially enhance the intelligence coverage of the policy-making levels of these organizations. A particular benefit of electronic surveillance in the Puerto Rican field could be the development of information identifying persons involved in terrorist activities. Communications intelligence coverage and travel control measures could be improved to provide greater awareness of the travel and other activities of individuals of security interest. Through the establishment of additional informant coverage on college campuses, the involvement of these organizations in the radicalization of students could be assessed with increased accuracy.

PART TWO
RESTRAINTS ON INTELLIGENCE COLLECTION

The Committee noted that the President had made it clear that he desired full consideration be given to any regulations, policies, or procedures which tend to limit the effectiveness of domestic intelligence collection. The Committee further noted that the President wanted the pros and cons of such restraints clearly set forth so that the President will be able to decide whether or not a change in current policies, practices, or procedures should be made.

During meetings of the Committee, a variety of limitations and restraints were discussed. All of the agencies involved, Defense Intelligence Agency (DIA), the three military counterintelligence services, the Central Intelligence Agency (CIA), the National Security Agency (NSA), and the Federal Bureau of Investigation (FBI), participated in these considerations.

In the light of the directives furnished to the Committee by the White House, the subject matters hereinafter set forth were reviewed for the consideration and decision of the President.

I. Specific Operational Restraints

A. INTERPRETIVE RESTRAINT ON COMMUNICATIONS INTELLIGENCE

Preliminary Discussion

Nature of Restriction

Advantages of Maintaining Restriction

Advantages of Relaxing Restriction
[still-classified section missing here]

B. ELECTRONIC SURVEILLANCES AND PENETRATIONS

Preliminary Discussion

The limited number of electronic surveillances and penetrations substantially restricts the collection of valuable intelligence information of material importance to the entire intelligence community.

Nature of Restrictions

Electronic surveillances have been used on a selective basis. Restrictions, initiated at the highest levels of the Executive Branch, arose as a result of the condemnation of these techniques by civil rights groups, Congressional concern for invasion of privacy, and the possibility of their adverse effect on criminal prosecutions.

Advantages of Maintaining Restrictions

1. Disclosure and embarrassment to the using agency and/or the United States is always possible since such techniques often require that the services or advice of outside personnel be used in the process of installation.

2. [still-classified section missing here]

3. Certain elements of the press in the United States and abroad would undoubtedly seize upon disclosure of electronic coverage in an effort to discredit the United States.

4. The monitoring of electronic surveillances requires considerable manpower and, where foreign establishments are involved, the language resources of the agencies could be severely taxed.

Advantages of Relaxing Restrictions

1. The U. S. Government has an overriding obligation to use every available scientific means to detect and neutralize forces which pose a direct threat to the Nation.

2. Every major intelligence service in the world, including those of the communist bloc, use such techniques as an essential part of their operations, and it is believed the general public would support their use by the United States for the same purpose.

3. The President historically has had the authority to act in matters of national security. In addition, Title III of the Omnibus Crime Control and Safe Streets Act of 1968 provides a statutory basis.

4. Intelligence data from electronic coverage is not readily obtainable from other techniques or sources. Such data includes information which might assist in formulating foreign policy decisions, information leading to the identification of intelligence and/or espionage principals and could well include the first indication of intention to commit hostile action against the United States.

5. Acquisition of such material from COMINT without benefit of the assistance which electronic surveillance techniques can provide, if possible at all, would be extremely expensive. Therefore, this approach could result in considerable dollar savings compared to collection methods.

DECISION: Electronic Surveillances and Penetrations

_____ Present procedures should be changed to permit intensification of coverage of individuals and groups in the United States who pose a major threat to the internal security.

_____ Present procedures should be changed to permit intensification of coverage [still-classified section missing here].

_____ More information is needed.

NOTE: The FBI does not wish to change its present procedure of selective coverage on major internal security threats as it believes this coverage is adequate at this time. The FBI would not oppose other agencies seeking authority of the Attorney General for coverage required by them and thereafter instituting such coverage themselves.

C. MAIL COVERAGE

Preliminary Discussion

The use of mail covers can result in the collection of valuable information relating to contacts between U. S. nationals and foreign governments and intelligence services. CIA and the military investigative agencies have found this information particularly helpful in the past. Essentially, there are two types of mail coverage: routine coverage is legal, while the second—covert coverage—is not. Routine coverage involves recording information from the face of envelopes. It is available, legally, to any duly authorized Federal or state investigative agency submitting a written request to the Post Office Department and has been used frequently by the military intelligence services. Covert mail coverage, also known as "sophisticated mail coverage," or "flaps and seals," entails surreptitious screening and may include opening and examination of domestic or foreign mail. This technique is based on high-level cooperation of top echelon postal officials.

Nature of Restrictions

Covert coverage has been discontinued while routine coverage has been reduced primarily as an outgrowth of publicity arising from disclosure of routine mail coverage during legal proceedings and publicity afforded this matter in Congressional hearings involving accusations of governmental invasion of privacy.

Advantages of Maintaining Restrictions

Routine Coverage:

1. Although this coverage is legal, charges of invasion of privacy, no matter how ill-founded, are possible.
2. This coverage depends on the cooperation of rank-and-file postal employees and is, therefore, more susceptible to compromise.

Covert Coverage:

1. Coverage directed against diplomatic establishments, if disclosed, could have adverse diplomatic repercussions.
2. This coverage, not having sanction of law, runs the risk of any illicit act magnified by the involvement of a Government agency.
3. Information secured from such coverage could not be used for prosecutive purposes.

Advantages of Relaxing Restrictions

Routine Coverage:

1. Legal mail coverage is used daily by both local and many Federal authorities in criminal investigations. The use of this technique should be available to permit coverage of individuals and groups in the United States who pose a threat to the internal security.

Covert Coverage:

1. High-level postal authorities have, in the past, provided complete cooperation and have maintained full security of this program.
2. This technique involves negligible risk of compromise. Only high echelon postal authorities know of its existence, and personnel involved are highly trained, trustworthy, and under complete control of the intelligence agency.
3. This coverage has been extremely successful in producing hard-core and authentic intelligence which is not obtainable from any other source. An example is a case involving the interception of a letter to a [still-classified section missing here] establishment in [still-classified section missing here] The writer offered to sell information to the [still-classified section missing here] and enclosed a sample of information available to him. Analysis determined that the writer could have given [still-classified section missing here] information which might have been more damaging.

DECISION: Mail Coverage

_____ Present restrictions on both types of mail coverage should be continued.
_____ Restrictions on legal coverage should be removed.

_____ Present restrictions on covert coverage should be relaxed on selected targets of priority foreign intelligence and internal security interest.

_____ More information is needed.

NOTE: The FBI is opposed to implementing any covert mail coverage because it is clearly illegal and it is likely that, if done, information would leak out of the Post Office to the press and serious damage would be done to the intelligence community. The FBI has no objection to legal mail coverage providing it is done on a carefully controlled and selective basis in both criminal and security matters.

D. SURREPTITIOUS ENTRY

Preliminary Discussion [still-classified section missing here]

Nature of Restrictions

Use of surreptitious entry, also referred to as "anonymous sources" and "black bag jobs," has been virtually eliminated. [still-classified section missing here]

Advantages of Maintaining Restrictions

1. The activity involves illegal entry and trespass.
2. Information which is obtained through this technique could not be used for prosecutive purposes.
3. The public disclosure of this technique would result in widespread publicity and embarrassment. The news media would portray the incident as a flagrant violation of civil rights

Advantages of Relaxing Restrictions

1. Operations of this type are performed by a small number of carefully trained and selected personnel under strict supervision. The technique is implemented only after full security is assured. It has been used in the past with highly successful results and without adverse effects.
2. Benefits accruing from this technique in the past have been innumerable [still-classified section missing here].
3. In the past this technique, when used against subversives, has produced valuable intelligence material.

DECISION: Surreptitious Entry

_____ Present restrictions should be continued.

_____ Present restrictions should be modified to permit procurement

_____ Present restrictions should also be modified to permit selective use of this technique against other urgent and high priority internal security targets.

_____ More information is needed.

NOTE: The FBI is opposed to surreptitious entry [still-classified section missing here]

E. DEVELOPMENT OF CAMPUS SOURCES

Preliminary Discussion

Public disclosure of CIA links with the National Student Association and the subsequent issuance of the Katzenbach Report have contributed to a climate adverse to intelligence-type activity on college campuses and with student-related groups. It should be noted that the Katzenbach Report itself does not specifically restrain CIA from developing positive or counterintelligence sources to work on targets abroad.

Restrictions currently in force limit certain other elements of the intelligence community access to some of the most troublesome areas: campuses, college faculties, foreign and domestic youth groups, leftist journalists, and black militants. It is recognized that these are prime targets of communist intelligence services and that the opportunity for foreign communist exploitation increases in proportion to the weakness of a U.S. counter-intelligence effort.

Nature of Restrictions

The need for great circumspection in making contacts with students, faculty members, and employees of institutions of learning is widely recognized. However, the requirements of the intelligence community for increased information in this area is obvious from the concern of the White House at the absence of hard information about the plans and programs of campus and student-related militant organizations. At the present time no sources are developed among secondary school students and, with respect to colleges and universities, sources are developed only among individuals who have reached legal age, with few exceptions. This policy is designed to minimize the possibility of embarrassment and adverse publicity, including charges of infringement of academic freedom.

Advantages of Maintaining Restrictions

1. Students, faculty members, and others connected with educational institutions are frequently sensitive to and hostile towards any Government activity which smacks of infringement on academic freedom. They are prone to publicize inquiries by governmental agencies and the resulting publicity can often be misleading in portraying the Government's interest.

2. Students are frequently immature and unpredictable. They cannot be relied on to maintain confidences or to act with discretion to the same extent as adult sources.

Advantages of Relaxing Restrictions

1. To a substantial degree, militant New Left and antiwar groups in the United States are comprised of students, faculty members, and others connected with educational institutions. To a corresponding degree, effective coverage of these groups and activities depends upon development of knowledgeable sources in the categories named. In this connection, the military services have capabilities which could be of value to the FBI.

2. Much of the violence and disorders which have occurred on college campuses have been of a hastily planned nature. Unless sources are available within the student bodies, it is virtually impossible to develop advance information concerning such violence.

3. The development of sources among students affiliated with New Left elements affords a unique opportunity to cultivate informant prospects who may rise to positions of leadership in the revolutionary movement or otherwise become of great long-range value.

4. The extraordinary and unprecedented wave of destruction which has swept U. S. campuses in the past several months and which in some respects represents a virtual effort to overthrow our system provides a clear justification for the development of campus informants in the interest of national security.

5. Contacts with students will make it possible to obtain information about travel abroad by U. S. students and about attendance at international conferences.

DECISION: Development of Campus Sources

_____ Present restrictions on development of campus and student-related sources should be continued.

_____ Present restrictions should be relaxed to permit expanded coverage of violence-prone campus and student-related groups.

_____ CIA coverage of American students (and others) traveling abroad or living abroad should be increased.

_____ More information is needed.

NOTE: The FBI is opposed to removing any present controls and restrictions relating to the development of campus sources. To do so would severely jeopardize its investigations and could result in leaks to the press which would be damaging and which could result in charges that investigative agencies are interfering with academic freedom.

F. USE OF MILITARY UNDERCOVER AGENTS

Preliminary Discussion

The use of undercover agents by the military services to develop domestic intelligence is currently limited to penetration of organizations whose membership includes military personnel and whose activities pose a direct threat to the military establishment. For example, although the Navy has approximately 54 Naval ROTC units and numerous classified Government contract projects on various campuses across the country, the Naval Investigative Service conducts no covert collection on college campuses. The same is true of the other military services.

Nature of Restrictions

The use of undercover agents by the military investigative services to develop domestic intelligence among civilian targets is believed beyond the statutory intent of the Congress as expressed in Title 10, U. S. Code, and in current resource authorizations. The Delimitations Agreement (1949 agreement signed by the FBI, Army, Navy and Air Force which delimits responsibility for each agency with regard to investigations of espionage, counterespionage, subversion and sabotage) reflects the current missions of the FBI and the military services. Further, there is a lack of assets to undertake this mission unless essential service-related counterintelligence missions are reduced. There is also concern for morale and disciplinary reactions within the services should the existence of such covert operations become known.

Advantages of Maintaining Restrictions

1. If the utilization of military counterintelligence in this mission is contrary to the intent of the Congress, discovery of employment may result in unfavorable legislation and further reductions in appropriations.

2. Lacking direct statutory authority, the use of the military services in this mission could result in legal action directed against the Executive Branch.

3. The use of military personnel to report on civilian activities for the benefit of civilian agencies will reduce the ability of the military services to meet service-connected intelligence responsibilities.

4. If expansion of the mission of the military services with regard to college campuses is to provide coverage of any significance, it will require corollary increases in resources.

5. Prosecutions for violations of law discovered in the course of military penetration of civilian organizations must be tried in civil courts. The providing of military witnesses will require complicated interdepartmental coordination to a much greater extent than the present and will serve, in the long run, to reduce security.

6. Disclosure that military counterintelligence agencies have been furnishing information obtained through this technique to nonmilitary investigative agencies with respect to civilian activities would certainly result in considerable adverse publicity. The Army's recent experience with former military intelligence personnel confirms this estimate. Since obligated service officers, first enlistees and draftees are drawn from a peer group in which reaction is most unfavorable, morale and disciplinary problems can be anticipated.

Advantages of Relaxing Restrictions

1. Lifting these restrictions would expand the scope of domestic intelligence collection efforts by diverting additional manpower and resources for the collection of information on college campuses and in the vicinity of military installations.

2. The use of undercover agents by the military counterintelligence agencies could be limited to localized targets where the threat is great and the likelihood of exposure minimal. Moreover, controlled use of trusted personnel leaving the service to return to college could expand the collection capabilities at an acceptable risk.

3. The military services have a certain number of personnel pursuing special academic courses on campuses and universities. Such personnel, who in many instances have already been investigated for security clearance, would represent a valuable pool of potential sources for reporting on subversive activities of campus and student-related groups.

DECISION: Use of Military Undercover Agents

_____ Present restrictions should be retained.

_____ The counterintelligence mission of the military services should be expanded to include the active collection of intelligence concerning student-related dissident activities, with provisions for a close coordination with the FBI.

_____ No change should be made in the current mission of the military counterintelligence services; however, present restrictions should be relaxed to permit the use of trusted military personnel as FBI assets in the collection of intelligence regarding student-related dissident activities.

_____ More information is needed.

NOTE: The FBI is opposed to the use of any military undercover agents to develop domestic intelligence information because this would be in violation of the Delimitations Agreement. The military services, joined by the FBI, oppose any modification of the Delimitations Agreement which would extend their jurisdiction beyond matters of interest to the Department of Defense.

II. Budget and Manpower Restrictions

The capability of member agencies, NSA, CIA, DIA, FBI, and the military counterintelligence services, to collect intelligence data is limited by available resources, particularly in terms of budget and/or qualified manpower. For some agencies fiscal limitations or recent cutbacks have been acute. Budgetary requirements for some agencies, other than the FBI, are reviewed and passed upon by officials who, in some instances, may not be fully informed concerning intelligence requirements.

The military services noted that cuts in budget requirements for counterintelligence activities have the effect of severely hampering the ability of these services to accomplish missions relating to coverage of threats to the national security. Budgetary deficiencies have occurred at a time when investigative work loads are increasing significantly.

Manpower limitations constitute a major restriction on the FBI's capabilities in the investigation of subversive activities. The problem is further complicated by the fact that, even if substantial numbers of Agents could be recruited on a crash basis, the time required to conduct background investigations and to provide essential training would mean several months' delay in personnel being available for use against the rapidly escalating subversive situation.

In the event, as a result of this report, additional collection requirements should be levied on the agencies involved, it would be necessary to provide for essential funding. For example, [still-classified section missing here]

DECISION: Budget and Manpower Restrictions

_____ Each agency should submit a detailed estimate as to projected manpower needs and other costs in the event the various investigative restraints herein are lifted.

_____ Each agency must operate within its current budgetary or manpower limitations, irrespective of action required as result of this report.

_____ More information is needed.

PART THREE
EVALUATION OF INTERAGENCY COORDINATION

I. CURRENT PROCEDURES TO EFFECT COORDINATION

There is currently no operational body or mechanism specifically charged with the overall analysis, coordination, and continuing evaluation of practices and policies governing the acquisition and dissemination of intelligence, the pooling of resources, and the correlation of operational activities in the domestic field.

Although a substantial exchange of intelligence and research material between certain of the interested agencies already exists, much remains to be done in the following areas: (1) the preparation of coordinated intelligence estimates in a format useful for policy formulation; (2) the coordination of intelligence collection resources of the member agencies and the establishment of clear-cut priorities for the various agencies; and (3) the coordination of the operational activities of member agencies in developing the required intelligence.

II. SUGGESTED MEASURES TO IMPROVE THE COORDINATION OF DOMESTIC INTELLIGENCE COLLECTION

It is believed that an interagency group on domestic intelligence should be established to effect coordination between the various member agencies. This group would define the specific requirements of the various agencies, provide regular evaluations of domestic intelligence, develop recommendations relative to policies governing operations in the field of domestic intelligence, and prepare periodic domestic intelligence estimates which would incorporate the results of the combined efforts of the entire intelligence community.

Membership in this group should consist of appropriate representatives named by the Directors of the Federal Bureau of Investigation, the Central Intelligence Agency, the National Security Agency, the Defense Intelligence Agency, and the counterintelligence agencies of the Departments of the Army, Navy, and Air Force. In addition, an appropriate representative of the White House would have membership. The committee would report periodically to the White House, and a White House staff representative would coordinate intelligence originating with this committee in the same manner as Dr. Henry Kissinger, Assistant to the President, coordinates foreign intelligence on behalf of the President. The chairman would be appointed by the President.

This interagency group would have authority to determine appropriate staff requirements and to implement these requirements, subject to the approval of the President, in order to meet the responsibilities and objectives described above.

DECISION: Permanent Interagency Group

_____ An ad hoc group consisting of the FBI, CIA, NSA, DIA, and the military counterintelligence agencies should be appointed and should serve as long as the President deems necessary, to provide evaluations of domestic intelligence, prepare periodic domestic intelligence estimates, and carry out the other objectives indicated above. The ad hoc group should be tasked to develop a permanent organization to carry out the objectives of this report.

_____ A permanent committee consisting of the FBI, CIA, NSA, DIA, and the military counterintelligence agencies should be appointed to provide evaluations of domestic intelligence, prepare periodic domestic intelligence estimates, and carry out the other objectives indicated above.

_____ No further action required.

_____ More information is needed.

NOTE: The FBI is opposed to the creation of a permanent committee for the purpose of providing evaluations of domestic intelligence, however, the FBI would approve of preparing periodic domestic intelligence estimates.

THE SENATE SELECT COMMITTEE ON INTELLIGENCE REPORTS ON THE ALDRICH AMES COUNTERINTELLIGENCE FAILURE, 1994

CONCLUSIONS AND RECOMMENDATIONS

Over the months since his arrest, it has become clear that Aldrich Hazen Ames caused more damage to the national security of the United States than any spy in the history of the CIA. Ten Soviet sources of the CIA and the FBI were executed as a result of Ames' treachery and others were imprisoned. Ames has admitted to compromising over 100 intelligence operations of the CIA, FBI, military departments, and allied governments, and there are likely others he does not specifically recall. Literally thousands of classified documents—on subjects ranging from U.S. defense capabilities to international narcotics trafficking—were turned over by Ames to his KGB handlers. Although the formal assessment of the damage cased by Ames has yet to be completed, his betrayal stands as the most egregious in American history.

Obviously, something went terribly wrong. For a CIA officer to carry on espionage activities without detection for almost nine years indicates, on its face, a failure of the system. As the Committee began to look into this failure, we found a bureaucracy which was excessively tolerant of serious personal and professional misconduct among its employees, where security was lax and ineffective. And we found a system and a culture unwilling and unable—particularly in the early years of Ames' betrayal—to face, assess, and investigate the catastrophic blow Ames had dealt to the core of its operations.

The system which permitted Ames' prolonged betrayal must be changed. The country cannot afford such calamities in the future, and the CIA cannot afford further erosion of the public's confidence. In the wake of the Cold War, the CIA still has an important mission to

Source: Excerpted from "An Assessment of the Aldrich H. Ames Espionage Case and Its Implications for U.S. Intelligence," *Staff Report,* Select Committee on Intelligence, U.S. Senate, 103d Cong., 2d. Sess. (November 1, 1994), pp. 53–72.

perform—a mission that is vital to the national security of the United States. Like all government agencies, the CIA ultimately depends upon the support of the American people and the Congress to carry out its unique functions and maintain its unique capabilities. To restore that confidence, the CIA must deal effectively with the serious deficiencies high-lighted by the Ames case.

In the discussion which follows, the Committee sets forth where we believe the system failed and what we believe should be done to correct it. In its action on the Intelligence Authorization Act for Fiscal Year 1995 (P.L. 103–359), the Committee undertook legis-lative remedies for many of these shortcomings by requiring coordination of counter-intelligence matters with the FBI and by providing authorized investigative agencies with new authority to obtain access to financial information and travel records of federal em-ployees who have access to classified information. While these legislative initiatives are an important beginning, far more is needed to correct the deficiencies evident in the Ames case than legislation alone can achieve.

In the end, regardless of what the Committee may recommend or what Congress may enact, fundamental change will come only if the Director of Central Intelligence, super-visors at all levels, and the employees of the CIA bring it about. The Committee intends to monitor the Agency's progress in this regard, but the leadership must come from within.

The Committee undertook its inquiry not for the purpose of assessing individual blame—which is the exclusive responsibility of the Executive branch—but rather to learn what had gone wrong and to evaluate the institutional lessons to be learned from the Ames case. Nevertheless, the Committee believes that the recent actions taken by the Director of Central Intelligence, R. James Woolsey, against past and current CIA officials implicated in the Ames case warrant comment.

On March 10 of this year, Director Woolsey appeared before the Committee in closed session to outline his interim responses to the Ames case. One area for reform which was cited by the Director was "management accountability." According to the Director: "[T]o my mind, this is very much at the heart of the entire matter." The Committee strongly shares this view.

Despite the CIA Inspector General's recommendation that 23 current and former CIA officials be held accountable for the Agency's failure to prevent and detect Ames espionage activities, Director Woolsey chose only to issue letters of reprimand to 11 individuals—7 retired and 4 current Agency employees. None of the individuals cited by the Inspector General was fired, demoted, suspended or even reassigned as a result of this case. In response to what was arguably the greatest managerial breakdown in the CIA's history, the disciplinary actions taken by the Director do not, in the collective experience and judgment of the Committee, constitute adequate "management accountability."

All Committee Members believe that the Director's disciplinary actions in this case are seriously inadequate and disproportionate to the magnitude of the problems identified in the Inspector General's report. It is clear, given the immense national security interests at stake, that there was "gross negligence"—both individually and institutionally—in creating and perpetuating the environment in which Ames was able to carry out his espionage activities for nine years without detection.

The Committee is concerned about the message that Director Woolsey's mild dis-ciplinary actions will send to the overwhelming majority of CIA employees who are dedi-cated, conscientious, patriotic, and hard-working professionals, many of whom are exposed daily to risk and hardship. For the current employees who were faulted by the Inspector

General for their role in the Ames case to remain in their grades and positions falls far short of the level of accountability expected by the Committee. Indeed, in the wake of the Director's decision, many professionals within the Intelligence Community have contacted the Committee to register the same sentiment.

As this report documents, the failures evident in the Ames case were numerous and egregious. While it might be argued that the majority of individuals cited by the Inspector General were guilty of acts of omission rather than commission, the seriousness of these omissions cannot be overstated. The failures of the individuals cited by the Inspector General led to the loss of virtually all of CIA's intelligence assets targeted against the Soviet Union at the height of the Cold War. Ten of these agents were executed. The inability of the CIA to get to the bottom of these losses in a timely way was itself a significant management failure.

If there is not a higher standard of accountability established by DCIs, then a repeat of the Ames tragedy becomes all the more likely. Management accountability within the Intelligence Community should be no less than the highest levels found elsewhere in the Executive branch. Director Woolsey's actions do not meet this standard.

Having noted in strong terms the magnitude of CIA's failures, the Committee would be remiss not to point out what went right. A traitor, responsible for heinous acts of espionage, was identified and convicted. He has been imprisoned for life. In the end, this was accomplished by the work of a small group of CIA and FBI personnel who took part in what became a long and arduous inquiry—for some, lasting almost nine years. At least one member of this group appears to have pushed from the very beginning to get to the bottom of the 1985 compromises. It was his impetus that eventually put the investigation back on track in 1991. Over time, the scope and pace of the investigation had taken many twists and turns, some caused by the KGB and some by internal factors beyond the control of the investigators themselves. The commentary which follows is not intended to diminish in any way what was ultimately accomplished by this dedicated group of investigators and analysts.

Finally, the Committee notes that its recommendations are based upon the situation that pertained through early 1994. Director Woolsey has promulgated some new policies since then and has announced his intention to institute still others. While the Committee believes in general that stronger measures are needed, it is too early to pass judgment on the Director's recent actions.

THE FAILURE TO "FIX" PAST COUNTERINTELLIGENCE PROBLEMS

The counterintelligence function at the CIA is weak and inherently flawed. Despite repeated internal and external reports which have recognized a longstanding cultural problem with the counterintelligence function, CIA managers have, judging from the Ames case, failed to fix it.

In particular, the Committee was struck by the number of internal and external studies undertaken after 1985—which became known as the "Year of the Spy" following the exposure of spies John Walker, Ronald Pelton, Edward Lee Howard, and Jonathan Pollard—which pointed out the systemic and deeply-rooted problems in the CIA's conduct of counterintelligence.

As summarized by the recent report of the CIA Inspector General, these internal and external reports over the years focused on common themes:

That a counterintelligence career was held in low esteem at the CIA and did not attract high caliber officers. This was, in part, because officers gained promotions by agent recruitments, not by analyzing problems in recruitment operations;

That there was an ambiguous division of responsibility for counterintelligence among CIA offices;

That counterintelligence information was not being shared properly among CIA components; and

That CIA was reluctant to share counterintelligence information fully and in a timely manner with the FBI. (IG Report, pp. 16–22)

The poor state of counterintelligence at the CIA in the mid-1980s can be explained in part by the reaction to the so-called "Angleton era." James Angleton had been the head of the Counterintelligence Staff of the CIA from 1954 until 1974 (when he was involuntarily retired by DCI William Colby). He became convinced that the KGB had penetrated the CIA. Accordingly, Angleton was suspicious of virtually every Soviet agent who was recruited by the CIA and suspicious of every CIA officer responsible for such recruitment. On occasion, his suspicions led to CIA officers being fired without adequate justification.

While several of the officers who had been unjustly fired were later compensated, the counterintelligence function was effectively undermined by the negative reaction to Angleton's relentless pursuit of spies, particularly within the Soviet-East European (SE) Division of the Directorate of Operations, which had the principal responsibility for recruiting Soviet agents for the CIA.

In addition, there appears to have been an excessive focus within the Directorate on the recruitment of intelligence sources to the exclusion of counterintelligence concerns. Few officers wanted to go into counterintelligence because promotions and recognition came from successful recruitments, not from questioning, or identifying problems with, ongoing operations. Further, there was an image of a "corporate elite" constructed among these officers which led them to dismiss too readily the possibility of a spy among them.

By all accounts, these attitudes were prevalent within the Directorate of Operations at the time Ames sabotaged the Agency's Soviet operations in the summer of 1985, and they greatly contributed to management's failure to focus upon the CIA employees who had had access to the compromised cases (as explained in detail below).

The CIA made some efforts to address these shortcomings after "the Year of the Spy," In 1988, the head of the counterintelligence staff was made an "Associate Deputy Director" in the Directorate of Operations, and was double-hatted as the head of a new Counterintelligence Center (CIC). The CIA and FBI also signed a new Memorandum of Understanding (MOU) in 1988, which provided, at least on paper, for improved sharing of information in counterintelligence cases.

But these new bureaucratic "trappings" for the counterintelligence function did not overcome the fundamental problems which continued to be cited in reports issued in the 1990s. Despite the formation of a "lead office" for counterintelligence and the 1988 MOU with the FBI, the sharing of counterintelligence information between CIA components and with the FBI continued to be a serious problem, as was clearly evident in the Ames case.

In conclusion, the Committee finds that, despite repeated internal and external reports which recognized a longstanding cultural problem in the counterintelligence function, the CIA failed to implement adequate solutions. Indeed, the Committee believes the fundamental problems persist.

Recommendation No. 1: The Director of Central Intelligence should revise the CIA's strategy for carrying out the counterintelligence function. The Director should institute measures to improve the effectiveness of counterintelligence to include (a) establishing as a requirement for promotion among officers of the Directorate of Operations, service in a counterintelligence or counterintelligence-related position during their careers; (2) establishing incentives for service in a counterintelligence position; (3) instituting effective and comprehensive counterintelligence training for all officers of the Directorate of Operations and for appropriate officers assigned elsewhere in the CIA; and (4) ensuring adequate access to ongoing foreign intelligence operations by those charged with the counterintelligence function. The Committee will make this a "special interest area" for purposes of oversight until it is satisfied the weaknesses noted above have been adequately addressed.

THE FAILURE TO DEAL WITH SUITABILITY PROBLEMS

As the Ames case all too clearly demonstrates, the CIA Directorate of Operations is too willing to dismiss, deny, or ignore suitability problems demonstrated by its officers.

From the outset of his career at the CIA, Ames demonstrated serious suitability problems which, over the years, should have led his supervisors to reassess his continued employment. These problems included drunkenness, disregard for security regulations, and sloppiness towards administrative requirements. In the years immediately before he began to commit espionage and during the rest of his career, his supervisors were aware of his personal and professional deficiencies, but did not make his problems part of his official record, nor act effectively to correct them. Despite his recognized unsuitability, there is little evidence that his assignments, activities, or access to sensitive information were in any way limited as a result.

Prior to Ames's assignment to the counterintelligence staff of the SE Division in 1983, his supervisor in Mexico City sent a message to CIA headquarters recommending that Ames be counseled for alcohol abuse when he returned. While Ames's supervisor recognized a chronic problem, the message to headquarters apparently stemmed from an incident which occurred at an official reception at the U.S. Embassy where Ames was drunk and became involved in a loud argument with a Cuban official. On another occasion, Ames was involved in a traffic accident in Mexico City and was so drunk he could not answer police question nor recognize the U.S. Embassy officer sent to help him. In fact, based upon recent interviews with his colleagues, Ames was notorious for long, alcoholic lunches, often slurring his speech when he returned to the office. None of this behavior prompted any serious effort to correct the problem while Ames was overseas, or when he later returned to CIA headquarters.

In April 1983, when CIA headquarters asked Ames's supervisors in Mexico City whether Ames qualified for a staff position in another Latin American country, they recommended against it, citing his alcohol problem, his failure to do financial accountings, and his generally poor performance. Nevertheless, six months later, when a former supervisor of Ames requested him to fill a position in the SE Division at headquarters—the most sensitive element of the Directorate of Operations—there is no indication that Ames' alcohol problem or poor performance were ever noted. Indeed, Ames was placed in a position which provided him access to the identities of virtually all of the Soviet intelligence officers by the CIA without his new supervisors being aware of the problems he had had in Mexico City.

The alcohol abuse counseling that Ames ultimately did receive upon his return to headquarters amounted to one conversation with a counselor, who, according to Ames, told him that his case was not a serious one when compared to many others in the Directorate of Operations.

In 1983, during the assignment in Mexico City, Ames also began an extra-marital relationship with a Colombian national, Rosario Casas Dupuy (hereinafter "Rosario"), herself a recruited asset of the CIA. Over time, the seriousness of their relationship became apparent to several of Ames's colleagues, but this never led to any action by Ames's supervisors, despite the fact that CIA regulations prohibit sexual relationships with re-cruited assets and require that reports of "close and continuing" relationships with foreign nationals be submitted by employees. Despite the security implications of this relationship, the violation of Agency regulations was ignored.

In fact, Ames did not file an official report concerning his relationship with Rosario until April 1984, four months after she came to the United States to live with him. Indeed, it appears that until their marriage in August 1985, Ames (still married to his first wife) and Rosario continued to live together, without any perceptible concern being registered by the CIA. While the counterintelligence staff recommended in February 1985, that in view of the anticipated marriage, Ames, be moved to a less sensitive position, nothing changed. Ames continued in the same position.

While his alcohol problem abated during this assignment to the SE Division—at least as a matter of attracting official attention—it resurfaced during his assignment in Rome. He was known among colleagues for his long, alcoholic lunches, for sleeping at his desk, for often slurred speech, and generally as a marginal performer. On one occasion, after an Embassy reception, he was so drunk that he passed out on a street and awakened in a hospital. While his supervisor was unhappy, this incident did not become part of Ames' record, nor does it appear that this episode led to counseling or any serious reevaluation of Ames' fitness for continued service. Indeed, the same supervisor extended Ames' tour in Rome for a third year.

Over his career, Ames repeatedly demonstrated carelessness and disdain for security requirements. In 1975, while on his way to meet a CIA source in New York, Ames left a briefcase of classified materials identifying the source on a subway train. Although the briefcase was ultimately recovered, it might well have compromised the source's rela-tionship with the CIA. In the fall of 1984, he brought Rosario to CIA housing where CIA undercover officers were staying, in violation of security regulations. In August 1985, he took her to the safe house where the Soviet defector Yurchenko was being debriefed, again in violation of security procedures. In Rome, he was known to prepare classified reports at home. During his assignments at CIA headquarters between 1989 and 1994, he was occasionally found in other CIA offices where he had no reason to be, and with materials he had no reason to have.

He was equally negligent throughout his career in complying with the administrative requirements imposed on officers of the Directorate of Operations, such as submitting financial accountings for the cases he was handling.

Despite these and other incidents, Ames never received a single official reprimand during his 31-year career at the CIA. Indeed, most of the incidents and shortcomings which have come to light since Ames was arrested were never made a matter of official record. Once on board, his fitness to serve in the Directorate of Operations was never reevaluated.

The Committee appreciates that intelligence officers of the Directorate of Operations are often placed in jobs and situations with stresses and strains that far exceed those of the average government employee. But these positions also demand self-control and personal discipline. Particularly in overseas assignments, it may be impossible to separate an intelligence officer's private life from his or her public, official one. A single misstep can prove his undoing or that of other officers.

It is the Committee's perception, which the Ames case confirms, that the Directorate of Operations has been far too willing to dismiss or ignore flagrant examples of personal misconduct among its officers. Excessive drinking and extra-marital relationships with sources have all too often been seen as part of the job, rather than as indicators of problems. Security concerns are too often dismissed as the bureaucratic whining of small-minded administrators. All too often an officer who has been through training, gone through the polygraph examination, and had an overseas assignment, is accepted as a "member of the club," whose fitness for assignments, promotions, and continued service becomes immune from challenge.

Director Woolsey, in a recent speech, said that the "culture" of the directorate must be changed. The Committee shares that view. Such change will not come solely by changing regulations or personnel. It will come only when supervisors at every level of the directorate take seriously their responsibilities as managers. Personal misconduct should be documented. Officers who do not meet acceptable standards of personal behavior should not be assigned to personal behavior should not be assigned to sensitive positions nor qualify for supervisory positions. Personal shortcomings should be factored into consideration of promotions and bonus awards. While officers with personal problems should be given an opportunity, as well as appropriate assistance, to rehabilitate themselves, failing that, their employment with the directorate, if not with the Agency itself, should be terminated.

Recommendation No. 2: The Director of Central Intelligence should ensure that where evidence of suitability problems comes to the attention of supervisors, it is made a matter of official record and factored into the consideration of assignments, promotions, and bonus awards; that efforts are made to counsel and provide assistance to the employee where indicated, and, if the problem persists over time, the employment of the individual is terminated. The Committee will make this a "special interest area" for purposes of oversight until it is satisfied these policies have been instituted and are being observed within the Directorate of Operations.

Recommendation No. 3: The Director of Central Intelligence should, in particular, take prompt and effective action to deal with what appears to be a widespread problem of alcohol abuse by ensuring that CIA employees experiencing such problems are identified and are put into effective counseling and/or treatment. During this period, these employees should be suspended from their duties until they have demonstrated to a qualified professional their fitness to return to service. Should their problems continue, their employment should be terminated.

Recommendation No. 4: The Director of Central Intelligence should institute, consistent with existing legal authority, an "up or out" policy for employees of the CIA, similar to that of the Foreign Service, without waiting for the report required by section 305 of the Intelligence Authorization Act for Fiscal Year 1995, pertaining to the Intelligence Community as a whole. Chronically poor performance should be grounds for dismissal from the Agency. If the Director decides not to institute such a policy and does not provide a persuasive rationale to the Committee for his decision, the Congress should enact legislation requiring such a policy during the next Congress.

Recommendation No. 5: The Director of Central Intelligence should review and revise the performance appraisal reporting system of the CIA, to include a review of the factors upon which employees are rated and the grading system which now exists, to institute a system which reflects more accurately job performance. Where supervisors are concerned, their rating should include an assessment of how well they have supervised the performance and development of their subordinates.

THE FAILURE TO COORDINATE EMPLOYEES' OPERATIONAL ACTIVITIES

The Ames case providers a striking example of CIA supervisors failing to critically evaluate the contacts of an operations officer—with known personal shortcomings and in an extremely sensitive position—with Soviet officials in 1984 and 1985. Further, the fact that Ames virtually ceased submitting reports of such contacts, in violation of standard Agency procedures, never became known to his SE Division supervisors or made part of his official record.

In 1984, while occupying a position within the SE Division which gave him access to the identities of Soviet agents working with the CIA and FBI, Ames, with the approval of his immediate supervisor, began making contacts with Soviet Embassy officials in Washington, D.C. According to testimony received by the Committee, it was not infrequent that Directorate of Operations Officers at CIA headquarters were asked to "help out" other CIA elements that had responsibility for establishing relationships and maintaining contacts with foreign individuals located in the Washington area.

The Committee has been advised that Ames's senior supervisors in the SE Division were unaware that he was having these meetings and would have disallowed them had they known.

In any event, to permit a person in Ames's position, and someone with the personal and professional shortcomings already noted, to meet alone with Soviet Embassy officials substantially increased the risk of the disaster that eventually occurred. It provided Ames with an opportunity that he otherwise may not have had, or may have had difficulty in contriving on his own.

After June 1985, after his espionage activities had begun, Ames repeatedly failed to submit reports of his contacts with Soviet officials. While his failure prompted complaints from the FBI, the CIA element that Ames was supporting failed to bring this to the attention of his supervisors in the SE Division, nor was it reflected in his official record. Again, had Ames' SE Division supervisors been aware of his failure to file these reports, it may have alerted them to a possible problem. Since the advancement of Directorate of Operations officers depends upon their official reporting, the failure to file such reports should have suggested something was amiss.

A similar failure occurred during his assignment in Rome. While his supervisor was aware that he was meeting along with Soviet officials in Rome (one of whom was Ames' KGB contact), Ames explained his failure to file reports of such meetings on the basis that he had obtained little worthwhile information. This apparently was enough to satisfy the supervisor.

Recommendation No. 6: The Director of Central Intelligence should revise the policies and procedures governing the operational activities of CIA officers to ensure that these activities are better supervised, controlled, coordinated, and documented.

THE FAILURE TO APPLY A STRUCTURED METHODOLOGY TO THE INVESTIGATION OF INTELLIGENCE COMPROMISES

The most puzzling deficiency in the Ames case was the failure, in the wake of the 1985–86 compromises, to aggressively investigate the possibility that CIA had been penetrated by a KGB spy.

Certainly by the fall of 1986, the CIA was aware that it had suffered a disaster of unprecedented proportions which was not explained by the defection of Edward Lee Howard. Within a matter of months, virtually its entire stable of Soviet agents had been imprisoned or executed. In the days of the Cold War, Soviet operations represented the Agency's principal *raison d'etre*. There were no operations which had greater importance to its mission. The CIA was left virtually to start from scratch, uncertain whether new operations would meet the same fate as its old ones.

To be sure, these compromises involved extremely sensitive agents. There was a need for discretion in terms of how the matter was handled. But this does not explain or excuse the Agency's tentative, tepid response. Initially, some CIA officers could not believe that the KGB would "roll up" all of CIA's sources at once if the KGB had a source in the CIA who was still in place. Taking some comfort that new operations appeared to be surviving, some believed the problem had gone away. But this in no way explains the seeming lack of urgency to get to the bottom of what had gone so drastically wrong.

The obvious place to begin would have been with the CIA employees who had had access to the information which had been compromised. At least one official in the SE Division made a strong plea to his supervisors at the time that they needed to "investigate it, not study it." But this did not happen. The CIA task force created in October 1986, undertook what was largely an analytical review of the compromised cases. The task force did oversee an Office of Security review of personnel who had served in Moscow, but no broader examination was made of all CIA officers who had had access to the compromised cases. No systematic effort was made to identify and investigate problem employees and their activities, as was eventually done in 1991–92.

Later, the CIA came to suspect that the KGB was running ploys against them, purposely suggesting reasons for the compromises other than a penetration of the CIA itself. Even then, however, any sense of urgency was lacking. CIA analysts waited for things to happen, for more information to surface. They continued to analyze and conjecture. There was no clear sense of purpose, no clear methodology, and no clear sense of what was required to get to the bottom of the compromises.

In a related counterintelligence investigation of a report suggesting that the KGB may have recruited a source in a particular office in the CIA, a CIA investigator conducted a systematic investigation of over 90 employees who were assigned to that office. The inquiry took more than year. But investigators did not conduct the same type of inquiry of the CIA employees who had had access to the information that was actually compromised in 1985 until 1991–1992.

The FBI was officially brought into the case in October 1986, when the CIA learned that two sources recruited by the FBI had been compromised. But the two agencies worked their investigations separately, despite the likelihood that the compromises were caused by the same source (whether it be human or technical).

While the FBI and CIA task forces regularly exchanged information on the compromises and on the progress of their respective analyses, they never performed a systematic assessment, together, of the CIA employees who had had access to the compromised information, until mid-1991.

Why CIA management during the 1986–1991 period did not attach more importance or urgency to getting to the bottom of the 1985 compromises is incomprehensible to the Committee. While CIA Director William Casey and Deputy Director for Operations (DDO) Clair George, who were in office at the time the compromises occurred, reportedly regarded them as "a huge problem," the Agency's response was to create a 4-person team to analyze the problem. No one believed there was a basis for bringing in investigators from the FBI at this juncture, apparently because CIA was unable to pin responsibility on a particular CIA employee.

While Casey and George became deeply enmeshed in the Iran-contra scandal in the fall of 1986 and spring of 1987, this circumstance does not explain, in the view of the Committee, why a problem so close to the heart of the CIA's mission was not given more attention by senior management. Indeed, once Casey and George departed the scene, it does not appear that their successors—either as DCI or as DDO—gave the inquiry any particular emphasis or priority. DCI William Webster, his deputy Robert M. Gates, and the new DDO Richard Stolz were briefed on the compromises in 1988, but did not delve deeply into either the nature of the problem (which was now several years old) or what the Agency was doing to resolve it.

Due to the extraordinary sensitivity of this inquiry, there was only one junior investigator from the Office of Security assigned to the case from 1985 until 1991. He was responsible for investigating all counterintelligence leads and reports coming in which involved CIA employees. After he began to develop information regarding Ames' unexplained affluence in the fall of 1989, he was diverted from this investigation for a nine-month period, first for training and then to handle other leads. There was no one else assigned to pick up the Ames leads. Nor was consideration given to having the FBI pick up the leads, despite the fact that the information now focused upon a particular CIA employee within the United States.

While the Committee believes that the investigator in question made a good faith effort to work the leads he was given, he was essentially self-trained and, because of the compartmented nature of the investigation, was given very little help and guidance. Overworked and overloaded, he did not use all of the investigative techniques he might have utilized to get at Ames' financial situation. Indeed, the statutory authority invoked by the CIA in 1992 to obtain access to Ames' bank records was available to the Agency in 1989. Had this authority been utilized at the time information was received concerning Ames's unexplained affluence, in might well have led to his detection at a much earlier stage. The investigator also apparently made no effort to develop information regarding Ames's unexplained affluence during his assignment in Rome. Efforts to verify the financial condition of Ames's in-laws in Bogota were shoddy and ineffective, producing inaccurate information which supported rather than exposed Ames's contrived explanation.

The Committee does not think it fair to hold the investigator assigned to the case solely responsible for these failures. CIA managers simply failed to assign enough investigators to such an important task and failed to provide them with sufficient legal and administrative support to ensure that all appropriate avenues would be explored and all appropriate investigative authorities utilized. Since the professional investigative expertise of the FBI was effectively spurned during this period, insufficient resources and expertise were brought to bear on the case.

The Committee believes that those in charge of the CIA during the 1986–1991 period—Director William Casey, Acting Director and later Deputy Director Robert Gates, Director William Webster, and Deputy Director and later Acting Director Richard Kerr— must ultimately bear the responsibility for the lack of an adequate investigative response to the 1985 compromises. Whatever they may have personally understood the situation to be, they were in charge. It was their responsibility to find out what was being done to resolve the 1985 compromises. Based upon the information available to the Committee, they failed to do so.

Their failure is especially disheartening when one realizes that the information developed in August 1992, which finally focused the investigation on Ames—correlating his bank deposits in 1985 and 1986 with his meetings with Soviet officials—was available to investigators since 1986. Unfortunately, no one asked for it, even when alerted to Ames's unexplained affluence in October 1989.

Although the 1985–86 compromises represented a unique situation for the CIA, the Ames case demonstrates the lack of a clear *modus operandi* for dealing with situations where intelligence sources are known to have been compromised.

Recommendation No. 7: The Director of Central Intelligence should establish procedures for dealing with intelligence compromises. At a minimum, these procedures should entail a systematic analysis of all employees with access to the relevant information and, if suspects are identified, provide an investigative methodology to determine whether there is evidence of unexplained affluence, unreported travel, unreported contacts, or other indicators of possible espionage. This type of systematic analysis should begin when a known compromise occurs, not after CIA has eliminated the possibility of a technical penetration, or after CIA has narrowed the range of possible suspects to one or two employees. Analysis and investigation should be undertaken on the basis of access and opportunity, and should not be delayed waiting for evidence on culpability.

Recommendation No. 8: Pursuant to section 811 of the Intelligence Authorization Act for Fiscal Year 1995, the FBI should be notified immediately of any case where it is learned that an intelligence source has been compromised to a foreign government, regardless of whether the CIA believes at the time that there is a basis for an FBI counterintelligence or criminal investigation of a particular employee or employees. The CIA should also coordinate with the FBI subsequent investigative actions involving employees potentially involved in the case in order not to prejudice later criminal or counterintelligence activities of the FBI and in order to benefit from the investigative assistance and expertise of the FBI.

Recommendation No. 9: The Director of Central Intelligence should require that all employees assigned as counterintelligence investigators have appropriate training, experience, and supervision which ensures, at a minimum, such investigators will be familiar with, and know how to utilize, the investigative authorities available to the CIA and the FBI.

Recommendation No. 10: CIA management must ensure that adequate analytical and investigative resources are assigned to counterintelligence cases, and that other kinds of staff assistance (e.g., legal support, administrative support) are made available. In turn, those involved in these cases must ensure that their needs are communicated to their supervisors. The Inspector General of the CIA should periodically assess the counter-intelligence cases of the CIA to ensure that adequate resources are being afforded to particular cases.

Recommendation No. 11: The status of significant counterintelligence investigations must be regularly briefed to senior Agency officials, including the Director of Central Intelligence. Such briefings should include an explanation of the resources and expertise being brought to bear upon a particular case.

THE FAILURE TO EXPEDITE THE INQUIRY AFTER 1991

The period after the CIA and FBI decided to join forces in June 1991—compared with the period between 1985 and 1991—was relatively intense and focused. For the first time, investigators conducted a systematic review of the CIA employees who had had access to the compromised information, and there was an intensive, productive effort to link Ames and other priority suspects to the compromises.

Yet even during this phase, the investigation took an inordinate amount of time and was plagued by past inefficiencies. The joint investigative unit still had only four people (two from each agency); and there was still a lone CIA investigator working with them. While members of the joint investigative unit did obtain support from the CIA Office of Security and the FBI Washington Metropolitan Field Office, they were still but a few people carrying an extraordinarily demanding workload.

In August 1991, the joint investigative unit developed a list of 29 CIA employees for priority scrutiny. Ames was at the top of the list.

Yet the first letters to go out to financial institutions requesting access to Ames's financial records did not go out until June 1992, almost 10 months later.

In August 1992, when investigators correlated the records of Ames's bank deposits with what was known about Ames's 1985 meetings at the Soviet Embassy, the joint investigative unit suspected they had their man. When they learned in October of Ames's Swiss bank accounts, their suspicions were confirmed.

But according to the Inspector General's report, this crucial information was not presented to FBI headquarters until January 1993. It was explained to the Committee that the joint investigative unit was looking at possible suspects in addition to Ames. But this still does not explain why significant information pertaining to Ames was not passed contemporaneously to the FBI, particularly given the presence of two FBI agents on the joint investigative unit.

On the basis of the work of the joint investigative unit—which culminated in the March 1993 Skylight/playactor report—the FBI assembled an investigative team and tasked the team members to acquaint themselves with the facts. The FBI began an intensive investigation of Ames shortly thereafter. The Committee was advised in the course of its investigation that FBI headquarters had determined that the earlier information developed on Ames by the joint investigative unit did not meet the standards for an intensive FBI investigation. The Committee believes, however, that there was ample evidence by October 1992, to reasonably suggest that Ames was acting in 1985 (and thereafter) as an agent of the Soviet Union. The FBI's hesitation resulted in a six-month delay before the FBI began to apply the full array of its investigative capabilities against Ames. Once applied, they produced impressive results. Indeed, the FBI investigative team from the Washington

Metropolitan Field Office, together with the CIA, did a superb job in bringing the investigation to a successful conclusion.

Recommendation No. 12: The Director of the FBI should ensure that adequate resources are applied to counterintelligence cases involving the CIA and other federal agencies, and that FBI headquarters is apprised immediately of significant case developments which could form the basis for the FBI's opening an intensive counterintelligence investigation.

Recommendation No. 13: The Attorney General and the Director of the FBI should review the FBI's guidelines for the conduct of counterintelligence investigations to determine whether clearer guidance is needed in determining whether a subject of a counterintelligence inquiry is acting as an agent of a foreign power.

FAILURE TO RESTRICT THE ASSIGNMENTS AND ACCESS TO SUSPECTS IN COUNTERINTELLIGENCE CASES

The Ames case reveals glaring weaknesses in the CIA's procedures for dealing with the career assignments of employees who are under suspicion for compromising intelligence operations. The CIA failed to restrict Ames's assignments and access even after information surfaced in 1989 which indicated Ames was a possible counterintelligence problem.

In September 1989, after a poor tour in Rome, which was known to the managers in the SE Division, his SE superiors allowed Ames to return to the SE Division and assigned him to the office supporting to all Soviet and East European operations in Europe, a position affording him broad access to sensitive information. He remained assigned to the SE Division until August 1990. During this period, investigators learned about Ames's unexplained affluence and developed information regarding several large bank deposits and a particularly large currency exchange. Yet none of this appears to have had any bearing on Ames's continued assignment or access during this period.

In fact, at the end of this assignment, notwithstanding his own poor performance record (he was then ranked 3rd from the bottom among 200 officers in his rating group), Ames was appointed to serve on a promotion board for mid-level CIA operations officers. This assignment gave him access to the personnel records of an entire class of mid-level CIA operations officers.

In October 1990, SE Division managers reassigned Ames to the Counterintelligence Center (CIC) because he had performed poorly and they wanted him out of the Division. Apparently, supervisors in the CIC knew Ames was a poor performer and were aware that questions had been raised about his unexplained affluence. Yet they believed they could manage the problem. After his arrest, these officials recognized that Ames' position had given him access to data which identified virtually every double agent operation controlled by the United States. It is unclear how or why this access was permitted. It is clear that despite the security concerns raised about Ames, his CIC supervisors did not ascertain or evaluate the extent of his access at the time.

In April 1991, while Ames was assigned to the CIC, the Office of Security carried out an updated background investigation of Ames. The results of this investigation were evaluated and shared with the investigator assigned to the special task force. Reflecting interviews with his co-workers in Rome and his Arlington, Virginia neighbors, the investigation produced information that Ames had frequent contacts in Rome with Soviet and

East European officials not fully explained by his work requirements, frequently violated security regulations by leaving his safe open and doing classified work at home, and lived far beyond his CIA salary in both Rome and Arlington. (One of those interviewed went so far as to say that he would not be surprised if Ames were a spy.)

Inexplicably, the CIA security officer who reviewed the investigative report evaluated it as "raising no CI concerns," and the task force investigator assigned to the case did not regard the report as providing any new information. Ames retained his security clearance and his job in the Counterintelligence Center, and no further action was taken to follow-up on the information developed in this report. Indeed, the special task force members viewed the investigative report, together with the favorable results of the April 1991, polygraph, as giving Ames "a clean bill of health."

In September 1991, despite having been "booted out" of the SE Division a year earlier, and despite the special task force inquiry then underway, Ames was allowed to return to the SE Division to conduct a special study of the KGB. While the study itself did not call for particularly sensitive access, Ames once again was given access to the personnel and records of the SE Division.

In December 1991, he was assigned to the Counternarcotics Center (CNC) where he remained until his arrest in 1994. This apparently was the first assignment made on the basis of the security concerns about Ames. But due to the sensitivity of the investigation into the 1985–86 compromises, CNC senior managers were not told of the investigation or the suspicions about Ames until the beginning of the FBI's intensive investigation in 1993. Even then, there was little or no effort made to evaluate and control the extent of Ames' access to classified information. Indeed, investigators later learned that Ames had computer access to a vast range of classified information that did not pertain to counternarcotics. Moreover, when a computer upgrade was installed in November 1993, it provided Ames with the capability to "download" vast quantities of information onto computer discs which he could take out of the building. Fortunately, Ames was arrested before he was able to pass these discs to his KGB handlers. But the fact that he was provided this capability at all at a time when his arrest was imminent is indicative of the CIA's lack of attention to this security problem.

Recommendation No. 14: The Director of Central Intelligence should establish procedures to inform current and prospective supervisors about employees under suspicion in counterintelligence cases. While the need to protect the secrecy of the investigation is essential, as well as the need to protect the employees themselves from unfair personnel actions, the assignment of employees under suspicion without frank consultations at the supervisory level increases the likelihood of serious compromises and leads to conflict between CIA elements.

Recommendation No. 15: The Director of Central Intelligence should issue procedures to require, in any case in which an employee is under suspicion for espionage or related activities, that a systematic evaluation be made of the employee's access to classified information, and that appropriate and timely actions be taken to limit such access. While care must obviously be taken to ensure that such actions do not tip off the employee that he or she is under suspicion, the failure to evaluate the access of an employee in these circumstances may eventually result in damage that might have been prevented.

Recommendation No. 16: The Director of Central Intelligence should establish more stringent criteria for CIA employees serving on promotion and assignment boards, which, among other things, prevent the appointment to such panels of employees with poor performance records or records of suitability problems.

DEFICIENCIES IN SECURITY PROCEDURES

The Ames case demonstrated numerous deficiencies in the CIA's use of the polygraph, its control over classified documents and materials, and its coordination of security and counterintelligence functions.

THE POLYGRAPH

Ames was able to pass polygraph examinations in 1986 and 1991 with relative ease. Although deeply involved in espionage activities, he was able to answer questions such as whether he worked for a foreign intelligence service, or had contacts with foreign nationals which he failed to report, without showing signs of deception.

The CIA Inspector General's report faults the 1986 examination, finding that the examiner was "too chummy" with Ames. When Ames showed a slight reaction to a question asking whether he had ever been "pitched," i.e., asked to work for a foreign intelligence service, the examiner appeared to readily accept his explanation that he was concerned about being "pitched" in his upcoming assignment in Rome.

The 1991 polygraph examination, according to the Inspector General's report, was deficient in that the examiners (there were two separate sessions) were not sufficiently familiar with the existing information on Ames' unexplained affluence, or with the information developed in the April 1991, background investigation of Ames. The examination was also deficient in that the investigator assigned to the special task force had not participated directly in the examination process, and there had been no prior planning in terms of how the CIA would handle the situation if Ames suddenly made damaging admissions.

According to Ames's debriefings, he did not take drugs or use any particular technique to pass the polygraph examinations. Acting on the advice of the KGB, he tried only to be cooperative and stay as calm as he could. Since he was acquainted with how polygraph examinations were conducted, he also was able to manipulate the process to prevent a "problem" from arising.

If Ames's account is true, it seems to indicate problems beyond those cited by the Inspector General's report, i.e. that examiners should be better informed and prepared. Indeed, it suggests that the CIA's reliance on the results of polygraph examinations needs to be far more circumspect than in the past.

Recommendation No. 17: The Director of Central Intelligence should tighten polygraph procedures to make the polygraph more useful. Such procedures should include random examinations instead of exams at regular intervals, with little or no prior notice, and variations in the polygraph technique. These procedures should also ensure that polygraph examinations involving employees under suspicion are carefully planned and constructed, and that appropriate prior notification is made to the Federal Bureau of Investigation if such cases have potential criminal implications. In addition, the Director should review the policies applicable to the training, supervision, and performance appraisal of polygraph examiners to ensure that polygraph examinations are conducted in a professional manner and produce optimum results.

Recommendation No. 18: The Director of Central Intelligence should institute a fundamental reevaluation of the polygraph as a part of CIA's security program. As the Ames case demonstrates, the polygraph cannot be relied upon with certainty to detect deception. This necessarily puts far more reliance on other aspects of the security process, e.g., background investigations, supervisory reporting, psychological testing, financial reporting, etc. The DCI's review should also include a reevaluation of the use of inconclusive polygraph test results. Even where the polygraph does indicate deception, such information is often useless unless damaging admissions are also obtained from the subject. The Committee believes that if an employee with access to particularly sensitive information does not make such admissions but continues to show deception to relevant questions after adequate testing, there should be additional investigation of the issues in question to attempt to resolve them. Should such investigation fail to do so, the CIA should have the latitude, without prejudice to the employee, to reassign him or her to less sensitive duties.

CONTROL OF CLASSIFIED DOCUMENTS AND MATERIALS

The Ames case also demonstrated gaps in the control of sensitive classified information. Ames was able—without detection—to walk out of CIA headquarters and the U.S. Embassy in Rome with bags and envelopes stuffed with classified documents and materials. Many of the classified documents he passed to his KGB handlers were copies of documents that were not under any system of accountability. Ames did not even have to make copies of them. In his last job in the Counternarcotics Center at the CIA, Ames was able to "download" a variety of classified documents onto computer discs and then simply remove them to his home. When he attended a conference in Turkey in 1993, he brought a lap-top computer to do work in his hotel room. This apparently raised no security concern among those familiar with the incident. He was also able to visit offices he had no reason to be in, and gain access to information he had no business seeing.

In the late 1970s, the CIA instituted a policy calling for random and unannounced spot-checks of personnel leaving Agency compounds. But the policy was discontinued soon thereafter due to the inconvenience caused to those subject to such searches.

Ames recounted later that his KGB handlers were amazed at his ability to gain access to sensitive operations and take large bundles of classified information out of CIA offices without arousing suspicion, a sad commentary on the laxness of security at the CIA.

Recommendation No. 19: The Director of Central Intelligence should reinstate the policy making persons leaving CIA facilities subject to random searches of their person and possessions, and require that such searches be conducted unannounced and periodically at selected locations. Such searches should be conducted frequently enough to serve as a deterrent without unduly hampering the operation of the facilities involved.

Recommendation No. 20: The Director of Central Intelligence should institute computer security measures to prevent employees from being able to "download" classified information onto computer diskettes and removing them from CIA facilities. In addition, existing policies for the introduction, accountability, dissemination, removal, and destruction of all forms of electronic media should be reevaluated. The ability of the CIA's security managers to "audit" specific computer-related functions in order to detect and monitor the actions of suspected offenders should be upgraded.

Recommendation No 21: The Director of Central Intelligence should institute a policy requiring employees to report to their supervisor any instance in which a CIA employee attempts to obtain classified information which the CIA employee has no apparent reason to know. In turn, supervisors should be required to report to the CIA Counterintelligence Center any such case where a plausible explanation for such a request cannot be ascertained by the supervisor.

Recommendation No. 22: The Director of Central Intelligence should institute new policies to improve the control of classified documents and materials within the CIA. In particular, the Directorate of Operations should undertake an immediate and comprehensive review of its practices and procedures for compartmenting information relating to clandestine operations to ensure that only those officers who absolutely need access can obtain such information. Further, the Directorate should establish and maintain a detailed, automated record of the access granted to each of its employees.

COORDINATION OF SECURITY AND COUNTERINTELLIGENCE

The Ames case demonstrated a serious division between security and counterintelligence activities in the CIA. Even though an investigator from the Office of Security (OS) participated in the investigation of the 1985–86 compromises under the auspices of the Counterintelligence Center (CIC), he failed to coordinate properly with OS with respect to Ames' 1991 polygraph examination. OS had initiated a background investigation of Ames in March 1991, but went ahead with the polygraph in April without the benefit of the background investigation. As it turned out, the background investigation provided significant information about Ames that was largely ignored by the investigator assigned to the CIC in light of Ames's passing the polygraph examination.

Citing senior security officials, the Inspector General's report noted there had always been a "fault line" in communications between the CIC and its predecessors, and the OS. The CIC had not always shared information regarding its counterintelligence investigations and had failed to make use of OS's investigative expertise. Indeed, the search to find the cause of the 1985 compromises might have moved more quickly from analysis to investigation if there had been better coordination between security and counterintelligence.

The Inspector General's report also found "a gradual degradation" of the resources and authority given the security function since 1985, concluding that "this degradation has adversely affected the Agency's ability to prevent and deter activities such as those engaged in by Ames. . . ." The Committee shares the view that this decline has been too great too precipitous. The Committee had recommended an increase in personnel security funding for the CIA and other agencies for Fiscal Year 1995, but was unable to sustain its initiative due to the lack of interest shown by the agencies involved.

Responding to the continuing problem of CIA offices failing to share pertinent information on CIA personnel with one another, Director Woolsey recently created a new Office of Personnel Security that combines elements of the old Office of Personnel, the Office of Medical Services, and the Office of Security. While this consolidation may facilitate the sharing of information regarding suitability problems, it may also hamper the exchange of counterintelligence information from the CIC and may further dilute the security function, particularly the expertise of security investigators.

The Committee believes that the personnel security function should be preserved with a separate office. Routine monitoring of Agency employees from a security perspective remains an important function and one that must be accomplished without carrying a presumption that persons are under suspicion. An effective personnel security program would deter potential traitors, limit the burden on counterintelligence investigators and result in faster, more effective counterintelligence investigations.

Recommendation No. 23: The Director of Central Intelligence should reexamine the decision to combine the Office of Security with the other elements of the CIA's new personnel center, and should ensure sufficient funding is provided to the personnel security function in Fiscal Year 1995 and in future years. The Director should also clarify the relationship between security and counterintelligence, specifying their respective functions and providing for effective coordination and cooperation between them.

FAILURE TO ADVISE THE OVERSIGHT COMMITTEES

The CIA failed to notify the congressional oversight committees in any meaningful way of the compromises of 1985–1986, as required by applicable law.

Indeed, in the hearings held annually on counterintelligence matters and in numerous staff briefings on the subject from 1985 until 1994, the massive compromises of 1985–86 were never once mentioned by representatives of the CIA or the FBI.

Based upon the recollections of individuals, there were two occasions when the 1985–86 compromises were alluded to in discussions with Members or staff of the Senate Select Committee on Intelligence (SSCI). The first mention came during a staff visit to Moscow in December 1988. The second occurred in 1992 during a visit to Moscow by two Members of the Committee. But on each occasion, the information provided was fragmentary and anecdotal and did not specifically address what was being done by the CIA about the problem. Informal staff efforts to follow-up on each of these conversations were put off by the CIA.

The Committee strongly believes that both the CIA and the FBI had an obligation to advise the oversight committees at the time of the 1985–86 compromises. Section 502 of the National Security Act of 1947 specifically requires intelligence agencies to report to the oversight committees "any significant intelligence failure." The compromises of 1985–86 resulted in a virtual collapse of CIA's Soviet operations at the height of the Cold War. According to the SE Division officer's memorandum of November, 1986, the evidence was at that point "overwhelming" and clearly indicated a problem of disastrous proportions. The oversight committees were responsible for funding the activities of the Directorate of Operations. They should have been formally notified pursuant to section 502 of the National Security Act of 1947.

THE NEED FOR CONTINUED FOLLOW-UP

Many of the problems identified by the Committee are deep-seated and pervasive, and will not be solved easily or quickly. Yet these problems are too important and too integral to the functioning of an agency with important national security responsibilities not to merit continuing and intensive scrutiny by both CIA managers and the congressional oversight committees.

While the Committee intends to make the CIA's response to this report an area of "special oversight interest" in the years ahead, the Committee also directs the Inspector General of the CIA to provide the Committee, through the Director of Central Intelligence, with a report no later than September 1, 1995, and annually thereafter, on the CIA's progress in responding to the recommendations contained in this report and to the continuing counterintelligence and security challenges that the CIA faces.

COUNTERTERRORISM, INTELLIGENCE, AND THE HART-RUDMAN COMMISSION, MARCH 2001

Editor's note: Former Senators Gary Hart (D-CO) and Warren Rudman (R-NH) led a Department of Defense study in the months before the 9/11 attacks that concluded the United States was vulnerable to just such a calamity. Reproduced here are the Commission's central thoughts on intelligence reform to strengthen America's antiterrorist stance.

ROAD MAP FOR NATIONAL SECURITY: IMPERATIVE FOR CHANGE

THE PHASE III REPORT OF THE U.S. COMMISSION ON NATIONAL SECURITY/21ST CENTURY MARCH 15, 2001

F. The Intelligence Community

The basic structure of the U.S. intelligence community does not require change. The community has implemented many of the recommendations for reform made by other studies. This Commission's focus is on those changes in intelligence policy, operations, and resources needed for the full implementation of recommendations found elsewhere within this report.

While the intelligence community is generally given high marks for timely and useful contributions to policymaking and crisis management, it failed to warn of Indian nuclear tests or to anticipate the rapidity of missile developments in Iran and North Korea. U.S.

Source: *Road Map for National Security: Imperative for Change*, U.S. Commission on National Security/21st Century (the Hart-Rudman Commission), Phase III Report (March 15, 2001), pp. 82–86.

intelligence has, at times, been unable to respond to the burgeoning requirements levied by more demanding consumers trying to cope with a more complex array of problems. Steep declines in human intelligence resources over the last decade have been forcing dangerous tradeoffs between coverage of important countries, regions, and functional challenges. Warfighters in theater are often frustrated because the granulated detail of intelligence that they need rarely gets to them, even though they know that it exists somewhere in the intelligence system.

It is a commonplace that the intelligence community lost its focus when the Berlin Wall fell. Since then, three other problems have compounded its challenges. First, the world is a more complex place, with more diffuse dangers requiring different kinds of intelligence and new means of acquiring them. Second, its resources—personnel and monetary—have been reduced. Third, the dangers of terrorism and proliferation, as well as ethnic conflicts and humanitarian emergencies, have led to a focus on providing warning and crisis management rather than long-term analysis.

The result of these three developments is an intelligence community that is more demand-driven than it was two decades ago. That demand is also more driven by military consumers and, therefore, what the intelligence community is doing is narrower and more short-term than it was two decades ago. Given the paucity of resources, this means that important regions and trends are not receiving adequate attention and that the more comprehensive analytical tasks that everyone agrees the intelligence community should be performing simply cannot be done properly.

This Commission has emphasized that *strategic planning* needs to be introduced throughout the national security institutions of the U.S. government. We have also emphasized the critical importance of *preventive diplomacy*. Both require an intelligence community that can support such innovations, *but current trends are leading in the opposite direction.*

This Commission has also stressed the increasing importance of diplomatic and especially economic components in U.S. statecraft. The intelligence community as a whole needs to maintain its level of effort in military domains, but also to do much more in economic domains. In a world where proprietary science and technology developments are increasingly the sinews of national power, the intelligence community needs to be concerned more than ever with U.S. technological security, not least in cyberspace. And here, too, the trends within the intelligence community point not toward, but away from, the country's essential needs. Resources devoted to handling such economic and technical issues are not increasing, but declining.

To respond to these challenges, some recommend strengthening the Director of Central Intelligence (DCI) through organizational changes, such as vesting greater budgetary authority in him and giving him greater control over community personnel. We believe, however, that current efforts to strengthen community management while maintaining the ongoing relationship between the DCI and the Secretary of Defense are bearing fruit. We recommend no major structural changes, but offer certain recommendations to strengthen the DCI's role and the efficiency of the process.

The National Security Act of 1947 gave the National Security Council responsibility for providing guidance with respect to intelligence functions. In practice, however, administrations have varied widely in their approach to this function—sometimes actively setting priorities for intelligence collection and analysis and sometimes focusing simply on coordinating intelligence response in times of crisis.

To achieve the strategy envisioned in our Phase II report, and to make the budgetary recommendations of this section most effective, more consistent attention must be paid to the setting of national intelligence priorities. To do this, we recommend the following:

36 The President should order the setting of national intelligence priorities through National Security Council guidance to the Director of Central Intelligence.

In recommending this, we echo the conclusion of the Commission on the Roles and Capabilities of the United States Intelligence Community (the Brown-Rudman Commission). While we do not want to dictate how future Presidents might use the National Security Council, we believe this is a crucial function that must be filled in some way. The President's authority to set strategic intelligence priorities should be exercised through continuous NSC engagement with the DCI, from which the DCI can establish appropriate collection and analysis priorities. Such an approach would ensure consistent policymaker input into the intelligence effort and, if policymakers come to feel a part of the intelligence process, it should enable greater support for the intelligence community, as well. We believe that this function would be best fulfilled by a true strategic planning staff at the NSC—as discussed in our recommendation 14. *The point is that policy and strategic guidance for intelligence should be formulated in tandem.*

We have emphasized the importance of securing the homeland in this new century and have urged, specifically in recommendation 4, that it be a higher intelligence priority. Making it so means greatly strengthening U.S. human intelligence (HUMINT) capability. This involves ensuring the quality of those entering the community's clandestine service, as well as the recruitment of foreign nationals as agents with the best chance of providing crucial information about terrorism and other threats to the homeland.

Along with the National Commission on Terrorism, we believe that guidelines for the recruitment of foreign nationals should be reviewed to ensure that, while respecting legal and human rights concerns, they maximize the intelligence community's ability to collect intelligence on terrorist plans and methods. We recognize the need to observe basic moral standards in all U.S. government conduct, but the people who can best help U.S. agents penetrate effectively into terrorist organizations, for example, are not liable to be model citizens of spotless virtue. Operative regulations in this respect must balance national security interests with concern for American values and principles. We therefore recommend the following:

37 The Director of Central Intelligence should emphasize the recruitment of human intelligence sources on terrorism as one of the intelligence community's highest priorities, and ensure that operational guidelines are balanced between security needs and respect for American values and principles.

The DCI must also give greater priority to the analysis of economic and science and technology trends where the U.S. intelligence community's capabilities are inadequate. While improvements have been made, especially in the wake of the Asian financial crisis, the global economic and scientific environments are changing so rapidly and dramatically that the United States needs to develop new tools merely to understand what is happening in the world. The Treasury Department has made important strides in this regard, but it has a long way to go. Treasury and CIA also need to coordinate better efforts in this critical area. We therefore recommend the following:

38 The intelligence community should place new emphasis on collection and analysis of economic and science/technology security concerns, and incorporate more open-source intelligence into analytical products. Congress should support this new emphasis by increasing significantly the National Foreign Intelligence Program (NFIP) budget for collection and analysis.

In order to maintain U.S. strength in traditional areas while building new capabilities, the President and the Congress should give priority to economic and science/technology intelligence. We need to increase overall funding in these areas significantly and the DCI needs to emphasize improvement in the collection and analysis of this intelligence. This will require, in turn, a major investment in the community's long-term analytical capacities, but these capacities are crucial in any event to supporting the strategic planning that we have emphasized throughout this report.

Better analysis in non-military areas also means ensuring that open-source intelligence is a vital part of all-source analysis. Many new challenges, but especially economic, scientific, and technological ones, call for greater attention to the wealth of openly available information. Analyses of the failure of the community to anticipate India's nuclear tests, when clear indications were available in open-source publications, demonstrate that this capability has relevance for traditional security issues as well.

We thus urge the strengthening of HUMINT capabilities, the broadening of analytical efforts across a range of issues, and the incorporation of more open-source information into all-source analysis. Meeting the nation's future intelligence needs, however, will also require changes in the community's technological capabilities.

Technological superiority has long been a hallmark of U.S. intelligence. Yet some agencies within the National Foreign Intelligence Program spend as little as three to four percent of their budget on all aspects of research and development, and as little as one percent on advanced research and development. This reflects a decline in overall intelligence expenditures in real terms, while salaries and benefits for intelligence personnel have been on the rise. Concerted effort is needed to ensure that research and development receive greater funding.

At the same time, the intelligence community must think about its technological capabilities in new ways. During the Cold War, the National Security Agency (NSA) and other agencies derived a great wealth of information through signals and communications intelligence. In today's Internet age, global networks, cable, and wireless communications are increasingly ubiquitous, with attendant improvements in encryption technologies. Together these trends make signal intelligence collection increasingly difficult. The United States must possess the best platforms and capabilities to ensure that it can collect necessary information consistent with respecting Americans' privacy. It must also have high-quality technical and scientific personnel able to respond to future challenges.

To achieve these ends, *we recommend that the DCI should provide the President a strategic assessment of the effectiveness of current technical intelligence capabilities to ensure the fullest range of collection across all intelligence domains, particularly as they relate to cyberspace and new communications technologies.*

Should the U.S. intelligence community lack a full-spectrum capability either in collection or analysis, the United States would forfeit the depth of intelligence coverage it enjoyed during the Cold War. Maintaining this edge will require greater funding and expertise in the information and communication sciences. We must also pursue innovative approaches with the private sector to establish access to new technologies as they become available.

This Commission, in sum, urges an overall increase in the NFIP budget to accommodate greater priority placed on nonmilitary intelligence challenges. Military intelligence needs also remain critical, however, so a simple reallocation of existing resources will not suffice. To ensure the continuing technological strength of the community, and to build cutting-edge intelligence platforms, there is no escaping the need for an increase in overall resources for the intelligence community.

THE 9/11 COMMISSION RECOMMENDATIONS ON INTELLIGENCE AND COUNTERTERRORISM, 2004

Editor's note: The 9/11 or Kean Commission (led by Republican former governor of New Jersey, Thomas H. Kean) reported in 2004 on its findings regarding the Al Qaeda terrorist attacks against the United States on September 11, 2001. Following are the Commission's main findings on how to organize the government differently to deal with the terrorist threat.

12 WHAT TO DO?
A GLOBAL STRATEGY

12.1 REFLECTING ON A GENERATIONAL CHALLENGE

Three years after 9/11, Americans are still thinking and talking about how to protect our nation in this new era. The national debate continues.

Countering terrorism has become, beyond any doubt, the top national security priority for the United States. This shift has occurred with the full support of the Congress, both major political parties, the media, and the American people.

The nation has committed enormous resources to national security and to countering terrorism. Between fiscal year 2001, the last budget adopted before 9/11, and the present fiscal year 2004, total federal spending on defense (including expenditures on both Iraq and Afghanistan), homeland security, and international affairs rose more than 50 percent, from $354 billion to about $547 billion. The United States has not experienced such a rapid surge in national security spending since the Korean War.[1]

This pattern has occurred before in American history. The United States faces a sudden crisis and summons a tremendous exertion of national energy. Then, as that surge

---

Source: *The 9/11 Commission Report: Final Report of the National Commission on Terrorist Attacks upon the United States* (New York: W.W. Norton, 2004), pp. 361–428, 562–67.

transforms the landscape, comes a time for reflection and reevaluation. Some programs and even agencies are discarded; others are invented or redesigned. Private firms and engaged citizens redefine their relationships with government, working through the processes of the American republic.

Now is the time for that reflection and reevaluation. The United States should consider *what to do*—the shape and objectives of a strategy. Americans should also consider *how to do it*—organizing their government in a different way.

DEFINING THE THREAT

In the post-9/11 world, threats are defined more by the fault lines within societies than by the territorial boundaries between them. From terrorism to global disease or environmental degradation, the challenges have become transnational rather than international. That is the defining quality of world politics in the twenty-first century.

National security used to be considered by studying foreign frontiers, weighing opposing groups of states, and measuring industrial might. To be dangerous, an enemy had to muster large armies. Threats emerged slowly, often visibly, as weapons were forged, armies conscripted, and units trained and moved into place. Because large states were more powerful, they also had more to lose. They could be deterred.

Now threats can emerge quickly. An organization like al Qaeda, headquartered in a country on the other side of the earth, in a region so poor that electricity or telephones were scarce, could nonetheless scheme to wield weapons of unprecedented destructive power in the largest cities of the United States.

In this sense, 9/11 has taught us that terrorism against American interests "over there" should be regarded just as we regard terrorism against America "over here." In this same sense, the American homeland is the planet.

But the enemy is not just "terrorism," some generic evil.[2] This vagueness blurs the strategy. The catastrophic threat at this moment in history is more specific. It is the threat posed by *Islamist* terrorism—especially the al Qaeda network, its affiliates, and its ideology.[3]

As we mentioned in chapter 2, Usama Bin Ladin and other Islamist terrorist leaders draw on a long tradition of extreme intolerance within one stream of Islam (a minority tradition), from at least Ibn Taimiyyah, through the founders of Wahhabism, through the Muslim Brotherhood, to Sayyid Qutb. That stream is motivated by religion and does not distinguish politics from religion, thus distorting both. It is further fed by grievances stressed by Bin Ladin and widely felt throughout the Muslim world—against the U.S. military presence in the Middle East, policies perceived as anti-Arab and anti-Muslim, and support of Israel. Bin Ladin and Islamist terrorists mean exactly what they say: to them America is the font of all evil, the "head of the snake," and it must be converted or destroyed.

It is not a position with which Americans can bargain or negotiate. With it there is no common ground—not even respect for life—on which to begin a dialogue. It can only be destroyed or utterly isolated.

Because the Muslim world has fallen behind the West politically, economically, and militarily for the past three centuries, and because few tolerant or secular Muslim democracies provide alternative models for the future, Bin Ladin's message finds receptive ears. It has attracted active support from thousands of disaffected young Muslims and resonates powerfully with a far larger number who do not actively support his methods. The resentment of America and the West is deep, even among leaders of relatively successful Muslim states.[4]

Tolerance, the rule of law, political and economic openness, the extension of greater opportunities to women—these cures must come from within Muslim societies themselves. The United States must support such developments.

But this process is likely to be measured in decades, not years. It is a process that will be violently opposed by Islamist terrorist organizations, both inside Muslim countries and in attacks on the United States and other Western nations. The United States finds itself caught up in a clash *within* a civilization. That clash arises from particular conditions in the Muslim world, conditions that spill over into expatriate Muslim communities in non-Muslim countries.

Our enemy is twofold: al Qaeda, a stateless network of terrorists that struck us on 9/11; and a radical ideological movement in the Islamic world, inspired in part by al Qaeda, which has spawned terrorist groups and violence across the globe. The first enemy is weakened, but continues to pose a grave threat. The second enemy is gathering, and will menace Americans and American interests long after Usama Bin Ladin and his cohorts are killed or captured. Thus our strategy must match our means to two ends: dismantling the al Qaeda network and prevailing in the longer term over the ideology that gives rise to Islamist terrorism.

Islam is not the enemy. It is not synonymous with terror. Nor does Islam teach terror. America and its friends oppose a perversion of Islam, not the great world faith itself. Lives guided by religious faith, including literal beliefs in holy scriptures, are common to every religion, and represent no threat to us.

Other religions have experienced violent internal struggles. With so many diverse adherents, every major religion will spawn violent zealots. Yet understanding and tolerance among people of different faiths can and must prevail.

The present transnational danger is Islamist terrorism. What is needed is a broad political-military strategy that rests on a firm tripod of policies to

- attack terrorists and their organizations;
- prevent the continued growth of Islamist terrorism; and
- protect against and prepare for terrorist attacks.

More Than a War on Terrorism

Terrorism is a tactic used by individuals and organizations to kill and destroy. Our efforts should be directed at those individuals and organizations.

Calling this struggle a war accurately describes the use of American and allied armed forces to find and destroy terrorist groups and their allies in the field, notably in Afghanistan. The language of war also evokes the mobilization for a national effort. Yet the strategy should be balanced.

The first phase of our post-9/11 efforts rightly included military action to topple the Taliban and pursue al Qaeda. This work continues. But long-term success demands the use of all elements of national power: diplomacy, intelligence, covert action, law enforcement, economic policy, foreign aid, public diplomacy, and homeland defense. If we favor one tool while neglecting others, we leave ourselves vulnerable and weaken our national effort.

Certainly the strategy should include offensive operations to counter terrorism. Terrorists should no longer find safe haven where their organizations can grow and flourish. America's strategy should be a coalition strategy, that includes Muslim nations as partners in its development and implementation.

Our effort should be accompanied by a preventive strategy that is as much, or more, political as it is military. The strategy must focus clearly on the Arab and Muslim world, in all its variety.

Our strategy should also include defenses. America can be attacked in many ways and has many vulnerabilities. No defenses are perfect. But risks must be calculated; hard choices must be made about allocating resources. Responsibilities for America's defense should be clearly defined. Planning does make a difference, identifying where a little money might have a large effect. Defenses also complicate the plans of attackers, increasing their risks of discovery and failure. Finally, the nation must prepare to deal with attacks that are not stopped.

MEASURING SUCCESS

What should Americans expect from their government in the struggle against Islamist terrorism? The goals seem unlimited: Defeat terrorism anywhere in the world. But Americans have also been told to expect the worst: An attack is probably coming; it may be terrible.

With such benchmarks, the justifications for action and spending seem limitless. Goals are good. Yet effective public policies also need concrete objectives. Agencies need to be able to measure success.

These measurements do not need to be quantitative: government cannot measure success in the ways that private firms can. But the targets should be specific enough so that reasonable observers—in the White House, the Congress, the media, or the general public—can judge whether or not the objectives have been attained.

Vague goals match an amorphous picture of the enemy. Al Qaeda and its affiliates are popularly described as being all over the world, adaptable, resilient, needing little higher-level organization, and capable of anything. The American people are thus given the picture of an omnipotent, unslayable hydra of destruction. This image lowers expectations for government effectiveness.

It should not lower them too far. Our report shows a determined and capable group of plotters. Yet the group was fragile, dependent on a few key personalities, and occasionally left vulnerable by the marginal, unstable people often attracted to such causes. The enemy made mistakes—like Khalid al Mihdhar's unauthorized departure from the United States that required him to enter the country again in July 2001, or the selection of Zacarias Moussaoui as a participant and Ramzi Binalshibh's transfer of money to him. The U.S. government was not able to capitalize on those mistakes in time to prevent 9/11.

We do not believe it is possible to defeat all terrorist attacks against Americans, every time and everywhere. A president should tell the American people:

- No president can promise that a catastrophic attack like that of 9/11 will not happen again. History has shown that even the most vigilant and expert agencies cannot always prevent determined, suicidal attackers from reaching a target.

- But the American people are entitled to expect their government to do its very best. They should expect that officials will have realistic objectives, clear guidance, and effective organization. They are entitled to see some standards for performance so they can judge, with the help of their elected representatives, whether the objectives are being met.

12.2 ATTACK TERRORISTS AND THEIR ORGANIZATIONS

The U.S. government, joined by other governments around the world, is working through intelligence, law enforcement, military, financial, and diplomatic channels to identify, disrupt, capture, or kill individual terrorists. This effort was going on before 9/11 and it continues on a vastly enlarged scale. But to catch terrorists, a U.S. or foreign agency needs to be able to find and reach them.

No Sanctuaries

The 9/11 attack was a complex international operation, the product of years of planning. Bombings like those in Bali in 2003 or Madrid in 2004, while able to take hundreds of lives, can be mounted locally. Their requirements are far more modest in size and complexity. They are more difficult to thwart. But the U.S. government must build the capacities to prevent a 9/11-scale plot from succeeding, and those capabilities will help greatly to cope with lesser but still devastating attacks.

A complex international terrorist operation aimed at launching a catastrophic attack cannot be mounted by just anyone in any place. Such operations appear to require

- time, space, and ability to perform competent planning and staff work;
- a command structure able to make necessary decisions and possessing the authority and contacts to assemble needed people, money, and materials;
- opportunity and space to recruit, train, and select operatives with the needed skills and dedication, providing the time and structure required to socialize them into the terrorist cause, judge their trustworthiness, and hone their skills;
- a logistics network able to securely manage the travel of operatives, move money, and transport resources (like explosives) where they need to go;
- access, in the case of certain weapons, to the special materials needed for a nuclear, chemical, radiological, or biological attack;
- reliable communications between coordinators and operatives; and
- opportunity to test the workability of the plan.

Many details in chapters 2, 5, and 7 illustrate the direct and indirect value of the Afghan sanctuary to al Qaeda in preparing the 9/11 attack and other operations. The organization cemented personal ties among veteran jihadists working together there for years. It had the operational space to gather and sift recruits, indoctrinating them in isolated, desert camps. It built up logistical networks, running through Pakistan and the United Arab Emirates.

Al Qaeda also exploited relatively lax internal security environments in Western countries, especially Germany. It considered the environment in the United States so hospitable that the 9/11 operatives used America as their staging area for further training and exercises—traveling into, out of, and around the country and complacently using their real names with little fear of capture.

To find sanctuary, terrorist organizations have fled to some of the least governed, most lawless places in the world. The intelligence community has prepared a world map that highlights possible terrorist havens, using no secret intelligence—just indicating areas that combine rugged terrain, weak governance, room to hide or receive supplies, and low population density with a town or city near enough to allow necessary interaction with the outside world. Large areas scattered around the world meet these criteria.[5]

In talking with American and foreign government officials and military officers on the front lines fighting terrorists today, we asked them: If you were a terrorist leader today, where would you locate your base? Some of the same places come up again and again on their lists:

- western Pakistan and the Pakistan-Afghanistan border region
- southern or western Afghanistan
- the Arabian Peninsula, especially Saudi Arabia and Yemen, and the nearby Horn of Africa, including Somalia and extending southwest into Kenya
- Southeast Asia, from Thailand to the southern Philippines to Indonesia
- West Africa, including Nigeria and Mali
- European cities with expatriate Muslim communities, especially cities in central and eastern Europe where security forces and border controls are less effective

In the twentieth century, strategists focused on the world's great industrial heartlands. In the twenty-first, the focus is in the opposite direction, toward remote regions and failing states. The United States has had to find ways to extend its reach, straining the limits of its influence.

Every policy decision we make needs to be seen through this lens. If, for example, Iraq becomes a failed state, it will go to the top of the list of places that are breeding grounds for attacks against Americans at home. Similarly, if we are paying insufficient attention to Afghanistan, the rule of the Taliban or warlords and narcotraffickers may reemerge and its countryside could once again offer refuge to al Qaeda, or its successor.

Recommendation: The U.S. government must identify and prioritize actual or potential terrorist sanctuaries. For each, it should have a realistic strategy to keep possible terrorists insecure and on the run, using all elements of national power. We should reach out, listen to, and work with other countries that can help.

We offer three illustrations that are particularly applicable today, in 2004: Pakistan, Afghanistan, and Saudi Arabia.

PAKISTAN

Pakistan's endemic poverty, widespread corruption, and often ineffective government create opportunities for Islamist recruitment. Poor education is a particular concern. Millions of families, especially those with little money, send their children to religious schools, or madrassahs. Many of these schools are the only opportunity available for an education, but some have been used as incubators for violent extremism. According to Karachi's police commander, there are 859 madrassahs teaching more than 200,000 youngsters in his city alone.[6]

It is hard to overstate the importance of Pakistan in the struggle against Islamist terrorism. Within Pakistan's borders are 150 million Muslims, scores of al Qaeda terrorists, many Taliban fighters, and—perhaps—Usama Bin Ladin. Pakistan possesses nuclear weapons and has come frighteningly close to war with nuclear-armed India over the disputed territory of Kashmir. A political battle among anti-American Islamic fundamentalists, the Pakistani military, and more moderate mainstream political forces has already spilled over into violence, and there have been repeated recent attempts to kill Pakistan's president, Pervez Musharraf.

In recent years, the United States has had three basic problems in its relationship with Pakistan:

- On terrorism, Pakistan helped nurture the Taliban. The Pakistani army and intelligence services, especially below the top ranks, have long been ambivalent about confronting Islamist extremists. Many in the government have sympathized with or provided support to the extremists. Musharraf agreed that Bin Ladin was bad. But before 9/11, preserving good relations with the Taliban took precedence.
- On proliferation, Musharraf has repeatedly said that Pakistan does not barter with its nuclear technology. But proliferation concerns have been long-standing and very serious. Most recently, the Pakistani government has claimed not to have known that one of its nuclear weapons developers, a national figure, was leading the most dangerous nuclear smuggling ring ever disclosed.
- Finally, Pakistan has made little progress toward the return of democratic rule at the national level, although that turbulent process does continue to function at the provincial level and the Pakistani press remains relatively free.

Immediately after 9/11, confronted by the United States with a stark choice, Pakistan made a strategic decision. Its government stood aside and allowed the U.S.-led coalition to destroy the Taliban regime. In other ways, Pakistan actively assisted: its authorities arrested more than 500 al Qaeda operatives and Taliban members, and Pakistani forces played a leading part in tracking down KSM, Abu Zubaydah, and other key al Qaeda figures.[7]

In the following two years, the Pakistani government tried to walk the fence, helping against al Qaeda while seeking to avoid a larger confrontation with Taliban remnants and other Islamic extremists. When al Qaeda and its Pakistani allies repeatedly tried to assassinate Musharraf, almost succeeding, the battle came home.

The country's vast unpoliced regions make Pakistan attractive to extremists seeking refuge and recruits and also provide a base for operations against coalition forces in Afghanistan. Almost all the 9/11 attackers traveled the north-south nexus of Kandahar–Quetta–Karachi. The Baluchistan region of Pakistan (KSM's ethnic home) and the sprawling city of Karachi remain centers of Islamist extremism where the U.S. and Pakistani security and intelligence presence has been weak. The U.S. consulate in Karachi is a makeshift fortress, reflecting the gravity of the surrounding threat.[8]

During the winter of 2003–2004, Musharraf made another strategic decision. He ordered the Pakistani army into the frontier provinces of northwest Pakistan along the Afghan border, where Bin Ladin and Ayman al Zawahiri have reportedly taken refuge. The army is confronting groups of al Qaeda fighters and their local allies in very difficult terrain.

On the other side of the frontier, U.S. forces in Afghanistan have found it challenging to organize effective joint operations, given Pakistan's limited capabilities and reluctance to permit U.S. military operations on its soil. Yet in 2004, it is clear that the Pakistani government is trying harder than ever before in the battle against Islamist terrorists.[9]

Acknowledging these problems and Musharraf's own part in the story, we believe that Musharraf's government represents the best hope for stability in Pakistan and Afghanistan.

- In an extraordinary public essay asking how Muslims can "drag ourselves out of the pit we find ourselves in, to raise ourselves up," Musharraf has called for a strategy of "enlightened moderation." The Muslim world, he said, should shun militancy and extremism; the West—and the United States in particular—should seek to resolve disputes with justice and help better the Muslim world.[10]
- Having come close to war in 2002 and 2003, Pakistan and India have recently made significant progress in peacefully discussing their longstanding differences. The United States has been and should remain a key supporter of that process.
- The constant refrain of Pakistanis is that the United States long treated them as allies of convenience. As the United States makes fresh commitments now, it should make promises it is prepared to keep, for years to come.

Recommendation: If Musharraf stands for enlightened moderation in a fight for his life and for the life of his country, the United States should be willing to make hard choices too, and make the difficult long-term commitment to the future of Pakistan. Sustaining the current scale of aid to Pakistan, the United States should support Pakistan's government in its struggle against extremists with a comprehensive effort that extends from military aid to support for better education, so long as Pakistan's leaders remain willing to make difficult choices of their own.

AFGHANISTAN

Afghanistan was the incubator for al Qaeda and for the 9/11 attacks. In the fall of 2001, the U.S.-led international coalition and its Afghan allies toppled the Taliban and ended the regime's protection of al Qaeda. Notable progress has been made. International cooperation has been strong, with a clear UN mandate and a NATO-led peacekeeping force (the International Security Assistance Force, or ISAF). More than 10,000 American soldiers are deployed today in Afghanistan, joined by soldiers from NATO allies and Muslim states. A central government has been established in Kabul, with a democratic constitution, new currency, and a new army. Most Afghans enjoy greater freedom, women and girls are emerging from subjugation, and 3 million children have returned to school. For the first time in many years, Afghans have reason to hope.[11]

But grave challenges remain. Taliban and al Qaeda fighters have regrouped in the south and southeast. Warlords control much of the country beyond Kabul, and the land is awash in weapons. Economic development remains a distant hope. The narcotics trade— long a massive sector of the Afghan economy—is again booming. Even the most hardened aid workers refuse to operate in many regions, and some warn that Afghanistan is near the brink of chaos.[12]

Battered Afghanistan has a chance. Elections are being prepared. It is revealing that in June 2004,Taliban fighters resorted to slaughtering 16 Afghans on a bus, apparently for no reason other than their boldness in carrying an unprecedented Afghan weapon: a voter registration card.

Afghanistan's president, Hamid Karzai, is brave and committed. He is trying to build genuinely national institutions that can overcome the tradition of allocating powers among ethnic communities. Yet even if his efforts are successful and elections bring a democratic government to Afghanistan, the United States faces some difficult choices.

After paying relatively little attention to rebuilding Afghanistan during the military campaign, U.S. policies changed noticeably during 2003. Greater consideration of the political dimension and congressional support for a substantial package of assistance signaled a longer-term commitment to Afghanistan's future. One Afghan regional official plaintively told us the country finally has a good government. He begged the United States to keep its promise and not abandon Afghanistan again, as it had in the 1990s. Another Afghan leader noted that if the United States leaves, "we will lose all that we have gained." [13]

Most difficult is to define the security mission in Afghanistan. There is continuing political controversy about whether military operations in Iraq have had any effect on the scale of America's commitment to the future of Afghanistan. The United States has largely stayed out of the central government's struggles with dissident warlords and it has largely avoided confronting the related problem of narcotrafficking. [14]

Recommendation: The President and the Congress deserve praise for their efforts in Afghanistan so far. Now the United States and the international community should make a long-term commitment to a secure and stable Afghanistan, in order to give the government a reasonable opportunity to improve the life of the Afghan people. Afghanistan must not again become a sanctuary for international crime and terrorism. The United States and the international community should help the Afghan government extend its authority over the country, with a strategy and nation-by-nation commitments to achieve their objectives.

- This is an ambitious recommendation. It would mean a redoubled effort to secure the country, disarm militias, and curtail the age of warlord rule. But the United States and NATO have already committed themselves to the future of this region—wisely, as the 9/11 story shows—and failed half-measures could be worse than useless.
- NATO in particular has made Afghanistan a test of the Alliance's ability to adapt to current security challenges of the future. NATO must pass this test. Currently, the United States and the international community envision enough support so that the central government can build a truly national army and extend essential infrastructure and minimum public services to major towns and regions. The effort relies in part on foreign civil-military teams, arranged under various national flags. The institutional commitments of NATO and the United Nations to these enterprises are weak. NATO member states are not following through; some of the other states around the world that have pledged assistance to Afghanistan are not fulfilling their pledges.
- The U.S. presence in Afghanistan is overwhelmingly oriented toward military and security work. The State Department presence is woefully understaffed, and the military mission is narrowly focused on al Qaeda and Taliban remnants in the south and southeast. The U.S. government can do its part if the international community decides on a joint effort to restore the rule of law and contain rampant crime and narcotics trafficking in this crossroads of Central Asia. [15]

We heard again and again that the money for assistance is allocated so rigidly that, on the ground, one U.S. agency often cannot improvise or pitch in to help another agency, even in small ways when a few thousand dollars could make a great difference.

The U.S. government should allocate money so that lower-level officials have more flexibility to get the job done across agency lines, adjusting to the circumstances they find in the field. This should include discretionary funds for expenditures by military units that often encounter opportunities to help the local population.

SAUDI ARABIA

Saudi Arabia has been a problematic ally in combating Islamic extremism. At the level of high policy, Saudi Arabia's leaders cooperated with American diplomatic initiatives aimed at the Taliban or Pakistan before 9/11. At the same time, Saudi Arabia's society was a place where al Qaeda raised money directly from individuals and through charities. It was the society that produced 15 of the 19 hijackers.

The Kingdom is one of the world's most religiously conservative societies, and its identity is closely bound to its religious links, especially its position as the guardian of Islam's two holiest sites. Charitable giving, or *zakat,* is one of the five pillars of Islam. It is broader and more pervasive than Western ideas of charity—functioning also as a form of income tax, educational assistance, foreign aid, and a source of political influence. The Western notion of the separation of civic and religious duty does not exist in Islamic cultures. Funding charitable works is an integral function of the governments in the Islamic world. It is so ingrained in Islamic culture that in Saudi Arabia, for example, a department within the Saudi Ministry of Finance and National Economy collects zakat directly, much as the U.S. Internal Revenue Service collects payroll withholding tax. Closely tied to zakat is the dedication of the government to propagating the Islamic faith, particularly the Wahhabi sect that flourishes in Saudi Arabia.

Traditionally, throughout the Muslim world, there is no formal oversight mechanism for donations. As Saudi wealth increased, the amounts contributed by individuals and the state grew dramatically. Substantial sums went to finance Islamic charities of every kind.

While Saudi domestic charities are regulated by the Ministry of Labor and Social Welfare, charities and international relief agencies, such as the World Assembly of Muslim Youth (WAMY), are currently regulated by the Ministry of Islamic Affairs. This ministry uses zakat and government funds to spread Wahhabi beliefs throughout the world, including in mosques and schools. Often these schools provide the only education available; even in affluent countries, Saudi-funded Wahhabi schools are often the only Islamic schools. Some Wahhabi-funded organizations have been exploited by extremists to further their goal of violent jihad against non-Muslims. One such organization has been the al Haramain Islamic Foundation; the assets of some branch offices have been frozen by the U.S. and Saudi governments.

Until 9/11, few Saudis would have considered government oversight of charitable donations necessary; many would have perceived it as interference in the exercise of their faith. At the same time, the government's ability to finance most state expenditures with energy revenues has delayed the need for a modern income tax system. As a result, there have been strong religious, cultural, and administrative barriers to monitoring charitable spending. That appears to be changing, however, now that the goal of violent jihad also extends to overthrowing Sunni governments (such as the House of Saud) that are not living up to the ideals of the Islamist extremists.[16]

The leaders of the United States and the rulers of Saudi Arabia have long had friendly relations, rooted in fundamentally common interests against the Soviet Union during the Cold War, in American hopes that Saudi oil supplies would stabilize the supply and price of oil in world markets, and in Saudi hopes that America could help protect the Kingdom against foreign threats.

In 1990, the Kingdom hosted U.S. armed forces before the first U.S.-led war against Iraq. American soldiers and airmen have given their lives to help protect Saudi Arabia. The Saudi government has difficulty acknowledging this. American military bases remained there until 2003, as part of an international commitment to contain Iraq.

For many years, leaders on both sides preferred to keep their ties quiet and behind the scenes. As a result, neither the U.S. nor the Saudi people appreciated all the dimensions of the bilateral relationship, including the Saudi role in U.S. strategies to promote the Middle East peace process. In each country, political figures find it difficult to publicly defend good relations with the other.

Today, mutual recriminations flow. Many Americans see Saudi Arabia as an enemy, not as an embattled ally. They perceive an autocratic government that oppresses women, dominated by a wealthy and indolent elite. Saudi contacts with American politicians are frequently invoked as accusations in partisan political arguments. Americans are often appalled by the intolerance, anti-Semitism, and anti-American arguments taught in schools and preached in mosques.

Saudis are angry too. Many educated Saudis who were sympathetic to America now perceive the United States as an unfriendly state. One Saudi reformer noted to us that the demonization of Saudi Arabia in the U.S. media gives ammunition to radicals, who accuse reformers of being U.S. lackeys. Tens of thousands of Saudis who once regularly traveled to (and often had homes in) the United States now go elsewhere.[17]

Among Saudis, the United States is seen as aligned with Israel in its conflict with the Palestinians, with whom Saudis ardently sympathize. Although Saudi Arabia's cooperation against terrorism improved to some extent after the September 11 attacks, significant problems remained. Many in the Kingdom initially reacted with disbelief and denial. In the following months, as the truth became clear, some leading Saudis quietly acknowledged the problem but still did not see their own regime as threatened, and thus often did not respond promptly to U.S. requests for help. Though Saddam Hussein was widely detested, many Saudis are sympathetic to the anti-U.S. insurgents in Iraq, although majorities also condemn jihadist attacks in the Kingdom.[18]

As in Pakistan, Yemen, and other countries, attitudes changed when the terrorism came home. Cooperation had already become significant, but after the bombings in Riyadh on May 12, 2003, it improved much more. The Kingdom openly discussed the problem of radicalism, criticized the terrorists as religiously deviant, reduced official support for religious activity overseas, closed suspect charitable foundations, and publicized arrests—very public moves for a government that has preferred to keep internal problems quiet.

The Kingdom of Saudi Arabia is now locked in mortal combat with al Qaeda. Saudi police are regularly being killed in shootouts with terrorists. In June 2004, the Saudi ambassador to the United States called publicly—in the Saudi press—for his government to wage a jihad of its own against the terrorists. "We must all, as a state and as a people, recognize the truth about these criminals," he declared, "[i]f we do not declare a general mobilization—we will lose this war on terrorism."[19]

Saudi Arabia is a troubled country. Although regarded as very wealthy, in fact per capita income has dropped from $28,000 at its height to the present level of about $8,000. Social and religious traditions complicate adjustment to modern economic activity and limit employment opportunities for young Saudis. Women find their education and employment sharply limited.

President Clinton offered us a perceptive analysis of Saudi Arabia, contending that fundamentally friendly rulers have been constrained by their desire to preserve the status quo. He, like others, made the case for pragmatic reform instead. He hopes the rulers will envision what they want their Kingdom to become in 10 or 20 years, and start a process in which their friends can help them change.[20]

There are signs that Saudi Arabia's royal family is trying to build a consensus for political reform, though uncertain about how fast and how far to go. Crown Prince Abdullah wants the Kingdom to join the World Trade Organization to accelerate economic liberalization. He has embraced the *Arab Human Development Report*, which was highly critical of the Arab world's political, economic, and social failings and called for greater economic and political reform.[21]

Cooperation with Saudi Arabia against Islamist terrorism is very much in the U.S. interest. Such cooperation can exist for a time largely in secret, as it does now, but it cannot grow and thrive there. Nor, on either side, can friendship be unconditional.

Recommendation: The problems in the U.S.-Saudi relationship must be confronted, openly. The United States and Saudi Arabia must determine if they can build a relationship that political leaders on both sides are prepared to publicly defend—a relationship about more than oil. It should include a shared commitment to political and economic reform, as Saudis make common cause with the outside world. It should include a shared interest in greater tolerance and cultural respect, translating into a commitment to fight the violent extremists who foment hatred.

12.3 PREVENT THE CONTINUED GROWTH OF ISLAMIST TERRORISM

In October 2003, reflecting on progress after two years of waging the global war on terrorism, Defense Secretary Donald Rumsfeld asked his advisers: "Are we capturing, killing or deterring and dissuading more terrorists every day than the madrassas and the radical clerics are recruiting, training and deploying against us? Does the US need to fashion a broad, integrated plan to stop the next generation of terrorists? The US is putting relatively little effort into a long-range plan, but we are putting a great deal of effort into trying to stop terrorists. The cost-benefit ratio is against us! Our cost is billions against the terrorists' costs of millions."[22]

These are the right questions. Our answer is that we need short-term action on a long-range strategy, one that invigorates our foreign policy with the attention that the President and Congress have given to the military and intelligence parts of the conflict against Islamist terrorism.

ENGAGE THE STRUGGLE OF IDEAS

The United States is heavily engaged in the Muslim world and will be for many years to come. This American engagement is resented. Polls in 2002 found that among America's friends, like Egypt—the recipient of more U.S. aid for the past 20 years than any other Muslim country—only 15 percent of the population had a favorable opinion of the United States. In Saudi Arabia the number was 12 percent. And two-thirds of those surveyed in 2003 in countries from Indonesia to Turkey (a NATO ally) were very or somewhat fearful that the United States may attack them.[23]

Support for the United States has plummeted. Polls taken in Islamic countries after 9/11 suggested that many or most people thought the United States was doing the right thing in its fight against terrorism; few people saw popular support for al Qaeda; half of those surveyed said that ordinary people had a favorable view of the United States. By 2003, polls showed that "the bottom has fallen out of support for America in most of the Muslim world. Negative views of the U.S. among Muslims, which had been largely limited to countries in the Middle East, have spread. . . . Since last summer, favorable ratings for the U.S. have fallen from 61% to 15% in Indonesia and from 71% to 38% among Muslims in Nigeria."[24]

Many of these views are at best uninformed about the United States and, at worst, informed by cartoonish stereotypes, the coarse expression of a fashionable "Occidentalism" among intellectuals who caricature U.S. values and policies. Local newspapers and the few influential satellite broadcasters—like al Jazeera—often reinforce the jihadist theme that portrays the United States as anti-Muslim.[25]

The small percentage of Muslims who are fully committed to Usama Bin Ladin's version of Islam are impervious to persuasion. It is among the large majority of Arabs and Muslims that we must encourage reform, freedom, democracy, and opportunity, even though our own promotion of these messages is limited in its effectiveness simply because we are its carriers. Muslims themselves will have to reflect upon such basic issues as the concept of jihad, the position of women, and the place of non-Muslim minorities. The United States can promote moderation, but cannot ensure its ascendancy. Only Muslims can do this.

The setting is diffcult. The combined gross domestic product of the 22 countries in the Arab League is less than the GDP of Spain. Forty percent of adult Arabs are illiterate, two-thirds of them women. One-third of the broader Middle East lives on less than two dollars a day. Less than 2 percent of the population has access to the Internet. The majority of older Arab youths have expressed a desire to emigrate to other countries, particularly those in Europe.[26]

In short, the United States has to help defeat an ideology, not just a group of people, and we must do so under difficult circumstances. How can the United States and its friends help moderate Muslims combat the extremist ideas?

Recommendation: The U.S. government must define what the message is, what it stands for. We should offer an example of moral leadership in the world, committed to treat people humanely, abide by the rule of law, and be generous and caring to our neighbors. America and Muslim friends can agree on respect for human dignity and opportunity. To Muslim parents, terrorists like Bin Ladin have nothing to offer their children but visions of violence and death. America and its friends have a crucial advantage—we can offer these parents a vision that might give their children a better future. If we heed the views of thoughtful leaders in the Arab and Muslim world, a moderate consensus can be found.

That vision of the future should stress life over death: individual educational and economic opportunity. This vision includes widespread political participation and contempt for indiscriminate violence. It includes respect for the rule of law, openness in discussing differences, and tolerance for opposing points of view.

Recommendation: Where Muslim governments, even those who are friends, do not respect these principles, the United States must stand for a better future. One of the lessons of the long Cold War was that short-term gains in cooperating with the most repressive and brutal governments were too often outweighed by long-term setbacks for America's stature and interests.

American foreign policy is part of the message. America's policy choices have consequences. Right or wrong, it is simply a fact that American policy regarding the Israeli-Palestinian conflict and American actions in Iraq are dominant staples of popular commentary across the Arab and Muslim world. That does not mean U.S. choices have been wrong. It means those choices must be integrated with America's message of opportunity to the Arab and Muslim world. Neither Israel nor the new Iraq will be safer if worldwide Islamist terrorism grows stronger.

The United States must do more to communicate its message. Reflecting on Bin Ladin's success in reaching Muslim audiences, Richard Holbrooke wondered, "How can a man in a cave outcommunicate the world's leading communications society?" Deputy Secretary of State Richard Armitage worried to us that Americans have been "exporting our fears and our anger," not our vision of opportunity and hope.[27]

Recommendation: Just as we did in the Cold War, we need to defend our ideals abroad vigorously. America does stand up for its values. The United States defended, and still defends, Muslims against tyrants and criminals in Somalia, Bosnia, Kosovo, Afghanistan, and Iraq. If the United States does not act aggressively to define itself in the Islamic world, the extremists will gladly do the job for us.

- **Recognizing that Arab and Muslim audiences rely on satellite television and radio, the government has begun some promising initiatives in television and radio broadcasting to the Arab world, Iran, and Afghanistan. These efforts are beginning to reach large audiences. The Broadcasting Board of Governors has asked for much larger resources. It should get them.**
- **The United States should rebuild the scholarship, exchange, and library programs that reach out to young people and offer them knowledge and hope. Where such assistance is provided, it should be identified as coming from the citizens of the United States.**

AN AGENDA OF OPPORTUNITY

The United States and its friends can stress educational and economic opportunity. The United Nations has rightly equated "literacy as freedom."

- The international community is moving toward setting a concrete goal—to cut the Middle East region's illiteracy rate in half by 2010, targeting women and girls and supporting programs for adult literacy.
- Unglamorous help is needed to support the basics, such as textbooks that translate more of the world's knowledge into local languages and libraries to house such materials. Education about the outside world, or other cultures, is weak.

- More vocational education is needed, too, in trades and business skills. The Middle East can also benefit from some of the programs to bridge the digital divide and increase Internet access that have already been developed for other regions of the world.

Education that teaches tolerance, the dignity and value of each individual, and respect for different beliefs is a key element in any global strategy to eliminate Islamist terrorism.

Recommendation: The U.S. government should offer to join with other nations in generously supporting a new International Youth Opportunity Fund. Funds will be spent directly for building and operating primary and secondary schools in those Muslim states that commit to sensibly investing their own money in public education.

Economic openness is essential. Terrorism is not caused by poverty. Indeed, many terrorists come from relatively well-off families. Yet when people lose hope, when societies break down, when countries fragment, the breeding grounds for terrorism are created. Backward economic policies and repressive political regimes slip into societies that are without hope, where ambition and passions have no constructive outlet.

The policies that support economic development and reform also have political implications. Economic and political liberties tend to be linked. Commerce, especially international commerce, requires ongoing cooperation and compromise, the exchange of ideas across cultures, and the peaceful resolution of differences through negotiation or the rule of law. Economic growth expands the middle class, a constituency for further reform. Successful economies rely on vibrant private sectors, which have an interest in curbing indiscriminate government power. Those who develop the practice of controlling their own economic destiny soon desire a voice in their communities and political societies.

The U.S. government has announced the goal of working toward a Middle East Free Trade Area, or MEFTA, by 2013. The United States has been seeking comprehensive free trade agreements (FTAs) with the Middle Eastern nations most firmly on the path to reform. The U.S.-Israeli FTA was enacted in 1985, and Congress implemented an FTA with Jordan in 2001. Both agreements have expanded trade and investment, thereby supporting domestic economic reform. In 2004, new FTAs were signed with Morocco and Bahrain, and are awaiting congressional approval. These models are drawing the interest of their neighbors. Muslim countries can become full participants in the rules-based global trading system, as the United States considers lowering its trade barriers with the poorest Arab nations.

Recommendation: A comprehensive U.S. Strategy to counter terrorism should include economic policies that encourage development, more open societies, and opportunities for people to improve the lives of their families and to enhance prospects for their children's future.

TURNING A NATIONAL STRATEGY INTO A COALITION STRATEGY

Practically every aspect of U.S. counterterrorism strategy relies on international cooperation. Since 9/11, these contacts concerning military, law enforcement, intelligence, travel and customs, and financial matters have expanded so dramatically, and often in an ad hoc way, that it is difficult to track these efforts, much less integrate them.

Recommendation: The United States should engage other nations in developing a comprehensive coalition strategy against Islamist terrorism. There are several multilateral institutions in which such issues should be addressed. But the most important policies should be discussed and coordinated in a flexible contact group of leading coalition governments. This is a good place, for example, to develop joint strategies for targeting terrorist travel, or for hammering out a common strategy for the places where terrorists may be finding sanctuary.

Presently the Muslim and Arab states meet with each other, in organizations such as the Islamic Conference and the Arab League. The Western states meet with each other in organizations such as NATO and the Group of Eight summit of leading industrial nations. A recent G-8 summit initiative to begin a dialogue about reform may be a start toward finding a place where leading Muslim states can discuss—and be seen to discuss—critical policy issues with the leading Western powers committed to the future of the Arab and Muslim world.

These new international efforts can create durable habits of visible cooperation, as states willing to step up to their responsibilities join together in constructive efforts to direct assistance and coordinate action.

Coalition warfare also requires coalition policies on what to do with enemy captives. Allegations that the United States abused prisoners in its custody make it harder to build the diplomatic, political, and military alliances the government will need. The United States should work with friends to develop mutually agreed-on principles for the detention and humane treatment of captured international terrorists who are not being held under a particular country's criminal laws. Countries such as Britain, Australia, and Muslim friends, are committed to fighting terrorists. America should be able to reconcile its views on how to balance humanity and security with our nation's commitment to these same goals.

The United States and some of its allies do not accept the application of full Geneva Convention treatment of prisoners of war to captured terrorists. Those Conventions establish a minimum set of standards for prisoners in internal conflicts. Since the international struggle against Islamist terrorism is not internal, those provisions do not formally apply, but they are commonly accepted as basic standards for humane treatment.

Recommendation: The United States should engage its friends to develop a common coalition approach toward the detention and humane treatment of captured terrorists. New principles might draw upon Article 3 of the Geneva Conventions on the law of armed conflict. That article was specifically designed for those cases in which the usual laws of war did not apply. Its minimum standards are generally accepted throughout the world as customary international law.

PROLIFERATION OF WEAPONS OF MASS DESTRUCTION

The greatest danger of another catastrophic attack in the United States will materialize if the world's most dangerous terrorists acquire the world's most dangerous weapons. As we note in chapter 2, al Qaeda has tried to acquire or make nuclear weapons for at least ten years. In chapter 4, we mentioned officials worriedly discussing, in 1998, reports that Bin Ladin's associates thought their leader was intent on carrying out a "Hiroshima."

These ambitions continue. In the public portion of his February 2004 worldwide threat assessment to Congress, DCI Tenet noted that Bin Ladin considered the acquisition of weapons of mass destruction to be a "religious obligation." He warned that al Qaeda "continues to pursue its strategic goal of obtaining a nuclear capability." Tenet added that "more than two dozen other terrorist groups are pursuing CBRN [chemical, biological, radiological, and nuclear] materials."[28]

A nuclear bomb can be built with a relatively small amount of nuclear material. A trained nuclear engineer with an amount of highly enriched uranium or plutonium about the size of a grapefruit or an orange, together with commercially available material, could fashion a nuclear device that would fit in a van like the one Ramzi Yousef parked in the garage of the World Trade Center in 1993. Such a bomb would level Lower Manhattan.[29]

The coalition strategies we have discussed to combat Islamist terrorism should therefore be combined with a parallel, vital effort to prevent and counter the proliferation of weapons of mass destruction (WMD). We recommend several initiatives in this area.

STRENGTHEN COUNTERPROLIFERATION EFFORTS.

While efforts to shut down Libya's illegal nuclear program have been generally successful, Pakistan's illicit trade and the nuclear smuggling networks of Pakistani scientist A.Q. Khan have revealed that the spread of nuclear weapons is a problem of global dimensions. Attempts to deal with Iran's nuclear program are still underway. Therefore, the United States should work with the international community to develop laws and an international legal regime with universal jurisdiction to enable the capture, interdiction, and prosecution of such smugglers by any state in the world where they do not disclose their activities.

EXPAND THE PROLIFERATION SECURITY INITIATIVE.

In May 2003, the Bush administration announced the Proliferation Security Initiative (PSI): nations in a willing partnership combining their national capabilities to use military, economic, and diplomatic tools to interdict threatening shipments of WMD and missile-related technology.

The PSI can be more effective if it uses intelligence and planning resources of the NATO alliance. Moreover, PSI membership should be open to non-NATO countries. Russia and China should be encouraged to participate.

SUPPORT THE COOPERATIVE THREAT REDUCTION PROGRAM.

Outside experts are deeply worried about the U.S. government's commitment and approach to securing the weapons and highly dangerous materials still scattered in Russia and other countries of the Soviet Union. The government's main instrument in this area, the Cooperative Threat Reduction Program (usually referred to as "Nunn-Lugar," after the senators who sponsored the legislation in 1991), is now in need of expansion, improvement, and resources. The U.S. government has recently redoubled its international commitments to support this program, and we recommend that the United States do all it can, if Russia and other countries will do their part. The government should weigh the value of this investment against the catastrophic cost America would face should such weapons find their way to the terrorists who are so anxious to acquire them.

Recommendation: Our report shows that al Qaeda has tried to acquire or make weapons of mass destruction for at least ten years. There is no doubt the United States

would be a prime target. **Preventing the proliferation of these weapons warrants a maximum effort—by strengthening counterproliferation efforts, expanding the Proliferation Security Initiative, and supporting the Cooperative Threat Reduction program.**

TARGETING TERRORIST MONEY

The general public sees attacks on terrorist finance as a way to "starve the terrorists of money." So, initially, did the U.S. government. After 9/11, the United States took aggressive actions to designate terrorist financiers and freeze their money, in the United States and through resolutions of the United Nations. These actions appeared to have little effect and, when confronted by legal challenges, the United States and the United Nations were often forced to unfreeze assets.

The difficulty, understood later, was that even if the intelligence community might "link" someone to a terrorist group through acquaintances or communications, the task of tracing the money from that individual to the terrorist group, or otherwise showing complicity, was far more difficult. It was harder still to do so without disclosing secrets.

These early missteps made other countries unwilling to freeze assets or otherwise act merely on the basis of a U.S. action. Multilateral freezing mechanisms now require waiting periods before being put into effect, eliminating the element of surprise and thus virtually ensuring that little money is actually frozen. Worldwide asset freezes have not been adequately enforced and have been easily circumvented, often within weeks, by simple methods.

But trying to starve the terrorists of money is like trying to catch one kind of fish by draining the ocean. A better strategy has evolved since those early months, as the government learned more about how al Qaeda raises, moves, and spends money.

Recommendation: Vigorous efforts to track terrorist financing must remain front and center in U.S. counterterrorism efforts. The government has recognized that information about terrorist money helps us to understand their networks, search them out, and disrupt their operations. Intelligence and law enforcement have targeted the relatively small number of financial facilitators—individuals al Qaeda relied on for their ability to raise and deliver money—at the core of al Qaeda's revenue stream. These efforts have worked. The death or capture of several important facilitators has decreased the amount of money available to al Qaeda and has increased its costs and difficulty in raising and moving that money. Captures have additionally provided a windfall of intelligence that can be used to continue the cycle of disruption.

The U.S. financial community and some international financial institutions have generally provided law enforcement and intelligence agencies with extraordinary cooperation, particularly in supplying information to support quickly developing investigations. Obvious vulnerabilities in the U.S. financial system have been corrected. The United States has been less successful in persuading other countries to adopt financial regulations that would permit the tracing of financial transactions.

Public designation of terrorist financiers and organizations is still part of the fight, but it is not the primary weapon. Designations are instead a form of diplomacy, as governments join together to identify named individuals and groups as terrorists. They also prevent open fundraising. Some charities that have been identified as likely avenues for terrorist financing have seen their donations diminish and their activities come under more scrutiny, and others have been put out of business, although controlling overseas branches of Gulf-area charities remains a challenge. The Saudi crackdown after the May 2003 terrorist attacks in Riyadh has apparently reduced the funds available to al Qaeda—perhaps drastically—but it is too soon to know if this reduction will last.

Though progress apparently has been made, terrorists have shown considerable creativity in their methods of moving money. If al Qaeda is replaced by smaller, decentralized terrorist groups, the premise behind the government's efforts—that terrorists need a financial support network—may become outdated. Moreover, some terrorist operations do not rely on outside sources of money and may now be self-funding, either through legitimate employment or low-level criminal activity.[30]

12.4 PROTECT AGAINST AND PREPARE FOR TERRORIST ATTACKS

In the nearly three years since 9/11, Americans have become better protected against terrorist attack. Some of the changes are due to government action, such as new precautions to protect aircraft. A portion can be attributed to the sheer scale of spending and effort. Publicity and the vigilance of ordinary Americans also make a difference.

But the President and other officials acknowledge that although Americans may be safer, they are not safe. Our report shows that the terrorists analyze defenses. They plan accordingly. Defenses cannot achieve perfect safety. They make targets harder to attack successfully, and they deter attacks by making capture more likely. Just increasing the attacker's odds of failure may make the difference between a plan attempted, or a plan discarded. The enemy also may have to develop more elaborate plans, thereby increasing the danger of exposure or defeat.

Protective measures also prepare for the attacks that may get through, containing the damage and saving lives.

TERRORIST TRAVEL

More than 500 million people annually cross U.S. borders at legal entry points, about 330 million of them noncitizens. Another 500,000 or more enter illegally without inspection across America's thousands of miles of land borders or remain in the country past the expiration of their permitted stay. The challenge for national security in an age of terrorism is to prevent the very few people who may pose overwhelming risks from entering or remaining in the United States undetected.[31]

In the decade before September 11, 2001, border security—encompassing travel, entry, and immigration—was not seen as a national security matter. Public figures voiced concern about the "war on drugs," the right level and kind of immigration, problems along the southwest border, migration crises originating in the Caribbean and elsewhere, or the growing criminal traffic in humans. The immigration system as a whole was widely viewed as increasingly dysfunctional and badly in need of reform. In national security circles, however, only smuggling of weapons of mass destruction carried weight, not the entry of terrorists who might use such weapons or the presence of associated foreign-born terrorists.

For terrorists, travel documents are as important as weapons. Terrorists must travel clandestinely to meet, train, plan, case targets, and gain access to attack. To them, international travel presents great danger, because they must surface to pass through regulated channels, present themselves to border security officials, or attempt to circumvent inspection points.

In their travels, terrorists use evasive methods, such as altered and counterfeit passports and visas, specific travel methods and routes, liaisons with corrupt government officials, human smuggling networks, supportive travel agencies, and immigration and identity fraud. These can sometimes be detected.

Before 9/11, no agency of the U.S. government systematically analyzed terrorists' travel strategies. Had they done so, they could have discovered the ways in which the terrorist predecessors to al Qaeda had been systematically but detectably exploiting weaknesses in our border security since the early 1990s.

We found that as many as 15 of the 19 hijackers were potentially vulnerable to interception by border authorities. Analyzing their characteristic travel documents and travel patterns could have allowed authorities to intercept 4 to 15 hijackers and more effective use of information available in U.S. government databases could have identified up to 3 hijackers.[32]

Looking back, we can also see that the routine operations of our immigration laws—that is, aspects of those laws not specifically aimed at protecting against terrorism—inevitably shaped al Qaeda's planning and opportunities. Because they were deemed not to be bona fide tourists or students as they claimed, five conspirators that we know of tried to get visas and failed, and one was denied entry by an inspector. We also found that had the immigration system set a higher bar for determining whether individuals are who or what they claim to be—and ensuring routine consequences for violations—it could potentially have excluded, removed, or come into further contact with several hijackers who did not appear to meet the terms for admitting short-term visitors.[33]

Our investigation showed that two systemic weaknesses came together in our border system's inability to contribute to an effective defense against the 9/11 attacks: a lack of well-developed counterterrorism measures as a part of border security and an immigration system not able to deliver on its basic commitments, much less support counterterrorism. These weaknesses have been reduced but are far from being overcome.

Recommendation: Targeting travel is at least as powerful a weapon against terrorists as targeting their money. The United States should combine terrorist travel intelligence, operations, and law enforcement in a strategy to intercept terrorists, find terrorist travel facilitators, and constrain terrorist mobility.

Since 9/11, significant improvements have been made to create an integrated watchlist that makes terrorist name information available to border and law enforcement authorities. However, in the already difficult process of merging border agencies in the new Department of Homeland Security—"changing the engine while flying" as one official put it[34]—new insights into terrorist travel have not yet been integrated into the front lines of border security.

The small terrorist travel intelligence collection and analysis program currently in place has produced disproportionately useful results. It should be expanded. Since officials at the borders encounter travelers and their documents first and investigate travel facilitators, they must work closely with intelligence officials.

Internationally and in the United States, constraining terrorist travel should become a vital part of counterterrorism strategy. Better technology and training to detect terrorist travel documents are the most important immediate steps to reduce America's vulnerability to clandestine entry. Every stage of our border and immigration system should have as a part of its operations the detection of terrorist indicators on travel documents. Information systems able to authenticate travel documents and detect potential terrorist indicators should be used at consulates, at primary border inspection lines, in immigration services offices, and in intelligence and enforcement units. All frontline personnel should receive some training. Dedicated specialists and ongoing linkages with the intelligence community are also required. The Homeland Security Department's Directorate of Information Analysis and Infrastructure Protection should receive more resources to accomplish its mission as the bridge between the frontline border agencies and the rest of the government counterterrorism community.

A BIOMETRIC SCREENING SYSTEM

When people travel internationally, they usually move through defined channels, or portals. They may seek to acquire a passport. They may apply for a visa. They stop at ticket counters, gates, and exit controls at airports and seaports. Upon arrival, they pass through inspection points. They may transit to another gate to get on an airplane. Once inside the country, they may seek another form of identification and try to enter a government or private facility. They may seek to change immigration status in order to remain.

Each of these checkpoints or portals is a screening—a chance to establish that people are who they say they are and are seeking access for their stated purpose, to intercept identifiable suspects, and to take effective action.

The job of protection is shared among these many defined checkpoints. By taking advantage of them all, we need not depend on any one point in the system to do the whole job. The challenge is to see the common problem across agencies and functions and develop a conceptual framework—an architecture—for an effective screening system.[35]

Throughout government, and indeed in private enterprise, agencies and firms at these portals confront recurring judgments that balance security, efficiency, and civil liberties. These problems should be addressed systemically, not in an ad hoc, fragmented way. For example:

WHAT INFORMATION IS AN INDIVIDUAL REQUIRED TO PRESENT AND IN WHAT FORM?

A fundamental problem, now beginning to be addressed, is the lack of standardized information in "feeder" documents used in identifying individuals. Biometric identifiers that measure unique physical characteristics, such as facial features, fingerprints, or iris scans, and reduce them to digitized, numerical statements called algorithms, are just beginning to be used. Travel history, however, is still recorded in passports with entry-exit stamps called cachets, which al Qaeda has trained its operatives to forge and use to conceal their terrorist activities.

HOW WILL THE INDIVIDUAL AND THE INFORMATION BE CHECKED?

There are many databases just in the United States—for terrorist, criminal, and immigration history, as well as financial information, for instance. Each is set up for different purposes and stores different kinds of data, under varying rules of access. Nor is access always guaranteed. Acquiring information held by foreign governments may require painstaking negotiations, and records that are not yet digitized are difficult to search or analyze. The development of terrorist indicators has hardly begun, and behavioral cues remain important.

WHO WILL SCREEN INDIVIDUALS, AND WHAT WILL THEY BE TRAINED TO DO?

A wide range of border, immigration, and law enforcement officials encounter visitors and immigrants and they are given little training in terrorist travel intelligence. Fraudulent travel documents, for instance, are usually returned to travelers who are denied entry without further examination for terrorist trademarks, investigation as to their source, or legal process.

WHAT ARE THE CONSEQUENCES OF FINDING A SUSPICIOUS INDICATOR, AND WHO WILL TAKE ACTION?

One risk is that responses may be ineffective or produce no further information. Four of the 9/11 attackers were pulled into secondary border inspection, but then admitted. More than half of the 19 hijackers were flagged by the Federal Aviation Administration's profiling system when they arrived for their flights, but the consequence was that bags, not people, were checked. Competing risks include "false positives," or the danger that rules may be applied with insufficient training or judgment. Overreactions can impose high costs too— on individuals, our economy, and our beliefs about justice.

- A special note on the importance of trusting subjective judgment: One potential hijacker was turned back by an immigration inspector as he tried to enter the United States. The inspector relied on intuitive experience to ask questions more than he relied on any objective factor that could be detected by "scores" or a machine. Good people who have worked in such jobs for a long time understand this phenomenon well. Other evidence we obtained confirmed the importance of letting experienced gate agents or security screeners ask questions and use their judgment. This is not an invitation to arbitrary exclusions. But any effective system has to grant some scope, perhaps in a little extra inspection or one more check, to the instincts and discretion of well trained human beings.

Recommendation: The U.S. border security system should be integrated into a larger network of screening points that includes our transportation system and access to vital facilities, such as nuclear reactors. The President should direct the Department of Homeland Security to lead the effort to design a comprehensive screening system, addressing common problems and setting common standards with systemwide goals in mind. Extending those standards among other governments could dramatically strengthen America and the world's collective ability to intercept individuals who pose catastrophic threats.

We advocate a system for screening, not categorical profiling. A screening system looks for particular, identifiable suspects or indicators of risk. It does not involve guesswork about who might be dangerous. It requires frontline border officials who have the tools and resources to establish that people are who they say they are, intercept identifiable suspects, and disrupt terrorist operations.

THE U.S. BORDER SCREENING SYSTEM

The border and immigration system of the United States must remain a visible manifestation of our belief in freedom, democracy, global economic growth, and the rule of law, yet serve equally well as a vital element of counterterrorism. Integrating terrorist travel information in the ways we have described is the most immediate need. But the underlying system must also be sound.

Since September 11, the United States has built the first phase of a biometric screening program, called US VISIT (the United States Visitor and Immigrant Status Indicator Technology program). It takes two bioretric identifiers—digital photographs and prints of two index fingers—from travelers. False identities are used by terrorists to avoid being detected on a watchlist. These biometric identifiers make such evasions far more difficult.

So far, however, only visitors who acquire visas to travel to the United States are covered. While visitors from "visa waiver" countries will be added to the program, beginning this year, covered travelers will still constitute only about 12 percent of all non-citizens crossing U.S. borders. Moreover, exit data are not uniformly collected and entry data are not fully automated. It is not clear the system can be installed before 2010, but even this timetable may be too slow, given the possible security dangers.[36]

- Americans should not be exempt from carrying biometric passports or otherwise enabling their identities to be securely verified when they enter the United States; nor should Canadians or Mexicans. Currently U.S. persons are exempt from carrying passports when returning from Canada, Mexico, and the Caribbean. The current system enables non-U.S. citizens to gain entry by showing minimal identification. The 9/11 experience shows that terrorists study and exploit America's vulnerabilities.
- To balance this measure, programs to speed known travelers should be a higher priority, permitting inspectors to focus on greater risks. The daily commuter should not be subject to the same measures as first-time travelers. An individual should be able to preenroll, with his or her identity verified in passage. Updates of database information and other checks can ensure ongoing reliability. The solution, requiring more research and development, is likely to combine radio frequency technology with biometric identifiers.[37]
- The current patchwork of border screening systems, including several frequent traveler programs, should be consolidated with the US VISIT system to enable the development of an integrated system, which in turn can become part of the wider screening plan we suggest.
- The program allowing individuals to travel from foreign countries through the United States to a third country, without having to obtain a U.S. visa, has been suspended. Because "transit without visa" can be exploited by terrorists to enter the United States, the program should not be reinstated unless and until transit passage areas can be fully secured to prevent passengers from illegally exiting the airport.

Inspectors adjudicating entries of the 9/11 hijackers lacked adequate information and knowledge of the rules. All points in the border system—from consular offices to immigration services offices—will need appropriate electronic access to an individual's file. Scattered units at Homeland Security and the State Department perform screening and data mining: instead, a government-wide team of border and transportation officials should be working together. A modern border and immigration system should combine a biometric entry-exit system with accessible files on visitors and immigrants, along with intelligence on indicators of terrorist travel.

Our border screening system should check people efficiently and welcome friends. Admitting large numbers of students, scholars, businesspeople, and tourists fuels our economy, cultural vitality, and political reach. There is evidence that the present system is disrupting travel to the United States. Overall, visa applications in 2003 were down over 32 percent since 2001. In the Middle East, they declined about 46 percent. Training and the design of security measures should be continuously adjusted.[38]

Recommendation: The Department of Homeland Security, properly supported by the Congress, should complete, as quickly as possible, a biometric entry-exit screening system, including a single system for speeding qualified travelers. It should be integrated with the system that provides benefits to foreigners seeking to stay in the United States. Linking biometric passports to good data systems and decisionmaking is a fundamental goal. No one can hide his or her debt by acquiring a credit card with a slightly different name. Yet today, a terrorist can defeat the link to electronic records by tossing away an old passport and slightly altering the name in the new one.

Completion of the entry-exit system is a major and expensive challenge. Biometrics have been introduced into an antiquated computer environment. Replacement of these systems and improved biometric systems will be required. Nonetheless, funding and completing a biometrics-based entry-exit system is an essential investment in our national security.

Exchanging terrorist information with other countries, consistent with privacy requirements, along with listings of lost and stolen passports, will have immediate security benefits. We should move toward real-time verification of passports with issuing authorities. The further away from our borders that screening occurs, the more security benefits we gain. At least some screening should occur before a passenger departs on a flight destined for the United States. We should also work with other countries to ensure effective inspection regimes at all airports.[39]

The international community arrives at international standards for the design of passports through the International Civil Aviation Organization (ICAO). The global standard for identification is a digital photograph; fingerprints are optional. We must work with others to improve passport standards and provide foreign assistance to countries that need help in making the transition.[40]

Recommendation: The U.S. government cannot meet its own obligations to the American people to prevent the entry of terrorists without a major effort to collaborate with other governments. We should do more to exchange terrorist information with trusted allies, and raise U.S. and global border security standards for travel and border crossing over the medium and long term through extensive international cooperation.

IMMIGRATION LAW AND ENFORCEMENT

Our borders and immigration system, including law enforcement, ought to send a message of welcome, tolerance, and justice to members of immigrant communities in the United States and in their countries of origin. We should reach out to immigrant communities. Good immigration services are one way of doing so that is valuable in every way— including intelligence.

It is elemental to border security to know who is coming into the country. Today more than 9 million people are in the United States outside the legal immigration system. We must also be able to monitor and respond to entrances between our ports of entry, working with Canada and Mexico as much as possible.

There is a growing role for state and local law enforcement agencies. They need more training and work with federal agencies so that they can cooperate more effectively with those federal authorities in identifying terrorist suspects.

All but one of the 9/11 hijackers acquired some form of U.S. identification document, some by fraud. Acquisition of these forms of identification would have assisted them in boarding commercial flights, renting cars, and other necessary activities.

Recommendation: Secure identification should begin in the United States. The federal government should set standards for the issuance of birth certificates and sources of identification, such as drivers licenses. Fraud in identification documents is no longer just a problem of theft. At many entry points to vulnerable facilities, including gates for boarding aircraft, sources of identification are the last opportunity to ensure that people are who they say they are and to check whether they are terrorists.[41]

STRATEGIES FOR AVIATION AND TRANSPORTATION SECURITY

The U.S. transportation system is vast and, in an open society, impossible to secure completely against terrorist attacks. There are hundreds of commercial airports, thousands of planes, and tens of thousands of daily flights carrying more than half a billion passengers a year. Millions of containers are imported annually through more than 300 sea and river ports served by more than 3,700 cargo and passenger terminals. About 6,000 agencies provide transit services through buses, subways, ferries, and light-rail service to about 14 million Americans each weekday.[42]

In November 2001, Congress passed and the President signed the Aviation and Transportation Security Act. This act created the Transportation Security Administration (TSA), which is now part of the Homeland Security Department. In November 2002, both the Homeland Security Act and the Maritime Transportation Security Act followed. These laws required the development of strategic plans to describe how the new department and TSA would provide security for critical parts of the U.S. transportation sector.

Over 90 percent of the nation's $5.3 billion annual investment in the TSA goes to aviation—to fight the last war. The money has been spent mainly to meet congressional mandates to federalize the security checkpoint screeners and to deploy existing security methods and technologies at airports. The current efforts do not yet reflect a forward-looking strategic plan systematically analyzing assets, risks, costs, and benefits. Lacking such a plan, we are not convinced that our transportation security resources are being allocated to the greatest risks in a cost-effective way.

- Major vulnerabilities still exist in cargo and general aviation security. These, together with inadequate screening and access controls, continue to present aviation security challenges.
- While commercial aviation remains a possible target, terrorists may turn their attention to other modes. Opportunities to do harm are as great, or greater, in maritime or surface transportation. Initiatives to secure shipping containers have just begun. Surface transportation systems such as railroads and mass transit remain hard to protect because they are so accessible and extensive.

Despite congressional deadlines, the TSA has developed neither an integrated strategic plan for the transportation sector nor specific plans for the various modes—air, sea, and ground.

Recommendation: Hard choices must be made in allocating limited resources. The U.S. government should identify and evaluate the transportation assets that need to be protected, set risk-based priorities for defending them, select the most practical and cost-effective ways of doing so, and then develop a plan, budget, and funding to implement the effort. The plan should assign roles and missions to the relevant authorities (federal, state, regional, and local) and to private stakeholders. In measuring effectiveness, perfection is unattainable. But terrorists should perceive that potential targets are defended. They may be deterred by a significant chance of failure.

Congress should set a specific date for the completion of these plans and hold the Department of Homeland Security and TSA accountable for achieving them.

The most powerful investments may be for improvements in technologies with applications across the transportation modes, such as scanning technologies designed to screen containers that can be transported by plane, ship, truck, or rail. Though such technologies are becoming available now, widespread deployment is still years away.

In the meantime, the best protective measures may be to combine improved methods of identifying and tracking the high-risk containers, operators, and facilities that require added scrutiny with further efforts to integrate intelligence analysis, effective procedures for transmitting threat information to transportation authorities, and vigilance by transportation authorities and the public.

A Layered Security System

No single security measure is foolproof. Accordingly, the TSA must have multiple layers of security in place to defeat the more plausible and dangerous forms of attack against public transportation.

- The plan must take into consideration the full array of possible enemy tactics, such as use of insiders, suicide terrorism, or standoff attack. Each layer must be effective in its own right. Each must be supported by other layers that are redundant and coordinated.
- The TSA should be able to identify for Congress the array of potential terrorist attacks, the layers of security in place, and the reliability provided by each layer. TSA must develop a plan as described above to improve weak individual layers and the effectiveness of the layered systems it deploys.

On 9/11, the 19 hijackers were screened by a computer-assisted screening system called CAPPS. More than half were identified for further inspection, which applied only to their checked luggage.

Under current practices, air carriers enforce government orders to stop certain known and suspected terrorists from boarding commercial flights and to apply secondary screening procedures to others. The "no-fly" and "automatic selectee" lists include only those individuals who the U.S. government believes pose a direct threat of attacking aviation.

Because air carriers implement the program, concerns about sharing intelligence information with private firms and foreign countries keep the U.S. government from listing all terrorist and terrorist suspects who should be included. The TSA has planned to take over this function when it deploys a new screening system to take the place of CAPPS. The deployment of this system has been delayed because of claims it may violate civil liberties.

Recommendation: Improved use of "no-fly" and "automatic selectee" lists should not be delayed while the argument about a successor to CAPPS continues. This screening function should be performed by the TSA, and it should utilize the larger set of watchlists maintained by the federal government. Air carriers should be required to supply the information needed to test and implement this new system.

CAPPS is still part of the screening process, still profiling passengers, with the consequences of selection now including personal searches of the individual and carry-on bags. The TSA is dealing with the kind of screening issues that are being encountered by other agencies. As we mentioned earlier, these screening issues need to be elevated for high-level attention and addressed promptly by the government. Working through these problems can help clear the way for the TSA's screening improvements and would help many other agencies too.

The next layer is the screening checkpoint itself. As the screening system tries to stop dangerous people, the checkpoint needs to be able to find dangerous items. Two reforms are needed soon: (1) screening people for explosives, not just their carry-on bags, and (2) improving screener performance.

Recommendation: The TSA and the Congress must give priority attention to improving the ability of screening checkpoints to detect explosives on passengers. As a start, each individual selected for special screening should be screened for explosives. Further, the TSA should conduct a human factors study, a method often used in the private sector, to understand problems in screener performance and set attainable objectives for individual screeners and for the checkpoints where screening takes place.

Concerns also remain regarding the screening and transport of checked bags and cargo. More attention and resources should be directed to reducing or mitigating the threat posed by explosives in vessels' cargo holds. The TSA should expedite the installation of advanced (in-line) baggage-screening equipment. Because the aviation industry will derive substantial benefits from this deployment, it should pay a fair share of the costs. The TSA should require that every passenger aircraft carrying cargo must deploy at least one hardened container to carry any suspect cargo. TSA also needs to intensify its efforts to identify, track, and appropriately screen potentially dangerous cargo in both the aviation and maritime sectors.

THE PROTECTION OF CIVIL LIBERTIES

Many of our recommendations call for the government to increase its presence in our lives—for example, by creating standards for the issuance of forms of identification, by better securing our borders, by sharing information gathered by many different agencies. We also recommend the consolidation of authority over the now far-flung entities constituting the intelligence community. The Patriot Act vests substantial powers in our federal government. We have seen the government use the immigration laws as a tool in its counterterrorism effort. Even without the changes we recommend, the American public has vested enormous authority in the U.S. government.

At our first public hearing on March 31, 2003, we noted the need for balance as our government responds to the real and ongoing threat of terrorist attacks. The terrorists have used our open society against us. In wartime, government calls for greater powers, and then the need for those powers recedes after the war ends. This struggle will go on. Therefore, while protecting our homeland, Americans should be mindful of threats to vital personal and civil liberties. This balancing is no easy task, but we must constantly strive to keep it right.

This shift of power and authority to the government calls for an enhanced system of checks and balances to protect the precious liberties that are vital to our way of life. We therefore make three recommendations.

First, as we will discuss in chapter 13, to open up the sharing of information across so many agencies and with the private sector, the President should take responsibility for determining what information can be shared by which agencies and under what conditions. Protection of privacy rights should be one key element of this determination.

Recommendation: As the President determines the guidelines for information sharing among government agencies and by those agencies with the private sector, he should safeguard the privacy of individuals about whom information is shared.

Second, Congress responded, in the immediate aftermath of 9/11, with the Patriot Act, which vested substantial new powers in the investigative agencies of the government. Some of the most controversial provisions of the Patriot Act are to "sunset" at the end of 2005. Many of the act's provisions are relatively noncontroversial, updating America's surveillance laws to reflect technological developments in a digital age. Some executive actions that have been criticized are unrelated to the Patriot Act. The provisions in the act that facilitate the sharing of information among intelligence agencies and between law enforcement and intelligence appear, on balance, to be beneficial. Because of concerns regarding the shifting balance of power to the government, we think that a full and informed debate on the Patriot Act would be healthy.

Recommendation: The burden of proof for retaining a particular governmental power should be on the executive, to explain (a) that the power actually materially enhances security and (b) that there is adequate supervision of the executive's use of the powers to ensure protection of civil liberties. If the power is granted, there must be adequate guidelines and oversight to properly confine its use.

Third, during the course of our inquiry, we were told that there is no office within the government whose job it is to look across the government at the actions we are taking to protect ourselves to ensure that liberty concerns are appropriately considered. If, as we recommend, there is substantial change in the way we collect and share intelligence, there should be a voice within the executive branch for those concerns. Many agencies have privacy offices, albeit of limited scope. The Intelligence Oversight Board of the President's Foreign Intelligence Advisory Board has, in the past, had the job of overseeing certain activities of the intelligence community.

Recommendation: At this time of increased and consolidated government authority, there should be a board within the executive branch to oversee adherence to the guidelines we recommend and the commitment the government makes to defend our civil liberties.

We must find ways of reconciling security with liberty, since the success of one helps protect the other. The choice between security and liberty is a false choice, as nothing is more likely to endanger America's liberties than the success of a terrorist attack at home. Our history has shown us that insecurity threatens liberty. Yet, if our liberties are curtailed, we lose the values that we are struggling to defend.

SETTING PRIORITIES FOR NATIONAL PREPAREDNESS

Before 9/11, no executive department had, as its first priority, the job of defending America from domestic attack. That changed with the 2002 creation of the Department of Homeland Security. This department now has the lead responsibility for problems that feature so prominently in the 9/11 story, such as protecting borders, securing transportation and other parts of our critical infrastructure, organizing emergency assistance, and working with the private sector to assess vulnerabilities.

Throughout the government, nothing has been harder for officials—executive or legislative—than to set priorities, making hard choices in allocating limited resources. These difficulties have certainly afflicted the Department of Homeland Security, hamstrung by its many congressional overseers. In delivering assistance to state and local governments, we heard—especially in New York—about imbalances in the allocation of money. The argument concentrates on two questions.

First, how much money should be set aside for criteria not directly related to risk? Currently a major portion of the billions of dollars appropriated for state and local assistance is allocated so that each state gets a certain amount, or an allocation based on its population—wherever they live.

Recommendation: Homeland security assistance should be based strictly on an assessment of risks and vulnerabilities. Now, in 2004, Washington, D.C., and New York City are certainly at the top of any such list. We understand the contention that every state and city needs to have some minimum infrastructure for emergency response. But federal homeland security assistance should not remain a program for general revenue sharing. It should supplement state and local resources based on the risks or vulnerabilities that merit additional support. Congress should not use this money as a pork barrel.

The second question is, Can useful criteria to measure risk and vulnerability be developed that assess all the many variables? The allocation of funds should be based on an assessment of threats and vulnerabilities. That assessment should consider such factors as population, population density, vulnerability, and the presence of critical infrastructure within each state. In addition, the federal government should require each state receiving federal emergency preparedness funds to provide an analysis based on the same criteria to justify the distribution of funds in that state.

In a free-for-all over money, it is understandable that representatives will work to protect the interests of their home states or districts. But this issue is too important for politics as usual to prevail. Resources must be allocated according to vulnerabilities. We recommend that a panel of security experts be convened to develop written benchmarks for evaluating community needs. We further recommend that federal homeland security funds be allocated in accordance with those benchmarks, and that states be required to abide by those benchmarks in disbursing the federal funds. The benchmarks will be imperfect and subjective; they will continually evolve. But hard choices must be made. Those who would allocate money on a different basis should then defend their view of the national interest.

COMMAND, CONTROL, AND COMMUNICATIONS

The attacks on 9/11 demonstrated that even the most robust emergency response capabilities can be overwhelmed if an attack is large enough. Teamwork, collaboration, and cooperation at an incident site are critical to a successful response. Key decisionmakers who are represented at the incident command level help to ensure an effective response, the efficient use of resources, and responder safety. Regular joint training at all levels is, moreover, essential to ensuring close coordination during an actual incident.

Recommendation: Emergency response agencies nationwide should adopt the Incident Command System (ICS). When multiple agencies or multiple jurisdictions are involved, they should adopt a unified command. Both are proven frameworks for emergency response. We strongly support the decision that federal homeland security funding will be contingent, as of October 1, 2004, upon the adoption and regular use of ICS and unified command procedures. In the future, the Department of Homeland Security should consider making funding contingent on aggressive and realistic training in accordance with ICS and unified command procedures.

The attacks of September 11, 2001 overwhelmed the response capacity of most of the local jurisdictions where the hijacked airliners crashed. While many jurisdictions have established mutual aid compacts, a serious obstacle to multi-jurisdictional response has been the lack of indemnification for mutual-aid responders in areas such as the National Capital Region.

Public safety organizations, chief administrative officers, state emergency management agencies, and the Department of Homeland Security should develop a regional focus within the emergency responder community and promote multi-jurisdictional mutual assistance compacts. Where such compacts already exist, training in accordance with their terms should be required. Congress should pass legislation to remedy the long-standing indemnification and liability impediments to the provision of public safety mutual aid in the National Capital Region and where applicable throughout the nation.

The inability to communicate was a critical element at the World Trade Center, Pentagon, and Somerset County, Pennsylvania, crash sites, where multiple agencies and multiple jurisdictions responded. The occurrence of this problem at three very different sites is strong evidence that compatible and adequate communications among public safety organizations at the local, state, and federal levels remains an important problem.

Recommendation: Congress should support pending legislation which provides for the expedited and increased assignment of radio spectrum for public safety purposes. Furthermore, high-risk urban areas such as New York City and Washington, D.C., should establish signal corps units to ensure communications connectivity between and among civilian authorities, local first responders, and the National Guard. Federal funding of such units should be given high priority by Congress.

PRIVATE-SECTOR PREPAREDNESS

The mandate of the Department of Homeland Security does not end with government; the department is also responsible for working with the private sector to ensure preparedness. This is entirely appropriate, for the private sector controls 85 percent of the critical infrastructure in the nation. Indeed, unless a terrorist's target is a military or other secure government facility, the "first" first responders will almost certainly be civilians. Homeland security and national preparedness therefore often begins with the private sector.

Preparedness in the private sector and public sector for rescue, restart, and recovery of operations should include (1) a plan for evacuation, (2) adequate communications capabilities, and (3) a plan for continuity of operations. As we examined the emergency response to 9/11, witness after witness told us that despite 9/11, the private sector remains largely unprepared for a terrorist attack. We were also advised that the lack of a widely embraced private-sector preparedness standard was a principal contributing factor to this lack of preparedness.

We responded by asking the American National Standards Institute (ANSI) to develop a consensus on a "National Standard for Preparedness" for the private sector. ANSI convened safety, security, and business continuity experts from a wide range of industries and associations, as well as from federal, state, and local government stakeholders, to consider the need for standards for private sector emergency preparedness and business continuity.

The result of these sessions was ANSI's recommendation that the Commission endorse a voluntary National Preparedness Standard. Based on the existing American National Standard on Disaster/Emergency Management and Business Continuity Programs (NFPA 1600), the proposed National Preparedness Standard establishes a common set of criteria and terminology for preparedness, disaster management, emergency management, and business continuity programs. The experience of the private sector in the World Trade Center emergency demonstrated the need for these standards.

Recommendation: We endorse the American National Standards Institute's recommended standard for private preparedness. We were encouraged by Secretary Tom Ridge's praise of the standard, and urge the Department of Homeland Security to promote its adoption. We also encourage the insurance and credit-rating industries to look closely at a company's compliance with the ANSI standard in assessing its insurability and creditworthiness. We believe that compliance with the standard should define the standard of care owed by a company to its employees and the public for legal purposes. Private-sector preparedness is not a luxury; it is a cost of doing business in the post-9/11 world. It is ignored at a tremendous potential cost in lives, money, and national security.

NOTES

1. For spending totals, see David Baumann, "Accounting for the Deficit," *National Journal*, June 12, 2004, p. 1852 (combining categories for defense discretionary, homeland security, and international affairs).

2. White House press release, "National Strategy for Combating Terrorism," Feb. 2003 (online at www.whitehouse.gov/news/releases/2003/02/20030214-7.html).

3. "Islamist terrorism is an immediate derivative of *Islamism.* This term distinguishes itself from *Islamic* by the fact that the latter refers to a religion and culture in existence over a millennium, whereas the first is a political/religious phenomenon linked to the great events of the 20th century. Furthermore Islamists define themselves as 'Islamiyyoun/Islamists' precisely to differentiate themselves from 'Muslimun/Muslims.' . . . Islamism is defined as 'an Islamic militant, anti-democratic movement, bearing a holistic vision of Islam whose final aim is the restoration of the caliphate.' " Mehdi Mozaffari, "Bin Laden and Islamist Terrorism," *Militaert Tidsskrift*, vol. 131 (Mar. 2002), p. 1 (online at www.mirkflem.pup.blueyonder.co.uk/pdf/islamistterrorism.pdf). The Islamist movement, born about 1940, is a product of the modern world, influenced by Marxist-Leninist concepts about revolutionary organization. "Islamists consider Islam to be as much a religion as an 'ideology,' a neologism which they introduced and which remains anathema to the ulamas (the clerical scholars)." Olivier Roy, *The Failure of Political Islam*, trans. Carol Volk (Harvard Univ. Press, 1994), p. 3. Facing political limits by the end of the 1990s, the extremist wing of the Islamist movement "rejected the democratic references invoked by the moderates; and as a result, raw terrorism in its most spectacular and destructive form became its main option for reviving armed struggle in the new millennium." Gilles Kepel, *Jihad: The Trail of Political Islam*, trans. Anthony Roberts (Harvard Univ. Press, 2002), p. 14.

4. Opening the Islamic Conference of Muslim leaders from around the world on October 16, 2003, then Malaysian prime minister Mahathir Mohamad said: "Today we, the whole Muslim *ummah* [community of believers] are treated with contempt and dishonour. Our religion is denigrated. Our holy places desecrated. Our countries are occupied. Our people are starved and killed. None of our countries are truly independent. We are under pressure to conform to our oppressors' wishes about how we should behave, how we should govern our lands, how we should think even." He added: "There is a feeling of hopelessness among the Muslim countries and their people. They feel that they can do nothing right. They believe that things can only get worse. The Muslims will forever be oppressed and dominated by the Europeans and Jews." The prime minister's argument was that the Muslims should gather their assets, not striking back blindly, but instead planning a thoughtful, long-term strategy to defeat their worldwide enemies, which he argued were controlled by the Jews. "But today the Jews rule the world by proxy. They get others to fight and die for them." Speech at the Opening of the Tenth Session of the Islamic Summit Conference, Oct. 16, 2003 (online at www.oicsummit2003.Org.my/speech_03.php).

5. CIA map, "Possible Remove Havens for Terrorist and Other Illicit Activity," May 2003.

6. For the numbers, see Tariq interview (Oct. 20, 2003).

7. For Pakistan playing a key role in apprehending 500 terrorists, see Richard Armitage testimony, Mar. 23, 2004.

8. For Pakistan's unpoliced areas, see Tasneem Noorani interview (Oct. 27, 2003).

9. Pakistanis and Afghanis interviews (Oct. 2003); DOD Special Operations Command and Central Command briefings (Sept. 15–16, 2004); U.S. intelligence official interview (July 9, 2004).

10. Pervez Musharraf. "A Plea for Enlightened Moderation: Muslims Must Raise Themselves Up Through Individual Achievement and Socioeconomic Emancipation," *Washington Post*, June 1, 2004, p. A23.

11. For a review of ISAF's role, see NATO report, "NATO in Afghanistan," updated July 9, 2004 (online at www.nato.int/issues/afghanistan).

12. United States Institute of Peace report, "Establishing the Rule of Law in Afghanistan," Mar. 2004, pp. 1–3 (online at www.usip.org/pubs/specialreports/sr117.html).

13. For the change, see Lakhdar Brahimi interview (Oct. 24, 2003); U.S. officials in Afghanistan interview (Oct. 2003). For the request that the United States remain, see Kandahar province local leaders interview (Oct. 21, 2003). For the effect of the United States leaving, see Karim Khalili interview (Oct. 23, 2003).

14. Some have criticized the Bush administration for neglecting Afghanistan because of Iraq. Others, including General Franks, say that the size of the U.S. military commitment in Afghanistan has not been compromised by the commitments in Iraq. We have not investigated the issue and cannot offer a judgment on it.

15. Even if the U.S. forces, stretched thin, are reluctant to take on this role, "a limited, but extremely useful, change in the military mandate would involve intelligence sharing with civilian law enforcement and a willingness to take action against drug warehouses and heroin laboratories." United States Institute of Peace report, "Establishing the Rule of Law in Afghanistan," Mar. 2004, p. 17.

16. For barriers to Saudi monitoring of charities, see, e.g., Robert Jordan interview (Jan. 14, 2004); David Aufhauser interview (Feb. 12, 2004).

17. For the Saudi reformer's view, see Members of *majles al-shura* interview (Oct. 14, 2003).

18. Neil MacFarquhar, "Saudis Support a Jihad in Iraq, Not Back Home," *New York Times*, Apr. 23, 2004, p. A1.

19. Prince Bandar Bin Sultan, "A Diplomat's Call for War," *Washington Post*, June 6, 2004, p. B4 (translation of original in *Al-Watan*, June 2, 2004).

20. President Clinton meeting (Apr. 8, 2004).

21. For Jordan's initiatives, see testimony of William Burns before the Subcommittee on the Middle East and Central Asia of the House International Relations Committee, Mar. 19, 2003 (online at www.house.gov/international_relations/108/burn0319.htm). For the report, see United Nations Development Programme report. *Arab Human Development Report 2003: Building a Knowledge Society* (United Nations, 2003) (online at www.miftah.org/Doc/Reports/Englishcomplete2003.pdf).

22. DOD memo, Rumsfeld to Myers, Wolfowitz, Pace, and Feith, "Global War on Terrorism." Oct. 16, 2003 (online at www.usatoday.com/news/washington/executive/rumsfeld-memo.htm).

23. For the statistics, see James Zogby, *What Arabs Think: Values, Beliefs, and Concerns* (Zogby International, 2002). For fear of a U.S. attack, see Pew Global Attitudes Project report, *Views of a Changing World: June 2003* (Pew Research Center for the People and the Press, 2003), p. 2. In our interviews, current and former U.S. officials dealing with the Middle East corroborated these findings.

24. For polling soon after 9/11, see Pew Research Center for the People and the Press report, "America Admired, Yet Its New Vulnerability Seen as Good Thing, Say Opinion Leaders; Little Support for Expanding War on Terrorism" (online at http://people-press.org/reports/print.php3? ReportID=145). For the quotation, see Pew Global Attitudes Project report, "War With Iraq Further Divides Global Publics But World Embraces Democratic Values and Free Markets," June 3, 2003 (online at www.pewtrusts.com/ideas/ideas_item.cfm?content_item_id=1645&content_type_id=7).

25. For the Occidentalist "creed of Islamist revolutionaries," see, e.g., Avishai Margalit and Ian Baruma, *Occidentalism: The West in the Eyes of Its Enemies* (Penguin Press, 2004).

26. We draw these statistics, significantly, from the U.S. government's working paper circulated in April 2004 to G-8 "sherpas" in preparation for the 2004 G-8 summit. The paper was leaked and published in *Al-Hayat*. "U.S. Working Paper for G-8 Sherpas," *Al-Hayat*, Feb. 13, 2004 (online at   http://english.daralhayat.com/Spec/02-2004/Article-20040213-ac40bdaf-c0a8-01ed-004e-5e7ac 897d678/story.html).

27. Richard Holbrooke, "Get the Message Out," *Washington Post*, Oct. 28, 2001, p. B7; Richard Armitage Interview (Jan. 12, 2004).

28. Testimony of George Tenet, "The Worldwide Threat 2004: Challenges in a Changing Global Context," before the Senate Select Committee on Intelligence, Feb. 24, 2004.

29. U.S. Department of Energy Advisory Board report, "A Report Card on the Department of Energy's Non-proliferation Programs with Russia," Jan. 10, 2001, p. vi.

30. For terrorists being self-funding, see United Nations report, "Second Report of the [UN] Monitoring Group, Pursuant to Security Council Resolution 1390," Sept. 19, 2002, p. 13.

31. For legal entry, see White House report, Office of Homeland Security, "The National Strategy for Homeland Security," July 2002, p. 20 (online at www.whitehouse.gov/homeland/book/index.html). For illegal entry, see Chicago Council on Foreign Relations task force report, *Keeping the Promise: Immigration Proposals from the Heartland* (Chicago Council on Foreign Relations, 2004), p. 28.

32. The names of at least three of the hijackers (Nawaf al Hazmi, Salem al Hazmi, and Khalid al Mihdhar) were in information systems of the intelligence community and thus potentially could have been watchlisted. Had they been watchlisted, the connections to terrorism could have been exposed at the time they applied for a visa or at the port of entry. The names of at least three of the hijackers (Nawaf al Hazmi, Salem al Hazmi, and Khalid al Mihdhar), were in information systems of the intelligence community and thus potentially could have been watchlisted. Had they been watchlisted, their terrorist affiliations could have been exposed either at the time they applied for a visa or at the port of entry. Two of the hijackers (Satam al Suqami and Abdul Aziz al Omari) presented passports manipulated in a fraudulent manner that has subsequently been associated with al Qaeda. Based on our review of their visa and travel histories, we believe it possible that as many as eleven additional hijackers (Wail al Shehri, Waleed al Shehri, Mohand al Shehri, Hani Hanjour, Majed Moqed, Nawaf al Hazmi, Hamza al Ghamdi, Ahmed al Ghamdi, Saeed al Ghamdi, Ahmed al Nami, and Ahmad al Haznawi) held passports containing these same fraudulent features, but their passports have not been found so we cannot be sure. Khalid al Mihdhar and Salem al Hazmi presented passports with a suspicious indicator of Islamic extremism. There is reason to believe that the passports of three other hijackers (Nawaf al Hazmi, Ahmed al Nami, and Ahmad al Haznawi) issued in the same Saudi passport office may have contained this same indicator; however, their passports have not been found, so we cannot be sure.

33. Khallad Bin Attash, Ramzi Binalshibh, Zakariya Essabar, Ali Abdul Aziz Ali, and Saeed al Ghamdi (not the individual by the same name who became a hijacker) tried to get visas and failed. Kahtani was unable to prove his admissibility and withdrew his application for admission after an immigration inspector remained unpersuaded that he was a tourist. All the hijackers whose visa applications we reviewed arguably could have been denied visas because their applications were not filled out completely. Had State visa officials routinely had a practice of acquiring more information in such cases, they likely would have found more grounds for denial. For example, three hijackers made statements on their visa applications that could have been proved false by U.S. government records (Hani Hanjour, Saeed al Ghamdi, and Khalid al Mihdhar), and many lied about their employment or educational status. Two hijackers could have been denied admission at the port of entry based on violations of immigration rules governing terms of admission—Mohamed Atta overstayed his tourist visa and then failed to present a proper vocational school visa when he entered in January 2001: Ziad Jarrah attended school in June 2000 without properly adjusting his immigration status, an action that violated his immigration status and rendered him inadmissible on each of his six subsequent reentries into the United States between June 2000 and August 5, 2001. There were possible grounds to deny entry to a third hijacker (Marwan al Shehhi). One hijacker violated his immigration status by failing to enroll as a student after entry (Hani Hanjour); two hijackers overstayed their terms of admission by four and eight months respectively (Satam al Suqami and Nawaf al Hazmi). Atta and Shehhi attended a flight school (Huffman Aviation) that the Justice Department's Inspector General concluded should not have been certified to accept foreign students, see DOJ Inspector General's report, "The INS' Contacts with Two September 11 Terrorists: A Review of the INS's Admissions of Atta and Shehhi, its Processing of their Change of Status Applications, and its Efforts to Track Foreign Students in the United States," May 20, 2002.

34. John Gordon interview (May 13, 2004).

35. For a description of a layering approach, see Stephen Flynn, *American the Vulnerable: How the U.S. Has Failed to Secure the Homeland and Protect Its People from Terrorism* (Harper-Collins, 2004), p. 69.

36. The logical and timely rollout of such a program is hampered by an astonishingly long list of congressional mandates. The system originated in the Illegal Immigration Reform and Immigrant Responsibility Act of 1996 and applied to all non-U.S. citizens who enter or exit the United States at any port of entry. Pub. L. No. 104–208, 110 Stat. 3009 (1996), § 110. The Data Management Improvement Act of 2000 altered this mandate by incorporating a requirement for a searchable centralized database, limiting the government's ability to require new data from certain travelers and setting a series of implementation deadlines. Pub. L. No. 106–215, 114 Stat. 337 (2000), § 2(a). The USA PATRIOT Act mandated that the Attorney General and Secretary of State "particularly focus" on having the entry-exit system include biometrics and tamper-resistant travel documents readable at all ports of entry. Pub. L. No. 107–56, 115 Stat. 272 (2001), § 1008(a). In the Enhanced Border Security and Visa Entry Reform Act, Congress directed that, not later than October 26, 2004, the attorney general and the secretary of state issue to all non-U.S. citizens only machine-readable, tamper-resistant visas and other travel and entry documents that use biometric identifiers and install equipment at all U.S. ports of entry to allow biometric authentication of such documents. Pub. L. No. 107–173, 116 Stat. 543 (2002), § 303(b). The Act also required that increased security still facilitate the free flow of commerce and travel. Ibid. § 102(a)(1)(C). The administration has requested a delay of two years for the requirement of tamper-proof passports. Testimony of Thomas Ridge before the House Judiciary Committee, Apr. 21, 2004 (online at www.dhs.gov/dhspublic/display?theme=45&content=3498&print=true). Program planners have set a goal of collecting information, confirming identity, providing information about foreign nationals throughout the entire immigration system, and ultimately enabling each point in the system to assess the lawfulness of travel and any security risks.

37. There are at least three registered traveler programs underway, at different points in the system, designed and run by two different agencies in the Department of Homeland Security (outside the U.S.VISIT system), which must ultimately be the basis for access to the United States.

38. For the statistics, see DOS report, "Workload Statistics by Post Regions for All Visa Classes" June 18, 2004. One post-9/11 screening process, known as Condor, has conducted over 130,000 extra name-checks. DOS letter, Karl Hofmann to the Commission, Apr. 5, 2004. The checks have caused significant delays in some cases but have never resulted in visas being denied on terrorism grounds. For a discussion of visa delays, see General Accounting Office report, "Border Security: Improvements Needed to Reduce Time Taken to Adjudicate Visas for Science Students and Scholars," Feb. 2004. We do not know all the reasons why visa applications have dropped so significantly. Several factors beyond the visa process itself include the National Security Entry-Exit Registration System, which requires additional screening processes for certain groups from Arab and Muslim countries; the Iraq war; and perhaps cyclical economic factors. For the cost to the United States of visa backlogs, see National Foreign Trade Council report, "Visa Backlog Costs U.S. Exporters More than $30 Billion Since 2002, New Study Finds," June 2, 2004 (online at www.nftc.org/newsflash/newsflash.asp?Mode=View&articleid=1686&Category=All).

39. These issues are on the G-8 agenda. White House press release, "G-8 Secure and Facilitated Travel Initiative (SAFTI)," June 9, 2004 (online at www.whitehouse.gov/news/releases/2004/06/20040609-51.html). Lax passport issuance standards are among the vulnerabilities exploited by terrorists, possibly including two of the 9/11 hijackers. Three models exist for strengthened prescreening: (1) better screening by airlines, such as the use of improved document authentication technology: (2) posting of border agents or inspectors in foreign airports to work cooperatively with foreign counterparts; and (3) establishing a full preinspection regime, such as now exists for travel to the United States from Canada and Ireland. All three models should be pursued, in addition to electronic prescreening.

40. Among the more important problems to address is that of varying transliterations of the same name. For example, the current lack of a single convention for transliterating Arabic names enabled the 19 hijackers to vary the spelling of their names to defeat name-based watchlist systems and confuse any potential efforts to locate them. While the gradual introduction of biometric identifiers will help, that process will take years, and a name match will always be useful. The ICAO

should discuss the adoption of a standard requiring a digital code for all names that need to be translated into the Roman alphabet, ensuring one common spelling for all countries.

41. On achieving more reliable identification, see Markle Foundation task force report, *Creating a Trusted Information Network for Homeland Security* (Markle Foundation, 2003), p. 72 (online at www.markle.org).

42. General Accounting Office report, *Mass Transit: Federal Action Could Help Transit Agencies Address Security Challenges*, GAO-03-263, Dec. 2002 (online at www.gao.gov/new.items/d03263.pdf).

13 HOW TO DO IT? A DIFFERENT WAY OF ORGANIZING THE GOVERNMENT

As presently configured, the national security institutions of the U.S. government are still the institutions constructed to win the Cold War. The United States confronts a very different world today. Instead of facing a few very dangerous adversaries, the United States confronts a number of less visible challenges that surpass the boundaries of traditional nation-states and call for quick, imaginative, and agile responses.

The men and women of the World War II generation rose to the challenges of the 1940s and 1950s. They restructured the government so that it could protect the country. That is now the job of the generation that experienced 9/11. Those attacks showed, emphatically, that ways of doing business rooted in a different era are just not good enough. Americans should not settle for incremental, ad hoc adjustments to a system designed generations ago for a world that no longer exists.

We recommend significant changes in the organization of the government. We know that the quality of the people is more important than the quality of the wiring diagrams. Some of the saddest aspects of the 9/11 story are the outstanding efforts of so many individual officials straining, often without success, against the boundaries of the possible. Good people can overcome bad structures. They should not have to.

The United States has the resources and the people. The government should combine them more effectively, achieving unity of effort. We offer five major recommendations to do that:

- unifying strategic intelligence and operational planning against Islamist terrorists across the foreign-domestic divide with a National Counterterrorism Center;
- unifying the intelligence community with a new National Intelligence Director;
- unifying the many participants in the counterterrorism effort and their knowledge in a network-based information-sharing system that transcends traditional governmental boundaries;
- unifying and strengthening congressional oversight to improve quality and accountability; and
- strengthening the FBI and homeland defenders.

13.1 UNITY OF EFFORT ACROSS THE FOREIGN-DOMESTIC DIVIDE

JOINT ACTION

Much of the public commentary about the 9/11 attacks has dealt with "lost opportunities," some of which we reviewed in chapter 11. These are often characterized as problems of "watchlisting," of "information sharing," or of "connecting the dots." In chapter 11 we explained that these labels are too narrow. They describe the symptoms, not the disease.

In each of our examples, no one was firmly in charge of managing the case and able to draw relevant intelligence from anywhere in the government, assign responsibilities across the agencies (foreign or domestic), track progress, and quickly bring obstacles up to the level where they could be resolved. Responsibility and accountability were diffuse.

The agencies cooperated, some of the time. But even such cooperation as there was is not the same thing as joint action. When agencies cooperate, one defines the problem and seeks help with it. When they act jointly, the problem and options for action are defined differently from the start. Individuals from different backgrounds come together in analyzing a case and planning how to manage it.

In our hearings we regularly asked witnesses: Who is the quarterback? The other players are in their positions, doing their jobs. But who is calling the play that assigns roles to help them execute as a team?

Since 9/11, those issues have not been resolved. In some ways joint work has gotten better, and in some ways worse. The effort of fighting terrorism has flooded over many of the usual agency boundaries because of its sheer quantity and energy. Attitudes have changed. Officials are keenly conscious of trying to avoid the mistakes of 9/11. They try to share information. They circulate—even to the President—practically every reported threat, however dubious.

Partly because of all this effort, the challenge of coordinating it has multiplied. Before 9/11, the CIA was plainly the lead agency confronting al Qaeda. The FBI played a very secondary role. The engagement of the departments of Defense and State was more episodic.

- Today the CIA is still central. But the FBI is much more active, along with other parts of the Justice Department.
- The Defense Department effort is now enormous. Three of its unified commands, each headed by a four-star general, have counterterrorism as a primary mission: Special Operations Command, Central Command (both headquartered in Florida), and Northern Command (headquartered in Colorado).
- A new Department of Homeland Security combines formidable resources in border and transportation security, along with analysis of domestic vulnerability and other tasks.
- The State Department has the lead on many of the foreign policy tasks we described in chapter 12.
- At the White House, the National Security Council (NSC) now is joined by a parallel presidential advisory structure, fhe Homeland Security Council.

So far we have mentioned two reasons for joint action—the virtue of joint planning and the advantage of having someone in charge to ensure a unified effort. There is a third: the simple shortage of experts with sufficient skills. The limited pool of critical experts—for example, skilled counterterrorism analysts and linguists—is being depleted. Expanding these capabilities will require not just money, but time.

Primary responsibility for terrorism analysis has been assigned to the Terrorist Threat Integration Center (TTIC), created in 2003, based at the CIA headquarters but staffed with representatives of many agencies, reporting directly to the Director of Central Intelligence. Yet the CIA houses another intelligence "fusion" center: the Counterterrorist Center that played such a key role before 9/11. A third major analytic unit is at Defense, in the Defense Intelligence Agency. A fourth, concentrating more on homeland vulnerabilities, is at the Department of Homeland Security. The FBI is in the process of building the analytic capability it has long lacked, and it also has the Terrorist Screening Center.[1]

The U.S. government cannot afford so much duplication of effort. There are not enough experienced experts to go around. The duplication also places extra demands on already hard-pressed single-source national technical intelligence collectors like the National Security Agency.

COMBINING JOINT INTELLIGENCE AND JOINT ACTION

A "smart" government would *integrate* all sources of information to see the enemy as a whole. Integrated all-source analysis should also inform and shape strategies to collect more intelligence. Yet the Terrorist Threat Integration Center, while it has primary responsibility for terrorism analysis, is formally proscribed from having any oversight or operational authority and is not part of any operational entity, other than reporting to the director of central intelligence.[2]

The government now tries to handle the problem of joint management, informed by analysis of intelligence from all sources, in two ways.

- First, agencies with lead responsibility for certain problems have constructed their own interagency entities and task forces in order to get cooperation. The Counterterrorist Center at CIA, for example, recruits liaison officers from throughout the intelligence community. The military's Central Command has its own interagency center, recruiting liaison officers from all the agencies from which it might need help. The FBI has joint Terrorism Task Forces in 84 locations to coordinate the activities of other agencies when action may be required.
- Second, the problem of joint operational planning is often passed to the White House, where the NSC staff tries to play this role. The national security staff at the White House (both NSC and new Homeland Security Council staff) has already become 50 percent larger since 9/11. But our impression, after talking to serving officials, is that even this enlarged staff is consumed by meetings on day-to-day issues, sifting each day's threat information and trying to coordinate everyday operations.

Even as it crowds into every square inch of available office space, the NSC staff is still not sized or funded to be an executive agency. In chapter 3 we described some of the problems that arose in the 1980s when a White House staff, constitutionally insulated from the usual mechanisms of oversight, became involved in direct operations. During the 1990s Richard Clarke occasionally tried to exercise such authority, sometimes successfully, but often causing friction.

Yet a subtler and more serious danger is that as the NSC staff is consumed by these day-to-day tasks, it has less capacity to find the time and detachment needed to advise a president on larger policy issues. That means less time to work on major new initiatives, help with legislative management to steer needed bills through Congress, and track the design and implementation of the strategic plans for regions, countries, and issues that we discuss in chapter 12.

Much of the job of operational coordination remains with the agencies, especially the CIA. There DCI Tenet and his chief aides ran interagency meetings nearly every day to coordinate much of the government's day-to-day work. The DCI insisted he did not make policy and only oversaw its implementation. In the struggle against terrorism these distinctions seem increasingly artificial. Also, as the DCI becomes a lead coordinator of the government's operations, it becomes harder to play all the position's other roles, including that of analyst in chief.

The problem is nearly intractable because of the way the government is currently structured. Lines of operational authority run to the expanding executive departments, and they are guarded for understandable reasons: the DCI commands the CIA's personnel overseas; the secretary of defense will not yield to others in conveying commands to military forces; the justice Department will not give up the responsibility of deciding whether to seek arrest warrants. But the result is that each agency or department needs its own intelligence apparatus to support the performance of its duties. It is hard to "break down stovepipes" when there are so many stoves that are legally and politically entitled to have cast-iron pipes of their own.

Recalling the Goldwater-Nichols legislation of 1986, Secretary Rumsfeld reminded us that to achieve better joint capability, each of the armed services had to "give up some of their turf and authorities and prerogatives." Today, he said, the executive branch is "stove-piped much like the four services were nearly 20 years ago." He wondered if it might be appropriate to ask agencies to "give up some of their existing turf and authority in exchange for a stronger, faster, more efficient government wide joint effort."[3] Privately, other key officials have made the same point to us.

We therefore propose a new institution: a civilian-led unified joint command for counterterrorism. It should combine strategic intelligence and joint operational planning.

In the Pentagon's Joint Staff, which serves the chairman of the joint Chiefs of Staff, intelligence is handled by the J-2 directorate, operational planning by J-3, and overall policy by J-5. Our concept combines the J-2 and J-3 functions (intelligence and operational planning) in one agency, keeping overall policy coordination where it belongs, in the National Security Council.

Recommendation: We recommend the establishment of a National Counterterrorism Center (NCTC), built on the foundation of the existing Terrorist Threat Integration Center (TTIC). Breaking the older mold of national government organization, this NCTC should be a center for joint operational planning *and* joint intelligence, staffed by personnel from the various agencies. The head of the NCTC should have authority to evaluate the performance of the people assigned to the Center.

- Such a joint center should be developed in the same spirit that guided the military's creation of unified joint commands, or the shaping of earlier national agencies like the National Reconnaissance Office, which was formed to organize the work of the CIA and several defense agencies in space.

  NCTC—Intelligence. The NCTC should lead strategic analysis, pooling all-source intelligence, foreign and domestic, about transnational terrorist organizations with global reach. It should develop *net* assessments (comparing enemy capabilities and intentions against U.S. defenses and countermeasures). It should also provide warning. It should do this work by drawing on the efforts of the CIA, FBI, Homeland Security, and other departments and agencies. It should task collection requirements both inside and outside the United States.
- The intelligence function (J-2) should build on the existing TTIC structure and remain distinct, as a national intelligence center, within the NCTC. As the government's principal knowledge bank on Islamist terrorism, with the main responsibility for strategic analysis and net assessment, it should absorb a significant

portion of the analytical talent now residing in the CIA's Counterterrorist Center and the DIA's Joint Intelligence Task Force—Combatting Terrorism (JITF-CT).

NCTC—Operations. The NCTC should perform joint planning. The plans would assign operational responsibilities to lead agencies, such as State, the CIA, the FBI, Defense and its combatant commands, Homeland Security, and other agencies. The NCTC should *not* direct the actual execution of these operations, leaving that job to the agencies. The NCTC would then track implementation; it would look across the foreign-domestic divide and across agency boundaries, updating plans to follow through on cases.[4]

- The joint operational planning function (J-3) will be new to the TTIC structure. The NCTC can draw on analogous work now being done in the CIA and every other involved department of the government, as well as reaching out to knowledgeable officials in state and local agencies throughout the United States.
- The NCTC should *not* be a policymaking body. Its operations and planning should follow the policy direction of the president and the National Security Council.

Consider this hypothetical case. The NSA discovers that a suspected terrorist is traveling to Bangkok and Kuala Lumpur. The NCTC should draw on joint intelligence resources, including its own NSA counterterrorism experts, to analyze the identities and possible destinations of these individuals. Informed by this analysis, the NCTC would then organize and plan the management of the case, drawing on the talents and differing kinds of experience among the several agency representatives assigned to it—assigning tasks to the CIA overseas, to Homeland Security watching entry points into the United States, and to the FBI. If military assistance might be needed, the Special Operations Command could be asked to develop an appropriate concept for such an operation. The NCTC would be accountable for tracking the progress of the case, ensuring that the plan evolved with it, and integrating the information into a warning. The NCTC would be responsible for being sure that intelligence gathered from the activities in the field became part of the government's institutional memory about Islamist terrorist personalities, organizations, and possible means of attack.

In each case the involved agency would make its own senior managers aware of what it was being asked to do. If those agency heads objected, and the issue could not easily be resolved, then the disagreement about roles and missions could be brought before the National Security Council and the president.

NCTC—Authorities. The head of the NCTC should be appointed by the president, and should be equivalent in rank to a deputy head of a cabinet department. The head of the NCTC would report to the national intelligence director, an office whose creation we recommend below, placed in the Executive Office of the President. The head of the NCTC would thus also report indirectly to the president. This official's nomination should be confirmed by the Senate and he or she should testify to the Congress, as is the case now with other statutory presidential offices, like the U.S. trade representative.

- To avoid the fate of other entities with great nominal authority and little real power, the head of the NCTC must have the right to concur in the choices of personnel to lead the operating entities of the departments and agencies focused on counterterrorism, specifically including the head of the Counterterrorist Center, the head of the FBI's Counterterrorism Division, the commanders of the Defense Department's Special Operations Command and Northern Command, and the State Department's coordinator for counterterrorism.[5] The head of the NCTC should also work with the director of the Office of Management and Budget in developing the president's counterterrorism budget.
- There are precedents for surrendering authority for joint planning while preserving an agency's operational control. In the international context, NATO commanders may get line authority over forces assigned by other nations. In U.S. unified commands, commanders plan operations that may involve units belonging to one of the services. In each case, procedures are worked out, formal and informal, to define the limits of the joint commander's authority.

The most serious disadvantage of the NCTC is the reverse of its greatest virtue. The struggle against Islamist terrorism is so important that any clear-cut centralization of authority to manage and be accountable for it may concentrate too much power in one place. The proposed NCTC would be given the authority of planning the activities of other agencies. Law or executive order must define the scope of such line authority.

The NCTC would not eliminate interagency policy disputes. These would still go to the National Security Council. To improve coordination at the White House, we believe the existing Homeland Security Council should soon be merged into a single National Security Council. The creation of the NCTC should help the NSC staff concentrate on its core duties of assisting the president and supporting interdepartmental policymaking.

We recognize that this is a new and difficult idea precisely because the authorities we recommend for the NCTC really would, as Secretary Rumsfeld foresaw, ask strong agencies to "give up some of their turf and authority in exchange for a stronger, faster, more efficient government wide joint effort." Countering transnational Islamist terrorism will test whether the U.S. government can fashion more flexible models of management needed to deal with the twenty-first-century world.

An argument against change is that the nation is at war, and cannot afford to reorganize in midstream. But some of the main innovations of the 1940s and 1950s, including the creation of the Joint Chiefs of Staff and even the construction of the Pentagon itself, were undertaken in the midst of war. Surely the country cannot wait until the struggle against Islamist terrorism is over.

"Surprise, when it happens to a government, is likely to be a complicated, diffuse, bureaucratic thing. It includes neglect of responsibility, but also responsibility so poorly defined or so ambiguously delegated that action gets lost."[6] That comment was made more than 40 years ago, about Pearl Harbor. We hope another commission, writing in the future about another attack, does not again find this quotation to be so apt.

13.2 UNITY OF EFFORT IN THE INTELLIGENCE COMMUNITY

In our first section, we concentrated on counterterrorism, discussing how to combine the analysis of information from all sources of intelligence with the joint planning of operations that draw on that analysis. In this section, we step back from looking just at the counterterrorism problem. We reflect on whether the government is organized adequately to direct resources and build the intelligence capabilities it will need not just for countering terrorism, but for the broader range of national security challenges in the decades ahead.

THE NEED FOR A CHANGE

During the Cold War, intelligence agencies did not depend on seamless integration to track and count the thousands of military targets—such as tanks and missiles—fielded by the Soviet Union and other adversary states. Each agency concentrated on its specialized mission, acquiring its own information and then sharing it via formal, finished reports. The Department of Defense had given birth to and dominated the main agencies for technical collection of intelligence. Resources were shifted at an incremental pace, coping with challenges that arose over years, even decades.

We summarized the resulting organization of the intelligence community in chapter 3. It is outlined below.

Members of the U.S. Intelligence Community

Office of the Director of Central Intelligence, which includes the Office of the Deputy Director of Central Intelligence for Community Management, the Community Management Staff, the Terrorism Threat Integration Center, the National Intelligence Council, and other community offices

The Central Intelligence Agency (CIA), which performs human source collection, all-source analysis, and advanced science and technology

National intelligence agencies:
- National Security Agency (NSA), which performs signals collection and analysis
- National Geospatial-Intelligence Agency (NGA), which performs imagery collection and analysis
- National Reconnaissance Office (NRO), which develops, acquires, and launches space systems for intelligence collection
- Other national reconnaissance programs

Departmental intelligence agencies:
- Defense Intelligence Agency (DIA) of the Department of Defense
- Intelligence entities of the Army, Navy, Air Force, and Marines
- Bureau of Intelligence and Research (INR) of the Department of State
- Office of Terrorism and Finance Intelligence of the Department of Treasury
- Office of Intelligence and the Counterterrorism and Counterintelligence Divisions of the Federal Bureau of Investigation of the Department of Justice
- Office of Intelligence of the Department of Energy
- Directorate of Information Analysis and Infrastructure Protection (IAIP) and Directorate of Coast Guard Intelligence of the Department of Homeland Security

The need to restructure the intelligence community grows out of six problems that have become apparent before and after 9/11:

- *Structural barriers to performing joint intelligence work.* National intelligence is still organized around the collection disciplines of the home agencies, not the joint mission. The importance of integrated, all-source analysis cannot be overstated. Without it, it is not possible to "connect the dots." No one component holds all the relevant information.By contrast, in organizing national defense, the Goldwater-Nichols legislation of 1986 created joint commands for operations in the field, the Unified Command Plan. The services—the Army, Navy, Air Force, and Marine Corps—organize, train, and equip their people and units to perform their missions. Then they assign personnel and units to the joint combatant commander, like the commanding general of the Central Command (CENTCOM). The Goldwater-Nichols Act required officers to serve tours outside their service in order to win promotion. The culture of the Defense Department was transformed, its collective mind-set moved from service-specific to 'joint," and its operations became more integrated.[7]
- *Lack of common standards and practices across the foreign-domestic divide.* The leadership of the intelligence community should be able to pool information gathered overseas with information gathered in the United States, holding the work—wherever it is done—to a common standard of quality in how it is collected, processed (e.g., translated), reported, shared, and analyzed. A common set of personnel standards for intelligence can create a group of professionals better able to operate in joint activities, transcending their own service-specific mind-sets.
- *Divided management of national intelligence capabilities.* While the CIA was once "central" to our national intelligence capabilities, following the end of the Cold War it has been less able to influence the use of the nation's imagery and signals intelligence capabilities in three national agencies housed within the Department of Defense: the National Security Agency, the National Geospatial-Intelligence Agency, and the National Reconnaissance Office. One of the lessons learned from the 1991 Gulf War was the value of national intelligence systems (satellites in particular) in precision warfare. Since that war, the department has appropriately drawn these agencies into its transformation of the military. Helping to orchestrate this transformation is the under secretary of defense for intelligence, a position established by Congress after 9/11. An unintended consequence of these developments has been the far greater demand made by Defense on technical systems, leaving the DCI less able to influence how these technical resources are allocated and used.
- *Weak capacity to set priorities and move resources.* The agencies are mainly organized around what they collect or the way they collect it. But the priorities for collection are national. As the DCI makes hard choices about moving resources, he or she must have the power to reach across agencies and reallocate effort.
- *Too many jobs.* The DCI now has at least three jobs. He is expected to run a particular agency, the CIA. He is expected to manage the loose confederation of agencies that is the intelligence community. He is expected to be the analyst in chief for the government, sifting evidence and directly briefing the President as his principal intelligence adviser. No recent DCI has been able to do all three effectively. Usually what loses out is management of the intelligence community, a

difficult task even in the best case because the DCI's current authorities are weak. With so much to do, the DCI often has not used even the authority he has.

- *Too complex and secret.* Over the decades, the agencies and the rules surrounding the intelligence community have accumulated to a depth that practically defies public comprehension. There are now 15 agencies or parts of agencies in the intelligence community. The community and the DCI's authorities have become arcane matters, understood only by initiates after long study. Even the most basic information about how much money is actually allocated to or within the intelligence community and most of its key components is shrouded from public view.

The current DCI is responsible for community performance but lacks the three authorities critical for any agency head or chief executive officer: (1) control over purse strings, (2) the ability to hire or fire senior managers, and (3) the ability to set standards for the information infrastructure and personnel.[8]

The only budget power of the DCI over agencies other than the CIA lies in coordinating the budget requests of the various intelligence agencies into a single program for submission to Congress. The overall funding request of the 15 intelligence entities in this program is then presented to the president and Congress in 15 separate volumes.

When Congress passes an appropriations bill to allocate money to intelligence agencies, most of their funding is hidden in the Defense Department in order to keep intelligence spending secret. Therefore, although the House and Senate Intelligence committees are the authorizing committees for funding of the intelligence community, the final budget review is handled in the Defense Subcommittee of the Appropriations committees. Those committees have no subcommittees just for intelligence, and only a few members and staff review the requests.

The appropriations for the CIA and the national intelligence agencies—NSA, NGA, and NRO—are then given to the secretary of defense. The secretary transfers the CIA's money to the DCI but disburses the national agencies' money directly. Money for the FBI's national security components falls within the appropriations for Commerce, Justice, and State and goes to the attorney general.[9]

In addition, the DCI lacks hire-and-fire authority over most of the intelligence community's senior managers. For the national intelligence agencies housed in the Defense Department, the secretary of defense must seek the DCI's concurrence regarding the nomination of these directors, who are presidentially appointed. But the secretary may submit recommendations to the president without receiving this concurrence. The DCI cannot fire these officials. The DCI has even less influence over the head of the FBI's national security component, who is appointed by the attorney general in consultation with the DCI.[10]

COMBINING JOINT WORK WITH STRONGER MANAGEMENT

We have received recommendations on the topic of intelligence reform from many sources. Other commissions have been over this same ground. Thoughtful bills have been introduced, most recently a bill by the chairman of the House Intelligence Committee Porter Goss (R-Fla.), and another by the ranking minority member, Jane Harman (D-Calif.). In the Senate, Senators Bob Graham (D-Fla.) and Dianne Feinstein (D-Calif.) have introduced reform proposals as well. Past efforts have foundered, because the president did not support them; because the DCI, the secretary of defense, or both opposed them; and because some proposals lacked merit. We have tried to take stock of these experiences, and borrow from strong elements in many of the ideas that have already been developed by others.

Recommendation: The current position of Director of Central Intelligence should be replaced by a National Intelligence Director with two main areas of responsibility: (1) to oversee national intelligence centers on specific subjects of interest across the U.S. government and (2) to manage the national intelligence program and oversee the agencies that contribute to it.

First, the National Intelligence Director should oversee *national intelligence centers* to provide all-source analysis and plan intelligence operations for the whole government on major problems.

- One such problem is counterterrorism. In this case, we believe that the center should be the intelligence entity (formerly TTIC) inside the National Counterterrorism Center we have proposed. It would sit there alongside the operations management unit we described earlier, with both making up the NCTC, in the Executive Office of the President. Other national intelligence centers—for instance, on counterproliferation, crime and narcotics, and China—would be housed in whatever department or agency is best suited for them.
- The National Intelligence Director would retain the present DCI's role as the principal intelligence adviser to the president. We hope the president will come to look directly to the directors of the national intelligence centers to provide all-source analysis in their areas of responsibility, balancing the advice of these intelligence chiefs against the contrasting viewpoints that may be offered by department heads at State, Defense, Homeland Security, Justice, and other agencies.

Second, the National Intelligence Director should manage the national intelligence program and oversee the component agencies of the intelligence community. (See diagram.)[11]

- The National Intelligence Director would submit a unified budget for national intelligence that reflects priorities chosen by the National Security Council, an appropriate balance among the varieties of technical and human intelligence collection, and analysis. He or she would receive an appropriation for national intelligence and apportion the funds to the appropriate agencies, in line with that budget, and with authority to reprogram funds among the national intelligence agencies to meet any new priority (as counterterrorism was in the 1990s). The National Intelligence Director should approve and submit nominations to the president of the individuals who would lead the CIA, DIA, FBI Intelligence Office, NSA, NGA, NRO, Information Analysis and Infrastructure Protection Directorate of the Department of Homeland Security, and other national intelligence capabilities.[12]
- The National Intelligence Director would manage this national effort with the help of three deputies, each of whom would also hold a key position in one of the component agencies.[13]
  - foreign intelligence (the head of the CIA)
  - defense intelligence (the under secretary of defense for intelligence)[14]
  - homeland intelligence (the FBI's executive assistant director for intelligence or the under secretary of homeland security for information analysis and infrastructure protection)

Other agencies in the intelligence community would coordinate their work within each of these three areas, largely staying housed in the same departments or agencies that support them now.

Returning to the analogy of the Defense Department's organization, these three deputies—like the leaders of the Army, Navy, Air Force, or Marines—would have the job of acquiring the systems, training the people, and executing the operations planned by the national intelligence centers.

And, just as the combatant commanders also report to the secretary of defense, the directors of the national intelligence centers—e.g., for counterproliferation, crime and narcotics, and the rest—also would report to the National Intelligence Director.

- The Defense Department's military intelligence programs—the joint military intelligence program (JMIP) and the tactical intelligence and related activities program (TIARA)—would remain part of that department's responsibility.
- The National Intelligence Director would set personnel policies to establish standards for education and training and facilitate assignments at the national intelligence centers and across agency lines. The National Intelligence Director also would set information sharing and information technology policies to maximize data sharing, as well as policies to protect the security of information.
- Too many agencies now have an opportunity to say no to change. The National Intelligence Director should participate in an NSC executive committee that can resolve differences in priorities among the agencies and bring the major disputes to the president for decision.

The National Intelligence Director should be located in the Executive Office of the President. This official, who would be confirmed by the Senate and would testify before Congress, would have a relatively small staff of several hundred people, taking the place of the existing community management offices housed at the CIA.

In managing the whole community, the National Intelligence Director is still providing a service function. With the partial exception of his or her responsibilities for overseeing the NCTC, the National Intelligence Director should support the consumers of national intelligence—the president and policymaking advisers such as the secretaries of state, defense, and homeland security and the attorney general.

We are wary of too easily equating government management problems with those of the private sector. But we have noticed that some very large private firms rely on a powerful CEO who has significant control over how money is spent and can hire or fire leaders of the major divisions, assisted by a relatively modest staff, while leaving responsibility for execution in the operating divisions.

There are disadvantages to separating the position of National Intelligence Director from the job of heading the CIA. For example, the National Intelligence Director will not head a major agency of his or her own and may have a weaker base of support. But we believe that these disadvantages are outweighed by several other considerations:

- The National Intelligence Director must be able to directly oversee intelligence collection inside the United States. Yet law and custom has counseled against giving such a plain domestic role to the head of the CIA.

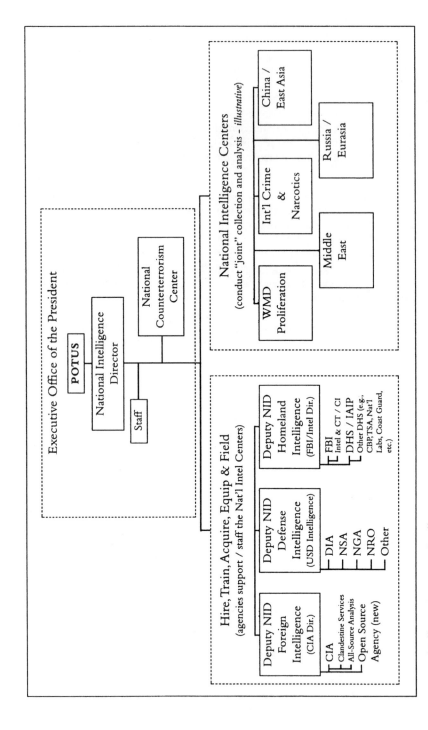

Executive Office of the President

POTUS

National Intelligence Director

Staff

National Counterterrorism Center

National Intelligence Centers
(conduct "joint" collection and analysis – *illustrative*)

WMD Proliferation

Int'l Crime & Narcotics

China / East Asia

Middle East

Russia / Eurasia

Hire, Train, Acquire, Equip & Field
(agencies support / staff the Nat'l Intel Centers)

Deputy NID Foreign Intelligence (CIA Dir.)

CIA
Clandestine Services
All-Source Analysis
Open Source Agency (new)

Deputy NID Defense Intelligence (USD Intelligence)

DIA
NSA
NGA
NRO
Other

Deputy NID Homeland Intelligence (FBI/Intel Dir.)

FBI
Intel & CT / CI
DHS / IAIP
Other DHS (e.g., CBP,TSA, Nat'l Labs, Coast Guard, etc.)

Unity of Effort in Managing Intelligence

- The CIA will be one among several claimants for funds in setting national priorities. The National Intelligence Director should not be both one of the advocates and the judge of them all.
- Covert operations tend to be highly tactical, requiring close attention. The National Intelligence Director should rely on the relevant joint mission center to oversee these details, helping to coordinate closely with the White House. The CIA will be able to concentrate on building the capabilities to carry out such operations and on providing the personnel who will be directing and executing such operations in the field.
- Rebuilding the analytic and human intelligence collection capabilities of the CIA should be a full-time effort, and the director of the CIA should focus on extending its comparative advantages.

Recommendation: The CIA Director should emphasize (a) rebuilding the CIA's analytic capabilities; (b) transforming the clandestine service by building its human intelligence capabilities; (c) developing a stronger language program, with high standards and sufficient financial incentives; (d) renewing emphasis on recruiting diversity among operations officers so they can blend more easily in foreign cities; (e) ensuring a seamless relationship between human source collection and signals collection at the operational level; and (f) stressing a better balance between unilateral and liaison operations.

The CIA should retain responsibility for the direction and execution of clandestine and covert operations, as assigned by the relevant national intelligence center and authorized by the National Intelligence Director and the president. This would include propaganda, renditions, and nonmilitary disruption. We believe, however, that one important area of responsibility should change.

Recommendation: Lead responsibility for directing and executing paramilitary operations, whether clandestine or covert, should shift to the Defense Department. There it should be consolidated with the capabilities for training, direction, and execution of such operations already being developed in the Special Operations Command.

- Before 9/11, the CIA did not invest in developing a robust capability to conduct paramilitary operations with U.S. personnel. It relied on proxies instead, organized by CIA operatives without the requisite military training. The results were unsatisfactory.
- Whether the price is measured in either money or people, the United States cannot afford to build two separate capabilities for carrying out secret military operations, secretly operating standoff missiles, and secretly training foreign military or paramilitary forces. The United States should concentrate responsibility and necessary legal authorities in one entity.
- The post-9/11 Afghanistan precedent of using joint CIA-military teams for covert and clandestine operations was a good one. We believe this proposal to be consistent with it. Each agency would concentrate on its comparative advantages in building capabilities for joint missions. The operation itself would be planned in common.
- The CIA has a reputation for agility in operations. The military has a reputation for being methodical and cumbersome. We do not know if these stereotypes match current reality; they may also be one more symptom of the civil-military

misunderstandings we described in chapter 4. It is a problem to be resolved in policy guidance and agency management, not in the creation of redundant, overlapping capabilities and authorities in such sensitive work. The CIA's experts should be integrated into the military's training, exercises, and planning. To quote a CIA official now serving in the field: "One fight, one team."

Recommendation: Finally, to combat the secrecy and complexity we have described, the overall amounts of money being appropriated for national intelligence and to its component agencies should no longer be kept secret. Congress should pass a separate appropriations act for intelligence, defending the broad allocation of how these tens of billions of dollars have been assigned among the varieties of intelligence work.

The specifics of the intelligence appropriation would remain classified, as they are today. Opponents of declassification argue that America's enemies could learn about intelligence capabilities by tracking the top-line appropriations figure. Yet the top-line figure by itself provides little insight into U.S. intelligence sources and methods. The U.S. government readily provides copious information about spending on its military forces, including military intelligence. The intelligence community should not be subject to that much disclosure. But when even aggregate categorical numbers remain hidden, it is hard to judge priorities and foster accountability.

13.3 UNITY OF EFFORT IN SHARING INFORMATION

INFORMATION SHARING

We have already stressed the importance of intelligence analysis that can draw on all relevant sources of information. The biggest impediment to all-source analysis—to a greater likelihood of connecting the dots—is the human or systemic resistance to sharing information.

The U.S. government has access to a vast amount of information. When databases not usually thought of as "intelligence," such as customs or immigration information, are included, the storehouse is immense. But the U.S. government has a weak system for processing and using what it has. In interviews around the government, official after official urged us to call attention to frustrations with the unglamorous "back office" side of government operations.

In the 9/11 story, for example, we sometimes see examples of information that could be accessed—like the undistributed NSA information that would have helped identify Nawaf al Hazmi in January 2000. But someone had to ask for it. In that case, no one did. Or, as in the episodes we describe in chapter 8, the information is distributed, but in a compartmented channel. Or the information is available, and someone does ask, but it cannot be shared.

What all these stories have in common is a system that requires a demonstrated "need to know" before sharing. This approach assumes it is possible to know, in advance, who will need to use the information. Such a system implicitly assumes that the risk of inadvertent disclosure outweighs the benefits of wider sharing. Those Cold War assumptions are no longer appropriate. The culture of agencies feeling they own the information they gathered at taxpayer expense must be replaced by a culture in which the agencies instead feel they have a duty to the information—to repay the taxpayers' investment by making that information available.

Each intelligence agency has its own security practices, outgrowths of the Cold War. We certainly understand the reason for these practices. Counterintelligence concerns are still real, even if the old Soviet enemy has been replaced by other spies.

But the security concerns need to be weighed against the costs. Current security requirements nurture overclassification and excessive compartmentation of information among agencies. Each agency's incentive structure opposes sharing, with risks (criminal, civil, and internal administrative sanctions) but few rewards for sharing information. No one has to pay the long-term costs of over-classifying information, though these costs—even in literal financial terms—are substantial. There are no punishments for *not* sharing information. Agencies uphold a "need-to-know" culture of information protection rather than promoting a "need-to-share" culture of integration.[15]

Recommendation: Information procedures should provide incentives for sharing, to restore a better balance between security and shared knowledge.

Intelligence gathered about transnational terrorism should be processed, turned into reports, and distributed according to the same quality standards, whether it is collected in Pakistan or in Texas.

The logical objection is that sources and methods may vary greatly in different locations. We therefore propose that when a report is first created, its data be separated from the sources and methods by which they are obtained. The report should begin with the information in its most shareable, but still meaningful, form. Therefore the maximum number of recipients can access some form of that information. If knowledge of further details becomes important, any user can query further, with access granted or denied according to the rules set for the network—and with queries leaving an audit trail in order to determine who accessed the information. But the questions may not come at all unless experts at the "edge" of the network can readily discover the clues that prompt to them.[16]

We propose that information be shared horizontally, across new networks that transcend individual agencies.

- The current system is structured on an old mainframe, or hub-and-spoke, concept. In this older approach, each agency has its own database. Agency users send information to the database and then can retrieve it from the database.
- A decentralized network model, the concept behind much of the information revolution, shares data horizontally too. Agencies would still have their own databases, but those databases would be searchable across agency lines. In this system, secrets are protected through the design of the network and an "information rights management" approach that controls access to the data, not access to the whole network. An outstanding conceptual framework for this kind of "trusted information network" has been developed by a task force of leading professionals in national security, information technology, and law assembled by the Markle Foundation. Its report has been widely discussed throughout the U.S. government, but has not yet been converted into action.[17]

Recommendation: The president should lead the government-wide effort to bring the major national security institutions into the information revolution. He should

coordinate the resolution of the legal, policy, and technical issues across agencies to create a "trusted information network."

- No one agency can do it alone. Well-meaning agency officials are under tremendous pressure to update their systems. Alone, they may only be able to modernize the stovepipes, not replace them.
- Only presidential leadership can develop government-wide concepts and standards. Currently, no one is doing this job. Backed by the Office of Management and Budget, a new National Intelligence Director empowered to set common standards for information use throughout the community, and a secretary of homeland security who helps extend the system to public agencies and relevant private-sector databases, a government-wide initiative can succeed.
- White House leadership is also needed because the policy and legal issues are harder than the technical ones. The necessary technology already exists. What does not are the rules for acquiring, accessing, sharing, and using the vast stores of public and private data that may be available. When information sharing works, it is a powerful tool. Therefore the sharing and uses of information must be guided by a set of practical policy guidelines that simultaneously empower and constrain officials, telling them clearly what is and is not permitted.

"This is government acting in new ways, to face new threats," the most recent Markle report explains. "And while such change is necessary, it must be accomplished while engendering the people's trust that privacy and other civil liberties are being protected, that businesses are not being unduly burdened with requests for extraneous or useless information, that taxpayer money is being well spent, and that, ultimately, the network will be effective in protecting our security." The authors add: "Leadership is emerging from all levels of government and from many places in the private sector. What is needed now is a plan to accelerate these efforts, and public debate and consensus on the goals."[18] ...

13.5 ORGANIZING AMERICA'S DEFENSES IN THE UNITED STATES

THE FUTURE ROLE OF THE FBI

We have considered proposals for a new agency dedicated to intelligence collection in the United States. Some call this a proposal for an "American MI-5," although the analogy is weak—the actual British Security Service is a relatively small worldwide agency that combines duties assigned in the U.S. government to the Terrorist Threat Integration Center, the CIA, the FBI, and the Department of Homeland Security.

The concern about the FBI is that it has long favored its criminal justice mission over its national security mission. Part of the reason for this is the demand around the country for FBI help on criminal matters. The FBI was criticized, rightly, for the overzealous domestic intelligence investigations disclosed during the 1970s. The pendulum swung away from those types of investigations during the 1980s and 1990s, though the FBI maintained an active counterintelligence function and was the lead agency for the investigation of foreign terrorist groups operating inside the United States.

We do not recommend the creation of a new domestic intelligence agency. It is not needed if our other recommendations are adopted—to establish a strong national intelligence center, part of the NCTC, that will oversee counterterrorism intelligence work, foreign and domestic, and to create a National Intelligence Director who can set and enforce standards for the collection, processing, and reporting of information.

Under the structures we recommend, the FBI's role is focused, but still vital. The FBI does need to be able to direct its thousands of agents and other employees to collect intelligence in America's cities and towns—interviewing informants, conducting surveillance and searches, tracking individuals, working collaboratively with local authorities, and doing so with meticulous attention to detail and compliance with the law. The FBI's job in the streets of the United States would thus be a domestic equivalent, operating under the U.S. Constitution and quite different laws and rules, to the job of the CIA's operations officers abroad.

Creating a new domestic intelligence agency has other drawbacks.

- The FBI is accustomed to carrying out sensitive intelligence collection operations in compliance with the law. If a new domestic intelligence agency were outside of the Department of Justice, the process of legal oversight—never easy—could become even more difficult. Abuses of civil liberties could create a backlash that would impair the collection of needed intelligence.
- Creating a new domestic intelligence agency would divert attention of the officials most responsible for current counterterrorism efforts while the threat remains high. Putting a new player into the mix of federal agencies with counterterrorism responsibilities would exacerbate existing information-sharing problems.
- A new domestic intelligence agency would need to acquire assets and personnel. The FBI already has 28,000 employees; 56 field offices, 400 satellite offices, and 47 legal attaché offices; a laboratory, operations center, and training facility; an existing network of informants, cooperating defendants, and other sources; and relationships with state and local law enforcement, the CIA, and foreign intelligence and law enforcement agencies.
- Counterterrorism investigations in the United States very quickly become matters that involve violations of criminal law and possible law enforcement action. Because the FBI can have agents working criminal matters and agents working intelligence investigations concerning the same international terrorism target, the full range of investigative tools against a suspected terrorist can be considered within one agency. The removal of "the wall" that existed before 9/11 between intelligence and law enforcement has opened up new opportunities for cooperative action within the FBI.
- Counterterrorism investigations often overlap or are cued by other criminal investigations, such as money laundering or the smuggling of contraband. In the field, the close connection to criminal work has many benefits.

Our recommendation to leave counterterrorism intelligence collection in the United States with the FBI still depends on an assessment that the FBI—if it makes an all-out effort to institutionalize change—can do the job. As we mentioned in chapter 3, we have been impressed by the determination that agents display in tracking down details, patiently going the extra mile and working the extra month, to put facts in the place of speculation. In our report we have shown how agents in Phoenix, Minneapolis, and New York displayed initiative in pressing their investigations.

FBI agents and analysts in the field need to have sustained support and dedicated resources to become stronger intelligence officers. They need to be rewarded for acquiring informants and for gathering and disseminating information differently and more broadly than usual in a traditional criminal investigation. FBI employees need to report and analyze what they have learned in ways the Bureau has never done before.

Under Director Robert Mueller, the Bureau has made significant progress in improving its intelligence capabilities. It now has an Office of Intelligence, overseen by the top tier of FBI management. Field intelligence groups have been created in all field offices to put FBI priorities and the emphasis on intelligence into practice. Advances have been made in improving the Bureau's information technology systems and in increasing connectivity and information sharing with intelligence community agencies.

Director Mueller has also recognized that the FBI's reforms are far from complete. He has outlined a number of areas where added measures may be necessary. Specifically, he has recognized that the FBI needs to recruit from a broader pool of candidates, that agents and analysts working on national security matters require specialized training, and that agents should specialize within programs after obtaining a generalist foundation. The FBI is developing career tracks for agents to specialize in counterterrorism/counterintelligence, cyber crimes, criminal investigations, or intelligence. It is establishing a program for certifying agents as intelligence officers, a certification that will be a prerequisite for promotion to the senior ranks of the Bureau. New training programs have been instituted for intelligence-related subjects.

The Director of the FBI has proposed creating an Intelligence Directorate as a further refinement of the FBI intelligence program. This directorate would include units for intelligence planning and policy and for the direction of analysts and linguists.

We want to ensure that the Bureau's shift to a preventive counterterrorism posture is more fully institutionalized so that it survives beyond Director Mueller's tenure. We have found that in the past the Bureau has announced its willingness to reform and restructure itself to address transnational security threats, but has fallen short—failing to effect the necessary institutional and cultural changes organization-wide. We want to ensure that this does not happen again. Despite having found acceptance of the Director's clear message that counterterrorism is now the FBI's top priority, two years after 9/11 we also found gaps between some of the announced reforms and the reality in the field. We are concerned that management in the field offices still can allocate people and resources to local concerns that diverge from the national security mission. This system could revert to a focus on lower-priority criminal justice cases over national security requirements.

Recommendation: A specialized and integrated national security workforce should be established at the FBI consisting of agents, analysts, linguists, and surveillance specialists who are recruited, trained, rewarded, and retained to ensure the development of an institutional culture imbued with a deep expertise in intelligence and national security.

- The president, by executive order or directive, should direct the FBI to develop this intelligence cadre.
- Recognizing that cross-fertilization between the criminal justice and national security disciplines is vital to the success of both missions, all new agents should receive basic training in both areas. Furthermore, new agents should begin their careers with meaningful assignments in both areas.

- Agents and analysts should then specialize in one of these disciplines and have the option to work such matters for their entire career with the Bureau. Certain advanced training courses and assignments to other intelligence agencies should be required to advance within the national security discipline.
- In the interest of cross-fertilization, all senior FBI managers, including those working on law enforcement matters, should be certified intelligence officers.
- The FBI should fully implement a recruiting, hiring, and selection process for agents and analysts that enhances its ability to target and attract individuals with educational and professional backgrounds in intelligence, international relations, language, technology, and other relevant skills.
- The FBI should institute the integration of analysts, agents, linguists, and surveillance personnel in the field so that a dedicated team approach is brought to bear on national security intelligence operations.
- Each field office should have an official at the field office's deputy level for national security matters. This individual would have management oversight and ensure that the national priorities are carried out in the field.
- The FBI should align its budget structure according to its four main programs— intelligence, counterterrorism and counterintelligence, criminal, and criminal justice services—to ensure better transparency on program costs, management of resources, and protection of the intelligence program.[19]
- The FBI should report regularly to Congress in its semiannual program reviews designed to identify whether each field office is appropriately addressing FBI and national program priorities.
- The FBI should report regularly to Congress in detail on the qualifications, status, and roles of analysts in the field and at headquarters. Congress should ensure that analysts are afforded training and career opportunities on a par with those offered analysts in other intelligence community agencies.
- The Congress should make sure funding is available to accelerate the expansion of secure facilities in FBI field offices so as to increase their ability to use secure email systems and classified intelligence product exchanges. The Congress should monitor whether the FBI's information-sharing principles are implemented in practice.

The FBI is just a small fraction of the national law enforcement community in the United States, a community comprised mainly of state and local agencies. The network designed for sharing information, and the work of the FBI through local joint Terrorism Task Forces, should build a reciprocal relationship, in which state and local agents understand what information they are looking for and, in return, receive some of the information being developed about what is happening, or may happen, in their communities. In this relationship, the Department of Homeland Security also will play an important part.

The Homeland Security Act of 2002 gave the under secretary for information analysis and infrastructure protection broad responsibilities. In practice, this directorate has the job to map "terrorist threats to the homeland against our assessed vulnerabilities in order to drive our efforts to protect against terrorist threats."[20] These capabilities are still embryonic. The directorate has not yet developed the capacity to perform one of its assigned jobs, which is to assimilate and analyze information from Homeland Security's own component agencies, such as the Coast Guard, Secret Service, Transportation Security Administration, Immigration and Customs Enforcement, and Customs and Border

Protection. The secretary of homeland security must ensure that these components work with the Information Analysis and Infrastructure Protection Directorate so that this office can perform its mission.[21]

HOMELAND DEFENSE

At several points in our inquiry, we asked, "Who is responsible for defending us at home?" Our national defense at home is the responsibility, first, of the Department of Defense and, second, of the Department of Homeland Security. They must have clear delineations of responsibility and authority.

We found that NORAD, which had been given the responsibility for defending U.S. airspace, had construed that mission to focus on threats coming from outside America's borders. It did not adjust its focus even though the intelligence community had gathered intelligence on the possibility that terrorists might turn to hijacking and even use of planes as missiles. We have been assured that NORAD has now embraced the full mission. Northern Command has been established to assume responsibility for the defense of the domestic United States.

Recommendation: The Department of Defense and its oversight committees should regularly assess the adequacy of Northern Command's strategies and planning to defend the United States against military threats to the homeland.

The Department of Homeland Security was established to consolidate all of the domestic agencies responsible for securing America's borders and national infrastructure, most of which is in private hands. It should identify those elements of our transportation, energy, communications, financial, and other institutions that need to be protected, develop plans to protect that infrastructure, and exercise the mechanisms to enhance preparedness. This means going well beyond the preexisting jobs of the agencies that have been brought together inside the department.

Recommendation: The Department of Homeland Security and its oversight committees should regularly assess the types of threats the country faces to determine (a) the adequacy of the government's plans—and the progress against those plans—to protect America's critical infrastructure and (b) the readiness of the government to respond to the threats that the United States might face.

• • •

We look forward to a national debate on the merits of what we have recommended, and we will participate vigorously in that debate.

NOTES

1. The Bush administration clarified the respective missions of the different intelligence analysis centers in a letter sent by Secretary ridge, DCI Tenet, FBI Director Mueller, and TTIC Director Brennan to Senators Susan Collins and Carl Levin on April 13, 2004. The letter did not mention any element of the Department of Defense. It stated that the DCI would define what analytical resources he would transfer from the CTC to TTIC no later than June 1, 2004. DCI Tenet

subsequently told us that he decided that TTIC would have primary responsibility for terrorism analysis but that the CIA and the Defense Intelligence Agency would grow their own analysts. TTIC will have tasking authority over terrorism analysts in other intelligence agencies, although there will need to be a board to supervise deconfliction. George Tenet interview (July 2, 2004). We have not received any details regarding this plan.

2. "TTIC has no operational authority. However, TTIC has the authority to task collection and analysis from Intelligence Community agencies, the FBI, and DHS through tasking mechanisms we will create. The analytic work conducted at TTIC creates products that inform each of TTIC's partner elements, as well as other Federal departments and agencies as appropriate." Letter from Ridge and others to Collins and Levin, Apr. 13, 2004.

3. Donald Rumsfeld prepared statement, Mar. 23, 2004, p. 20.

4. In this conception, the NCTC should plan actions, assigning responsibilities for operational direction and execution to other agencies. It would be built on TTIC and would be supported by the intelligence community as TTIC is now. Whichever route is chosen, the scarce analytical resources now dispersed among TTIC, the Defense Intelligence Agency's Joint Interagency Task Force—Combatting Terrorism (JITF-CT), and the DCI's Counterterrorist Center (CTC) should be concentrated more effectively than they are now.

- The DCI's Counterterrorist Center would become a CIA unit, to handle the direction and execution of tasks assigned to the CIA. It could have detailees from other agencies, as it does now, to perform this operational mission. It would yield much of the broader, strategic analytic duties and personnel to the NCTC. The CTC would rely on the restructured CIA (discussed in section 13.2) to organize, train, and equip its personnel.
- Similarly, the FBI's Counterterrorism Division would remain, as now, the operational arm of the Bureau to combat terrorism. As it does now, it would work with other agencies in carrying out these missions, retaining the JTTF structure now in place. The Counterterrorism Division would rely on the FBI's Office of Intelligence to train and equip its personnel, helping to process and report the information gathered in the field.
- The Defense Department's unified commands—SOCOM, NORTHCOM, and CENTCOM—would be the joint operational centers taking on DOD tasks. Much of the excellent analytical talent that has been assembled in the Defense Intelligence Agency's JITF-CT should merge into the planned NCTC.
- The Department of Homeland Security's Directorate for Information Analysis and Infrastructure Protection should retain its core duties, but the NCTC should have the ultimate responsibility for producing *net* assessments that utilize Homeland Security's analysis of domestic vulnerabilities and integrate all-source analysis of foreign intelligence about the terrorist enemy.
- The State Department's counterterrorism office would be a critical participant in the NCTC's work, taking the lead in directing the execution of the counterterrorism foreign policy mission.

The proposed National Counterterrorism Center should offer one-stop shopping to agencies with counterterrorism and homeland security responsibilities. That is, it should be an authoritative reference base on the transnational terrorist organizations: their people, goals, strategies, capabilities, networks of contacts and support, the context in which they operate, and their characteristic habits across the life cycle of operations—recruitment, reconnaissance, target selection, logistics, and travel. For example, this Center would offer an integrated depiction of groups like al Qaeda or Hezbollah worldwide, overseas, and in the United States.

The NCTC will not eliminate the need for the executive departments to have their own analytic units. But it would enable agency-based analytic units to become smaller and more efficient. In particular, it would make it possible for these agency-based analytic units to concentrate on analysis that is tailored to their agency's specific responsibilities.

A useful analogy is in military intelligence. There, the Defense Intelligence Agency and the service production agencies (like the Army's National Ground Intelligence Center) are the institutional memory and reference source for enemy order of battle, enemy organization, and enemy equipment. Yet the Joint Staff and all the theater commands still have their own J-2s. They draw on the information they need, tailoring and applying it to their operational needs. As they learn more from their tactical operations, they pass intelligence of enduring value back up to the Defense Intelligence Agency and the services so it can be evaluated, form part of the institutional memory, and help guide future collection.

In our proposal, that reservoir of institutional memory about terrorist organizations would function for the government as a whole, and would be in the NCTC.

5. The head of the NCTC would thus help coordinate the operational side of these agencies, like the FBI's Counterterrorism Division. The intelligence side of these agencies, such as the FBI's Office of Intelligence, would be overseen by the National Intelligence Director we recommend later in this chapter.

6. The quotation goes on: "It includes gaps in intelligence, but also intelligence that, like a string of pearls too precious to wear, is too sensitive to give to those who need it. It includes the alarm that fails to work, but also the alarm that has gone off so often it has been disconnected. It includes the unalert watchman, but also the one who knows he'll be chewed out by his superior if he gets higher authority out of bed. It includes the contingencies that occur to no one, but also those that everyone assumes somebody else is taking care of. It includes straightforward procrastination, but also decisions protracted by internal disagreement. It includes, in addition, the inability of individual human beings to rise to the occasion until they are sure it is the occasion—which is usually too late. . . . Finally, as at Pearl Harbor, surprise may include some measure of genuine novelty introduced by the enemy, and some sheer bad luck." Thomas Schelling, foreword to Roberta Wohlstetter, *Pearl Harbor: Warning and Decision* (Stanford Univ. Press, 1962), p. viii.

7. For the Goldwater-Nichols Act, see Pub. L. No. 99–433, 100 Stat. 992 (1986). For a general discussion of the act, see Gordon Lederman, *Reorganizing the Joint Chiefs of Staff: The Goldwater-Nichols Act of 1986* (Greenwood, 1999); James Locher, *Victory on the Potomac: The Goldwater-Nichols Act Unifies the Pentagon* (Texas A&M Univ. Press, 2003).

8. For a history of the DCI's authority over the intelligence community, see CIA report, Michael Warner ed., *Central Intelligence; Origin and Evolution* (CIA Center for the Study of Intelligence, 2001). For the Director's view of his community authorities, see DCI directive, "Director of Central Intelligence Directive 1/1: The Authorities and Responsibilities of the Director of Central Intelligence as Head of the U.S. Intelligence Community," Nov. 19, 1998.

9. As Norman Augustine, former chairman of Lockheed Martin Corporation, writes regarding power in the government, "As in business, cash is king. If you are not in charge of your budget, you are not king." Norman Augustine, *Managing to Survive in Washington: A Beginner's Guide to High-Level Management in Government* (Center for Strategic and International Studies, 2000), p. 20.

10. For the DCI and the secretary of defense, see 50 U.S.C. § 403-6(a). If the director does not concur with the secretary's choice, then the secretary is required to notify the president of the director's nonconcurrence. Ibid. For the DCI and the attorney general, see 50 U.S.C. § 403-6(b)(3).

11. The new program would replace the existing National Foreign Intelligence Program.

12. Some smaller parts of the current intelligence community, such as the State Department's intelligence bureau and the Energy Department's intelligence entity, should not be funded out of the national intelligence program and should be the responsibility of their home departments.

13. The head of the NCTC should have the rank of a deputy national intelligence director, e.g., Executive Level II, but would have a different title.

14. If the organization of defense intelligence remains as it is now, the appropriate official would be the under secretary of defense for intelligence. If defense intelligence is reorganized to elevate the responsibilities of the director of the DIA, then that person might be the appropriate official.

15. For the information technology architecture, see Ruth David interview (June 10, 2003). For the necessity of moving from need-to-know to need-to-share, see James Steinberg testimony, Oct. 14,

2003. The Director still has to strategy for removing information-sharing barriers and—more than two years since 9/11—has only appointed a working group on the subject. George Tenet prepared statement, Mar. 24, 2004, p. 37.

16. The intelligence community currently makes information shareable by creating "tearline" reports, with the nonshareable information at the top and then, below the "tearline," the portion that recipients are told they can share. This proposal reverses that concept. All reports are created as tearline data, with the shareable information at the top and with added details accessible on a system that requires permissions or authentication.

17. See Markle Foundation Task Force report, *Creating a Trusted Information Network for Homeland Security* (Markle Foundation, 2003); Markle Foundation Task Force report, *Protecting America's Freedom in the Information Age* (Markle Foundation, 2002) (both online at www .markle.org).

18. Markle Foundation Task Force report, *Creating a Trusted Information Network*, p. 12. The pressing need for such guidelines was also spotlighted by the Technology and Privacy Advisory Committee appointed by Secretary Rumsfeld to advise the Department of Defense on the privacy implications of its Terrorism Information Awareness Program. Technology and Privacy Advisory Committee report, *Safeguarding Privacy in the Fight Against Terrorism* (2004) (online at www.sainc.com/tapac/TAPAC_Report_Final_5-10-04.pdf). We take no position on the particular recommendations offered in that report, but it raises issues that pertain to the government as a whole—not just to the Department of Defense.

19. This recommendation, and measures to assist the Bureau in developing its intelligence cadre, are included in the report accompanying the Commerce, Justice and State Appropriations Act for Fiscal Year 2005, passed by the House of Representatives on July 7, 2004. H.R. Rep. No. 108–576, 108th Cong., 2d sess. (2004), p. 22.

20. Letter from Ridge and others to Collins and Levin, Apr. 13, 2004.

21. For the directorate's current capability, see Patrick Hughes interview (Apr. 2, 2004).

THE SILBERMAN-ROBB COMMISSION RECOMMENDATIONS ON INTELLIGENCE AND WMDS IN IRAQ, 2005

Editor's Note: The Department of Defense Commission investigating the incorrect intelligence assessments about weapons of mass destruction in Iraq reported on its findings in 2005. Led by Judge Laurence Silberman and former Senator Chuck Robb (D-VA), the Silberman-Robb Commission offered a number of recommendations on how intelligence might be improved to avoid similar mistakes in the future with regard to WMDs and terrorist activities. This appendix summarizes the panel's key findings.

COMMISSION ON THE INTELLIGENCE CAPABILITIES OF THE UNITED STATES REGARDING WEAPONS OF MASS DESTRUCTION WASHINGTON, D.C. 20503

CO-CHAIRMEN:

THE HONORABLE
LAURENCE H. SILBERMAN

THE HONORABLE
CHARLES S. ROBB

March 31, 2005

Mr. President:

With this letter, we transmit the report of the Commission on the Intelligence Capabilities of the United States Regarding Weapons of Mass Destruction. Our unanimous report is based on a lengthy investigation, during which we interviewed hundreds of experts from inside and outside the Intelligence Community and reviewed thousands of documents. Our report offers 74 recommendations for improving the U.S. Intelligence Community (all

Source: The Silberman-Robb Commission, Washington, DC, 2005, pp. 399–428.

but a handful of which we believe can be implemented without statutory change). But among these recommendations a few points merit special emphasis.

We conclude that the Intelligence Community was dead wrong in almost all of its pre-war judgments about Iraq's weapons of mass destruction. This was a major intelligence failure. Its principal causes were the Intelligence Community's inability to collect good information about Iraq's WMD programs, serious errors in analyzing what information it could gather, and a failure to make clear just how much of its analysis was based on assumptions, rather than good evidence. On a matter off this importance, we simply cannot afford failures of this magnitude.

After a thorough review, the Commission found no indication that the Intelligence Community distorted the evidence regarding Iraq's weapons of mass destruction. What the intelligence professionals told you about Saddam Hussein's programs was what they believed. They were simply wrong.

As you asked, we looked as well beyond Iraq in our review of the Intelligence Community's capabilities. We conducted case studies of our intelligence agencies' recent performance assessing the risk of WMD in Libya and Afghanistan, and our current capabilities with respect to several of the world's most dangerous state and non-state proliferation threats. Out of this more comprehensive review, we report both bad news and good news. The bad news is that we still know disturbingly little about the weapons programs and even less about the intentions of many of our most dangerous adversaries. The good news is that we have had some solid intelligence successes—thanks largely to innovative and multi-agency collection techniques.

Our review has convinced us that the best hope for preventing future failures is dramatic change. We need an Intelligence Community that is truly integrated, far more imaginative and willing to run risks, open to a new generation of Americans, and receptive to new technologies.

We have summarized our principal recommendations for the entire Intelligence Community in the Overview of the report. Here, we focus on recommendations that we believe only you can effect if you choose to implement them:

- *Give the DNI powers—and backing—to match his responsibilities.*

In your public statement accompanying the announcement of Ambassador Negroponte's nomination as Director of National Intelligence (DNI), you have already moved in this direction. The new intelligence law makes the DNI responsible for integrating the 15 independent members of the Intelligence Community. But it gives him powers that are only relatively broader than before. The DNI cannot make this work unless he takes his legal authorities over the budget, programs, personnel, and priorities to the limit. It won't be easy to provide this leadership to the intelligence components of the Defense Department, or to the CIA. They are some of the government's most headstrong agencies. Sooner or later, they will try to run around—or over—the DNI. Then, only your determined backing will convince them that we cannot return to the old ways.

- *Bring the FBI all the way into the Intelligence Community.*

The FBI is one of the proudest and most independent agencies in the United States Government. It is on its way to becoming an effective intelligence agency, but it will never arrive if it insists on using only is own map. We recommend that you order an organizational reform of the Bureau that pulls all of its intelligence capabilities into one place and subjects them to the coordinating authority of the DNI—the same authority that the DNI exercises over Defense Department intelligence agencies. Under this recommendation, the counterterrorism and counterintelligence resources of the Bureau would become a single National Security Service inside the FBI. It would of course still be subject to the Attorney General's oversight and to current legal rules. The intelligence reform act almost accomplishes this task, but at crucial points it retreats into ambiguity. Without leadership from the DNI, the FBI is likely to continue escaping effective integration into the Intelligence Community.

- *Demand more of the Intelligence Community.*

The Intelligence Community needs to be pushed. It will not do its best unless it is pressed by polilcymakers—sometimes to the point of discomfort. Analysts must be pressed to explain how much they don't know; the collection agencies must be pressed to explain why they don't have better information on key topics. While policyinakers must be prepared to credit ntelligence that doesn't fit their preferences, no important intelligence assessment should be accepted without sharp questioning that forces the community to explain exactly how it came to that assessment and what alternatives might also be true. This is not "politicization"; it is a necessary part of the intelligence process. And in the end, it is the key to getting the best from an Intelligence Community that, at its best, knows how to do astonishing things.

- *Rethink the President's Daily Brief.*

The daily intelligence briefings given to you before the Iraq war were flawed. Through attention-grabbing headlines and repetition of questionable data, these briefings overstated the case that Iraq was rebuilding its WMD programs. There are many other aspects of the daily brief that deserve to be reconsidered as well, but we are reluctant to make categorical recommendations on a process that in the end must meet your needs, not our theories. On one point, however, we want to be specific: while the DNI must be ultimately responsible for the content of your daily briefing, we do not believe that the DNI ought to prepare, deliver, or even attend every briefing. For if the DNI is consumed by current intelligence, the long-term needs of the Intelligence Community will suffer.

* * *

There is no more important intelligence mission important intelligence than understanding the worst weapons that our enemies possess, and how they intend to use them against us. These are their deepest secrets, and unlocking them must be our highest priority. So far, despite some successes, our Intelligence Community has not been agile and innovative enough to provide the information that the nation needs. Other commissions and observers have said the same. We should not wait for another commission or another Administration to force widespread change in the Intelligence Community.

Very respectfully,

Laurence H. Silberman   Charles S. Robb
Co-Chairman   Co-Chairman

Richard C. Levin   John McCain   Henry S. Rowen   Walter B. Slocombe
William O. Studeman   Patricia M. Wald   Charles M. Vest

Lloyd Cutler
(Of Counsel)

OVERVIEW OF THE REPORT

INTRODUCTION

On the brink of war, and in front of the whole world, the United States government asserted that Saddam Hussein had reconstituted his nuclear weapons program, had biological weapons and mobile biological weapon production facilities, and had stockpiled and was producing chemical weapons. All of this was based on the assessments of the U.S. Intelligence Community. And not one bit of it could be confirmed when the war was over.

While the intelligence services of many other nations also thought that Iraq had weapons of mass destruction, in the end it was the United States that put its credibility on the line, making this one of the most public—and most damaging—intelligence failures in recent American history.

This failure was in large part the result of analytical shortcomings; intelligence analysts were too wedded to their assumptions about Saddam's intentions. But it was also a failure on the part of those who collect intelligence—CIA's and the Defense Intelligence Agency's (DIA) spies, the National Security Agency's (NSA) eavesdroppers, and the National Geospatial-Intelligence Agency's (NGA) imagery experts.[1] In the end, those agencies collected precious little intelligence for the analysts to analyze, and much of what they did collect was either worthless or misleading. Finally, it was a failure to communicate effectively with policymakers; the Intelligence Community didn't adequately explain just how little good intelligence it had—or how much its assessments were driven by assumptions and inferences rather than concrete evidence.

Was the failure in Iraq typical of the Community's performance? Or was Iraq, as one senior intelligence official told the Commission, a sort of "perfect storm"—a one-time breakdown caused by a rare confluence of events that conspired to create a bad result? In our view, it was neither.

The failures we found in Iraq are not repeated everywhere. The Intelligence Community played a key role, for example, in getting Libya to renounce weapons of mass destruction and in exposing the long-running A.Q. Khan nuclear proliferation network. It is engaged in imaginative, successful (and highly classified) operations in many parts of the world. Tactical support to counterterrorism efforts is excellent, and there are signs of a boldness that would have been unimaginable before September 11, 2001.

But neither was Iraq a "perfect storm." The flaws we found in the Intelligence Community's Iraq performance are still all too common. Across the board, the Intelligence Community knows disturbingly little about the nuclear programs of many of the world's most dangerous actors. In some cases, it knows less now than it did five or ten years ago. As for biological weapons, despite years of Presidential concern, the Intelligence Community has struggled to address this threat.

To be sure, the Intelligence Community is full of talented, dedicated people. But they seem to be working harder and harder just to maintain a *status quo* that is increasingly irrelevant to the new challenges presented by weapons of mass destruction. Our collection agencies are often unable to gather intelligence on the very things we care the most about.

---

[1] While we have attempted to write this report in a way that is accessible to those not acquainted with the world of intelligence, we have included a primer on the U.S. Intelligence Community at Appendix C of this report for readers who are new to the subject.

Too often, analysts simply accept these gaps; they do little to help collectors identify new opportunities, and they do not always tell decisionmakers just how limited their knowledge really is.

Taken together, these shortcomings reflect the Intelligence Community's struggle to confront an environment that has changed radically over the past decade. For almost 50 years after the passage of the National Security Act of 1947, the Intelligence Community's resources were overwhelmingly trained on a single threat—the Soviet Union, its nuclear arsenal, its massive conventional forces, and its activities around the world. By comparison, today's priority intelligence targets are greater in number (there are dozens of entities that could strike a devastating blow against the United States) and are often more diffuse in character (they include not only states but also nebulous transnational terror and pro-liferation networks). What's more, some of the weapons that would be most dangerous in the hands of terrorists or rogue nations are difficult to detect. Much of the technology, equipment, and materials necessary to develop biological and chemical weapons, for ex-ample, also has legitimate commercial applications. Biological weapons themselves can be built in small-scale facilities that are easy to conceal, and weapons-grade uranium can be effectively shielded from traditional detection techniques. At the same time, advances in technology have made the job of technical intelligence collection exceedingly difficult.

The demands of this new environment can only be met by broad and deep change in the Intelligence Community. The Intelligence Community we have today is buried beneath an avalanche of demands for "current intelligence"—the pressing need to meet the tactical requirements of the day. Current intelligence in support of military and other action is necessary, of course. But we also need an Intelligence Community with *strategic* cap-abilities: it must be equipped to develop long-term plans for penetrating today's difficult targets, and to identify political and social trends shaping the threats that lie over the horizon. We can imagine no threat that demands greater strategic focus from the In-telligence Community than that posed by nuclear, biological, and chemical weapons.

The Intelligence Community is also fragmented, loosely managed, and poorly co-ordinated; the 15 intelligence organizations are a "Community" in name only and rarely act with a unity of purpose. What we need is an Intelligence Community that is *integrated*: the Community's leadership must be capable of allocating and directing the Community's resources in a coordinated way. The strengths of our distinct collection agencies must be brought to bear together on the most difficult intelligence problems. At the same time we need a Community that preserves diversity of analysis, and that encourages structured debate among agencies and analysts over the interpretation of information.

Perhaps above all, the Intelligence Community is too slow to change the way it does business. It is reluctant to use new human and technical collection methods; it is behind the curve in applying cutting-edge technologies; and it has not adapted its personnel practices and incentives structures to fit the needs of a new job market. What we need is an In-telligence Community that is flexible—able to respond nimbly to an ever-shifting threat environment and to the rapid pace of today's technological changes.

In short, to succeed in confronting today's and tomorrow's threats, the Intelligence Community must be transformed—a goal that would be difficult to meet even in the best of all possible worlds. And we do not live in the best of worlds. The CIA and NSA may be sleek and omniscient in the movies, but in real life they and other intelligence agencies are vast government bureaucracies. They are bureaucracies filled with talented people and armed with sophisticated technological tools, but talent and tools do not suspend the iron laws of bureaucratic behavior. Like government bodies everywhere, intelligence agencies are prone to develop self-reinforcing, risk averse cultures that take outside advice badly. While laudable steps were taken to improve our intelligence agencies after September 11, 2001, the agencies have done less in response to the failures over Iraq, and we believe that many within those agencies do not accept the conclusion that we reached after our year of study: that the Community needs fundamental change if it is to successfully confront the threats of the 21st century.

We are not the first to say this. Indeed, commission after commission has identified some of the same fundamental failings we see in the Intelligence Community, usually to little effect. The Intelligence Community is a closed world, and many insiders admitted to us that *it has an almost perfect record of resisting external recommendations.*

But the present moment offers an unprecedented opportunity to overcome this resistance. About halfway through our inquiry, Congress passed the *Intelligence Reform and Terrorism Prevention Act of 2004*, which became a sort of a *dens ex machina* in our deliberations. The act created a Director of National Intelligence (DNI). The DNI's role could have been a purely coordinating position, with a limited staff and authority to match. Or it could have been something closer to a "Secretary of Intelligence," with full authority over the principal intelligence agencies and clear responsibility for their actions—which also might well have been consistent with a small bureaucratic superstructure. In the end, the DNI created by the intelligence reform legislation was neither of these things; the office is given broad responsibilities but only ambiguous authorities. While we might have chosen a different solution, we are not writing on a blank slate. So our focus has been in large part on how to make the new intelligence structure work, and in particular on giving the DNI tools (and support staff) to match his large responsibilities.

We are mindful, however, that there is a serious risk in creating too large a bureaucratic structure to serve the DNI: the risk that decisionmaking in the field, which sometimes requires quick action, will be improperly delayed. Balancing these two imperatives— necessary agility of operational execution and thoughtful coordination of intelligence activities—is, in our view, the DNI's greatest challenge.

In considering organizational issues, we did not delude ourselves that organizational structure alone can solve problems. More than many parts of government, the culture of the Intelligence Community is formed in the field, where organizational changes at headquarters are felt only lightly. We understand the limits of organizational change, and many of our recommendations go beyond organizational issues and would, if enacted, directly affect the way that intelligence is collected and analyzed. But we regret that we were not able to make such detailed proposals for some of the most important technical collection agencies, such as NSA and NGA. For those agencies, and for the many other issues that we could only touch upon, we must trust that our broader institutional recommendations will enable necessary reform. The DNI that we envision will have the budget and management tools to dig deep into the culture of each agency and to force changes where needed.

This Overview—and, in far more detail, the report that follows—offers our conclusions on what needs to be done. We begin by describing the results of our case studies— which include Iraq, Libya, Afghanistan, and others—and the lessons they teach about the Intelligence Community's current capabilities and weaknesses. We then offer our recommendations for reform based upon those lessons.

Three final notes before proceeding. First, our main tasks were to find out how the Intelligence Community erred in Iraq and to recommend changes to avoid such errors in the future. This is a task that often lends itself to hubris and to second-guessing, and we have been humbled by the difficult judgments that had to be made about Iraq and its weapons programs. We are humbled too by the complexity of the management and technical challenges intelligence professionals face today. We recommend substantial changes, and we believe deeply that such changes are necessary, but we recognize that other reasonable observers could come to a different view on some of these questions.

Second, no matter how much we improve the Intelligence Community, weapons of mass destruction will continue to pose an enormous threat. Intelligence will always be imperfect and, as history persuades us, surprise can never be completely prevented. Moreover, we cannot expect spies, satellites, and analysts to constitute our only defense. As our biological weapons recommendations make abundantly clear, all national capabilities—regulatory, military, and diplomatic—must be used to combat proliferation.

Finally, we emphasize two points about the scope of this Commission's charter, particularly with respect to the Iraq question. First, we were *not* asked to determine whether Saddam Hussein had weapons of mass destruction. That was the mandate of the Iraq Survey Group; our mission is to investigate the reasons why the Intelligence Community's pre-war assessments were so different from what the Iraq Survey Group found after the war. Second, we were not authorized to investigate how policymakers used the intelligence assessments they received from the Intelligence Community. Accordingly, while we interviewed a host of current and former policymakers during the course of our investigation, the purpose of those interviews was to learn about how the Intelligence Community reached and communicated its judgments about Iraq's weapons programs—not to review how policymakers subsequently used that information.

LOOKING BACK: CASE STUDIES IN FAILURE AND SUCCESS

Our first task was to evaluate the Intelligence Community's performance in assessing the nuclear, biological, and chemical weapons activities of three countries: Iraq, Afghanistan, and Libya. In addition, we studied U.S. capabilities against other pressing intelligence problems—including Iran, North Korea, Russia, China, and terrorism. We wanted a range of studies so we would not judge the Intelligence Community solely on its handling of Iraq, which was—however important—a single intelligence target. In all, the studies paint a representative picture. It is the picture of an Intelligence Community that urgently needs to be changed.

IRAQ: AN OVERVIEW

In October 2002, at the request of members of Congress, the National Intelligence Council produced a National Intelligence Estimate (NIE)—the most authoritative intelligence assessment produced by the Intelligence Community—which concluded that Iraq was reconstituting its nuclear weapons program and was actively pursuing a nuclear device. According to the exhaustive study of the Iraq Survey Group, this assessment was almost completely wrong. The NIE said that Iraq's biological weapons capability was larger and more advanced than before the Gulf War and that Iraq possessed mobile biological weapons production facilities. This was wrong. The NIE further stated that Iraq had renewed production of chemical weapons, including mustard, sarin, GF, and VX, and that it had accumulated chemical stockpiles of between 100 and 500 metric tons. All of this was also wrong. Finally, the NIE concluded that Iraq had unmanned aerial vehicles that were probably intended for the delivery of biological weapons, and ballistic missiles that had ranges greater than the United Nations' permitted 150 kilometer range. In truth, the aerial vehicles were not for biological weapons; some of Iraq's missiles were, however, capable of traveling more than 150 kilometers. The Intelligence Community's Iraq assessments were, in short, riddled with errors.

Contrary to what some defenders of the Intelligence Community have since asserted, these errors were *not* the result of a few harried months in 2002. Most of the fundamental errors were made and communicated to policymakers well before the now-infamous NIE of October 2002, and were not corrected in the months between the NIE and the start of the war. They were not isolated or random failings. Iraq had been an intelligence challenge at the forefront of U.S. attention for over a decade. It was a known adversary that had already fought one war with the United States and seemed increasingly likely to fight another. But, after ten years of effort, the Intelligence Community still had no good intelligence on the status of Iraq's weapons programs. Our full report examines these issues in detail. Here we limit our discussion to the central lessons to be learned from this episode.

The first lesson is that the Intelligence Community cannot analyze and disseminate information that it does not have. The Community's Iraq assessment was crippled by its inability to collect meaningful intelligence on Iraq's nuclear, biological, and chemical weapons programs. The second lesson follows from the first: lacking good intelligence, analysts and collectors fell back on old assumptions and inferences drawn from Iraq's past behavior and intentions.

The Intelligence Community had learned a hard lesson after the 1991 Gulf War, which revealed that the Intelligence Community's pre-war assessments had underestimated Iraq's nuclear program and had failed to identify all of its chemical weapons storage sites. Shaken by the magnitude of their errors, intelligence analysts were determined not to fall victim again to the same mistake. This tendency was only reinforced by later events. Saddam acted to the very end like a man with much to hide. And the dangers of underestimating our enemies were deeply underscored by the attacks of September 11, 2001.

Throughout the 1990s, therefore, the Intelligence Community assumed that Saddam's Iraq was up to no good—that Baghdad had maintained its nuclear, biological, and chemical technical expertise, had kept its biological and chemical weapons production capabilities, and possessed significant stockpiles of chemical agents and weapons precursors. Since Iraq's leadership had not changed since 1991, the Intelligence Community also believed that these capabilities would be further revved up as soon as inspectors left Iraq. Saddam's continuing cat-and-mouse parrying with international inspectors only hardened these assumptions.

These experiences contributed decisively to the Intelligence Community's erroneous National Intelligence Estimate of October 2002. That is not to say that its fears and assumptions were foolish or even unreasonable. At some point, however, these premises stopped being working hypotheses and became more or less unrebuttable conclusions; worse, the intelligence system became too willing to find confirmations of them in evidence that should have been recognized at the time to be of dubious reliability. Collectors and analysts too readily accepted any evidence that supported their theory that Iraq had stockpiles and was developing weapons programs, and they explained away or simply disregarded evidence that pointed in the other direction.

Even in hindsight, those assumptions have a powerful air of common sense. If the Intelligence Community's estimate and other pre-war intelligence had relied principally and explicitly on inferences the Community drew from Iraq's past conduct, the estimate would still have been wrong, but it would have been far more defensible. For good reason, it was hard to conclude that Saddam Hussein had indeed abandoned his weapons programs. But a central flaw of the NIE is that it took these defensible assumptions and swathed them in the mystique of intelligence, providing secret information that seemed to support them but was in fact nearly worthless, if not misleading. The NIE simply didn't communicate how weak the underlying intelligence was.

This was, moreover, a problem that was not limited to the NIE. Our review found that *after* the publication of the October 2002 NIE but *before* Secretary of State Colin Powell's February 2003 address to the United Nations, intelligence officials within the CIA failed to convey to policymakers new information casting serious doubt on the reliability of a human intelligence source known as "Curveball." This occurred despite the pivotal role Curveball's information played in the Intelligence Community's assessment of Iraq's biological weapons programs, and in spite of Secretary Powell's efforts to strip every dubious piece of information out of his proposed speech. In this instance, once again, the Intelligence Community failed to give policymakers a full understanding of the frailties of the intelligence on which they were relying.

Finally, we closely examined the possibility that intelligence analysts were pressured by policymakers to change their judgments about Iraq's nuclear, biological, and chemical weapons programs. The analysts who worked Iraqi weapons issues universally agreed that in no instance did political pressure cause them to skew or alter any of their analytical judgments. That said, it is hard to deny the conclusion that intelligence analysts worked in an environment that did not encourage skepticism about the conventional wisdom.

OTHER CASE STUDIES: AN OVERVIEW

Our remaining case studies present a more mixed picture. On the positive side, Libya is fundamentally a success story. The Intelligence Community assessed correctly the state of Libya's nuclear and chemical weapons programs, and the Intelligence Community's use of new techniques to penetrate the A.Q. Khan network allowed the U.S. government to pressure Libya into dismantling those programs. In counterterrorism, the Intelligence Community has made great strides since September 11, in particular with respect to tactical operations overseas. These successes stemmed from isolated efforts that need to be replicated in other areas of intelligence; in the case of Libya, from innovative collection techniques and, in the case of terrorism, from an impressive fusion of interagency intelligence capabilities.

But we also reviewed the state of the Intelligence Community's knowledge about the unconventional weapons programs of several countries that pose current proliferation threats, including Iran, North Korea, China, and Russia. We cannot discuss many of our findings from these studies in our unclassified report, but we can say here that we found that we have only limited access to critical information about several of these high-priority intelligence targets.

LESSONS LEARNED FROM THE CASE STUDIES

Our case studies revealed failures and successes that ran the gamut of the intelligence process. Although each of these studies is covered in far greater detail in the report itself, we include here a summary of the central lessons we drew from them.

Poor target development: not getting intelligence on the issues we care about most. You can't analyze intelligence that you don't have—and our case studies resoundingly demonstrate how little we know about some of our highest priority intelligence targets. It is clear that in today's context the traditional collection techniques employed by individual collection agencies have lost much of their power to surprise our adversaries. The successful penetrations of "hard targets" that we did find were usually the result either of an innovative collection technique or of a creative integration of collection capabilities across agencies. In general, however, the Intelligence Community has not developed the long-term, coordinated collection strategies that are necessary to penetrate today's intelligence targets.

Lack of rigorous analysis. Long after the Community's assessment of Iraq had begun to fall apart, one of the main drafters of the NIE told us that, if he had to grade it, he would still give the NIE an "A." By that, he presumably meant that the NIE fully met the standards for analysis that the Community had set for itself. That is the problem. The scope and quality of analysis has eroded badly in the Intelligence Community and it must be restored. In part, this is a matter of tradecraft and training; in part, too, it is a matter of expertise.

Analytic "tradecraft"—the way analysts think, research, evaluate evidence, write, and communicate—must be strengthened. In many instances, we found finished intelligence that was loosely reasoned, ill-supported, and poorly communicated. Perhaps most worrisome, we found too many analytic products that obscured how little the Intelligence Community actually *knew* about an issue and how much their conclusions rested on inference and assumptions. We believe these tendencies must be reversed if decisionmakers are to have confidence in the intelligence they receive. And equally important, analysts must be willing to admit what they don't know in order to focus future collection efforts. Conversely, policymakers must be prepared to accept uncertainties and qualifications in intelligence judgments and not expect greater precision than the evaluated data permits.

Good "tradecraft" without expertise, however, will only get you so far. Our case studies identified areas in which the Community's level of expertise was far below what it should be. In several instances, the Iraq assessments rested on failures of technical analysis that should have been obvious at the time—failure to understand facts about weapons technology, for example, or failures to detect obvious forgeries. Technical expertise, particularly relating to weapons systems, has fallen sharply in the past ten years. And in other areas, such as biotechnology, the Intelligence Community is well behind the private sector.

But the problem of expertise goes well beyond technical knowledge. During the Cold War, the Intelligence Community built up an impressive body of expertise on Soviet society, organization, and ideology, as well as on the Soviet threat. Regrettably, no equivalent talent pool exists today for the study of Islamic extremism. In some cases, the security clearance process limits the Intelligence Community's ability to recruit analysts with contacts among relevant groups and with experience living overseas. Similarly, some security rules limit the ways in which analysts can develop substantive expertise. Finally, poor training or bad habits lead analysts to rely too much on secret information and to use non-clandestine and public information too little. Nonclandestine sources of information are critical to understanding societal, cultural, and political trends, but they are insufficiently utilized.

Lack of political context—and imagination. The October 2002 NIE contained an extensive technical analysis of Iraq's suspected weapons programs but little serious analysis of the socio-political situation in Iraq, or the motives and intentions of Iraqi leadership-which, in a dictatorship like Iraq, really meant understanding Saddam. It seems unlikely to us that weapons experts used to combing reports for tidbits on technical programs would ever have asked: "Is Saddam bluffing?" or "Could he have decided to suspend his weapons programs until sanctions are lifted?" But an analyst steeped in Iraq's politics and culture at least *might* have asked those questions, and, of course, those turn out to be the questions that could have led the Intelligence Community closer to the truth. In that respect, the analysts displayed a lack of imagination. The Iraq example also reflects the Intelligence Community's increasing tendency to separate regional, technical, and (now) terrorism analysis—a trend that is being exacerbated by the gravitational pull toward centers like the National Counterterrorism Center (NCTC).

Overemphasis on and underperformance in daily intelligence products. As problematic as the October 2002 NIE was, it was not the Community's biggest analytic failure on Iraq. Even more misleading was the river of intelligence that flowed from the CIA to top policymakers over long periods of time—in the President's Daily Brief (PDB) and in its more widely distributed companion, the Senior Executive Intelligence Brief (SEIB). These daily reports were, if anything, more alarmist and less nuanced than the NIE. It was not that the intelligence was markedly different. Rather, it was that the PDBs and SEIBs, with their attention-grabbing headlines and drumbeat of repetition, left an impression of many corroborating reports where in fact there were very few sources. And in other instances, intelligence suggesting the existence of weapons programs was conveyed to senior policymakers, but later information casting doubt upon the validity of that intelligence was not. In ways both subtle and not so subtle, the daily reports seemed to be "selling" intelligence—in order to keep its customers, or at least the First Customer, interested.

Inadequate information sharing. There is little doubt that, at least in the context of counterterrorism, information sharing has improved substantially since September 11. This is in no small part due to the creation of the Terrorist Threat Integration Center (now NCTC) and the increased practice of housing collectors and analysts together, which provides a real-world solution to some of the bureaucratic and institutional barriers that exist between the big intelligence-collecting agencies. But in the three and a half years since September 11, this push to share information has not spread to other areas, including counterproliferation, where sharing is also badly needed. Furthermore, even in the counterterrorism context, information sharing still depends too much on physical co-location and personal relationships as opposed to integrated, Community-wide information networks. Equally problematic, individual departments and agencies continue to act as though they own the information they collect, forcing other agencies to pry information from them. Similarly, much information deemed "operational" by the CIA and FBI isn't routinely shared, even though analysts have repeatedly stressed its importance. All of this reveals that extensive work remains yet to be done.

Poor human intelligence. When the October 2002 NIE was written the United States had little human intelligence on Iraq's nuclear, biological, and chemical weapons programs and virtually no human intelligence on leadership intentions. While classification prevents us from getting into the details, the picture is much the same with respect to other dangerous threats. We recognize that espionage is always chancy at best; 50 years of pounding away at the Soviet Union resulted in only a handful of truly important human sources. Still, we have no choice but to do better. Old approaches to human intelligence alone are not the answer. Countries that threaten us are well aware of our human intelligence services' *modus operandi* and they know how to counter it. More of the same is unlikely to work. Innovation is needed. The CIA deserves credit for its efforts to discover and penetrate the A.Q. Khan network, and it needs to put more emphasis on other innovative human intelligence methods.

Worse than having no human sources is being seduced by a human source who is telling lies. In fact, the Community's position on Iraq's biological weapons program was largely determined by sources who were telling lies—most notably a source provided by a foreign intelligence service through the Defense Intelligence Agency. Why DIA and the rest of the Community didn't find out that the source was lying is a story of poor asset validation practices and the problems inherent in relying on semi-cooperative liaison services. That the NIE (and other reporting) didn't make clear to policymakers how heavily it relied on a single source that no American intelligence officer had ever met, and about whose reliability several intelligence professionals had expressed serious concern, is a damning comment on the Intelligence Community's practices.

The challenge to traditional signals intelligence. Signals intelligence—the interception of radio, telephone, and computer communications—has historically been a primary source of good intelligence. But changes in telecommunications technology have brought new challenges. This was the case in Iraq, where the Intelligence Community lost access to important aspects of Iraqi communications, and it remains the case elsewhere. We offer a brief additional discussion of some of the modern challenges facing signals intelligence in our classified report, but we cannot discuss this information in an unclassified format.

Regaining signals intelligence access must be a top priority. The collection agencies are working hard to restore some of the access that they have lost; and they've had some successes. And again, many of these recent steps in the right direction are the result of innovative examples of cross-agency cooperation. In addition, successful signals intelligence will require a sustained research and development effort to bring cutting-edge technology to operators and analysts. Success on this front will require greater willingness to accept financial costs, political risks, and even human casualties.

Declining utility of traditional imagery intelligence against unconventional weapons programs. The imagery collection systems that were designed largely to work against the Soviet Union's military didn't work very well against Iraq's unconventional weapons program, and our review found that they aren't working very well against other priority targets, either. That's because our adversaries are getting better at denial and deception, and because the threat is changing. Again, we offer details about the challenges to imagery intelligence in our classified report that we cannot provide here.

Making the problem even more difficult, there is little that traditional imagery can tell us about chemical and biological facilities. Biological and chemical weapons programs for the most part can exist inside commercial buildings with no suspicious signatures. This means that we can get piles of incredibly sharp photos of an adversary's chemical factories, and we still will not know much about its chemical weapons programs. We can still see a lot and imagery intelligence remains valuable in many contexts, including support to military operations and when used in conjunction with other collection disciplines—but too often what we can see doesn't tell us what we need to know about nuclear, biological, and chemical weapons.

Measurement and signature intelligence (MASINT) is not sufficiently developed. The collection of technologies known as MASINT, which includes a virtual grab bag of advanced collection and analytic methods, is not yet making a significant contribution to our intelligence efforts. In Iraq, MASINT played a negligible role. As in other contexts, we believe that the Intelligence Community should continue to pursue new technology aggressively—whether it is called MASINT, imagery, or signals intelligence. Innovation will be necessary to defeat our adversaries' denial and deception.

An absence of strong leadership. For over a year, despite unambiguous presidential direction, a turf battle raged between CIA's Counterterrorist Center (CTC) and the Terrorist Threat Integration Center (now NCTC). The two organizations fought over roles, responsibilities, and resources, and the Intelligence Community's leadership was unable to solve the problem. The intelligence reform act may put an end to this particular conflict, but we believe that the story reflects a larger, more pervasive problem within the Intelligence Community: the difficulty off making a decision and imposing the consequences on all agencies throughout the Community. Time and time again we have uncovered instances like this, where powerful agencies fight to a debilitating stalemate masked as consensus, because no one in the Community has been able to make a decision and then make it stick. The best hope for filling this gap is an empowered DNI.

LOOKING FORWARD:
OUR RECOMMENDATIONS FOR CHANGE

Our case studies collectively paint a picture of an Intelligence Community with serious deficiencies that span the intelligence process. Stated succinctly, it has too little *integration* and too little *innovation* to succeed in the 21st century. It rarely adopts integrated strategies for penetrating high-priority targets; decisiomnakers lack authority to resolve agency disputes; and it develops too few innovative ways of gathering intelligence.

This section summarizes our major recommendations on how to change this state of affairs so that full value can be derived from the many bright, dedicated, and deeply committed professionals within the Intelligence Community. We begin at the top, and suggest how to use the opportunity presented by the new intelligence reform legislation to bring better integration and management to the Intelligence Community. Our management recommendations are developed in greater detail in Chapter Six of our report. We next offer recommendations that would improve intelligence collection (Chapter 7) and analysis (Chapter 8). Then we examine several specific and important intelligence challenges-improving information sharing (Chapter 9); integrating domestic and foreign intelligence in a way that both satisfies national security imperatives and safeguards civil liberties (Chapter 10); organizing the Community's counterintelligence mission (Chapter 11); and a largely classified chapter on managing covert action (Chapter 12). We then devote a stand-alone chapter to examining the most dangerous unconventional weapons challenges the Intelligence Community faces today and offer specific prescriptions for improving our intelligence capabilities against these threats (Chapter 13).

LEADERSHIP AND MANAGEMENT: FORGING AN INTEGRATED
INTELLIGENCE COMMUNITY

A former senior Defense Department official described today's Intelligence Community as "not so much poorly managed as unmanaged." We agree. Everywhere we looked, we found important (and obvious) issues of interagency coordination that went unattended, sensible Community-wide proposals blocked by pockets of resistance, and critical disputes left to fester. Strong interagency cooperation was more likely to result from bilateral "treaties" between big agencies than from Community-level management. This ground was well-plowed by the 9/11 Commission and by several other important assessments of the Intelligence Community over the past decade.

In the chapter of our report devoted to management (Chapter 6), we offer detailed recommendations that we believe will equip the new Director of National Intelligence to forge today's loose confederation of 15 separate intelligence operations into a real, integrated Intelligence Community. A short summary of our more important management recommendations follows:

- **Strong leadership and management of the Intelligence Community are indispensable.** Virtually every senior intelligence official acknowledged the difficulty of leading and managing the Intelligence Community. Along with acting as the President's principal intelligence advisor, this will be the DNI's main job. His success in that job will determine the fate of many other necessary reforms. We thus recommend ways in which the DNI can use his limited, but not insignificant, authorities over money and people. No matter what, the DNI will not be able to run the Intelligence Community alone. He will need to create a management structure that allows him to see deep into the Intelligence Community's component agencies, and he will need to work closely with the other cabinet secretaries—especially the Secretary of Defense—for whom several Intelligence Community agencies also work. New procedures are particularly needed in the budget area, where today's Intelligence Community has a wholly inadequate Planning, Programming, and Budgeting System.
- **Organize around missions.** One of the most significant problems we identified in today's Intelligence Community is a lack of cross-Community focus on priority intelligence missions. By this, we mean that in most cases there is not one office, or one individual, who is responsible for making sure the Intelligence Community is doing all it can to collect and analyze intelligence on a subject like proliferation, or a country like Iran. Instead, intelligence agencies allocate their scarce resources among intelligence priorities in ways that seem sensible to them but are not optimal from a Community-wide perspective. The DNI needs management structures and processes that ensure a strategic, Community-level focus on priority intelligence missions. The specific device we propose is the creation of several "Mission Managers" on the DNI staff who are responsible for developing strategies for all aspects of intelligence relating to a priority intelligence target: the Mission Manager for China, for instance, would be responsible for driving collection on the China target, watching over China analysis, and serving as a clearinghouse for senior policymakers seeking China expertise.
- **Establish a National Counter Proliferation Center.** The new intelligence legislation creates one "national center"—the National Counterterrorism Center (NCTC)—and suggests the creation of a second, similar center devoted to counterproliferation issues. We agree that a National Counter Proliferation Center (NCPC) should be established but believe that it should be fundamentally different in character from the NCTC. The NCTC is practically a separate agency; its large staff is responsible not only for conducting counterterrorism analysis and intelligence gathering but also for "strategic operational planning" in support of counterterrorism policy. In contrast, we

believe that the NCPC should be a relatively small center (i.e., fewer than 100 people); it should primarily play a *management and coordination* function by overseeing analysis and collection on nuclear, biological, and chemical weapons across the Intelligence Community. In addition, although we agree that government-wide strategic planning is required to confront proliferation threats, we believe that entities other than the NCPC—such as a Joint Interagency Task Force we propose to coordinate interdiction efforts—should perform this function.

- ***Build a modern workforce.*** The intelligence reform legislation grants the DNI substantial personnel authorities. In our view, these authorities come none too soon. The Intelligence Community has difficulty recruiting and retaining individuals with critically important skill sets—such as technical and scientific expertise, and facility with foreign languages—and has not adapted well to the diverse cultures and settings in which today's intelligence experts must operate. We propose the creation of a new human resources authority in the Office of the DNI to develop Community-wide personnel policies and overcome these systemic shortcomings. We also offer specific proposals aimed at encouraging "joint" assignments between intelligence agencies, improving job training at all stages of an intelligence professional's career, and building a better personnel incentive structure.

- ***Create mechanisms for sustained oversight from outside the Intelligence Community—and for self-examination from the inside.*** Many sound past proposals for intelligence reform have withered on the vine. Either the Intelligence Community is inherently resistant to outside recommendations, or it lacks the institutional capacity to implement them. In either case, sustained external oversight is necessary. We recommend using the new Joint Intelligence Community Council—which comprises the DNI and the cabinet secretaries with intelligence responsibilities—as a high-level "consumer council." We also recommend the President's Foreign Intelligence Advisory Board play a more substantial advisory role. Like others before us, we suggest that the President urge Congress to reform its own procedures to provide better oversight. In particular, we recommend that the House and Senate intelligence committees create focused oversight subcommittees, that the Congress create an intelligence appropriations subcommittee and reduce the Intelligence Community's reliance on supplemental funding, and that the Senate intelligence committee be given the same authority over joint military intelligence programs and tactical intelligence programs that the House intelligence committee now exercises. Finally—and perhaps most importantly—we recommend that the DNI create mechanisms to ensure that the Intelligence Community conducts "lessons learned" and after-action studies so that it will be better equipped to identify its *own* strengths and weaknesses.

Additional Leadership and Management Recommendations

In addition to those described above, Chapter Six of our report offers recommendations concerning:

- How to build a coordinated process for "target development"—that is, the directing of collection resources toward priority intelligence subjects;

- How to spur innovation outside individual collection agencies;
- How the DNI might handle the difficult challenges of integrating intelligence from at home and abroad, and of coordinating activities and procedures with the Department of Defense; and
- How the DNI might organize the office of the DNI to fit needed leadership and management functions into the framework created by the intelligence reform legislation.

INTEGRATED AND INNOVATIVE COLLECTION

The intelligence failure in Iraq did not begin with faulty analysis. It began with a sweeping collection failure. The Intelligence Community simply couldn't collect good information about Iraq's nuclear, biological, or chemical programs. Regrettably, the same can be said today about other important targets, none of which will ever be easy targets—but we can and should do better.

Urging each individual collection agency to do a better job is not the answer. Where progress has been made against such targets, the key has usually been more integration and more innovation in collecting intelligence. As a result, we recommend the following:

- *Create a new Intelligence Community process for managing collection as an "integrated enterprise."* In order to gather intelligence effectively, the Intelligence Community must develop and buy sophisticated technical collection systems, create strategies for focusing those systems on priority targets, process and exploit the data that these systems collect, and plan for the acquisition of future systems. Today, each of these functions is performed primarily within individual collection agencies, often with little or no Community-level direction or interagency coordination. We propose that the DNI create what we call an "integrated collection enterprise" for the Intelligence Community—that is, a management structure in which the Community's decentralized collection capabilities are harmonized with intelligence priorities and deployed in a coordinated way.
- *Create a new Human Intelligence Directorate.* Both the Defense Department and the FBI are substantially increasing their human intelligence activities abroad, which heightens the risk that intelligence operations will not be properly co-ordinated with the CIA's human espionage operations, run by its Directorate of Operations (DO). The human intelligence activities of the Defense Department and the FBI should continue, but in the world of foreign espionage, a lack of co-ordination can have dangerous, even fatal, consequences. To address this pressing problem, we suggest the creation of a new Human Intelligence Directorate within the CIA, to which the present DO would be subordinate, to ensure the coordination of all U.S. agencies conducting human intelligence operations overseas. In addition to this coordination role, the Human Intelligence Directorate would serve as the focal point for Community-wide human intelligence issues, including helping to develop a national human intelligence strategy, broadening the scope of human intelligence activities, integrating (where appropriate) collection and reporting systems, and establishing Community-wide standards for training and tradecraft.

- *Develop innovative human intelligence techniques.* The CIA's Directorate of Operations is one of the Intelligence Community's elite and storied organizations. However, the DO has remained largely wedded to the traditional model—a model that does not meet the challenges posed by terrorist organizations and nations that are "denied areas" for U.S. personnel. Accordingly, we recommend the establishment of an "Innovation Center" within the CIA's new Human Intelligence Directorate—but *not* within the DO. This center would spur the use of new and nontraditional methods of collecting human intelligence. In the collection chapter of our report, we also detail several new methods for collecting human intelligence that in our judgment should either be explored or used more extensively.

- *Create an Open Source Directorate within the CIA.* We are convinced that analysts who use open source information can be more effective than those who don't. Regrettably, however, the Intelligence Community does not have an entity that collects, processes, and makes available to analysts the mass of open source information that is available in the world today. We therefore recommend the creation of an Open Source Directorate at the CIA. The directorate's mission would be to deploy sophisticated information technology to make open source information available across the Community. This would, at a minimum, mean gathering and storing digital newspapers and periodicals that are available only temporarily on the Internet and giving Intelligence Community staff easy (and secure) access to Internet materials. In addition, because we believe that part of the problem is analyst resistance, not lack of collection, we recommend that some of the new analysts allocated to CIA be specially trained to use open sources and then to act as open source "evange-analysts" who can jumpstart the open source initiative by showing its value in addressing particular analytic problems. All of this, we believe, will help improve the Intelligence Community's surprisingly poor "feel" for cultural and political issues in the countries that concern policymakers most. The Open Source Directorate should also be the primary test bed for new information technology because the security constraints—while substantial—are lower for open source than for classified material.

- *Reconsider MASINT.* Measurements and signatures can offer important intelligence about nuclear, biological, and chemical weapons. But the tools we use to collect these measurements and signatures—tools collectively referred to within the intelligence community as "MASINT"—do not obviously constitute a single discipline. In a world of specialized collection agencies, there is reason to suspect that these orphaned technologies may have been under-funded and under-utilized. We recommend that the DNI take responsibility for developing and coordinating new intelligence technologies, including those that now go under the title MASINT. This could be done by a special coordinator, or as part of the DNI's Office of Science and Technology. The DNI's office does not need to directly control MASINT collection. Rather, we recommend that individual collection agencies assume responsibility for aspects of MASINT that fall naturally into their bailiwicks. At the same time, the DNI's designated representative would promote and monitor the status of new technical intelligence programs throughout the Intelligence Community to ensure that they are fully implemented and given the necessary attention.

Additional Collection Recommendations

In addition to those described above, Chapter Seven of our report offers recommendations concerning:

- Developing new human and technical collection methods;
- Professionalizing human intelligence across the Intelligence Community;
- Creating a larger and better-trained human intelligence office cadre;
- Amending the Foreign Intelligence Surveillance Act to extend the duration of certain forms of electronic surveillance against non-U.S. persons, to ease administrative burdens on NSA and the Department of Justice; and
- Improving the protection of sources and methods by reducing authorized and unauthorized disclosures.

TRANSFORMING ANALYSIS

Integrated, innovative collection is just the beginning of what the Intelligence Community needs. Some of the reforms already discussed, particularly the DNI-level "Mission Managers," will improve analysis. But much more is needed. In particular, analytic expertise must be deepened, intelligence gaps reduced, and existing information made more usable—all of which would improve the quality of intelligence.

As an overarching point, however, the Intelligence Community must recognize the central role of analysts in the intelligence process. Needless to say, analysts are the people who analyze intelligence, put it in context, and communicate the intelligence to the people who need it. But in addition, analysts are the repositories for what the Intelligence Community *doesn't* know, and they must clearly convey these gaps to decisionmakers—as well as to collectors so that the Intelligence Community does everything it can to fill the holes. (Analysts will also play an increasingly prominent role in information security, as they "translate" intelligence from the most sensitive of sources to a variety of consumers, ranging from state and local first responders to senior policymakers.) To enable analysts to fulfill these roles, we recommend the following:

- *Empower Mission Managers to coordinate analytic efforts on a given topic.* The Mission Managers we propose would serve as the focal point for all aspects of the intelligence effort on a particular issue. They would be aware of the analytic expertise in various intelligence agencies, assess the quality of analytic products, identify strategic questions receiving inadequate attention, encourage alternative analysis, and ensure that dissenting views are expressed to intelligence users. When necessary, they would recommend that the DNI use his personnel authorities to move analysts to priority intelligence topics. At the same time, Mission Managers should *not* be responsible for providing a single, homogenized analytic product to decisionmakers; rather, Mission Managers should be responsible for encouraging alternative analysis and for ensuring that dissenting views are expressed to intelligence customers. In sum, Mission Managers should be able to find the right people and expertise and make sure that the right analysis, including alternative analysis, is getting done.

- *Strengthen long-term and strategic analysis.* The most common complaint we heard from analysts in the Intelligence Community was that the pressing demand for current intelligence "eats up everything else." Analysts cannot maintain their expertise if they cannot conduct long-term and strategic analysis. Because this malady is so pervasive and has proven so resistant to conventional solutions, we recommend establishing an organization to perform only long-term and strategic analysis under the National Intelligence Council, the Community's existing focal point for inter-agency long-term analytic efforts. The new unit could serve as a focal point for Community-wide alternative analysis, thereby complementing agency-specific efforts at independent analysis. And although some analysts in this organization would be permanently assigned, at least half would serve only temporarily and would come from all intelligence agencies, including NGA and NSA, as well as from outside the government. Such rotations would reinforce good tradecraft habits, as well as foster a greater sense of Community among analysts and spur collaboration on other projects.
- *Encourage diverse and independent analysis.* We believe that diverse and independent analysis—often referred to as "competitive analysis"—should come from many sources. As we have just noted, we recommend that our proposed long-term research and analysis unit, as well as the National Intelligence Council, conduct extensive independent analysis. In some circumstances there is also a place for a "devil's advocate"—someone appointed to challenge the consensus view. We also think it important that a not-for-profit "sponsored research institute" be created *outside* the Intelligence Community; such an institute would serve as a critical window into outside expertise, conduct its own research, and reach out to specialists, including academics and technical experts, business and industry leaders, and representatives from the nonprofit sector. Finally, the Intelligence Community should encourage independent analysis throughout its analytic ranks. In our view, this can best be accomplished through the preservation of dispersed analytic resources (as opposed to consolidation in large "centers"), active efforts by Mission Managers to promote independent analysis, and Community-wide training that instills the importance of such analysis.
- *Improve the rigor and "tradecraft" of analysis.* Our studies, and many observers, point to a decline in analytic rigor within the Intelligence Community. Analysts have suffered from weak leadership, insufficient training, and budget cutbacks that led to the loss of our best, most senior analysts. There is no quick fix for tradecraft problems. However, we recommend several steps: increasing analyst training; ensuring that managers and budget-writers allot time and resources for analysts to actually *get* trained; standardizing good tradecraft practices through the use of a National Intelligence University; creating structures and practices that increase competitive analysis; increasing managerial training for Intelligence Community supervisors; enabling joint and rotational assignment opportunities; ensuring that finished intelligence products are sufficiently transparent so that an analyst's reasoning is visible to intelligence customers; and implementing other changes in human resource policies—such as merit-based-pay—so that the best analysts are encouraged to stay in government service.
- *Communicating intelligence to policymakers.* The best intelligence in the world is worthless unless it is effectively and accurately communicated to those who need it.

The Iraq weapons of mass destruction case is a stark example. The daily reports sent to the President and senior policymakers discussing Iraq over many months proved to be disastrously one-sided. We thus offer recommendations on ways in which intelligence products can be enhanced, including how the President's Daily Brief (PDB) might be improved. In this regard, we suggest the elimination of the inherently misleading "headline" summaries in PDBs and other senior policymaker briefs, and that the DNI oversee production of the PDB. To accomplish this, we recommend the DNI create an analytic staff too small to routinely undertake drafting itself, but large enough to have background on many of the issues that are covered by the PDB. The goal would be to enable the DNI to coordinate and oversee the process, without requiring him to take on the heavy—and almost overwhelming—mantle of daily intelligence support to the President. Critically, the DNI's staff would also ensure that the PDB reflects alternative views from the Community to the greatest extent feasible.

We also recommend that the DNI take responsibility, with the President's concurrence, for the three primary sources of intelligence that now reach the President: the PDB, the President's Terrorism Threat Report—a companion publication produced by the NCTC and focused solely on terrorism-related issues—and the briefing by the Director of the FBI. We suggest that the DNI coordinate this intelligence in a manner that eliminates redundancies and ensures that only material that is necessary for the President be included. We think this last point is especially important because we have observed a disturbing trend whereby intelligence is passed to the President (as well as other senior policymakers) not because it requires high-level attention, but because passing the information "up the chain" provides individuals and organizations with bureaucratic cover.

- *Demand more from analysts.* We urge that policymakers actively probe and question analysts. In our view, such interaction is not "politicization." Analysts should expect such demanding and aggressive testing without—as a matter of principle and professionalism—allowing it to subvert their judgment.

Additional Analysis Recommendations

In addition to those described above, Chapter Eight of our report offers recommendations concerning:

- Developing technologies capable of exploiting large volumes of foreign language data without the need for human translations;
- Improving career-long analytical and managerial training;
- Creating a database for all finished intelligence, as well as adopting technology to update analysts and decisionmakers when intelligence judgments change;
- Improving the Intelligence Community's science, technology, and weapons expertise;
- Changing the way analysts are hired, promoted, and rewarded; and
- Institutionalizing "lessons learned" procedures to learn from past analytical successes and failures.

Information Sharing

While the new intelligence reform legislation correctly identifies information sharing as an area where major reforms are necessary, the steps it takes to address the problem raise as many questions as they answer. The legislation creates a new position—a "Program Manager" who sits outside of the Intelligence Community and reports directly to the President—responsible for creating an integrated, government-wide Information Sharing Environment for all "terrorism information." At the same time, the Director of National Intelligence is given responsibility for facilitating information sharing for *all* intelligence information *within* the Intelligence Community.

We believe that these two separate statutory information sharing efforts should be harmonized. We are less confident that any particular mechanism is optimal. Perhaps the least bad solution to this tricky problem—short of new legislation—is to require that the Program Manager report to the President *through* the DNI, and that the Information Sharing Environment be expanded to include all intelligence information, not just intelligence related to terrorism. In recommending this solution, however, we emphasize that information sharing cannot be understood merely as an Intelligence Community endeavor; whoever leads the effort to build the Information Sharing Environment must be sensitive to the importance of distributing necessary information to those who need it both in the non-intelligence components of the federal government, and to relevant state, local, and tribal authorities.

We also make specific recommendations concerning how best to implement the information sharing effort. Among these recommendations are: designating a single official under the DNI who will be responsible for both information sharing *and* information security, in order to break down cultural and policy barriers that have impeded the development of a shared information space; applying advanced technologies to the Information Sharing Environment to permit more expansive sharing with far greater security protections than currently exist in the Intelligence Community; and establishing clear and consistent Community-wide information sharing and security policies. Last but not least, we recommend that the DNI jettison the phrase "information sharing" itself, which merely reinforces the (incorrect) notion that information is the property of individual intelligence agencies, rather than of the government as a whole.

Finally, we believe it is essential to note the importance of protecting civil liberties in the context of information sharing. We believe that the intelligence reform act provides the framework for appropriate protection of civil liberties in this area, and that all information sharing must be done in accordance with Attorney General guidelines relating to "U.S. persons" information. At the same time, in our view the pursuit of privacy and national security is *not* a zero-sum game. In fact, as we describe in our report, many of the very same tools that provide counterintelligence protection can be equally valuable in protecting privacy.

Intelligence at Home: the FBI, Justice, and Homeland Security

Although the FBI has made strides in turning itself into a true collector and analyst of intelligence, it still has a long way to go. The Bureau, among other things, has set up Field Intelligence Groups in each of its 56 field offices and created an Executive Assistant Director for Intelligence with broad responsibility for the FBI's intelligence mission. Yet even FBI officials acknowledge that its collection and analysis capabilities will be a work in progress until at least 2010.

In our view, the biggest challenge is to make the FBI a full participant in the Intelligence Community. This is not just a matter of giving the Bureau new resources and new authority. It must also mean integrating the FBI into a Community that is subject to the DNI's coordination and leadership. Unfortunately, the intelligence reform legislation leaves the FBI's relationship to the DNI especially murky. We recommend that the President make clear that the FBI's intelligence activities are to be fully coordinated with the DNI and the rest of the Community.

- *Create a separate National Security Service within the FBI that includes the Bureau's Counterintelligence and Counterterrorismi Divisions, as well as the Directorate of Intelligence.* The intelligence reform act empowers the DNI to lead the Intelligence Community, which includes the FBI's "intelligence elements." Although the statute leaves the term ambiguous, we believe that "elements" must include *all* of the Bureau's national security-related components—the Intelligence Directorate *and* the Counterterrorism and Counterintelligence Divisions. Anything less and the DNI's ability to coordinate intelligence across our nation's borders will be dangerously inadequate.

    Simply granting the DNI authority over the Bureau's current Directorate of Intelligence is, we believe, insufficient. We say this because the Directorate of Intelligence has surprisingly little operational, personnel, and budgetary authority. Currently the directorate has no authority to initiate, terminate, or re-direct any collection or investigative operation in any of the FBI's 56 regional field offices that are scattered throughout the nation or within any of the four operational divisions (Counterintelligence, Counterterrorism, Cyber, and Criminal) at FBI Headquarters. Although the Directorate of Intelligence may "task" the field offices to collect against certain requirements, it has no direct authority to ensure that FBI resources actually carry out these requirements. Its "taskings" are really "askings." Nor does the directorate contain the great bulk of the FBI's intelligence analysts. And the directorate has no clear control over the Bureau's portion of the National Intelligence Program budget, which is largely spent by the Counterterrorism and Counterintelligence Divisions. In short, the intelligence directorate has few, if any, mechanisms for exercising direct authorities over FBI's intelligence collectors or analytic products. With a direct line of authority only to the Bureau's Directorate of Intelligence, the DNI cannot be ensured influence over the Bureau's national security functions, and the FBI will not be fully integrated into the Intelligence Community.

    We therefore recommend the creation of a separate National Security Service *within the FBI* that has full authority to manage, direct, and control all Headquarters and Field Office resources engaged in counterintelligence, counterterrorism, and foreign intelligence collection, investigations, operations, and analysis. Critically, this division would then be subject to the same DNI authorities as apply to such Defense agencies as NSA and NGA. Of equal importance, this structure would maintain the Attorney General's oversight of the FBI's activities to ensure the Bureau's compliance with U.S. law. In this sense, the Attorney General's role would be similar to that of the Secretary of Defense, who—even with the appointment of the DNI—continues to oversee Defense Department agencies within the Intelligence Community, like NSA and NGA.

- *Ensure better mechanisms for coordination and cooperation on foreign intelligence collection in the United States.* The expansion of the FBI's intelligence collection and reporting activities over the past few years has engendered turf battles between the CIA and the FBI that have already caused counterproductive conflicts both within and outside of the United States. In particular, the two agencies have clashed over the domestic collection of foreign intelligence—an area in which they have long shared responsibilities. We see no reason to change the status quo dramatically or to expand the FBI's authority over foreign intelligence gathering inside the United States. If unanticipated conflicts emerge, both agencies should be instructed to take their differences to the DNI for resolution. The two agencies' capabilities should complement, rather than compete with, one another. We also expect that such an integrated approach would continue to rely on the existing Attorney General guidelines, which carefully limit the way both agencies operate within the United States, and with regard to U.S. persons overseas. We believe that strong CIA/FBI cooperation and clear guidelines are essential for protection of civil liberties as well as for effective intelligence gathering.

- *Reorient the Department of Justice.* Every agency that has major responsibility for terrorism and intelligence has been overhauled in the past four years. With one exception: at the Department of Justice, the famous "wall" between intelligence and criminal law still lingers, at least on the organization charts. On one side is the Office of Intelligence Policy and Review, which handles Foreign Intelligence Surveillance Court orders—those court orders that permit wiretaps and physical searches for national security reasons. On the other side are two separate sections of the Criminal Division (Counterterrorism and Counterespionage), reporting to two separate Deputy Assistant Attorneys General. This organizational throwback to the 1990s scatters intelligence expertise throughout the Department and in some cases has contributed to errors that hampered intelligence gathering. A single office with responsibility for counterterrorism, counterintelligence, and intelligence investigations would ensure better communication and reduce the tendency to rebuild the wall along bureaucratic lines.

  We recommend that these three components (perhaps joined by a fourth Justice Department component that coordinates issues related to transnational crimes) be placed together under the authority of an Assistant Attorney General for National Security who would, like the Assistant Attorney General for the Criminal Division, report either directly to the Deputy Attorney General, or to a newly created Associate Attorney General responsible for both the National Security and Criminal Divisions.

- *Strengthen the Department of Homeland Security's relationship with the Intelligence Community.* The Department of Homeland Security is the primary repository of information about what passes in and out of the country—a critical participant in safeguarding the United States from nuclear, biological, or chemical attack. Yet, since its inception, Homeland Security has faced immense challenges in collecting information effectively, making it available to analysts and users both inside and outside the Department, and bringing intelligence support to law enforcement and first responders who seek to act on such information. We did not conduct a detailed study of Homeland Security's capabilities, but it is clear to us that the department faces challenges in all four roles it plays in the intelligence community—as collector, analyst, disseminator, and customer.

Among the obstacles confronting Homeland Security, we found during the course of our study that the Department's Immigration and Customs Enforcement still operates under an order inherited from the Treasury Department in the 1980s. The order requires high-level approval for virtually all information sharing and assistance to the Intelligence Community. We think this order should be rescinded, and we believe the DNI should carefully examine how Homeland Security works with the rest of the Intelligence Community.

COUNTERINTELLIGENCE

Every intelligence service on the planet wants to steal secrets from the last remaining superpower. But as other nations increase their intelligence operations against the United States, U.S. counterintelligence has been in a defensive crouch—fractured, narrowly focused, and lacking national direction. This may change as a result of the President's newly announced counterintelligence strategy. The good ideas in the strategy must, however, still be put into practice.

CIA does counterintelligence abroad, but its capabilities are limited. The FBI's counterintelligence efforts within the United States are well-staffed, but hardly strategic in their nature. Finally, the Defense Department's counterintelligence capabilities lack effective cross-department integration and direction. To address these concerns, we recommend four steps to strengthen counterintelligence: the empowerment of the nation's chief counterintelligence officer, the National Counterintelligence Executive (NCIX); the development of a new CIA capability for enhancing counterintelligence abroad; the centralization of the Defense Department's counterintelligence functions; and, as suggested earlier, bringing the FBI into the Intelligence Community to ensure that its robust counterintelligence capabilities are employed in line with the DNI's priorities. Moreover, all of these efforts must focus greater attention on the technical aspects of counterintelligence, as our adversaries shift from human spying to attempting to penetrate our information infrastructure.

COVERT ACTION

If used in a careful and limited way, covert action can serve as a more subtle and surgical tool than forms of acknowledged employment of U.S. power and influence. As part of our overall review of the Intelligence Community, we conducted a careful study of U.S. covert action capabilities. Our findings were included in a short, separate chapter of our classified report. Regrettably, this area is so heavily classified that we could not include a chapter on the subject in our unclassified report.

We will, however, state here—at a necessarily high level of generality—some of our overall conclusions on covert action. At the outset, we note that we found current covert action programs in the counterproliferation and counterterrorism areas to be energetic, innovative, and well-executed within the limits of their authority and funding. Yet some critically important programs are hobbled by lack of sustained strategic planning, insufficient commitment of resources on a long-term basis, and a disjointed management structure. In our classified report we suggest organizational changes that we believe would consolidate support functions for covert action and improve the management of covert action programs within the Intelligence Community; we are unable to provide further details on these recommendations, however, in this unclassified format.

ADDRESSING PROLIFERATION

So far, we have focused on improving the Intelligence Community writ large—on the theory that only a redesigned Community can substantially improve its performance in assessing the threat posed by weapons of mass destruction. But quite apart from the structural changes we have already recommended, the Intelligence Community also needs to change the way it approaches two of the greatest threats—biological weapons and new forms of nuclear proliferation.

BIOLOGICAL WEAPONS

The 2001 anthrax attacks on the United States killed five people, crippled mail delivery in several cities for a year, and imposed more than a billion dollars in decontamination costs. For all that, we were lucky. Biological weapons are cheaper and easier to acquire than nuclear weapons—and they could be more deadly. The threat is deeply troubling today; it will be more so tomorrow, when genetic modification techniques will allow the creation of even worse biological weapons. Most of the traditional Intelligence Community collection tools are of little or no use in tackling biological weapons. In our classified report, we discuss some of the specific challenges that confront our intelligence effort against the biological threat—but regrettably we cannot discuss them here.

Faced with a high-priority problem that does not yield to traditional methods, large parts of the Intelligence Community seem to have lowered their expectations and focused on other priorities. This is unacceptable. The Intelligence Community, and the government as a whole, needs to approach the problem with a new urgency and new strategies:

- *Work with the biological sciences community.* The Intelligence Community simply does not have the in-depth technical knowledge about biological weapons that it has about nuclear weapons. To close the expertise gap, the Community cannot rely on hiring biologists, whose knowledge and skills are extremely important, but whose depth and timeliness of expertise begins eroding as soon as they move from the laboratory to the intelligence profession. Instead, the DNI should create a Community Biodefense Initiative to institutionalize outreach to technical experts inside and outside of government. We describe specific components of this initiative in the body of our report.
- *Make targeted collection of biological weapons intelligence a priority within the Intelligence Community.* The Intelligence Community's collection woes starkly illustrate the need for more aggressive, targeted approaches to collection on biological threats. We recommend that the DNI create a deputy within the National Counter Proliferation Center who is specifically responsible for biological weapons; this deputy would ensure the implementation of a comprehensive biological weapons targeting strategy, which would entail gaining real-time access to non-

traditional sources of information, filtering open source data, and devising specific collection initiatives directed at the resulting targets.

• *Leverage regulation for biological weapons intelligence.* The United States should look outside of intelligence channels for enforcement mechanisms that can provide new avenues of international cooperation and resulting opportunities for intelligence collection on biological threats. In the corresponding chapter of our report, we recommend encouraging foreign criminalization of biological weapons development and establishing biosafety and biosecurity regulations under United Nations Security Council Resolution 1540. We also propose extending biosecurity and biosafety regulations to foreign institutions with commercial ties to the United States.

NUCLEAR WEAPONS

The intelligence challenge posed by nuclear weapons continues to evolve. The Intelligence Community must continue to monitor established nuclear states such as Russia and China, and at the same time face newer and potentially more daunting challenges like terrorist use of a nuclear weapon. But the focus of the U.S. Intelligence Community has historically been on the capabilities of large nation states. When applied to the problem of terrorist organizations and smaller states, many of our intelligence capabilities are inadequate.

The challenges posed by the new environment are well-illustrated by two aspects of nuclear proliferation. The first is the continuing challenge of monitoring insecure nuclear weapons and materials, or "loose nukes"—mainly in the former Soviet Union but also potentially in other nations. The second aspect is the appearance of non-state nuclear "brokers," such as the private proliferation network run by the Pakistani scientist A.Q. Khan. In Khan's case, innovative human intelligence efforts gave the United States access to this proliferation web. However, not only does the full scope of Khan's work remain unknown, but senior officials readily acknowledge that the Intelligence Community must know more about the private networks that support proliferation. The Intelligence Community must adapt to the changing threat.

INTELLIGENCE SUPPORT TO INTERDICTION

So far, the Intelligence Community has enjoyed a number of successes intercepting materials related to nuclear, biological, and chemical weapons (and their related delivery systems)—the process commonly referred to as "interdiction." But success has come at a cost. The Intelligence Community has focused so much energy on its own efforts that the Community shows less ambition and imagination in supporting other agencies that should play a large role in interdiction. Many other federal agencies could do more to interdict precursors, weapons components, and dangerous agents if they had effective intelligence support. We recommend several mechanisms to improve intelligence support to these agencies, most particularly the creation of a counterproliferation Joint Interagency Task Force modeled on similar entities that have proved successful in the counternarcotics context.

Moreover, since it may not be possible in all cases to identify proliferation shipments before they reach the United States, our last line of defense is detecting and stopping these shipments before they reach our border. Yet new sensor technologies have faced challenges. In the corresponding chapter of this report, we suggest how the Intelligence Community and Department of Homeland Security can work together on this issue.

Intelligence alone cannot solve the proliferation threat. But it may not have to. Information that spies and eavesdroppers would spend millions for and risk their lives to steal can sometimes be easily obtained by the right Customs, Treasury, or export control officials. The industries that support proliferation are subject to a host of regulatory regimes. But the agencies that regulate industry in these areas—Treasury, State, Homeland Security, and Commerce—do not think of themselves as engaged in the collection of intelligence, and the Intelligence Community only rarely appreciates the authorities and opportunities presented by regulatory regimes.

Given the challenges presented by quasi-governmental proliferation, the United States must leverage all of its capabilities to flag potential proliferators, gain insight into their activities, and interdict them, where appropriate. We therefore recommend a series of possible changes to existing regulatory regimes, all designed to improve insight into nuclear, biological, or chemical proliferation and enhance our ability to take action. These changes include negotiating ship boarding agreements that include tagging and tracking provisions to facilitate the surveillance of suspect vessels, taking steps to facilitate greater coordination between the Commerce Department (and Immigrations and Customs Enforcement) and the Intelligence Community, using Commerce Department and Customs and Border Protection regulations to facilitate information sharing about suspect cargo and persons and to justify related interdictions, and expanding the Treasury Department's authority to block assets of proliferators.

CONCLUSION

The harm done to American credibility by our all too public intelligence failings in Iraq will take years to undo. If there is good news it is this: without actually suffering a massive nuclear or biological attack, we have learned how badly the Intelligence Community can fail in struggling to understand the most important threats we face. We must use the lessons from those failings, and from our successes as well, to improve our intelligence for the future, and do so with a sense of urgency. We already have thousands of dedicated officers and many of the tools needed to do the job. With that in mind, we now turn first to what went wrong in Iraq, then to other intelligence cases, and finally to our detailed recommendations for action.

THE BUTLER REPORT ON WEAPONS OF MASS DESTRUCTION IN IRAQ, 2004

Editor's note: The British conducted their own inquiry into why its secret services—like the U.S. intelligence agencies—failed to estimate accurately that Saddam Hussein had abandoned his WMD program. Led by The Rt Hon Lord Butler of Brockwell KG GCB CVO, the British panel reported on July 14, 2004. It key findings related to intelligence and counterterrorism are presented below.

CHAPTER 1
THE NATURE AND USE OF INTELLIGENCE

"Much of the intelligence that we receive in war is contradictory, even more of it is plain wrong, and most of it is fairly dubious. What one can require of an officer, under these circumstances, is a certain degree of discrimination, which can only be gained from knowledge of men and affairs and from good judgement. The law of probability must be his guide."

[Clausewitz, On War, Vol 1, Bk 1, Ch VI]

1.1 INTRODUCTION

20. In view of the subject matter of our Review, and of what we have found in the course of it, we think that it may be helpful to the general reader to describe the nature of intelligence; the successive processes of validation, analysis and assessment which are necessary for using it properly; its limitations; and the risks which nevertheless remain.

Source: "Review of Intelligence on Weapons of Mass Destruction," *Report of a Committee of Privy Counsellors*, Chairman: Lord Butler, HC 898 (July 14, 2004), pp. 7–16, 29–36.

21. Governmental decisions and actions, at home and abroad, are based on many types of information. Most is openly available or compiled, much is published, and some is consciously provided by individuals, organisations or other governments in confidence. A great deal of such information may be accurate, or accurate enough in its own terms. But equally much is at best uninformed, while some is positively intended to mislead. To supplement their knowledge in areas of concern where information is for one reason or another inadequate, governments turn to secret sources. Information acquired against the wishes and (generally) without the knowledge of its originators or possessors is processed by collation with other material, validation, analysis and assessment and finally disseminated as 'intelligence.' To emphasise the point, the term 'secret intelligence' is often used (as, for instance, enshrined in the title of the Secret Intelligence Service), but in this Review we shall use the simple word 'intelligence.'

22. The protective security barriers which intelligence collectors have to penetrate are usually formidable, and particularly so in the case of programmes which are the subject of this Review. Nuclear, biological and chemical programmes are amongst the ultimate state secrets, controlled by layers of security protection going beyond those applied to conventional weapons. Those of the greatest concern to governments are usually embedded within a strong apparatus of state control. Few of the many people who are necessarily involved in such programmes have a view of more than their own immediate working environment, and very few have comprehensive knowledge of the arrangements for the control, storage, release and use of the resulting weapons. At every stage from initial research and development to deployed forces, nuclear, biological and chemical weapons and their delivery systems are treated as being of particular sensitivity, often to the extent of the establishment of special command and control arrangements in parallel with, but separate from, normal state or military channels.

1.2 COLLECTION

23. The UK has three intelligence and security agencies ('the agencies') responsible for the collection of intelligence[1]: the Secret Intelligence Service (SIS), the Security Service and Government Communications Headquarters (GCHQ). The Defence Intelligence Staff (DIS), part of the Ministry of Defence (MOD), also manages some intelligence collection, notably that of imagery, but its main function is all-source analysis and assessment and the production of collated results, primarily to serve MOD requirements.

24. There is a panoply of collection techniques to acquire intelligence which do not exactly correspond to inter-departmental organisational boundaries. The three main ones are signals intelligence (the product of interception, generally abbreviated to 'Sigint'); information from human sources such as classical espionage agents (which is conveniently described, by extension from the previous category, as 'Humint'): and photography, or more generally imagery ('Imint'). Signals intelligence and human intelligence are of widespread and general applicability. They can produce intelligence on any topic (for example, the intentions, plans, negotiations, activities and achievements of people involved in the development, acquisition, deployment and use of unconventional weapons), since ultimately the data they acquire stem from the

---

[1] They also have other functions not relevant here.

human beings involved. Imagery is more confined to the study of objects (buildings, aircraft, roads, topography), though modern techniques have extended its abilities (for example, infra-red photography can in some circumstances show where an object was, even though it may have gone by the time the photograph is taken).

25. There are also other, more specialised intelligence techniques, some of particular relevance to this Review[2]. For example, the development of nuclear explosives inevitably involves highly-radioactive materials, radiation from which may be detected. Leakage from facilities concerned with the development of chemical and biological agents, and deposits in testing areas, can provide characteristic indicators. Missile testing may involve the generation of considerable heat, which can be detected, and missiles may be tracked by radar.

26. In the case of the weapons covered by this Review, there is additionally another category of information which is frequently mentioned by the Joint Intelligence Committee (JIC) in its assessments. International inspection and enforcement bodies have been established, on a permanent basis (e.g. the International Atomic Energy Agency), or temporary basis (e.g. the United Nations Special Commission), to ensure compliance with international treaties or United Nations resolutions[3]. Some of the findings and reports of these bodies are published on an official basis to United Nations members and are of considerable importance. In Iraq between 1991 and 1998, in many ways they surpassed anything that national intelligence agencies could do, but since their work is carried out on behalf of the United Nations it can hardly be considered 'intelligence' by the definitions to which we are working. Data obtained in the course of work on export licensing can also be important.

1.3 VALIDATION

27. Intelligence, though it may not differ in type or, often, reliability from other forms of information used by governments, operates in a field of particular difficulty. By definition the data it is trying to provide have been deliberately concealed. Before the actual content of an intelligence report can be considered, the validity of the process which has led to its production must be confirmed. For imagery and signals intelligence this is not usually an issue, although even here the danger of deception must be considered. But for human intelligence the validation process is vital.

28. Human intelligence reports are usually available only at second-hand (for example, when the original informant talks to a case officer[4] who interprets—often literally— his words to construct an intelligence report), and maybe third- or fourth-hand (the original informant talks to a friend, who more or less indirectly talks to a case officer). Documentary or other physical evidence is often more compelling than the best oral reports[5], and has the advantage of being more accessible to specialised examination, but is usually more difficult to acquire. Conventional oral reporting can be difficult

---

[2] The term 'Masint' (Measurement and Signature Intelligence) has been coined for at least some of these techniques, though they lack the unifying themes which characterise Sigint and Humint.

[3] Such bodies often also have a wider operational role in the implementation of treaties or Security Council Resolutions.

[4] An official responsible for handling and receiving reports from human intelligence sources.

[5] Such evidence is no more immune to deception or fabrication than is oral testimony, though of a different type.

enough if all in the chain understand the subject under discussion. When the topic is unfamiliar to one or more of the people involved, as can be the case when details of (say) nuclear weapons design are at issue, there is always the chance of misunderstanding. There is in such cases a considerable load on the case officer to be familiar with the subject-matter and sufficiently expert in explaining it. It need only be added that often those involved in providing intelligence may for one reason or another have deliberately mis-represented (or at least concealed) their true identities, their country of origin or their employment to their interlocutors[6], to show how great is the need for careful evaluation of the validity of any information which eventually arrives.

29.   The validation of a reporting chain requires both care and time, and can generally only be conducted by the agency responsible for collection. The process is informed by the operational side of the agency, but must include a separate auditing element, which can consider cases objectively and quite apart from their apparent intelligence value. Has the informant been properly quoted, all the way along the chain? Does he have credible access to the facts he claims to know? Does he have the right knowledge to understand what he claims to be reporting? Could he be under opposition control, or be being fed information? Is he fabricating? Can the *bona fides*, activities, movements or locations attributed to those involved in acquiring or transmitting a report be checked? Do we understand the motivations of those involved, their private agenda[7], and hence the way in which their reports may be influenced by a desire to please or impress? How powerful is a wish for (in particular) financial reward? What, if any, distorting effect might such factors exert? Is there—at any stage—a deliberate intention to deceive? Generally speaking, the extent and depth of validation required will depend on the counter-intelligence sophistication of the target, although the complexity of the operational situation will affect the possibility of confusion, misrepresentation or deception.

1.4 ANALYSIS

30.   The validation process will often have involved consideration of the coherence and consistency of intelligence being provided by an informant, as one of the ways in which that source's reliability can be tested. But at the next stage, analysis, the factual material inside the intelligence report is examined in its own right. This stage may not be required where the material is self-explanatory, or it may be readily subsumed into assessment and conducted by the same people. But much intelligence is fragmentary or specialised and needs at least a conscious analytic stage. Analysis assembles individual intelligence reports into meaningful strands, whether weapons programmes, military operations or diplomatic policies. Intelligence reports take on meaning as they are put into context. Analysis is also the process required to convert complex technical evidence into descriptions of real-world objects or events.

31.   The department which receives the largest quantity of intelligence is the MOD, where analysis is carried out by the DIS[8] whose reports are distributed not only internally in

---

[6] The ultimate in such deceptions is the classic 'double agent,' who is infiltrated into an espionage network to discover, misinform, expose or pervert it.

[7] We have been assured that SIS has for half a century been viscerally wary of emigre organisations. We return to this below in the context of Iraq.

[8] The DIS also has other management and intelligence collection responsibilities.

the MOD but also to other relevant departments. Although the DIS is a component of the MOD, funded from the Defence Account and managed in accordance with defence priorities, it is a vital component of and contributor to the national intelligence machinery, and its priorities and work programme are linked with those of the Cabinet Office.

32.   Analysis can be conducted only by people expert in the subject matter—a severe limitation when the topic is as specialised as biological warfare or uranium enrichment, or the internal dynamics of terrorist cells or networks. A special danger here can be the failure to recognise just what particular expertise is required. The British intelligence assessment of the German V-2 rocket during the Second World War was hindered by the involvement of the main British rocket expert, who opined that the object visible on test-stands could not possibly be a rocket. The unrecognised problem was that he was an expert only on *solid powder* rockets, of the type that the UK had developed for short-range artillery. It was true that a solid firework of the size of the V-2 was, with the technology then available, impracticable. But the Germans had developed *liquid-propellant* rocket engines, with the combustion chamber fed by powerful turbo-pumps. On that subject, there were no British experts.

1.5 ASSESSMENT

33.   Assessment may be conducted separately from analysis or as an almost parallel process in the mind of the analyst. Intelligence reports often do not immediately fit into an established pattern, or extend a picture in the expected way. Assessment has to make choices, but in so doing runs the risk of selection that reinforces earlier conclusions. The risk is that uneven standards of proof may be applied; reports that fit the previous model are readily accepted, while contrary reports have to reach a higher threshold. This is not only perfectly understandable, it is the way perception normally operates. But in the intelligence world in which data are scanty, may be deliberately intended to confuse and may sometimes be more inadequate than can be appreciated, normal rules do not apply.

34.   In the UK, assessment is usually explicitly described as 'all-source.' Given the imperfections of intelligence, it is vital that every scrap of evidence be examined, from the most secret sources through confidential diplomatic reports to openly published data. Intelligence cannot be checked too often. Corroboration is always important but seldom simple, particularly in the case of intelligence on 'hard targets'[9] such as nuclear, biological or chemical weapons programmes or proliferation networks. The simple fact of having apparently coincident reports from multiple types of intelligence sources is not in itself enough. Although reports from different sources may say the same thing, they may not necessarily *confirm* one another. Is a human intelligence report that a factory has been put into operation confirmed by imagery showing trucks moving around it? Or are both merely based on the same thing—observation of physical external activity? Reporting of different but mutually consistent activities

---

[9] In a sense, almost all intelligence is conducted against 'hard targets.' If the information were readily available, it would not be necessary to call on intelligence resources to acquire it. But within the hierarchy of intelligence activities it is inevitable, given the protection afforded to nuclear, biological and chemical weapons programmes, that they are among the hardest targets.

can be complementary. This can build up knowledge to produce a picture which is more than the simple sum of the parts. But it may be false, if there is no link between the pieces other than the attractiveness of the resulting picture. Complementary information is not necessarily confirmatory information.

35. Multiple sources may conflict, and common sense has to be used in evaluation. A dozen captured soldiers may have provided mutually consistent and supportive reports about the availability of chemical weapons to their neighbouring battalion. But if these were flatly contradicted by a single report from a senior member of that battalion, which should be believed?

36. It is incorrect to say, as some commentators have done, that 'single source' intelligence is always suspect. A single photograph showing missiles on launchers, supporting a division deployed in the field, trumps any number of agent reports that missiles are not part of a division's order of battle. During the Second World War, innumerable Allied command decisions were taken on the basis of intelligence reports from a single *type* of source (signals intelligence, providing decrypts of high-level German and Japanese military plans and orders), and quite often (e.g. re-routing convoys in the middle of the Atlantic) important decisions had to be taken on the basis of a *single report*. As before, common sense and experience are the key.

37. Assessment must always be aware that there may be a deeper level of reality at which apparently independent sources have a common origin. Multiple sources may have been marshalled in a deception campaign, as the Allies did in Operation Fortitude before D-Day to mislead the German High Command about the location of the landings. Although deception on so grand a scale is rare, the chance of being deceived is in inverse proportion to the number of independent sources—which, for 'hard targets,' are few.

38. Many of the manifestations of nuclear, biological or chemical weapons programmes can have innocuous, or at least non-proscribed, explanations—the 'dual-use' problem. Nuclear developments can be for peaceful purposes. Technologies for the production of chemical and biological agents seldom diverge from those employed in normal civilian chemical or bio-chemical industries. And, in the case of missile development, some procurement and development activities may be permissible.

39. Thus, the recipients of intelligence have normally to make decisions on the basis of the balance of probabilities. That requires, first, the most effective deployment of all possible sources and, secondly, the most objective assessment possible, as unaffected as may be by motives and pressures which may distort judgement.

40. In the UK, central intelligence assessment is the responsibility of the Assessments Staff. This comprises some 30 senior and middle-ranking officials on secondment from other departments, within the Cabinet Office, together with secretarial and administrative support.

1.6 THE JOINT INTELLIGENCE COMMITTEE

41. The agencies and the DIS are brought together with important policy departments in the JIC[10]. The JIC was established in 1936 as a sub-committee of the Committee of

---

[10] For a fuller description see *National Intelligence Machinery*, HMSO 2001, which puts the JIC into context within the structures of Parliamentary and Cabinet government.

Imperial Defence. During the Second World War, it comprised the heads of the agencies and the three Services' Directors of Intelligence, under the chairmanship of a senior member of the Foreign Office and was joined by other relevant departments such as the Ministry of Economic Warfare, responsible for the Special Operations Executive.

42. The JIC has evolved since 1945. It became part of the Cabinet Office rather than of the Chiefs of Staff organisation in 1957. To the original membership of the JIC (intelligence producers, with users from MOD and the FCO) were added the Intelligence Co-ordinator when that post was established in 1968, the Treasury (1968), the Department of Trade and Industry (1997) and the Home Office (2000). Other departments attend when papers of relevance to them are taken. Representatives of the Australian, Canadian and United States intelligence communities also attend as appropriate. In 1993, the post of Chairman of the JIC and that of the Head of the Cabinet Office's Defence and Overseas Secretariat[11] were combined, the two posts remaining so until 1999. From 1992 to 2002, the chairmanship was combined with the post of Intelligence Co-ordinator. A new post of Security and Intelligence Co-ordinator was created in 2002, taking on the responsibilities of the previous Intelligence Co-ordinator together with wider responsibilities in the field of counter-terrorism and crisis management. The holder became a member of the JIC.

43. The JIC's main function[12], on which its regular weekly meetings are centred, is to provide:

Ministers and senior officials with co-ordinated intelligence assessments on a range of issues of immediate and long-term importance to national interests, primarily in the fields of security, defence and foreign affairs.

The Assessments Staff are central to this role, and the Chief of the Assessments Staff is a member of the JIC in his own right. With the assistance of other departments, the Assessments Staff draft the JIC assessments, which are usually debated at Current Intelligence Groups (CIGs) including experts in the subject before being submitted to the JIC. The JIC can itself ask the Assessments Staff to draft an assessment, but the process is usually triggered by a request from a policy department. The forward programme of assessments to be produced is issued three times a year, but is revised and, when necessary, overridden by matters of more immediate concern. The JIC thus brings together in regular meetings the most senior people responsible for intelligence collection, for intelligence assessment and for the use of intelligence in the main departments for which it is collected, in order to construct and issue assessments on the subjects of greatest current concern. The process is robust, and the assessments that result are respected and used at all levels of government.

44. Intelligence is disseminated at various levels and in different forms. The agencies send reports direct to users in departments and military commands; these reports are used by

---

[11] From 1984 to the end of 1993 the Chairman of the JIC was also the Prime Minister's Foreign Policy Adviser. This title was revived in September 2001 and assumed by the Head of the Defence and Overseas Secretariat.

[12] The JIC also has other responsibilities, for the establishment of intelligence collection priorities and monitoring of agency performance.

civil and military officials in their daily business, and some of them are selected and brought to Ministers' attention. The JIC's co-ordinated intelligence assessments, formally agreed at their weekly meetings, are sent to Ministers and senior officials. In addition the JIC produces Intelligence Updates and Immediate Assessments whenever required, which are sent to a standard distribution throughout government.

45. A feature of JIC assessments is that they contain single statements of position; unlike the practice in the US, there are no minority reports or noted dissents. When the intelligence is unclear or otherwise inadequate and the JIC at the end of its debate is still uncertain, it may report alternative interpretations of the facts before it such as they are; but in such cases all the membership agrees that the interpretations they are proposing are viable alternatives. The JIC does not (and this is borne out by our examination of several hundred JIC assessments in the course of our Review) characterise such alternatives as championed by individual members who disagree with colleagues' points of view. While the JIC has at times been criticised for its choice of language and the subtlety of the linguistic nuances and caveats it applies[13], it has responded that when the intelligence is ambiguous it should not be artificially simplified.

46. In the sometimes lengthy line that leads to the production of the JIC's output, all the components of the system—from collection through analysis and assessment to a well-briefed and educated readership—must function successfully. Problems can arise if the JIC has to make bricks without (enough) straw. Collection agencies may produce too little intelligence, or too much intelligence about the wrong subjects, or the right intelligence but too late to be of value. Although assessments generated under such circumstances may have proper caveats, with attention drawn to important gaps in knowledge and with the dubious steps in an argument clearly identified, they may reach misleading conclusions. Or—which is equally destructive of their purpose—even if they are correct they may be mistrusted. In either case, the reputation of the JIC product is at risk, and the Committee has on occasion refused to issue drafted papers which it has felt are not sufficiently supported by new intelligence or add nothing to the information already publicly available.

1.7 THE LIMITATIONS OF INTELLIGENCE

47. Intelligence merely provides techniques for improving the basis of knowledge. As with other techniques, it can be a dangerous tool if its limitations are not recognised by those who seek to use it.

48. The intelligence processes described above (validation, analysis, assessment) are designed to transform the raw material of intelligence so that it can be assimilated in the same way as other information provided to decision-makers at all levels of government. Validation should remove information which is unreliable (including reporting which has been deliberately inserted to mislead). Analysis should assemble fragmentary intelligence into coherent meaningful accounts. Assessment should put

---

[13] We have been told that some readers believe that important distinctions are intended between such phrases as "intelligence indicates...", "intelligence demonstrates..." and "intelligence shows...", or between "we assess that...", "we judge that..." and "we believe that...". We have also been told that there is in reality no established glossary, and that drafters and JIC members actually employ their natural language.

intelligence into a sensible real-world context and identify how it can affect policy-making. But there are limitations, some inherent and some practical on the scope of intelligence, which have to be recognised by its ultimate recipients if it is to be used wisely.

49.   The most important limitation on intelligence is its incompleteness. Much ingenuity and effort is spent on making secret information difficult to acquire and hard to analyse. Although the intelligence process may overcome such barriers, intelligence seldom acquires the full story. In fact, it is often, when first acquired, sporadic and patchy, and even after analysis may still be at best inferential.

50.   The very way that intelligence is presented can contribute to this misperception. The necessary protective security procedures with which intelligence is handled can reinforce a mystique of omniscience. Intelligence is not only—like many other sources—incomplete, it can be incomplete in undetectable ways. There is always pressure, at the assessment stage if not before, to create an internally consistent and intellectually satisfying picture. When intelligence becomes the dominant, or even the only, source of government information, it can become very difficult for the assessment process to establish a context and to recognise that there may be gaps in that picture.

51.   A hidden limitation of intelligence is its inability to transform a mystery into a secret. In principle, intelligence can be expected to uncover secrets. The enemy's order of battle may not be known, but it is knowable. The enemy's intentions may not be known, but they too are knowable. But mysteries are essentially unknowable: what a leader *truly* believes, or what his reaction would be in certain circumstances, cannot be known, but can only be judged. JIC judgements have to cover both secrets and mysteries. Judgement must still be informed by the best available information, which often means a contribution from intelligence. But it cannot import certainty.

52.   These limitations are best offset by ensuring that the ultimate users of intelligence, the decision-makers at all levels, properly understand its strengths and limitations and have the opportunity to acquire experience in handling it. It is not easy to do this while preserving the security of sensitive sources and methods. But unless intelligence is properly handled at this final stage, all preceding effort and expenditure is wasted.

1.8 RISKS TO GOOD ASSESSMENT

53.   It is a well-known phenomenon within intelligence communities that memory of past failures can cause over-estimation next time around. It is equally possible to be misled by past success. For 45 years of Cold War, the intelligence community's major task was to assess the intentions and capabilities of the Soviet Union and its satellite states[14]. As the details which had been sought became more accessible, first through *glasnost'* and explicit exchanges of data under international agreements and then fairly readily through open sources after the dissolution of the Soviet empire, most of the intelligence community's conclusions were vindicated—at least in the areas in

---

[14] The intelligence community did, of course, have many other tasks during this period ranging from the consequences of the withdrawal from empire through the many facets of the conflicts and confrontations in the Middle East to the Falklands War.

which it had spent the largest part of its efforts, the Soviet bloc's military equipment, capabilities and order of battle.

54. But it is risky to transfer one model to cases where that model will only partially apply. Against dictatorships, dependent upon personal or tribal loyalties and insensitive to international politics, an approach that worked well for a highly-structured, relatively cohesive state target is not necessarily applicable even though many aspects of the work may appear to be identical. The targets which the UK intelligence community needs to study most carefully today are those that structurally and culturally look least like the Government and society it serves. We return to this when we consider terrorism, at Chapter 3.

55. Risks in intelligence assessment will arise if this limitation is not readily recognised. There may be no choice but to apply the same intelligence processes, methods and resources to one target as were developed for and applied to others. But it is important to recognise that the resulting intelligence may need to be analysed and assessed in different ways.

56. A further risk is that of 'mirror-imaging'—the belief that can permeate some intelligence analysts that the practices and values of their own cultures are universal. The more diffuse range of security challenges of the 21st century means that it will not be possible to accumulate the breadth and depth of understanding which intelligence collectors, analysts and users built up over the years about the single subject of the Soviet Union. But the more alien the target, the more important is the ability of intelligence analysts to appreciate that their own assumptions do not necessarily apply everywhere. The motives and methods of non-state organisations built on a special interest (whether criminal, religious or political) can be particularly hard for members of a stable society to assess.

57. There is also the risk of 'group think'—the development of a 'prevailing wisdom.' Well-developed imagination at all stages of the intelligence process is required to overcome preconceptions. There is a case for encouraging it by providing for structured challenge, with established methods and procedures, often described as a 'Devil's advocate' or a 'red teaming' approach. This may also assist in countering another danger: when problems are many and diverse, on any one of them the number of experts can be dangerously small, and individual, possibly idiosyncratic, views may pass unchallenged.

58. One final point should be mentioned here, to which we return in our Conclusions. The assessment process must be informed by an understanding of policy-makers' requirements for information, but must avoid being so captured by policy objectives that it reports the world as policy-makers would wish it to be rather than as it is. The JIC is part (and an important part) of the UK's governmental machinery or it is nothing; but to have any value its product must be objective. The JIC has always been very conscious of this.

1.9 THE USE OF INTELLIGENCE

59. In addition to the use of intelligence to inform government policy, which we describe in Chapters 2 and 3, there are important applications in the enforcement of compliance with national law or international treaties and other obligations, in warning of untoward events, in the support of military and law enforcement operations, and in long-term planning for future national security capabilities. The British Government's machinery for the areas covered by our Review is described at Chapter 4.

CHAPTER 3 TERRORISM[1]

3.1 SCOPE

110. We have examined intelligence reports and assessments on the links between terrorism and chemical, biological, radiological and nuclear weapons, and the use made of that intelligence, from when it began in the early 1990s to emerge as a topic of interest to the Joint Intelligence Committee (JIC). For the purpose of illustrating the contribution made by intelligence to policy formulation by the Government and to actions taken on the basis of that policy, we have focussed on the scope and quality of intelligence reports and assessments on the use by terrorists and extremists of unconventional weapons, and the extent to which they were validated by subsequent discoveries in Afghanistan. To avoid prejudicing current operations, we do not cover in this Report more recent intelligence assessments or findings.

3.2 THE PERIOD UP TO 1995

111. In the late 1980s, the possibility that terrorist groups might seek to use unconventional weapons was considered remote. In surveys of nuclear, biological and chemical weapons proliferation in 1989, the JIC dealt briefly with the possibility that such technology might be used by terrorists:

We believe that even the most sophisticated and well-organised terrorist group is highly unlikely to be able to steal and then detonate a nuclear weapon with the foreseeable future. . . . At present the most feasible terrorist nuclear incident would probably be a credible hoax. A terrorist threat to detonate a nuclear device would be difficult to dismiss entirely in view of the increasing number of producers of fissile material in a variety of countries and the problems of accounting fully for all material produced. Terrorists might see a seemingly plausible and preferably well publicized warning of an imminent nuclear attack as potentially a very effective means of blackmailing governments. [JIC, July 1989]

and:

We have no intelligence that any terrorist group makes CBW agents, possesses any such agents or is currently contemplating attacks using CBW agents or other toxic chemicals. The use of CBW agents by terrorists would generate widespread fear and could cause large numbers of casualties. The mere threat of such use could be sufficient to cause panic.

A terrorist would need only small quantities of CW agents. The simpler ones could in principle be made by anyone with a knowledge of A-level chemistry using readily obtainable materials. We believe that terrorist organizations could also readily obtain and handle without surmountable difficulty, suitable bacteria, viruses and certain toxins.

Although CBW proliferation undoubtedly increases the risk that CBW agents could be stolen by or even supplied to terrorists by state sponsors . . . this prospect must be viewed against a

---

[1] This section is limited to intelligence on the use by terrorists of chemical, biological, radiological and nuclear weapons. The large majority of terrorist actions employ conventional armaments and explosives, and are not relevant to this Review.

background where many suitable agents can be manufactured in small quantities using easily available materials. So as far as terrorism is concerned, proliferation (if it comes about) may not necessarily be much affected by the actions of States with the relevant capability. [JIC, 26 June 1989]

112. The main strands in this assessment set the standard for the next few years. There was no credible evidence of terrorist interest in nuclear, biological or chemical weapons; hoaxes and threats might be more disuptive than actual use; terrorists were very unlikely to be able to acquire nuclear devices; and the fact that some states possessed nuclear, biological or chemical weapons was unlikely to affect the risk of their use by terrorists.

113. In April 1992[2], in its first assessment specifically on the threat of attacks by terrorists using chemical, biological, radiological or nuclear weapons, the JIC considered the technical options, but emphasised the difficulties which were thought likely to render such methods unattractive options for terrorist groups:

They may be deterred by the danger to their own members, or by the risk of alienating the public and especially their own supporters. They may also fear that an attack would cause international outrage leading to determined efforts on an international scale to bring them to book. By contrast, conventional weapons are cheaper, easier to procure, and offer equal or greater effectiveness against traditional targets (such as prominent individuals, members of the security forces, government buildings). [JIC, 23 April 1992]

This, too, was to become a feature of JIC assessments; for most terrorist uses, conventional weapons were better.

114. By October 1994, there had been a number of media reports—some correct—of fissile material being available on the black market. In the first of several such studies, the JIC did not consider that these affected its overall assessment:

Despite the possibility which now exists of obtaining fissile material, it is extremely unlikely that a terrorist group could produce even a crude nuclear device; nor is there any evidence that any group has contemplated the use of nuclear weapons. A more plausible scenario might be the dispersal of radioactive materials by conventional explosives or other means to achieve radiological contamination. The actual danger to the public from radioactivity would probably be small—smaller in some cases than to the terrorists. But such an attack (or its threat) could be highly effective in causing panic and public concern.

We believe that terrorists would not be able to acquire or deploy a nuclear weapon; radiological attacks are possible but unlikely. Attacks involving chemical or biological agents are also unlikely, though use of toxic chemical substances (for which there are some limited precedents) remains a possibility. [JIC, 13–19 October 1994]

3.3 1995–1997

115. By June 1995, the JIC was assessing the threat posed by Islamist extremists; the terrorist threat was spreading outside the Middle East. The JIC commented on the use

---

[2] It was also in 1992 that a Kurdish terrorist group tried to poison the water supply of a Turkish airbase using cyanide.

of suicide tactics, a strand which was subsequently to become significant in such assessments:

Selective interpretation of the Muslim faith enables such groups to justify terrorist violence and to recruit 'martyrs' for suicide attacks. [JIC, 8 June 1995]

116. However, the first serious use of chemicals by terrorists was not by Islamist extremists. The sarin gas attack in the Tokyo underground by the Aum Shinrikyo sect came in March 1995[3]. In a 1996 assessment of the nuclear, biological and chemical threat to the UK[4] (which responded to the G7 declaration at the Lyons summit in June that year that special attention should be paid to the threat of use of nuclear, biological and chemical materials for terrorist purposes) the JIC stuck to its previous line, though noting the Aum Shinrikyo attack:

There is no indication of any terrorist or other group showing interest in the use of nuclear, biological or chemical (NBC) materials against the UK. For a number of reasons, conventional weapons are likely to remain more attractive for terrorist purposes. But last year's nerve agent attack in Tokyo will have heightened interest and, with ever more NBC information publicly available, hoaxes threatening NBC use are likely to become more difficult to assess. [JIC, 4 July 1996]

3.4 1998–1999

117. Usama bin Laden first became known as a high-profile supporter of Islamist extremism while fighting against Soviet forces in Afghanistan during the 1980s. Expelled from Saudi Arabia in 1991 and from Sudan in 1996, he returned to Afghanistan. Evidence of his interest in unconventional weapons accumulated, and was summarised by the JIC in November 1998:

He has a long-standing interest in the potential terrorist use of CBR materials, and recent intelligence suggests his ideas about using toxic materials are maturing and being developed in more detail. . . . There is also secret reporting that he may have obtained some CB material—and that he is interested in nuclear materials. We assess that he lacks the expertise or facilities even to begin making a nuclear weapon, but he might seek to make a radiological device. [JIC, 25 November 1998]

118. Seven months later, in June 1999, the JIC had received more intelligence, and re-assessed the threat from Usama bin Laden's organisation accordingly:

Most of UBL's planned attacks would use conventional terrorist weapons. But he continues to seek chemical, biological, radiological and nuclear material and to develop a capability for its terrorist use. There is insufficient evidence to conclude that he has yet acquired radiological or nuclear material. In contrast, we now assess that his followers have access to some unspecified

---

[3] The sect had carried out sporadic and unsuccessful open-air attacks using a range of agents since 1990. One attack (using sarin) in Matsumoto in June 1994 caused 7 deaths and 264 people were hospitalised. These earlier attacks were little noticed outside Japan.

[4] Because of its limited ambit this paper did not take note of the then recent Chechen guerrilla operation to place minute quantities of caesium-137 in a Moscow park.

chemical or biological material. Some have received basic training in its use against individuals or in confined spaces.

In April a leading Egyptian terrorist, apparently believing the information was already known to the authorities, told an Egyptian court the UBL had CB 'weapons' which he would use against US or Israeli targets. [JIC, 9 June 1999]

Intelligence reports of bin Laden's associates falling for nuclear materiel frauds suggested, however, that they were not well advised on nuclear matters.

119. A month later, in July 1999, the JIC explained an important change in one of the major assumptions underpinning its previous assessments—some terrorists were no longer reluctant to cause mass casualties, for example some Islamist extremist terrorists and Aum Shinrikyo:

Over the 1990s there has been significant increase in the quantity and quality of intelligence that some terrorists are interested in CBRN—and particularly in chemical and biological—materials as weapons. The risk of a CBRN terrorist incident has risen, albeit from a low base. In part this increase reflects the rise of Islamic extremism and ethnic hatred as terrorist motivations: some of the terrorists thus motivated are less constrained by considerations such as public support, casualties among innocent bystanders, or the prospect of retaliation. It may also reflect the increasing availability of information about making and using CB materials, and t he publicity attracted by major incidents and hoaxes. Whether the attacker's aim is political or economic blackmail, or severe disruption, society's vulnerability to terrorist attack from CB or radiological materials is high, exacerbated by the lack of a tried and tested CB counter-terrorist response in some countries. [JIC, 15 July 1999]

120. In the same assessment, the JIC made its own judgement, in the absence of specific intelligence, that Usama bin Laden had after several years been successful in acquiring non-conventional weapons. That judgement was later shown to be correct:

There have been important developments in [Islamist extremist] *terrorism. It has become clear that Usama Bin Laden has been seeking CBRN materials . . . His wealth permits him to fund procurement, training and experimentation to an extent unmatched by other terrorists. . . . Given the quality and quantity of intelligence about his interest in CB materials, the length of time he has sought them, and the relative ease with which they can be made, we assess that he has by now acquired or made at least modest quantities of CB materials—even if their exact nature and effectiveness are unclear. The significance of his possession of CB materials is that, in contrast to other terrorists interested in CB, he wishes to target US, British and other interests worldwide. There is also intelligence on training in the use of chemicals as weapons in a terrorist camp in Afghanistan, although it is not yet clear if this is under Bin Laden's auspices. The CB threat is likely to be higher abroad than in the UK, reflecting the location of Bin Laden and his allies, the vulnerability of potential targets, and the effectiveness of local security authorities. Targets may include British official sites or related facilities overseas. That said, Bin Laden's attacks remain more likely to employ conventional weapons than CB materials.* [JIC, 15 July 1999]

121. However the JIC still retained its overall conclusion, that:

. . . the indications of terrorist interest in CBRN materials have yet to be matched by a comparable amount of evidence about possession and intent to use CBRN. Most terrorists continue to favour

conventional weapons, as easier to use, more reliable, safer and more controllable than CBRN materials. [JIC, 15 July 1999]

3.5 2000–2001

122. By January 2000, in an assessment of conventional threats, the JIC summarised bin Laden's aspirations for non-conventional weapons:

UBL retains his interest in obtaining chemical, biological, radiological and nuclear (CBRN) materials and expertise. In autumn 1999 there was intelligence that he had recruited ... chemicals specialists. ... Our assessment remains that UBL has some toxic chemical or biological materials, and an understanding of their utility as terrorist weapons. But we have yet to see hard intelligence that he possesses genuine nuclear material. [JIC, 12 January 2000]

123. By August 2000, the JIC was clear that, although there were other Islamist extremist groups[5] with an interest in non-conventional weapons, Usama bin Laden posed the most severe threat:

Some [Islamist extremist groups] *are interested in exploring the use of chemical or biological materials as weapons. In the forefront is UBL...* [JIC, 9 August 2000]

124. In January 2001, the JIC reported at length on the terrorist threat from unconventional weapons and emphasised the unique nature of the threat from Usama bin Laden:

The actual threat does not match the media hype. Almost all the available intelligence refers to terrorist interest in CB materials, rather than to specific attack plans. There is no credible intelligence that any terrorist except UBL has the capability or serious intent to explore the use of weapons-grade nuclear materials—nor, except for Chechen extremists, radiological material. Terrorists interested in CB are generally those least constrained by public opinion or their members' or supporters' sensitivities. Their resources and targets tend to be abroad rather than in Britain, so the risk of attacks using toxic materials has always been greater overseas.

UBL has sought CBRN materials for use as terrorist weapons. ... From his public statements and interviews it is clear that he believes it is legitimate to use them as weapons and his wealth has allowed him to fund procurement, experimentation and training. There is plentiful intelligence that this interest is sustained, mostly relating to toxic materials.

In 1999 he sought equipment for a chemical weapons lab in Afghanistan, and claimed already to have ... experts working there. [JIC, 10 January 2001]

3.6 THE AFTERMATH OF 9/11

125. In an important paper shortly after the attacks of 11 September 2001, the JIC made clear the way in which Usama bin Laden's philosophy, combined with suicide attacks, had changed the calculus of threat. This assessment summarised the new security

---

[5] The JIC was a year later to comment that the word 'groups' can be misleading in the context of Islamist extremist terrorists. *"There are established groups in different countries, usually working to a national agenda, but the networks associated with UBL are changeable ad hoc groupings of individuals who share his agenda, and who may come together only for a particular operation. Nevertheless, 'groups' is used as a short form for want of another available term."*

challenge which, as we describe further in the context of Iraq at Chapter 5, was to become dominant in the thinking of British Ministers—the desire of terrorists and extremists to cause casualties on a massive scale, undeterred by the fear of alienating the public or their own supporters that had been noted as a constraining factor in JIC assessments in the early 1990s or by considerations of personal survival. To this fundamental shift in the JIC's judgement on the likely motivation and goals of terrorists and extremists was added a corresponding shift in its conclusions about the attractiveness of nuclear, biological or chemical weapons. Thus, in September 2001 the JIC noted that:

Many defensive and preventive measures taken against terrorism (such as ensuring that passenger and luggage travel together) still presuppose that the terrorist will want to survive the attack. But suicide attackers, especially those backed by sophisticated planning and pursuing non-negotiable objectives, negate many security measures and widen society's vulnerability. New strategies are required to counter the threat of terrorists willing, or even eager, to sacrifice their lives as martyrs in Islamic extremist or other causes—although there can be no complete protection against them.

In the context of UBL's jihad, casualties and destruction could be an end in themselves as much as a means to an end (Footnote: UBL's stated objective is to secure US withdrawal from the Middle East or, failing that, to provoke a reaction which would further demonise the US in the eyes of Muslims and destabilise moderate Arab states that he perceives as un-Islamic). He has no interest in negotiation and there is no indication that he can be deterred. [JIC, 18 September 2001]

126. The JIC also went on in this paper to note Usama bin Laden's interest in nuclear devices.
127. The British Government's dossier of 4 October 2001[6], which attributed the attacks of 11 September 2001 to Usama bin Laden, also reflected the attractiveness to him of nuclear, biological and chemical weapons, saying that:

From the early 1990s Usama bin Laden has sought to obtain nuclear and chemical materials for use as weapons of terror.

and reminding its readership that:

When asked in 1998 about obtaining chemical or nuclear weapons he said "acquiring such weapons for the defence of Muslims (was) a religious duty". [Government's dosssier, 4 October 2001]

3.7 INTELLIGENCE ON UBL'S CAPABILITIES AND ITS VALIDATION

128. A considerable quantity of evidence of Usama bin Laden's capabilities in the nuclear, biological and chemical fields was uncovered after the US-led military action in Afghanistan in October 2001. This section compares these discoveries with JIC judgements beforehand.

---

[6] "Responsibility for the Terrorist Atrocities in the United States, 11 September 2001".

NUCLEAR

129. In 1999, the JIC reported Usama bin Laden's claims to be setting up a laboratory in Afghanistan. Following the collapse of the Taliban regime, in January 2002 the United Nations Security Council listed a former Pakistani nuclear scientist Bashir Mahmoud as associated with the Taliban or Al Qaida.

CHEMICAL

130. Intelligence reporting from 1999 onwards testified to the activities of Abu Khabbab, an explosives and chemicals expert who ran training courses which included information on how to make and use poisons. This was confirmed by discoveries in Afghanistan such as a video showing chemical experiments being carried out on animals, and by the finding of numerous training manuals.

BIOLOGICAL

131. In 1999, the JIC reported that:

> *In February 1999 one of his followers claimed that UBL intended to attack US and UK targets in India, Indonesia and the US, by using means which even the US could not counter, implying the use of chemical or biological material.* [JIC, 9 June 1999]

132. Some work with biological agents was also attributed to Abu Khabbab, though the evidence was not detailed. However, the JIC's judgement that Al Qaida was developing biological weapons was confirmed by the discovery in Afghanistan of the Kandahar laboratory, and evidence that scientists had been recruited.

3.8 INTELLIGENCE RESPONSES TO INTERNATIONAL TERRORISM

133. Few of the measures being taken by the Government to improve the response to the terrorist threat are unique to attacks using chemical, biological, radiological and nuclear materials. The threat is international, and has motivated intelligence organisations to intensify both national and international collaboration on an unprecedented scale. **All of the UK intelligence agencies are developing new techniques, and we have seen clear evidence that they are co-operating at all levels.**

134. The most obvious embodiment of enhanced inter-departmental co-operation in the UK is the Joint Terrorism Analysis Centre (JTAC). This is a multi-agency organisation, hosted by the Security Service but staffed by personnel seconded from all of the agencies, law enforcement organisations and relevant departments. Its staff retain links to their parent departments and, operating on a round-the-clock basis, pool information to produce continuous assessments of threats within the UK, to British interests abroad and of terrorist activities generally. **JTAC has now been operating for over a year and has proved a success.**

135. The Security Service and Home Office are improving public education, through web sites and by other means, for both long-term and immediate appreciation of terrorist threats.

136. **International counter-terrorism collaboration has also been significantly enhanced in the past six or seven years. Though we understand that other countries have not yet achieved the same level of inter-departmental synthesis, considerable developments have taken place. Staff of the UK intelligence and security agencies are today in much wider contact with their opposite numbers throughout the world.** We have, for example, been briefed on a recent successful counter-terrorist operation which involved eight different countries working together. **We note these initiatives, but remain concerned that the procedures of the international community are still not sufficiently aligned to match the threat.**

GLOSSARY

ACCM	Alternative or Compensatory Control Measure
AFIO	Association of Former Intelligence Officers
AG	Attorney General
Aman	Agaf ha-Modi'in (Israeli military intelligence)
ANC	African National Congress
BDA	Battle Damage Assessment
BfV	Bundesamt für Verfassungsschutz (German equivalent of the FBI)
BMD	Ballistic Missile Defense
BND	Bundesnachrichtendienst (German foreign intelligence service)
BSO	Black September Organization
BW	Biological Weapons
CA	Covert Action
CAS	Covert Action Staff (CIA)
CBW	Chemical/Biological Warfare
CCP	Consolidated Cryptographic Program
CDA	Congressionally Directed Action
CE	Counterespionage
CHAOS	Code name for CIA illegal domestic spying
CI	Counterintelligence
CIA	Central Intelligence Agency
CIFA	Counterintelligence Field Activity
CIG	Central Intelligence Group
CMS	Community Management Staff
CNC	Crime and Narcotics Center (CIA)

COINTELPRO	FBI Counterintelligence Program
COMINT	Communications Intelligence
Corona	Codename for first U.S. spy satellite system
COS	Chief of Station (CIA)
COSPO	Community Open Source Program Office
CPA	Covert Political Action
CPSU	Communist Party of the Soviet Union
CSI	Committee on Intelligence Services (Britain)
CT	Counterterrorism
CTC	Counterterrorism Center (CIA)
CW	Chemical Weapons
D & D	Denial and Deception
DARP	Defense Airborne Reconnaissance Program
DAS	Deputy Assistant Secretary
DBA	Dominant Battlefield Awareness
DC	Deputies Committee (NSC)
DCD	Domestic Contact Division (CIA)
DCI	Director of Central Intelligence
D/CIA	Director of Central Intelligence Agency
DDA	Deputy Director of Administration (CIA)
DDCI	Deputy Director for Central Intelligence (DDCI)
DD/CIA	Deputy Director, Central Intelligence Agency
DDO	Deputy Director for Operations (CIA)
DDP	Deputy Director for Plans (CIA)
DDS&T	Deputy Director for Science and Technology (CIA)
DEA	Drug Enforcement Administration
DGSE	Directorie Génerale de la Sécurité Extérieure (French intelligence service)
DHS	Department of Homeland Security
DI	Directorate of Intelligence (CIA)
DIA	Defense Intelligence Agency
DIA/Humint	Defense Humint Service
DINSUM	*Defense Intelligence Summary*
DNI	Director of National Intelligence
DO	Directorate of Operations
DoD	Department of Defense
DOD	Domestic Operations Division (CIA)
DOE	Department of Energy
DOJ	Department of Justice
DOT	Department of Treasury
DOS	Department of State
DP	Directorate of Plans (CIA)
DST	Directoire de Surveillance Territore (France)
ECHR	European Convention of Human Rights

ELINT	Electronic Intelligence
ENIGMA	Code machine used by the Germans during World War II
EO	Executive Order
EOP	Executive Office of the President
ETF	Environmental Task Force (CIA)
FARC	Fuerzas Armadas Revolucionarias in Colombia
FBI	Federal Bureau of Investigation
FBIS	Foreign Broadcast Information Service
FISA	Foreign Intelligence Surveillance Act (1978)
FNLA	National Front for the Liberation of Angola
FOIA	Freedom of Information Act
FRD	Foreign Resources Division (CIA)
FSB	Federal'naya Sluzba Besnopasnoti (Federal Security Service, Russia)
GAO	General Accountability Office (Congress)
GCHQ	Government Communications Headquarters (the British NSA)
GEO	Geosynchronous Orbit
GEOINT	Geospatial Intelligence
GRU	Soviet Military Intelligence
GSG	German Counterterrorism Service
HEO	High Elliptical Orbit
HPSCI	House Permanent Select Committee on Intelligence
HUAC	House Un-American Activities Committee
HUMINT	Human Intelligence (assets)
I & W	Indicators and Warning
IAEA	International Atomic Energy Agency
IAF	Israel Air Force
IC	Intelligence Community
ICS	Intelligence Community Staff
IDF	Israeli Defense Force
IG	Inspector General
IMINT	Imagery Intelligence (photographs)
INR	Bureau of Intelligence and Research (Department of State)
INTELINK	An intelligence community computer information system
INTs	Collection disciplines (IMINT, SIGINT, OSINT, HUMINT, MASINT)
IOB	Intelligence Oversight Board (White House)
ISA	Israeli Security Agency
ISC	Intelligence and Security Committee (U.K.)
ISI	Inter-Services Intelligence (Pakistani intelligence agency)
IT	Information Technology
JCAE	Joint Committee on Atomic Energy
JCS	Joint Chiefs of Staff
JIC	Joint Intelligence Committee (U.K.)

JSOC	Joint Special Operations Command
JSTARS	Joint Surveillance Target Attack Radar Systems
KGB	Soviet Secret Police
KH	Keyhole (satellite)
LTTE	Tamil Tigers of Tamil Elam
MAGIC	Allied code-breaking operations against the Japanese in the World War II
MASINT	Measurement and Signatures Intelligence
MI5	Security Service (U.K.)
MI6	Secret Intelligence Service (U.K.)
MON	Memoranda of Notification
MONGOOSE	Code name for CIA covert actions against Fidel Castro of Cuba (1961–62)
Mossad	Israeli Intelligence Service
MPLA	Popular Movement for the Liberation of Angola
NAACP	National Association for the Advancement of Colored People
NBC	Nuclear, Biological, and Chemical (Weapons)
NCS	National Clandestine Service
NCIC	National Counterintelligence Center
NCTC	National Counterterrorism Center
NED	National Endowment for Democracy
NFIB	National Foreign Intelligence Board
NFIC	National Foreign Intelligence Council
NFIP	National Foreign Intelligence Program
NGA	National Geospatial-Intelligence Agency
NGO	Nongovernmental organization
NIA	National Intelligence Authority
NIC	National Intelligence Council
NID	*National Intelligence Daily*
NIE	National Intelligence Estimate
NIO	National Intelligence Officer
NOC	Nonofficial Cover
NPIC	National Photographic Interpretation Center
NRO	National Reconnaissance Office
NSA	National Security Agency
NSC	National Security Council (White House)
NSCID	National Security Council Intelligence Directive
NTM	National Technical Means
OB	Order of Battle
OC	Official Cover
ODNI	Office of the Director of National Intelligence
OMB	Office of Management and Budget
ONI	Office of Naval Intelligence

OPC	Office of Policy Coordination
OSD	Office of the Secretary of Defense
OSINT	Open-Source Intelligence
OSS	Office of Strategic Services
P & E	Processing and Exploitation
PDB	*President's Daily Brief*
PFIAB	President's Foreign Intelligence Advisory Board (White House)
PFLP	Popular Front for the Liberation of Palestine
PIJ	Palestinian Islamic Jihad
PLO	Palestine Liberation Organization
PM	Paramilitary
PRO	Public Record Office (U.K.)
RADINT	Radar Intelligence
RFE	Radio Free Europe
RL	Radio Liberty
SA	Special Activities Division (DO/CIA)
SAS	Special Air Service (U.K.)
SBS	Special Boat Service (U.K.)
SDO	Support to Diplomatic Operations
SHAMROCK	Code name for illegal NSA interception of cables
SIG	Senior Interagency Group
SIGINT	Signals Intelligence
SIS	Secret Intelligence Service (U.K., also known as MI6)
SISDE	Italian Intelligence Service
SMO	Support to Military Operations
SMS	Secretary's *Morning Summary* (Department of State)
SNIE	Special National Intelligence Estimate
SO	Special Operations (CIA)
SOCOM	Special Operations Command (Department of Defense)
SOE	Special Operations Executive (U.K.)
SOG	Special Operations Group (DO/CIA)
SOVA	Office of Soviet Analysis (CIA)
SSCI	Senate Select Committee on Intelligence
SVR	Russian Foreign Intelligence Service
TECHINT	Technical Intelligence
TELINT	Telemetery Intelligence
TIARA	Tactical Intelligence and Related Activities
TPED	Tasking, Processing, Exploitation, and Dissemination
UAV	Unmanned Aerial Vehicle (drone)
ULTRA	Code name for the Allied operation that deciphered the German ENIGMA code in World War II
UN	United Nations
UNITA	National Union for the Total Independence of Angola

UNSCOM	United Nations Special Commission
USIB	United States Intelligence Board
USTR	United States Trade Representative
VCI	Viet Cong Infrastructure
VENONA	Code name for SIGINT intercepts against Soviet spying in America
VOA	Voice of America
VX	A deadly nerve agent used in chemical weapons
WMD	Weapons of mass destruction

INDEX

Abdallah-Azzam Brigades, Al Qaeda affiliated group, 173

Abel, Rudolf, Russian spy, 36–37, 66–67

Abwehr spies, German espionage, 32

Accountability politics: congressional oversight, 115–16; deference to president, 116; domestic intelligence gathering, 120–21; media oversight of intelligence, 116–17; responsibility, 114–15; secrecy, 115. *See also* Political games

Adams, Arthur, military-industrial spy, 31

Afghanistan, 9/11 Commission, 250–52

African Americans, Federal Bureau of Investigation (FBI) agents, 87

Agenda politics: domestic intelligence gathering, 118; intelligence as tool or instrument of policy, 113–14; intelligence not always welcomed, 112; intelligence not determining policy, 111–12; intelligence to be contested and competitive, 112–13; leaks, 114; self-interest, 111–14. *See also* Political games

Aldrich Ames counterintelligence failure, Senate Select Committee, 220–37

Al-Khansaa, Palestinian role model for girls, 165

al-Khansaa, online periodical, 170

All-source collection: advanced technology, 146; Allied strategy defeating Hitler, 143; countering terrorism, 140, 143; data fusion and age of terror, 146–49; increasing complex analysis, 145

Al Qaeda: espionage, 46; female suicide bombings, 158–59; Geneva Conventions and war on terrorism, 135; investigating sympathizers, 69. *See also* Women of Al Qaeda

Al-Rantissi, Rascha, widow choosing political action, 167

American Bill of Rights, 80–81

American civil liberties, 119

American Communist Party, 57

Americans, distaste for federal government intrusion, 149

America's defenses, 9/11 Commission, 294–98

Ames, Aldrich: espionage, 40–41, 42–43; luck in counterintelligence, 67; Senate Select Committee on counterintelligence failure, 220–37; treason, 10–11

Analysis: data mining and data, 151; intelligence, for war on terrorism, 135–36

Anderson, Malcolm, FBI-Europol issue, 78

André, John, spy execution, 27

Angleton, James Jesus, 10

Anti-lynching law, campaign for federal, by NAACP, 81

Antiwar activists, Huston Plan, 199–200

Arab Americans, Federal Bureau of Investigation (FBI) agents, 87–88

Aroud, Malika, Al Qaeda terrorist, 176

Atomic bomb: Klaus Fuchs, 33–34; Soviet espionage, 31

Atomic Energy Commission, Fuchs and Soviet atomic research, 33

Atomic research, monitoring Oppenheimer, 32–33

Attorney General, Judiciary Act of 1789 creating office, 83

Barnett, David, 38

Belgium, suicide attack of Muriel Degauque, 173–74

Bentley, Elizabeth: defector, 15, 21, 24, 31, 34; Soviet espionage, 60, 61–62

Biddle, Attorney General Francis, approving wiretapping, 57

Bin Laden, Osama: counterintelligence investigation, 69; covert operations, 134

Biometric screening system, 9/11 Commission, 263–64

Black Chamber, Code and Cipher Bureau, 28, 29

Black extremist movement, internal security threat, 203–5

Black Panther Party, 203

Bold employee, Europol, 88

Bonaparte, Attorney General Charles, Bureau of Investigation, 53

Boosterism, U.S. intelligence history, 83–84, 85

Boosting, concept of collection, 142–43

Boyce, Christopher, 38–39

British elections, Moscow's efforts to influence, 139

Bruggeman, Willy, 76

Bunyan, Tom, 76–77

Bureau of Investigation, Theodore Roosevelt's, 81

Bush administration: access to intelligence, 112–13; symbolic politics, 101–4

Butler Report, weapons of mass destruction, 330–47

Canada, U.S.-Canadian police cooperation, 78

Castro government, operations by, 43–44

Central Intelligence Agency (CIA): covertly killing and detaining terrorist suspects, 133–34; foreign intelligence liaison service, 130; 1950s Doolittle inquiry, 87; public relations embarrassment, 110–11; war on terrorism, 135–36

Chambers, Whittaker: counterintelligence failure, 64–65; spy, 29

Chechen suicide bombings, women, 158

Chicago: inferencing engines, 152; law enforcement surveillance, 148

Chichayev, Ivan, VENONA code-named ROSS, 20

China, spying for, 42, 45

Church Committee: excerpt from, 183–91; investigating intelligence abuses, 38

Civil liberties concern, Europe, 85–86

Civil liberties Statewatch, FBI-Europol issue, 76–77

Civil War, lessons of American history, 83

Clarke, Charles, data retention measure, 86

Classification, counterintelligence technique, 6–7

Classified Information Procedures Act, espionage, 39

Code and Cipher Bureau, Black Chamber, 28, 29

Coercion, female suicide bombers, 167–68

COINTELPRO project (FBI), counterintelligence, 36

Cold War, CIA's human operations, 129. See also VENONA and Cold War

Collection: espionage, 143, 155 n.13; intelligence, for war on terrorism, 135–36

Collection boosting, 142–43

Comintern, Moscow's efforts to influence British elections, 139

Communications, terrorists, 144–45

Communications Act of 1934, banning wiretapping, 55

Communications security, counterintelligence technique, 6

Communist Party: COINTELPRO project, 36; internal security threat, 208

Communist Party of Great Britain: MI5's penetration, 139–40

Compartmentation, counterintelligence technique, 6–7

Competition, connection with secrecy, 141–42, 154 n.6

COMPIC program, Hollywood film industry, 60

COMRAP (Comintern Apparatus), FBI counterintelligence operation, 58–59

Congress, oversight of intelligence community, 115

Constitution: Europol, 77–78; FBI history, 80–81; Fourth Amendment to U.S., 119

Consumer safety alerts, symbolic politics, 104

Cook, Fred, critical study of FBI, 90

Coordinating intelligence agency, Europol, 86

Coplon, Judith: background, 21–22; code name SIMA, 21; Federal Bureau of Investigation files, 57; Soviet espionage, 60–61; VENONA project, 16, 35

Counterespionage, counterintelligence, 186–87

Counterintelligence, age of terror, 140–46; assumptions of, theory, 8–9; classification and compartmentation, 6–7; communications security, 6; defector, 188; definition, 183–84; description, 141; excerpt from Church Committee report, 183–91; facility security, 6; in-service personnel security, 6; Moscow's efforts to influence British

elections, 139; organization, 189–91; penetration and double agent, 187–88; pre-employment personnel security, 5–6; primary functions, 5; product, 186; prosecuting traitors, 7–8; security and espionage, 186–87; signals intelligence, 7; sources of treason, 11; surprise, 141, 154 n.4; techniques, 5–8; threat, 184–86; trust, 9–11; trust assumption, 11; trust-distrust paradox, 11

Counterintelligence Field Activity (CIFA), expansion, 148–49

Counterterrorism: data fusion and management facing, analysts, 151; Hart-Rudman Commission, 238–42; intelligence for, 144–46

Counterterrorism Center (CTC): intelligence collection, 132–33; team inside CIA, 127

Covert action: suspected terrorists, 133–34; war on terrorism, 135–36

Crises, U.S. intelligence boosterism, 83–84

Criticism for intelligence failures, symbolic politics deflecting, 104

Cuban government, operations by, 43–44

Cultural rules, women in terrorist organizations, 161–62, 165

Currie, Lauchlin, VENONA, 15, 23

Cybernetics: assumptions about theory, 9; intelligence theory, 4–5

The Daily Telegraph, critique of FBI-Europol issue, 77

Dangle operation, spy catching, 38

Data analysis, intelligence, 151

Data mining, intelligence, 151

Détente, 37–38

Defense Department, Counterintelligence Field Activity (CIFA), 148–49

Degauque, Muriel, suicide attack in Belgium, 173–74

Den Tredje Vågen, Europol image, 84

Department of Homeland Security: intelligence collection and data fusion, 147; missions, 106–7; resource politics, 106–7; symbolic politics, 102

Direction finding (DF), boosting within single discipline, 142–43
Director of National Intelligence (DNI): 9/11 Commission, 108; resource politics, 108; symbolic politics, 102; war on terrorism, 135–36
Disch, William, supplying obsolete blueprints, 29
Division of Military Information, 27–28
Domestic alliances, surveillance and communications, 146, 155 n.20
Domestic groups, law enforcement officials, 148
Domestic intelligence gathering: accountability politics, 120–21; agenda politics, 118; gathering, 117–22; recurring patterns, 117–18; resource politics, 121–22; symbolic politics, 119–20
Domestic spying, National Security Agency (NSA), 120–22
Doolittle inquiry 1950s, central intelligence agency (CIA), 87
Double agent, counterintelligence, 187–88
Dragnet raids, controversial actions, 54
Drug Enforcement Administration (DEA), policing drugs, 78, 89–90
Drug prohibition, Federal Bureau of Investigation (FBI), 89–90
Dunn, Newton: Europol opposition, 90; pamphlet Europe Needs an FBI, 79–80
Duquesne case, Federal Bureau of Investigation (FBI) success, 56

East Bloc, spying for, 41–42, 44
Economic espionage, investigations, 45–46
Espionage Act of 1917, Congress passing, 28
Ethno-religious profiling, 69–70
Europe: American and European exchange of ideas, 74–75; civil liberties concern, 85–86; cultural threat by United States, 76
European Drugs Unit, drug prohibition, 89
European Federal Bureau of Investigation (FBI): constitutional impracticality,

77–78; national sovereignty, 77; pamphlet Europe Needs an FBI, 79–80; paternity debate of FBI-Europol issue, 78–79; perceptions of FBI-Europol issue, 76–77; reasons for inquiring into idea of, 73–74; resentment of American power, 76; states' rights in America, 77; Statewatch's critique, 76–77; unpopularity of G.W. Bush administration, 76. See also Europol
European Union (EU): Europol, 73; freedom of information provision, 86; harmonization of laws, 82; national sovereignty, 76; oversight of federal police, 91
Europe Needs An FBI, (Dunn), 79–80
Europol: bold employee, 88; coordinating intelligence agency, 86; defending against charges of prejudice, 88; history, 73–74; image in movies, 84–85; jihadism and racial justice, 88–97; opposition, 90; oversight, 90–91; political generalizations, 90–91; proposed constitution, 77–78; racial issues, 88–89; ratification of protocols, 82–83; recruitment problems, 87; strategic assessment of Storbeck, 84
Europol Protocol of 1996, 77
Euskadi Ta Askatasuna (ETA), Basque separatist organization, 158
Exploitation, female suicide bombers, 167–68

Facility security, counterintelligence technique, 6
The Falcon and the Snowman (Lindsey), 38–39
Fatawa, women of Al Qaeda, 168–69
Federal Bureau of Investigation (FBI): budget, 30; Bureau of Investigation predecessor, 81; constitutional and legal facets of history, 80–82; counterintelligence failures, 58–60; diversity problem, 92; establishment, 53; Gestapo phobia, 85–86, 91; Hoover wanting to emulate Scotland Yard, 75; luck in counterintelligence, 65, 67; Mann

Act 1911, 81; monitoring Latin and South America, 55–56; oversight, 90–91; Palmer raids, 54; perceived fascist and communist threat, 54–55; political generalizations, 90–91; political profiling, 69–70; racial issues, 87–88; reorganization, 110; sensitivity of intelligence investigations, 55; shift to intelligence investigations, 54; Two Prohibitions hypothesis, 89–90; wartime investigations, 54; White Slavery Act, 81; wiretapping, 55. *See also* Europol

Federal Emergency Management Agency (FEMA), resource politics, 109–10

Federal government, events boosting power of, 82

Female terrorism: advantages for terrorist organization, 163; alternative to traditional gender roles, 160; capacity for mobilizing support, 163; eagerly going to deaths, 159; formative stages, 163–64; fulfilling traditional male duties, 160–61; gender-based oppression, 160; ideology becoming tranquilizer, 165; motivations, 159; Palestinian, 164–68; social, cultural, and religious rules, 161–62; tactical change by terrorist organization, 162–63; Tamil women in Sri Lanka, 162; total submission in male-dominated terrorist organization, 161; vengeance, 161. *See also* Women

Fish, Hamilton, 29

Foreign and domestic agencies, 9/11 Commission, 279–84

Foreign and national security policy: "all politics is local," 99, 100; "politics stops at water's edge," 99–100. *See also* Political games

Foreign Intelligence Surveillance Act of 1978 (FISA): methods, 39, 155–56 n.22; passage, 120, 147

Foreign Intelligence Surveillance Court, 119–20

Freedom of information provision, European Union, 86

Fuchs, Klaus: spying for Soviets, 33–34; VENONA identifying, 15, 16–17, 20–21, 23

Fuerzas Armadas Revolucionarias in Columbia (FARC), women combatants, 158

Geneva Conventions, war on terrorism, 135

German espionage operations, Federal Bureau of Investigation (FBI), 56

German paternity, FBI-Europol issue, 78–79

German saboteur case, Federal Bureau of Investigation (FBI) success, 56–57

"Gestapo phobia," 85, 91

Global Salafi Jihad, ideology, 169, 178 n.1. *See also* Women of Al Qaeda

Global terrorism, symbolic politics, 101

Gold, Harry, 29, 35, 62

Golos, Jacob, 31

Greek government, spying for, 42

Greenglass, David, 57, 62

Griebl, Dr. Ignatz, 30

Hajj ritual, women's Jihad, 170, 180 n.52

Hamas: female terrorism, 164; women as suicide bombers, 166

Hamour, Thawiya, exploitation, 168

Hanssen, Robert: counterintelligence, 67–68; espionage, 40–41, 44

Hart-Rudman Commission, 238–42

Hearst, Patty, 158

Hiskey, Arthur, Manhattan Project, 33

Hiskey, Clarence, 31

Hiss, Alger, 60–61, 64–65

Hollywood film industry: code-named COMPIC, 60; image of Europol, 84–85

Holmuradova, Dilnoza, 172–73

Hospitals, counterintelligence, 152

House Un-American Activities Committee (HUAC), 36

Human intelligence (HUMINT): boosting, 143, 155 n.13; Central Intelligence Agency (CIA), 129–31; collection type, 142

Hurricane Katrina: law enforcement surveillance, 148; resource politics, 109–10

Hussein, Saddam, female suicide bombings, 172

Huston Plan: antiwar activists, 199–200; black extremist movement, 203–5; current intelligence collection procedures, 201–2; evaluation of interagency coordination, 218–19; intelligence services of communist countries, 206–7; internal security threat, 198–209; new left terrorist groups, 200–201; restraints of intelligence collection, 210–17; revolutionary groups, 208–9; student protest groups, 198–99; youthful anti-Vietnam war protesters, 192

Ideology: global Salafi Jihad, 168–70, 178 n.1; Palestinian female terrorism, 165

Idris, Wafa: coercion, 167–68; Palestinian female terrorist, 165

Industrial espionage, investigations, 45–46

Inferencing engines, automated data analysis, 152

Information sharing, 9/11 Commission, 292–94

In-service personnel security, counterintelligence technique, 6

Intelligence: agenda politics, 111–14; all-source collection, 142; all-source data fusion for countering terrorism, 143; American and European exchange of ideas, 74–75; boosterism, 83–84, 85; boosting collection disciplines, 143; collection types, 142; connection between competition and secrecy, 141–42, 154 n.6; data fusion for counterterrorism, 152; data mining and data analysis, 151; definitions, 2–3; doctors and hospitals, 152; domestic, gathering, 117–22; domestic context for, collection and data fusion, 147–49; enlisting private sector, 152–53; for counterterrorism, 144–46; Hart-Rudman Commission, 238–42; Latin origins of

word, 2, 3; national security and, 3; nature of, in age of terror, 140–46; oversight, 92; role of, 141–42; role of all-source, and advanced technology, 146; smart buildings, 152–53; terrorists within democracies, 149–50; theories, 3–5; thinking ahead, 151; Total Information Awareness, 149, 150–51; understanding external enemies, 100

Intelligence collection: current procedures, 201–2; domestic context, 147–49; restraints, 210–17

Intelligence community: Al Qaeda surprise attacks, 127; analyzing terrorists intentions, plans, and capabilities, 132–33; Central Intelligence Agency (CIA) running human operations, 129–31; covertly killing and detaining suspected terrorists, 133–34; human intelligence (HUMINT), 129–31; National Security Agency (NSA) intercepting communications, 129, 131; 9/11 Commission, 284–92; role of CIA, 128–29; signals intelligence (SIGINT), 129–31; stealing terrorists' secrets, 129–31; strengthening collection, analysis and covert action for war on terrorism, 135–36; terrorism, 128; U.S. at war with Al Qaeda, 127–28

Intelligence failures, symbolic politics deflecting criticism, 104

Intelligence policy. See Political games

Intelligence Reform and Terrorism Act of 2004: resource politics, 108–9, 111; symbolic politics, 102

Intelligence theories: cybernetics, 4–5; Johnson theory, 3, 4; Kahn theory, 3–4

Intercepted communication: cipher-breaking, 155 n.13; technical intelligence (TECHINT), 143

Interdepartmental Intelligence Committee, (Franklin Roosevelt's), 30

Internal security threat, Huston Plan, 198–209

Interstate commerce crimes, 53

Iraq: female suicide bombings, 158–59, 172; policy and case for war, 112–13; Silberman-Robb Commission, 302–329

Iraqi suicide bombers, female, in Amman, Jordan, 173

Israel, spying for, 46

Jackson, Attorney General Robert, approving wiretapping, 57

Jemaah Islamiah, Al Qaeda affiliate, 176

Jihad, reinterpreted for women, 175

Jihadism, Europol, 88–97

Johnson, Loch K.: assumptions of counter-intelligence theory, 8–9; intelligence theory, 3, 4

Judiciary Act of 1789, office of attorney general, 83

Kahn, David: assumptions of counter-intelligence theory, 8–9; intelligence theory, 3–4

Kampiles, William, surveillance satellite data, 38

Khaled, Leila, Popular Front for the Liberation of Palestine (PFLP), 158

KH-11 military surveillance, espionage, 38

Khlopkova, Olga V., VENONA code-named JULIA, 22–23

Kohl, Chancellor Helmut, FBI-Europol issue, 73, 75, 78–79

Korovin, Nikolai, VENONA project, 18–19

Kravchenko, Victor, 58, 59–60

Krivitsky, General Walter, 31–32

Ku Klux Klan terrorism, special agents in Justice Department, 87

Kurdish Workers Party (PKK): alternative gender role for women, 160; female suicide bombings, 158

Laghriff, Imame and Sana, suicide attack plot, 172

Latin and South America, FBI monitoring, 55–56

Law enforcement: Hurricane Katrina, 148; local responsibility, 83; officials investigating domestic groups, 148

Lawrence, Ernest O., atomic research for War Department, 32

Leaks, agenda politics, 114

Lincoln, President Abraham, 81

Lindsey, Robert, *The Falcon and the Snowman*, 38–39

Lipka, Robert Stephan, 43

Local empowerment, personal communications, 146, 155 n.20

Local responsibility, law enforcement, 83

Lunev, Stanislav, 8

Maclean, Donald, VENONA code-named HOMER, 19–21, 23

Mahaydali, Sana, female suicide bomber, 158

Malik Suicidal Brigades, Al Qaeda affiliated group, 173

Manhattan Project: Arthur Hiskey, 33; military intelligence, 62–63

Manila government, spying for, 41

Mann Act, 53, 81

Markelov, Valery I., 37

Marriage alliances, Jemaah Islamiah, 176

Martin, William H., 37

Martyrdom, Palestinian female terrorists, 165–66

MASK, MI5's penetration of Communist Party of Great Britain, 139–40

May, Allan Nunn, 33–34

Media: images of women terrorists, 162–63; intelligence oversight, 116–17

Meinhof, Ulrike, female terrorist, 158

MI5, penetration of Communist Party of Great Britain, 139–40

Military Information Section, intelligence collection, 28

Mission to Moscow, pro-Soviet film, 60

Mitchell, Bernon F., 37

Modin, Yuri, VENONA, 16, 17, 18

Monet, Jean-Claude, policing, 79

Muslims: Europol, 88; Federal Bureau of Investigation (FBI), 87–88

My Silent War (Philby), 16

Nanotechnology, micro-energy systems in buildings, 152

Narcotics prohibition, Federal Bureau of Investigation (FBI), 89–90

National Association of the Advancement of Colored People (NAACP), campaign for federal anti-lynching law, 81

National Counterterrorism Center: intelligence collection and data fusion, 147; terrorism suspects, 119

National security: foreign and, policy, 99–100; intelligence and, 3

National Security Agency (NSA): domestic spying program, 120–22; intercepting communications, 131

National sovereignty, European union (EU), 76

National Student Strike (NSS), 198

Nazi Germany, security threat, 57

Nelson, Steve: communist party activist, 58; House Un-American Activities Committee (HUAC), 36; military-industrial spy, 31, 32

New left terrorist groups, Huston Plan, 200–201

9/11 Commission: Afghanistan, 250–52; attack terrorists and organizations, 247–54; congressional oversight of intelligence, 115–16; defining threat, 244–45; Director of National Intelligence, 108, 135–36; measuring success, 246–47; more than war on terror, 245–46; organizing America's defenses, 294–98; Pakistan, 248–50; preventing continued growth of Islamist terrorism, 254–60; problem of intelligence sharing, 107; protecting and preparing for terrorist attacks, 261–73; recommendations on intelligence and counterterrorism, 243–93; Saudi Arabia, 252–54; symbolic politics, 102–3; unity of effort, 284–98

Occhipinti, John D., U.S.-Canadian police cooperation, 78

Open-source intelligence (OSINT), collection type, 142, 154 n.7

Oppenheimer, J. Robert, 32–33

Organized crime, European Union (EU), 82

Organizing America's defenses, 9/11 Commission, 294–98

Ovakimian, Gaik, 31

Oversight: congressional, of intelligence, 115–16; intelligence functions, 92

Pakistan, 9/11 Commission, 248–50

Palestinian female terrorism: Al-Khansaa as role model, 165; choosing political action, 167; coercion and exploitation, 167–68; Hamas and female suicide bombers, 166; ideology, 165; incidence of female suicide bombers, 168; Jamila Shanti, 166; loss by Israeli countermeasures, 166–67; martyrdom expansion to include women, 165–66; Palestinian Islamic Jihad (PIJ), 166; patriotism, 164–65; Rascha al-Rantissi, 167; respect, honor, and self-esteem, 168; roles of Palestinian mothers, 164–65; Tahani Titit, 168; Thawiya Hamour, 168; Wafa Idris, 165

Palestinian Islamic Jihad (PIJ), recruiting women, 166

Palestinian mothers, roles of, 164–65

Palmer raids, controversial actions, 54

Parliamentary oversight, Federal Bureau of Investigation (FBI), 90–91

Paskalian, Sarkis O., 37

Patriotism, female terrorism, 164–65

Pedersen, Søren Kragh, 73

Pelton, Ronald, 40

Perl, William, conviction using VENONA, 35–36

Personnel security, counterintelligence technique, 5–6

Philby, Kim: Bentley's defection, 62; code-named STANLEY, 18, 19; *My Silent War*, 16

Philippines, spying for, 41

Police, U.S.-Canadian, cooperation, 78

Policing, American and European exchange of ideas, 74–75

Policy, foreign and national security, 99–100

Policy makers, intelligence and self-interest, 113–14

Political action, Palestinian women choosing, 167

Political games: accountability politics, 114–17; agenda politics, 111–14; domestic intelligence gathering, 117–22; resource politics, 105–11; symbolic politics, 100–105

Political profiling, counterintelligence, 69–70

Politics, drug policing, 89–90

Popular Front for the Liberation of Palestine (PFLP), Leila Khaled, 158

Pre-employment personnel security, counterintelligence technique, 5–6

Private sector, counterintelligence, 152–53

Proliferation of weapons of mass destruction, 9/11 Commission, 258–59

Propaganda, images of women terrorists, 162–63

Prosecuting traitors, counterintelligence technique, 7–8

Protection of civil liberties, 9/11 Commission, 270–71

Publicity, FBI's director, 84; FBI's Hoover, 84

Public reassurances, symbolic politics, 100–103

Puerto Rican Nationalist Extremist Groups, internal security threat, 208

Racial issues: Europol, 88–89; Federal Bureau of Investigation (FBI), 87–88

Recruitment, Europol, 87

Red Army Faction, female terrorists, 158

Religious rules, women in terrorist organizations, 161–62

Remington, William Walter, information to Bentley, 34

Resource politics: Congress and bureaucratic forces dominating, 105–6; Department of Homeland Security, 106–7; Director of National Intelligence, 108; domestic intelligence gathering, 121–22; Federal Emergency Management Agency (FEMA) and Hurricane Katrina, 109–10; Intelligence Reform and Terrorism Prevention Act of 2004, 108–9, 111; organizations, 106; Silberman-Robb Committee, 110. *See also* Political games

Responsibility, intelligence, 114–15

Roosevelt, Eleanor, FBI photocopying correspondence, 60

Roosevelt, Franklin D.: Interdepartmental Intelligence Committee, 30; perceived fascist and communist threat, 54–55

Roosevelt, President Theodore, Bureau of Investigation, 81

Rosenberg, Ethel and Julius: crime of century, 63; Soviet espionage, 60–61, 62; VENONA, 15, 17, 35

Rumrich, Guenther Gustave, 30, 56

Salafi Jihad, women of Al Qaeda, 168–69

Satellite intelligence, espionage, 38–39

Saudi Arabia, 9/11 Commission, 252–54

Scotland Yard, FBI director Hoover wanting to emulate, 75

Sebold, William G., handling Nazi ring, 30–31

Secrecy: accountability politics, 115; connection with competition, 141–42, 154 n.6

September 11, 2001, intelligence after terrorist attacks, 45. *See also* 9/11 Commission

Sexual violence, Tamil women as survivors of, 162

Shahids, martyrs for Allah, 164

Shanti, Jamila, Women's Activist Division of Palestinian Islamic movement, 166

Shevchenko, Andrei: military-industrial spy, 31; Soviet espionage, 33

Shishkin, Mikhail, code-named ADAM in VENONA, 17, 20

Signals intelligence: counterintelligence technique, 7; National Security Agency (NSA), 129, 131

Silberman-Robb Committee: intelligence and weapons of mass destruction in Iraq, 302–329; watchdog organization, 110 Slackers in New York City, controversial actions, 54

"Slam dunk," case for war in Iraq (2002), 113, 124 n.30

Smart buildings, counterintelligence, 152–53

Socialist Workers Party, internal security threat, 208

Social rules, women in terrorist organizations, 161–62

Sombolay, Albert, 41

Soubra, Zakaria, Al Qaeda sympathizer, 69

South Africa, spying for, 41

Soviet espionage, VENONA project, 23–24. *See also* VENONA and Cold War

Soviet *Sputnik*, 36

Spy catching in United States: Abwehr spies, 32; Aldrich Ames, 40–41, 42–43; Al Qaeda operatives, 46; arrest of John A. Walker Jr., 40; atomic bomb project, 31, 33–34; Classified Information Procedures Act, 39; Code and Cipher Bureau, 28; COINTELPRO project against Communist Party, 36; defector Elizabeth Bentley, 15, 21, 24, 34; defense information to Soviet Union, 36–37; defunct East Bloc, 41–42, 44; diplomatic environment of détente preventing, 37–38; economic and industrial espionage, 45–46; effect of terrorist attacks of September 11, 2001, 45; Espionage Act of 1917, 28; espionage in 1980s, 39–41; espionage in other countries against U.S., 41–44; execution of John André, 27; FBI handling Nazi ring, 30–31; Fish committee, 29; Foreign Intelligence Surveillance Act of 1978 (FISA), 39; Interdepartmental Intelligence Committee, 30; KH-11 military surveillance satellite and William Kampiles, 38; Klaus Fuchs, 33–34; Manhattan Project and Hiskey, 33; military as recruiting ground, 42; Military Information Section, 28; monitoring atomic researchers Oppenheimer and Lawrence, 32–33; Nazi Germany, 32; NSA communications specialist Ronald Pelton, 40; operations by Castro's government, 43–44; prosecution of Christopher Boyce, 38–39; prosecution of David Barnett, 38; Robert Hanssen, 40–41, 44; spying for Israel, 46; USA-PATRIOT Act, 39; VENONA project, 34–35; War Department's Division of Military Information, 27–28; without statute of limitations, 43

Spying program: human intelligence (HUMINT), 143, 155 n.13; National Security Agency (NSA) domestic, 120–22

Sri Lanka: bombings by Tamil Tigers of Tamil Elam (LTTE), 158; Tamil women as survivors of sexual violence, 162

Statewatch, FBI-Europol issue, 76–77

Steganography, embedding sensitive information, 145

Storbeck, Jürgen, 84

Student protest groups, Huston Plan, 198–99

Suicide terrorism, female attackers, 157–59

Surprise, extension of counterintelligence, 141, 154 n.4

Surveillance technologies, development and use, 145–46

Suspected terrorists, covertly killing and detaining, 133–34

Symbionese Liberation Army (SLA), female terrorists, 158

Symbolic politics: 9/11 Commission, 103; attention and reaffirmation, 103; blaming others for future problems, 104–5; deflecting criticism for intelligence failures, 104; domestic intelligence gathering, 119–20; favoring aggressive collection policies, 101; global terrorism, 101; reassuring public about administration, 101–3; words and images, 100–101. *See also* Political games

Taiwan, industrial espionage, 46; spying for, 41

Tamil Tigers of Tamil Elam (LTTE): women as survivors of sexual violence, 162; women combatants, 158

Tanzim, female terrorism, 164

Teapot Dome scandal, 54
Technical intelligence (TECHINT):
    collection type, 142; intercepted
    communications, 143
Technology, counterterrorism mission, 145
Terrorism: debate and controversy of term,
    128; intelligence for counterterrorism,
    144–46; meaning and usage, 157,
    177 n.1
Terrorism Threat Integration Center,
    intelligence collection and data fusion,
    147
Terrorist attacks: commercial surveillance
    technology, 145–46; intelligence
    following, 45
Terrorists: analyzing intentions, plans,
    and capabilities, 132–33; covertly killing
    and detaining suspects, 133–34; stealing
    secrets of, 129–31; steganography, 145
Terrorist travel, 9/11 Commission, 261–63
Terror organizations: advantages of female
    suicide bombers, 163; female partici-
    pation, 163–64
Theories, assumptions of counter-
    intelligence theory, 8–9; cybernetics,
    4–5; David Kahn and Loch K. Johnson,
    3–4; intelligence, 3–5
Total Information Awareness (TIA): data
    mining and analysis, 150; fusing data
    for crisis management, 150–51; project,
    149
Traitors, prosecuting, 7–8
Treason, sources of, 11
Truman administration, counterintelligence,
    61

United States: American and European
    exchange of ideas, 74–75; U.S.-
    Canadian police cooperation, 78. See
    also Spy catching in United States
Unmanned aerial vehicles (UAVs), killing
    Al Qaeda operatives, 134
USA-PATRIOT Act: expanded
    surveillance authority, 68, 117, 118;
    passage, 39, 46
U.S. border screening system, 9/11
    Commission, 265–66

U.S. intelligence, boosterism, 83–84, 85.
    See also Intelligence
U.S. Secret Service, Lincoln and creation
    of, 81

Van Deman, Ralph, Military Information
    Section, 28
Venceremos Brigade (VB), 198
VENONA and Cold War: British and
    American counterintelligence, 15;
    British Government Communications
    Headquarters (GCHQ), 17; code-named
    CHARLES, 16, 17, 19, 21; compromised
    Soviet cipher system, 15–16; defector
    Elizabeth Bentley, 15, 21, 24; Donald
    Maclead code-named HOMER, 19–21,
    23; FBI counterintelligence failure, 63;
    Flora Wovschin code-named ZORA,
    22–23; Guy Burgess, 17–21; Harry Gold,
    16, 17; identification of Klaus Fuchs,
    15, 16–17, 20–21, 23; identifying spies,
    34–35; Ivan Chichayev code-named
    ROSS, 20; Judith Coplon (code-name
    SIMA), 16, 21–22; Julius and Ethyl
    Rosenberg, 15, 17, 35; Mikhail Shishkin,
    17, 20; My Silent War (Philby), 16;
    Olga V. Khlopkova code-named JULIA,
    22–23; Philby code-named STANLEY,
    18, 19; rezident Nikolai Korovin, 18–19;
    Signals Intelligence Service (SIS), 29;
    wartime military intelligence program,
    62; Yuri Modin, 16, 17, 18
Verbruggen, Frank, FBI-Drug
    Enforcement Agency (DEA), 78,
    89–90
Violence organizations, role of women,
    162

Walker, John A. Jr.: motives for spying, 67;
    spy arrest, 40
War imagery, symbolic politics, 101
War on drugs, Federal Bureau of
    Investigation (FBI), 89–90
War on terrorism: covertly killing and
    detaining suspected terrorists, 133–34;
    Geneva Conventions, 135; 9/11
    Commission, 245–46; strengthening

War on terrorism (*continued*)
  intelligence collection, analysis and
  covert action, 135–36
Weapons of mass destruction: Butler
  Report on, 330–47; 9/11 Commission,
  258–59; Silberman-Robb Commission,
  302–29
Weatherman terrorist group, Huston Plan,
  200–201
Weinberg, Joseph, 31
White, Harry Dexter, VENONA, 15, 23
White Slave Traffic Act, enactment,
  53, 81
Wiesband, William, VENONA leak, 16
Wiretapping: Communications ACT of
  1934, 55; FBI requests approving,
  57–58
Women: Chechen campaign of suicide
  bombings, 158; motives of, and
  organization, 159–64; suicide terrorism,
  157–59; terrorist groups in Western
  Europe, 158; terrorist groups throughout
  history, 157. *See also* Female terrorism
Women in Al Qaeda: development of
  suicide bombers in Iraq, 172; Dilnoza
  Holmuradova, 172–73; female bomber
  at wedding in Amman, Jordan, 173;
  Imame and Sana Laghriff, 172; Jemaah
  Islamiah and marriage alliances, 176;
  Jihad reinterpreted for women, 175;
  Malika Aroud, 176; Muriel Degauque in
  Belgium, 173–74; recruiting, 175;
  responsibility of male relatives, 171;
  supporting and helping their men, 171;
  terrorist attack in Egypt, 173; websites
  advising participation, 171–72
Women of Al Qaeda: *fatawa*, 168–69; *hajj*
  ritual, 170, 180 n.52; ideology of global
  Salafi Jihad, 168–70; importance of
  female support, 170; role, 169; role in
  Jihad, 170; suicide bombers, 168–69;
  victims of infidels, 169–70
Women's Information Bureau of Al
  Qaeda, 170
Words, symbolic politics, 100–105
World War II, boosting powers of federal
  government, 82
Wovschin, Flora, VENONA code-named
  ZORA, 22–23

Yardley, Herbert, Code and Cipher Bureau,
  28, 29

ABOUT THE EDITOR AND CONTRIBUTORS

EDITOR

Loch K. Johnson is Regents Professor of Public and International Affairs at the University of Georgia and author of several books and over 100 articles on U.S. intelligence and national security. His books include *The Making of International Agreements* (1984); *A Season of Inquiry* (1985); *Through the Straits of Armageddon* (1987, coedited with Paul Diehl); *Decisions of the Highest Order* (1988, coedited with Karl F. Inderfurth); *America's Secret Power* (1989); *Runoff Elections in the United States* (1993, coauthored with Charles S. Bullock III); *America as a World Power* (1995); *Secret Agencies* (1996); *Bombs, Bugs, Drugs, and Thugs* (2000); *Fateful Decisions* (2004, coedited with Karl F. Inderfurth); *Strategic Intelligence* (2004, coedited with James J. Wirtz); *Who's Watching the Spies?* (2005, coauthored with Hans Born and Ian Leigh); *American Foreign Policy* (2005, coauthored with Daniel Papp and John Endicott); and *Seven Sins of American Foreign* Policy (2007). He has served as special assistant to the chair of the Senate Select Committee on Intelligence (1975–76), staff director of the House Subcommittee on Intelligence Oversight (1977–79), and special assistant to the chair of the Aspin-Brown Commission on Intelligence (1995–96). In 1969–70, he was an American Political Science Association Congressional Fellow. He has served as secretary of the American Political Science Association and President of the International Studies Association, South. Born in New Zealand and educated at the University of California, Johnson has taught at the University of Georgia since 1979, winning its Meigs Professorship for meritorious teaching and its Owens Award for outstanding accomplishments in the field of social science research. In 2000, he led the founding of the School of Public and

368 ABOUT THE EDITOR AND CONTRIBUTORS

International Affairs at the University of Georgia. He is the senior editor of the international journal *Intelligence and National Security*.

CONTRIBUTORS

Matthew M. Aid is Managing Director in the Washington, DC, office of Citigate Global Intelligence and Security and coeditor of *Secrets of Signals Intelligence During the Cold War and Beyond* (2001).

James E. Baker sits on the U.S. Court of Appeals for the Armed Forces. He previously served as Special Assistant to the President and Legal Adviser to the National Security Council and as Deputy Legal Adviser to the NSC. He has also served as Counsel to the President's Foreign Intelligence Advisory Board, an attorney at the Department of State, a legislative aide to Senator Daniel Patrick Moynihan, and as a Marine Corps infantry officer. He is the coauthor with Michael Reisman of *Regulating Covert Action* (Yale University Press, 1992).

David M. Barrett is Associate Professor of Political Science at Villanova University and author of *Congress and the CIA* (Kansas, 2005).

Hans Born is a senior fellow in democratic governance of the security sector at the Geneva Centre for Democratic Control of the Armed Forces (DCAF). He is an external member of the crisis management and security policy faculty of the Federal Institute of Technology and a guest lecturer on governing nuclear weapons at the UN Disarmament Fellowship Programme. He has written, co-authored, and co-edited various books on international relations and security policy, including the Inter-Parliamentary Union Handbook on *Parliamentary Oversight of the Security Sector: Principles, Mechanisms and Practices* (Geneva: IPU/DCAF, 2003, translated in 30 languages); *Making Intelligence Accountable: Legal Standards and Best Practice for Oversight of Intelligence Agencies* (Oslo: Publishing House of the Parliament of Norway, 2005, translated in 10 languages); *Who is Watching the Spies? Establishing Intelligence Agency Accountability* (Dulles, VA: Potomac Publishers, 2005); *Civil-Military Relations in Europe: Learning from Crisis and Institutional Change* (London: Routledge, 2006); and *The Double Democratic Deficit: Parliamentary Accountability and the Use of Force under International Auspices* (London: Ashgate Publishers: Aldershot).

A. Denis Clift is President of the Department of Defense Joint Military Intelligence College. He was born in New York City and educated at Friends Seminary, Phillips Exeter Academy (1954), Stanford University (B.A., 1958), and the London School of Economics and Political Science (M.Sc., 1967). He began a career of public service as a naval officer in the Eisenhower and Kennedy administrations and has served in military and civilian capacities in ten administrations, including thirteen successive years in the Executive Office of the President and the White House. From 1971–76, he served on the National Security

Council staff. From 1974–76, he was head of President Ford's National Security Council staff for the Soviet Union and Eastern and Western Europe. From 1977–81, he was Assistant for National Security Affairs to the Vice President. From 1991–94, he was Chief of Staff, Defense Intelligence Agency. From 1963–66, he was the editor of the U.S. Naval Institute *Proceedings*. His published fiction and nonfiction include the novel *A Death in Geneva* (Ballantine Books, Random House), *Our World in Antarctica* (Rand McNally), *With Presidents to the Summit* (George Mason University Press), and *Clift Notes: Intelligence and the Nation's Security* (JMIC Writing Center Press).

William J. Daugherty holds a doctorate in government from the Claremont Graduate School and is Associate Professor of government at Armstrong Atlantic State University in Savannah, Georgia. A retired senior officer in the CIA, he is also the author of *In the Shadow of the Ayatollah: A CIA Hostage in Iran* (Annapolis, 2001) and *Executive Secrets: Covert Action and the Presidency* (Kentucky, 2004).

Jack Davis served in the CIA from 1956 to 1990 as analyst, manager, and teacher of analysts. He now is an independent contractor with the Agency, specializing in analytic methodology. He is a frequent contributor to the journal *Studies in Intelligence*.

Stuart Farson is Lecturer, Political Science Department, Simon Fraser University, Vancouver/Surrey, Canada. He is a former Secretary-Treasurer of the Canadian Association for Security and Intelligence Studies, and served as Director of Research for the Special Committee of the House Commons (Canada) on the Review of the Canadian Security Intelligence Service Act and the Security Offences Act. He has numerous articles on security, intelligence, and policing issues and is the coeditor of *Security and Intelligence in a Changing World* (with David Stafford and Wesley K. Wark, Cass, 1991).

Timothy Gibbs is a final-year doctoral student in history at Robinson College, Cambridge University, and a member of the Cambridge University Intelligence Seminar. He is also a former Visiting Scholar at the University of Georgia. His doctoral dissertation, titled *British and American Intelligence and the Atom Spies*, was submitted in the summer of 2006 and was supervised by Professor Christopher Andrew.

Peter Gill is Reader in Politics and Security, Liverpool John Moores University, Liverpool, United Kingdom. He is coauthor of *Introduction to Politics* (1988, 2nd ed.) and *Intelligence in an Insecure World* (2006). He is currently researching the control and oversight of domestic security in intelligence agencies.

Harold M. Greenberg graduated with a B.A. in history from Yale University in 2005. At Yale, he participated in the Studies in Grand Strategy program, and he has recently published research on CIA covert action in the 1950s. He now works as a legislative aide in the U.S. House of Representatives.

Daniel S. Gressang IV is Professor at the Joint Military Intelligence College (JMIC) in Washington, DC, and serves concurrently as the National Security Agency/National Cryptologic School of Liaison to JMIC. He has researched, written, and lectured extensively on terrorism and counterinsurgency. His research focuses primarily on the application of complex adaptive systems perspectives to understanding the dynamics of terror and other forms of unconventional warfare. In 2004, he was designated Intelligence Community Officer by the Director of Central Intelligence.

Glenn Hastedt received his doctorate in political science from Indiana University. Until recently he was Professor and Chair of the Political Science Department at James Madison University. He is now chair of the Justice Studies Department there. Among his publications is *American Foreign Policy: Past, Present, Future*, 6th ed. (Prentice Hall).

John Hollister Hedley, during more than thirty years at CIA, edited the *President's Daily Brief*, briefed the *PDB* at the White House, served as Managing Editor of the *National Intelligence Daily*, and was Chairman of the CIA's Publications Review Board. Now retired, Hedley has taught intelligence at Georgetown University and serves as a consultant to the National Intelligence Council and the Center for the Study of Intelligence.

Michael Herman served from 1952 to 1987 in Britain's Government Communications Headquarters, with secondments to the Cabinet Office and the Ministry of Defence. Since retirement he has written extensively on intelligence matters, with official clearance. He has had academic affiliations with Nuffield and St. Antony's Colleges in Oxford and is Founder Director of the Oxford Intelligence Group and Honorary Departmental Fellow at Aberystwyth University. In 2005 he received the degree of Honorary D.Litt from Nottingham University. He is a leading British intelligence scholar and author of *Intelligence Power in Peace and War* (Cambridge, 2001).

Frederick P. Hitz is Lecturer (Diplomat in Residence) in Public and International Affairs, Woodrow Wilson School, Princeton University.

Max M. Holland is the author of *The Kennedy Assassination Tapes* (Knopf, 2004).

Arthur S. Hulnick is Associate Professor of International Relations at Boston University. He is a veteran of thirty-five years of intelligence service, including seven years in Air Force Intelligence and twenty-eight years in the CIA. He is author of *Fixing the Spy Machine* (Praeger, 1999) and *Keeping Us Safe* (Praeger, 2004).

Rhodri Jeffreys-Jones is Professor of American History at the University of Edinburgh. The author of several books on intelligence history, he is currently completing a study of the FBI.

Ephraim Kahana is Professor of Political Science and faculty member in the Western Galilee College, Acre, Israel. He teaches courses on international relations, national security and intelligence, and foreign policy in the National Security Program in the University of Haifa. Kahana has written numerous papers on intelligence and foreign policy. His most recent book is the *Historical Dictionary of Israeli Intelligence* (2006).

Patrick Radden Keefe is a graduate of the School of Law at Yale University and is presently a Fellow with the Century Foundation in New York City. He is the author of *Chatter: Uncovering the Echelon Surveillance Network and the Secret World of Global Eavesdropping* (Random House, 2006), and has published essays in *The New York Review of Books*, *The New York Times Magazine*, the *New York Times*, the *Boston Globe*, the *Yale Journal of International Law*, *Legal Affairs*, *Slate*, and *Wired*. He has been a Marshall Scholar and a 2003 fellow at the Dorothy and Lewis B. Cullman Center for Scholars and Writers at the New York Public Library.

Jennifer D. Kibbe is Assistant Professor of Government at Franklin and Marshall College. Between 2002 and 2004, she was a postdoctoral fellow at the Brookings Institution. Her research interests include U.S. foreign policy, intelligence and covert action, presidential decision making, and political psychology. She has published work on U.S. policy in Iraq and the Middle East, and the military's involvement in covert actions.

Katharina von Knop is a doctoral candidate in Political Science at Leopold-Franzens University in Innsbruck, Austria, specializing in counter- and antiterrorism, and coeditor with Heinrich Neisser and Martin van Creveld of *Countering Modern Terrorism: History, Current Issues, and Future Threats* (2005).

Lawrence J. Lamanna is a doctoral candidate in the School of Public and International Affairs at the University of Georgia. He holds an M.A. from Yale University and a B.A. from the University of Notre Dame.

Ian Leigh is Professor of Law and Codirector of the Human Rights Centre at the University of Durham. He lives in Durham, England.

Kristin M. Lord is Associate Dean at George Washington University's Elliott School of International Affairs. In 2005–2006, she was a Council on Foreign Relations International Affairs Fellow and Special Adviser to the Under Secretary of State for Democracy and Global Affairs. Lord is the author of *The Perils and Promise of Global Transparency: Why the Information Revolution May Not Lead to Security Democracy or Peace* (SUNY Press, 2006); coeditor, with Bernard I. Finel, of *Power and Conflict in the Age of Transparency* (Palgrave Macmillan, 2000); and the author of numerous book chapters, articles, and papers on international politics and security. Lord received her doctorate in government from Georgetown University.

Minh A. Luong is Assistant Director of International Security Studies at Yale University, where he teaches in the Department of History. He also serves as adjunct Assistant Professor of Public Policy at the Taubman Center at Brown University.

Cynthia M. Nolan earned a doctorate at American University in the School of International Service, researching intelligence oversight. She is a former officer in the Directorate of Operations in the CIA and has published in the *International Journal of Intelligence and Counterintelligence*.

Kevin A. O'Brien is a former research associate with the Canadian Institute of Strategic Studies and is currently a senior analyst for RAND Europe.

Mark Phythian is Professor of International Security and Director of the History and Governance Research Institute at the University of Wolverhampton, United Kingdom. He is the author of *Intelligence in an Insecure World* (2006, with Peter Gill), *The Politics of British Arms Sales Since 1964* (2000), and *Arming Iraq* (1997), as well as numerous journal articles on intelligence and security issues.

Harry Howe Ransom is Professor Emeritus of Political Science at Vanderbilt University. He has a B.A. from Vanderbilt and an M.A. and Ph.D. from Princeton University. He was a Congressional Fellow of the American Political Science Association and a Fellow of the Woodrow Wilson International Center for Scholars. He taught at Princeton, Vassar College, Michigan State University, Harvard University, and the University of Leeds. His books include *Central Intelligence and National Security* (1958), *Can American Democracy Survive Cold War?* (1963), and *The Intelligence Establishment* (1970).

Jeffrey T. Richelson is Senior Fellow with the National Security Archive in Washington, DC, and author of *The Wizards of Langley*, *The U.S. Intelligence Community*, *A Century of Spies*, and *America's Eyes in Space*, as well as numerous articles on intelligence activities. He received his doctorate in political science from the University of Rochester and has taught at the University of Texas, Austin, and the American University, Washington, DC. He lives in Los Angeles.

Jerel A. Rosati is Professor of Political Science and International Studies at the University of South Carolina since 1982. His area of specialization is the theory and practice of foreign policy, focusing on the U.S. policy-making process, decision-making theory, and the political psychological study of human cognition. He is the author and editor of five books and over forty articles and chapters. He has received numerous outstanding teaching awards. He has been Visiting Professor at Somalia National University in Mogadishu and Visiting Scholar at China's Foreign Affairs College in Beijing. He also has been a Research Associate in the Foreign Affairs and National Defense Division of the Library of Congress's Congressional Research Service, President of the International

Studies Association's Foreign Policy Analysis Section, and President of the Southern region of the International Studies Association.

Richard L. Russell is Professor of national security studies at the National Defense University. He is also an adjunct associate professor in the Security Studies Program and research associate in the Institute for the Study of Diplomacy at Georgetown University. He previously served as a CIA political-military analyst. Russell is the author of *Weapons Proliferation and War in the Greater Middle East: Strategic Contest* (2005).

Frederick A. O. Schwarz Jr. received an A.B. from Harvard University and J.D. from Harvard Law School, where he was an editor of the *Law Review*. After a year's clerkship with Hon. J. Edward Lumbard, U.S. Court of Appeals for the Second Circuit, he worked one year for the Nigerian government as Assistant Commissioner for Law Revision under a Ford Foundation grant. He joined the New York City law firm of Cravath, Swaine and Moore in 1963 and was elected a partner in 1969. From 1975 through mid-1976, he served as Chief Counsel to the Senate Select Committee to Study Government Operations with Respect to Intelligence Activities (the Church Committee); from 1982–89, he served as Corporation Counsel and head of the Law Department of the City of New York. In 1989, he chaired the New York City Charter Revision Commission.

James M. Scott is Professor and Chair of the Department of Political Science at Oklahoma State University. His areas of specialization include foreign policy analysis and international relations, with particular emphasis on U.S. foreign policy making and the domestic sources of foreign policy. He is author or editor of four books, over forty articles, book chapters, review essays, and other publications. He has been President of the Foreign Policy Analysis section and President of the Midwest region of the International Studies Association, where he has also served as conference organizer for both sections and has been a two-time winner of the Klingberg Award for Outstanding Faculty Paper at the ISA Midwest Annual Meeting. Since 1996, he has received over two dozen awards from students and peers for his outstanding teaching and research, including his institution's highest awards for scholarship in 2000 and 2001. Since 2005, he has been Director of the Democracy and World Politics Summer Research Program, a National Science Foundation Research Experience for Undergraduates.

Len Scott is Professor of International Politics at the University of Wales, Aberystwyth, where he is Director of the Centre for Intelligence and International Security Studies. Among his recent publications are *Understanding Intelligence in the Twenty-First Century: Journeys in Shadows* (2004, coedited with Peter Jackson) and *Planning Armageddon: Britain, the United States and the Command of Nuclear Forces, 1943–1964* (2000, coedited with Stephen Twigge).

Katherine A. S. Sibley is Professor and Chair of the History Department at St. Joseph's University. She is currently working on a biography of Florence Kling

Harding, titled *America's First Feminist First Lady*. Sibley's work will revise the typical portrait of Mrs. Harding as manipulative, unhappy wife, casting new light on her public and private life. In 2004, Sibley published *Red Spies in America: Stolen Secrets and the Dawn of the Cold War* with the University Press of Kansas. She is also the author of *The Cold War* (1998) and *Loans and Legitimacy: The Evolution of Soviet-American Relations, 1919–1933* (1996). Her work has appeared in journals including *American Communist History*, *Peace and Change*, and *Diplomatic History*, and she also serves as book review editor for *Intelligence and National Security*. She is a three-term Commonwealth Speaker for the Pennsylvania Humanities Council.

Jennifer Sims is Director of Intelligence Studies and Visiting Professor in the Security Studies Program at Georgetown University's Edmund A. Walsh School of Foreign Service. She also consults for the U.S. government and private sector on homeland security and intelligence related matters. Prior to this, Sims was Research Professor at Johns Hopkins University's Nitze School of Advanced International Studies in Washington, DC (Fall 2001–Summer 2003). She has served as defense and foreign policy adviser to Senator John Danforth (1990–94), a professional staff member of the Senate Select Committee on Intelligence (1991–94), Deputy Assistant Secretary of State for Intelligence Coordination (1994–98), and as the Department of State's first Coordinator for Intelligence Resources and Planning in the office of the Under Secretary for Management. In 1998 Sims was awarded the U.S. Intelligence Community's Distinguished Service Medal. She received her B.A. degree from Oberlin College and her M.A. and Ph.D. in national security studies from Johns Hopkins University in 1978 and 1985, respectively. She is the author of a number of books and articles on intelligence and arms control. The most recent of these include "Foreign Intelligence Liaison: Devils, Deals and Details," *International Journal of Intelligence and Counterintelligence Affairs* (Summer 2006); *Transforming US Intelligence*, coedited with Burton Gerber (Georgetown University Press, 2005); "Transforming U.S. Espionage: A Contrarian's Approach," *Georgetown Journal of International Affairs* (Winter/Spring 2005); "Domestic Factors in Arms Control: The U.S. Case," in Jeffrey A Larson (ed.), *Arms Control: Cooperative Security in a Changing Environment* (Lynne Rienner, 2002); "What Is Intelligence? Information for Decision-Makers," in Roy Godson, Ernest R. May, and Gary Schmitt, *U.S. Intelligence at the Crossroads* (Brassey's, 1995); "The Cambridge Approach Reconsidered," *Daedalus* 120 (Winter 1991); and *Icarus Restrained: An Intellectual History of American Arms Control* (Westview Press, 1990).

Robert David Steele is CEO of OSS.Net, an international open source intelligence provider. As the son of an oilman, a Marine Corps infantry officer, and a clandestine intelligence case officer for the CIA, he has spent over twenty years abroad in Asia and Central and South America. As a civilian intelligence officer he spent three back-to-back tours overseas, including one tour as one of the first officers assigned full-time to terrorism, and three headquarters tours in offensive counterintelligence, advanced information technology, and satellite program management. He resigned from the CIA in 1988 to be the senior civilian founder of the Marine Corps Intelligence Command. He resigned from the Marines in 1993. He is the author of three works on intelligence, as well as the editor of a book on peacekeeping intelligence. He has earned graduate degrees in international relations and public administration, is a graduate of the Naval War College, and has a certificate in Intelligence Policy. He is also a graduate of the Marine Corps Command and Staff Course and of the CIA's Mid-Career Course 101.

John D. Stempel is Senior Professor of International Relations at the University of Kentucky's Patterson School of Diplomacy and International Commerce, where he was Associate Director (1988–93) and Director (1993–2003). He came to the University of Kentucky following a 24-year career in the U.S. Foreign Service. There he focused on political and economic affairs, with overseas assignments in Africa (Guinea, Burundi, Zambia), Iran, and India, concluding with three years as U.S. Consul General in Madras. His Middle East service (1975–79) in Tehran provided the material for his book *Inside the Iranian Revolution*. His subsequent academic writings have focused on religion and diplomacy, intelligence and diplomacy, and American views of negotiation. His Washington assignments featured duty for both the State and Defense Departments, including a two-year tour as Director of the State Department's Crisis Center. He has taught at George Washington and American Universities, plus two years as Diplomat in Residence at the U.S. Naval Academy, Annapolis. Stemple is a member of the New York Council on Foreign Relations and is listed in *Who's Who in the World* and *Who's Who in America*. He holds an A.B. degree from Princeton University and M.A. and Ph.D. degrees from the University of California at Berkeley.

Stan A. Taylor is an Emeritus Professor of Political Science at Brigham Young University in Provo, Utah. He has taught in England, Wales, and New Zealand and in 2006 was a visiting professor at the University of Otago in Dunedin, New Zealand. He is founder of the David M. Kennedy Center for International Studies at Brigham Young University. He writes frequently on intelligence, national security, and U.S. foreign policy.

Athan Theoharis is Professor of History at Marquette University whose research has focused on government secrecy, Cold War politics, and the history of the FBI. He is the author, coauthor, and editor of eighteen books, including *The FBI and American Democracy* (2004), *Chasing Spies* (2002), *A Culture of Secrecy* (1998), and *The FBI: A Comprehensive Reference Guide* (1998). He has received numerous awards, including the American Bar Association's Gavel Award and selection as a fellow by the Wisconsin Academy of Arts, Sciences, and Letters.

Gregory F. Treverton is senior analyst at the RAND Corporation. Earlier, he directed RAND's Intelligence Policy Center and its International Security and Defense Policy Center, and he is Associate Dean of the Pardee RAND Graduate School. His recent work has examined at terrorism, intelligence, and law enforcement, with a special interest in new forms of public-private partnership. He has served in government for the first Senate Select Committee on Intelligence, handling Europe for the National Security Council, and most recently as vice chair of the National Intelligence Council, overseeing the writing of America's National Intelligence Estimates. He holds an A.B. *summa cum laude* from Princeton University, a master's in public policy, and Ph.D. in economics and politics from Harvard University. His latest books are *Reshaping National Intelligence for an Age of Information* (Cambridge University Press, 2001), and *New Challenges, New Tools for Defense Decisionmaking* (edited, RAND, 2003).

Michael A. Turner is a political scientist who has taught international relations and national security matters in San Diego, California, for the past twelve years. Before that, he spent over fifteen years in various positions within the CIA. Turner is the author of *Why Secret Intelligence Fails* (2005; 2006) and the *Historical Dictionary of United States Intelligence* (2006).

Michael Warner serves as Historian for the Office of the Director of National Intelligence.

Nigel West is a military historian specializing in security and intelligence topics. He is the European editor of the *World Intelligence Review* and is on the faculty at the Center for Counterintelligence and Security Studies in Washington, DC. He is the author of more than two dozen works of nonfiction and recently edited *Guy Liddell Diaries*.

Reg Whitaker is Distinguished Research Professor Emeritus, York University, and Adjunct Professor of Political Science, University of Victoria, Canada. He has written extensively on Canadian and international security and intelligence issues.

James J. Wirtz is Professor in the Department of National Security Affairs at the Naval Postgraduate School, Monterey, California. He is Section Chair of the Intelligence Studies Section of the International Studies Association and President of the International Security and Arms Control Section of the American Political Science Association. Wirtz is the series editor for *Initiatives in Strategic Studies: Issues and Policies*, published by Palgrave Macmillan.

Amy B. Zegart is Associate Professor of Public Policy at the University of California, Los Angeles. A specialist on national and homeland security, she has served on the National Security Council staff, as a foreign policy advisor to the Bush-Cheney 2000 presidential campaign, and as a consultant to California state and local homeland security agencies. She has published articles in leading academic journals, including *International Security* and *Political Science Quarterly*, and is the author of *Flawed by Design: The Origins of the CIA, JCS, and NSC* (Stanford, 1999). She received her Ph.D. in political science from Stanford, where she studied under Condoleezza Rice, and an A.B. in East Asian Studies from Harvard University.